Martha Graham's Cold War

Martha Graham's Cold War

The Dance of American Diplomacy

VICTORIA PHILLIPS

OXFORD

UNIVERSITY PRESS

OXFORD
UNIVERSITY PRESS

Oxford University Press is a department of the University of Oxford. It furthers
the University's objective of excellence in research, scholarship, and education
by publishing worldwide. Oxford is a registered trade mark of Oxford University
Press in the UK and certain other countries.

Published in the United States of America by Oxford University Press
198 Madison Avenue, New York, NY 10016, United States of America.

Library of Congress Cataloging-in-Publication Data

Names: Phillips, Victoria, author. | Phillips, Victoria.
Strange commodity of cultural exchange.
Title: Martha Graham's Cold War : the dance of American diplomacy /
[Victoria Phillips].
Description: New York, NY : Oxford University Press, [2020] |
Revision of author's thesis (doctoral)—Columbia University, 2013,
titled Strange commodity of cultural exchange : Martha Graham and
the State Department on tour, 1955–1987. | Includes bibliographical references and index.
Identifiers: LCCN 2019035357 (print) | LCCN 2019035358 (ebook) |
ISBN 9780190610364 (hardback) | ISBN 9780190610388 (epub) |
ISBN 9780190610371 (updf) | ISBN 9780190610395 (oso)
Subjects: LCSH: Graham, Martha—Travel. | Graham, Martha—Political and social views. |
Modern dance—Political aspects—United States—History—20th century. |
Cultural diplomacy—United States—History—20th century. |
Cold War—Social aspects—United States. | Politics and culture—United States. |
United States—Foreign relations—1945–1989.
Classification: LCC GV1785.G7 P55 2020 (print) | LCC GV1785.G7 (ebook) |
DDC 792.802/8—dc23
LC record available at https://lccn.loc.gov/2019035357
LC ebook record available at https://lccn.loc.gov/2019035358

1 3 5 7 9 8 6 4 2

Printed by Integrated Books International, United States of America

And just to stop internal mayhem, we dispatched Martha Graham:
That's what we call cultural exchange.
No commodity is quite so strange as this thing called cultural exchange.
— *The Real Ambassadors*
by Iola and Dave Brubeck
in collaboration with Louis Armstrong

Contents

Prologue

An American Ambassador on the Tarmac

At 8:25 a.m. on October 17, 1955, the sleek Japanese Airlines jet carrying Martha Graham's modern dance company touched down outside Tokyo, and the dancers descended onto the red carpet, the men wearing pressed suits and slim ties, the women wearing New Look dresses and carrying white gloves. Throngs pressed against the airport barricades, waving Japanese and American flags to greet them.[1] Graham wore a fitted dark travel dress that hugged her slim figure, a chunky golden necklace, and gloves—looking every bit the part of the "High Priestess of Modern Dance in America," as she was billed in advance publicity.[2] As she waved, looking out over the crowd, walking assuredly across the tarmac, large metal cameras popped. Luminaries greeted her, even hugging her, thus breaking with Japanese protocol. Children handed her more bouquets than she could hold. She leaned down, straight-backed, and smiled, a woman in the midst of a grand performance. After all, as she had declared, "Center stage is wherever I am." And she arrived as a modern American, "The Picasso of Modern Dance."

Embarking on her first State Department–sponsored tour of what President Dwight D. Eisenhower considered the world's "domino nations," those most likely to topple to communism, Martha Graham was situated in the nexus of Cold War geopolitics. The Chinese "domino" had fallen in 1949, and the United States feared that the southern half of Korea, as well as Thailand, Malaysia, Indonesia, Burma, and India—all countries Graham would visit on this tour—would follow. In public speeches about the "fall" of the Pacific, Eisenhower called Japan the "mega-domino," and said that "losing Japan" would turn the surrounding area into a "communist lake."[3] Japanese leaders were re-examining the "reforms" of the occupation period. A United States country report stated, "A sentiment which has repeatedly been referred to as 'anti-Americanism' would seem to prevail." There was "alarm" with the "elevated status held by Marxism among [university] students and professors." The theater and performing arts were "marked with

Martha Graham's Cold War. Victoria Phillips, Oxford University Press 2020. © Oxford University Press.
DOI: 10.1093/oso/9780190610364.001.0001

Leftist and Communist influence." Indeed, the report added, "In such fields it is extremely difficult to find influential persons [or 'molders of opinions'] who could pass the security and visa requirements necessary [to come to the United States]."[4] In this tense atmosphere, Eisenhower's administration sent Graham abroad in the hope that her American dance modernism, with its "universality," would promote America's cause with reinvigorated messages of freedom and democracy. As US government officials watched the planning of the Bandung Conference in 1954, a gathering of newly decolonized or decolonizing nations, Graham was being considered as an export to regions including Asia and the Middle East. Thus Tokyo became the first stop on the grueling tour, which would last through February 1956, culminating in Iran. The company then moved to Israel with foundation funding from Bethsabée de Rothschild of the famous banking family for which a boulevard in the business heart of Tel Aviv had been named. Graham would bring the art of American modern dance, and the power of American Cold War values, to nations that the United States wanted to impress further into its cause.

Culture met political aims, as private met public needs, and apolitical ideology served politics. During Eisenhower's "Crusade for Freedom" campaign, launched in 1950 as a private organization to support cultural activities in Europe, yet covertly associated with numerous governmental agencies including the Central Intelligence Agency (CIA), he called for the celebration of American tenets like "freedom" and the "dignity of the individual" to combat "Soviet lies." Graham embodied her country's drive for a freedom that celebrated the power of the individual with her dance works and techniques that had developed independently during the interwar period.[5] By the early 1950s, modernism had been firmly linked to the political aims of the United States, and Graham had become directly involved. *Perspectives USA*, a magazine which was funded by the Ford Foundation to entice European elites to the American side, yet which also worked beside the CIA's own publishing ventures, had published an article by George Kennan, the famed diplomat known as the "Father of Cold War Containment," on the use of modernism and its arts as propaganda to fight the Soviets.[6] The journal then promoted Graham and her dance as a celebration of "man and his individuality" with a technique linked to Picasso and the groundbreaking modern visual artists.[7] The United States Information Agency (USIS) advance publicity throughout Asia and the Middle East repeatedly celebrated Graham as the "Picasso" of dance with her repertory of choreographic art.[8] She brought the modern, "with a variety of works never before seen"—a marked contrast to the traditional czarist tales in the ballets Galina Ulanova and her fellow Bolshoi dancers would present on tours preceding Graham.[9] Graham arrived with the full support of the political and cultural elites armed with modernism as a Cold War weapon.

Upon her company's arrival, Graham stopped on the tarmac in Japan to speak to the crowd. Behind the female leader stood her diverse troupe and crew: well-coiffed women who could trace their lineage to the *Mayflower* next to African American men in suits and ties; Jewish women beside Christian women; a Filipino American alongside a man who had fought and flown fighter planes in World War II. With no direct flights in the 1950s, the group had flown from New York to California, where they boarded a Japanese Airlines plane headed first to Hawaii, and then to Wake Island to refuel. While the stewardesses had changed into casual kimonos for the long flight across the Pacific, Graham insisted that her female dancers wear their silk stockings, pumps, dresses, and suits for the duration.[10] Although exhausted, they had emerged on the tarmac as stars. The dancers' bodies were a diplomatic expression of Graham's distinctly American "New Look" and groundbreaking modernist language that sought to express human "universals."

Reporters leaned in to hear her words, scribbling on small white pads, then looking up to take note of the star herself as Graham declared in her quiet but strong voice that she could cross borders with dance, "the first language."[11] While radio, film, plays, libraries, books, and public appearances by diplomats demanded verbal commonalities, dance stood with art and music as a form that transcended language barriers; indeed, Graham's choreographic genius embedded the nonverbal arts of dramatic expression, art, and music. She used her dancers' bodies and her own as the star to tell abstracted stories that united the Western canon, religion, and the American frontier to create new archetypes for global consumption. Yet to convey both those classic and classically American myths effectively in the context of a State Department tour, Graham first had to establish herself as a modernist. Her well-received reflection on love, its passion, joy, and purity, *Diversion of Angels*, exemplified her melding of "pure art" and modernism to express human "universals." Based on a painting by modern artist Wassily Kandinsky, only the distilled emotion remained.[12] Continuing her press conference, Graham pronounced that all the works in her repertory could create an "opening of doors that have not been opened before."[13] While artistically referring to "the human spirit," Graham's geography demonstrated US geopolitical aims.

In Japan, where the United States was starting to lose the tight grip that it had in the immediate postwar era, Graham and her modernist dance would be competing directly against the codified Soviet ballet, a "literal war of dance between the United States and the Soviet Union," according to the Japanese press.[14] Russian ballerina Galina Ulanova had just completed a tour of the region, and the public had also seen Ulanova's brilliance on-screen.[15] The Soviet ballet traditionally featured corseted women in tutus with arched feet bound in pointe shoes, dancing tales of swans and princes. Yet the Russian star had arrived in Tokyo with only a small group of dancers; Graham, by contrast, had brought seventeen dancers, although the press reported an even more robust twenty-eight. Why had Ulanova not brought such a large team?, wondered Japanese reporters, critics, and even diplomats. Was Japan not important enough to warrant a full production? Perhaps seeking to show inclusiveness, the Russians used Japanese performers to fill in the lesser parts and supply the corps de ballet. Making matters worse, the Japanese nationals onstage failed in the eyes of the Japanese critics, causing some humiliation.[16] Standing in front of the Japanese aircraft, Graham claimed that with ten years of training, she could use "any body" in her freed yet disciplined modernist technique, setting her strategy apart from that of Soviets, whose bodies were measured from childhood and trained for uniformity. On the tarmac, Graham, standing side by side with her diverse, free, and yet highly trained dancers, announced, "Only through discipline, free creation is born."[17]

Graham's iconic modern dance, she explained to reporters, "supplement[s] the classic dance with the requirements of the modern age so that it will develop into a new classic."[18] With Graham center stage, her diverse bodies told complex human stories of psychological angst and redemption through Greek myths, biblical tales, and stories of the American frontier (known as "Americana"), all set in the context of her ability to abstract "universal" emotions into Picasso-esque moving art. Whereas the Soviet dancers appeared in nineteenth-century classical works associated with a long-overthrown monarchy, Graham and her large company showcased a range of works including Night Journey, the Greek tale of Oedipus made famous by modern psychology, yet told by Graham through the voice of Jocasta, his mother and lover, through memory and flashback. Other stories of timeless human struggles included the Greek myth of Medea, a scorned princess of great intelligence who seeks revenge, originally dramatized by Euripides. Seraphic Dialogue celebrated Joan of Arc, the political martyr turned religious saint. These archetypes were collected and performed alongside

Americana and the frontier Bride in *Appalachian Spring*. Graham played the leads, and the Greek chorus and pioneer townspeople would include women who were Jewish, African American, *Mayflower* American, and Asian American, all working together. Balletic tales of nobles and the monarchy were tagged as czarist and Soviet but also served as a possible reminder to Japanese audiences of the alliance of elites that had led them disastrously into war, a conflict that ended with the bombings of Hiroshima and Nagasaki almost exactly ten years earlier. Graham used her dance vocabulary to retell age-old tales that accessed human frailties and triumphs of the spirit. Her narrative works featured female protagonists who moved the psychological drama forward, accessing human psychology, memory, and thus "universal" truths through freedom of expression brought by modern American democracy. Newspapers faithfully reported that Graham was the "New Classic."[19]

Yet Graham had an American propaganda mission to fulfill. "Entertainment which does not also carry a political message should be reduced to a minimum," a USIS memo circulated before the trip directed.[20] Thus Americana and *Appalachian Spring*, which promoted the power of the frontier through the figures of the Bride, her Husbandman, the Preacher, the Pioneer Woman, and the Followers, became a centerpiece. Expansionist in scope, the work argued for the promise brought by the United States and manifest destiny. The Pulitzer Prize–winning score by Aaron Copland, featuring the Shaker song "Simple Gifts" with the lyrics, "'Tis a gift to be free," helped make it a fitting work to propagate America's vision of its own values through the equation of Graham with an idealized America. The dance work, initially titled "Ballet for Martha," became a staple of the Graham company's government-sponsored tours, and through 1956 *Appalachian Spring* closed the final show in each international city the company visited.

While USIS required Americana, the United States promoted its messages of democracy and inclusion via other works as well. Thus, Graham's works demonstrate what I call "cultural convergences," or a modernized infusion of host-country elements into American cultural exports, a syncretism that USIS would promote via both public and private outlets.[21] Like all the other works on tour that included a stage set, *Appalachian Spring* featured the work of Japanese American artist Isamu Noguchi, whose collaborations with Graham aroused much interest in Japan, and argued for the inclusionary ethos of the United States as a "melting pot." That morning at the Tokyo airport, Graham acknowledged the designer and his influences, noting her desire to visit Japanese gardens, which Noguchi had described as the embodiment of the doctrine of Zen Buddhism, so that she could understand his mastery of modernist space and the sets within which she danced.[22] The Japanese influence would meld with a European-American story when Graham, as the Bride onstage at Tokyo's New Empire Theatre, sat on the abstracted Noguchi rocking chair in *Appalachian Spring*'s proscenium frontier. The designer had constructed a modernist farmhouse, a preacher's pulpit, and a fence that marked the new couple's land. One Japanese critic, highly impressed at what the dancer and Japanese American designer had accomplished, wrote that, in comparison, "Even the *best* of [Russian] ballet is very pale stuff."[23]

In these 1955 appearances in Japan, Graham's work not only triumphed over Ulanova's Soviet ballet tour but also displaced such German artists as Mary Wigman, the progenitors of much of Japanese modern dance. During the interwar period, Japanese dancers and choreographers Michio Ito and Baku Ishii had trained in Germany and influenced the rise of a Japanese modern dance.[24] Many Japanese dancers subsequently went to Germany to train, clearly a response to the performances. Nonetheless, before Graham's arrival in 1955, USIS-led publicity announced that Harald Kreutzberg, Wigman's student, had been the first "modern dancer" to appear in Japan before World War II, and that he had disappointed the Japanese (a response not reflected in the actual reviews from the 1930s).[25] Although Graham had worked with Ito in New York and he had introduced Graham to Noguchi during the interwar period, Ito returned to Japan, and publicity remained silent about their relationship. The celebration of her American modernist roots that included Japanese American Noguchi thus undermined the idea of an independent Japanese modern dance related to totalitarian or fascist influences. Denying the power of the Germans, Graham directly associated her American dance with Eastern influences, emphasizing that she revered pure Asian forms. Numerous reviewers noted that her technique and theatricality seemed to be derived from yoga or Noh, although they did not trace her back directly through the "orientalism" of Denishawn, the California troupe from which she had emerged, and which had toured Asia during the interwar years. Her alliance to modernism and her integration of Asian forms seemed to be drawn out of historical thin air, but it was effective as a means of making her work appear American in origin while drawing on Asian sensibilities.

In marked contrast to the Soviet ballet company and stagings—where the locally hired Japanese dancers had looked out of place—Graham integrated bodies and artistic practices into her works through her troupe and design team. As the consummate ambassador, she also adjusted her presentation to meet local needs and sensibilities. Because the bare sole of a foot should not be flexed in front of a respected person in Japan and much of Asia, in her lecture-demonstrations during which she explained the technique as her dancers performed, the dancers angled their bodies and demonstrated the training technique as she explored the importance of the freed and thus bared foot. Graham well understood local customs as a diplomat yet also remained true to her technique, which stressed the body's connection to the soil. Newspapers reported on the enthusiasm of local young dancers for the American modernist technique, which was strikingly new yet infused with enduring Japanese cultural elements.[26] With Graham as the medium of exchange, the United States could show interest in other cultural traditions while also demonstrating how American artists could reinterpret them to create a new, modern art that transcended cultural boundaries for both the elite and the youth who would carry the Graham technique to new generations of dancers, choreographers, and diplomats.

Publicity for Graham's performances was molded to fit government needs to promote not just American ideals of freedom but also American power. A Japanese poster of Graham portrayed her with uncharacteristic Rita Hayworth–like hair, positioned with her fist raised to the side like the iconic World War II poster of Rosie the Riveter, with a slit dress that showed a cut, muscular thigh.[27] Merging political and private-sector power, Graham became an ambassador for American foundation and business exchanges, always remaining steadfast in her connection to American philanthropy and industry. Tour programs noted that *Appalachian Spring* was a commissioned work, and cultural sponsorships by host-nation organizations and governments were met side by side by American corporate sponsors. One program stated, prominently on the inside front cover, "Martha Graham is a star of the American Modern Dance and Chevrolet is the Star of General Motors."[28]

Graham and her company became vital people-to-people diplomats on the ground, joining with Japanese people from elites and students to shopkeeps. The company and crew learned local dance forms, shopped for ancient artifacts, and attended receptions and dinners with elites. They understood the vital importance of these exchanges and had been well-trained by the government and Graham herself. Graham set the model: in her press conference, she declared that she had always wanted to come to Japan, not just to perform but to experience "Japanese dance first, and drama, then the gardens, ancient architecture and picture-scrolls on the soil of Japan."[29] A Japanese celebration of Graham took place under the auspices of the Japan Art Dance Association. Graham and her troupe sat in folding chairs on manicured grass and watched the display of Japanese dance along with three hundred guests. The "High Priestess of Modern Dance" was positioned for the cameras in the center of the front row, draped in an Asian embroidered shawl as she represented the United States. In addition to shopping for cloth, Graham loved jade and searched antique stores for relics to bring home; her dancers looked at beautiful pottery and brought home masks and fans decorated in gold and blood red.[30] On another day, her dancers, one more stunning than the next, rode in a motorcade down avenues that had been completely reconstructed since the war. The troupe attended a welcome party as well as an embassy dinner where dancers were required by Graham to eat everything despite their performing schedule, even the quail eggs.[31] Graham and her dancers thrived in what the USIS called the "cocktail circuit of diplomacy."[32]

However effective an ambassador, Graham began her first government tour in Japan dealing with issues that would plague her for the next forty years: her age and her gender. Although she was born in 1894, the press announced upon her landing in 1955 that she was fifty-two years old. While she celebrated the fact that, as an American woman, she could create a new dance and run a company, she was pictured in newspapers sitting demurely for the press over a hibachi grill in a Japanese home.[33] Back at home in New York, she rarely, if ever, cooked, and was quite defiant about the fact to some.[34] Although a divorcée once passionately in love and married to the man who had originated the role of the Husbandman in *Appalachian Spring*, she was billed as "Miss Graham." She was the sole leader of a company and the star of her works, which always centered female protagonists, but Graham seemed as easily practiced as a woman at a tea, carrying gloves and demanding that her female company members do the same. The public relations events and newspaper photographs that presented Graham to the Japanese expressed the paradoxes of powerful women in Cold War America. A single woman could create art, lead a company, and tour the world, but first and foremost, she had to project the acceptable ideals of the era, including the "New Look" of youthful maturity and traditional gendered household roles, however unreflective of the ambassador herself.

The company's performances reached the Japanese elites whom the State Department had targeted and immediately engaged them in an "imagined community" of international cultural sophisticates.[35] Because Graham was a "Person of Supreme Intelligence," according to the Japanese reporters covering her arrival, she would "bring a big insightment [sic] and development in the Japanese circles."[36] With Graham's abstract expressionism, classical and biblical allusions, and creative embrace of Americana, she seduced the intelligentsia and political leaders into an imagined international community of modernist thinkers. The elite engagement seemed to work. By closing night of the Japanese leg of Graham's tour in early November, a final review noted that members of the imperial family followed the US ambassador and "distinguished guests" as the group "rose to its feet and cheered."[37]

Graham became a manifestation of what government strategists and politicians called "trickle-down diplomacy." With the establishment's international bonds reinforced with culture, so the thinking surely went, international leaders would join with the Americans to enact pro-US policy. Graham's rhetoric followed suit, and although the press wrote that she showed a deep knowledge of literature and culture, she herself noted that her work could be understood by anyone because it held "universals" in the language of the dance—a vocabulary that could be understood despite any boundaries of knowledge or traditions. Although the specific references were elite, the language could be accessible to all. Indeed, the nonelitist inclusion of the general population was of growing concern to the American high-art modernist project. A telegram the US embassy sent to the State Department emphasized the delight of the audience in Japan writ large: "Large numbers of people stood in the aisles at every performance and the final curtain brought a thunderous ovation of applause, cheers, exploding firecrackers, confetti, serpentine, and flowers."[38] Graham saved a backstage photograph with her stage manager and a Japanese workman in front of the Noguchi frontier home from *Appalachian Spring*, covered in the fallen confetti and streamers, with stray petals by their feet.[39]

By the end of the performances, newspapers announced that, in the Soviet-US "dance competition" between "living national treasures," the Americans were the clear victors, the true purveyors of innovation, intelligence, and largesse.[40] Graham established the validity of a dance system freed from the yokes of tradition, which allowed her to express humanity through her narratives, rather than through old-fashioned, if technically demanding, czarist fairy tales. The social aspects of the tour became a distinct American success. An embassy official wrote to the State Department that at one reception, the Soviet diplomats themselves got involved: "Even the Russians turned out," he exclaimed.[41]

The cultural Cold War waged by Graham engaged political issues beyond communism versus democracy, guiding leaders toward a postwar era of cooperation. A cable noted that one prominent critic of America who had felt that the United States placed excessive emphasis on military materiel for Japan said to an embassy representative after the performance, "Your country has sent us 'Honest Jon' (atomic rocket launcher). Now send us a teacher who can teach Miss Graham's modern dance to the Japanese!"[42] With Japan having recently marked the tenth anniversary of the American atomic bombings with memorials and gatherings, Graham's visit was the culmination of a decade-long reformulation of Japan's internal political life by the United States. During the postwar US occupation of Japan, the US had rewritten the Japanese constitution, disallowed armament, and demanded that Japan host military bases for American soldiers and armaments.[43] Graham embodied the tenets of "empire by invitation," as the Japanese asked for the American modern form to be taught and to mold the bodies of its young citizens.[44]

Appalachian Spring closed the tour in Japan to thunderous applause and the seeming enchantment of "hearts and minds."[45] Local reporters felt that Graham showed "the movement of the heart." The *Nippon Times* reported, "Without a doubt, [Graham's performance] will go down in theatrical history here as a landmark."[46] A Japanese diplomat gushed, "Miss Graham's performances have greatly advanced [American] prestige."[47] Yet even as these Japanese critics and audience members celebrated the dancer and her all-American yet "universal" dances, others remained cognizant of the project's ultimate aims. One critic remarked that "the patriotic placing of American national interest at the end with *Appalachian Spring*" served "to underscore the diplomatic nature of this cultural mission."[48] Graham's dances were modernist and seemingly apolitical art as creatures of Cold War politics.

Introduction

When they sensed internal mayhem / They sent out Martha Graham
/ That's what we call cultural exchange . . .
Nothing is quite so strange / As this thing called cultural exchange
—Dave and Iola Brubeck with Louis Armstrong

"I am not a propagandist," declared Martha Graham upon landing in India in 1955. "My dances are not political."[1] Yet between 1955 and 1987, under every president from Dwight D. Eisenhower through Ronald Reagan, Graham and her troupe traveled under government auspices to upwards of twenty-five countries, with gala events planned under George H. W. Bush in Moscow, St. Petersburg, and Soviet bloc countries in November 1989.[2] She was honored or fêted at the White House by each president from Franklin D. Roosevelt through George H. W. Bush, and she formed alliances with first ladies from Eleanor Roosevelt to Jackie Kennedy, Betty Ford, and Barbara Bush. From Eisenhower's "domino nations" in 1955, behind the Iron Curtain, covertly and in plain sight to Israel beginning in 1956 and the broader Middle East with the "Jimmy Carter Goodwill Tour," to East Berlin in 1987, and to Soviet Russia and bloc nations just before the fall of the Wall, Graham landed in Cold War hotspots where the United States sought to exert influence. In 1955, while Japan was the "mega-domino," India was of particular concern as a lead nation in the foundation of the Bandung Conference, which sought nonalignment for nations in Asia and Africa in the Soviet-US rivalry. John Foster Dulles, Eisenhower's powerful secretary of state, famously announced that neutrality was "immoral and shortsighted." Thus the opera *The Real Ambassadors* (1962), written by leading artists deployed by the government for its programs abroad—Dave and Iola Brubeck with Louis Armstrong— poked fun at the clear political intent of the tours with the refrain, "When they sensed internal mayhem / They sent out Martha Graham / That's what we call cultural exchange," adding, "Nothing is quite so strange / As this thing called cultural exchange."[3]

Martha Graham's Cold War. Victoria Phillips, Oxford University Press 2020. © Oxford University Press.
DOI: 10.1093/oso/9780190610364.001.0001

Graham disavowed political attachments: indeed, understanding what she said she was *not* is often a way to understand Graham as a person and as an actor in US diplomatic history. Not political, she also disavowed herself as a modernist, feminist, and American missionary. Yet as an American female ambassador touring the globe during the Cold War with her modern dance, she represented classic American freedoms and thus defended and encouraged US interests abroad. She posited as uniquely American the ability to create an individualistic—and thus "free"—dance technique. With her modernism, with Eisenhower's hearts and minds "stripped to the bones," as her dance was described, she accessed a universal, born in America; she could create an imagined community of sophisticates under the "trickle-down" theory of cultural diplomacy. If the intelligentsia embraced and celebrated this imagined community, the people would follow. As an integral part of the project, she viewed her dance and repertory as offering what I call "cultural convergences" that were paradoxically invited into her universal freed expression, with Japanese techniques featured in Asia, the Old Testament in Israel, European myths and history in Europe, and Russian defectors in Moscow.[4] As a modernist who was also a female ambassador, she demonstrated the principle of freedom of speech, and her multiracial troupe demonstrated an unspoken and contested freedom posited in response to the communist dissemination of news about a racist America. Her works demonstrated freedom of religion, and her company demonstrated not only freedom "from" want but also freedom "to" want with local shopping expeditions.[5]

During the Cold War, this government export model changed over time to target youth, and by 1974, one diplomat called Graham's modernism historic and even old-fashioned. Yet Graham's message remained consistent between her first White House performance in 1937 of *Frontier*, the presentation of a pioneer woman responding to a horn calling for war and celebrating the barren American land, to her planned tour under President George H. W. Bush in 1989 that would feature a remade "premiere" of *American Document*, featuring Hollywood icon Liza Minnelli and the words of Walt Whitman and Abraham Lincoln alongside a film of Soviet ballet defector Mikhail Baryshnikov, who had played Graham's frontier Husbandman a few years earlier. She promoted American ideals associated with freedom and democracy, and thus capitalism, as "universal" yet "made in America"—even as those ideals caused controversy and conflict. As a nonliberationist woman who was feminine yet always center stage, she could deliver potent messages in "soft power" and depoliticized terms.

This book examines Graham's enduring influence as a female ambassador who performed American freedoms with modernism in dance on the global Cold War stage. "No idea is more fundamental to Americans' sense of themselves as individuals and as a nation than freedom," writes the historian Eric Foner.[6] Graham, as a diplomat, choreographer, dancer, and company manager, used her construction of American freedom to culturally proclaim the launch of the United States as a reliable postwar global leader. The Western-led idealism embedded in Graham's works would age with time; the promotion of the United States in the 1950s as a supremely modern country, and thus represented by the modern dance, metamorphosed over nearly four decades into the celebration of this dance as iconic, traditional, even codified, Hollywood-esque, and conservative. Under the banner of American freedom, modernism met modernization in politics and culture, and both aged, ossified, and sparked increasing if sporadic and unpredictable dissent alongside ideas of imagined communities. Yet because Graham's central tenet was a dedication to freedom available only in a democracy, she bridged administrations from the interwar years through the Cold War, Democratic to Republican. Although Graham's projections on behalf of the government can seem heavy-handed, particularly as she engages with nationalism with her Americana and orientalism with cultural convergences, her metaphoric message continues to ring clear in her solo work *Frontier*: she called for walls among people to be torn down in the name of American freedom.

* * *

I came to this topic through my own childhood experiences as a dancer and a child of the 1960s protest movements. At the age of eight, in 1968, after I had been rejected for promotion to the next level of modern dance because I was overweight and lacked coordination, my mother enrolled me in French baroque dance classes. I was one of three children in the class, and one of the others quickly dropped out. By the process of elimination, I became proof positive that any child could learn and perform a minuet from the period of Louis XIV, and my performing career began at the Lincoln Center Performing Arts Library. I learned to read the exacting Beauchamp-Feuillet notation, slowly mastered a gavotte, and was laced into my corset as I began to slim down. As the child of Harvard-trained Upper West Side New York liberals, I attended the Walden School. Andrew Young, who was murdered while registering voters in the South, was our most celebrated alumnus. The social studies curriculum emphasized attendance at antiwar demonstrations over dates and facts. My two lives, dance and politics, seemed completely separate. Exacting French dance training after school and weekend performances mingled with peace marches and protests and the view of Harlem burning as politicians and heroes were murdered. My first direct political memory of a president's face was on a black-and-white television with metal rabbit ears on top to boost reception as Richard M. Nixon resigned, with my mother cheering "Right on" in the background.

When I saw the Graham company perform in 1976, I thought, "I want to do that." Graham's charisma drew me in, and from the abstract works to the Greek myths, the human drama gripped me. The Walden School welcomed my passion, and I skipped morning classes to pursue independent studies in Greek myth and theater. As a teenager in Martha Graham's New York townhouse, in class each morning the dance felt just as it looked. In *Diversion of Angels*, the explication of love, I was joy. I was hooked. After I graduated from high school, with most of my junior and senior years spent in the Graham studios or the theater, my parents—more Harvard than Upper West Side— were dismayed to learn that I would not be attending college. While working as a waitress, I took company class, learned the repertory, and began to know whenever Graham would teach class: the building vibrated with her presence, and a vase of flowers would appear on the piano. I also had my own memory of Graham's apolitical professions, having been at the studio when the company was about to leave on its Jimmy Carter Goodwill Tour, just after the Camp David Accords, the import of which I was completely unaware. She and the dancers spoke of the trip as an international performing opportunity, or even just a paying job, but surely not as a diplomatic cause. Although I stopped dancing several years later because of injuries and age, Martha Graham, her choreography, her curious intellect and desire to innovate, and her paths into the world remain with me. Never forget, one of Graham's star dancers admonished me just before her death, "Graham is a genius."

When I entered the doctoral program at Columbia University while raising a family and after a career on Wall Street, I intended to write about the relationship of American modern dance to communism during the interwar period. But then the Graham archives at the Library of Congress opened. When I saw letters to Graham from George Kennan, father of containment and then ambassador to Yugoslavia, and Eleanor Dulles, the sister of Secretary of State John Foster and director of the CIA Allen under Eisenhower—as well as memos seemingly penned by Henry Kissinger, National Security Adviser and later Secretary of State under Richard M. Nixon and, after the president's resignation, Secretary of State under Gerald R. Ford—I asked, if she was so apolitical, as she always claimed, why were all of these figures engaged with her? Why a plethora of United States Information Agency (USIS) government reports on her touring activities? After more than a decade of research in archives and libraries in the United States, the Middle East, and Europe, I found the very political biography of Martha Graham.

* * *

The research behind this book probes beyond official and traditional archives, although those sources form the core of the research. I read Graham's papers held at the Library of Congress and by Martha Graham Resources in New York City alongside government documents used by foreign policy and Cold War experts, as well as foundation and corporate records. Freedom of Information Act (FOIA) requests revealed previously classified or suppressed information, including Graham's file at the Federal Bureau of Investigation (FBI), which contained the only complete survey of her tours through the early 1980s. Yet her report, requested several times using all possible names, opens her story in the 1970s despite her "fellow traveler" activities in support of the pro-communist fundraising efforts for the Spanish Civil War during the interwar years in New York. A brief reference to the FBI documentation of her pro-communist, if pro-democratic, performances in support of medical assistance during the Spanish Civil War can be found at the National Security Archive. The rest of her file remains lost or missing. Surveillance reports on the historical actors, also obtained through FOIAs, offer new perspectives on events and the people involved. In addition, working backward, I queried all presidential records from 1935 through 1990, as well as the private papers of diplomats. Numerous foreign and host country government archives have also provided documents and news reports. If I had another fifteen years, I would make my final stop in Moscow to look for the Soviet documents detailing the tour that never took place.

More important, Graham company members, company officials, and government representatives saved their papers and letters, including the negative reviews of performances not preserved in official archives, and shared their memories. The dancers generously offered me vivid memories in oral histories and interviews. Numerous government officials and cultural attachés have given testimony about what they call "propaganda" and

"Americana" as cultural diplomacy to influence foreign policy outcomes. Finally, Graham's choreographic oeuvre—including the abstracted works, *Appalachian Spring*, and stories from the Western canon told from the perspective of female protagonists—provides evidence when analyzed as visual text. Cross-reading this myriad of sources leads to new conclusions about Martha Graham, American cultural diplomacy during the Cold War, and the history of American dance as a means of promoting American freedom and democracy abroad.

* * *

This book places Martha Graham and modern dance at the center of Cold War American cultural and political history because government representatives understood that dance—particularly modern dance—was second only to music in its effectiveness and impact in foreign markets as a necessarily apolitical agent in both aligned and nonaligned nations.[7] Graham's public denial of her political work as a modern artist for the United States is a direct signal of Cold War politics in action: like the export of abstract visual art, her choreography and persona met the US government's anti-Soviet "informational" or propaganda needs precisely because her work could be promoted as modernist, a free form disallowed by artists in the Soviet Union, independently created, and apolitical.[8]

Although "propaganda" has become a sullied term, when Graham was first sent into the field, it remained in use by policy experts as "the planned dissemination of news, information, special arguments designed to influence the beliefs, thoughts, and actions of a specific group"; this definition is followed in *Martha Graham's Cold War*.[9] During the Cold War, the source of propaganda became vital: overt propaganda was white, covert was black, and a third class emerged: gray. Although Graham became a white, sometimes gray, part of State Department activities in the 1960s and 1970s, in the 1950s she was distinctly gray psychological warfare as an apolitical agent. Under Reagan in Berlin, she was gray-black, unattributed to the government but surely supported as she crossed into the communist sector of Berlin.

The link of apolitical aesthetic modernism to the American Cold War project to export freedom is not a new study among historians; modern American visual art during the Cold War "self-propagandized itself as a champion of eternal humanist freedom."[10] Like the visual artists, Graham represented a pure depiction of the enduring American idea "of freedom as a universal human birthright."[11] Yet dance became additive: Graham incorporated music, sculpture, drama, movement, and bodies into the visual experience. And in contrast to the static work of visual artists, her dance technique could demonstrate that freedom was anathema to anarchy or a childlike technique in a postwar battle with the Soviets.

Modern art could be redemptive and push political narratives of freedom forward, even in the face of shifts in communist policies over time. During the interwar and through World War II, the Nazi regime had condemned "degenerate art" including Picasso's work in its denunciations. The Stalinist suppression of the Russian burgeoning and profound nonrepresentational art, replaced by socialist realism and "dictator chic" decorative works, made the use of Graham's progressive abstraction, which exposed experience using the individual mind, rather than the eye that demands consensus, a seemingly obvious choice. Both wartime and postwar totalitarian leaders could be condemned as neophytes. Yet Graham remained increasingly pertinent even after the death of Stalin and a seeming thaw. While the Soviet Nikita S. Khrushchev denounced Stalin and seemed to embrace "peaceful co-existence" and some domestic freedoms, he likened the technique of the modern artist to a misbehaved child with a canvas, stating, "This is just a mess" and describing modern-type dances as "indecent" when people "wiggle a certain section of the anatomy." Yet during Graham's public lecture-demonstrations and speeches, she undeniably proved that her modern dance demanded highly disciplined training as the dancers contorted their pelvises in contraction and release, jumped in the air, and split upside down.[12] In addition, her choreographic choices demonstrated that Western ideals could be held as universal truths once they were extracted by a modernist and "stripped to the bones," as she said. Khrushchev proclaimed at the end of his tirade against modernism, "Art should ennoble the individual," and, in a twist, Graham fulfilled this proclamation with her heroic characters.[13]

Although numerous writers have explored why and how American abstract expressionism and literary modernism were ideal "weapons of the Cold War" as apolitical agents with readable political implications, cultural histories of Cold War diplomacy have overlooked modern dance as a discrete subject, and its leaders as singular diplomats. Historians favor art, jazz, orchestral music, rock and roll, film, sports, literature, ballet, and even children as "weapons."[14] Cultural histories of diplomacy have deepened an understanding of the Cold War, but enduring figures such as Graham and the specificity of her modern dance need to be firmly integrated into Cold War political and strategic narratives.[15]

But what did it mean to be "modern" both artistically and politically? Fredric Jameson writes, "Perhaps it might be better to admit that the notions that cluster around the word 'modern' are as unavoidable as they are unacceptable."[16] Graham herself declared that she was not "modern": she famously said, "Modern dance dates so quickly. That is why I always use the term 'contemporary'—it is of its time."[17] Yet Graham allowed the publicity arm of the government, her own publicists, and the likes of Henry Luce, the author of "The American Century" and publisher of *Life* magazine, to use that very word to describe her dance in the international markets when she represented the United States. Indeed, she was promoted as "Forever Modern" in 1974 on the Asian tour ending in Saigon as performance met politics and she closed just months before the North Vietnamese took over the city. Despite her denials, Graham herself said she attempted to emulate the abstraction of Kandinsky, and thus she became the "Dancing Picasso" in international field publicity. Self-references to modernists framed the a-modernist.

Regarding the appreciation of modern art, Graham's links to the visual artists served her well. Both the Soviets and the Western elites professed their inability to understand modern art, yet American diplomats celebrated its freedom and gave agency to the viewer, sophisticated or not, whereas the Soviets condemned its laxity. Diplomats discussed art easily. According to Khrushchev, he and British prime minister R. Anthony Eden were in agreement. When the British leader asked Khrushchev about a piece of abstract art, Khrushchev recalled, "I said I didn't understand it. He said he didn't understand it either, and asked me what I thought about Picasso. I said I didn't understand Picasso, and he said he couldn't understand Picasso either."[18] Indeed, George Kennan, the "Father of Containment," lectured at the Museum of Modern Art (MoMA) on diplomacy, and later opened an exhibit of abstract art in Yugoslavia, telling those attending the opening ceremony that, for him, "a considerable part of modern art does not reveal its meaning."[19] Yet the Soviet Ministry of Culture was reprimanded for spending even "a kopeck" on modern art, with exclamations of "Phooey," and asking, "Who are your parents?," in response to the promotion of capitalistic "so-called 'free-world'" and "amoral" art by "jackasses."[20] In opposition, Kennan asked his audience to find their own meaning and to use free will; he concluded, "I am well aware that this meaning [of abstraction] is visible to people whose acquaintance with art is far deeper than my own and for this reason I am wholly prepared to believe that it exists."[21] The exhibit was thronged with crowds, according to reports. Like Kennan, Graham seduced the audience with permission to experience modernism freely. When Graham was asked, "Will you be upset if the audience does not understand?," she responded, "I am not interested whether they understand or not. I am only interested if they feel it." She continued, "And it's on that basis that I've tried to reveal—through women, through whatever means I had available— the quickening of people's sensitivity."[22] Of the goal, the Soviet leader would agree with Graham that great art finds "the essence" and "inspires a person." Seeing opportunity, the Russian-trained Kennan used his platform at MoMA to call for American cultural diplomacy to enter "walled off" bloc countries and enable peoples of Russia that were "stagnant and sterile" to experience, as Graham would conclude of her Cold War tours, "the opening of doors that have not been opened before."[23]

General physical principles can be associated with the modern dance form, yet the issues are complex. "Modern dance" is a sticky container term loaded with import as a "free" form of movement that embodied a "universal" human experience, with high-art movement constrained only by the imagination of the choreographer and the physical limitations of the body reacting to the gravitational pull of the earth. Deploying the avant-garde, Loïe Fuller bared her legs and feet using theatrical techniques, lighting, and fabrics. Isadora Duncan and Mary Wigman used breath, the flexible torso, bare feet, and multidimensional spatial planes to indicate a connection to the earth and a respect for the physical properties of gravity's dynamic pull on the body. This dance utilized space in numerous dimensions allowed by physical movement, unconstrained by corsets and shoes. Graham's modernist technique seeded itself in the most elemental and indeed "universal" aspect of human life: the breath, and also in its greatest drama, the orgasm. Alongside claims of freedom, Graham's technique was highly codified and then exported to train bodies internationally in the universally derived yet highly American style. From a Foucauldian perspective, the Graham technique could be theorized as an American colonizing of the foreign body under the rubric of creating freedom. Paradoxes of modernism's freedom abound. What becomes most important over time is how the term became useful like a fly catcher.

While many have framed modern dance by what it is not—that is, nonballetic—Graham complicates this definition because she called her choreographic works ballets and used balletic principles and techniques. While studying at her studio, dancers had to hide their pointe shoes at the bottom of their dance bags lest the ribbons show, yet arabesques had to be stretched and lean, leaps high, and legs split parallel to the floor over time. Unlike the exalted artifices of Soviet ballet, which was seeded in Europe and demanded the curation of beauty with the first government institute formed in France under Louis XIV, Graham's bare feet and sometimes painfully contorted movements were deeply and immediately human. The leg only moved from the torso's contraction and release, which held meaning. No gesture, however spectacular and stretched, went unmotivated by the core. Breath, with its subsequent movement, was the essence of communication.

Although both the Soviet and Graham ballets used narrative drama to fuel numerous creations, Graham did not use linear time, and stories were framed with flashback, memory, and personal experience, Freudian and Jungian in the retelling. With a firm technical base, much like the representational surrealism of Salvador Dalí, Graham told human dramas. Indeed, the use of psychoanalytic techniques to understand a universal core of humanity in artistic expression engaged key Western concepts in the Cold War. While Graham quietly promoted the power of psychology through a catharsis experienced by her characters onstage, with individual analysis often used in the 1950s to promote conformity to Western values, this approach contradicted the Soviet understanding of the realization of well-being.[24] Graham showed a deep respect for classical ballet's core, yet not for its storytelling approach. *Swan Lake* was such a well-known work, fashioned from Russian folk tales with music by Pyotr Ilyich Tchaikovsky, that the ballet was shown to Soviet citizens on television to distract the population from unpleasant current events or to mark the death of a leader. Of this classic in particular, Graham said, "I believe Petipa must have studied swans for his *Swan Lake*. To witness the swan in water spinning into itself, you can understand the fouettés he created for the Black Swan. And in nature it is the black swan that is the most dangerous." Yet her "hypnotic" black swan would be different, she claimed, concluding that Rotbart's sexuality would take the white and make it black through seduction, concluding that the essence of the work showed that "sexuality is still the most powerful lure and manipulation."[25] Graham reduced even Soviet classics used as government propaganda to their core with psychoanalytical conclusions about human motivations.

However, while people within the State Department and the CIA, and some in the Executive Office of the President, may have applauded an export as highbrow as Graham's modern dance, Congress and even President Truman mirrored the perceived dilettantism of the Nazis and the Soviets regarding modernist art and preferred the ballet, if anything, to show American expertise. Congress repeatedly investigated government funding for modern exports and tried to shut it down as communistic or ill-advised, at best. Regarding nonballetic performances, some American officials wanted "Cowboy and Indian" shows for India and American Indian dances for the Germans, who loved Karl May's frontier novels. Critics argued that with modern dance, "people would think Americans go around barefoot" and asked, "Is Martha Too Sexy for Export?" Yet in Washington those who were educated together in prep schools and Ivy League institutions sent modernist projects using a complex web of women and men who worked in the public and private sectors (often hopping from one to the other), who provided diplomatic liaisons, press contacts, and funding from their own personal bank accounts, as well as influencing a maze of agencies and bureaus both domestically and internationally, all of which would shape the trajectory of dance as diplomacy in international markets.

Modern dance, specifically the work of Martha Graham, forms a lens through which to view the Cold War as a battle for the mantle of the politically "modern." Indeed, in using the word "modernization," the American political theorists claimed they borrowed the term from the art world.[26] In the late nineteenth century, modernity developed from "Enlightenment values," including civilization, progress, and development.[27] In the United States, social scientists argued that the process of modernization derived from freedom, and thus democracy and capitalism; the Soviets claimed to have the modern technology to bring all people into a better, communist world. Propaganda surrounding these issues became vital because the foundational tenets were shared by the United States and the Soviet Union, despite Cold War constructions of "the other" as enemy in a bipolar ideological world. Essential to the concept of "modernization" for the American theorists was the Enlightenment belief in a "universal" utopia, and thus, they concluded, "being western without the onus of following the west." Traveling from nation to nation, Graham followed this injunction that political theorists then borrowed from the artists and modeled the idea of finding a distinct voice in dance through individual freedom, all the time using an American-embodied modernist art technique to achieve universally desirable results.

The question of modernization necessarily included the problem of commerce, or money, and its role in achieving successful projects; funding for the tours exemplifies the paradox of capitalism's representation vis-à-vis communism in cultural exports. Under capitalism, the artist did not rely on the state as a patron, and thus he or she could create freely; under communism, the state paid for and thus directed and controlled output. Artists representing freedom through democracy could not be directly tied to the state as Soviet artists were. Yet the US government funded cultural exports. On Graham's first tour in 1955, the State Department masked its funding in programs and distributed literature. As an artist working in a democratic nation whose foreign tours were enabled by the state and its agencies, Graham repeatedly had to prove her creative independence with claims that she had no link to a capitalistic ideology mandated or molded by the government. In addition to donations from philanthropists and foundations, covertly government-funded institutions in the United States and host nations paid Graham's way as well. Indeed, when she received the Medal of Freedom from President Gerald R. Ford, she claimed that she had funded herself during the Depression with bank loans; she had not relied on government support available to artists under Franklin Roosevelt's Works Progress Administration. While Graham's posturing directly supported the Ford administration's arts funding objectives, where private donations were matched by public grants, the Graham company surely would have folded in the mid-1970s without its government-funded work; public support from Betty Ford, who had briefly danced with the company; and grants from the National Endowment for the Arts. A combination of private, overt public, and sporadic covert government support enabled Graham to float her company for decades and followed the structure of many American modernization projects in the countries visited by the woman herself, who took center stage.

* * *

Throughout this text, "isms" abound. As discussed earlier, the execution of modernism relies on the pretext of universalism. The desire to deploy cultural convergences leads to orientalism and the resulting exposé of nationalism and religiosity in the United States. Racism and feminism come as vital corollaries that must be addressed here, yet they are subjects for books on their own. Attached to feminism is the centrality of the woman in Graham's dramas and the stigma of "soft power"; this engages the political history of "Big Women" and their networks during the Cold War. All this in a narrative that spans decades and makes stops in more than twenty-five nations, whose names and languages and borders, much less political alliances, change over time. "I'll be a dilettante!" I pleaded when my PhD adviser, Eric Foner, suggested that I take this on. "Nonsense," he replied. "You're a tourist."

Graham's heroines demonstrated the force of human passions and the spirit, advertised by both Graham and USIS as "universal," and she depicted characters lifted from Western civilization and showed progress through the well-developed, highly technical, modernized yet freed body. Anticolonial nationalism and "identity politics" seemed at odds with those who sought universalist ideologies, particularly in contested nations outside of the bipolar spheres.[28] Graham bridged this gap by integrating what diplomats understood as host country culture, or cultural convergences, into her programming and publicity in order to promote mutual understanding.[29] Theaters became "contact zones," where one could construct an American imperialist and orientalist project, yet exchange was not one-way.[30] Graham's government exports were cosponsored by host country governments, foundations, and individuals, and supplemented by box office receipts from local audiences. The country-by-country emphasis worked, sometimes improbably, particularly given the rise of critiques of cultural imperialism with Edward Said's groundbreaking *Orientalism* in the 1970s, the midpoint of Graham's touring years.

Unexpected successes took place when the use of host country forms seemed to echo local traditions, which becomes logical in the context of discussions of modernism framed by contests between ideologies of universalism and nationalism in political structures. In 1955, local reports in communist-contested Indonesia declared that Graham's works "showed the influence of Eastern dances." In the desire to show a literal bond between "East and West," the genetic heritage of Graham's Japanese American set designer, Isamu Noguchi, became ripe for promotion.[31] Graham retold and modernized Greek myths in Greece, the narrative of the Catholic Joan of Arc in Poland and Western Europe, the biblical story of the Jewish Judith who beheaded an invading general in Israel, and the history of the glamorous and tragic Cleopatra in Egypt. In the end, it often worked: a reviewer concluded, "Martha Graham, through her art, is helping to bring people together."[32]

Along with established archetypes—from the abstraction of human emotion with the Woman in White, Red, and Yellow who signified three aspects of love, to figures from Greek mythology, to the Bible, and icons from the Middle East—Graham added new female characters from the American frontier. Reflecting the "frontier thesis" expressed by historian Frederick Jackson Turner just after Graham's birth, which argued that Americans were uniquely created and generationally recreated by the experience and power of their land, the Bride and Pioneering Woman joined Jocasta, Medea, Judith, and Cleopatra as timeless figures whose stories held human truths. Although Graham's Americana sometimes backfired or seemed heavy-handed, her pioneers also worked in improbable places. In 1954, the year before Graham arrived in the recently decolonized or decolonizing nations in Asia, USIS strategically promoted the British colonial heritage of the United States in order "to establish a basis of understanding." In 1955, *Appalachian Spring* brought a story of decolonization and political freedom to the former American colony of the Philippines and to British Singapore; onstage, the Bride and Husbandman explored the land frontier—after their ancestors had fought against colonization by the British—an approach that nations which had been subject to Western imperialism could seem to appreciate. The program for *Appalachian Spring* on that tour featured a photo of Graham as the Bride, clad in a layered frontier dress; the opposite page featured a line drawing of George Washington next to his cherry tree, looking westward. Not unexpectedly, in 1974, the embassy in the formerly American-colonized Philippines asked that the work not be performed.

At first blush, Graham's dance could immediately seem dated and ineffective as pro-democratic propaganda by the 1970s. Yet it often worked, even if in unexpected ways. Lebanese dancers heralded *Appalachian Spring* when it was performed in Jordan because America's story included reunification. Lebanon was struggling with civil war, and the pro-American Christian dancers sent to Amman courtesy of the American government found hope and uplift in Graham, her work, and the example brought by the United States. While the US government flew the Graham dancers in a military jet from Israel to Egypt, landing with great fanfare as the Americans again united the two countries with Camp David aplomb, the sets and costumes traveled in trucks across the desert; at the border, Israeli stagehands passed the frontier farmhouse, fence, and rocking chair by hand over the divide to Egyptian workers. Afterward, they sat together, drinking a Coke. Improbably, Americana was back in play in the Middle East.

A few years later, paired with the presidential cowboy motif, Graham took her company to East Berlin under Reagan with *Frontier*. While her African American soloist performed the tale of freedom wearing a long dress and pioneer's bib in front of a fence as a part of the 750th anniversary of Berlin in the east, Reagan called for the communists to "tear down this wall" in front of the Berlin Wall as a part of the celebration in the west. First Lady Nancy Reagan was featured in a West German photo op wearing a cowboy hat as she blew out the candles on a tiered birthday cake bearing the sugar fondant numbers "750th" to promote reunification, Western-style. Ironically, Graham's perpetuation of frontierism through the late 1980s lost her a tour as the Soviet Union crumbled, and under Bush, the United States pulled back from heavy-handed Americana to allow events to unfold. She was scheduled to tour in November 1989, but the Berlin Wall fell just before her planned departure.

Religious freedom as a part of this American frontier came to the forefront of cultural diplomacy under Eisenhower, yet Graham, wriggling out of any direct Christian references in her work, declared on a later tour, "I am not a missionary." The Wandering Preacher in *Appalachian Spring* and his Followers had proclaimed freedom of religion on the American frontier in the domino nations under Eisenhower and Nixon. The stories of Judith and Joan of Arc used biblical and religious tales to fight the Kremlin's "atheists" in Germany and Poland, and the pioneer became merely a metaphor under Kennedy. Yet on future tours with the revival of religious fervor under Jimmy Carter with the Camp David Accords–inspired Goodwill Tour, publicity for *Appalachian Spring* shifted and programs billed the dance as a story of "The Promised Land," giving a biblical and yet territorial cast to its description, with pioneers onstage gesturing over the land to be taken just past theaters in Jerusalem and Tel Aviv. After the defection of Soviet ballet star Rudolf Nureyev, Graham created two ballets for him, and while wooing the White House with a gala presentation of Americana in New York, Graham cast Mikhail Baryshnikov as the frontier Husbandman who was married to his Bride, famously played by Graham, by The Preacher, performed by Nureyev himself.

Yet, like religious freedom, American freedom was "a cruel mockery" for some US citizens, and the Soviet Union used the Cold War "Achilles heel" of race relations to denounce Western capitalism. Graham combatted charges of American racism through the diversity of her dancers and her own statements and actions, seeking to overcome her country's contradictions.

From the start of her career in the 1920s, as a matter of personal conviction, Graham was committed to racial and ethnic diversity in her casting. Upon leaving the Denishawn dance company in the 1920s, Graham hired Jewish dancers, who were subject to Aryan quotas, even in the United States in "free dance" casting. In the 1930s, she spoke out against the Nazi persecution of the Jewish people in a direct exchange with Hitler's propaganda minister. During World War II, she hired a Japanese dancer who had been released from an American internment camp. In 1951, Graham hired dancers Mary Hinkson and Matt Turney, both of African American descent.[33] She challenged American racism when she refused to tour the South not just because of African American segregation but because her Japanese dancer was also targeted by signage that demanded that each race go in a separate place. She asked, "Which way do I go?" These women populated Graham's frontier in *Appalachian Spring* and played the Woman in White with her Caucasian male partner, embodying the essence of pure love. After Graham's retirement, the starring roles in her Greek tragedies could be played by an Asian, Jewish, African American, or Mayflower American woman.

The Graham company's long record of diversity became a post–World War II propaganda tool. Her Jewish dancers performed in Germany and the new state of Israel; in the Cold War, Asian dancers hit Asia; African American dancers danced duets with Caucasian partners. In the Philippines, her Filipino dancer was spotlighted in interviews encouraged by USIS. Although choreographer George Balanchine was heralded in 1957 for his interracial partnering in *Agon*, Graham had been staging interracial duets for years. Performing for President Lyndon B. Johnson and his wife Lady Bird in the White House in 1969, Graham chose Hinkson and her own longtime stage partner, Bertram Ross, a white Jewish man, to portray the purity of love in *Diversion of Angels*. In 1974 on a tour of Asia, a Japanese star of the Graham company who played Clytemnestra was booked on popular television interview programs. Graham's company performed in East Berlin under the Ronald Reagan administration, where an African American woman portrayed the Pioneer in *Frontier*. Yet Graham became most useful not because she demonstrated integration while on tour or in politically charged moments, but rather because of the stand she had taken against racism writ large throughout her career. Graham's multiracial casting and the public appearances of Graham's dancers, as well as Graham's own words in speeches, writings, and radio shows, countered Soviet charges of American racism.

Graham used female characters and sexual power to fuel her work, and although this would be associated with a feminist sensibility, she denied this influence. She said, "I've tried to reveal—through women," and her handlers proclaimed in USIS-produced bulletins, "Woman's soul is on stage," during international tours. Yet Graham claimed that she was "baffled" by "liberationist" women, surely also referring to the suffragettes of her early adulthood, and the subsequent feminist movement, adding for effect, "I had no affiliation with it."[34]

As an apolitical woman in modern dance, Graham could translate the tenets of Western civilization with the American dance language, using powerful female characters to transmit political ideas through psychological revelations, which was what the government needed. In the 1950s, USIS reports questioned whether the use of "emotion in output" in informational publicity about America would lead to a gain in credibility for the United States; it was possible, the agency staffers maintained, that women could transmit political ideas through psychological revelations. Graham proved them right. Unlike the female figures of Soviet classical ballet, her choreographed characters were not fantastical or naïve. Graham's works showed human drama through the stories of women from Greek myth, religious history, and the American frontier, all of which allowed American modern dance to demonstrate the nation's ability to describe timeless emotions through the new high-art form, one that displaced Europe and Russia's staid body with the highly trained, riveting pelvis of the modern woman, adding a new archetype to the Western canon.

Graham demonstrated Western norms in the political arena and simultaneously attached her work to the modernist rubric; thus, the expressions of sexuality, both female and male, that infused her technique and works became acceptable and even celebrated on the international stage. On tours, Graham arrived in a city with the women in her company wearing pressed dresses and holding white gloves, but once onstage, they performed deep pelvic contractions and releases, which were the sexually based center of her technique. To educate the unschooled or provincial populations that might perceive base eroticism in such movements, publicity consistently championed her work as high art, and she performed lecture-demonstrations that were considered "the best propaganda to date" by some government officials. The psychological underpinnings of Graham's choreography portrayed the demons of man from a woman's perspective. Graham ultimately used sexually explicit physicality to depict the triumph of the human spirit despite the cruelty of human actions. For example, during *Errand into the Maze*, the scantily clad Minotaur jumps over her, split legged, as she writhes on the floor just before she vanquishes him; in *Night Journey*, as Jocasta she has mock sex with Oedipus, her son, on a modernist bed; in *Clytemnestra*, Graham, as the Mycenaean queen, has a drunken evening of sex with her young lover in a loincloth. With works that centered on female protagonists, Graham could use modernist psychology and sexuality to address the problems of humankind in a resonating, woman-centered voice.

Although Graham's female and male torsos writhed in contraction and release, and women were the center of the dramas, the men also drew attention. As would be seen in the United States in 1962 and again in 1979, it was the choice of costumes for the male body that attracted government ire, particularly in *Phaedra*. Although the women were split legged and contracting, they were generally clothed in dresses, many of which reached the floor. Thus, the nude male body drew shock and disapproval in the context of a female-centered art. While women grew increasingly exposed over time, with Jocasta's early Cold War evening-length costume contrasted with the later glittering nude unitard for Clytemnestra in the disco era's Egyptomania, the men always wore scant costumes from the opening early mythic pieces. Yet in works of Americana, men matched women and donned Puritan wear and even shoes to cover the bared foot.

In the final analysis, it was not merely Graham's modern dance or her protagonists that promoted the United States abroad; the charisma and detailed use of protocol Graham brought as a female diplomat made her an enduring genius of the international "soft power" stage—despite the fact that she claimed that she was not a feminist, and "the movement didn't touch me."[35] Again, I challenge the legend herself to unpack her particular power as a woman diplomat who represented American interests abroad until her death. I claim this book as a political, old-fashioned "Big Women's" Cold War biography. Graham died and the Soviet Union disintegrated within weeks of one another in 1991. As a testament to her power as a diplomat, and the American waning of interest in cultural diplomacy when the war was thought to have been won, the Graham company did not book another large-scale government-sponsored tour. The woman was indeed needed, center stage.

Graham was an elite political activist and global American diplomat in the context of recognized female power brokers, including Eleanor Roosevelt, Eleanor Dulles, and Clare Boothe Luce. Graham wielded political power with her connections to a series of prototypical first ladies occupying the East

Wing of the White House, including Jackie Kennedy, Betty Ford, and Barbara Bush. On government tours as early as 1962, Graham was advertised as "The First Lady of Modern Dance." She worked with female philanthropists, including Elizabeth Sprague Coolidge, Bethsabée de Rothschild, and Lila Atkinson Wallace, and such underrecognized political women and philanthropists as Virginia Inness-Brown.[36] The study of women in the diplomatic field is expanding, and Graham demonstrates that cultural figures must be included.

Graham was one of the few female artists of her generation to be chosen as a significant player in the Cold War, thus putting her among the ranks of female diplomats of the era. The literature of the period's cultural diplomacy has focused on male protagonists from Jackson Pollock and Dizzy Gillespie to the "Miracle" Olympic hockey team of 1980 and Nobel Prize–winning author William Faulkner. Studies on Cold War dance usually center on the defection of male ballet stars or the work of George Balanchine and José Limón. But as a woman, Graham held a particular type of power. Before the term "soft power" was invented, Graham embodied its seductive elements with her dances. She espoused the complexities of an Americanized and modernized diplomatic agenda in speeches, on radio broadcasts and television, and at cocktail parties, saying that the purpose of her performances was the "interchange of ideas" while she promoted the timeless power of the American Western frontier and the United States itself.[37]

Because of the intricate public and private mechanisms at work to create and export cultural products during the Cold War, both domestically and internationally, connections among women became paramount, even as they led to men. The story of Martha Graham displays the intricacies of State Department projects on the ground: she could not be firmly identified as an agent of the state because of her varied alliances. Funding for the Graham tours exhibits the commingling of public and private sectors in elite projects for international purposes. The covert and overt links of agencies, public and private, and the individuals who inhabit them both show that the close identification of "who is doing what to whom" is vital in the history of cultural diplomacy.

To build and perform works that appeared in the international market, Graham formed bonds with powerful women from the start of her career. After First Lady Eleanor Roosevelt saw Graham's work at the Neighborhood Playhouse, founded by Alice and Irene Lewisohn, she invited Graham to perform *Frontier* at the White House in 1937. Elizabeth Sprague Coolidge commissioned *Appalachian Spring*, which premiered at the Library of Congress in 1944. Bethsabée de Rothschild underwrote Graham's first European tours in the 1950s, traveled with the company, and later supported Graham in Israel with a platform to teach her technique and perform the repertory. In 1955, Virginia Inness-Brown, a wealthy and independent woman, oversaw the committee that exported dance for the State Department; she continued to support Graham in the 1960s. In 1957, Eleanor Dulles brought Graham to Berlin. Lila Acheson Wallace of *Reader's Digest*, an undercovered publication vital to information dissemination in Cold War politics, bought Graham a building for her school and almost certainly brokered the Sackler Foundation's commission of the dance *Frescoes* for the opening of the Temple of Dendur at the Metropolitan Museum of Art in 1978. During the Kennedy administration, Jacqueline Kennedy Onassis became a strong advocate for Graham. After the 1962 tour, for decades she hosted galas, lent her name to events, and later became Graham's editor for the posthumously published autobiography at Doubleday.[38] Criss-crossing over time, forward-looking female political leaders and philanthropists created and maintained Graham's potent sustainability as an export. Graham, bringing her benefactors the soft power of cultural products in a female package, worked as an indomitable force with her cadre of powerful women, who introduced her to their men.

* * *

Each chapter of *Martha Graham's Cold War: The Dance of American Diplomacy* follows the chronology and geography of her tours, while foregrounding a specific aspect of the book's argument. The chapters progress according to her schedule because the geography of Graham's tours as a representational American product for export challenges the traditional bipolar view of Cold War cultural diplomacy as a pure fight against the Soviets—a challenge that engages historians.[39] The anti-Soviet enterprise and the ideology of freedom have been presented as the grand narratives framing the Cold War, but country-by-country analysis of Graham's decades-spanning efforts argues against such readings.

The chapters are driven by the archives and their silences, that is, the archival gaps. Although Martha Graham toured, or planned a tour, for the State Department under every president, Republican or Democrat, from Eisenhower to George H. W. Bush, she declared herself apolitical. Although called the "Picasso of Modern Dance" and even "Forever Modern" in government publicity, surely approved by her, she claimed that her work was not modern; it was contemporary. Bringing modernized religious works to the globe during the Cold War against the Soviet atheists, she declared, "I am not a missionary." Then, although hers was one of the few female-led companies to tour the globe, certainly due to her skills as an ambassador as well as a performer and company manager, and the founder of an increasingly hegemonic dance technique globally that was based on the actions of the female pelvis, she declared she was not a feminist. Indeed, what she said she was not provides the map to find what she was, and how she waged an international Cold War with modernism in the name of freedom. The final Bush tour was not included in the original book manuscript because it did not take place; I found it by accident on the internet and pursued it with the gracious help of the Bush Library archivists and Linda Hodes, who scouted the Soviet bloc countries and Russia for Graham in 1988.

Chapter 1 explores the history of modern dance and how it became a useful Cold War export as a "victor's history," which displaced the early German dominance and proclaimed its American origins at a time when a USIS report declared that "the US should replace European countries as a model civilization."[40] The chapter traces the political roots of modern dance from Isadora Duncan in Moscow through the lasting impact of free dance innovators Mary Wigman and Michio Ito in the United States, despite the historical postwar silencing of the German and Japanese artists with their connection to totalitarian and fascist states. As a *Mayflower* descendant, Graham was integral to the promotion of the United States as the "land of the free." The tenets of abstraction, which had been infused into the dance form during the interwar period and included an ideal of expressing a human universal, were promoted as a language born in America of an American icon, Martha Graham. USIS literature avowed that exported cultural products should rewrite the tenets of what they called "Western Civilization" in American terms for the international market, and Martha Graham hit the mark.

Chapter 2 explores Graham's first tour after its initial leg in Japan from the "mega-domino" of the domino nations through decolonized and decolonizing nations that also sought the much-feared status of political nonalignment in Bandung, Indonesia. Landing after the Bandung Conference, in 1955 and 1956 Graham established her political power both with the resounding success of her performances and with her work as an ambassador as Eisenhower's National Security Agency oversaw her deployment. Although the choreography met with resistance in some newly decolonizing nations, especially in India, where dancers were exploring various freed modern dance forms as a voice of political independence, overall the tour offered Graham credibility in the field, which would resonate through the end of the Cold War. Graham triumphed as an ambassador on the "cocktail circuit of diplomacy" as she and her company mingled at embassy events. The United States was placed on the cultural stage with the aid of Martha Graham, her dance, and her persona.

Chapter 3 analyzes Graham's solo 1957 performance in West Germany at the opening of Eleanor Dulles's Congress Hall, which demonstrates the potency of Graham's direct connections to the government and the private sector. She used connections to Dulles; to Inness-Brown, who served both on the American government American National Theater and Academy (ANTA) committee that made deployment decisions, the private German-American Benjamin Franklin board funded the project, and its Convocations Committee that chose the artists who performed at the opening; and Clare Boothe Luce, whose husband would report on Graham's work in *Life* magazine. Graham would again cross paths with the actress Lillian Gish, who had also studied at Denishawn during the interwar years, and with Mary Wigman, the German dance pioneer. Both the 1955 and 1957 tours demonstrate the way in which notable public- and private-sector women supported the Graham tours. Through the deployment, Graham became connected to the Congress for Cultural Freedom, which circled back with funding by the CIA for cultural events, such as those in Berlin, that featured Graham. Although Graham received poor reviews in Berlin as pushback against American claims of sovereignty over the modern dance, which further backfired in the face of Mary Wigman's regeneration and the ovations for her *Rite of Spring* performed days later with Graham in the audience, the two tours solidified Graham's political reach and impact, and ultimately began to seal her political legacy.

In 1962, the rumblings of resistance to the Graham project became manifest while she remained potent as a figure of American cultural power, which is the subject of chapter 4. The failure and successes of that year's tour were neither straightforward, consistent, nor entire. Problems in Germany should have been anticipated given the reception in Berlin in 1957, yet lessons were not learned. While scholars have conflated success in Poland and Yugoslavia, the dancers and reviews show otherwise. In Poland, despite Graham's repertory that emphasized religious works to ally with the repressed Catholic population and fight Soviet domination, dancers were followed and tightly monitored; reviews were decimating. But poor reception was offset by successes in Yugoslavia, where Kennan had sponsored an exhibit of modern American art proposed by his cultural attaché, Francis Mason, who later became the chair of Graham's company board. The art exhibit had drawn unprecedented crowds, paving the way for Graham to tour with her modernist dance. In Greece, audiences adored the Greek dramas and the retelling of their myths, despite deep trepidation among dancers that they were interpreting Greek myths for the Greeks. Graham's age and "exhaustion," a code word for her alcohol-induced unreliability, began to seep into government reports, yet her ability to rejuvenate herself and charm diplomats remained front and center. Engaging with the politics of neutrality, in which propaganda could not attack but rather had to promote, Graham's American modern dance was revered by critics in Finland. *Appalachian Spring* and overt Americana were left at home. With "free" dance having been fueled during the interwar by the Germans in the United States, in Finland, as it had been in Israel, Graham's sophisticated American modern technique in the Cold War held enduring twentieth-century messages about totalitarian leaders and the outcome of such alliances. In arcs of decline and rise, with the steep declines offset by recoveries, the 1962 venture nonetheless marked the end of Graham's large international tours as a performer.

Chapter 5 explores the decline and rise of Graham attributable to a combination of the decline of modernism in dance, her age as a performer, her growing instability related to alcohol, and the increasing desire of the US government to target youth with its export projects. Fighting to remain relevant with works that had stressed sexuality under the rubric of advanced modernism on the 1962 tour, Graham met government backlash after having suffered some European disdain for a seemingly old-fashioned approach. Using backlash to her advantage, Graham played the press in the name of freedom. Yet Graham, like her modernism, was clearly aging, and funding was growing thin. Although her company was invited to perform at the White House under Johnson, and she secured some funding in Portugal, Graham declined on the political and international scene. Despite successes in Israel and the United States, critical support for her performances noted her failing body, private support waned, and public support was curtailed. After Graham's retirement from the stage in 1969, with the help of numerous men (including Bertram Ross, Ben Garber, Francis Mason, and Ron Protas), she reappeared on the government's radar screen. Without Graham, cultural diplomacy had moved forward. The chapter chronicles Graham's improbable and spectacular recovery as she battled her addiction to alcohol and triumphed, albeit with the possibility of prescribed drugs, particularly given the history of her arthritis pain. Using her past political traction, Graham tapped into the international rumblings that concerned the White House. Graham and her team planned the second Asian tour, two years after Richard Nixon visited China. With an eye on the Soviets, she began to work with its balletic defectors to free their bodies with her American modern choreography. Performing as the matriarch, if not the protagonist on the proscenium, Graham took center stage as she presided over a spectacularly new young and highly trained company.

The tours from 1974 through 1987, explored in chapters 6 through 9, highlight Graham as an ambassador and not as a performer, at a time when she became framed as an icon. In chapter 6, I examine how the 1974 tour, planned under Nixon and executed under Ford, with Secretary of State Henry Kissinger as the guiding force, demonstrates the power of embedded government bureaucracy: while memos back to the State Department made the tour seem as though it was a resounding success, private musings by a State Department official show otherwise. Graham was a seamless cultural diplomat for Kissinger, who had political aspirations in Asia that transcended Nixon and carried into the Ford administration. Meanwhile, Graham's own objectives overlapped with those of First Lady Betty Ford.

Chapter 7 demonstrates how the two political women needed and used each other in a heady time during which audiences and the public relished the male Soviet ballet stars who had defected to the United States. Graham and Betty Ford used "domestic cultural diplomacy" to fight communism.[41] While domestic and international support were theoretically separate, the categories bled into each other as the National Endowment for the Arts increasingly supported artistic endeavors that could be sent abroad. The Soviet defectors worked with Graham and Ford to promote modernism as a representation of American freedom, however aged. Engaging the history of New York and the glitz of galas, discos, and designers, this chapter demonstrates how domestic cultural moves were ultimately inspired by international battles.

In 1978, with strong publicity created by the Ford connection buoying Graham, the Sackler Foundation commissioned a new work that was particularly well-suited for the needs of the Carter administration in the Middle East, the subject of chapter 8. Drawing on a disco-bejeweled Egyptomania that gripped the public imagination, Graham choreographed *Frescoes*, the story of Cleopatra, for the opening of the Sackler Wing at the Metropolitan

Museum of Art that held the newly installed Temple of Dendur, brought to the United States under the guidance of Kennedy Onassis. With the help of Lila Acheson Wallace, American and Egyptian cultural representatives discussed a tour at the opening. In 1979, the improbable and American orientalist choreography became celebrated in Middle Eastern host countries that were targeted by the Carter administration: Israel, Egypt, and Jordan.

Chapter 9 examines 1987, a year that brought Graham's relationship with the executive branch full circle as both she and President Reagan used old-fashioned frontier tropes to fight communism. Although modern dance had become codified, iconic, and old by this point in the late twentieth century, Graham retained her diplomatic utility when she expressed the aims and ideals of freedom and favored the destruction of barriers and walls between peoples. Although, in East Berlin, communist reviewers ignored her *Frontier* and claimed that the mythic works demonstrated the angst caused by capitalism, Graham had done her job. She had joined with Reagan to promote the American ideal of freedom during the 750th anniversary of the divided city. Her dancer performed in front of a fence, as did Reagan in front of a wall. Graham concluded her autobiography remembering that the German modernist and Nazi collaborator Mary Wigman had understood the frontier as a series of barriers, not as an expression of the power of the individual.

After this tour, in the book's Coda, Graham returned to the White House under President George H. W. Bush. Barbara Bush arranged for a performance of *Frontier* at the White House, and Graham's advance people scouted Soviet bloc countries, Moscow, and St. Petersburg for a November 1989 tour. Barbara Bush served as chair for Graham's "premiere" of *American Document*, although the work initially premiered in 1938. During the Cold War version, Graham's lead male was the Soviet defector looking for artistic freedom, Baryshnikov. While he performed the American modern dance, he spoke lines from American documents that espoused freedom. The script included Abraham Lincoln, a favorite Cold War trope to promote the United States; Walt Whitman; and numerous others. Although in the 1930s the work had been heralded by the leftist press for its critique of the United States, in the 1980s Graham "premiered" the work as a celebration of the nation with Soviet defectors speaking for her. In a letter to the White House, Graham wrote that she would take the former Soviet ballet star back to the Soviet Union in a film shown as a part of her performances. Barbara Bush liked Graham and her work, but the president was not as enthusiastic. While no evidence has yet been found regarding the cancellation, November's tour did not take place. Heavy-handed Americana did not go hand in hand with the Bush White House strategies. Yet Graham herself reflected on the promise of American freedoms in the context of Berlin and perhaps communism as a triumph for open frontiers of the mind and the destruction of walls that barred communication and exchange among peoples. Kennan, the father of containment who staunchly supported cultural exchange as a tool of psychological warfare, was redeemed as the youth dismantled bricks and streamed over the wall. With the end of the Cold War, cultural exchange had done its work. The totalitarian nationalist walls—physical, political, and cultural— that both Kennan and Graham abhorred seemed to have crumbled.

The paradox of an individualistic American artistic construction promoted as a universally applicable approach consistently plagued Graham with critical international audiences, however modern, or however eager some were to join the movement. Graham passed away in 1991 with the official end of the Cold War, and its government agencies for exchange were reconfigured over time and tucked into departments: it seemed that the war had been won. With walls down, the immeasurable power of cultural diplomacy was exactly that, but only in wartime for Americans, and thus put to rest. Yet keeping herself ever-contemporary and never "past-tense" modern, always center stage, Graham vaulted herself into twenty-first-century politics with the failed attempts of the final tour. When her scout left Moscow in 1988, she shared a plane home with a golf course designer who worked for Donald Trump; as the only Americans, they spoke about their work as they waited to board the plane home with hopes for the future. The American president elected in 2016 had tried to do real estate deals while Graham planned her cultural tour, both promoting the power of Americana in architecture and dance. Remaining ever-contemporary, withering Graham-style diplomacy has been made relevant again—even just as a study—as Mr. Trump seemingly twists Cold War elements to make America "great again" who tweeted nuclear threats, while improbably sidling up to a John le Carré leader of Russia and his cohort. Despite Graham's disavowals—propagandist, modernist, missionary, feminist—she never denied the power of the United States and its ideals of freedom, truth, and democracy, however flawed in practice. She worked for the performance of these politics, the taking down of physical "barriers" as walls of the mind, and then "the opening of doors that have not been opened before," as she understood it in Turner's terms, in the geography of the American land, the inclusion of people from other nations, and in the spirit.[42]

1

How Martha Graham Became a Cultural Ambassador

Modernist on the Frontier

> I had the idea of a frontier in my mind as a frontier of exploration.
> —Martha Graham

Writing about cultural diplomacy the year before Martha Graham left on her maiden tour, the United States Information Agency (USIS) concluded, "Events should be planned and 'planted' to implement propaganda themes."[1] Graham obliged, and during the tarmac press conference in Manila in 1955, she declared that "through new art forms," *Appalachian Spring* and her repertory captured "the mood, the life, and the dream of America."[2] Indeed, in a propaganda show, the American ambassador celebrated the universality of freedom and national sovereignty in the United States' own former protectorate, the Philippines.[3] In painting, music, literature, and film, the idea of "the modern" became an essential part of Cold War politics and diplomacy to promote American ideology with soft-power implants. Graham stepped forward with her modern dance. Unpacking the telling of modern dance history and Graham's position as the "Picasso" and "First Lady of Modern Dance" reveals how Graham's tours became useful to the United States government and its officials.

After World War II, the origins of modern dance had been rewritten by American critics and artists as a victor's history. This revisionist framework enabled Graham to become a potent Cold War propagandist. Although a formal definition of "modern dance" printed in interwar books in the United States began with critical references to the pre–World War I Germans, with dancers seeking to create a distinctive medium informed by modernist tenets and German culture through a concept of the "free dance," post–World War

Martha Graham's Cold War. Victoria Phillips, Oxford University Press 2020. © Oxford University Press.
DOI: 10.1093/oso/9780190610364.001.0001

II scholars asserted that modernism could have emerged only from the "land of the free," the United States.[4] Despite the fact that Graham had watched, studied, and worked with the Germans and the Japanese during the interwar period, American critics downplayed those nations' contributions in the wake of the Allies' wartime victory. Certain tenets of modernism that had been built into the discipline of dance in the early twentieth-century prewar period—particularly freedom and universalism found through an exploration of the human psyche—became particularly important in the Cold War "psychwar" campaigns to win "hearts and minds" to the side of the United States with a Westernized notion of "universal freedom."

* * *

Until the end of the twentieth century, the formal modern dance canon often began with the American-born Isadora Duncan and her work with bared feet, the freed solar plexus, and writings such as "I See America Dancing."[5] Yet before the start of the twentieth century and during the interwar period, modernism's seeds included artists in Europe, Asia, and Russia, as well as the Americas—a global movement.[6] Indeed, the early artists from the United States, Loïe Fuller and Isadora Duncan, both of whom are celebrated as "firsts" in modern dance, left the country to find recognition in Europe and Russia. Logically, the aesthetic appreciation of experimentation in dance lay across the ocean. For the purposes of this book and some nod to brevity, I forgo a discussion of the historiography of dance scholarship to concentrate on the significant figures who were rewritten, or written out, as a part of the description of Graham and her dance by critics, scholars, government agencies, and Graham herself.

Germany and Japan, having both seeded a freed dance but then fought against the victorious Allied Powers in World War II, were written out of the Western historical narrative with which Graham engaged. Yet she landed in both nations during her maiden and immediately subsequent postwar international engagements. The German Mary Wigman, often referenced in Graham publicity and reviews, came from a larger early twentieth-century movement of dancers, critics, choreographers, and theoreticians, including her mentor, Rudolf von Laban.[7] The Japanese also made a significant prewar contribution to modern dance by way of dancers like Michio Ito, who had trained in Germany and then deeply influenced Graham. Ito had been a participant in Hellerau, a creative planned community, including a theater, founded in 1909 near Dresden, Germany. Architects joined with artists, and their festivals were attended by the progressive elite.[8] Wigman was a key part of the enterprise and an influence on Ito. Indeed, before World War I, he had begun to think about a "theatre for the future" in Germany and brought this idea to New York, where he worked with Graham and the American moderns. Relying on the ideas of Ted Shawn of Denishawn and Ito, they would create the Dance Repertory Theatre.

In Munich in 1913, a breakthrough took place when Wigman performed her iconic work *Hexentanz*, or *Witch Dance*. Using a mask that defined the face with deep lines, she sat on the floor in silence. Legs together, she presented her hands to the audience, fingers spread wide. Cymbal-like sounds crashed. Reaching up first with one arm, her fingers like a claw, she extended the other arm high, then in alternation: one-two, one-two. Later, she took her arms and pried her legs apart, only to cross herself with one arm, then the other. She pounded the floor with her feet and turned herself in circles. To see a woman's body in such jagged, provocative motion onstage was as radical as beholding a cubist portrait or a futurist poem of fragments. "Absolutely revolutionary," declared critics.[9] Wigman became immersed in the written work of German philosopher Friedrich Nietzsche and in 1917 performed "musical interludes" to Nietzsche's composition at the opening of a "DaDa Evening" at the Galerie Corie.[10] She and others studied Picasso and abstraction. After World War I ended, Wigman's student Harald Kreutzberg, among others, traveled to the United States, performing solos and other works with his partner. The German-influenced Ito came to New York, used Japanese forms to codify a new technique, trained American dancers, and choreographed full productions.[11] Although during the interwar period Graham choreographed works that experimented with elements used in *Witch Dance*, read Nietzsche—choreographing works in his name as did Wigman—and worked directly with Ito, Graham's modernism was declared distinctly American for the international Cold War market. Indeed, Graham herself had begun this move during the interwar years with her own declarations in which she refuted foreign influences to find her own dance exceptionalism. Yet as she developed, she borrowed from others, which, paradoxically, she would not deny, declaring, "I am a thief." But she added, "I only steal from the best." Ever the innovator, she then transformed stolen artistry into her own works, declaring it hers alone and distinctly American.[12]

According to numerous critics, American modern dance began with Isadora Duncan and her "prophetic love of America" with its "mighty songs" from the "Pacific over the plains," "the swing or curves of the Rocky Mountains," "the vibration of the American soul striving upward through labor to harmonious life." However, during the Cold War, critics overlooked Duncan's connection to the Soviet Union and belief in communist ideology. The history of modernist moves in Soviet dance began before the October Revolution and Duncan. Yet after taking power in 1917, Vladimir Lenin aspired to create a state-sponsored dance culture for the people. Ironically, the postrevolutionary Soviet state understood the "mother of modern dance" to be an American: Duncan. In their view, she was a humanist cultural messenger, misunderstood by Americans themselves, whose art form could be adopted for political purposes. Duncan's dance became a symbol of emancipation.[13] The tenets of her free, expressive style critiqued and condemned the old czarist European ballet. Lenin himself applauded Duncan when she performed in Moscow's Bolshoi Theatre to celebrate the fourth anniversary of the October Revolution.[14] After she returned to the United States, the Soviets sent her a telegram: "The Russian government can alone understand you. Come to us; we will make you a school."[15] She enthusiastically took the offer. In Boston, after Duncan brandished a red scarf in support of the Bolsheviks, she was banned from the city.[16]

In 1925, the Soviet government closed down all dance schools except Duncan's and the Bolshoi and opened the State Academy of Art Science, which focused on techniques to perform "propaganda through dance," demanding the use of "artistic movement to campaign for revolutionary ideas."[17] So important was Duncan deemed to the early Soviet project that newspapers were not permitted to publish anything but enthusiastic notices of her performances. Yet when Lenin died, so did the support for the dance revolutionary.[18] Duncan, well past her prime, returned to the West and passed away in a dramatic flash in France in 1927, the same year that modern dance became firmly recognized as a movement by New York arbiters of taste.[19]

Just weeks after her death, the New York Herald Tribune published Duncan's last article, "I See America Dancing," surely written as an attempt to ingratiate herself to enable a return to her home country. In it, she bid dancers to look to the American West in order "to dance the language of our pioneers, the fortitude of our heroes."[20] Duncan's grandmother bore her mother in a covered wagon allegedly during a "smoking gun" battle with "the Redskins." Her dance came not from the Greeks or Europe, although she admitted influence, but rather from "the solar plexus, the temporal home of the soul, upward to the Star Spangled Banner of the great sky." Ironically writing from France, Americans, she penned, must not engage with the "minuet" or "ballet," but "rather let them come forth with great strides, leaps and bounds, with lifted forehead and far-spread arms, to dance the language of our pioneers, the fortitude of our heroes." The Communist legacy was easily overwritten for critics and historians who remembered her as the "Mother of Modern Dance," not an artist declaring "I am Red," but rather an American who embraced the pioneer spirit and its archetypal heroes and heroines who danced to the sounds of Walt Whitman.

In the late 1920s, Graham was well aware of Duncan's travels and international developments, but she had not yet achieved her own "modern" voice in movement and writing. Before coming to New York to break out on her own, Graham had studied in California and toured the United States with Ruth St. Denis and Ted Shawn's Denishawn company. From the study of yoga to the commingling of Japanese Noh, Indian headpieces and saris, mock-Egyptian draped robes, and even ballet, Graham had been infused with the theatricality of the "other" in her study of new dance forms. Her mentors had drawn on the Egyptomania sweeping the nation in the 1920s to formulate dances that used a melange of Asian and Middle Eastern forms and costumes. While she worshipped Ruth St. Denis, Ted Shawn embraced her as a dancer and cast her in solos. He taught ballet as well as what was titled "Greek forms," but specialized in works based on the American frontier that famously displayed Native American headpieces. Graham gained theatrical notoriety as his partner in *Xochitl*, a picture of which would appear in USIS publicity in the 1970s.

At the Denishawn school, Graham learned the "Individuality System," in which it was believed that "each pupil has some one thing which is unique." Graham was transfixed by the idea that "whatever medium of expression is chosen, this is that pupil's message to the world."[21] It was a message she would adopt and theatricalize for the world stage. While touring with Denishawn, Graham saw a Kandinsky painting, saying upon seeing his work for the first time—in a story that became lore—"Someday I will make a dance like that."[22] Even though Kandinsky did not hang in the museum where she recalled seeing the work, Graham became intellectually driven by modernism, which led to *Lamentation* and eventually a work after Kandinsky, *Diversion of Angels*, a signature work on tours.[23] Louis Horst, composer and musician at Denishawn, as well as Graham's mentor and lover, encouraged her to go to New York to find her voice. Yet Denishawn would loom large.

The Denishawn company's tour to "the Orient" from 1925 through 1926 must have been professionally devastating for Graham, who was left behind, particularly since her sister was taken on tour along with Doris Humphrey, who would become a Cold War arbiter of taste and training for the modern dance. As the company prepared the repertory to travel, Graham learned that another dancer would play the lead that Shawn had created for her in *Xochitl*.[24] The tour publicity began by boasting that twenty thousand people gathered in the United States at the port to celebrate the departure of Denishawn by ship. If Graham was not standing in the throngs, surely she saw the publicity photo at home. As the company toured Asia, performing in most of the regions that Graham would tour thirty years later, it celebrated its success with a continuing series of glossy bulletins "from the flowery peninsulas and the spice islands," sent back to supporters in the United States.[25] Graham would have seen all, as well as letters from her sister from the tour sent to their mother.[26]

The Denishawn tour set the narrative for Graham's own later tours of Asia, in 1955 and 1974, with Humphrey offering advice on the earlier tour. In a striking parallel, in September 1925, Denishawn opened at the Imperial Theatre in Japan, where Graham would open with her company exactly three decades later. Graham's sister, who worked with Graham as an administrator in later years, and Humphrey performed with the company in Japan, the Philippines, Singapore, the Federated Malay States, and India— all places where Graham would tour—but Denishawn also went to China, whereas due to the political Cold War climate, Graham would only venture to Hong Kong. Press reports from Japan in 1925 were precursors of reports from Graham's own tour thirty years later with publicity sent home such as, "The dancers convinced Japanese that America is now creating its own art."[27] The publicity shot that Denishawn sent home from the Taj Mahal— St. Denis and Shawn dressed as oriental actors in front of the monument— parallels the photograph taken of Graham and her dancers in the same spot, yet all in "New Look" Western dress, down to the gloves.[28] Although the source of the funding for the Denishawn tour remains unknown, the company and its members were received by diplomats and local hosts, as was Graham. Akin to the meticulous reports that USIS would later compile on Graham, exacting reports followed Denishawn performances: the Nizam of Hyderabad attended every night of the Denishawn season in his kingdom. The Denishawn company met with local dancers and watched their technique, toured ancient sites, and shopped, as would the Graham dancers.[29]

In the repertory offerings, Denishawn made use of the cultural convergences to show mutual understanding that would come to dominate Graham's publicity and tours during the Cold War. In India, Denishawn's Miss Ruth performed "Dance of the Black and Gold Sari." A dancer wrote in her diary, "[The Indian dancer] puts on [jewels] of black and gold and wraps herself in a sari" and performs the "lovely turns and quick jumps which Miss Ruth does."[30] While this direct cultural appropriation may appear unseemly in the twenty-first century, it was reported that an Indian woman in the audience remarked, "Why she [Miss Ruth] puts on her sari far better than I can." Another critic commented on the performance of the American translation of an Indian dance in India: "While being an accurate presentation of the real thing, it is at the same time more colorful, more beautiful and infinitely more pleasing to the eye."[31] As Graham would be in later decades, these dancers were celebrated for their understanding of the host nation exactly *because* of the appropriation. Shawn did a Japanese spear dance in Japan and visited the Shiva Temple in the costume of Nataraja, the Lord of the Dance, and dressed as the god, implanted himself into the shrine for the photograph. St. Denis performed as Quan Yin, the Chinese goddess of mercy, in China.[32] Works "inspired by the art forms of ancient Egypt" traveled to Egypt.[33] Furthermore, as Graham would reiterate decades later, papers reported of Denishawn, "They have danced through the barriers of language."[34]

As would be the case on the Graham tours, the Denishawn programming used orientalism, while it also celebrated what would come to be called Americana. Shawn's "American Sketches" included "Invocation to the Thunderbird," "Boston Fancy 1854," "Around the Hall in Texas," and even "The Gringo Tango," alongside the heralded *Xochitl*.[35] While these works were representational and not abstracted as were Graham's, she would follow her mentors with repertory that melded Asian forms for Asia, European for Europe, and Middle Eastern and biblical for the Middle East and Israel, and then join these figures with those found on the American frontier in an evening of dance performances. Headlines sent home lauded the Denishawn troupe as "America's Unofficial Ambassadors."[36] Graham would make that cultural exchange official.

* * *

In 1927, because of the growing recognition in the United States of what would come to be called the modern dance, the leading New York newspapers hired dance critics to provide analysis of the new art for the burgeoning audiences; they studied Graham along with her international forerunners.[37] John Martin of the *New York Times* led the establishment of a modern dance canon with his performance reviews, lectures, and books, and significant writers joined him at other publications. In Martin's early articles, he wrote about the "freedom" of the new "non-ballet type of dancing" *brought to America* by the Germans. In "Over America the Dance Wave Sweeps," Martin showed two almost identical pictures, one of an American and the other of a German, illustrating the "New German Influence in American Dancing."[38] He credited the rise in the new American movement to the German "national background of musical genius and . . . penchant for philosophical thinking," which "furnished a fertile soil for the germination of a new art." According to Martin, modern dance promised a return to the "heart and soul of human intercourse," as well as "religion, philosophy, [and] ethics," and thus showed promise for artists in all nations to find a universal kinesthetic expression.[39] Yet the moment had not yet arrived. Although some performances in New York by Americans demonstrated "the modern spirit," the critic asserted that the new dance was "more fully stabilized" and "highly perfected" in Germany.[40]

Graham was surely irked by the attention the *New York Times* gave to the Germans, particularly since she remained critically tainted by her early "orientalist" training in California and her use of drapery rather than innovation. She observed Mary Wigman's student Harald Kreutzberg when he came to the United States to perform as he rehearsed in her own studio while Louis Horst worked with him. Of German descent himself, Horst could speak to Kreutzberg in their native tongue and likely discussed the philosophy behind the new German dance. Graham followed their intellectual study of Nietzsche, even making dances parallel to Wigman's in which she celebrated the scholar.[41] As the Germans had looked to Picasso, so Graham reviewed abstraction and recalled Kandinsky. In 1928, perhaps referring to Graham and Horst, Martin noted that American dancers had studied the Germans "through diligent book study at home," but that the new dance "insurgency" in the United States was still "more in the nature of a distinct rumble than of a present storm."[42] Although Martin wrote that in a 1928 concert Graham bade "farewell" to her Denishawn style, he noted that she had gone over "wholeheartedly to the new German technique."[43] He wrote about Nietzsche's inspiration for the dance, linking the philosophical roots of Mary Wigman to Graham's study. Contrasting the two women, he described Graham as "a veritable chameleon in changing her style and method."[44] He unfavorably compared Graham with Kreutzberg, highlighting the repeated "bravos" and "encores" for Kreutzberg before noting, "When [Graham] misses, she misses completely."[45]

Looking for inspiration and performing opportunities, Graham performed in Ito's productions in the late 1920s and shared concert programs with him in New York at the McDowell Center, the Neighborhood Playhouse, and various theaters on Broadway. Ito introduced Graham to other modernist artists, including Isamu Noguchi, who was then struggling as a sculptor. Noguchi crafted a bust of Graham, which brought him recognition in a gallery showing.[46] The two would form an enduring partnership, beginning in 1935 with Noguchi's construction of the stage set for Graham's seminal work *Frontier*.

By 1929, Wigman had become a defining part of "the modern dance" in New York through her students. John Martin described Ito and the German practitioners as "the progressive modern dancers" who "dedicated themselves to the attainment of the abstract."[47] Graham continued to make some "crowd pleasing" works in which she posed in oriental-style draperies, and she named her pieces after Asian artistic techniques such as *Study in Lacquer*. Yet in 1929, she also choreographed *Heretic*, which used a heavier and starker approach to movement and subject matter, exploring the woman as rebel. Departing from drapes and headpieces, Graham's stark angled figures were hugged by jersey.[48] In December, Martin began to concede. Although he opened "The Dance: Modernism," writing that the German dance "brings to the fore once more questions of the 'absolute' dance, modernism, abstractness," and cited their "advanced method," he continued, "The question of modernism, however, is a much larger one than the performance of any single individual," thus "making a shibboleth of modernism." He proceeded to make a bow to Graham, reporting that with some of her new work, "The close relationship between her esthetic and that of contemporary painting has frequently been noted."[49] Graham was searching, learning, and assembling the pieces of her own modern dance, struggling to find her voice, and critics took note.

Still, Graham could not shake the Germans. Kreutzberg's partner described Graham's work in a letter: "There is a dancer who looked so much like Wigman, that she might be her twin." While Graham was making inroads into the discovery of a new form of abstract dance, nonrepresentational like the painters, that also embodied an American individualist approach, she also fell back into a reliance on the orientalist theatricality she had practiced as a young woman. Martin continued to sporadically conclude that the American modern dance was inferior to its German counterpart.[50] The absolute revolt had not yet taken place.

* * *

The first American example of "modern forms of the art" occurred at the opening of the Dance Repertory Theatre in 1930, gushed John Martin.[51] The series of collaborative performances included programs by Martha Graham and others in the field, including Doris Humphrey, under the organizational leadership of Graham's Louis Horst.[52] The theory behind the season, which included only American performers, was to ferment a new theater of the dance that had been imagined by Michio Ito and Graham's early teacher and partner, Ted Shawn. Inspired by the German model, Ito brought plans for a dance theater to New York in the 1920s, which Martin had praised in the *Times*.[53] Ted Shawn published a call for a dance theater, a place to explore the American voice.[54] In 1930, reflecting the convergence of those who had influenced Graham from the abstract artists to the Germans, Ito, Shawn, Horst, and Martin, a *Times* review put Graham at the forefront of the emerging American choreographers, with the premiere of *Lamentation* under the umbrella of the Dance Repertory Theatre. *Lamentation* demonstrated what modern dance historians have come to see as the tenets of abstraction at work. Using the physicality of breath, contraction, and release, Graham writhed and stretched in a jersey cloth in a solo that eliminated the who, why, where, and when of a narrative. Her solo spoke only to the what: grief. Graham described *Lamentation*'s expression of grief as a "universal" emotion.[55] At the conclusion of the Dance Repertory Theatre's first season, Martin extolled its success despite earlier reservations, noting that with Graham's new work, "the American dance has come of age."[56]

Like other dancers who came before her, Graham took pen to page and published her writings. The 1930 publication of Oliver Sayler's *Revolt in the Arts*, which included a chapter by Graham, politicized the arts and demanded a new approach—whether in film, theater, photography, the graphic arts, literature, or dance. The volume's dance contributors emphasized the need for a national expression, be it modernist, expressive, or balletic.[57] In Graham's article, "Seeking an American Art of the Dance," which Martin praised in his review of the book as "brilliant," she struck back at critics who associated her work with the Germans and lashed out against the Japanese: "German dance, nearest to us of all, dangerously near, [is] the voice of a determined, tired, but forever mentally undefeated people," she wrote, referring to World War I.[58] Here, Graham alluded to a rising German nationalism, which she saw as an unacceptable aesthetic force on foreign soil. She similarly critiqued "the Oriental dance" and "its hieratic symbolic gesture," calling it "least comprehensible of all" and "impossible of assimilation because of its involved philosophy."[59] Graham declared that if Americans dug into their soil for inspiration, looking to the pioneer spirit, the human experience manifesting itself would become as borderless as the imagined American frontier and, thus, "universal." Just as the Germans had explored the foundations of their intellectual traditions to create a revolutionary form, Graham seemed to follow Isadora Duncan and Ted Shawn as she delved into the American Southwest as a symbol of the frontier and American exceptionalism.

Graham's words echoed the "frontier thesis" of historian Frederick Jackson Turner, with whom she would have likely been familiar, consummate reader that she was. Graham's power as an intellectual fueled her works from the start of her career. Searching for material to inspire her choreography, Graham inundated herself in research, particularly historical works. Martha Hill remembered of their early years: "She was like a young scholar. There would be piles of books around. Martha would go to the library on the weekends if she wanted to research. There she was with her glasses on like a little student with all these books around."[60] In his seminal work, Turner claimed that although the land frontier had closed, the American spirit had been forever molded by the experience of land expansion. Indeed, in the early twentieth century when Graham was growing up and studying at school, "the frontier thesis became the most familiar model of American history, the one learned in school, extolled by politicians, and screened each Saturday afternoon at the Bijou."[61] Although there is no direct proof that Graham read Turner's book, her own biography reflects his thesis. She was born in Allegheny, Pennsylvania, and her family moved to California when she was a teenager. She vividly recalled the train ride west and discussed "the hold the frontier had always had on me as an American, a symbol of a journey into the unknown. . . . I had the idea of frontier in my mind as a frontier of exploration, a frontier of discovery."[62] After arriving at Denishawn in California, she learned of Ted Shawn's writings, also surely influenced by Turner. Shawn wrote about the closing of the land frontier and the opening of the spiritual one, echoing Turner as he wrote, "There is nothing left for us to conquer so far as the natural wilderness of this continent are [sic] concerned, but the wilderness of our national art consciousness is producing just now its great pioneers."[63] Turner called America's opportunities "limitless," and American dance would be built by its pioneers "on universal lines," according to Shawn, which would be adopted by Duncan "from sea to shining sea" and then proclaimed by Graham internationally during the Cold War.[64]

* * *

Yet even after the heralded *Lamentation* closed in theaters in the winter of 1930, and despite the artistic merit and nationalist confidence expressed by Graham in her dance and writings, the ever-mercurial John Martin again argued that American dance had not yet established its presence as an international competitor. Graham continued to choreograph and write, digging into individualism and American narratives. When Mary Wigman arrived for a much-vaunted tour of the United States in the summer of 1930, Martin gushed that she deserved "the lion's share of the credit for the virtues of the modern movement."[65] Wigman noticed the aesthetic kinship of the American modern dance with that of Germany, referring to the experimental dance art as "amerikanischer Ausdruckstanz," or an American version of German expressionist dance.[66] Wigman's influence on the modern dance in the United States continued with the opening of her New York school in 1931, and a second acclaimed tour. While Wigman wanted her work to be known as "contemporary," and not modern—a phrase used by Martin to describe the abstract visual artists in 1929 and a stance later echoed by Graham—critics in the United States and internationally continued to refer to Wigman's work as "modern."[67]

The American moderns mounted a second Dance Repertory Theatre season on Broadway in 1931, and Graham's sparkling new *Primitive Mysteries* celebrated the power of the American Southwest, where she had traveled to study Native American dances and religions. She had attempted to ingratiate herself into the salon of philanthropist Mabel Dodge Luhan, where she could rub shoulders with Georgia O'Keeffe, D. H. Lawrence, and Carl Jung, the psychiatrist who developed concepts of personality, archetypes, and the collective unconscious from Freud that would deeply inform Graham's work, as well as her own psychoanalytic journey. In *Primitive Mysteries*, Graham performed on an abstracted Native American pueblo as the Virgin Mary, set in the context of American Indian ritual dances. Although Graham had wanted a painting by Georgia O'Keeffe as a backdrop, the painter declined the offer (O'Keeffe reportedly rolled her eyes when Graham arrived in New Mexico). Only stark lighting set the stage. Graham's work met with audience raves and accolades from the *Times* critic. Couching his review in the context of Graham's "ups and downs," Martin reported that after *Primitive Mysteries*, the audience did not merely shout "bravo"—the applause became "an expression of a mass of people whose emotional tension found spontaneous release."[68] He raved, "Here is a composition which must be ranked among the choreographic masterpieces of the modern dance movement."[69] While the American effort to institutionalize an annual collective season of dance collapsed after the 1931 series, the works and the artists presented during the Dance Repertory Theatre seasons would come to define the American modern dance.[70]

In 1931, a series of lectures at the New School for Social Research in New York City—organized with the ever-present John Martin—provided new institutional support for American choreographers. The series attempted to codify American modernism through discussions and academic inquiry with presentations by key thinkers in art, literature, architecture, and the performing arts.[71] Martin knew of the German Tanzkongress sessions in 1927, 1928, and 1930, which had furthered a parallel aim.[72] Martin's own lectures introduced modern dance and the choreographers at its vanguard to the American intelligentsia and provided the basis for his first book, *The Modern Dance*.[73] He announced that the chief aim of these choreographers was "the expression of an inner compulsion."[74] The idea that an audience could be educated into appreciation for the form would follow Graham in the Cold War, with her lecture-demonstrations, radio broadcasts on the government-sponsored Voice of America, the extensive USIS-arranged print coverage of her tours, and eventually television programming. In New York during the interwar years, the cultural stage was set.

As the Depression ravaged on, many working artists became more closely associated with the left. Numerous artists and writers, dancers and musicians, directors, actors, photographers, and filmmakers either joined the Communist Party or allied themselves with its program as "fellow travelers." After American representatives at the 1932 Workers Cultural Federation returned from the Moscow convention, they declared "Art Is a Weapon," and artists in numerous genres, forming a loose "cultural front," claimed that their work could also serve as a political propaganda weapon. In New York, dancers added their own slant to the new slogan, boasting, "Dance Is a Weapon." [75]

With the deepening of the Great Depression and in the wake of World War I isolationism, nationalism became a driving force. Graham followed naturally with her educational background. In 1935, she penned "The American Dance" for Martin's collection. Ironically in a volume dedicated to understanding a universalist, abstract form of art, Graham opened the essay with a nationalist battle cry: "To the American Dancer I say: 'Know our country.'"[76] Graham placed "Know our country" in quotes, thus referencing Turner directly. As Turner developed his frontier thesis, he wrote, "When State and country history shall be studied in the light of world history, we shall begin to know our country."[77] In this essay, Turner also expressed that the German influence on the United States was a "germ," and the essence of the nation's people and "American colonization" must be found on the land frontier and the experience of westward expansion.[78] Graham wrote out the Germans and directly echoed Turner when she spoke about her pioneer ancestors, concluding in her essay that began with Turner, "We don't have land frontiers anymore. We do have the frontier inside."[79] That same year, drawing on her readings, writings, her *Mayflower* heritage, and her travels to California, Graham choreographed *Frontier*.[80]

As the curtain rose in this work, Graham stood in front of Isamu Noguchi's abstracted fence with ropes extending from it to etch the West's vast mountains. In silence, Graham rose with an inhale, and the exhale brought her torso to the left, then to the right; her arm swept over the empty space in a single, wide gesture as the music began. Side battements swept her skirt through arcs. She returned to the fence and arched her spine backward, supplicant to the sky. As the work progressed, tiny parallel steps then marked the straight lines of plowed fields. The dance ended as Graham placed her bent leg on the fence, standing in profile, again marking the land with her arm's reach. This female pioneer attested to the power of every citizen to take part in building a nation. Graham was met with audience cheers.[81] Reviewing *Frontier* for the *Times*, Martin called the "deeply felt and simply projected" work "the finest note of Miss Graham's career." Margaret Lloyd, a reporter who would define the modern dance as distinctly American after the war, announced after seeing the work that summer that *Frontier* showed "dance history in the making."[82]

In the 1930s, Graham worked alongside other American artists who were searching for an expression of their country in the arts.[83] They sought what the myth of the American West promised: disentanglement from the European, renewal through an engagement with the land, a dialogue between

West and East to create unique American products, a return to fundamental forms, and the unleashing of the power and promise of the individual. With *Frontier* and her pioneer as an archetype, Graham clearly articulated the conflation of the abstracted and universal "human" with the "American" which had concerned her from the start of her training and career as a dancer, choreographer, and critic. Perhaps building on her study of Jung, Graham looked to archetypes to access "universal consciousness." Jung had first written of his concept of the archetype in *Instinct and the Unconscious*. Published in 1919, the book put forth that a shared human condition can be found in the individual. Thus, accessing Jung, Graham stated in her writings that through American modern dance one could find a human universal.[84] *Frontier* could tell a larger story not bounded by geography, but relevant to all. And in her desire to separate herself from her European and Asian influences, Graham refuted those forebears entirely. She equated herself with the American frontier and asserted in another 1935 article, "The modern American dance began here."[85]

Nationalistic tensions in Germany and the United States grew and were further reflected in the modern dance internationally. In the year of *Frontier*'s premiere, Adolf Hitler broke the Treaty of Versailles by beginning to rearm Germany. The swastika officially became the centerpiece of the new German national flag. Crowds of ordinary Germans, including women in tears and young children, raised their arms to salute their leader and his Nazi Party as he passed in motorcades. That same year, Mary Wigman, in her book *Deutsche Tanzkunst*, wrote about "the call of the blood" and emphasized "the question of true Germanness in regard to the arts."[86] Also in 1935, Horst's *Dance Observer* reported that Wigman was "under the direct control of Joseph Goebbels, *Reichsminister für Volksaufklärung und Propaganda*," or minister of propaganda for the Nazi regime. Within a year, the Wigman School would be renamed for Hanya Holm, German but not recognized as allied with the state; Holm would stay in the United States, where she continued as a leader of American modern dance and choreographed popular Broadway musicals.[87]

While citizens migrated across the United States and clamored for work to pay for food, shelter, and even minimal healthcare, Franklin D. Roosevelt's Works Progress Administration (WPA), which offered Americans paid employment, gave rise to the WPA's Federal One arts program, and many of these artists "stepping left" went on the government payroll. The Federal Theatre Program employed artists, writers, directors, actors, and dancers who needed paying jobs; they would entertain and educate the public. Although initially dance was not a separate unit, Hallie Flanagan, the woman who ran Federal One, acknowledged, "It is impossible to think of the modern theatre without thinking of the dance." Thus, dance became a recognized and independent government-sponsored enterprise in the United States.[88]

In order to work for Federal One, like the other WPA programs, artists had to establish economic hardship and go on "relief" first; but once Flanagan set up the program's Dance Unit, that requirement was waived for some of the Dance Repertory Theatre moderns, including Doris Humphrey. With forward-thinking artists who had been trained to "step left," projects abounded with multiracial works, and even a musical with an opening number that showed top-hatted capitalists toppling off human pyramids onstage. Although Martha Graham participated in the cultural front, choreographing protest works and later showing support for the pro-democratic communists during Spanish Civil War fundraisers in New York, she chose not to accept any funding from the federal government. Conveniently free of government influence through funding, she later claimed that she preferred to finance her performances independently through contributions and even bank loans, which were scarce during the Depression.[89]

In 1935, Roosevelt also signed a congressional charter that created the American National Theater and Academy (ANTA), an organization that would join the private and public sectors to form a national theater.[90] The document contained a short clause that would allow the State Department to export culture internationally under the ANTA umbrella.[91] The stage was set for dance as diplomacy, although it would be four years before Roosevelt used what some of his WPA performers had called "dance as a weapon" to fight the Nazis in Latin America.

In the theatrical sphere, John Martin and Martha Graham continued to battle over the Americanness of modern dance. In Martin's book *America Dancing: The Background and Personalities of the Modern Dance* (1936), he wrote, "It is by contagion rather than logic that the word 'modern' has got itself attached to the particular type of dance which has come to life as a characteristic American expression."[92] He asserted that Wigman's importance could not be diminished by the rise of the Americans and the problem of Germany: her name should be a "subtitle for modern dance."[93] On the other side, Graham continued to commingle modernist artistic ideology with American nationalism. During a lecture and performance that year, she set her lecture in the context of a performance of *Frontier*, even while she spoke in terms of a "universalism" in her dances. Graham explained that her own technique represented an attempt to access truth about "mankind," whose narrative took place on the frontier because of its symbolic ties to freedom and boundless creativity, and in dance through the movement of the torso in contraction and release.[94]

With nationalist rumblings, and Mary Wigman sketching mass celebratory choreography for the 1936 Olympics in Germany, Graham received an invitation: Joseph Goebbels, the head of the Nazi Olympic Committee, and Rudolf von Laban, Wigman's mentor, invited Graham to participate in a festival the week before the athletic games started in Berlin.[95] The Nazis sought to use the theoretically apolitical Olympic games as a demonstration of political power and supremacy through sportsmanship.[96] Even though Hitler had denounced modernist painters as "incompetents, cheats and madmen," the German expressionist dancers were initially brought into his fold.[97] In the United States, debates raged among officials and athletes about a possible American boycott.[98] Yet for Graham, a performance in Germany could have marked her as an international leader of modern dance in the very country that had allegedly established the form. Yet she did not hesitate in declining the invitation and replied only to Laban. "I would find it impossible to dance in Germany at the present time," she began. "So many artists whom I respect and admire have been persecuted, have been deprived of their right to work, and for such unsatisfactory and ridiculous reasons, that I should consider it impossible to identify myself, by accepting the invitation, with the regime that has made such things possible." Having hired Jewish dancers when many in the United States would not, she noted that many of her dancers would not be welcomed.[99] Numerous newspapers in the United States reported on Graham's refusal to participate in the festival and quoted her letter approvingly.[100] With her refusal, Graham made a dramatic political statement that would be remembered and later used during American denazification efforts in Germany at the start of the Cold War.[101]

The circles of political ironies flowed over the modernist rubric from the interwar period and etched themselves on Cold War cultural exports. Wigman sketched circle after circle within the stadium in a beige-papered notebook to celebrate the omnipresent power of the Nazi regime.[102] Ironically, that summer, Goebbels also planned the *Große Deutsche Kunstausstellung* (Great German Art Exhibition) and *Entartete Kunst* (Degenerate Art Exhibition) to show citizens the "decay" of the Weimar era.[103] "Racially pure" art would be contrasted with the products of Dadaism and modernists, including Picasso, who attacked German "decency."[104] Even modernist architecture was drawn into the fray of dance as politics as Hitler ordered that flat-roofed modernist buildings created by modernist Walter Gropius be given more "traditionally German" thatched replacements.[105] A Communist, Gropius fled Germany for America. He later taught at Harvard, where he trained Hugh Stubbins, the architect of Congress Hall, a 1957 monument to anti-Communist freedom in Berlin, just across from the Nazi Reichstag, the pseudo-parliament of the Third Reich. Graham would perform at the opening ceremonies of the hall with her work and a commissioned score by a German composer banned by the Nazis. Wigman participated in the Nazi spectacle, and some of Wigman's dancers fled across Europe or into Palestine, setting in motion a German-based yet universal "free dance" that sought to express nationalist ideals in territories Graham would tour during the Cold War, from Finland to Israel.

* * *

In 1937, Graham became the first modern dancer to perform at the White House when she presented *Frontier* for Franklin and Eleanor Roosevelt as well as members of the cabinet after a Friday evening dinner. After seeing Graham's work in New York months earlier at the Neighborhood Playhouse, founded by philanthropists Alice and Irene Lewisohn, Eleanor Roosevelt became drawn to Graham. In Roosevelt's syndicated column, "My Day," she noted Graham's "strength and direction."[106] The women had much in common: they both abhorred the Nazis, made antifascist statements in support of the democratically elected Communists during the Spanish Civil War, supported the power of the arts, and believed in ethnic and racial integration. Before the event, the first lady had advised Graham that there would be a number of people in attendance worth meeting—a perfect opportunity to make government contacts for the future.[107]

Standing on a rickety platform in the gilded State Dining Room, Graham wore a pioneer woman's dress and stood with one bare foot on a makeshift fence. Looking out over the nation's leaders, she imagined a vast frontier and the promise of the American West. With a language that used no words, she described in dance what she wrote about, the America "whose meaning was inexhaustible, whose purpose was infinite."[108] In the practiced side sweep, her leg went so high that her foot almost grazed the dining room chandelier.[109] Although the Office of Protocol was concerned about her bare feet, the president's guests applauded heartily at the end.[110] After the performance,

Eleanor Roosevelt noted Graham's "perfect control" and the "devotion on the part of the artist."[111] Graham had arrived on the American political stage.[112]

The next year, the Roosevelt administration created the Division of Cultural Relations at the State Department. The president divided South America from the rest of the international arena and named Nelson Rockefeller, who was not yet thirty, head of the Office of the Coordinator of Inter-American Affairs (CIAA).[113] Rockefeller, a son of the industrialist John D. Rockefeller Jr., understood the power of modernism through his deep involvement with the Museum of Modern Art (MoMA), with Abby Rockefeller, his philanthropist mother, at the helm. Funding for artistic exports relied on business and philanthropic leaders like Rockefeller to underwrite and manage the projects because the largely isolationist Congress found cultural propaganda suspicious, at best.[114] Rockefeller used the term "total war" to describe the use of culture as a propaganda tool—a term that would later be used to describe the Cold War itself, with cultural diplomacy one front in that all-points conflict.[115]

On the domestic front, in 1939 members of both the WPA Federal Theatre Program and the Dance Unit were called before Congress and condemned for encouraging communistic leanings in audiences. The WPA production *Revolt of the Beaver*, in which "Worker Beavers" carried weapons in their lunchboxes to protest against the capitalists, especially attracted the ire of Congress.[116] Indeed, one dancer who had performed under the banner "Dance Is a Weapon" played a beaver with a gun in her lunchbox in the show. Other accusations of subversion included the commingling of African American and white women—a sure sign of Communist influence to crusaders in Washington. Artistic philistinism also prevailed among the elected officials: they sought to call Christopher Marlowe to the stand for his subversive plays, unaware that he was a contemporary of Shakespeare. Eleanor Roosevelt sat with Hallie Flanagan during the hearings to show support for the arts, yet most of the programs were shut down.

However, Franklin Roosevelt would not be deterred on the international front, which benefited Graham. For the president, modernism itself became a burgeoning American propaganda arsenal, with Rockefeller executing the White House agenda with a new program of cultural exports. In 1939, Roosevelt delivered a nationally broadcast speech at MoMA, with its Rockefeller connections, in which the president made the link explicit between American art and international interests. After equating modern art with civilization, Roosevelt declared, "What we call freedom in politics results in freedom in the arts."[117] He then spoke of world peace, thus linking it to political and artistic freedom. American freedom and morality were firmly connected to modernism by the president.[118]

Just after Roosevelt's remarks, Graham and her company were invited to perform *Tribute to Peace* for the 1939 World's Fair opening ceremonies with the president and his first lady. The Roosevelts sat in the front row as the American modern dance represented the nation on the "world's" stage. The press described Graham's company in messianic terms: "On a wide platform, built as an altar to peace and which stood halfway between the President's reviewing stand and the first row of an audience of 60,000 people, Martha Graham's company of twenty danced a solemn impressive tribute."[119] Graham was now working in lockstep with the White House, as she would for decades to follow.

* * *

When Rockefeller began his work with Roosevelt to export dance in 1940, he applied the president's "Good Neighbor" approach to cultural diplomacy to fight fascism and the Germans. "Cultural relations means simply that you are interested in what your neighbor is thinking and doing," Rockefeller wrote, adding, "You hope that he is similarly interested in you."[120] Nonverbal arts such as music and dance became vital as a way to reach elites and leaders as well as the performance-going public in Latin America with the embodiment of cultural convergences. The CIAA exported symphonic pieces that would appeal to European sensibilities in Latin America and brought arts that demonstrated American interest in South America through new compositions that reinterpreted "folk themes," however misplaced Mexican references and Spanish-language declarations became in Brazil.[121] In dance, Rockefeller exported the American Ballet Caravan with the help of dance impresario Lincoln Kirstein, a friend and former Harvard classmate. In 1933, Kirstein had brought George Balanchine from the Soviet Union to the United States to encourage the development of ballet, and he had also overseen two ballet companies, each featuring a diverse selection of choreographers who presented both avant-garde ballets and American-themed works.[122]

In April 1941, Kirstein signed a contract with the CIAA to send thirty-five dancers, two pianists, two singers, a conductor, and a technical staff to Latin America along with Balanchine, who choreographed new works especially for the tour.[123] In order to promote the idea of unity through people-to-people exchange and overcome what Kirstein referred to as the "language barrier," the company hired three Mexican choreographers as well as a Cuban.[124] Following the interwar propaganda arts strategy under Roosevelt and Rockefeller, Kirstein's Ballet Caravan performed works of Americana yet also showed choreography that incorporated European and South American traditions. The repertory included choreography that conveyed central messages that would underlie future tours by Graham and others: the association of the United States with cultural sophistication; Americana and the use of folk; and the commingling of local forms with American dance, to embody cultural convergences between the host country and the United States as a foundation for alliances.[125] Announcements of the ballet programs and reviews of the works appeared in newspapers carrying advertisements for German products emblazoned with swastikas.

With the success of this tour, despite some glitches, both American dance and modernism held promise. Dance as diplomacy had influenced cultural attitudes in Latin America among elites who could fall to the Nazis, a source of deep concern given the escalation of war in Europe.[126] The State Department continued to explore possibilities for further tours, and Graham herself was on the government's radar screen as the leader of an eligible company.[127] But that December, when the Japanese bombed Pearl Harbor and the United States declared war on Japan and Germany, soft-power cultural tours seemed less viable. Rockefeller compared wars to an iceberg: three-tenths above the water represented the military fight; the other seven-tenths, invisible to the eye, demanded "psychological phases of total war."[128] Yet the need to transport troops and war materiel took priority over sending dancers, stagehands, and sets to perform before foreign audiences. Hard power trumped soft in the hot war that engulfed the world.

Yet Rockefeller did not go unheeded, and as commander of the European Theater, General Dwight D. Eisenhower created the Psychological Warfare Branch, which worked with the Office of War Information (OWI) in Washington.[129] While radio broadcasts, posters, print, and other propaganda better suited wartime, members of the State Department, encouraged by Rockefeller, likewise knew the United States would eventually need the performing arts.[130] The OWI found Graham attractive: her lineage could be traced back to the *Mayflower*, and she had opposed the Nazis. Although she showed tremendous promise as an American icon for export, the OWI worried that her modernist form would be understood only by knowledgeable audiences. In addition, her strongest repertory did not encompass the full range of offerings required to make her a successful avatar beyond the elite in America. But in the fall of 1944, Graham showed strong potential for propaganda efforts with her newest work, *Appalachian Spring*.

Graham's *Appalachian Spring*, with a score by Aaron Copland, premiered at the Library of Congress with funding by Elizabeth Sprague Coolidge. First known as *Ballet for Martha*, it delivered a high-art yet accessible American message. The archetypal characters, nineteenth-century Americans celebrating on their wedding day and reflecting on their past and future, performed American nationalism. The dance opens with stillness: Copland's sparse notes accompany the lights rising on Noguchi's abstracted Pennsylvania farmhouse. A planked wall, angled poles, and several steps indicate a home. A simple rocking chair rests inside the house, and a bench sits outside. Upstage, a preacher's pulpit is a tipped wooden sphere. Downstage, an angled log fence encloses the space. The Preacher enters alone with a walk that Graham described as "a Sunday stroll"; his character was called the "Wandering Preacher" in press releases and "The Revivalist (a man of God)" in programs for the premiere.[131] The Preacher proclaimed the access to freedom of religion with his four Followers. The Pioneering Woman enters next, majestic and aloof, and sits in the rocking chair. According to Graham, the Pioneering Woman became "the protagonist of all that happens here. She possesses our thoughts." The Husbandman, a new homeowner, walks to the house, stroking it in awe. Initially Graham called him "The Citizen," describing him as "a power to be reckoned with, a man who brings reform."[132] The Citizen presented a model for people exploring rights in new nation-states. Such a work was ripe for export.

The following April, Franklin Roosevelt's sudden death meant that Graham's ally, Eleanor, moved out of the White House. Graham celebrated her fifty-first birthday the next month, determined to work that summer on creating new pieces and training students for the future. Although the war in Asia had not ended, the Soviets had quickly become the new problem during negotiations in Potsdam, Germany, where Harry S. Truman, the new president, "casually" mentioned the new American bomb to Stalin in the context of rising tensions about the division of Germany and its occupied territories among the victors.[133] Graham worked over the summer with students, and in August, after a bitter summer of battles against the Japanese, the war was finally over. The Allied victory was ensured when Truman ordered the use of atomic bombs, killing hundreds of thousands in Hiroshima and Nagasaki, melting the skin from the bones of those who survived, infecting generations with radiation, and demonstrating American prowess to the Soviets.

As the United States entered an uneasy postwar period, Graham's pioneering Bride seemed the perfect symbol for the nation as women who had worked in factories and plants seemed destined to return to less public lives at home.[134] Although 1945 was a barren year for Graham choreographically, Aaron Copland won the Pulitzer Prize for Appalachian Spring. With the Cold War taking shape, Copland's score took on greater resonance as cultural diplomacy: he became one of the first American composers whose music was played for the Soviet people by the American government–run radio project, Voice of America (VOA).[135] Appalachian Spring opened evening programs with its American folk refrain "'Tis a gift to be free." During the war, radio had become a potent cultural weapon; this would continue in the Cold War with programming that sought to engage the international public with music, language lessons, comedy, and game shows, as well as news broadcasts that brought "truth." At VOA, Francis Mason interviewed Graham for international broadcasts, and Graham showed magnetic charisma. Mason would become a diplomat, promoted Graham to government officials, and served as chair of the board of directors of Graham's company, finally bailing out the company when it needed loans most with his own savings. Keenly aware of the international prospects for her work, Graham wrote to a potential donor, "[The company] no longer belongs to me alone but has assumed the demands of public property. It has entered a field where greater and more meaningful things are expected of it."[136] Partnering with Copland and influential arbiters of taste, Graham offered promising material for export—and she knew this.

Graham's hope for a government-sponsored international tour may also have been spurred that year by the State Department's funding of a New York exhibition and tour of modern art paintings titled Advancing Modern Art. With leftover funds from the war, the OWI bought modernist paintings, becoming the State Department's "collector."[137] After a showing at the esteemed Metropolitan Museum in the new cultural capital of the world, New York, the paintings would go to Latin America, following the interwar pattern, and then to Europe.[138] Yet the New York opening did not receive the unmitigated accolades that had been expected when politics met the modern. The New York Times reported on "people making cracks" about the State Department's "extremely modern" approach to art, despite its postwar support for old-fashioned British colonialism when it came to politics. On the opposite aisle, other critics remarked that "the people overseas [were] thirsting for the latest in American-born modern art." Yet Congress halted the State Department exhibit, considering the art "too modern."[139] Indeed, mirroring investigations begun by the House Committee on Un-American Activities (HUAC) and foreshadowing McCarthyism, one newspaper reported that the State Department was infused with Communists because modern art was communistic. "The pictures had too red a tinge," noted one reporter. In response, the State Department created a committee to investigate if the paintings "really are art." Some works were halted in Prague; another section, which was still touring Latin America, was suspended in Haiti. Although a memo to Nelson Rockefeller from the director of MoMA associated the government's withdrawal from the art exhibition with Hitler's likening of modern artists to degenerates, government resistance to modernism did not bode well for Graham's hopes of government patronage.[140]

The battle over modernism and the equation of modern artists with Communists continued to rage, with "Donderoism" ascendant in Congress. Representative George Dondero of Michigan derided modern art and declared that Soviet Russia had used "art as a weapon in the powerlust drive of international communism."[141] He named seventeen of the government-sponsored artists as known to have "affiliations with Left-Wing movements."[142] Graham surely had to be cognizant of her past association with communist movements when she supported medical aid for the Loyalists during the Spanish Civil War. Although she performed the nationalist *Frontier* at benefits, a dance that fought against the tenets of Stalinist communism in its emphasis on the power of the individual voice in a democratic nation, the FBI had nonetheless collected information on her due to the company she kept.[143]

In the midst of these artistic controversies, in 1947 the diplomat George Kennan dispatched the "Long Telegram" from Moscow to his superiors at the State Department; it described the Soviet threat and proposed a strategy for countering it. Kennan's views, which were soon adopted by the Truman administration, became known as the containment policy. If the Soviets were contained, so the theory argued, Russia's new bloc of Eastern European allies would implode. Often neglected is Kennan's keen understanding of the importance of culture and cultural exchange to quicken the implosion. Kennan's work was fueled by a cultural knowledge of Russia that included dance.[144] In the chapter of his memoirs about the Long Telegram, Kennan reflected on Russian dance, noting the cultural power of ballet and the failure of Sovietized modern dance with its American mother, Isadora Duncan.

Joseph Stalin, Lenin's successor, loved ballet, and the freed modernist strain of dance in the Soviet Union was buried as the famous classical ballets regained prominence, along with the new school of socialist realism. In 1932, the Soviet newspaper *Pravda* announced, "Art, the object of which is to serve the masses, cannot be other than realistic."[145] Abstraction in art, architecture, and dance indicated "Western decadence" and "degeneracy."[146] With Duncan discredited, Stalin almost never missed a premiere of the Bolshoi Ballet, although the leader eschewed the czar's center box.[147] Indeed, showing proletarian equality, "diplomats, tank drivers, and pilots" sat together and enjoyed the lavishly staged evenings of classical dance.[148] While Kennan wrote from the Soviet Union, he arranged for James F. Byrnes, the visiting American secretary of state, to attend a performance of the Soviet classical ballet in Moscow. Kennan recalled that the "orchestra were all in their places waiting to strike up the national anthems." Politics aside, Kennan described the performance as "first rate."[149] Yet soon afterward, while visiting a circus, he came across what he recognized as Duncan's leftover "expressive" dance in a "terrible" performance that prefaced an exhibition of a man putting his head in a lion's mouth.[150] Kennan well understood that the Soviets could not compete with the likes of Martha Graham, and the father of containment would deploy Graham behind the Iron Curtain.

The escalation of the Cold War during the 1940s marked by Kennan's telegram demanded innovative tactics to create, manage, and fund all shades of American propaganda. The Fulbright Act and the United States Information and Educational Exchange Act funded cultural diplomacy.[151] Diplomats stressed to Congress that sophisticated cultural products that were distinctly American could counteract Soviet accusations that the United States was an immature and uncouth world leader. William Benton, the assistant secretary of state for public affairs, told Congress that "one of the manifestations of our adolescence is that we neglect the power of ideas, and the importance of symbols in international relations."[152] He asserted that even military officers understood the need for cultural propaganda more than Congress because the generals had witnessed warfare and thus were "quicker to see these issues."[153] Dwight Eisenhower, who had ordered the filming of Nazi concentration camps and had the footage shown to troops, was immediately drawn into the project. He joined the privately funded Free Europe Committee, which had deep-pocketed support from the CIA, to fund Radio Free Europe to broadcast news and cultural programming into Soviet-controlled nations. The Soviet Union was using the high arts to demonstrate its sophistication to the international public, but Congress so far had approved appropriations only for export expenditures of radio, commercial trade fairs, motion picture, and people-to-people exchanges.[154] As Congress offered only a meager budget for high culture, Eisenhower, Rockefeller, and other advocates of cultural diplomacy had to turn toward foundations, private individuals, and industry for financial support.

* * *

In 1947, Martha Graham became directly involved in early Cold War experiments with dance as pro-American propaganda. Theoretically, Graham offered a range of new works that situated her in the firmament of modernism and further established her as the kind of artist the United States could effectively export as an exemplar of American performing arts. *Appalachian Spring* was followed by *Hérodiade*, based on the writings of Stéphane Mallarmé, the nineteenth-century symbolist poet known for complex, intricate language and obscure references.[155] Graham's increasing range of cultural products challenged OWI doubts about her limited repertory. Nonetheless, her time had not yet arrived, with modernism in question and a somewhat inexperienced, certainly publicly discredited State Department when it came to its export of modernism. Yet the State Department believed that the arts could be used to showcase American cultural power at a summer youth festival in Prague in 1947, and ANTA asked the modernist Graham to join the export project alongside ballet's representative Lucia Chase, the Ballet Theatre company director, philanthropist, and ballerina.[156] ANTA's newly formed Dance Committee then became the American Dance Committee and added Rockefeller's Lincoln Kirstein and *Times* critic John Martin, among other dance luminaries and modernists.[157]

Although the youth festival was supposedly designed to encourage peace, the State Department reversed course and declared that calls for peace were Soviet propaganda, and hopes of an immediate international performance were dashed. Suspecting Communist machinations in Prague, and encountering continued congressional suspicion of cultural programming, State withdrew its support for the delegation. Most American Dance Committee representatives quit immediately, including Graham. Of the US dance companies scheduled to attend, only the New Dance Group, which had earlier Communist attachments, sent a small group of amateur folk dancers who practiced in the bowels of the ship to Europe. Yet eighty-one thousand people from seventy-one nations attended the festival, and the Soviets sent their ballet stars along with "an entire corps de ballet." American leftists proclaimed that the United States showed a "sad lack of official support and professional talent."[158] A *New York Times* reporter likewise commented that "Soviet Russia had 'stolen the show.'" Blame fell on the State Department.[159] The Communists scored a propaganda bonanza in the field of dance with the Sovietized ballet. The United States could not yet fully compete with an American ballet, but desperately needed a dance counterpoint. Modern dance stood in the wings.

* * *

The key moment that defined modern dance as distinctly American, and thus primed for export, was the 1949 publication of *The Borzoi Book of Modern Dance* by *Christian Science Monitor* critic Margaret Lloyd. This substantial volume reviewed dancers and dance companies in the nascent discipline of modern dance. Lloyd challenged Martin's defense of the German tradition and dismissed the early choreographers: "Because of the obscuration that befell [Wigman's] art during the Nazi reign of terror, it seems advisable here to refer to her career in the past tense." She added, reflecting language she had used as a critic years earlier while championing Graham's *Frontier*, "We think of 'frontier' as an opening up, as a vista into something new. Mary Wigman, hearing the word for the first time, thought it meant a barrier." Lloyd pushed back against accusations that the New Dance Group was communistic, despite its history and participation in Prague. "There are no communists left in the modern dance today," she wrote, opening their entry. Decades later, one dancer recalled of the New Dance Group and the McCarthy era: "She was trying to protect us."[160] Modern dance redefined by Lloyd, and thus to the academy, was deeply American and democratic. She concluded, "More is the modern dance ascribable to the bright land of its birth—a land where freedom and democracy are ideals; where traditions of human decency prevail; a land where all races are learning to work out their destiny together; a land of great spaces and mighty projects."[161]

* * *

Despite the increasing legitimacy of modern dance as a distinctly American art form that had ideals of freedom and thus democracy deeply embedded in it, Martha Graham's potential as a cultural export dimmed in 1950 after a series of poorly received performances. Graham's first European tour, sponsored by Bethsabée de Rothschild, a German-Jewish and Israeli philanthropist, sought to place Graham's work before the international, artistic, and political intelligentsia. But in Paris, the first stop, the critical reception was poor. *Le Monde* offered disparaging comments about Graham's works and their "strange interpretations," "extravagant gestures," and dancers who "move and grimace without apparent reason."[162] *Le Parisien Libéré* presented a more balanced review, noting that Eleanor Roosevelt liked Graham's work but finally concluding that the evening's dances were "bizarre."[163] After a knee injury in Paris, Graham canceled the tour. She returned devastated, retreating with Rothschild from the public eye; newspapers in the United States, however, remained supportive, with one of them declaring that such modern American work was "too advanced" for the French.[164] Yet ANTA reports on "Martha Graham's failures" filtered back to the State Department.[165]

Adding to Graham's government woes, under Truman, ballet rather than modern dance took center stage as a dance propaganda tool to fight the Soviets. The new president had famously called modern art "merely the vaporings of half-baked lazy people." Like Stalin, Truman himself liked ballet. He hoped for the creation of a "National Ballet" that would take its place in Washington, DC, alongside the National Gallery of Art.[166] Touring was particularly important in Europe, where the president believed that "communist groups ... naturally oppose American artists at any point whenever possible." He was told that the United States had stumbled badly in France with the American Ballet Company, a company led by Ruth Page, which was viewed as a government export, although it was not. Horrified critics called the poor performances "shocking," noting that the audience demanded, "Curtain! Curtain!" Advisers asked Truman to "act quickly" to export Lucia Chase's Ballet Theatre (BT) into the international arena.[167] Truman liked the idea, and the White House coordinated with the secretary of defense for touring air transport: according to Truman's assistant, BT would make a major contribution to the effort of "combatting foreign misconceptions about the materialistic nature of American civilization."[168] The government and the company scrambled for funds, procuring support by offering to perform for army troops stationed abroad, and Truman committed to the export.[169] Although the tour was nearly canceled because of the burgeoning tensions in Korea in 1950, BT performed throughout West Germany and Latin America over a five-month period under the name American National Ballet Theatre.[170]

Using a system that would be paralleled on a larger scale during the Cold War, the army, air force, and other agencies participated directly in non-combat international cultural deployments despite congressional disdain, and because of congressional scrutiny of State Department spending that would limit these much-needed projects in the field. In West Germany, the dancers stayed in army housing and performed for officers, soldiers, and German civilians. Although it could not lend planes for transport out of the United States because its military hardware had to supply the Korean War, the air force offered support to the group when it was not in the United States with housing and transport.[171] The paperwork for the tour contains veiled references to "private funding" consistently in quotations, so it seemed to some that the CIA was also involved (in later years, "private backing" was often the euphemism for this financial support).[172] Thus, numerous branches of government coordinated forces to present the United States as culturally significant to fight the Cold War abroad. Indeed, Secretary of Defense Louis Johnson agreed with the State Department and other agencies and deemed such cultural exports "to be in the national interest."[173] The response to the tour was cabled home: "GENUINE OVATIONS. AUDIENCE STOMPED AND CHEERED."[174]

Despite Graham's disastrous European 1950 tour, and Truman's opinions on modernism, the year also offered her greater official visibility. The president himself celebrated Graham as one of the "Six Outstanding American Women" at the Women's National Press Club, applauding her contribution as a national female leader who created a new language of dance.[175] Presidential recognition for her efforts gave Graham renewed hope of a diplomatic mission, a prospect that was very much on her mind. "I only wanted to go [abroad] if there could be some good accrue from it as far as [foreign] relations are concerned," she mused.[176]

* * *

With the fall of China to communism and the Korean War bringing Asia into high relief, in 1951, Rockefeller went to Japan with John Foster Dulles. Rockefeller traveled as a so-called cultural envoy at the same time that the State Department was negotiating a peace treaty between Japan and the Allied Powers, a pact that would officially end World War II and terminate Japan's standing as an imperial power. Tensions were high: the Japanese agreed to disarm their military in return for American protection, but the pact met resistance among some Japanese as an American imperialist project.[177] One Japanese businessman advised the State Department delegation that "there is too much of the 'tooth-paste approach' in the American method," referring to the flood of American consumer goods in postwar occupied Japan. The United States, he said, needed high-class cultural exports to propagate its values—exports that were neither ingested nor used as a vehicle to Americanize through commercialized hygiene.[178]

Once he was back in the United States, Rockefeller sent a report to Dulles that emphasized the need to woo the elite with culture. Since a "relatively small segment of the population" would "determine the course that Japan is to take in the years ahead," he wrote, "[i]t is believed that maximum results in the cultural field can be obtained by working particularly with this group."[179] At the same time, USIS set forth a similar theory that if the elites could be persuaded, the rest would follow.[180] This would become known as "trickle-down diplomacy." But how would someone communicate cultural values without a shared language? The nonverbal medium of dance, which included visual arts and music with stage sets and compositions, became essential as a form of communication. Indeed, "special groups," as Rockefeller put it, might be particularly interested in modern dance.[181] American cultural diplomacy could transcend toothpaste with highbrow art and American modernist dance. Graham's relationship with Noguchi had become culturally mainstream with the Pulitzer Prize having gone to *Ballet for Martha*, or *Appalachian Spring*.

Yet modernist art remained a controversial national export when, again in 1952, Congressman Dondero again equated modernist art with communism, calling modern art "'the latest link' in a chain of a Moscow-inspired controversy to communize [Americans]."[182] Two years later, as a supporter of the zealously anti-communist Senator Joseph McCarthy, Dondero told a newspaper interviewer that modern art "does not glorify our beautiful country, our cheerful and smiling people." He continued, "It is therefore opposed to our government and those who promote it are our enemies."[183] But the intelligentsia had made their political mark for some in the State Department and other agencies: modern art was a propaganda weapon that used freedom of expression as a central tenet to promote the fruits of democracy abroad. Because of the American Cold War equation of Nazis and Soviets in terms of their contemptuous treatment of modern art and artists, American modernists provided a singular weapon of the Cold War, despite domestic congressional posturings.[184] Yet it took time and a soft-power military intervention.

With culture needed to fight the war of ideologies, and the former general and pro–private sector propaganda president firmly in office, in 1954 President Dwight D. Eisenhower created the Emergency Fund for Cultural Affairs, which supported international cultural diplomacy; dance and modernism remained on the export radar.[185] While in the private sector and then as president, Eisenhower had proved his dedication to cultural diplomacy, and then created USIS. He brought Nelson Rockefeller back into government service, giving him responsibility as a special assistant in the White House for new diplomatic projects to "increase understanding and cooperation."[186] The success of Roosevelt's American Ballet Caravan and Truman's American National Ballet Theatre (ANBT), as well as Rockefeller's role in them, had not been forgotten. Lincoln Kirstein wrote Rockefeller, "After all, it was you who started this whole scheme of waging peace by the exportation of art as far back as 1941; I know what foresight, what courage it took."[187] In addition, a memo describing ANTA noted that it "has demonstrated to the Government how the theatre can serve the Nation in peacetime on international levels." In characteristically cryptic form, it continued, "Too long to enumerate here are [ANTA's] daily services to the State Department and other government agencies," which had included the review of culture in the international fields.[188] Showing a dedication to the dance arts, Eisenhower personally wrote to ANBT's Lucia Chase and asked that her ballet company become known as American Ballet Theatre (ABT), to clarify in both the domestic and international markets that it represented the nation.[189]

Eisenhower and his secretary of state John Foster Dulles created a strategic infrastructure that would coordinate cultural exports. The Operations Coordinating Board (OCB) synchronized "departmental execution of national security policies" and created the Working Group for Cultural Activities, which became the Cultural Presentations Committee (CPC).[190] Rockefeller sat on the OCB, which had ultimate oversight over cultural exports.[191] A State Department designee chaired the CPC, which included representatives from the Department of Defense, the CIA (then run by John Foster Dulles's brother Allen), and the National Security Council. Yet the agencies understood that their board members were not equipped to choose specific artists or handle the delicate negotiations of bookings, and that they needed private citizen experts to validate the apolitical nature of the touring selections. ANTA became the mechanism to work through these details, with separate panels in music, theater, and dance. Despite the centrality of ANTA, which officially reviewed and funded exports, the State Department and the OCB still had to give the final stamp of approval.[192] USIS would become "responsible for exploiting and publicizing" cultural events "in order to increase the psychological impact on the host country."[193]

In 1954, the OCB's Working Group for Cultural Activities engaged in projects that included government and nongovernmental players. As a member of the OCB, Nelson Rockefeller participated in developing new projects. Individuals in the private sector, including Virginia Inness-Brown, who would chair or co-chair the ANTA panels, lobbied individual philanthropists for financial support. Inness-Brown was particularly intrigued by the power of dance as a nonverbal and thus cross-cultural form. Under her watch and funding, Kirstein's newly formed New York City Ballet performed in the Salute to France festival in June 1954, to great accolades.[194] In the competition with Moscow and its government-sponsored dance, the US private-public model worked particularly well as propaganda. Now American artists—and particularly Graham, who had never worked on government projects such as the WPA—could firmly declare their independence and freedom as an American staple of production.

After the successful reception of Kirstein's ballet companies during the interwar period in Latin America and the Cold War in Europe, and the recognized failure of Graham in Paris, the OCB experimented first in Latin America with the modern dancer José Limón and his company in 1954. As a Mexican-born American, Limón seemed an ideal cultural ambassador, although the government again seemed to conflate Mexico with Latin America writ large.[195] Yet his choreography underscored the unique character of American modern dance—it could be practiced by anyone who trained with discipline—while also demonstrating his international cultural sophistication, with works such as The Moor's Pavane, inspired by Shakespeare's Othello. His affinity for Mexican stories was evident with La Malinche, which was set in his homeland during the sixteenth-century Spanish invasion. Although he did not present Americana, Limón adeptly demonstrated the power of modernism in the United States and its attachment to the ideals of Western civilization, as well as the cultural convergences that stemmed from a shared heritage. Speaking in his native Spanish to audiences in Latin America, Limón said, "We are all Americans. We are not afraid to declare ourselves, and have done so in dance."[196]

In 1954, the Graham company again traveled overseas without government support, yet its leader was aware that the State Department had its eye on her.[197] Political connections continued to reap dividends: in the Hague,

Queen Juliana of the Netherlands and her daughter Princess Irene had met Graham several years earlier with Eleanor Roosevelt in New York, and they visited backstage to offer their congratulations on her well-received performances.[198] The American embassy in London sent dispatches back to the State Department describing Graham's choreography as "an instrument of all human emotions" and noted some critical success during the season.[199] The embassy's reports quoted reviewers who reflected on the "intellectual and literary elements and the hidden symbolism" of her works. Memos noted that appreciating Graham's choreography required "a thoughtful approach and repeated viewing" or even "an almost superhuman and spasmodic effort of a great intellect."[200] The State Department continued to emphasize programming "for adaption to the elite audience," USIS molded publicity for cultural presentations for "specific target groups," and thus Graham continued to show potential.[201] Nevertheless, there was general suspicion that Graham's claims that modern dance was "American" would draw raised eyebrows among the culturally savvy British who knew the European landscape. One London reviewer, for instance, reported that "the core of Martha Graham's art is to be found in the school of Mary Wigman."[202]

At the same time, the cultural diplomacy programs faced resistance from a continually dubious House and Senate. In addition, Senator Joseph McCarthy had accused the State Department and USIS of harboring Communists. Thus, in 1954, a USIS self-evaluation study outlined the reasons that targeting educated audiences had become increasingly important. Anecdotal reports and embassy chatter further buttressed the argument for the exports of the modern arts.[203] Graham's work proved effective because it spoke to "bourgeoisie" and "elite" audiences. Projects that targeted politicians, intellectuals, artists, and others became important as a positive reflection of "the decadent part of mankind."[204]

Although USIS could demonstrate the effectiveness of artistic projects for a select international group of elite leaders and their wives, congressional oversight committees preferred supporting trade fairs over sending cultural groups abroad. Yet merely promoting trade fairs and other broad-based events that directly spoke to the fruits of capitalism fed into the Soviet accusations of American cultural depravity and its addiction to consumer delights. While the Department of Commerce boasted thirty-four people working in its "economic diplomacy division," as well as additional part-time employees, State had only "two and a half people" working on cultural exports in 1954.[205] By necessity, its "staff unit" worked with ANTA and "other organizations."[206]

In late 1954, the OCB considered funding for a Martha Graham tour and set forth a schedule of countries for her company to visit in Asia, focusing on Eisenhower's "domino" nations. Yet, as one historian concludes, "[I]t all started in Bandung."[207] What came to be known as the Bandung Conference in Indonesia, where Graham would land, both in 1955, brought together the leaders of decolonized or decolonizing nations whose citizens represented almost two-thirds of the global population.[208] Although the agenda of the conference centered on asserting national independence against an imperial past, with Europe at the forefront, and the Soviet Union a threatening power, the United States became the new "global imperialist power that had to be resisted at all costs."[209] As Richard Wright defiantly reported, "It brought together for the first time representatives of a billion and a half people . . . for a meeting at which delegates of the Western peoples were excluded."[210] Despite its imperial past, Japan was allowed in.[211] Inflamed by the non-Western race implications, Eisenhower's Foster Dulles also became increasingly apoplectic about the politics of nonalignment and neutrality: the conference organizers ranged from "socialist but neutral" to "anticommunist and pro-West" to experimenters with "Arab socialism."[212] Outbursts could be heard in Washington that "Western civilization is outnumbered."[213]

While the Graham tour was funded in 1954—before the conference—neither the tour nor Bandung was spontaneous. A myriad of significant crises, meetings, and treaties affecting the region were negotiated during the Eisenhower administration and required political attention. As the OCB planned funding and tentative locations for Graham's tour, the idea for Bandung was generated at the Colombo Conference. In December, Secretary of State Dulles expressed strong apprehensions, and his brother, Allen, oversaw reports.[214] Indeed, Bandung was viewed with "special alarm" by the OCB.[215] In February 1955, the OCB formed another special working group to draw up US objectives at Bandung as locations for touring were negotiated for Graham.[216] International leaders' distaste for John Foster Dulles's saber-rattling was well-understood, making him a "menace," and "narrow-minded"; regarding race, he was "bigoted."[217] Yet because countries either were neutral or showed allegiance to both sides, alienating their leaders by condemning the communists seemed to some American diplomats as counterproductive, and, despite Dulles, "attention turned to predicting the issues that would be raised and briefing friendly delegations on how to respond to them."[218] A "soft-power" approach would also be taken. Exports that showed the value and promise of the United States in positive terms would respond to Bandung attendees' concerns in a "friendly" manner.

Graham brought this dance, and Dulles could be softened. The conference was divided into economic, political, and cultural committees.[219] Newly decolonized, decolonizing, and firmly independent nations sought economic modernization, and thus economic aid, be it capitalistic or communistic; decolonization and issues of imperialism would frame the conference; the hodgepodge of ideological combinations needed to be addressed.[220] Race and "bigotry" were on the agenda, as well as the question of Israel and Palestine. The OCB sent Graham to each of the organizing nations of the Bandung Conference, known as the "Colombo Powers" of India, Burma, Indonesia, Ceylon, and Pakistan. She brought American modern dance, modernization of the body, and, with *Appalachian Spring*, the celebratory story of the frontier after the pioneers ridded themselves of the British Empire. The cultural landscape was marked with a new home for the couple-to-be, as a universal to be celebrated and overseen by an African American Pioneering Woman, as all danced to the refrain "'Tis a gift to be free."

Initially the OCB scheduled Graham's tour to start in Japan and move to Korea, the mega-domino followed by the former war zone now divided, where hot war had embroiled the peninsula, sent home Americans in body bags, and ended in a stalemate for the United States. Graham and her company would then travel to Taiwan, the Philippines, Hong Kong, Indonesia, Singapore, Thailand, Ceylon, Malaya, Burma, India, Pakistan, Egypt, and Lebanon, all nations attached to Bandung. Graham might continue to other countries where the government feared Soviet influence would take hold, including the nations Truman had singled out with his Kennan-inspired "Truman Doctrine": Turkey and Greece, as well as Yugoslavia, which aligned with the Bandung leaders as Josip B. Tito negotiated with the leaders of India and Egypt to found the Non-Aligned Movement.[221] When not directly countering the Soviets, Graham would challenge the totalitarianism associated with communism in Asia, the Middle East, and Eastern Europe, using culture to sway nonbelievers and, particularly, the ever-defiant neutral nations to the American side. While initially Iran was not considered as a tour location, despite the American "Operation Ajax" with the British in 1953 to firmly install the Shah, US diplomats and the followers of the Shah appreciated both the power of oil and the aesthetics of modern art. Government officials noted, "The political situation during these past few months, with a new Government in power, has created difficulties . . . It should be emphasized that in each case the choice [of a cultural export] is made because the individual is well placed to serve our purpose."[222] Israel did not appear in early discussions, with officials later noting that Rothschild funded the tour, emphasizing, "Local tour was not under the auspices of the Fund or of ANTA."[223] With the decision about the region effectively made by Eisenhower's OCB before the Dance Panel met to formalize the tour, the government approved Martha Graham's modern dance.[224]

When the Dance Panel first met to review Limón and discuss Graham, Virginia Inness-Brown served as chair. Inness-Brown reported on the "very cordial" reactions to Limón and his work in Latin America and "equally enthusiastic" embassy comments.[225] She noted USIS reports that the Limón company received favorable press, even "roaring success" in leftist newspapers.[226] She reported to the carefully chosen dance experts who made up the panel, which met in New York, the epicenter of dance after World War II and arguably the world's cultural capital.[227] The use of this group of private-sector experts was meant to prove to people at home and abroad that the United States would allow independent, knowledgeable, and creative minds to guide governmental decisions about cultural exports, as opposed to imposing government mandates from above. Inness-Brown, a handsome woman with a long face, arched eyebrows, gleaming eyes, and dark hair that she styled to hit the nape of her neck, was known to most only as a noted New York socialite. She held a staunch belief in the power of culture as diplomacy, which she acted on through her philanthropy, supporting strategic artistic exports supported by the State Department, but not necessarily by Congress. Thanks to her social prominence and work as a private citizen to support executive branch aims, Inness-Brown served as the cultural conduit representing music, theater, and dance between Eisenhower, the State Department, and what the Dance Panel members referred to as "Washington."[228]

Prominent on the panel was the familiar figure of Lincoln Kirstein. After numerous iterations, with the New York City Ballet he had created yet another sparkling new company of dancers possessed of unprecedented, distinctly American technical prowess. Walter Terry, the earthbound *New York Herald Tribune* dance critic, gave credibility to the committee's decisions as an objective reviewer. ABT's Lucia Chase was elegant, opinionated, and fierce; she expressed her ideas about programming choices without reserve, despite her company's desperate need to survive via government funding. Martha Hill had worked with Graham and was now director of the Juilliard School, which trained upcoming dancers and choreographers: she represented the voice of education. Also on the panel was Bethsabée de Rothschild, who, while she showed no favorites outwardly, was a friend of Graham's and had kept the leading lady working after the 1950 tour; in turn, Graham made sure the rather dowdy Rothschild became coiffed and designed. John Martin was notably absent. Although he had celebrated the diplomatic success of Limón, he disparaged any involvement with political projects that could be deemed incestuous.[229] While all the Dance Panel members championed individual interests, they understood their objectives that demanded private expert advice for a state-driven export for psychwar purposes.[230] Inness-Brown would state that the government would consult the panel "whenever possible," but that "in cases where the State Department, for its own reasons," decided on a particular export, the membership would have to defer.[231] They were ready.

Tour stops were modified over time with ever-changing Cold War politics, but logistics also determined locations. Relying on the organization created by Franklin Roosevelt, the State Department dispatched ANTA to explore performance spaces, accommodations, and public reception prospects for the artists, as well as potential local sponsorship. Before the final approval of Graham's destinations, the State Department's Near Eastern and Far Eastern booking office reported back on poor theater conditions in certain locales. Many venues with proscenium stages had been transformed into movie theaters. Graham's team followed; Craig Barton, as her advance man, reviewed the theaters, accommodations, and transport issues for dancers, sets, and costumes.[232] He would be responsible to Graham, yet would also file reports with ANTA and USIS. Eventually, they settled on stops in twelve countries and territories, starting in Japan and ending in Iran. Graham volunteered to go to Cambodia, but the offer was rejected. Taiwan and Hong Kong were deleted. Egypt and Lebanon were dropped because of violence on the ground. Graham herself wanted to go to Egypt and believed there was funding from the University of Cairo. Sino-Western strains regarding the funding of the Aswan Dam and Egypt's increasing demonstration of leadership in the 1955 conference would have made it an ideal location to woo newly installed power brokers. But violent student demonstrations at the university and an assassination attempt against Egyptian strongman Gamal Abdel Nasser made the country too precarious for the dancers, according to the State Department.[233] Dramatic newsreels about the "communist threat" in Lebanon hit the United States, showing students storming the American University of Beirut in protest against "Western Imperialism." Although the activists were more concerned with Israel than capitalism, students threw stones and climbed gates, with footage showing one dead on the ground. Voice-overs for the American public described a city mired in student factions of communist-inspired anti-American violence.[234] With continued developments in the list of attendees at Bandung, Malaya and Iran were added to the official roster.

Israel continued to present geopolitical problems after its founding in 1947, and questions of political recognition ignited complex diplomatic tensions for the United States and the Bandung nations. The OCB thus let the known Jewish philanthropist and Dance Panel member Rothschild step forward to pay for a final leg after Iran, to Israel. As a new state that emerged in the Middle East as a result of World War II, Israel wanted a seat at the Bandung table, which would theoretically follow "the universality of issuing invitations to every independent state within the Asian and African continents![235] Yet after the initial planning meeting in 1954 and during subsequent gatherings, the Arab League Council voiced dissent on the Israel question. The council dictated, "It is known that this conference is a regional one. It has been the policy of Arab states not to participate in any regional conference where Israel is represented."[236] The issue of the Palestinians became central; despite India's and Burma's recognition of Israel, the conference could not survive an Arab boycott. Thus the "universal" invitation was extended "with minor variations and modifications."[237] Questions of manifest destiny and claims to the land frontier that could be heard at Bandung would continue to engage diplomats throughout the Graham tours, as they recognized the import of her performances in Tel Aviv and Jerusalem. Regarding Bandung inclusion, Israeli diplomats housed in both cities lamented that "it remains a melancholy fact that the troublesome Palestinian question has been allowed to contaminate one more international pot of ointment."[238] Although Palestinians had initially been denied entry into the Bandung Conference as stateless delegates, a Palestinian representative took part in the Political Committee's proceedings during which he described "Israel's territorial designs" and "territorial crimes."[239] While Burma felt that "it was not chivalrous to discuss the question [of territorial claims] when Israel was not present," the same consideration would not be offered the Palestinians by the West at Camp David two decades later; Graham would present her frontier tale as a part of the agreement in Egypt and Israel.[240] In 1955, with Bandung wrapping up, American government funding for a Western-aligned Arab nation, no funding for a nonaligned country, and private funding for Israel with embassy support,

Graham entered the region and its politics where she would stay through 1979, with her legacy echoing.

As specific cities and theaters were negotiated, the desire to show host nations that American artists were not created by government funding meant that Graham became a conduit for business and foundation exchanges; private-sector and local funding served government propaganda needs but also relieved the American taxpayer of some of the cost, which would be attacked by Congress. USIS recommended that arts programming not be associated with the State Department, or it would appear state-sponsored and thus communistic. Rather, groups should appear to be sponsored by American business, host-country institutions, or joint-operated foundations. In Graham's tour programs, advertisements boasting the modern efficiency of American products such as General Electric refrigerators and promoting high-end airlines appeared alongside descriptions of her choreographed works.[241] Graham also crossed cultures with her business alliances. In Abadan, Iran, Graham "performed under the sponsorship" of the Iranian Oil Refining Company.[242] The State Department garnered private support in Israel and Iran from individuals as well as the Israel-America and Iran-America foundations, showing cultural cooperation and shared purpose; indeed, some of these foundations were supported by covert American government funding during the Cold War.[243] Eisenhower stated that he wanted his administration to achieve "more bang for the buck," and the Dance Panel deployments were constructed accordingly, "in order for the government to get its money's worth."[244]

Yet Graham was savvy from the start with her maneuvers to get increased support. For Graham, according to those closest to her, "everything is totally calculated."[245] Graham played her cards: although in December 1954 it was reported that Graham "said she would like to go to the Orient," and, indeed, the OCB had already funded her stops there, at the start of 1955 she had balked and demanded a strictly European tour. Yet the greatest areas of concern expressed by the Dance Panel, with OCB funding in hand as understood by some, were "the Near East and the Far East."[246] After surveying the locations, Graham then insisted on a better financial package: twice the amount offered to Lucia Chase's ballet company for its tour in 1950, and three times the funding Limón had recently received.[247] When the panel met formally in New York to consider Graham's final locations and funding, New York had just endured a long and cold winter, with temperatures frequently dropping below zero. Yet on that day, according to airport reports, skies were crisp and blue. The air of spring promise surely matched the panelists' optimism about the new venture. Politics, like the March wind, was at their backs.[248] There was a Cold War to be won. The panel sweetened the deal for her tour through what it called "the Orient."[249] Off Graham would go to Asia and the Middle East with her modern dance, an ambassador for America in a global Cold War.[250]

2

"The New Home of Men"

Modern Americana Goes to Asia and the Middle East

When American dance, American thought, American theatre, music, painting, poetry, novels, opera and American teaching have captivated the imagination of the peoples of the rest of the hemisphere and become part of its cultural store and its spiritual formation, then the U.S. will be, without dispute, the lighthouse which was France; it will become the new home of men.[1]

—Operations Coordination memo, 1955–1956

The first shock of the Martha Graham company's tour came from the telephone calls the dancers received in their hotel rooms as they packed their practice clothes and souvenirs, leaving Japan as celebrities: they would no longer be going to Seoul the next day.[2] The company had looked forward to seeing a city that, after the Korean War, had been on American minds. They had hoped to venture into the country's mountain landscapes, with their crystal-clear streams, and see the bowed temples of Mount Seorak. But instead they were just to pack up, stay inside, and wait for the next call.

For the tour's advance man, Craig Barton, the Korean cancellation did not come as a total surprise. The logistical issues in Korea seemed daunting from first blush. During Barton's reconnaissance trip to Seoul, he stepped off the plane and soon realized—after people drifted away—that no one was there to meet him; he was, in his words, "stranded at that primitive little airport." After attempts to contact the sponsors and the embassy, he realized that "nobody even *knew* we were coming." Shuttled to a hotel, he waited for three days to meet with officials; the American embassy provided no assistance because it was "short handed" and "swamped." As plans seemed to crumble, Barton grew insistent and even threatening, warning Korean officials that "Martha Graham is a great world name and your irresponsibility in dropping her will make every international news service in the world."[3] As negotiations moved forward, money for the tour promised from Korean partners was not materializing. The Asia Foundation, linked to the CIA, and the Korean-American Foundation, another possible CIA conduit, had been cited as "private"

Martha Graham's Cold War. Victoria Phillips, Oxford University Press 2020. © Oxford University Press.
DOI: 10.1093/oso/9780190610364.001.0001

donors for touring support; they offered less than expected.[4] Negotiations continued after Barton departed.

Despite the issues on the ground, American officials expected a good response to Graham's work as much-needed postwar Cold War trickle-down diplomacy in the divided nation. Korea loomed large in the era's geopolitics: the conflict between North and South, capitalism and communism, had ended just two years earlier. A State Department debriefing memo noted, "This viable [South Korean] democracy [brought by] the United States—important to USIA objectives—is something which will be watched by other countries in Asia."[5] The country, like Germany and Vietnam, was divided. Seoul, like Berlin, remained war-ravaged. Such devastation was a propaganda problem for the West.[6] The US military was omnipresent, with its cars and troop carriers and compounds, and armed soldiers walking on the streets in their green fatigues. "Many Koreans have been erroneously influenced and misunderstood US policy completely," stated a report, continuing, "It is, therefore, vital that Korean groups which will affect the future of the country should be given opportunities to understand the United States."[7] Indeed, the South Korean military, governmental, and cultural elite seemed enthusiastic about hosting renowned American arts figures like Martha Graham. In early negotiations for the company's performances in Seoul, the US Army requested that military personnel be included in the audience as they had been for American ballet performances in Germany.[8] State noted that cultural "acts" had to have an "international reputation" and "important names." The US government at home, for its part, had high expectations for the impact of American cultural exports. "Korea is now intensely interested in catching up with the rest of the world and is looking to the US as the country that can lead them into the modern age," the debriefing continued.[9] Because Barton understood that the State Department's representatives "thought it was important enough to play [in Korea] under any circumstances," he persisted, ultimately arranging a venue and performance dates. Although a State Department memo on cultural exchange stated that issues of "war debt" were hampering tours, Barton had seemingly managed financial and currency exchange support.[10]

Despite overtures and ideas, the logistical problems were exacerbated by politics in Korea as Graham and her dancers left the United States for Japan. After the dancers landed in Tokyo, the political situation between South Korea and the United States started deteriorating rapidly, thus complicating the already strained conditions. While Graham was performing in Japan, the Korean president said that the US Chamber of Commerce had "shamed Korea before the world" over economic issues, and the American ambassador to Korea resigned; memos about economic "saber-rattling" and American troop levels circulated.[11] On November 9, the day before dancers got their hurried cancellation calls, the assistant secretary of state for Far Eastern affairs wrote to Washington that the Korean president "at times appears irrational and irresponsible" and could "fabricate an incident" to create international "mayhem."[12] But the State Department anticipated negotiations, not reactions, and Graham could help "soothe" all. However the following day, the Korean government froze all dollar assets except those earmarked for economic revitalization: the Graham company couldn't get paid for the tour. As the dancers waited for instructions, Barton wondered "how much more uncoordinated Washington could get with its own projects."[13]

After the unexpected break, during which the company toured, shopped, and scavenged for familiar foods, they boarded another plane to Manila, the capital of the Philippines, where the USIS publicity machine went full throttle to celebrate American values and accomplishments through the dance of Martha Graham. Cold War decolonization meant work needed to be done. The Filipino-US history was long, complicated, and fraught: in 1903, with the Philippines having endured Spanish rule, President William McKinley justified the American annexation as a "gift from God" because Filipinos were "unfit for self-government." Unrest lasted until 1913, when President Woodrow Wilson promised gradual independence. Although soft-power moves in English-language education and the outlawing of the use of a Spanish-language national anthem caused some backlash, American colonial rule held through the 1930s. After the Japanese occupation during World War II, in 1946 the nation gained independence on July 4, the same date as the American day of independence, 170 years later. The postwar American flag was lowered, and the flag of the Philippines was raised; the day came to be known as Filipino-American Friendship Day. Yet an alliance with the United States was complicated by the history of imperialist domination that had been well exposed on racial and cultural fronts.[14]

In line with American goals, when the dancers arrived, the *Manila Times* wrote that Graham had created a dance that "transcended national boundaries" and "brought people together."[15] In photographs that emphasized their high cheekbones, perfectly coiffed hair, and sparkling eyes, Graham's women and men continued to present themselves as racially diverse American movie stars. In a nod to cultural convergences, the dancers included one Filipina, pictured by the press as she kneeled and introduced Graham in a photo. In addition to showing racial and national inclusion, the Graham group had to dispel any myth of the "ugly American," politically inept and culturally insensitive. The American-led press commented on "the freshness and youth of the dancers and their simple, unpretentious charm."[16]

Graham was a successful cultural ambassador and propagandist because her promotion of the United States was seemingly apolitical; defined by the tenet of abstraction to find essence, modernism equated her work with humanism and thus universal ideas. Newspapers initially featured Graham's *Diversion of Angels*, a reflection on love based on a painting by Wassily Kandinsky; in this abstract work, only the distilled emotion of love remains. The Woman in Red, the Woman in White, and the Woman in Yellow describe three aspects of love: passion, serenity, and playful joy. It was the only dance in which Graham did not perform center stage; three female bodies, all central, drove the work. The piece begins with the Woman in White upstage center. With the first musical chords, her partner raises his hand, and his outstretched fingers form a halo over her head. She dances as a serene and lyrical centerpiece with long extensions and a perfect ballet penché replete with arched feet. From the right wing, the Woman in Red crosses on a diagonal in a series of off-center tilts on one leg. No ballerina could maintain such a pose. Red tilts and steps, tilts and steps, each tilt a perfect replication of the last. She holds the final tilt, her body lifted to demi-pointe by the torso's contraction, and then exits downstage. In her signature moment, Red crosses diagonally, which takes her flying from upstage to downstage in a movement both entirely grounded in the legs and freed in the body: it replicated the slash of red Graham saw in the Kandinsky painting.[17] The Woman in Yellow finds a playful camaraderie with her partner in split leaps and jumps. In one moment, the dancer jumps onto her partner's shoulder, and they spin offstage. The chorus of men and women race with arms pushing through the air like sparklers, and legs extended in cartwheels; they melt into scooped positions that they hold with a powerful technical finesse to make a backdrop for the three central characters. Graham showed that, like ballet stars, her dancers could perform arabesques and lifts, but hers were modern, unique, never before seen, cutting-edge. There was no set, no backdrop. The dance set the stage. Taking Kandinsky's writings and his textured use of color as inspiration, Graham used the modernist body as a brushstroke and found "that shaft of intimacy."[18] A reporter concluded of Graham, "She has established modernism in dance."[19]

As a master of modernist abstraction, Graham carried the intellectual weight to reinterpret the greatest narratives from the Western canon that would be well known by elites in the audiences. *Night Journey*, her retelling of the tale of Oedipus, was a standard part of her repertory and played in all the cities she would visit on her diplomatic dance tour. Graham fractured the linear narrative to dwell in the psyche of Jocasta, Oedipus's mother and the role Graham would dance, dominated by flashback and relived trauma, guilt, and redemption.

Night Journey begins before the curtain rises. The dramatic, foreboding music, written for Graham by William Schuman, commences while the audience sits in darkness. Graham's work begins with Jocasta's death, as she relives her life's drama through fractured memories. The publicity photo for this work showed Graham strangling herself with a rope that represented the umbilical cord to her child, and the familial psychic ties that would ultimately kill her. Jocasta faces the Noguchi sculpture that will be her bed where she unwittingly has sex with her son, whom she unknowingly married. The blind prophet Tiresias stands upstage on the other side of the bed. He extends his staff forward, then up, and brings it down to the ground with a heavy thud. He repeats this movement and then stabs his staff into the loop of Jocasta's rope. Jocasta turns to the audience and split falls to the ground.

A chorus of women proceed onstage wearing long dresses, with clinging tops and fabric that flows from the crest of the hipbone to the ground. Their sinewy wire headpieces, a modernist take on the images that adorn ancient Greek pottery, sparkle when the dancers hit the light just right. As the torsos of the chorus dancers contract, the sleek curves strike with force, yet when their legs sweep outward, the fabric of their dresses flows in arcs and curves. The chorus enters, slapping their spread legs. In another moment, they throb with heavy angled lunges, eyes covered, torsos scooped. Then, foretelling the queen's fate, the dancers use clawed hands to simulate ripping out their eyes, heart, and womb in hard-hitting gestures. Their bodies abruptly fold inward as they slap their hipbones with cupped hands, fall backward, and hit the floor. They recover into spirals, then back up to their knees and feet. Jocasta and Oedipus move slowly, serenely, until the moment of revelation. Jocasta takes the rope and again crosses it over her neck and frames her face. Graham held the audience rapt with performances. As the curtain descended and rose, she and her dancers emerged to receive ovations, bravos, and unrequited calls for encores.

Graham further added ideas of religious freedom—also tied to politics—with her iconic work *Seraphic Dialogue* (1955), the story of Joan of Arc. Freedom of religion in America was a central Cold War propaganda trope because it had infused the language of the myths of the men of the *Mayflower* landing, from which Graham was descended. A local newspaper, fed stories by USIS, reported on Graham's status as a descendent of the pilgrim Miles Standish: "Three hundred and thirty-five years ago, a group of Puritans dissatisfied with the British church arrived in America on the Mayflower."[20] Because the United States had found its origins in an escape from tyranny—religious, political, and economic—the use of religious references, rhetoric, and propaganda infused the ideological Cold War. As the Puritan-built "City upon a Hill," based on Matthew 5:16, the United States clashed with the Marxist notion of religion as "the opiate of the masses."[21]

Christian tropes had long infused American national Cold War rhetoric, and had direct interwar links to freedom with Roosevelt's "Four Freedoms." Harry Truman had used pious language to promote his doctrine of containment in Turkey and Greece when he declared, "God has created us and brought us to our present position of power and strength for some great purpose."[22] His assistant secretary of state, who headed the Information Service, a precursor to the United States Information Agency, believed that religion-based advocacy could become "communism's greatest foe." Dwight Eisenhower had drawn on the expertise of John Foster Dulles, his secretary of state, who brought prayer to the White House cabinet meetings. After being baptized ten days after becoming president, Eisenhower inserted the words "In God We Trust" onto paper money, the postwar symbol of American financial hegemony in the face of the Communist system. Karl Marx opposed religious institutions as a "quick fix" for a systemic problem; the United States claimed an attachment to Judeo-Christian freedom to worship as deeply American, extending this even to Muslim and Buddhist practices. Yet God was also politicized and militarized. During his Flag Day speech, the five-star general turned president said that with the words "under God" inserted in the "Pledge of Allegiance," "We shall constantly strengthen those spiritual weapons which forever will be our country's most powerful resource in peace and war." Eisenhower stated that the greatest weapon against communism was the West's "ultimate appeal to the soul."[23]

Seraphic Dialogue explores the three aspects of Saint Joan of Arc—Maid, Warrior, and Martyr—with three separate female dancers.[24] The dance retells a story of political and religious persecution, drawing on the idea of a universal human narrative in which the righteous become victimized. Promoting the idea of Joan as an everywoman despite her European and Catholic historical roots, Graham said, "I had no grounds to go on except what I imagined went on in her heart."[25] She projected the character's multi-faceted nature when she hears the voices of Saint Catherine, Saint Michael, and Saint Margaret, and her own in martyrdom.[26] The Noguchi set became an integral part of the dance. Graham described the set as "a cathedral without limitations, like no other cathedral in the world."[27] Noguchi called it "his geometry of faith."[28] Although posited as a *Mayflower* descendant, Graham told the story of a Catholic saint embedded in a Japanese set for the audiences.

Despite their political import, Graham did not choose protagonists with the government in mind. Always "contemporary," Graham's focus on Saint Joan arose not just from intellectual curiosity or a ready identification with a dramatic historical female figure.[29] In the 1950s, religious books populated the bestseller lists.[30] Joan's story became compelling in the post-Holocaust atomic age. As a martyr who saved the French from conquest by England, Joan was thus a voice of national independence, a postwar theme in the Bandung or domino nations as the old colonial powers withdrew. She embodied "the peculiar blend of the visionary and the military."[31] This message would have rung true for many from Warsaw to Tel Aviv, and certainly in the nations seeking independence where Graham landed. Yet like Graham, Joan claimed herself apolitical. When asked during her trial if victory was for the "flag," Joan had responded that it was "all for the Lord."[32] Here, too, publicity underscored American claims to inclusiveness; the African American Matt Turney played Joan, the Warrior, which USIS featured in publicity shots. While Moscow promoted images of the American use of the atomic bomb and harped on US warmongering, surely aided by Dulles's rhetoric, Eisenhower himself linked religious piety, or democratic freedoms, with peace: "The pursuit of peace is at once our religious obligation and our national policy."[33] Graham's Saint Joan worked on numerous levels to embed ideas abroad, and the choreographer's imagination worked in lockstep with her nation.[34]

Having established herself as a humanist under the umbrella of abstraction and a dance form that brought universals and cultural archetypes readable to all, Graham introduced the frontier narrative as a subset of the established canon and used her frontier to counter Soviet propaganda of an imperialist, racist America. Despite the fact that the United States had been the colonial ruler of the Philippines for half a century, President Eisenhower declared, "The whole of our history is anti-colonial."[35] Engaging American rhetoric about its own anticolonial history, USIS reminded the citizens of the newly independent Philippines about America's own status as a British colony, as a way "to establish a basis of understanding and sympathy with subject peoples."[36] *Appalachian Spring*'s frontier tale told the history of a nation that had achieved freedom and prosperity after the defeat of the British Empire, offering decolonizing countries a blueprint with the postindependence success of a vast former British colony, the United States itself. Another souvenir booklet for *Appalachian Spring* featured a line drawing of a statue of George Washington, hand on his sword as he looked out over the horizon, providing thematic guidance and a readable blueprint for newly forming governments.[37] In a bid to promote the idea of racial equality available to all American citizens, the friendly press followed USIS guidance and noted that Matt Turney was an "attractive Negro girl" who played the Pioneering Woman, as well as Joan of Arc.[38]

Overall, the company received huge ovations in the Philippines. The modernist tactic worked: a review noted that with Graham's use of the "human body . . . [s]he delivers a shock not unlike that of an initial confrontation of modern painting."[39] Reports back to the United States from USIS followed: "Although modern dance, as such, was practically unknown, the public acceptance and enthusiasm for the company's performances were immediate and overwhelming."[40] While the *Manila Chronicle* had been darkly critical of the policies of the US government, critics praised the State Department for bringing Graham and "the genius who conceived the idea of sending out to all parts of the world . . . the best American dance companies . . . [who] deserves more than routine commendation." Writing of Graham's performances, the newsman reported that the dance "proved that the United States is not a nest of materialism that it has always been said to be."[41]

* * *

After the first two legs of the tour, the company began a grueling series of shorter stops through Asia and the Middle East. While Graham had proved herself an ideal cultural ambassador in Japan and the Philippines, she was beginning to show signs of wear. She held strong at performances, lectures, company classes, dinners, and cocktail parties, but the strain was evident behind the scenes. At one point, the company manager cabled the American consulate in Calcutta that Graham couldn't "sustain [the] present grind."[42] Although her age was never directly mentioned, she managed a company, acted as diplomat, and performed as the young Bride at age sixty-one. Reports also noted her "exhaustion," which later became a code word for excessive drinking. Performances in Thailand began on November 21 and lasted three days. On Thanksgiving night, the embassy did all it could to stave off the fatigue and homesickness that also hit company members. Hosted in the elaborate home of the ambassador, they ate small roasted quails, or something they understood to be birds, in place of turkey.[43]

On the way to Malaya, the company performed in Singapore, where the value of offstage appearances became paramount. The United States sought to keep both resource-rich countries within the Western sphere: Singapore had rubber; Malaya, tin and gold mines. Both countries had been colonized by Britain—with a brief interlude of Japanese occupation. Some anticolonial sentiment in Singapore was assuaged by elections in 1948 and 1951, but with few allowed to register to vote, the British colonial administration remained dominant. Yet by the spring of 1955, with automatic voter registration, newly formed political parties with labor and leftist ties won seats, and the leader of the Labour Front became the first chief minister of Singapore.[44] To reinforce capitalistic democracy, *Appalachian Spring* could play well in Singapore and Malaya with their history of being colonized by the British, with the local elites educated in the Western canon and Greek myths. Yet the works backfired: in Singapore, USIS reported that most of Graham's audience was "expatriate, two-thirds of whom walked out during [the] first interval." The embassy had not stacked the audience according to plan; the British had not favored Graham's modernism in London in 1954. Thus, offstage appearances remained vital to assert American values to the Singapore elite: the report also noted congenial opportunities for the women in the company to meet with female leaders and influential wives.[45] Graham made personal appearances, sat for radio interviews, and socialized at women's luncheons. According to USIS research, the question of female leadership carried "world wide appeal," and Graham met the challenge in Singapore.[46] Graham and her dancers were "all valuable assets in representational settings" for the State Department.[47]

In addition to private meetings, the value of the lecture-demonstration became palpable. Audiences in Singapore expressed "delight" at seeing the troupe of young, sleek dancers demonstrate the Graham technique as she explained its principles. Her show quickly became recognized as a vital part of the government's package for export. Graham declared that her version of *Night Journey*, the story of Oedipus told by Jocasta, was "stripped to its bones." While the acceptance of the acute sexuality of her works seemed incomprehensible, perhaps offensive in a number of the countries she visited, it was this claim to the modernist tradition steeped in the myth-based canon that allowed critics and the audience an intellectual understanding of her project, as she explained in lectures during the day. In addition, Graham spoke to young local dancers who could be receptive to a modernist technique that they could then use to develop their own choreography. The State Department heartily approved of this one-to-one contact with local youth, viewing it as vital to the project.[48] Graham would leave, but the Graham technique would be practiced and put to use as nations decolonized and artists found new cultural expressions, seeded in a technique mythologized as American yet applicable to all.

Moving on to Malaya, in Penang, Graham performed as the star of the modern dance, but not as a dancer, presenting the lecture-demonstrations only. Programming was adjusted to give her some rest. Establishing a mantra that would be used in later tours, she was billed as the "High Priestess" of dance, who was "worshipped" by her young company. The men and women were shown in newspaper photos in black practice clothes that hugged the shape of their finely tuned muscles. Graham sat at the side of the stage explaining the fundamentals of her dance and the American "tradition" of "innovation" in which disciplined knowledge met the youthful joy of creation with a frontier ethos. The company members brought freshness and physical beauty to the rooms, close enough for the audience to touch, holding positions unthinkably off-balance without a wobble. The State Department reported, "Miss Graham, whose name is synonymous with American modern dance, points out that new sensibilities are born in mankind as time goes on."[49]

Graham was revitalized after the performance break in Malaya, and the company moved on to Indonesia, the nation that had hosted the Bandung Conference. Like the other places Graham had visited, Indonesia had a complicated colonial history that included Japanese occupation during World War II. After the end of the war, the Indonesian people declared independence, yet the Dutch attempted to regain control with British support, leading to an armed conflict that ended in 1949 only after pressure from the international community, including the United States. Although the country became the United States of Indonesia, ideological ferment persisted, and

1955 election posters showed numerous images, including the hammer and sickle.[50] The region remained unstable and was a hotbed of US government activity and interest. Not unexpectedly, the CIA reported as Graham's sleek planes landed.[51] Graham always used two planes: one for the company and another cargo plane for the sets and costumes. Eisenhower's administration was known to use clandestine cameras to take aerial shots over contested areas.[52] A CIA memo noted that her planes had successfully entered the Indonesian airspace and were approved by its government without usual clearances.[53]

At the Jakarta airport, crowds flocked around Graham when she and the company arrived. Graham was back onstage as a full performer, not merely a narrator, for the two days of shows. She gave her usual introduction and thanks on the tarmac. Throngs pressed to see her on the street. Newspapers featured the dancers in a motorcade, smiling and waving to expectant crowds standing three deep. Student tickets for performances sold out in twenty minutes.[54] The press, tired of the US assertion of Hollywood-style economic and military might, reported, "We have had too little opportunity to convince ourselves that besides [America's] cheap films, the domineering attitude of Americans as regards political, military and commercial matters and the like, America has also another aspect." Yet in a soft-power win for the United States, the article moved on to discuss Graham specifically: "In day-to-day activities we are fed up with the waves of 'Americanism,' so that the coming here of Martha Graham is a relief, since her creations have convinced us that America . . . is in the possession of much that should deserve our attention."[55] Graham, indeed, soothed international mayhem—for the moment.

In Indonesia, the State Department's pro-nationalist and anticolonial message bolstered the American partnership with host sponsors: empire by invitation was at work by the end of the two days of appearances.[56] Reporters wrote that Graham's performances marked the "first time an Indonesian [sponsor] has ever had a chance to bring anything to Indonesia."[57] The press noted that the Netherlands, the longtime colonial ruler, had imported high art only for the Dutch intelligentsia, reserving it for "limited and private audiences," thus excluding the Indonesians themselves. Because the modern dance was marketed not as an American phenomenon but as a universal form, it seemingly offered host nations an opportunity to establish and embrace their own connection to the future of the arts in the postwar era through the economics of aesthetic cultural convergence. At the conclusion of the Graham company's visit, the editor of the *Times of Indonesia* wrote, "If

ever this paper came perilously close to forgetting its policy of leaning neither to the East nor to the West, it was during the Martha Graham week, because this talented woman presented something of the United States that we
could wholeheartedly approve of."[58] Operations Coordination Board progress reports back in Washington touted the fact that Graham performances
had swayed audiences toward the United States.[59]

* * *

As she had in Japan, in Burma, the next leg of the tour, Graham went up
against the Soviets. This time, she directly followed politicians, not a ballerina. Her political import seemed to be growing as soft-power gained traction. The embassy in Burma stated, "It was particularly fortunate that the
GRAHAM company performed so shortly after the visit of the Soviet leaders,
[Communist Party secretary Nikita] Khrushchev and [Premier Nikolai]
Bulganin, as it kept very favorable publicity about the United States on the
front pages of the Burmese newspapers and showed that our country had not
lost interest in Burma."[60] Burma had become a British colony in the 1820s,
and anticolonial movements erupted immediately that later included Marxist
followers, particularly during the interwar period. During World War II,
when Burma was occupied by the Japanese, antifascist movements included
some that aligned with the Soviet Union, while the Japanese also offered
empty promises of freedom from colonial rule. Three years after the war, the
British granted independence, and the new nation saw continued insurgen-
cies by Communist groups. Yet in the spirit of Bandung, the Burmese government wanted to retain its independence from foreign interference, East
or West.[61] Graham promoted an American-Burmese alliance through the
arts, which demonstrated a political commitment that the United States had
made to Burma; as with all neutral and nonaligned countries, such an approach seemed more effective than taking an openly anti-Soviet stance.[62]

While politics met performance, the troupe struggled with unexpected
local issues. At one stop, the troupe found there was no dressing room,
and after a particularly difficult performance, the ever-poised dancer Ethel
Winter threw her costume on to the dirt floor in frustration and stamped
on it.[63] Graham looked at her, astonished, as Winter feared retribution. Yet
Graham merely remarked, "Good girl, Ethel." Unbeknownst to Winter,
Graham watched with future casting in mind. Despite their inspirational
power in some cases, things kept going wrong. Bethsabée de Rothschild,

designated as "costume mistress," yet certainly not adept with an iron, burned an *Appalachian Spring* Follower's dress (luckily, there was an extra one). Bills of lading show massive delays and political complexity, and customs officials kept sets just within reach for performances as they arrived within an hour of the curtain.[64]

Ignoring the touring drama, USIS reports could often be deceptively dry and neutral regarding Graham's engagement with the population, and unreported people-to-people relationships undeniably increased the success of the tour. A report on the stop in the capital city of Rangoon, for instance, merely noted that the Graham company "gave open-air performances for five successive nights before audiences of about 4,000 persons each night." But this only scratches the surface. When the Graham company stage manager arrived to shepherd the sets and prepare to hang the lights for a rehearsal, he found there was no stage—just a field and a pile of teak.[65] Corralling a group of local workers, some of them excited but others reluctant, he went to work to build a stage, hang a makeshift curtain, and mount sets. By the time the dancers arrived, the staging was nearly completed—enough so that rehearsals could take place. For opening night, in the front local dignitaries, embassy officials, and the ever-watchful members of USIS sat in lavish padded armchairs. Toward the back, inelegant folding chairs were offered to those less fortunate. They all solemnly watched the performances closely.[66] Yet included in the audience were Buddhist monks, apparently uninvited, and unseated. They perched in the trees and watched in fascination. Each time a female dancer touched a male, or a male dancer touched a female, and they turned upside down, the monks laughed and laughed. Rather than feeling indignation at the sensual display, as might be expected by the Americans, they were fascinated, engaged. The dancers were distracted by the reaction, but they kept going.[67] While at times failures went unreported in official documents, so did perplexing successes.

* * *

The next leg of the tour was in South Asia, taking the company to India, Ceylon, back to India, and then to Pakistan. This region was fraught with political tension, with overlapping communities clashing at newly established borders. In 1947, when Britain dismantled its empire by partitioning it into predominantly Hindu India and majority Muslim Pakistan, more than a million people died, and the two nations went to war. Although a formal ceasefire was declared in 1949, battles and conflicts continued. In addition, as a powerful and nonaligned nation seen to be playing "both sides," India became a particular problem for the United States; thus, Graham visited the nation twice. The United States provided India with monetary aid and food support, particularly after 1950, at the same time that the Soviet Union contributed modernizing technology, know-how, and loans. Prime Minister Jawaharlal Nehru positioned himself as a leader of the Third World and worked with both sides, stating that India would never accept the "attachment of political strings to aid."[68] Nonalignment conferences and gatherings had begun to brew, and cultural diplomacy was needed. A State Department memo from New Delhi began, "The role of an overseas information service is primarily that of achieving agreed upon foreign policy objectives through psychological and informational means." A USIS study titled "American Values with Which Indians Can Identify Themselves" reflected the frustration with capitalistic cultural deployments, stating glibly, "The presentation of America as a country of solved problems and Kohler plumbing is not only ineffective but actually psychologically impossible to grasp."[69]

The year 1955 brought the conference and a renewed show of Soviet friendship with India, as Nehru visited Moscow in June, and Bulganin and Khrushchev returned the favor in November and December in India just before Graham's arrival. As Graham's dance was planned, Eisenhower and Nehru struggled with each other over ideas of "colonialism, communism and nationalism."[70] A USIS "Summary of Propaganda Policy" listed the unit's objectives in India. First was the acceptance of democratic concepts; second was acceptance for US foreign policies. Teaching the Indians "the best traditions of our American history" would achieve propaganda ends.[71] Graham conveniently arrived with *Appalachian Spring*.

Although the use of *Appalachian Spring* in India could seem too direct a comment on the country's current situation with distinct pro-American messages, a USIS survey from just two years prior gave reason to think that it would resonate. USIS hired an Indian social scientist, who had prepared a questionnaire that asked Indians, "What subjects about America or Americans are you most interested in?" The answer was "Americana."[72] Working soft power along with empire by invitation, Graham brought the Indians what they seemed to want.

The definition of "Americana," however, grew increasingly contested, which became problematic with the export of *Appalachian Spring*. Three years before Graham's deployment, the USIS-India study, titled "Some

Clarification of the Word 'Americana,'" opened, "Although several evaluation studies point to a demand for more 'Americana' in our USIS output, little
is known as to what is really meant by the word."[73] Graham's work served
as a point-by-point answer to the survey of the audience that would watch
her dance. First, the report noted an interest in "Physical Characteristics of
[the United States]" on the list of curiosities for Indians. *Appalachian Spring*
was perfect for the task: it opened with a bare stage that described the vast
US landscape in modernist terms and depicted the way in which the land
was tamed in a democratic capitalistic state with a fence and home. Next
on the list of Americana-style interests were "Physical Characteristics of
People" and "Standard of Living." Both aspects of American life were well
represented by Graham's multiracial dancers and the stage, which showed
both the outside and the inside of the American home with the transparency of modernism. Fourth on the list was "American Home Life," with
"Husband and Wife Relationship" as the top subcategory. *Appalachian Spring*
revolves around the courtship, marriage, and integration of the Husband
and Bride into American life. Sixth was "Women," including "Women's political and social advance; pioneer women in women's rights," and questions
about working women.[74] Graham's Pioneering Woman was a representative
of the nation, the spirit of freedom and order, exemplifying the American
emancipated woman and personifying her as the United States itself; on
tour and for the film, the Pioneering Woman was played by an African
American. And Indians sought information about "Religion" and "different religions, different sects of Christians, workings of a church, functions
of church in American life, separate or common churches for Negros and
whites, freedom of religion." The Preacher, and even his antics, showed both
godliness and tolerance of religions on the frontier. Indians also wanted to
know about American "Recreation," including "Pick nicks, festivals, fun-
fair."[75] *Appalachian Spring* showed a square dance in the town. In addition to
"Folk," Indians wanted to know more about American "Art, Music, Drama,
etc." Aaron Copland brought the prize-winning score. Thus, even though
the government's promotional arm wasn't quite sure how to define the word
"Americana," they knew it when they saw Graham in *Appalachian Spring*.

* * *

Amid mishaps and exhaustion followed by respite, when the company
landed in India on the first tour, ready to perform *Appalachian Spring* as the

celebratory crowd-pleaser, they were again serenaded. The famed choreographer Uday Shankar, who brought Western dance to India and remade the art form, greeted Graham at the airport with a wide smile and flowers. His legacy had been firmly established; as early as 1935, he was celebrated as "a messenger of goodwill and culture of India, [and also] an ambassador and propagandist on behalf of Indian art and culture."[76] After he toured New York in 1937 with his company of more than 120 dancers and musicians, newspapers reported, "He is something quite extraordinary among the numerous dance recitalists," using the adjectives "genuine" and "brilliant."[77] He had toured the United States in 1950 and been celebrated at Constitution Hall in Washington, DC.[78] The people-to-people stage was set: one established master was meeting another on the red carpet, now in India. Yet Graham always merged culture with politics; also meeting the American icon on the tarmac were the Indian finance minister and the chief justice.

Despite USIS research and advance publicity plans, India's leftists contested Graham and her all-American message. Although the mainstream press in Calcutta, which had been fully supplied with pro-Graham publicity, called *Appalachian Spring* "a delightful piece of Americana," the left-wing press was not as enthusiastic.[79] The propaganda intrinsic to *Appalachian Spring* seemed transparently pro-American as a pseudo-folk work with a pro-American political message. Indian choreographers, with their version of artistic nationalism, had been experimenting with modernism and folk forms to express their own developing dance and politics as they threw off the bonds of the British. One reviewer, for instance, criticized Graham's hosts for booking her on the same evening as a performance of Indian dance.[80]

While it seemingly had little to do with Graham's high art, the politics of "folk" art forms and Left-Right, proletariat-bourgeois claims were palpable in the context of the fights for "hearts and minds" in the Cold War. Both the Americans and the Soviets declared their dedication to the needs of the people; a homegrown nationalism could be built on a return to folk culture. From Appalachia to Romania, folk dance and references to its traditions based on "the people" became politically essential and contested cultural propaganda vehicles over time. Here in India, Shankar had adapted modern theatrical techniques to local dance and demonstrated what he called an "immaculate professional approach."[81] Taking a different path from the Indian dance master, Shanti Bardhan, a younger colleague of Shankar, became a part of a new generation of choreographers inspired by socialist themes under the sponsorship of the Indian People's Theatre Association (IPTA). Bardhan used untrained dancers alongside those trained by Shankar and drew on Indian folk themes to create dances that spoke to people "from the bottom up" versus the top-down trickle-down diplomacy engaged by the Americans in the early Cold War.[82] The IPTA subscribed to "the indigenous folk model of theatre, music and dance for inspiration and expression," having "its roots deep down in the cultural awakening of the masses of India."[83]

In *Appalachian Spring*, Graham made a sharp distinction between her modernist treatment of folk material and the approach taken by leftist dancers in the United States, which was also reflected by the new Indian dancers. Graham had "abstracted" folk dances on the frontier stage set by the modernist Noguchi with Copland's score and had not taken it to Prague in 1947, whereas New Dance Group dancers in the United States had bucked State Department warnings and performed actual folk dances in the bloc nation's festival. In the United States, New Dance Group leader Sophie Maslow had made leftist-leaning works such as *Folksay*, which showed farmers with their thumbs in their work clothes dancing to harmonicas.[84] The dedication of these choreographers to political protest made them unacceptable for export by the State Department, even as they directly evoked the lives of everyday American people from factory workers to small farmers using dance and the homespun tunes of musicians like Woody Guthrie and Pete Seeger.[85] With *Appalachian Spring*, Graham asserted that American folk material could be modernized and transformed into theatrical high art. Yet efforts did not always pay off in balancing folk with the abstract. While an American official attending a Graham performance appreciated the folkish "pantomime" in *Appalachian Spring*, an Indian reporter wrote, "There must be something wrong with a gesture language that escapes one's grasp so totally. [*Appalachian Spring*] was like listening to an actor whose words cannot be heard in the stalls."[86]

Like the tarmac reunion, dancegoers and critics in India would have equated Graham with Shankar. Graham's highly trained dancers and Shankar's legacy stood in contrast with the use of untrained dancers associated with socialistic projects created by Shankar's student, Bardhan. Although USIS-inspired press reported that at Graham company performances Shankar stood up shouting "Brava! Brava!" from the front row, clash often seemed more common than convergence in India. An independent Indian critic wrote that *Night Journey* "was [a] wrong conception to show the lovemaking between mother and son on stage."[87] The Western cultural references to Sophocles and Freud were not appreciated. Another critic added that *Cave of the Heart*, the story of Medea, was a "jungle of movements that ought to be shunned"—a scathing denunciation of the idea that Graham's work evoked classical civilization in a way that modern, international elite audiences could appreciate, even if British-trained ones in colonized or formerly colonized nations.[88]

It was in India during a press conference that Graham was most potently challenged as a propagandist for the United States regarding race relations. Before Graham left on tour, the New York press had emphasized that "women and men of color" were "supporting Miss Graham."[89] She was a known supporter of racial equality in the United States with her history of Jewish, Japanese, and African American inclusion. While in India, when questioned about racism in the United States and asked why she didn't speak out against it in her choreography, Graham insisted that all her dances spoke to the "brotherhood of mankind."[90] Dancers reported tension. The leftist reporters did not seem impressed. Even with Matt Turney playing the Pioneering Woman, *Appalachian Spring* and American folk remained contested topics at best, propaganda at worst.

Throughout the Asian tour, Graham and her company were sent to countries in which the American government "sensed internal mayhem," and the India-Pakistan leg fell in line with expectations. Company members had to be sneaked out of the hotel in Bombay under guard at five in the morning because of rioting nearby.[91] Nonetheless, Graham and her company attended teas and performances of local dance groups. Yet the cultural ambassador and her deputies were charming and effective at myriad official functions. They visited Adyar, headquarters of the Theosophical Society in the city of Madras, and met with gurus and dancers.[92] At other locations, Graham was shown appreciating Indian "folk" dance at live demonstrations and expressed her delight with such performances for the press. In Agra, the "All Nations Society of Culture and Art" sponsored her stay at the Taj Mahal Hotel. The entire company was then photographed in front of the Taj Mahal. Graham's luminous dancers of all colors and backgrounds, clothed in perfectly fit American New Look styles, stood smiling in front of an emperor's magnificent mausoleum for the soon-to-be famous postcard picture.[93] The ancient stories of Graham's dances played in the evenings echoed the language of enduring grandeur that stood behind them by day in the photographs sent home.

Before returning to India a second time, the company performed on Christmas Day in Dacca, Pakistan. In 1954, the year before Graham arrived, the United States signed a treaty recognizing Pakistan as an ally, and India cultivated relations with the Soviet Union to counter the American move. While he was still in New York putting together the schedule, Graham's advance man, Barton, wrote that Karachi would be a "dead end."[94] But the capital city of Pakistan remained on the itinerary; politics, first and foremost, determined performance locations. "Hope no one notices," he wrote in response.[95] Even as they exchanged small presents and received letters from home via the consulate, the dancers were reaching both emotional and physical exhaustion. Barton's wish seemed to have come true regarding the performances; with Christmas Day shows, few press reports made it to the translators.

* * *

The company closed the State Department leg of the tour in Tehran after having stopped in Abadan, in Iran's southwest. Graham was well aware of the strategic importance of Iran to the United States with the American- and British-sponsored coup having occurred just two years earlier, in 1953.[96] The Persian elites, once again securely in power, were deeply apprecia-tive of artistic modernism. Bowing to the politics of finance and artistry, the American government and the Iranian oil industry jointly sponsored Graham's performances. Guests invited to her performances included leaders in government, industry, education, and culture. In Iran, some theaters had as few as five hundred seats, which allowed the nation's elite to be seated strategically in the theater and to mingle with one another at champagne intermissions and after the performance.[97] Wives of business leaders sponsored postperformance suppers for the dance company.[98] On some days, according to reports, "nothing was accomplished except social-izing."[99] American representatives were fully satisfied with the impact of Graham and her social outreach offstage. The company manager remarked, "The [US] Ambassador announced that as far as he is concerned if the the-atre burned down and Martha never performed, a tremendous thing had been accomplished."[100]

Leaders in Iran, who boasted important collections of modern art, engaged in heated conversations about Graham's works and her use of the body.[101] Initially, Graham described the applause the dancers received as "a nervous kind of response"; nevertheless, her performances sold out, and sponsors clamored for more dates.[102] Graham's depiction of love and eroticism was advertised as an evocation of common human emotions that, abstracted, connected her to the modernist form. In a radio speech delivered in Tehran, Graham reinforced this view, saying, "The language of dance is the universal language of the world. It is the language of gesture that proceeds from men's hearts . . . of the soul."[103] Iranian elites and the Iranian public embraced the argument. So many flower petals rained down on the company during the final curtain call that Graham complained later about the difficulty of walking offstage without slipping. At the conclusion of the season and the final tour performance of *Appalachian Spring*, the Shah's son presented her with a medal.

Graham wanted to leave her mark on the next generation as well. A local radio station asked Graham to describe what she wished to say to the youth of Iran. Even though the CIA and British intelligence had recently reinstalled the Shah as head of state, Graham emphasized, in general and easily sanctioned terms, her very American belief that the world's students had to act as democratically empowered individuals free of politics: "My advice would be—have a dream, keep to that dream and make that dream come into manifestation."[104] Yet ballet schools were opened with Soviet teachers who also taught Russian folk dances. The Iranian National Ballet Company began in 1956. Tehran became a center of dance that fused Iranian dances with classical ballet technique brought by the Soviets.[105] Indeed, as Graham approached the region in the 1970s, but skipped over Iran, her advice would come to backfire as politics engaged freethinking students who had not joined the American side.

* * *

After Graham completed her performances in Iran, the company proceeded to Israel, where, as mentioned previously, Bethsabée de Rothschild underwrote the expenses for a multi-week extension of the tour along with the American Fund for Israel Institutions. Although it was a "private" tour, the government noted, "At the request of the Foundation, the Embassy extended the usual range of facilitative services accorded an attraction sponsored by the President's Fund, including the patronage of Ambassador and Mrs. Lawson."[106] President Truman had recognized the State of Israel in 1948, and Graham's proposed visit showed American support, however veiled. Like the question of Israel's participation in the Bandung Conference, the postwar formation of new states brought a myriad of problems for those claiming to champion "universal rights" in geopolitical terms. Thus Gertrude Macy, a private citizen and Broadway theatrical producer who later ran ANTA's productions, brokered the details of the deal between Rothschild, Graham's business manager, and the Israeli state.[107] The American Fund for Israel Institutions circumvented any currency problems. The foundation also strongly promoted Israeli settlements, and thus *Appalachian Spring* would have rung true as a narrative that explicitly promoted the expansion of a nation into "empty" lands. Although Graham had included the figure of an American Indian in *American Document*, an earlier interwar work that was critical of the government, in *Appalachian Spring* she finally deleted the character of Pocahontas, clearing the frontier. In like terms, the Israeli government was interested in promoting the regeneration of the desert as an unoccupied place.[108] Private support for Graham from a Rothschild whose family boasted an eponymous boulevard, multiple businesses, and foundations in Israel was key to bringing her to this country, with other citizens working for the production.

Despite Rothschild's support, Graham had to be vetted by the Israeli government before entering the country. Because the US government was not officially brokering the deal, Graham had to make her case in an independent appeal. While her application for entry reads much the same as the text in Graham's programs, Graham herself was credited with having written a section in Hebrew.[109] Indeed, the sophisticated choice of words underlies a framing of her deep commitment to the project by a skilled translator. The passage "written by Graham" is heavily crafted, with the word for "faith" chosen for its connotation of "trust." Other examples abound. Graham wrote, in translation back to English:

> I am a dancer and that means for me that I believe we learn by having faith [or trust]. Whether it means learning the art of dance or learning how to live, in both cases we discuss the same principle in both cases there's a need of precise realization of defined acts, physical and intellectual, that from them will be derived—the form of achievement, the sense of self-existence, and spiritual satisfaction, so a person can be, in a certain territory, the athlete of God.

Accessing the political moment and the seemingly miraculous Israeli survival after attacks by Arab states, Graham wrote, "Faith means repetition, repetition and again repetition, crushing obstacles; it means also faith in having a vision and will." She referenced the Torah, saying, "This kind of faith [trust] has to be the kind of faith that Abraham had in God's promise."[110] Dance, for Graham, was the ultimate tool through which to express shared experiences Her personal alliances were heartfelt and became useful to the US government as a private vehicle of political support.

Although the State Department had not underwritten this portion of the tour, it remained involved, continuing to orchestrate travel details and promulgate Graham's message. Representatives at the American Fund, a private foundation that supported Graham, had close contacts at the American embassy, and the ambassador and cultural attaché received the Graham company as though it had been deployed by the American state.[111] USIS continued to support Graham with direct advance and current publicity as though Graham were on a government-sponsored tour leg.[112]

As was the case in the United States, but with deeper political twists and turns, modern dance in Israel had been inspired by the German expressive dance during the interwar period, which had political consequences for cultural deployments in the Cold War. While the area was ruled by the British, German Jewish dancers came to Palestine to escape the Nazi threat. When Mary Wigman exiled Jewish dancers from her school and company in Germany, some went to Israel. Much like the women who seeded the political dance in New York in the 1930s, these women used Wigman's teachings to create a wholly Israeli dance. In the tradition of union halls where many Jewish women performed in New York, the women in Israel used this dance to express Zionist ideals and danced on newly founded kibbutzim. When adapting Wigman's techniques, the Jewish women in New York and in Palestine did not see a contradiction in her attachment to the Nazi state. They recognized the expressive possibilities of accessing the freed body.[113] Ruth Eshel recalls:

> The first generation emerged in the beginning of the 1920s. A few dancers—they wanted to make something original that was Israeli. Then from 1933 to 1936, suddenly a big wave of people who fled Nazi Germany, and some of them were dancers . . . they brought with them avant-garde dance. After World War I, Europe had collapsed, and *Ausdruckstanz* dance here flourished with Arab-Israeli subjects. Culture flourished here [in Israel].[114]

Like the New Dance Group founders, dancers who trained in the Wigman style and then used it for political expression were not schooled in the physical rigor demanded by the Graham technique.

As in America's modern dance historiography, when Graham arrived in Israel, she would again displace German-based expressive dance, in its adaptation to serve local political needs, with the "universal" American-based modern dance. As in the United States and in India, Graham's codified technique fought leftist "free" dance; in Israel, the political dancers felt scoffed at and considered "fat" and "bent-kneed" by those who sought freedom through skilled technique under Graham. Graham's project met with resistance from those who had trained under the German dancers in Israel, ironically considered the political activists who supported the new state. The German Jewish tradition in dance attempted to hold firm as an intellectually based artistic medium that supported indigenous political ideals based on folk and the expressions of the individual. With the start of nation-building and new political alliances, "Dance groups suddenly started to come in both from Europe and America. And then came Martha Graham. People were shocked. From that moment nobody wanted to dance *Ausdruckstanz* anymore. That generation was all about Martha Graham."[115]

Given the strength of Israel's political alliance with the United States, the mixed reviews her company received there were unexpected. Liberal Israelis who had fought for nationhood, having won it just seven years earlier, could find meaning in a narrative of political and religious heroism, male and female. So it was not surprising that Graham's *Seraphic Dialogue*, which centered on the idea of a heroine-saint vanquishing a religiously powerful conqueror, received critical acclaim. Yet for the citizens of this new Middle Eastern nation, the USIS emphasis on Graham's Asian themes and repertory backfired. Graham's audiences found her other dances "too Japanese in appearance." The myth-based works did not resonate: *Cave of the Heart* seemed merely "acrobatic"; Jocasta in the story of Oedipus was seen as a "dancer-mime." Oedipus himself fared worse: the character was "like the Tarzan of the movies" to reviewers.[116] For a nation founded on the tenets of the Bible, the works based on Greek mythology looked like old-fashioned cinema with an Asian twist. Yet because Graham had a wide variety of dances in her repertory, performances overall could boast triumph in each location because officials filtered information sent back to the United States. Failures were easily buried by USIS, which quoted rave reviews most frequently.

Like other American consumer goods that entered Israel, Graham lent a sophisticated edge to cultural products that were embraced by Israelis. One dancer recalls, "The first time we saw American products [in Israel upon independence] we were fascinated. Suddenly everything that was made here looked very provincial."[117] Audiences were distinctly perceived as budding elitists in search of American modernized chic. A cartoon published in Israel at the time showed a couple in front of the theater with the American and Israeli flags behind them. The man, poised in the cartoon as an Israeli diplomat in a trench coat, escorted a woman in fancy evening attire out of the theater with Graham on the marquee. The woman said to the man, "In dancing I don't understand too much, but the important thing is that everybody saw me there."[118] Graham and Rothschild as choreographer and cultural leader would displace the Germans and socialists in Israel, as Graham had in the United States seven years earlier. Government reports lauded the season as "extremely successful, [a] most widely acclaimed attraction"[119] and "particularly valuable contribution to country objectives." Of "most vital importance" was "the application of American methods in the particular field with which the grantee is concerned."[120] Within years, Rothschild would launch a Graham school and then dance company with Graham technique and repertory as its backbone; it would become recognized by the Israeli government as a national institution.

* * *

With its failures as well as successes, Graham's 1955–1956 tour was hailed as a triumph back at home in the press. The *Mirror*'s "Washington Merry-Go-Round" column, which had quoted Truman disparaging modern art in 1950, announced that Dizzy Gillespie's American jazz and Graham's modern dance were "this country's best propaganda to date."[121] Upon her return to New York, Graham received a coveted award from *Dance Magazine*, given to her for creating "a bond with the Orient through the medium of dance" because she spoke with a "universal language" and "communicat[ed] the oneness of human experience."[122] Although domestic publicity about the recently completed tour only obliquely mentioned State Department involvement, Graham became recognized in the United States for her international work representing the nation. Just as her words, actions, and theater paralleled the foreign policy rhetoric and specific aims of the Eisenhower administration, so, too, did her fundamental outlook on America, modernism, and human freedom. American propagandistic goals intersected naturally with her art. She spoke easily of Eisenhower's "soul of mankind," the kind of philosophical attitude that infused her choreography. Graham's success abroad became a nationwide story, one whose resonance would propel her on future tours because her belief was homegrown and resolute.

Upon Graham's return from all tours, the State Department and the CIA vetted her in Washington, and some dancers filed reports along with the stage manager and support team.[123] A company member on this tour wrote, "I believe that Martha Graham was the perfect person to send on such a mission." Remarking that Graham had to answer "difficult questions" (these went unmentioned, but certainly had to do with race, gender, and American politics), the dancer concluded, "Never could one find a better diplomat."[124] State Department and executive branch involvement became clear. Documents demonstrate Graham's importance to the CIA for both security and artistic purposes. While the presence of cameras under cargo planes comes as no surprise, the agency was waging cultural wars it described as "the battle for Picasso's mind" in the international market of ideas. Covert funding of American foundations, magazines, journals, films, and exhibitions sought to engage the international intellectual with democratic principles. The CIA had an interest in the State Department cultural work from 1951, "although it was very quietly done." The Agency "visited with people" who were traveling and performing on behalf of the government and asked them "to put certain questions to [a] foreign dignitary during lunch or dinner."[125] Graham was an ideal muse. The greatest minds globally could be examined and slowly turned to the American side in the theater, over teas, at the dinner table, and during the cocktail hour.[126]

Yet in the public government funding sphere, Graham faced charges that her cultural diplomacy was elitist. Reading reports of her tour, the leaders of the Dance Panel complained that "poorer people" could not understand modern dance.[127] The committee's minutes stated that "one [diplomatic] post" had reservations about Graham's company's reception by "the natives" and that future performers should be "less esoteric." In response, a representative of the panel announced, "We are investigating the possibilities of a Wild West Show for the Far East with rodeo events, stage coach hold-ups, trick riding, etc."[128] These moves would bring her closer to the more clandestine forces of government in 1957 with her tour to West Berlin as the elite continued to see the value of her diplomacy.

The elite remained attached to Graham, however. In May 1956, Graham visited with Eleanor Roosevelt to regale her and her friends with stories from the tour. This was not just a private social event. Roosevelt, a champion of the United Nations, wrote in her syndicated newspaper column: "There is no doubt that if you like people and go to foreign countries with a desire to learn as much as possible, the people in those countries like you in return and you get much from your visit." Graham had "gained a deep understanding of the needs and longings of people in the Far East and Middle East," which she had brought home.[129] Later that summer, Roosevelt continued her reflections and support for Graham in the public sphere. "As a nation we are apt to take up the fads of the moment," Roosevelt explained to her readers, adding, "These fads fade quickly, but the enduring things are the really beautiful developments, such as those . . . Martha Graham creates today."[130]

On her first State Department–sponsored tour, Graham and government agencies had successfully allied with politicians, foundations, international businesses, and the intelligentsia to enact trickle-down diplomacy. They emerged from the tour as reliable partners who could, together, create goodwill and sway elite opinion in America's favor while maintaining the appearance of a timeless universalism befitting the image of an idealized United States. This modernist construct fell in lockstep with Cold War hyperbole—America had made the modern dance. Graham established herself as an effective ambassador who represented national interests. "Can a dancer win battles in the cold war?," asked the *Herald Tribune* of Martha Graham about her first State Department tour. "Martha Graham appears to be doing just that without benefit of weapons, politics or loans, but with her art," the reporter answered his rhetorical question, adding, "She is serving her country brilliantly."[131]

3

"Dedicated to Freedom"

Martha Graham in Berlin, 1957

> They say that the two primary arts are dance and architecture.
>
> —Martha Graham

Waving to the gathered dignitaries like a visiting monarch, Martha Graham descended the steel steps of a Pan American airplane onto the requisite carpeted tarmac, now in West Berlin, the epicenter of Cold War contention between the United States and the Soviet Union. Photographers popped pictures, surely blinding her for a moment, but the surefooted American modern dancer never looked down. On this cloudy September afternoon in 1957, Graham arrived to perform during a nine-day celebration of the opening of Congress Hall, an American-designed modernist building that, with its transparent glass walls, luminous curved roof, and reflecting pool, was an aggressive and forthright "symbol of the Free World," according to the German press, situated just one hundred yards from the line dividing West Berlin from East, liberal democracy from communism.[1] "We should have the freedom of modern dancing as well as that of speech," Graham declared on her first government tour in two years; she embodied the modern impulse and the ideal of freedom that came with it.[2]

The Americans planning the inauguration of Congress Hall understood that with Martha Graham, they had a cultural ambassador who was "dedicated to freedom."[3] While the Dance Panel had suggested other dancers and choreographers, Graham had been selected by the Congress Hall Board Committee in conjunction with the CIA-backed Congress for Cultural Freedom (CCF), led by Norman Lasky, to open the ceremonies. With Dance Panel Graham backer Virginia Inness-Brown serving on the Congress Hall Board, Planning Committee, and the Dance Panel, Graham secured round-about approval.

Martha Graham's Cold War. Victoria Phillips, Oxford University Press 2020. © Oxford University Press.
DOI: 10.1093/oso/9780190610364.001.0001

For her press conference in Berlin, Graham appeared in a fur stole, a single string of pearls, and a dress that showed off her lean silhouette. Although the sixty-two-year-old dancer and choreographer had once described herself as possessing "odd dark looks," she walked, dressed, and talked like a Hollywood movie star. Leaning slightly forward into a microphone before a battery of reporters, she paused after phrases so as to entice her audience. "Modern dance," she told the press, "is a freedom of the body."[4] Graham's innovative technique proved that artists in the United States could experiment and create art without censorship or state support, unlike the German Mary Wigman, who had choreographed for the 1936 summer Olympics in Berlin under the Nazis. While promoting denazification in the former capital of the Third Reich, Graham also became a potent symbol of anticommunism. The Nazis had called modern art "degenerate," and the Soviets had shut down modernism for public consumption. In both cases, modern artists were persecuted and went underground. American publicity easily linked the two totalitarian regimes when promoting modern artists from the United States abroad. For Graham and her sponsors, freedom of the body was a part of a heroic freedom in the West.[5]

A day after her press conference, photographers took candid shots of Graham walking alongside Eleanor Dulles, the mastermind of Congress Hall. Dulles wore her slightly dowdy cloth coat as she walked just ahead of Graham in her tailored outfit. As special assistant to the director of German affairs in the State Department, Eleanor Dulles wielded power in Berlin despite the misgivings of her brother, Secretary of State John Foster Dulles. She seemed to operate more comfortably with her other brother, Allen, who was Eisenhower's director of the CIA. At sixty-two, Eleanor Dulles was a handsome woman with high, rounded cheekbones and bobbed silver hair, her blue eyes bright behind thick, round glasses. Like Graham, she donned pearls for photographs. While Graham wore fur stoles, Dulles transversed Berlin and Washington in her simple wool coat. Although Graham arrived in some countries in a dramatic veiled hat, Dulles always wore her signature pillbox hat, with its curved shape and upward-tilted brim. In an early rendering of Congress Hall, with its innovative design featuring a distinctive bowed roof, the architect penciled in the words "Eleanor's Hat." West Berliners, accordingly, dubbed the building "Frau Dulles' Hut."[6] Two Cold War matriarchs: one diplomat, one artistic innovator. One worked behind the scenes, the other performed on the stage.

* * *

By the time she greeted Graham, Dulles had been involved with Berlin in some capacity for more than a decade. She initially encountered a city in dire straits and geopolitical crosshairs. In 1947, the raw winter cold only made the ruins, homelessness, and starvation of the people in the Western sector, occupied by British, French, and American troops, more glaring. Dulles wrote about Berlin's "total devastation." In 1948, while administering the Marshall Plan in the war-divided Austria, she monitored the Soviet Union's attempt to exacerbate the region's problems and starve out Berlin's Western sector, an effort that was finally thwarted when American planes filled with food swept in low over the city's rubble-ridden apartment buildings, landing seconds apart on war-tattered, overgrown runways. "Operation Parachute" famously dropped chocolate bars for children. Not only did the Berlin airlift bring much-needed food, but the rescue endeavor also aroused anti-communist sentiment and inspired respect for the daring Americans who protected the other Western-occupied nations.[7] Eleanor Dulles officially arrived in Berlin in 1953 under the Eisenhower administration. She was encouraged by American operatives to "put an American kitchen in the center of Berlin"; thanking them for the suggestions, she said she would "add it to our list."[8] She did not, and began planning Congress Hall instead. Championed by James Riddleberger, the influential head of the German bureau, and slipped in before her brother became secretary of state, she became the head of a wholly new creation, the "Berlin desk," where she fought for food and housing with such vehemence that she became known as "the Mother of Berlin."[9]

Congress Hall was the first brainchild of her Berlin desk. Dulles had always been aware of the power of culture. In the early 1950s, she had watched as the Communists planned the Stalin-Allee area of East Berlin, the zone occupied by the Soviets under the Four Power Agreement at the end of World War II. Architects designed eight-story apartment buildings in adherence to the Stalinist architectural style, or "socialist classicism," on a broad avenue named in honor of the Soviet Union's leader.[10] Despite the grand arches and elaborate cornices, this elaborate complex was trumpeted as a housing, shopping, and entertainment center for "the common man." As the project proceeded, the East Berlin government mounted posters of the intimidatingly impressive buildings under construction alongside photographs of the charred parks and still-skeletal buildings of West Berlin. Indeed, the Western Zone remained a debris-strewn landscape. The once-lavish Tiergarten was barren. The world-renowned zoo had only one elephant left, and the trees had been used as firewood. As an outpost of the West, Berlin had become a propaganda nightmare.[11] Stalin-Allee became the flagship of Soviet power and East German reconstruction with its advertised "luxurious" apartments for "plain workers," as well as shops, restaurants, cafes, a tourist hotel, and a cinema.

But the complex was not without controversy, which Dulles well understood. East Germany (the German Democratic Republic [GDR]) had borne the brunt of Stalinization exerted upon Soviet bloc countries. The regime's critics met with systematic torture. The "common man" suffered from a shortage of consumer goods and a ban on electricity in the evenings, and farmers had their land seized by the government. Emigration from the East to the West reached a peak in early 1953, and Berlin became central to the East-West crossing. In response to the crisis, the East German Communist Central Committee mandated increasingly systematic changes for workers building Stalin-Allee, including a 10 percent increase in work quotas with no corresponding rise in salary. On June 16, 1953, with Dulles's arrival, the workers rioted. Troops in the GDR, employing tanks mounted with large-caliber cannons and rotating guns, quashed the uprising with a violent show of force.

Nevertheless, in defiance, protests rippled through East Berlin and the East German countryside the next day. Using food stockpiles obtained through funds commandeered from her brother Foster in Washington, Eleanor Dulles offered free food packages to anyone with an East German identity card. The East German government ordered its people not to take the handouts. Dulles understood that the propaganda worked either way: giving free food won hearts, minds, and stomachs; troops stationed to prevent people from obtaining much-needed sustenance could be photographed for American propaganda purposes.[12] It was a win-win. According to the Communists, Dulles herself had abetted these protests with her brother and the CIA, "stirring up new gangster acts of sabotage."[13] She denied the charges, citing her dedication to culture and the people of Berlin.

In 1955, while Graham and her company toured Asia, West Germany had joined the North Atlantic Treaty Organization (NATO) and confirmed its solidarity with the United States and its allies. In response, the GDR joined the Warsaw Pact, the Soviet-led military alliance.[14] The division of Germany underscored the political polarization of Europe in the mid-1950s: nations on the continent joined NATO or the Warsaw Pact, as capitalist or communist.[15] While the neutrality of Switzerland could be considered expedient for the United States, and embedded in its national history, nonaligned nations in Europe would become a cause for concern.[16] Surrounded by East German territory, West Berlin remained an isolated outpost, one that required both economic and propaganda support from the United States.

Unlike Graham, who would proclaim her nonpolitical status as an artist, Dulles could not escape her connection to her brothers, as well as to the CIA and State Department's foreign policies, connections that were well advertised by the Soviets. As Graham was wrapping up her tour of Iran in early 1956, Eleanor was accused of working with Allen to mastermind "Operation Stopwatch/Gold," a tunnel built between East and West Berlin to intercept Soviet communications. From inside the tunnel, CIA and British intelligence agents tapped and recorded Soviet messages. Yet, in Berlin, the Soviets knew about the tunnel from the time it was built; they used an "accidental" discovery, replete with a film crew, as anti-Western propaganda. While Eleanor Dulles had been in Austria, a similar tunnel had been built in Vienna with success. Having to repair diplomatic relations between East and West in Germany, Eleanor Dulles declared in exasperation, perhaps also covering her own tracks, "It's all Allen's fault."[17] She began a concerted and relentless effort to get Congress Hall finished by September 1957 so that it could house the INTERBRAU project, an international architectural exhibition, to demonstrate American cultural finesse.[18] The new hall would sit on the border of the Soviet sector within view of the famous and crumbling Reichstag, constructed in 1894 to house the Imperial Diet of the German Empire, and best known as a symbol of the Nazi suspension of individual rights and an execution. At the time, the borders between East and West allowed easy crossovers from one sector of the city to another, so East Berlin officials would be visiting the exhibition and her hall. Politics met architectural performance.

* * *

Just as Graham denied ties to women's suffrage and liberation movements, Eleanor Dulles proclaimed, "I am not a feminist."[19] While Graham took center stage, Dulles would later reflect on her power, "In order to take an authoritative position, one has to arrange an invisible promotion."[20] Thus, Dulles deployed a group of men to design and create the Congress Hall in her image, positioning herself as a silent partner in the effort. By 1956, the Benjamin Franklin Foundation (BFF) had been established to finance the project. It received some funding from American foundations, philanthropists, and the Irving Trust Bank, whose headquarters had been designed by the Dulles-anointed chairman of the BFF, architect Ralph Walker. During meetings, participants asserted that corporations such as Kodak, the groundbreaking photography company, should give the project money "without making any business propaganda."[21] In addition, Dulles was able to get support from the Department of State. Because she traveled back and forth from Germany to the United States, she was able to request money in cables she sent from Berlin. By the time they were decoded in Washington, she would be home to approve the expenditures. Indeed, in one request for fifteen million dollars that was marked "Dulles only" (meaning one brother or the other), she authorized the amount and then some, also being a Dulles. CIA front organizations became involved.[22] The German government also chipped in.

Dulles and Walker chose Hugh Stubbins as the architect of Congress Hall. Stubbins, an American, had studied with the German modernist Walter Gropius at Harvard, thus creating a cultural convergence between the United States and the country it sought to influence.[23] Early newspaper reports noted Stubbins's work under Gropius, the founder of the Bauhaus school who fled Nazi Germany in the 1930s; pointedly, these reports did not mention that Gropius had left because he was a communist sympathizer. The appointment became known as "a gesture of goodwill towards the Germans" who supported democracy and freedom of thought.[24] John Foster Dulles, now working with his sister, proclaimed that the proposed hall demonstrated "the exchange of ideas."[25] The architectural legacy of Congress Hall aimed to foster positive diplomatic relations by highlighting shared aesthetics and values between the United States and denazified Germany.

Eleanor Dulles focused on the export of assertively American culture as a tool of foreign policy. As she concluded a speech at a 1956 women's Republican luncheon in New York, she proclaimed, "In this last decade, there has been a growing awareness that art, music, and literature can carry the word of human aspiration more than political speeches or more factual explanations." In the United States, meeting with often skeptical legislators as well as female leaders, she underscored the power of modernism as a Cold War weapon in the divided European landscape.[26] Dulles knew that the Congress Hall project would demonstrate her power as a cultural diplomat. Although the Soviets accused Dulles of using the project as a cover for further covert activities, she countered these arguments by celebrating the building itself. The architecturally unparalleled modernist edifice, with its luminous, curved roof, would be what she later called a "shining beacon beaming towards the East."[27]

Modern architecture under the American eye acted as a symbol of American political and cultural life, with its glass walls demonstrating the transparency of democracy, open spaces that allowed for free discussion, and conference rooms with round tables designed to encourage democratic conversations.[28] Although German engineers said the curved roof in Stubbins's design would never hold, the Americans insisted on moving forward with the innovative plan. The theater in Congress Hall would boast fine acoustics and a modern stage. Dulles under the cover of the BFF guided the architectural design and meticulously planned opening ceremony performances to communicate the ideas that Dulles wanted to convey to the West and East Germans, and, as she said, to the "Kremlin."[29] Martha Graham wholeheartedly embraced Eleanor Dulles's point of view, and the two made a perfect rhetorical match while one performed center stage and the other produced from offstage.

As the building neared completion, opening ceremonies had to be carefully planned. Dulles met in the high-ceilinged, oak-paneled dining room of New York's University Club with Shepard Stone, a veteran of wartime military intelligence and the CIA who had worked with her in Germany. She mandated that the hall's programming promote American, and thus democratic, "freedom of thought." Stone advised Dulles to meet with Melvin Lasky, an esteemed anti-communist intellectual and journalist who had founded the CIA-funded publication *Der Monat* in Germany, which deployed the works of intellectuals for elite German consumption.[30] Its first publication appeared several months after the start of the Berlin airlift, with CIA and Ford Foundation funding.[31] Ford would later be tapped for Congress Hall funding, as well.[32] Plans accelerated.

Lasky wrote Dulles that because Congress Hall had conference rooms and a twelve-hundred-seat theater, the opening ceremony should include both symposia and performances for elite leaders, which would be led and dominated by Americans. His committee would invite these speakers and artists as well as a few dozen German "writers, thinkers, et al." for roundtable discussions that would encourage Germans to replace their typical rulebound meetings with more democratic interactions modeled by American leaders. "In this way the conference produces 'concrete results'; things 'happen,'" he continued. Indeed, this was the plan: cultural diplomacy would plant the seeds of democratic thinking among the German intelligentsia, in a continuing effort to woo them into mutually productive alliances with the West.[33] After meeting with Dulles, the thin, long-faced Lasky became the general chairman of the opening ceremony board. Lasky's CCF offered meeting space to the Congress Hall committee. Graham also received direct CCF funding for her company.[34]

With the Lasky appointment and accompanying covert finances in place, BFF chair Ralph Walker announced that the CCF would run presentations because, as it was "financed by special funds," it had the leeway to create programming as it wished.[35] Dulles agreed: "Since Berlin was to be a symbol of freedom on the continent, we tried to get a special allotment for the [opening] celebration."[36] Lasky then recruited Virginia Inness-Brown to decide on artistic deployments for the Congress Hall festivities. As a leader of the ANTA-linked panels in dance, theater, and music, and known to Eisenhower, Inness-Brown knew how to maneuver. Within months, she was promoted to chair of the Convocation Committee for the BFF— unbeknownst to her domestic ANTA Dance Panel.[37] Whether in the design of the building, the presentation of modern dance, or invitations to other American artists, the BFF-CCF committee sought to foster work that could be universalized: modern American genres were to rewrite prewar European approaches, and modernism restored what Graham so often called "the soul of mankind." With a small stage, Graham—a powerful soloist—would fill the space. Women led the team. Inness-Brown wanted Graham.

Although it was never discussed at Dance Panel meetings, on the cultural front the Soviets had taken the West by storm in the fall of 1956 through a tour by the theoretically apolitical Bolshoi Ballet, and the Americans felt that they needed their own act with which to counter such star power. London newspapers gushed about the power of the Soviets.[38] The lessening threat of Donderoism and even McCarthyism, along with a track record of successes, now allowed the American arts to be more visible. State consequently began to take greater control over cultural export activities. During a Dance Panel meeting, a government representative announced, "The requirements which we now have are that any group will go where and when the Department requires."[39] Although ABT had gone to Germany in 1950, both private Dance Panel representatives and the State Department felt that ABT was not "strong enough" to compete with the Soviets after their tour. Panel members followed suit and requested that Lucia Chase, the head of ABT, adopt several star dancers from other companies for the tour because "bringing ballet to Russia is like bringing a report card." Chase retorted, "If you want to choose a Company, start your own."[40] Although Dulles and Chase had been classmates at Bryn Mawr, the ballet was not strong enough for Berlin. Modern dance had a clear advantage because it was an apples-to-oranges fight. And Graham carried the weight of high drama as a supremely charismatic figure, center stage.

With the Berlin desk, the CIA, and State all working with similar agendas, Lasky's Berlin Congress Hall inauguration committee knew it needed modern dance. Graham fought with newly defined terms when West met East. She had begun calling her works ballets, and during her 1957 Berlin trip, she was in the process of choreographing her first and only modern evening-length work, *Clytemnestra*. The Lasky group knew that audiences understood that the American modernist ballet, unlike Soviet classical ballet, was not, as a critic noted, "steeped in nineteenth-century European tradition," but rather was "innovative and contemporary."[41] This became vital as Washington's cultural officials looked for "transference" from cultural messages to conclusions about American politics and economics.

During the Dance Panel's April 1957 meeting in New York, five months before the opening of Congress Hall, Virginia Inness-Brown asked her committee for suggestions for the venue's inaugural ceremony—a seeming embrace of democratic principles, even though the decision had already been largely made. The onstage offerings had to complement the inauguration's gala spirit while unabashedly demonstrating American high-art cultural prowess, challenging early German forays into modernism, promoting denazification, and using American modernism to assert the universal power of freedom, and thus liberal democracy. The committee bandied around various ideas. José Limón had toured Latin America; as a Mexican-born modern choreographer, he was a great ambassador and celebrated the artistic freedom offered by America. Other considerations included the appearance of what the panel termed a "Negro Ballerina," whose presence would prove that the United States was not the racist nation the Soviets depicted. Martha Graham's name came up briefly. Finally, someone on the panel suggested an American cowboy-and-Indian show. The committee discussed the suggestion. Inness-Brown made no comment on this proposal, and discussions moved on to other areas.[42]

At the following month's meeting, Inness-Brown brought up Congress Hall again, and committee members made other suggestions. Inness-Brown interjected that since José Limón would be on tour, Martha Graham should perform, and suggested the solo *Judith*. While she did not say why, her choice of the artist and the dance was deliberate. With a set designed by Isamu Noguchi that included a stripped-down tent that looked like bones, a glittering headpiece and chunky pearls for Graham, and music composed by the German William Schuman specifically for Graham, *Judith* seemed to be a sophisticated, innovative, and ideologically bold statement of American modernism and its apolitical politics. Yet the Biblical character of Judith had saved the Jewish people, the Noguchi set used a mustard yellow cloth for the Berlin performance only—representing the color of the stars sewn on the clothes of Jewish people in the streets and then in concentration camps—and Schuman's compositions had been banned by the Nazis. Without taking a vote on Inness-Brown's proposal, the usually opinionated committee again moved on to other issues. With Eleanor Dulles and Melvin Lasky behind her, Inness-Brown neatly included yet circumvented the private-sector experts and designated Martha Graham to represent modern dance at the opening of the new Cold War American outpost in West Berlin.

Tapping other culturally powerful women, the Dulles-Lasky committee also chose Agnes de Mille, choreographer for ABT and the Broadway hit *Oklahoma!,* as well as the niece of staunchly anti-communist Hollywood filmmaker Cecil B. de Mille; Lillian Gish, known as "the First Lady of American Cinema"; and the African American soprano Ethel Waters.[43] The writer and diplomat Clare Boothe Luce would speak at the opening ceremonies and represent the political accomplishments of women while addressing American democratic principles. She had worked as an editor at *Vanity Fair* before becoming a playwright, served in the House of Representatives, and became ambassador to Italy, where she successfully worked to suppress communist movements.[44] She was also the wife of *Time-Life* founder Henry Luce, whose *Architectural Digest* supported international modernist projects such as Congress Hall as beacons of democratic freedom of expression. When architect Ralph Walker was not available to represent BFF in public ceremonies, Inness-Brown stood in his place, putting one more woman on the dais.[45] Graham's modern art, her aplomb as an ambassador, and her divaesque stature harmonized with the women included in the programming and execution of the project.

Yet in Eleanor Dulles's view, men had to appear center stage in the West-East battle if the West were to make an impact. The topics of the symposia reflected the American concerns: "The Old World and the New" ("Die Alte und die Neue Welt") and "Europe and America: The Strength of the Unfettered Mind."[46] The events in the meeting halls were dominated by male-led panels in science and technology, including American sociologists, philosophers, and architects. Theatrical productions featured works by Thornton Wilder, Tennessee Williams, Eugene O'Neill, and "musical artist" Charles Ives. Virgil Thomson conducted music played by the Juilliard String Quartet and the Berlin Orchestra; he also conducted Martha Graham's music for her performance. The Berlin orchestra played music by Igor Stravinsky, the composer of *Rite of Spring* and an émigré to America who had been celebrated by Walter Gropius, the mentor of architect Hugh Stubbins. Indeed, in 1930, Graham had performed as "The Chosen One" in a production of *Rite of Spring* at the Metropolitan Opera House and earned press accolades, while it was noted that she had, uncharacteristically, not created the choreography that she performed.[47] Roundtable discussants included Noguchi, who designed the set for Graham's *Judith* and *Frontier*.[48] Although few women were included in photographs of the roundtable events, Graham could be seen amid a long table of male speakers as she holds headphones to her ears.[49]

With Virgil Thompson conducting *Judith* behind her onstage, Graham and the biblical figure would represent the United States with modernism and a politico-religious message.[50] Although Copland's *Appalachian Spring*, once called *Ballet for Martha* by the composer, would be played at Congress Hall as an orchestral score, Graham and her company would not perform the choreography. The stage did not have traditional wings and would not support a full production of the work, with its complicated entrances, exits, and stage crossings. While Graham could have performed excerpted solos from the work (something she despised), the biblically based *Judith* would reinforce the American value of freedom of religion that was central to the organizers' agenda.[51]

Dulles's and Graham's ancestors would have been a part of the eighteenth-century American zeitgeist among the elites who promoted freedom of religion alongside political freedom and democracy. John Foster Dulles, whose father was a Presbyterian minister, felt that religion was the Soviets' "Achilles heel" because they were atheists who demanded an alliance of the "people" with the false god of communism.[52] Eleanor Dulles saw Berlin as a "spiritual center" and tapped into an appreciation of the transcendent aspect of expression in the arts.[53] Following her family's religious and political beliefs, Eleanor Dulles quoted scripture when speaking about Congress Hall, deliberately referencing the "City upon a Hill" metaphor, ensuring that the building inscription read, "Let your light shine before men that they may see your good works."[54] The Benjamin Franklin quotation that the designers displayed in the Congress Hall foyer was also directly religious: "God grant that not only the love of liberty but a thorough knowledge of the rights of man may pervade all the nations of the earth."[55] Like the Dulles siblings, Graham was trained in Presbyterian scripture as a child, however much she was scolded for dancing in church. She was also trained in the teachings of the Catholic Church from her nanny and father. Graham's own charismatic proclamations that her modern choreography showed the "struggle between good and evil" and shone "the light of freedom" were exactly what Dulles, her brothers, the president, and the Congress Hall opening ceremony committee wanted to hear.[56]

The American effort to encourage the denazification of Germany, remind the population of the Nazi extermination of more than six million Jews, and equate the Soviets with the Nazis in the European imagination made religion-based morality a particularly important element of the opening ceremonies, and thus of Graham's performance. American Cold War propaganda consistently framed parallels between the Nazi and Soviet regimes as totalitarian, godless, and even anti-Semitic. When Graham landed in West Berlin, she boldly announced that she explored "the soul of man," just as American Cold Warriors in the United States proclaimed that the United States held "the soul of mankind."[57] Eleanor Dulles surely approved, as would have Clare Boothe Luce. Both had been committed to eradicating all remnants of Nazi Germany, particularly targeting the elites who would sit in the contained theater in full-dress attire. Dulles believed in the power of the prewar German intellectual tradition, and after the death of her grandfather, also a Protestant minister, she had married a Romance-language professor who was Jewish. He had committed suicide in 1934, and she remained committed to his legacy as a Jewish scholar. Luce, along with her famed husband, took a stand against the Nazis both artistically and politically. She wrote a heralded Broadway play, *Margin for Error*, which brought Nazi atrocities to light. Martha Graham as Judith and the new Congress Hall would both embody American freedom in the body of a woman in the shadow of the Nazi Reichstag that sat, crumbling, on the Soviet side of Berlin.[58]

* * *

Graham's presence in West Berlin provoked memories of her early condemnation of the totalitarian and genocidal Nazi state.[59] Graham's rejection of Rudolf von Laban's invitation to perform at the 1936 Summer Olympics was well remembered by many in the German artistic community, the intelligentsia, and the German dignitaries in the audience.[60] The publicity that appeared before Graham's arrival in Berlin emphasized her condemnation of the Nazi persecution of the Jewish people by reporting on her alliances with Israel. To promote Graham as a cultural diplomat, the US government produced thick-papered, gilded publicity booklets that employed highly selective information and shaded truths. Graham's seventy-five-word biography, written in German, began by reminding readers of her status in the United States, and then took unexpected turns. The program claimed that Graham had toured Europe, the "Orient," and Israel for the State Department.[61] While she certainly had been to Asian nations under government aegis, any claim that Graham was sponsored by the State Department in Europe speaks to the murkiness of State Department activities. As noted earlier, Bethsabée de Rothschild underwrote the European tours in the early 1950s and the last leg of the Asian tour in Israel. Yet Graham, promoted as an artist celebrated in Europe and Israel under American auspices, gained a peculiar and undeniable postwar German currency as she presented her pro-Jewish work in West Berlin, just in view of the Reichstag in the Soviet-controlled East. Just as Americans linked the Soviets and the Nazis in their rejection of modernism, so, too, did they on the basis of anti-Jewish discrimination given the policies and pogroms of Stalin.[62]

As the lights rise on the stage, the first thing the audience hears is the dramatic opening of the score, commissioned for *Judith* specifically, which immediately served the pro-modernist, anti-Nazi agenda with an experiential moment for the audience even before Graham moved. With its dramatic yet modernist undertones immediately recognizable, William Schuman's composition exemplified the prewar power of the German intellectual and cultural heritage.[63] It had been banned by the Third Reich, and Schuman staunchly believed that the horror of the Holocaust must never be forgotten. Just as Graham shared anti-Nazi feelings with Dulles and Luce, Graham would write to Schuman recalling her 1936 refusal to appear at the Olympics festival.[64] The choreographer and the composer were culturally, aesthetically, and politically allied. Graham performed as a strong symbol of anti-Nazi beliefs.

With its biblical origin and its inevitable political implications, the story of Graham's *Judith* was a momentous work to perform in Berlin. Judith, an undercover agent of sorts on behalf of the Hebrews, tempts the opposing general Holofernes with the promise of sex and information about her people and thereby gains access to his tent. The leader lies inside the tent in a drunken stupor, but in Graham's dance, he is never seen. In the biblical story, after decapitating Holofernes, Judith brought his head to the Israelites. In Graham's dance, she emerges from the tent with golden laurels of peace that catch the light and shimmer, a final image that Graham transformed from the biblical original for political purposes. The woman triumphed with the rhetoric of Eisenhowerian "peace," with the symbol of laurels sculpted by Noguchi for the end of the performance. The Soviets had claimed "peace" as a part of their propaganda offensive against the West as "warmongers" who had dropped the nuclear bomb. Eisenhower had countered with his propaganda blitz, "Atoms for Peace." Graham allied with Eisenhower's campaigns when she shook the gilded leaves that hooked the light just so.

To enhance the propaganda value of *Judith*, Graham altered the set. In earlier presentations in the United States, Holofernes's tent had been draped with a royal purple sheath. However, for her Berlin performance, the fabric was a mustard yellow. When Bertram Ross, Graham's lead male dancer, asked her if she realized that this was the color of the Star of David that Jews had to wear under Nazi Germany, Graham was "overjoyed." In addition, pictures show that Graham erected screens on the Berlin stage in order to shield the dance from the gestures of the orchestra; these screens were plastered with the shade of yellow. Ross later wrote, "I was pleased that Martha chose to take [*Judith*] to Germany, and told her how right it was that she was going to Germany with a dance about a nice Jewish girl who saved her people."[65] Just as Congress Hall represented the promise of Western liberal democracy, Graham's choreographic oeuvre reminded the German people of their past collective sins and helped them expiate them.[66]

Graham believed herself to be taking center stage in Germany as a modernist hegemon. Although in the United States she had consistently denied that Mary Wigman had influenced her work, in Cold War West Germany she said that German dance had shared roots with the United States in that it expressed "love, fear and other movements of the soul."[67] Yet advance publicity for Graham's German performances defined Graham as "the master of the expressionist dance," a term generally reserved for the German manifestation.[68] With her preeminence having previously been established, Graham expected to prevail as the leader of a "universal" art, built in America and brought to the Germans, who had, in fact, brought expressionist dance to the Americans decades earlier.

* * *

Before Graham performed, Congress Hall opened with great fanfare. A newspaper headline announced, "Berlin—A Symbol of the West."[69] Hugh Stubbins's daughter cracked a champagne bottle against the Congress Hall cornerstone, christening the edifice the "house of free speech." The bottle's thick glass exploded like a firework, and the champagne soaked the young woman's belted A-line dress. The tall, thick men in raincoats looking on were national leaders, celebrated artists, and political experts from West Germany, the United States, and even East Berlin. Reporters called it "the first time in history" that a building was christened as if it were a new ship.[70] In the West, articles about Stubbins and the arrival of performers, dignitaries, and officials saturated newspapers.[71] A "Kongresshalle" stamp featured an elegant rendering of the building that transmitted its image from Berlin throughout West Germany.[72] USIS distributed tickets for the performances to East Germans through America House, and estimated that more than 25 percent had gone to East German elites.[73] Those unable to gain admission to the ceremonies could visit the exhibition *A Nation of Many Nations* (*Volk Aus Vielen Volkern*), where all panels and programs were printed in both English and German.

Despite the damp weather that evening, men, women, and even children from both the West and the East leaned against barricades to watch the celebratory procession as it entered the floodlit building. Congress Hall seemed to be a full circle of glowing amber as the lights hit the reflecting pool, which doubled the effect of the building's architecture. The audience filed up the wide steps that led into the fantastical and undeniably modern building. Was it a spaceship? A cloud? A fighter jet? Or just Eleanor's Hat? Those in the crowd who could get near enough pressed against the long glass windows to glimpse the stars and dignitaries inside. Women wearing evening gowns with long trains walked arm in arm with men in perfectly fitted tuxedos. The dignitaries, members of the intelligentsia, and invited guests mounted the sweeping interior double stairways that were flanked by two rectangular pools of water. Fountains sprang into the air. The audience entered the warm wood walls of the auditorium where Graham would perform. The rounded space seemed comfortable and embracing, with the staircase carpeted with light gray to contrast with the vivid blue velour of the seats.

At the gala opening, soprano Eileen Farrell opened the evening with the arioso to *Esther* by George Frideric Handel, a musical choice and performance that underscored the intellectual gravity of the proceedings. Her voice resonated in low and noble registers within the hall's modern acoustical system. Next, several of the luminaries present took the stage. After brief speeches by BFF chair Walker and the mayor of Berlin, Clare Boothe

Luce took the stage as the evening's keynote speaker. Luce was arguably the most publicly eloquent and forcefully pro-American female cold warrior in the world. Beautiful, charismatic, elegant, and serene in her double row of pearls and a tailored suit that hugged her torso and arched down from her waist, Luce rose from her seat onstage, walked to the podium, and put on her glasses. Dulles, Innes-Brown, and Graham sat in the audience, waiting. Now would come the words that would crystallize their mission.[74]

In her speech, "Berlin, Symbol of the West," Luce echoed the messages brought by Graham under Dulles. "Congress Hall is an eloquent symbol, embodying through its form, the attitudes of the Western peoples of our time," she said. She cited the classical metropolis of Rome as an example of a city like Berlin with a name that would survive through the ages. The Cold War could be won if American artists could lay claim to the enduring meanings and values of the masterpieces of Western civilization, both artistically and architecturally. Modern dance was a perfect medium for that effort; it set aside words in favor of the global language of the body in order to become both universal and specific. Portraying the great female hero of the Bible, Graham, as Judith, would embody the tenets of the building and the aims of the United States.[75]

Once the singing and speeches ended, "the cocktail circuit of diplomacy" began in full force. After passing through a prebanquet receiving line that included Dulles, Luce, and Innes-Brown, Graham, wearing a tasteful, sequined evening gown, moved on to cocktails. Graham's great-grandmother had trained her in the social graces as a child. Graham moved into the banquet hall and took her place at a U-shaped table adorned with a centerpiece of low flowers. Graham knew how to hold conversations with the person to her right during the first course, then to her left. Dulles sat at the head of the group as hostess, facing the group of American and German leaders.[76]

The following day, articles reviewed the building and noted the "select" group in attendance at the opening. Newspapers embraced the intended theme: "Berlin's New Landmark: A Lasting Symbol of German-American Cooperation," read the headline in one German daily.[77] Keeping with the tone of American arguments about freedom of religion, the editorial board of Berlin's *Telegraf* called the building "a monument to the spirit."[78] Yet cartoons criticized the lavish opening as a contradiction of the idea that Congress Hall represented democracy for the common man. One contained a sketch of Uncle Sam holding up a pillbox hat studded with daisies. Another showed a police officer pushing his hand against a man in a trench coat, denying him admission as ladies and gentlemen ascended the steps in the background in gowns with trains that draped the modernist steps.[79]

That evening, Graham prepared to take the stage at Congress Hall. Because the modern, curved stage had no wings, she had to warm her body for the performance—contracting, releasing, stretching, and breathing—in an anteroom. Graham wore a costume whose modern style and accoutrements complemented the gowns of the evening's female guests. Her sweeping dress, which hugged her lean torso and fanned out to the floor from her hipbones, her spiraled headpiece, her large gilt pearls, and the glimmering, Noguchi-designed props all refracted the glamour of the crowd. Graham's success seemed assured in the elegant, modern hall, with her heralded dance, her dramatic costume, the sculptured set, and the famed Virgil Thomson poised to conduct Schuman's foreboding score. As she entered, she did not look at the audience. No one in the auditorium stirred as she walked silently and commandingly onto the stage. Behind her, Thomson brought his baton up and suspended it in space. Graham moved just before his wand hit its lower stroke. The moment before the music began belongs to the dancer, she believed; the eye is slower than the music. To arrive with the sound, Graham moved first on what she called the "and" count—"and one," she would say silently before she began. Graham moved, and then Schuman's music struck its first note.[80]

Austere and severe, Graham executed wide sweeping steps and supplicatory arms, reaching, writhing, as the young and seductive Judith, who had readied herself to decapitate the enemy general. Graham's torso rounded, sharply contracting with the anguish of the heroine as she decided to forgo her own sexual passion for Holofernes and kill him to save her people from oppression and death. Reaching for the sky, and then bending and shooting down to the floor, she expressed the enormity of her task. Moving across the stage into the tent, Graham bourréed on her knees, one knee against the other, skimming the floor, a figure grounded yet smooth, a gold Noguchi-designed knife in hand. She took a sudden plunge into the mustard yellow velvet. The audience knew that Judith's sword would slice through the neck of the drunken, sleeping general, unseen, unheard. Graham made a headlong return out of the tent to reveal not the bloody triumph of a severed head but instead interwoven branches of metallic laurel—a wreath that highlighted her head and neck pieces, and which celebrated peace. She and the music finished with knowing command.[81]

After a long moment of silence, she was met with polite applause. The woman who had become used to standing ovations took a deep bow, showing the back of her neck, despite the delayed and muted response. As Graham stood tall again and prepared for a second bow, Mary Wigman made her way down the aisle, ascended the stage, and embraced Graham. Now, as the two matriarchs of modern dance reunited, the audience leapt to its feet, and applause rose to a roar.[82]

The reviews echoed the underwhelmed response of the audience. "Unfortunately [Graham] failed to achieve the maximum effect," began one reporter the next day. Her "pantomimic style is very limited in the idiom of the dance," concluded another. *Judith* was likened to an "archaic ceremony." The seduction of Holofernes was described as "swinging and dragging steps" with "beseeching gestures." Critics understood Graham's contractions as merely a "bending and rearing body." A reviewer noted that it was "surprising and alienating" to see a dancing style "which is perceived in Germany as simple and immediate"; Graham seemed to him to be "strange and foreign." Slighting Graham with a nod toward Wigman, another writer concluded that the United States, represented by Graham and the architecture of Congress Hall itself, did not show "real originality." Back at home, the *New York Times* euphemistically concluded, "The critics were not altogether favorable."[83]

Despite the disappointing reception, Graham pressed forward. At the postperformance cocktail reception, Graham wore a gilded dress and spoke demurely to a man in a thin tie as the cameras clicked away. She moved from guest to guest, grand and demure as ever.[84] In the following days, she spoke at symposia with aplomb. At an event moderated by Melvin Lasky, Graham sat in a well-cut dark dress at a long table covered in a white tablecloth, the only woman among a sea of men in flawless suits with perfectly placed pocket handkerchiefs. She listened intently to Lasky's words, seeming to rise slightly from her seat in her response. Yet at the end of the table, one gentleman in a baggy brownish suit sat slumped in his chair, looking at his fingers.[85]

Several days later, Graham attended the performance of Mary Wigman's choreography for *Rite of Spring*, with its dramatic and revolutionary rhythmic structure and music by Igor Stravinsky, who was in attendance at the Congress Hall festivities. The work was first performed in Paris in 1913, with choreography by the famed ballet dancer Vaslav Nijinsky, and met with near riots by the audience both cheering and booing the work. In it, a maiden, or "The Chosen One," is sacrificed. When the ballet was set in New York in 1930, Graham had wanted to choreograph but was offered only the lead role.[86] She had dreamed of making a work for the score, but Leopold Stokowski, the famed producer, "did not think [she] had enough experience."[87] Indeed, Alfred Stieglitz, Georgia O'Keeffe's mentor, had told Graham that despite the critical accolades she received, the role of The Chosen One was "beneath [her] strength as a dancer."[88] Graham, however, remembered her dance of death as an intense rebirth on the Metropolitan stage in 1930. Although she would rise to modernist fame a month later with the premiere of Lamentation, the sense of bitterness became undeniable: "I had known the music for years," she mused.[89] Now, she watched Wigman's maiden wrapped in rope, subtly spinning, shaking. In comparison to Wigman's fresh, stark interpretation, Graham's Medea, Jocasta, and Judith seemed dated, overly dramatic. Wigman's choreography was stripped to its bones; her Chosen One, wrapped in rope, was vibrant, relevant. Wigman received rave reviews for her Rite, revitalizing the form of what was being called by the press "German modern dance." Wigman trumped the American diva and choreographer. Even the press in the United States declared that Wigman's Rite of Spring showed that "Berlin is rapidly forging to the front as a modern dance center." Once thought to be a relic of the Weimar and Nazi past, Wigman was reborn. Compared with Wigman's work, in the eyes of the Germans and many international critics, Graham's dance languished as old-fashioned and outdated.[90]

At the conclusion of the week's opening festivities, Eleanor Dulles deemed the Congress Hall project a success. In cables back to her brother at the State Department, she boasted that 95 percent of the publicity was positive.[91]

* * *

Returning to New York, Graham found a diplomatically polite but brief, perhaps curt, note from Dulles thanking her for her participation.[92] Dulles said that the Congress Hall committee was "fortunate to find such a reputable modern American dancer." Graham was not accustomed to being thanked for being "reputable." She was a "Priestess," lauded as "Picasso," known for her dynamic charisma as "The First Lady."[93]

During the next Dance Panel meeting, Inness-Brown reported to the committee simply that the opening ceremonies of Congress Hall included Graham's performance of Judith—suppressing the verdict of the reviews and noting that the performance should be considered a success because "25 percent–50 percent of the audience came from the Eastern sector to attend." Although Graham had indeed lured the Communist-allied elites to the Western sector and executed her part as an anti-communist American propaganda offensive, the critical results were not as hoped.[94]

When Graham returned to her studio, "things were not the same." According to Bertram Ross, her working rhythm had fallen apart. She was "changed." Wigman had brought the house down with the famous avant-garde score Graham had not been allowed to use; Graham's modernism in *Judith* looked pantomimic and even old-fashioned. Graham could only achieve a standing ovation with the help of Wigman, whose influence Graham had spent decades denying, and in Germany, which she understood to be steeped in the blood and ashes of the tortured, gassed, and burned. In New York, Graham struggled with her three-act ballet, *Clytemnestra*. And alcohol was always waiting in the wings, a soothing companion for her quick, creatively jagged mind, and a balm to her insecurity. In the months that followed her Berlin appearance, she began drinking more heavily and became unable to cobble together the remaining pieces of her latest work. During her frequent absences from the studio, her tall, muscled men and increasingly lean women spun themselves to the ground, improvising their parts in order to complete the work. Yet, ever determined, Graham would enter the studio at key moments to direct the work.[95]

As always, Graham struggled against her insecurities and found inspiration and redemption. On April 1, 1958, *Clytemnestra* premiered on Broadway as the world's first three-act modern ballet, including both a prologue and an epilogue.[96] It was a full-evening work, and not a twenty- or thirty-minute interlude, a structure that until then seemed to delimit modernism in dance. It defined Graham as the leading creator of the genre.[97] The ballet opened with a scene set in Hades, where the titular protagonist attempted to discover why she had been dishonored and damned; it became a reflection on guilt, anger, jealousy, and love. After Helen of Troy appears, Clytemnestra imagines the rape of Troy. She recalls the sacrifice of her daughter, Iphigenia, which had allowed Agamemnon to sail to war. She envisions Orestes and Electra plotting her death. When Cassandra enters, foretelling the coming of doom, Clytemnestra becomes possessed by the desire for vengeance. In parts II and III, Graham showed Clytemnestra with her lover, her reaction to the fall of Troy, and the return of her husband. Clytemnestra and her lover sit at the front of the stage planning the murder of Agamemnon. Her lover gestures across the landscape in much the same way as the Husbandman surveyed the frontier for the Bride in *Appalachian Spring*. Yet the gesture, showing a couple looking toward the future in 1944, transformed from hope of renewal to the realization of murder by 1958.

As Clytemnestra, the almost sixty-four-year-old Graham sat through much of the work and watched the scenes unfold, yet her dramatic moments showed her power as a performer, actress, and chronicler of undying truths, some of which were deeply personal. Indeed, using her alcoholic bouts as creative fuel, Graham choreographed a "Drunk Scene" for the work. After imbibing with her lover, Clytemnestra dreams that her son will murder her. In a red sheath, she relives onstage the shivers, sweats, and chills of a recovery from a severe and prolonged use of the alluring sedative of wine. Graham employed simple and starkly graphic movements to unearth the conflicts of the human psyche and the physical horrors that accompany it, including her own. The night tremors and guilt of a woman who acted on her own instincts and resentments fed by the seductive passions fueled by alcohol became theatrical gold. Graham functioned as her own archetype as she bared her soul on stage.

American critics raved. John Martin wrote in the *New York Times* that *Clytemnestra* was "a work of giant stature" and marveled at the "extraordinary skill with which the whole essence of the Oresteia has been manipulated."[98] "Epic," "monumental," a "whirlwind," declared other reviewers. Despite her own stated desire to be known as "contemporary," she earned the title "A Modern Master." The *New York Herald Tribune*'s Walter Terry equated the dance with such great theatrical works of Western civilization as "the great Oresteia," Strauss's *Elektra*, and *Death of a Salesman*.[99] Audiences demanded that Graham extend the run of the new production.

Of her part as Clytemnestra and perhaps her artistic comeback as well, Graham said in an interview, "A dancer's instrument is his body bounded by birth and death." A government report used quotes from both Martin and Terry as evidence of Graham's power to represent America again.[100] In West Berlin, after having given all she could to the cause of freedom for an audience that did not entirely appreciate her dance or its meanings, Graham now triumphed as the revengeful queen.[101]

4

The Aging of a Star in Camelot

Israel, Europe, and "Behind the Iron Curtain," 1962

And if the world goes really wacky, we'll get John to send out Jackie /
That's what we call cultural exchange.
                                    —Dave and Iola Brubeck with Louis Armstrong

"It takes me ten years to make a dancer," Martha Graham declared during her lectures, and by 1961, at age sixty-seven, she had created an internationally recognized generation of stars who could tour in her full-length ballet, *Clytemnestra*.[1] Her company was stunning and technically powerful as they performed with the matriarch of modern dance, its "Picasso," as they readied to tour for a new, young president. John F. Kennedy and his wife, Jacqueline, marked a generation of urbane and sparkling new modern leaders who stood in sharp contrast to the golf-playing Dwight Eisenhower and his wife, Mamie, as well as former vice president Richard Nixon. Nixon had been Kennedy's opponent in the 1960 presidential election, and his upper lip famously showed beads of sweat during the first televised debate as he faced off against his cool, handsome opponent. Youth and charisma now counted: politics met performance.

Despite Graham's poor reception in Berlin, and the muted letter from Eleanor Dulles, Washington continued to court Graham. In 1958, the White House invited Graham to join a State Department conference in Washington to address the Soviet threat and international economic policy in Asia. Graham accepted the White House invitation and spent several days with political figures including former President Truman, the Dulles brothers, President Eisenhower, and Vice President Nixon.[2] In 1959, the State Department considered modern dance for the Moscow exhibition, the location of the great "Kitchen Debate" between Nixon and Khrushchev in front of the gleaming yellow American kitchen, replete with a housewife in her

Martha Graham's Cold War. Victoria Phillips, Oxford University Press 2020. © Oxford University Press.
DOI: 10.1093/oso/9780190610364.001.0001

apron. Noted was the import of dance personalities at such events when the modern icon would sit "with six or eight intellectuals who are interested in dance [and talk] over lunch or dinner." Indeed, "[Cultural] officers take it out of their own pockets in order to entertain" the modern dance leaders because they were considered "extremely useful persons."[3] Yet the exhibition became known for the American kitchen, consumer goods, and the glamor brought by high fashion in the West.

In 1961, the State Department filed a report on culture and the value of non-verbal communication: "We have taken the cream of some crops. We have quite naturally selected first those things which knew no language barrier, such as music and dance." While American ballet companies had shown great expertise, the modern ballet presented by Robbins was of huge import as was modernism. According to the State Department, after seeing Robbins the Yugoslavs proclaimed, ' "You [in America] are the wave of the future. You are really presenting us with something that is revolutionary, in the way of the dance, and when we see Russia and its classical ballet, which hasn't changed one bit in generations, we can only look to [America] for guidance and we believe that'—then *transferring their frame of reference*—'this is true of a great many things that America stands for.' This is good to hear, when you get this reaction from something which is basically a cultural manifestation [emphasis mine]."[4] The government valued cultural exports because the messages embedded in the apolitical presentations allowed for the 'transference' of these ideas into larger conclusions about the United States writ large: its freedoms, politics, economics. It brought bloc countries closer to the American fold.

Thus under the Kennedys, in 1962, Graham and her twenty glowing dancers—as well as support staff; an orchestra; complex, shimmery sets; costumes; and even a long roll of linoleum to cover splintery stages—toured under the aegis of the United States Cultural Program, the American National Theater and Academy, and the Department of State in Greece and Turkey, Yugoslavia (which had received Robbins), Poland, Sweden, West Germany, Finland, the Netherlands, and Norway, traversing a complex geographic puzzle of territories contested between East and West. While wooing bloc nations, Graham engaged with the Bandung issues of nonalignment, as well as old-fashioned wartime European neutrality refashioned by the Cold War. Yet the tour would start in Israel, where the first tour under Eisenhower had ended, again courtesy of Bethsabée de Rothschild.[5] Although this leg of the tour did not officially receive direct government or State Department funding, Graham and her company were again supported by USIS publicity as they spent a month performing in Israel "under the patronage" of the United States ambassador in Tel Aviv.[6]

Graham projected what the Kennedy administration needed as a cultural export to further the American message abroad. As the West and East Wing planned this tour, foreign conflicts loomed large, and the president needed to build his credibility as a statesman while maintaining his appeal as a bristling new force in Washington. While his youthful charisma drew domestic voters to the polls, in international spheres he appeared diplomatically immature; he lacked the critical postwar stature brought by the former president and general to the emerging superpower. Tensions between the United States and the Soviet Union had escalated as a result of Kennedy's Bay of Pigs invasion of Cuba in March 1961; that botched effort only increased the legitimacy of Soviet influence.[7] While Soviet premier Nikita Khrushchev wrote Kennedy demanding a stop to "armed aggression" in the name of "the peace of the whole world," Kennedy claimed that the Americans fought for freedom and the self-determination of Cubans.[8] His sentiments rang hollow internationally. In June, seeking people-to-people diplomacy, the still idealistic statesman met with Khrushchev for the first time during a summit in Vienna. The location held Cold War meaning: in postwar negotiations, Austria had been divided between West and East; subsequently, the United States and Soviet Union had granted the nation the legal status of neutrality in 1955.

Neutrality had a long European legal history. During the Cold War, contested and malleable diplomatic alignments, or theoretical issues of neutrality, neutralism, and nonalignment, or, as I encapsulate the three, antialignment, would ricochet across the continent, causing mayhem and hot encounters.[9] In 1948, the Czech move to build a Balkan Federation had led to Soviet suppression and domination. In 1956, Bandung fizzled, the Soviets suppressed Hungary with military force, and Moscow quieted Poland's rebels. Nevertheless, by 1961 the Yugoslav leader Josip Tito had taken to the fore of an antialignment strategy and, for both powers, threatened to disrupt Finland, Germany, and others understood to be neutrals, nonaligned, or divided.

Experts scripted the Kennedy-Khrushchev Vienna Summit discussions to focus on the postwar division of Germany, where Graham would also perform the next year, and the implications of new treaties in Berlin, where she had performed near the ever-porous East-West border.[10] Yet the two men launched into ideology, off the American script, which the president had been advised not to do. Kennedy admitted later, "He beat the hell out of me," ..., "He savaged me."[11] Khrushchev remarked that after the summit Kennedy looked "anxious" and "deeply upset", adding for his own effect, "But there was nothing I could do to help him," concluding, "Politics is a merciless business."[12]

With the sudden construction of the Berlin Wall that August, although Kennedy appeared weak and inept in the face of the East German communist bravado, Khrushchev also found himself at the mercy of politics with the East German move.[13] Both men found themselves on the defensive, heightening the tension and the demand for diplomacy. On September 1, many of the Bandung nations gathered in Belgrade, Yugoslavia, to discuss neutralism and the formulation of the Non-Aligned Movement (NAM) under the leadership of Yugoslavia, India, and Egypt. Tensions about the antialigners escalated in Washington and Moscow, and soft power met hard demonstrations. On the opening day of the Belgrade conference, the Soviet Union conducted the first of thirty-one nuclear tests to follow, and nations were aghast.[14] Moving into the fall, Finnish president Urho Kekkonen, an experienced statesman, made a state visit to Washington to meet Kennedy, who felt optimistic about alliances with the nonaligned.[15] Although Finland had tacitly cooperated with the Soviet Union, its much larger neighbor, its aim was to remain neutral in order to enjoy economic exchange with Europe and the West. Later, as the Finn vacationed in Hawaii, the "Note" crisis ensued in which the Soviets demanded Finnish military cooperation.[16] On the day Moscow passed the note, it exploded a test hydrogen bomb known as Tsar Bomba: the blast was three thousand times as powerful as the explosion over Hiroshima; the fireball was five miles wide.[17] Beleaguered by Soviet aggression and undercut by blunders, Kennedy seemed unseasoned and even puerile as the leader of the free world. Sophisticated cultural diplomacy could help him shed this image and show that optimistic, if unseasoned, energy and global moral gravitas could coexist. As an iconic and seasoned apolitical American diplomat backed by a youthful, impeccably trained team, Graham could fit the bill.

The new president was dedicated to international exchange as a means to advance the American agenda abroad, quietly buttressed with steely soft-power tactics by his culturally sophisticated wife; together, the first couple reshaped trends set by earlier administrations. Like Rockefeller and Roosevelt, Kennedy sent American cultural exchange to Latin America, with

the Alliance for Progress program in 1961. Mirroring the cultural fascination with Turner's thesis and the power of the frontier echoed in presidential addresses from Woodrow Wilson to create a unified peace, Kennedy
used frontier tropes when he announced the program's initiation.[18] Like
Roosevelt, Kennedy and his New Frontier would employ Graham to express
these aims through her dance. In these efforts, Kennedy surrounded himself with people he considered to be "the best and the brightest."[19] Secretary
of State Dean Rusk had worked at the Rockefeller Foundation, where John
Foster Dulles had served, and Rusk had learned from Nelson Rockefeller
about the importance of high-art culture as a tool of influence during times
of "total war" that demanded cultural propaganda. According to Rusk's office, Kennedy's boost to Eisenhower's programs with the new Mutual
Educational and Cultural Act would "lift educational and cultural affairs
to a new position of potential influence in our foreign relations."[20] Echoing
Eisenhower in words and then with Graham, Kennedy proclaimed that
the exchange programs were the preeminent example "in recent history of
beating swords into plowshares, of having some benefit come to humanity
out of the destruction of war."[21] While, in the White House, a dead-end paper
trail silences the first lady, a powerful relationship in later years betrays an alliance between this first lady and Graham. Indeed, as had Eleanor Roosevelt,
Jacqueline Kennedy would become a consummate supporter of Graham at
performances and in print, even after the death of both husbands. While
Roosevelt had attended performances in Europe and written for newspapers
to promote Graham, Kennedy Onassis would embrace the dancer, wearing
sequined dresses to Graham galas that carried the Kennedy name on the
marquee; she would also edit Graham's last book at war Doubleday in 1991.
Both Graham and Kennedy Onassis appreciated the architecture of fashion,
design, and graceful diplomacy and exploited the political opportunities
offered by its soft-power spotlight.

Meanwhile, Kennedy allied with George Kennan, whom he named ambassador to Yugoslavia, the home of NAM. Speaking at New York's Museum
of Modern Art, Kennan again showed his dedication to modern art as diplomacy. The father of containment proclaimed that modernism had "universal
appeal among the artists and intellectuals, not only in the non-Communist
world, but even in the Communist world." He equated American "freedom
of expression" and the "initiative of artistic expression" with the political
goals of fighting Soviet accusations of American "materialism" and asserting
Western principles. Kennan declared that American artistic modernism

could "transcend the barriers of language"; his statement mirrored Graham's own pronunciations about the language of dance and her work. "The spine is your body's tree of life," she said. The dancer's body "says what words cannot." Graham found the eternal, the universal, in the lines "You will know the language / Of my wordless poems."[22] Graham and Kennan would join together on the European stage in theaters and embassy events because, as Kennan remarked to his MoMA audience, elites "must evaluate and interpret advanced ideas to the general public," gesturing to the trickle-down diplomacy essential to modern dance and wordless cultural exchange using Graham's American language.

The American modernist genre became increasingly vital as anti-Communist propaganda that spring. As Graham prepared to go "behind the Iron Curtain," as dancers called it, and beyond, the legendary Bolshoi arrived in New York: it had not been seen in the United States since 1959, when it took the dance world by storm.[23] Yet as the Soviet ballet had garnered publicity in the West for its striking technique, a method steeped in European tradition, Graham would soon land in Soviet territories to display her strikingly polished modern technique executed by individual and racially diverse bodies, unavailable to cookie-cutter pale ballet dancers, however high their legs and arched their feet. Graham's American modern dance used a method of free expression that the Soviets had abandoned during the interwar years—and then added technical finesse. For Kennan, as a cultural figure who advised Kennedy and had written under Roosevelt about the importance of ballet in the Soviet Union versus the paltry position of leftover expressive modern attempts in dance, the lineup of Graham versus the Bolshoi would have seemed to promise a win.

* * *

Specific, rigorous preparations for the tour began in New York, Washington, and the host nations. In New York, the young Graham dancers started each day with the mandated morning company class. They lined up in rows wearing leotards and footless tights—no colored leg warmers, draped shawls, knee pads, or anything to distract from the simple elegance of each body. They stood straight-necked, backs slightly arched, tall like Amazons, with feet in parallel as Graham entered. As she took the front of the room, before the mirrors, in silent unison they drew one leg behind the other and sank to the floor before the matriarch. In her deep commanding tone, Graham

said, "And one." The dancers moved, executing the floor work with preci-
sion, spinning on hip bones and arching to the sky after contracting in grief,
knowing exactly what came next in ritual procession until she noticed you,
noticed something different, and it changed for the next time, a little higher,
deeper, perhaps taller and faster; she was still grasping for the human.

In this same studio, the dancers gathered to learn about the State
Department mandates: how to interact with the public, etiquette for embassy dinners, and so on. They also watched a brief film describing Turkey.[24]
Sexuality entered the discussion, too, because there were concerns about the
men in the company engaging in behavior that would make them vulnerable
to blackmail.[25] Dancers understood they would be followed, watched, and
listened to, particularly "behind the Iron Curtain," and thus behavior had to
be "all-American" all the time. While the rest of the world was starting to
sport blue jeans, and there was even trading in denim on the black market in
Eastern bloc countries, the female company members knew they would need
to resurrect their white gloves, flared skirts, and heels in order to descend
the steel steps after grueling flights, perfectly manicured on the tarmac as
1950s New Look diplomats who now could rely on Jackie's comportment as a
model under the new president.

By the 1960s the idea of modernism and the legend of Martha Graham
made the framing of American innovation paradoxical. The ironies of the
"modern" dance and its choreography had come full circle for some with
Doris Humphrey's *The Art of Making Dances*, a book published in 1958.[26]
Humphrey delineated rules for creating "good" and "bad" modern dances,
offering diagrams and flow charts, thus puncturing the illusory bubble
of individual artistic agency in high-art American modern dance. While
deeply challenged by the postmodernists led by former Graham soloist and
Appalachian Spring's first frontier Preacher, Merce Cunningham, many mainstream critics and most private-sector arbiters of dance taste who advised the
government were classical modernists who largely followed Humphrey. As a
"contemporary" choreographer, in her words, Graham had to produce new
works that would shock, yet as a modernist before the critics and government, she performed on Broadway in a traditional theatrical setting, using
her recognized and now hegemonic training vocabulary. A corroding maturity was catching up with modernism in dance, and thus with Graham. Her
dancers were sparkling new, yet trained in a highly codified method. As a
performer, center stage, Graham had been heralded for her command of her
audience, but the very longevity of her stage career could also make her seem

antiquated and grandiose to some. For "the modern," rigid laws and an elderly body meant certain death, particularly in a decade that was increasingly
celebrating the power of youth and rebellion as a mandate of freedom.

Battling to be contemporary and modern in New York, Graham
choreographed *Phaedra*, which merged her Greek myth classicism with
youthful power and increasingly overt sexuality to ensure that her dances
were perceived as fresh and relevant, yet artistically highbrow. Her use of
classic source material enabled her to push boundaries while maintaining
cultural credibility, particularly important for touring purposes. Phaedra had
appeared in the works of Euripides, Jean Racine, and Jean-Philippe Rameau,
who composed for Louis XV, the French monarch who had established the
first formal ballet academy. In the narrative, the Cretan princess Phaedra,
the wife of the aging Theseus, falls in love with her stepson, Hippolytus, who
rejects her. Aphrodite imbues Phaedra with sexual desire and hateful resent-
ment; she resorts to deceit, revenge, and suicide. Under Graham's watch,
the story drew attention to her young, virtuosic team in tight costumes performing in provocative set pieces. Determined to keep "center stage" at age
sixty-eight, Graham deployed the modernist narrative technique she had
used with the story of Oedipus in *Night Journey*: she played the aged Phaedra
in a long gown as she recalled the tragedy, yet in *Phaedra* her young stars
performed the events being remembered. Having stomped on her costume
during the first government tour, Ethel Winter played Aphrodite in skintight leotard and footless tights, at one point hanging herself from a set piece
looking like the internals of the female anatomy, then facing the audience
head-on, only to spread her legs to the audience at 180 degrees, opening
her own anatomy for view were it not for the leotard. At the opening night,
Graham herself described *Phaedra* as a "phantasmagoria of desire."[27]

The New York critical reaction was mixed, with concerns about Graham's
age picked up by some in Washington as USIS decided what to use for
publicity on the upcoming tour. The *New York Herald Tribune* described
Phaedra's "erotic vision" as "tremendously sensual."[28] The costumes revealed
"physical desire." Graham's women were "so beautiful in form and face, so
sensuous."[29] The movement was so provocative that "the traditional tired
business man would need to look no further" (understood in the 1960s as a
euphemism for those seeking erotic visual stimulation).[30] Reviewers also singled out Graham's "virile" male dancers, who showed "masculine prowess" as
they danced "only in near nude loincloths."[31] Finally, the Noguchi set contributed to the heightened eroticism of the piece: "A panel revealed "Hippolytus's

[male] physical attributes" in a "teasing fashion" near Phaedra's bed.[32] The myth told the story of the evils of desire and the doom that faced those who succumbed—yet not without first exposing desire itself. Although the sexual nature of the work brought in both "tired businessmen" and energetic younger audiences, it also drew attention to the contrast between the vital and youthful dancers and the aging diva who clung to center stage. According to some, Graham "was not in her best dance form."[33] A government memo plainly told American diplomats that this should be Graham's last tour as a performer under government auspices: "Martha Graham is getting older and the time approaches when her personal performance would detract considerably from the quality of the show."[34] Although Graham positioned herself firmly center stage surrounded by youthful dancers, others were hoping for a farewell tour.

Graham's other new work that season, *Secular Games*, celebrated the younger members of the company, and, as in *Diversion of Angels*, Graham did not appear, except after the work concluded to take a bow for the now requisite standing ovation. Graham's choreography had previously featured women in roles that demanded technical expertise but also required an emotional or spiritual journey. In *Secular Games*, with the dancers' "seductive eyes and suggestive bodies," the women met the power of the again noted "virile" men in a technical show.[35] Although *Secular Games* was criticized for its eroticism, its "sexual aspects" were excused thanks to the display of the dancers' technique. "The fresh erotic presentation is a masterpiece," concluded one critic.[36] Along with *Diversion of Angels*, it would go out on tour as the second piece in which Graham did not dance.

Politics as well as the power of American modernism dictated touring repertory choices managed from Washington in coordination with Graham. A section of a government memo titled "Selection" suggested that Graham bring works derived from Greek mythology and the abstracted masterpiece "crowd stopper" *Diversion of Angels*, the work inspired by Kandinsky. Creating the aura of "the new," the just-premiered *Phaedra* and *Secular Games* were added to this roster. Yet in a different twist, the repertory for the 1962 tour overtly emphasized religious themes, which achieved several aims. As in Berlin, 1957, the character of Judith would reference the Jews and the legacy of the Holocaust in Germany, and Israel would host the premiere of the reworked piece. In order to combat the specter of Soviet atheism in Europe, particularly in Poland, the known work *Embattled Garden*, the story of the Garden of Eden, joined the Catholic Joan of Arc and *Seraphic*

Dialogue. In addition, *Acrobats of God* joined the roster as another piece in which Graham did not dance but did appear onstage. Choreographed in 1960, the work used religious references to exhibit the youth of the dancers as "acrobats," with Graham sidelined in jumps, lifts, and splits to the floor, yet playing "God" onstage as director-choreographer in a bid to humor.

Acrobats of God, with its title from "the early church fathers," according to Graham, was her "fanfare for dance as an *arta* celebration in honor of the trials and tribulations, the discipline, denials, glories and delights of a dancer's world."[37] She refers to her dancers as "acrobats of God," in the context of the Old Testament and Abraham. The program notes state that she took this title from those religious leaders "who subjected themselves to the discipline of the desert, the *athletae Dei*." Graham also implied that the training of the body was a training of the soul with discipline and prayer, study, solitude, and confession in "Christlike habits," referencing Paul in 1 Timothy and Romans. Audiences would see her athletes in training to become gods and goddesses spin to the floor, tilt, and leap in a piece named for the phrase. Graham herself "plays God," comically reining in her dancers, assisted by a man with a whip. The *Herald Tribune* relished the piece, lavishing praise on "all manner of fantastic lifts, balances, jumps, turns, and related feats of skill," the "fabulous body techniques" of the dancers, and Graham's choreographic skill "that made you fall in love with it."[38] The *Christian Science Monitor* gushed, "*Acrobats of God* is a beautiful thing," adding, "We can only watch and marvel as this glorious company goes through its incredible paces."[39] While relishing the "delicious" work, Martin of the *New York Times* took the dance as politics and wrote that Graham's new work and season were "an occasion for jubilation" because of "its sorely needed reassurance about the status of America . . . with [Graham's art] as a medium of its greatness."[40] While he had refused to join the government-led Dance Panel, Martin remained a patriot who championed the nation with Graham, and the reviews made it back to Washington.

As noted earlier, the "godless" communists were ever-present in Cold War propaganda that emanated from the State Department, USIS, Voice of America (VOA), and Radio Free Europe/Radio Liberty (RFE/RL-CIA), and Graham's biography was thus manipulated for tours. Government-sponsored outlets consistently sought to "mobilize the great spiritual and moral resources" of God-fearing people who existed in Soviet bloc states. VOA broadcasts into Europe attacked godlessness and coupled the Soviets with the Nazis, linking irreligious tyrannies.[41] The Communists were a product of "atheism," and thus "barbarism and totalitarianism."[42] If Eastern Europe were liberated, the "pseudo-Gods of the Kremlin" would be vanquished.[43] RFE/RL studies emphasized the importance of religious programming, and broadcasts followed in turn. Kennedy's election, as a Catholic, took on new meaning. Although Protestants still dominated the upper echelons of government in the United States, during the Cold War a "new American civil religion" came into being for political purposes, incorporating Catholic, Jewish, and, internationally, even Muslim practices.[44] Eisenhower's words became increasingly liberalized as the Cold War escalated as a struggle for the soul of modern man.[45]

Graham's program notes, crafted by USIS before she departed, reflected this effort to pose American "civil religion" against state atheism; her being a descendant of *Mayflower* settlers had been perfect fodder under Eisenhower but did not tell the entire story under Kennedy, and her knowledge of the Old Testament and Catholic teachings took precedence over her Puritan ties. Graham was the child of an interfaith marriage: her Protestant mother with roots going back to the founding of Massachusetts had married an Irish Catholic. Despite the strict influence of Graham's puritanical maternal grandmother, she was raised by a Catholic nanny. Graham seemed to ally most directly with her Protestant background in publicity, yet she was deeply affected by her Irish nanny and her father and their attachment to the Catholic Church: "a place of ceremony, mystery, blessing." Graham loved "the formality, the ritual, and the discipline ... the almost incomprehensible message" of the Catholic Church.[46] She identified with the physicality, mysticism, and "livingness of the body" she found in the Catholic Church, as well as stories from the Old Testament.[47] Yet she recalled a letter from her Catholic father, in which he wrote, "Martha, you must keep an open soul."[48] Graham referenced ideas of religious freedom in her family as a microcosm of the United States: her father told her that she would become "a woman of the world who is able to choose her own religion."[49] Graham celebrated freedom to practice, and was thus recognized by the government.[50]

George Kennan's work under Roosevelt would inform the Kennedy administration's deployment of Graham not only regarding modernism, but also the use of religion as a weapon. In 1945, Kennan had observed that "the religious feelings of the Russian masses represented a potentially incalculable danger to the Soviet government."[51] When he advised on strategies of covert propaganda, Kennan understood the power of religion and an Americanized Judeo-Christianity in thwarting Soviet expansionism, and Graham would perform for him in Belgrade. Yet the company's next stop, Poland, was particularly fraught: fifty million Catholics throughout Eastern Europe, mostly Poles, had been brought into the Soviet sphere when the Iron Curtain came down. Although Stalin had believed in a dedication to the state, he made overtures to Pope Pius XII, which the pontiff and his advisers resisted.[52] Religion, and particularly Catholicism, thus became the perfect glue to bind anti-Soviet rebels to American democratic aims.

Preparing for the tour, programming would be distributed by USIS and shown in host countries; it emphasized Graham's status and attachment to fundamental human beliefs, which included faith, while avoiding fealty to any specific religion. Graham's technique had been codified, and host nations' well-to-do learned about her innovative technique in *A Dancer's World*, a film screened in movie theaters and on television. USIS noted that "the principles of the school seem to have become a law."[53] Her works were derived from "the laws of human nature."[54] In addition, Graham spoke about her philosophy of dance, of life couched in religious terms, making proclamations about "the state of the soul" in a taped interview with Kennedy's new USIS director, Edward R. Murrow, for his Cold War radio show "This I Believe." The program featured prominent Americans discussing their personal philosophies "in the hope that they may strengthen your beliefs so that your life may be richer, fuller, happier" and included numerous interviews with African Americans and musicians who would also tour. In the program that would be broadcast by USIS to prepare nations for her arrival, Graham explained that a dancer must have "the kind of faith that Abraham had: 'Therein he staggered not at the promise of God through unbelief.' "[55] Her dancers were "acrobats of God," she said, referencing the piece they would perform on tour. Murrow always concluded by acknowledging the individuality and political independence of his guests. "Those are the personal beliefs of Martha Graham," he reminded listeners who would hear the government radio program.[56]

Like the deletion of Graham's *Mayflower* heritage in place of religious references, this time Graham did not bring Americana. With his New Frontier slogan, Kennedy had set the stage for the export of repertory to include frontier narratives, and like Graham, he had looked to the opportunities offered by the metaphor. Still, he envisioned a wholly different territory than that of any pioneer narrative of the American West, such as *Appalachian Spring*. "Beyond that frontier," he said, "are uncharted areas of science and space."[57] It was his New Frontier. Graham's West, with its provincial territorial barriers and fences, was a part of a mythic past, no longer directly applicable. Moreover, the work had already been described as "ideological propaganda" by critics, hardly the baggage needed by the young administration defined by its own resized symbols.[58] The celebration of American modernism and religious freedom stood in for the overt depiction of the prairie house and the frontier Preacher.

* * *

The Graham company touring extravaganza began in Israel to perform the repertory and premiere *Legend of Judith* in Tel Aviv. Since Graham's 1956 performances in Israel, she had returned often and remained ideologically close to Rothschild, who had immigrated there. An Israeli dancer recalled, "Batsheva [Rothschild] came to Israel from New York and Paris, and she believed that after the Holocaust she wanted to do an Aliyah [ascent towards Jerusalem]." For Jews in the post-Holocaust diaspora, this "act of going up" or "making Aliyah," by moving to the Land of Israel and building a new state, followed one of the most basic tenets of Zionism. Rather than a prewar aspiration in the Jewish imagination, the establishment of the State of Israel meant that the Law of Return gave Jews and their descendants automatic citizenship and legal claim to the land. The dancer concluded, "[Rothschild] pushed Martha toward this idealism."[59] After Graham's first season in 1956, she returned to Israel often and became well-known because even when caught in the country during armed conflicts or skirmishes, she refused to leave. "Good friends never leave good friends in trouble," she told the dancers in Israel, even as they hid in makeshift studio bathrooms that promised the cover of piping.[60] In 1958 the Israeli Ministry of Education had invited Rothschild to become chair of its newly created Dance Division, and Rothschild imported Graham to teach the first summer course. Graham had become a legend, linking herself to her *Judith*. The Graham technique became the government-sanctioned form of dance training, much to the chagrin of the German-trained dancers who believed that they possessed the "true" Israeli dance that was embedded in traditions that transcended the Holocaust and statehood, but used German-based free dance and socialist roots for expression.[61] Together in Israel, Graham and Rothschild found "a new spirit, new beginning."[62]

As mentioned earlier, the State Department did not overtly fund this initial leg of the tour, on the grounds that it did not want to be seen siding overtly with Israel. Nevertheless, State's fingerprints could still be seen.

Although Kennedy took a decidedly pro-Israel position by combating Soviet influence among Arab countries, he had to tread carefully. European allies needed Middle Eastern oil.[63] Graham's performance of a biblically themed work in Israel, however, was the ideal cultural message to send. Graham's story about the Jewish heroine who saves her people brought the horrors of any totalitarian rule into high relief, especially since the United States had likened Soviet atrocities to Nazi terrors against the Jews, and both were positioned in American propaganda as areligious regarding biblical teachings. Thus, once she had arrived in Israel, the embassy hosted Graham, and government operatives assisted her with press and publicity. Typical of cultural private-public partnerships, "pickup tours" could be more easily rationalized by government promoters. As with ABT under Truman in 1950, private funding got the dancers to Europe, and army planes and housing took over once they were there. Rothschild's sponsorship allowed the government to pay only for Graham's transport within Europe.

Despite Graham's familiarity with the terrain, upon the company's arrival in 1962 all was not quite right with her. This unease would permeate the tour as she wrestled with age, appearance, and her own frailties alongside her understanding of the importance of diplomacy and her role as ambassador for America. In many respects, the stock shot of the company in front of a sleek, modern airplane—this time an Israeli jet—was like its predecessors: a racially diverse group of well-tailored dancers stood on the steel steps and on the tarmac, exhibiting their poise and sleek physiques. Youth, like the airplane, was glossy and modern. But Graham was nowhere to be found in this picture celebrating their arrival in Israel. Making room for the modern image, she uncharacteristically stood away from the eye of the camera, offstage.

Yet under the watchful eye of Rothschild, Graham would triumph with well-planned cultural convergences onstage. While preparing for the tour in New York, Graham rechoreographed the solo *Judith* into a group work, *Legend of Judith*, and incorporated Israeli artists into her restaging. By design, the new piece featured neither the Schuman composition nor the Noguchi set and props. Instead, Graham used music by Mordecai Seter, a Russian-born Israeli composer, with a set by Dani Karavan: both men had biographies that were useful as propaganda in programs distributed to the audiences in Tel Aviv and Jerusalem.

After suffering pogroms and other acts of anti-Semitism, Seter's family had fled the Soviet Union for Israel, an Aliyah. Both as an individual and as a composer, Seter embodied the persecution of Jews in the Soviet Union

and the creative freedom to be found in Israel as a citizen. In correspondence reminiscent of the creation of *Appalachian Spring* with composer
Copland and the renaming of *Ballet for Martha*, Graham had suggested to
Seter that they change the name of the work to follow words of triumph, this
time uttered by Judith: "I will sing unto the Lord a new song." Graham noted
that Judith "for so many means a woman who killed," but, she emphasized,
"They forget the reason."[64] The reason was deeply political: Judith had saved
the Israeli people from military domination and persecution. As with the
Holocaust, this history must not be forgotten. Graham wrote Seter that she
was considering choreographed references to the traditional Shabbat ritual
in which women light candles. In a return letter, he suggested that the choreography include "women pursued by soldiers, etc."[65] Graham replied that she
would use a quotation from Judith to frame the work, "For God breaketh the
battles: for among the camps in the midst of the people He hath delivered me
out of the hands that persecuted me."[66] As they continued to create via mail,
Graham wrote that the biblical legend kept her awake nights: "I only hope
I can do justice to it." Anticipating the work in Israel in the coming months to
complete the project, she concluded, "I hope and pray that God will be with
us all and that it will be for all of us a period of exultation in joy."[67]

Dani Karavan, an artist who was also creating sculptures for the Court
of Justice in Tel Aviv, designed the set.[68] Graham had seen his work during
a 1961 trip to Israel, telling him, "I want to dance in your sculpture. I want
you to design a set for me." Rothschild's foundation immediately funded the
project. In a letter, Graham discussed the personal and political import of
the piece and its character. As with Saint Joan and others in her suitcase of
female archetypes, only through the personal could Graham communicate
the political. She wrote, "I also had the feeling that [Karavan] felt the stress
[of the choreography] was a little too much on the personal side of Judith
and her relationships and not enough on the side that she was acting for her
people." She continued, "I think, however, that no one who lives in legend
can do anything except in a deeply personal way. One must face the ultimate
large pattern through the small but very intense one experienced through actual inner conflict and triumph."[69] Cultural archetypes could only be formulated using the specifics of their humanity, a Jungian tenet that had fueled her
approach to the tale of Oedipus and Saint Joan, as well as her frontier Bride.

Once they were settled in Israel, Graham and the company rehearsed
for several days. The dancers struggled to execute the choreography
constructed in the bare New York studio within the new set in Israel that

they had never seen. Yet Graham wrote, "Suddenly in one extraordinary moment, all the parts [came] together." She and Seter sat together as the company met the challenges: "Only once in a lifetime is one lucky enough to witness such a happening. Seter and I were left speechless with our emotions, and inspired."[70] The use of Israeli artists enraptured stagehands and the theater's workmen, who, according to the press, wept when they saw the set they had constructed with Graham walking through it in rehearsal.[71] Yet unreported troubles plagued the company. Rehearsal time was limited. Bertram Ross, who danced Holofernes (the character appeared onstage in this revised version of the dance), was out with a bad back for three days. One dancer fractured her ankle, and another was dropped on her head after a difficult lift went wrong.[72] Seter, who was conducting all evenings, conducted every dance other than his own "about ten times faster" than usual. Tempo was key to performance success: Graham repeatedly shouted at him to calm down.[73]

When the company's Israeli engagement formally began in October 1962, critics deeply appreciated Graham's professionalism and craft.[74] Meanwhile, a Cold War drama played out in the Western Hemisphere that month. Graham's time in Israel coincided with the Cuban Missile Crisis, the thirteen-day standoff over the installation of nuclear-armed Soviet missiles in Cuba. For the general public and diplomats in Washington, nuclear Armageddon seemed impossibly near. One Washington diplomat piled his four children and their mother into the family's station wagon, drove them to his home in the Iowa cornfields on Friday night, and drove back to the nation's capital, where he resumed his work, not missing a single workday.[75] The threat was real to all in the know. Yet no one cabled the dancers, even after Kennedy's televised speech. In Israel, frantic calls by parents to the dancers were met by surprise: they had not heard the news in briefings or the international press.[76] They were dancing. In the context of turmoil, Graham had made her mark on the state cultural power brokers, in both the public and private sectors. Embassy events and parties took place to celebrate the matriarch and her company. Graham can be seen in photos fondly squeezing the Israeli ambassador's cheek during an American diplomatic event.

Promoting the tour to the American public and Congress, and despite extensive State Department, USIS, ANTA, and other agency pre-planning, the *New York Herald Tribune* reported on the "hefty savings" for the taxpayer because the State Department had "acted quickly" to get Graham to

Europe once they learned of her sponsorship to travel to Israel.[77] Politically protected and seeming like a bargain, Graham now began her official State Department work.

* * *

In Greece, Graham had to counter the threat of communism and celebrate democracy with myths born in the country itself, yet modernized by an American. Fifteen years earlier, Truman, inspired by Kennan's ideas of Soviet containment, had announced that without American aid, Greece and Turkey, Graham's next two stops, would become overrun by Communists. While both countries remained outside the Soviet sphere of influence, tensions continued. Although Greece's bloody civil war was now ten years past, it was still very much on people's minds. In Washington the previous year, at a state luncheon with Kennedy, the prime minister had underscored the importance of American aid to maintaining stability.[78] When the company arrived in Greece, Graham and her members feared artistic backlash. Would audiences feel that she had appropriated their national heritage through the use of ancient myths?[79]

As it turned out, the people of Athens showed just the opposite reaction: "Greek audiences saw the implacability of the classical gods recreated with depth and vigor unmatched since ancient times."[80] They adored *Clytemnestra*, deeply appreciating how Graham had adapted their own stories with a modern idiom that could be understood without the written word. Cultural convergences gained increasing credibility as the performances attracted a larger public than usual for Graham. One theater had raked seating, and tickets were priced affordably. The company connected deeply to the Greek youth who filled the theaters. Even taxi drivers saw the show. Graham left an "indelible impression on all who attended performances," and "her dignity and artistry greatly impressed the more than 20 newspaper reporters."[81] Graham triumphed as a cultural export in the eyes of critics, audiences of all classes and generations, and the State Department.[82] Although one report foreshadowed the future stops and noted of Graham that "her performance was not quite up to its usual standards," the tour was off to a magnificent start.[83]

In Turkey, the next stop, Graham's shows did not attract as broad of an audience: theaters were stocked with elites. Reviews there emphasized the political import of the personalities in attendance, as well as the social aspects of the performances. The political front was fraught: highly contested nuclear weapons were stationed in Turkey, and "Operation Red Sheepskin" left behind American military–trained and clandestine forces to fight Soviet and leftist moves on the ground.[84] The Americans needed to maintain a cultural presence in Turkey to cloak military aims, as well as to encourage leaders to join their geopolitical anti-Soviet project. The *Daily News* noted the presence of the Turkish prime minister and a host of political and cultural personalities seated with American diplomats and the military elite. Its "Social Corner" reported that the audience was "full of beautifully dressed women in mink and jewels."[85] Despite the presence of a few people in "cable-knit sweaters," the lobby was celebrated as a "fashion show."[86] In addition to political ties, cooperation with business seemed paramount: Graham's programs, which helped defray the cost of performances, featured advertisements for "reduced fares" for airline travelers within contested areas of the Middle East, American refrigerators, and the Turkish arm of Mobil Oil.[87] History became important: while her company was noted for its youth, publicity featured Graham as a longtime American ambassador, noting that she danced for President Roosevelt in 1937 and was cited by President Truman, who had vowed to protect Turkey, as a 1950 "Woman of the Year."[88]

The embassy party in Ankara displayed another aspect of the Graham company's usefulness for government officials: the clandestine cover offered by social gatherings. When the Graham company performed, a crisis between Turkey and Cyprus, in which the Kennedy administration had been involved, was coming to a head.[89] On the night of the reception in Ankara, according to dancer Marni Thomas, "It was supposed to look like there was a big party going on, and there was a big meeting going on about Cyprus. And it was covering the thing with the [Graham] company downstairs."[90] The party took place with larger political negotiations just rooms away. Diplomats could come and go, seemingly on American soil in the embassy for a glass of postperformance champagne and canapés. On tours, it was rumored that unknown men appeared to "assist" the company with various tasks that were already well taken care of. Upon departure, one man appeared at the airport seeming to be in charge of handing out plane tickets, a task that was easily accomplished by the company manager in the past.

What dancers called the "behind the Iron Curtain" portion of the tour came next, with stops in Yugoslavia and Poland. The roots of the trip can be traced to Francis Mason and Kennan, with Mason serving as cultural attaché for Kennan in Belgrade and later chairman of the Graham company's board. Even before Kennan's arrival, Mason had written a letter to Graham in 1957, urging her to consider performing in Yugoslavia.[91] Yet the time was not ripe, and Graham was chosen for Berlin. Although Mason had left the post as cultural attaché by the time the modern dance artist arrived, while in Yugoslavia he had a key role in arranging for an exhibition of modern art to travel to Belgrade under Kennan.[92] Speaking at the opening of the exhibit of modernist art in Yugoslavia, the pro-modernist ambassador emphasized Americanist mantras and encouraged the gallery goers to view the art on their own terms, freely.[93] Self-deprecating and savvy, he remained a superb diplomat.[94] People lined up in droves to see the works. The success spawned more projects. A *Herald Tribune* story, "Embassy of Good Will, a U.S. Art Show in Red Poland," described the success in Belgrade and reported that another avant-garde exhibit would be headed to Poland in 1962, just months before Graham was slated to arrive there.[95]

Although former British prime minister Winston Churchill had defined Yugoslavia as being "behind the Iron Curtain" in 1946, in 1948 Yugoslavian president Josip Tito, the "little Stalin" who espoused the ideals of communism, shrugged off Soviet backing. Yugoslavia was officially expelled from the Cominform, the group of Soviet bloc nations initially established in 1947 to fight the Marshall Plan and to resist "the plans of American imperialist expansion and aggression in all spheres."[96] Tito played both sides and kept the State Department guessing about his alliances. His "globetrotting" in the 1950s positioned him as a leader of the Non-Aligned Movement; in fact, Tito seemed "instrumental" in transforming the aspirations expressed in Bandung in 1955 to concrete proposals.[97] While the United States saw neutralism as "immoral" and as a possible "springboard towards Western disintegration," this stance had begun to ease with the realities of the nuclear age Cold War, particularly on the European continent. As time went on, even John Foster Dulles, Eisenhower's secretary of state, had said it was "prudent to help Yugoslavia, so long as it remains determined to maintain genuine independence."[98]

George Kennan, Kennedy's ambassador, was friendly with Tito—too much so for some. The 1961 NAM meeting in Belgrade was understood as a nonmilitary alliance in opposition to joining NATO or the Warsaw Pact in the "long aftermath" of the Soviet political election coup in Czechoslovakia, the 1956 events in Hungary and the Suez Canal, conflicts in Asia, and the Congo Crisis where the Cold War again turned hot.[99] Indeed, at the United Nations Tito took the high ground. As the "belligerent powers" grew inflamed with one another, he recalled, "It became necessary to douse the fire." He claimed that the uncommitted NAM leaders "found ourselves playing the role of firemen. . . . We began consulting about what should be done to prevent things from escalating further," an attitude that did not make him popular with either Washington or Moscow.[100] Under Kennan's watch in Belgrade, using soft power to combat the heat, the United States and Yugoslavia signed a cultural agreement in 1961. American spending on cultural exports to this Balkan nation more than doubled.[101] Politicians in Washington continued to complain that while the United States had given Yugoslavia more than $3 billion since the war, Tito still worked to undermine American interests.[102] He may not have been a reliable partner, but Yugoslavia allowed American intelligence services to operate on its territory. With Kennedy ideologically attuned to decolonization and freedom's ideals, and the specter of a doubling of new UN nations between 1945 and 1961 with seventy-eight countries unaligned with either the United States or the Soviet Union, Kennedy sent congratulatory letters after the NAM in Belgrade. Yet the State Department quickly disavowed his sentiments, at which point Kennan had to soothe the State Department–inflicted wounds using language typical of the region and touring problems: "The U.S. is not doubting [Yugoslavia's] non-alignment."[103]

Because the Cold War was a battle of ideals, when faced with the double-negative paradox-ridden complexities of neutralism and nonalignment, never mind the historically based European legalities of neutrality, propaganda became ever more vital. The active weapons of this war (except in Asia and proxy wars) were not guns and tanks but rather cultural ideas and sympathies, with the use of radio, films, music, theater, literature, libraries, visual arts, television, and dance as a means of delivery. The geography to be taken was the geography of the mind, individual by individual, contact moment by contact zone, and the unallied mind demanded a particular approach.[104] With the memory of Bandung, the career State Department and USIS officers would have looked to the gathering for propaganda strategies when approaching the NAM in the 1960s. Regarding this American propaganda at a conference to which they were not welcomed at the table, Dulles had noted that "the voice of freedom should be able to blanket the voice of Communism." He urged those in Washington at USIS and the CIA to use "imaginative thinking" when attempting to sway uncommitted states to the Western side. Thus USIS developed an "affirmative attitude" in the uncommitted toward the "free world."[105] Rather than anti-communist propaganda, USIS used positive images of the United States and the taste of Pepsi to sway the neutral, nonaligned, and antialignment delegates to Western ways. People-to-people contact and "private discussions and meetings" grew in importance because representatives could show "less restraint" in conversations and not appear to be "mouthpieces" of the American government.[106] After a seeming win at Bandung for the Americans, with the movement dissipating over time, those at USIS had "convinced themselves that [affirmative attitude] propaganda had contributed significantly to neutralizing the ideological threat caused by neutralism."[107] In neutralizing neutralism, officers floated the idea of writing a "how-to" handbook for addressing the peculiarities of propaganda for the uncommitted. However "self-delusional" historians judge the self-evaluation of USIS, in 1961 the agency felt it was at the top of its game with the neutral and nonaligned political elite: negative propaganda engaged dissent; positive propaganda was the ultimate seductive use of soft power. Thus, the seeming apolitical neutrality of Graham grew in strategic importance exponentially, even if by 1961 modernism was getting old.

On the cultural side in Yugoslavia, by 1961, although Tito had allowed USIS to "popularize the American lifestyle and Western democracy," the government well understood the problematic nature of American propaganda.[108] This informed understanding fueled critical reactions to Graham. While the Yugoslav public was "not aware of the political and ideological background of American cultural activities," a report found that "the subtle and covered up nature of the United States propaganda is, at its core, subversive."[109] Nevertheless, exchange continued and even thrived with Graham a part of the project that included libraries, publications, lectures, films, exhibitions, and even requests from the Yugoslav government itself for an international school for students in Belgrade, where the American choreographer and her company would perform.[110] With its complexities, empire by invitation was at work, and Graham was on the ground.

The Yugoslav stop was grueling and demanded that Graham be on her best behavior as a diplomat. A Soviet ballet company was set to appear in Belgrade the day after Graham's performance, raising the stakes even further. When the company landed on November 15, Graham held her usual press conference. The following morning, she led a lecture-demonstration to explain the fundamentals of her dance to a select audience, including ballet masters and critics, who would soon see the Soviet ballerinas onstage.[111] After the opening night performance, Kennan invited Graham to the embassy for the requisite cocktail party and dinner with dignitaries and embassy officials. Unfortunately for Graham, Kennan missed both the performance and the reception because he had the flu.[112] Still, many Yugoslav officials did attend, from cultural leaders in government to the political secretariat for foreign affairs, to the head of foreign trade. In addition, representatives from the British and French embassies were on the guest list. The Polish embassy sent an emissary, perhaps in anticipation of the company's next stop.[113] As representatives of Kennedy, the Graham company members relished the opportunity to participate in people-to-people exchange. Not only at parties but also during informal social gatherings, the dancers interacted with artists in conversation and exchange, "instead of just going to the theater, rehearsing the show."[114] As outlined by the lessons learned at Bandung, as informal representatives they thrived in Yugoslavia under the watch of the State Department and USIS in personal conversations as well as public events.

Reviews translated by USIS for Washington's "eyes" were positive but mixed, as might be predicted from the reviews Graham had received in New York and the Yugoslavian awareness of cultural propaganda. Graham's age, especially in contrast to her youthful company, loomed larger: although she was a great choreographer with a spectacular crew, she failed to deliver as a dancer. *Seraphic Dialogue* received rave reviews for its "perfectly realized," "mystic-religious" drama.[115] Performing *Secular Games*, the company showed "the perfect mastering of technique."[116] A critic exclaimed, "We marveled [at] the perfect movements of her dancers."[117] Yet another review criticized its American "modernity" and noted that the work "borders on becoming monotonous."[118] Falling in line with some New York critics and internal State Department musings, a reviewer remarked that Graham, despite her exemplary acting skills, was "lacking youthful freshness."[119] Yet even as Graham's novelty waned, her star power remained undeniable. On closing night, after thirty curtain calls, the audience chanted, "Mar-tha, Mar-tha."[120] At the conclusion of the performances, one newspaper celebrated the individual qualities of each dancer, ultimately concluding, "The center of the whole group is Martha Graham."[121]

When Graham and the company arrived in Poland, the political implications of the tour became undeniable. The government had scheduled "Ballet Martha Graham" in 1962 alongside the "Leningrad Ballet," a communist Vietnamese group, the East's "Berliner Ensemble," and "The Hungarian State Folk Ensemble."[122] West met East.

The USIS publicity wooed the Polish elite, and the Polish government impinged on the dancers' freedoms to walk on the streets, shop, or even go to the ladies' rooms unescorted. In the grand hotel hallways, which had a particular Soviet smell of industrial cleaners, uniformed women sat in chairs watching the dancers come and go, taking stock of their movements—even between rooms. It was the company's "first experience with a Soviet organization of any kind," according to Linda Hodes, a star Graham dancer who had been with the company on the 1955–56 tour as well.[123] While the stop had promised the possibilities of exchange with Polish youth, it was not to be.

Poland, unlike Yugoslavia, remained a part of the Soviet bloc. Although political protests there had been suppressed by the Soviets and local communists, the nature of Poland's cultural history showed promise for the United States. Despite the specter of rolling tanks in Eastern Europe after World War II, the Soviets had used their own soft-power propaganda techniques to create "the invented community of the new communist nation" and used culture from magazines to architecture in order to draw nations formerly allied with the Nazis or the West into the Communist sphere.[124] However, the Soviets demanded that the Polish people renounce national holidays and other celebrations that did not show direct fidelity to the Kremlin. Most important, religion had proved a deep point of contention. In Catholic Poland, "churches had been turned into museums of atheism."[125] After the death of Stalin in 1953, however, a Soviet-Polish "middle ground" was achieved. Although the 1956 uprising in Poznań brought riots against the government and led to civilian deaths, Władysław Gomułka, who had been a popular leader until 1948, returned to power, which encouraged a softening of rules against Polish culture. He encouraged a "Polish way to socialism."[126] Thus began the "Thaw," named for a book that denounced those who followed Stalinist socialist realism, and the United States had an opening. Henry Luce's *Time* magazine opened a 1956 article on Poland with a quotation from the nineteenth-century Prussian statesman Otto von Bismarck: "Russia seems impregnable, but she is not all. Poland is her weak spot."[127]

While a 1956 "agreement on cultural cooperation" between Poland and the USSR stipulated cooperation in literature, fine arts, music, theater, film, television, and radio, by 1958, American jeans were a hit, and the Thaw allowed the rise of American jazz.[128] In 1959, Vice President Nixon had visited Warsaw, the US government reopened a consulate in Poznań, and a Fulbright exchange program began.[129] The American government identified Poland as "a model for other regimes to emulate in pursuing independence from Moscow" and deployed cultural diplomacy accordingly. Indeed, exchange grew to the point that one expert referred to it as the "invasion of the Americans."[130]

For the United States, looser Soviet control suggested that cultural diplomacy would have an impact, and it sent the American Ballet Theatre, photography exhibits, and modernist author William Faulkner to Poland.[131] In a 1960 campaign speech to the Polish-American Congress, Kennedy announced, "As long as we in the United States continue to maintain our strength, and send out rays of freedom around the world, then in my judgment the situation behind the Iron Curtain can only be regarded as a temporary one."[132] Kennedy's "rays of freedom" included RFE broadcasts to Poland, sending messages of freedom under democracy. Unlike Yugoslavia, which had even considered hosting a radio tower to receive foreign broadcasts, listening to the Western station was still considered subversive and punishable in Poland, and RFE's signals were jammed.[133] Nevertheless, by the early 1960s, Poland was becoming "a window to the West."[134]

In Washington, the Polish embassy worked on cultural exchange with the United States.[135] While the Poles wanted American performers, and distributed magazines from *Opera News* to *Musical America*, the American cultural diplomats pushed alliances with the Polish American community in people-to-people exchanges.[136] In 1961, Virginia Inness-Brown visited Poland as the United States specialist to the Bureau of Educational and Cultural Affairs, garnering herself a report by the Polish state on her activities.[137] Following a Polish official who stressed the need for "a 'girly cover'" to promote Soviet magazines (ballerinas such as the Russian Galina Ulanova were considered "girly" bait), Martha Graham, with the highbrow sex appeal of her work and youthful company, could claim to bring what the Polish population asked for, to representing American modern dance versus Soviet ballet.[138] In addition, just as the Polish communist cultural agencies were targeting the youth, USIS presented the Graham dancers to engage the young. Publicity for her performances in Poland included numerous photographs of split-legged women being drawn across the floor by muscled, barefooted men in loincloths.[139]

However well planned and thought out, before the Graham dancers left on the tour, the Polish embassy in Washington had become increasingly concerned about American-Polish contact after several cultural "incidents" during the US tour of the Polish State Folk Group dancers. When they arrived in the United States, members of the folk group were approached by Polish Americans who reportedly asked the Poles to defect to the United States and told them, "Eat, children, eat. Because you do not have [this good food] in Poland." The Americans then asked the Poles, "Have you even seen such fridges and TVs before?" In Buffalo, New York, according to the Poles, the group was "threatened" and told the show would be canceled if they did not all attend church services. Only nine members went, apparently infuriating the Americans.[140] Warsaw may not have been pleased to welcome the potentially subversive American dancers.

As always, the schedule in Poland served diplomatic needs: after the now requisite press conference upon arrival, the entire company attended an evening violin concert starting at 7:30 p.m., followed by dinner. Graham and the dancers then had to arrive at the theater for morning rehearsals. Their own opening night was followed by a two-hour reception at the embassy for the entire company. The exhaustion showed even before the schedule started: Graham was pictured in newspapers wearing a warm fur hat in the airport, slightly Soviet in its style, with her eyes wandering down toward the microphone, seeming to be a bit lazy.[141]

One dancer remembers that the "lush embassy party" was not at all in keeping with the lifestyle of the Polish people that the dancers would be shown in the following days on circumscribed guided tours.[142] Unlike Yugoslavia, where the dancers had been encouraged to interact with the people independently, in Warsaw, company members were marched onto a bus for sightseeing. "There was a lot of propaganda that they took us through," Hodes recalls. As they passed by bleak, Soviet-style gray buildings, their guides presented nuggets of information such as, "This is where the head of all of Poland lives with five other families in the same apartment." As they whisked past, "We saw people waiting in line to get milk in a store where you could see there wasn't anything in the window." She continued:

> We were told not to go shopping; we were given very little per diem because everything was arranged for us. For instance, there was nothing to buy anyway. I always went shopping on tour, and I would walk down the streets. The store windows didn't have things in them, or maybe there was one refrigerator in the window or one fur coat or whatever they sold. But there was nothing in the store. We were told not to—if we were approached by anyone in the street—sell blue jeans or anything like that, not to deal with them.[143]

Hodes concluded: "Everybody was nervous and feeling very undone by all of the pressure of the propaganda."[144]

Yet, in Warsaw, the subtle American propaganda effect could not have been better. Graham and her company performed in a theater named for Stalin, with architecture reminiscent of his repressive era; student demonstrations against the Soviet regime had taken place there just a year earlier.[145] The ornate, "crude towering specimen of Stalinist gothic" stood in sharp contrast to American modernism and the youthful dancers. While the tour in Europe largely included gilded theaters with raked stages, the experience in Poland seemed most striking. Marni Thomas, a seasoned performer, noted, "The place was huge, so it felt like you were reaching."[146] In 1961, the young protesters had gathered in front of the tribute to Stalin and "brought color and fashion blazing into the city; they met in small groups, recited poetry, listened to jazz, and discussed art." At the festival's culmination, abstract art appeared in Warsaw's Arsenal: "The paintings roared off the walls, not so much imitating Western trends as vividly (if 'desperately') 'making up for lost time.' "[147] Graham stood in contrast to the Stalinist architecture, as had the modern art and the brightly clad protesters playing jazz. As in Berlin, architecture again met politics in the dance of diplomacy.

In Poland, Graham's repertory focused on freedom through religious programming, with *Seraphic Dialogue* featured during evening performances instead of *Appalachian Spring*. The Second Vatican Council had just urged Catholics to return to the church for spiritual renewal, and thus freedom to worship had become a potent message, particularly because of new evidence of the Communist crackdown on Polish Catholics.[148] After *Seraphic Dialogue*, evenings continued with *Embattled Garden*, the spirited and accessible story of the Garden of Eden. The adventures among the characters—Adam, Eve, Lilith (Adam's first wife in Jewish works), and the serpent—seemed less driven by the drama and angst of the Old Testament story than Graham's other biblical works. Graham retained the seductive core of the story, but she created a satiric, playful work, with stark pink, black, and red costumes; highly stylized sexual movements; and a multi-level, cutting-edge set by Noguchi. Graham's version of the story of the Fall foreshadowed mischief with risqué movements rather than a tragic Fall of Man that demanded repentance. *Acrobats of God* closed evenings rather than the usual fare on the 1962 tour, *Diversion of Angels*. The press noted the title's reference to the devotion of "monks in a monastery," parroting the New York review that appeared in the *Christian Science Monitor*, surely sent to them by USIS.[149] With the pieces working together, Graham brought the

seriousness of revelation in worship alongside a light work with an unmistakable religious theme.

Critical reactions in Poland were mixed. Some singled out *Secular
Games* because of its "particular brilliance," one calling it "a really modern
dance."[150] Yet another reviewer found the dancers in the work to be "devoid of any emotion" in the "automatic mechanism of their movements."[151]
A third critic, reflecting the American messaging, said the work's "American
style . . . determines its modernity," theoretically a positive reflection.[152]
Yet the author simultaneously noted Graham's advanced age, criticized the
music, and castigated Graham's works for a "disarray of invention."[153] The
commingling of youth with age hit particularly hard with *Phaedra*: it was "an
orgy the like of which we have never seen in the form of a ballet," yet also
"the one that dates the choreographer."[154] Hodes remembered the reception
as "fairly good," adding, "I think it was all subdued; the whole place was very
subdued." No chants of "Mar-tha" were reported.[155]

A State Department summary of the event noted that Polish impressions
were a matter of "individual reaction," and thus Graham created critical controversy. USIS reported that the Graham company dancers were celebrated
for their "discipline and control, physical dexterity, balance, co-ordination,
elasticity and softness of movement" and "the concentration of the dancer
of the inner feeling," which produced "remarkable results," particularly
during lecture-demonstrations. Yet the choreography and Graham herself
did not fare as well. The works produced "a certain monotony bordering on
boredom," due to "stereotyped" movements. Ironically, the USIS-proclaimed
modernity of Graham backfired because audiences in Poland felt they already knew about modernism in dance due to their exposure to modern art
as well as Jerome Robbins's work with his touring company, Ballets U.S.A.
The Graham vocabulary, although seemingly modern or new, was already
dated on first viewing for the culturally sophisticated. Other reviewers
complained about the excessive intellectualism of the work. "Less of philosophy and more of dancing!," the State Department summary concluded.
Graham's modernization of the religious stories seemed old-fashioned in
the end. Unreported by State, a magazine for Catholics celebrated *Seraphic
Dialogue* among other works by Graham, "a modern choreographer [who]
inspires us with enthusiasm and admiration for vivid, fresh and unexpected
beauty."[156] Cables back to the State Department nevertheless emphasized
that "numerous representatives of diplomatic missions were present" at the

performances.[157] The depth and breadth of political figures and the intelligentsia in attendance were appreciated as a win.

Left unreported by the State Department were remarks made in the review that appeared in *Nowa Kultura* (The New Culture Magazine), a Polish weekly that represented itself as the pinnacle of "The New" in the arts, and a second review by Jerzy Waldorff, an iconic Polish music and arts critic. In one of the worst notices received by Graham in any country, East or West, *Nowa Kultura* observed that Graham "left a lot of disappointment . . . like a [Hollywood] movie whose artistic value is too small." Referring to the dramatic effect of the choreography, the author continued, "All this ingenious motion composition serves simply nothing, and gives no subtext to engage imagination or thought." Regarding the religious problem, the article reported, "The dances created the effect [of] dead and soulless images." The well-considered *Seraphic Dialogue* met specific hostility. Noguchi's set, his "geometry of faith," was not interpreted as such: "When [Saint Joan] is being taken to the sky by the saints, [the set] glows with the flickering, unreal light of [truck] headlights." Of the new music, an important genre for the Polish elite who championed their connections to the Polish genius Frédéric Chopin, the Graham compositions were "embarrassing, naïve songs that cannot inspire any contemporary choreographer." And of the choreography, the review concluded, "Compositions were as naïve as the music. And this naïveté leads to the *end* of any kind of art."[158] According to this review, Graham had failed at every level for those who considered themselves a part of the sophisticated Polish elite. She was not new, seemed like a cheap American movie or car, did not engage the intellect or promote religious freedom, and was intrinsically naive. According to *Nowa Kultura*, Graham signaled the end of the aged hegemonic American modernism, not a new beginning.

In "*Towary na eksport*" [Goods for Export], published by *Świat* [The World], a weekly magazine dedicated to socio-political, cultural, scientific, and economic topics, Waldorff discussed the Graham performances in Warsaw. The summary read, "Criticism of Marta Graham's performance. Lack of neatness. Unaesthetic selection of postures. . . Audience reaction." He opened, "I can't convince myself of [the import of] the dance called liberated [or free or modern]! I am comforted that I'm not alone and this genre of dance went out of fashion [lost its popularity] a long time ago [in Europe]." After recalling the history of the free dance from Duncan through Laban, he addressed the modern technique promoted by Graham, which he called "lunacy"; the movements were "heavy," "clumsy," and "awkward." Regarding plot and meaning, he wrote, "I only saw a few people in nice costumes throbbing convulsively around the stage and with particular pleasure rolling around on the floor. Only later I learnt from the summary that they wanted to show the heroism and martyrdom of Joan D'Arc."[159] If audiences wanted to experience sophisticated American modernism, they were advised to see ABT's work and Jerome Robbins, not Graham. As a Polish tastemaker, the reviewer's criticisms would have been significant to the Polish elites and to those at the embassy monitoring cultural presentations.

The company had Thanksgiving dinner at the embassy in Poland before departing. Graham had charmed the diplomats despite the mixed critical reception, and officials were unaware of the scathing article to come. It was floated that some in the State Department now wanted to extend the tour to other locations after the final stop. Falling in line with State Department thinking about bloc nations, they may have been considering Czechoslovakia, another site of dissent and Soviet repression where Graham would plan to perform in 1991. Yet doing so would put the company on tour through Christmas. Votes by the dancers determined that the tour end as planned. Thanksgiving in Poland and the entire experience there were bad enough. Although small birds may have been all they ate, a few remember that someone found a turkey.[160]

After Poland, the company proceeded to Sweden for two performances in Stockholm. Photographs reveal the growing wear and tear not only on Graham but also on the company. The normal framed photos of the dancers in front of the airplane, poised and chic, disappeared. Instead, the dancers were shown walking from planes in disorganized lines. While the women remained in dresses and high heels, the dancers all seemed to be carrying something in their arms as they hurried toward the terminal, darting out of the cold. They were certainly not posed for the shot.[161] Photos in the newspapers would feature Graham as she had appeared in the 1950s, or in long shots, in which only her silhouette could be seen. The use of a blackened cutout silhouette would later become a fixture of her publicity.

Although Sweden was neutral and less politically fraught, its status was distinctly European in origin and thus did not seem a threat to American interests. The United States considered Sweden a "Western neutral" because it had participated in the Marshall Plan and accepted Western aid.[162] In that northern capital, Graham showed that, despite her age, her performances did have a particular appeal for youth. Critics remembered her from a previous tour, in 1954. Thus, her technique and the woman herself were not presented

by USIS as "new," and her dancers impressed the audiences. Critics celebrated her electricity as a performer, despite her "difficulties sliding on her
knees with splits."[163] Yet at embassy parties, she seemed to recover, and stood
with seemingly captivated dignitaries and women in fur stoles who listened
intently to her words.[164]

The movie-star qualities of the Graham dancers captivated young Swedes
even if the woman did not. The beauty and sexuality of Graham's dancers
positioned them as artistic, athletic, and sensual, yet still appropriate for the
culturally sophisticated. According to dancer Marni Thomas, "In Sweden the
audience fell in love with Bob Powell and at the curtain call—there must have
been eleven curtain calls—the teenagers were screaming, 'Bob! Bob! Bob!'
And they were all waiting when he would come out [after performances]."[165]
As throngs had pushed against barricades to see Graham in 1955, they now
stood at the backstage door to garner autographs from her dancers. However
popular her dancers in loincloths, according to the press, "for an audience
which nowadays knows what Martha Graham's contribution has meant for
choreography in our time," the performances were understood to be the culmination of a "worldwide farewell tour."[166]

When the company landed in West Germany, the dancers were again
photographed candidly as they walked as a dense group heading to the terminal, smiling at the gathered press corps. Graham stood on the cold tarmac
wearing an elegant fur hat and divaesque sunglasses (seemingly unnecessary,
given the weather), speaking to a dignitary who was there to greet her. Yet in
newspapers, a close-up showed her holding her dachshund, looking withered, her almost plastic-looking cheekbones and fleshy neck, folded over
upon itself.[167] As she and her technique came under attack for being aged
and old-fashioned to the seasoned German dance intelligentsia, she found
solace in alcohol, which increasingly showed its effect on her art, her body,
and her face, and would undermine her value as an ambassador.

West Germany had become the front line of the Cold War. Yet, unlike
Berlin, the cities Graham visited had experienced the *Wirtschaftswunder*,
or "economic miracle," with strong postwar demand met by a drop in un-
employment. When the tour was planned, the State Department could not
have known there would be pro-democracy, anti-Nazi youth uprisings with
her arrival, but the timing would seem to work. Graham landed in the midst
of the "*Der Spiegel* Incident," with mass demonstrations, especially among
the youth, who blamed their parents for their Nazi-linked dishonesty and
demanded a change from the *Obrigkeitsstaat* (authoritarian state) to a

modern democracy. Yet Graham's age, the codification of her technique, and her now understood artistic roots that connected her to Weimar Germany made her more a part of the establishment than a harbinger of contemporary modernism and a new movement. The dances Graham brought, unfortunately for her, were received as the lingerings of the past. She was seen as old-fashioned, a companion to the former Wigman, Graham's mythic tales and all-American technique not attuned to the moment. While the youth renewal should have worked in favor of the Americans, it backfired.

Reviews brought to the fore the direct conflict of cultural hegemony between American and German dance. The Germans did not identify Graham as the leader of a universal or global art form, and USIS publicity thus seemed offensive. Five years earlier in Berlin, Mary Wigman had triumphed over Graham with her *Rite of Spring*. West Germany had found its own voice, and Graham's choreographic dicta came across as artistically imperialist. Kurt Jooss, the German master who had choreographed *The Green Table* during the interwar, a piece that dramatized the evils of warfare, had become the recognized leader of Tanztheater and was known as "Papa Jooss" to young German dance students and choreographers.[168] Unlike Wigman, he had not collaborated with the Nazis and had been forced to flee Germany in 1933 after refusing to expunge Jewish dancers from his company. Gret Palucca, Wigman's student and later rival, had also brought striking new innovations to German modern dance.[169] By 1962, German critics were again ready to take on the Americans. In reviews, Graham was seen less as a visionary than as a dancer whose work poorly mimicked that of the Germans—indeed, several papers called her "the American Mary Wigman." Graham was also negatively compared to Palucca, a truly "contemporary" choreographer unlike the modernist Graham, who only claimed to be contemporary. Graham's dance, another critic remarked, had its meaning and its use, but had become merely peripheral to the advancement of the art.[170] One writer asked, "[Can] Graham's company be anything else but a museum?"[171]

Other issues abounded and would even follow Graham back to the United States. One reporter scoffed at the moralistic presentation of Graham by USIS, particularly with the religiously themed works that seemed to put across American religious piety as propaganda in the face of *Phaedra*. In Munich, where the theater was half empty, the issue of a dated elitism hit hard; a critic there wrote, "The decor and the costumes are described as distinctively American, the latter could as well be found on Fifth Avenue."[172] A report to USIS noted that the performances didn't attract Germany's most influential people, but instead social strivers trying to edge themselves into an elitist group, or "others who pretended to belong to one or the other of these groups."[173] Young people seemed lost in the mix. One report noted that while in the past, Graham could count on the elite, in Germany, she was selling to the "Want-to-Be's." Adding to the problems, during a performance two American congresspeople who had come to see "America's Best Propaganda to Date," according to the column "Washington Merry-Go-Round" in the 1950s, walked out in the middle of *Phaedra*, horrified by its sexuality.

In response to the difficulties of the grueling tour and some painful criticism, the diva spiraled downward. Dancers knew of her alcohol problem but did not feel they could intervene to stop her, only to help when they could. Critical euphemisms proliferated. "Graham's first performances appeared clumsy," offered one reporter. "Exhaustion" and "clumsiness" became known descriptors.[174] Graham either took reviews to heart (even though she claimed not to read them), was just feeling her failing body, or was suffering from the progression of alcoholism. One evening, preparing to play Clytemnestra in her signature work, Graham sat in her dressing room and stared into the mirror. "Her hair was down, she didn't have any makeup on, and she was drinking," remembered Thomas.[175] They brought her coffee. Another night when she got onstage, she fell into the wings, disappeared for a moment, and then fell back onstage.[176] During *Acrobats of God*, dancers would direct her, murmuring, "Martha, get over to the left," or "Martha, come over here." Her lead male dancer, Bertram Ross, recalls moving her limbs. Nor did the drinking stop after evening performances: "She was still drunk the next day."[177] This stumble was duly noted because of the importance of the highly valued lecture-demonstrations. While in the 1950s she had been able to use the "cocktail circuit of diplomacy" to her advantage, by 1962 alcohol had consumed her as dancer and as a diplomat. Certainly, foreign service and USIS representatives could not fail to notice, and they wrote home about her "exhaustion."[178]

Nonetheless, the ever-resilient Graham seemed able to dry out for spells, and for the remainder of the tour, she did. Graham arrived in Finland, the next leg, looking noticeably older yet coherent. Press photos showed Graham looking downward, hair pulled back and thinning—an unusual photographic stance for the star. In images of her lecturing about her dance, her outstretched hands revealed the shriveling skin that would eventually crumple around her arthritic hands, fingers swollen and joints bunioned. In other candid shots, her cheekbones look sunken, her face almost mummified and thick-skinned. Yet the diva pressed forward with her still dazzling team.

The State Department had added the leg to Finland as plans were being finalized for the tour in June 1962, and the export became a state-to-state project.[179] In 1961, Finland found itself at the geopolitical crossroads with its shared border with the Soviet Union; thus the State Department would not serve Finland hard or hot antipropaganda but rather Graham's soft and coercive cultural offerings in line with the nation's status as neutral, and its attempts at nonalignment alongside the antialignment of Yugoslavia. Because of the World War II cooperation with Nazi Germany and the 1944 Finnish-German defeat by the Soviet army, Finland lost territory on its border with Russia, had stiff reparation payments to Moscow, and hosted a Soviet naval base. Yet a "Line" was established in which the Soviets tolerated and then even celebrated neutrality if the Finns allowed an active Communist Party, and refrained from military, covert, and economic alliances with the West. While Moscow demanded that Finland fall in line with bloc countries such as Hungary and Romania with the Friendship, Cooperation, and Assistance Agreement, the Finns looked to the 1948 Soviet coup in Czechoslovakia, which had signed such an agreement. Finland negotiated a less onerous agreement with the Soviets. Yet particularly after the death of Stalin, independent, sometimes informal contacts began to form between Finland and the nonaligned Yugoslavia, which also shared a border with Russia. The Soviets prevented Finland from joining the United Nations until 1955, and in 1956 Finland abstained from official UN discussions of the Hungarian Revolution, to the dismay of many Finns. Given the violence of Moscow's actions against its own bloc nations, official Finnish "neutrality" seemed like a show of support for their "cold neighbours" to the general population. Yet in 1956 Finland joined the UN troops that brought together men from Yugoslavia, India, Indonesia, Norway, Poland, and Sweden, all Graham territories, when the UN Emergency Force, under the banner "Uniting for Peace," called for the withdrawal of Israeli, French, and British forces from occupied territories in the Suez Canal.[180] Khrushchev referred to Finland as a model of neutrality, a "zone of peace," and thus President Urho Kekkonen was seen as one of Moscow's "agents" by some in the West.[181]

Yet by 1960 the Finns had begun actively cooperating with the United States, assisting CIA intelligence gathering and hosting cultural institutions such as the Finnish American Center.[182] Adding greater hope, in 1961 Finland negotiated an agreement with the European Free Trade Association: it wanted to liberalize internal policies and economic ties with the West.[183] That fall, Kekkonen made the first official Finnish head of state visit to the

United States and was warmly greeted by Kennedy and the ever-glamorous first lady, a bouquet in hand, on the White House South Lawn, where Kekkonen and his wife landed by helicopter during heavily scripted "Arrival Ceremonies."[184] After being feted at the White House, Kekkonen traveled to the UN. Yet Finland was drawn out of its much-protected neutrality during the Note Crisis, just after Kekkonen met with Canadians and the queen of England and vacationed in Hawaii, when its powerful neighbor sent a "note" proposing that Finland and the Soviet Union begin discussions to secure mutual defense against threats against the West given the situation in West Germany. As previously mentioned, on the day Moscow sent the note, it exploded Tsar Bomba for effect.[185] Kekkonen met with Khrushchev and reached an agreement suspending military negotiations unless political tensions in northern Europe and Germany grew worse.[186] In a bid to soothe the wary West, in December Kekkonen allowed the defection of a Russian diplomat in Helsinki.[187] If cheered by the defection, Kennedy remained concerned about the impact of the Soviet Union on Finland and the resulting effect on other nations in the region, including neutral Sweden and the divided Germany, Norway, and the Netherlands, all visited by Graham. In a bid to people-to-people diplomacy, Kennedy and Kekkonen corresponded on the anniversary of Finland's independence, and Kennedy offered congratulatory remarks on the Finn's re-election.[188] The stage was quickly set for Graham.[189]

Finland's dance history also tied it to earlier American moves in Israel. In 1908, Isadora Duncan had visited Helsinki. Mary Wigman performed there in 1926, and politico-dance currents took hold. While Finnish references to the German influence are muted in current history, and the Finnish school of German Marta Bröyer opened in 1931 was not explored, pictures of her work show a deep connection to Laban and Wigman.[190] The Finnish Maggie Gripenberg oversaw the Finnicization of the "free dance" through the 1940s and the outbreak of war, but the alliance with the German tradition certainly reflected Finland's wartime alignment with the Nazis. Like the German-influenced dancers in Israel on the kibbutz, these performers were not rigorously trained and did not perform in grand theaters. In contrast, the Finnish National Ballet, founded in 1922, was appreciated by an elite audience and toured internationally, and was strongly influenced by the Soviet traditions and training.[191] The free dance form continued to exert influence through the 1950s. Duncan was no longer significant, and Wigman had been discredited in Finland. The free dance was seen to show "amateurism."[192] In 1958, ABT represented the United States against soloists of the Bolshoi and

Kirov at an "exceptional ballet event in Helsinki."[193] According to critics, the Soviets won. Although ABT's Soviet tour in 1960 met with accolades, Graham's remained an apples-to-oranges fight. The Soviets had no oranges. Before Graham arrived, USIS flooded the press comparing her company with the Kirov Ballet, Balanchine and his New York City Ballet, and the heritage of Isadora Duncan.[194] The Finnish American Center held a symposium on Graham for cultural power brokers, and it circulated *A Dancers World*, a film starring Graham as she spoke about her dance, and company members as they performed her technique.

Graham arrived with diplomatic fanfare, and during her press conference she introduced her company members, immediately referring to her group as "The United Nations of Dance," representing nineteen different countries. She immediately invoked the politics of national sovereignty, neutrality, and peace well understood by the Finns: Finland had initially been denied the option of joining the UN, then "forced" into an uncomfortable "neutral" position, later finding redemption by joining troops in a peace mission. She continued that "our purpose will have been achieved" if "we will be able to inspire you in an everlasting way." A newspaper duly reported to the public the next day, quoting Graham, "'The United Nations of Dance'—Martha Graham arrives with the company."[195] The opening jab at the Communists by Graham was encouraged by a critic later in the run who brought politics directly into dance, writing, "With her coeval, she tried to reveal something new out of that which was considered frigidly and un-emotional Russian, so-called classical ballet." The reference to the "cold neighbors" harkens directly back to the UN stance the Finns seemed forced to take by Moscow. As noted by one scholar, "Here, the geopolitics are transparent."[196]

When the opening night curtain rose, the theater seating had been prearranged to include Kekkonen along with the American ambassador, diplomats, and the cultural intelligentsia—all of whom would have normally only be seen at the ballet.[197] Local reviews were erratic, but audiences clearly cheered Graham. Graham's style was celebrated as "divine" and "holy." In some cases, however, the religious overtones of the dances were not appreciated. *Seraphic Dialogue* was not a popular opening, with one critic deeming it a "disappointment" and its sacred elements "a little strange."[198] *Diversion of Angels*, which had been heralded elsewhere, did not excite all the Finns. Although for some the work carried the evening, another reviewer took the figures Red, White, and Yellow as "women in evening dress who fall flat on the ground."[199] In addition, Finnish audiences felt that Graham's works were overly obscure and carried an "intellectual element" that threatened to "paralyze her genius."[200] What Graham had once celebrated as the universal and nonverbal "language of dance" now required schooling. Some reviews contradicted themselves, condemning American dance modernism overall while they celebrated a particular work and acknowledged Graham as the master. USIS flew into action, flooding the newspapers with explanations of Graham's works and the wires with translation after translation back to the United States that *Legend of Judith* was appreciated internationally.[201]

As with the displacement of the German-based "free dance" in Israel with the Graham technique, Graham's codified technique showed the promise of a professionalized modern dance that could take hold in Finland even after the departure of the company. One critic saw "nuances" that "originated" from "European free dance," but "[Graham's] dance is closest to being divine."[202] He continued that Finnish "dancers only imitate what has already been made familiar by free dance many years ago." He wrote that the "so-called free dance has already for many, many years been literally a hobby pursuit here in Finland."[203] He concluded, "Therefore the visit of Martha Graham and her dance group was indeed a significant and inspiring experience."[204] While it was not a pure win for the Americans, her influence showed promise. "The great artist and her superb collaborators were thanked with ovations by an enthusiastic audience," concluded one USIS-translated review.[205]

For the penultimate leg of the tour that December, publicity in the Netherlands, associated Graham directly with the US government and the Kennedys themselves, hailing her as the "First Lady" of American dance. But the tension over Graham's age remained: publicity pictures in newspapers featured the young dynamic dancers in motion; photos of Graham herself were recycled from the 1955–56 tour of Asia for newspapers. The Dutch reviews were so mixed that they even bordered on the illogical. Reviews celebrated the youthful dancers and the dance genius leading them before going on to criticize specific works. A review translated by USIS from *De Groene Amsterdammer*, an Amsterdam weekly, epitomized the tone of other press reviews during the season. Graham was a genius "by no means past her pinnacle" with her technically dazzling dancers and a long career that embodied the evolution of modern dance with her "stunningly expressive form." However, with *Legend of Judith*, her dancers "juggled" with sets that detracted from the dance, which relied on symbolism that was "impossible" to understand. *Phaedra* and its sexuality seemed "pretty much forced" and looked like "some laboratory research work." The critic called Graham's work "over-intellectual and perverse," but at least not "obscene." Despite barbs, the review ended by celebrating Graham, whose work was "highly expressive of man's inner life."[206] Other Dutch reviews celebrated Graham as an "important personality" who presumably would soon retire due to her advancing age.[207] Although one show was completely sold out, a social democratic newspaper attributed this success to the fact that Graham herself would never appear again: "It is bitter to see a God fall from his pedestal. But also Gods do not remain forever."[208]

The press reviews summarized by USIS began to get more obviously slanted in excerpts toward the positive. In a Dutch article on Graham excerpted by USIS, bureaucrats translated only two sentences about Graham's "great influence" and the company's "technical perfection" with a technique that could "demonstrate that American inventiveness can achieve superior results," all from an article revealingly titled "Renewal of the Dance and Its Limitations."[209]

* * *

As Graham was winding down the tour, meetings took place to dismantle ANTA's relationship with the government for touring operations. As it had been left out in Finland, so would it be cut out of future planning. Accusations flew that "incredible fiascos" had resulted from ANTA's decisions, including sending out "cheap" shows, as well as "homosexuals," "dope pushers" and the like, as American ambassadors. "It was all just a sordid mess," according to one ANTA member. Graham and her failures were not discussed, but they were certainly implicated in the demolition of ANTA's institutional influence. In addition, Graham faced scrutiny over *Phaedra*—unfavorable government reports quoted responses in the field to its gratuitous sexuality. But it was not the title character, with her legs spread to the audience, that sparked the negative attention. Graham's male dancers had been warned not to engage in homosexual relations while on tour, and yet the loincloths worn by male dancers as commanded by Graham provoked controversy. Oddly, the era of sexual revolution brought a heightened awareness of indiscretion to tours as the male dancers appeared in public and on the stage. Government reports on the Graham tour would, in the end, spark an investigation by Congress.

* * *

Of the final stop in Norway, little is found in Graham's scrapbooks save a letter from the Foreign Service stating that it could not send a set of reviews to the company because it was "so voluminous and good that we wanted the Department to know the widespread positive impact good performances can produce."[210] Washington worried that Norway's dedication to the West was not solid; it had joined NATO in 1949 while also offering Moscow assurances that it would not accept troops unless under direct attack. Some saw the potential danger in a couched alignment, and thus Norway hit the State Department agenda.[211] Yet the final reports were not shared.

Although Graham again expressed interest in continuing in Europe after Norway to perform either for the State Department or under independent funding, dancers had families—husbands, boyfriends, girlfriends, children, parents—to return home to.[212] Graham had no husband, no family, no children; indeed, she had even taken to calling her bottles of alcohol her children, rocking them and singing, "my babies, my babies," in rehearsals.[213] Embassy and USIS reports certainly did not warrant an increase in the budget to keep the Martha Graham company in the field. Nor did Graham's decline over the life of the tour bode well for future engagements. Those who wanted to go home to their families for Christmas firmly won out.

Back in New York, the press continued to champion Graham as an ambassador, although this impulse would be moderated by Washington. The *New York Herald Tribune* lauded her tour. In *Dance and Dancers* magazine, Clive Barnes wrote a two-page spread about it.[214] In a syndicated column, critic John Chamberlain followed Cold War battle lines by pitting the Bolshoi against Graham's company and reported on the "propaganda" value of dance. Although a politically potent dance war "may seem a little silly" to some, Chamberlain argued that the subtleties of the conflict counted. The "battle for men's minds" used as its weapons entrechats on one side and contraction and release on the other. While the Soviets proved the merits of technical finesse, Graham proved that the United States could pioneer a new approach to movement that demonstrated both creativity and technical power. In addition, Graham had "taken to certain countries of the Old World a number of remarkable modern interpretations of their oldest legends."[215] Chamberlain championed her success in bringing *Legend of Judith* to Israel and *Clytemnestra* to Athens.

Yet the Washington press revealed that Graham was being shouldered aside in favor of new, younger choreographers who also served urgent diplomatic needs—particularly the African American Alvin Ailey—and

New York followed. In the *Washington Post*, the article "Artists Give Views of Audiences Abroad" opened with Graham boldly stating, "I am the face of America." Indeed, her face was featured at the top of the page. However, it was clear that her signature jet-black hair, bun just over the top, was thinning—the deep comb marks could be seen in the pixilated photo. And while her necklace was in place, her jacket flap looked slightly undone. Her brows were arched high, framing eyes that stared distantly and slightly off to one side, the right lid drooping ever so slightly.[216] The article continued and distinctly featured the words of Alvin Ailey as he described his 1962 State Department tour to the Far East and Australia. In response, the *New York Times* praised Ailey as a "rising star," concluding that "the Department of State has completely overlooked the tremendous cultural bond that we might build with other countries by exporting one of our major and most authentic and most vital treasures, an American Negro dance company."[217] Ailey's company was quickly becoming the avatar of American modernism with youth, daring, and a new "Americana" on its side with the energy of gospel music treated as authentic folk in *Revelations,* his stunning work that brought crowds to their feet. The contrast between Ailey's *Revelations* and Graham's *Appalachian Spring* could not be more striking.

In another blow to Graham's bid to be the enduring vibrant, ever self-renewing modernist genius, a summary prepared for the State Department compared her unfavorably to the more experimental ballet choreographers George Balanchine and Jerome Robbins—equating them all as modernists. Balanchine was captivating, the summary said. Robbins's company, Ballets U.S.A., was more accessible in its approach to modernism in dance, as had been evidenced in Poland. Youth appreciated its vigorous and new energy. While Graham dances presented a codified American modernism, critics deemed Robbins's offerings "so much richer."[218] Thus, in an ironic twist, modernism in pointe shoes, with bound feet and lithe female bodies, was triumphing over the barefoot freedom of expression for the growing target audience: the youth. This strategy had begun to displace "trickle-down" tactics.

In a USIS summary memo, Graham had become, according to translated press reports, "the old lady of modern dance." USIS clearly outlined Graham's shortcomings: "Some sympathetic hints that Miss Graham should now be content to rest on her 'laurels' and retire from active performances were evident."[219] *Phaedra* had "worn out symbols."[220] Despite the cables to Israel from Yugoslavia, the newly restaged *Legend of Judith* was "doomed to be forgotten soon and completely." The internal report cited Graham's "pretense to modernity" with works that "were not really that modern." USIS concluded, "We have experienced a rather withered modernity of the 30's."[221]

Having landed in New York to celebrate Christmas in her apartment, Graham drank more and more heavily. With the new year, she missed rehearsals. Dancers would wait for her, practicing on their own. A guard would be posted at the door in case she showed up. As soon as she entered, her dancers would fall into lines, ready to follow her instructions and hear her wisdom, which, however confused, rambling, and disjointed it may have been, persisted. When asked why she was late, she would often blame phone calls from "Washington."[222] But Washington was no longer calling.

5

Triumphing over "Exhaustion," 1963–1974

"She may be too tired to tour again," announced a State Department official at a meeting to discuss Martha Graham's 1962 tour.[1] Performance shots of Graham's *Phaedra* showed her as the aging protagonist in a long, bejeweled cocktail dress costume, with an extended leg inarticulate and bent, foot unpointed, its rounded, bunioned joints in evidence. Airbrushed press photos showed her elegant face, with long eyelashes and theatrically painted eyes, but her neck betrayed her age.[2] In Washington, although details of her alcohol abuse were not discussed, officials concluded that in her recent tour, Graham had "saturated" Europe.[3] Despite her currency as the high priestess who commanded a dance troupe still appreciated by critics—as well as teens who thronged at backstage entrances and chanted for the handsome men like rock stars—Graham had become a liability both as a performer and as a reliable ambassador with her "museum" of modern dance.

Yet private-sector cultural ambassadors and some government officials had long memories, back to the early Cold War years and the success of dance as diplomacy with private-public funding, under-the-radar performances, and pickup tours. Graham had demonstrated experience despite and because of her age. Virginia Inness-Brown, who had funded dance at the Edinburgh Festival in 1954, served as the chair of the ANTA dance, music, and theater panels, privately advised Eisenhower, became a central player in the planning of Congress Hall events, and assisted Kennedy's efforts in Poland, remained on the new administration's advisory panel. From the early Cold War and the humiliation at the Prague Festival in 1947, when American leftist folk dancers competed with Soviet ballet stars, the US government remained aware of the import of mass cultural gatherings. In 1954, Inness-Brown had started her international dance work by raising private money and cooperating with various branches of government to send troupes to the Edinburgh Festival in Scotland. The CIA-funded Congress for Cultural Freedom, which, like Inness-Brown, had been involved in planning the Congress Hall cultural events, had been allied with the Edinburgh Festival since 1950.[4] A State Department report credited the 1954 festival's success

Martha Graham's Cold War. Victoria Phillips, Oxford University Press 2020. © Oxford University Press.
DOI: 10.1093/oso/9780190610364.001.0001

with providing inspiration for Eisenhower's Emergency Fund, which provided the template for the export mechanisms used by Kennedywho, like Eisenhower, had exported Graham.[5]

Graham remained on some government watch lists with her legendary successes that proved the power of culture. In 1963, the CIA took note when Graham was discussed in Congress. "Culture is the only international language," began Edgar M. Bronfman, a member of the Seagram's family and a champion of cultural diplomacy. "It is understood by all people, everywhere." He continued:

> In the battle for men's minds, now going on, this international language plays a vital role. As an example, just consider the statement that Prime Minister Nehru of India once made to Martha Graham, leading American dancer. He said to Miss Graham, "Your dancing and artistry will do more than all the planes and dollars in gaining understanding of the United States."[6]

Funding emerged for Graham to appear at the August 1963 Edinburgh Festival, with appearances to follow in London in early September.[7]

While the Edinburgh Festival was important to the government, in general the State Department did not fund appearances because the population was largely not the "target group" or "opinion makers . . . intellectuals, teachers, and important government officials." In addition, "we have no control over them." Seating was random so that people could not be seated next to specific interlocutors. Although the Unites States could "compete in a friendly peaceful way," a report countered. "And right there is the trouble [because we are] sharing the limelight. We are considered and criticized against other offerings, not as an interesting American manifestation." Because the local embassies and consulates wanted to "show the flag," State concluded, "We would of course include festivals and all like convocations whenever possible in our regular tours."[8]

Graham needed the work, and she accepted the offer to appear at the festival, although it did not place her center stage. It would get her back to Europe. At the festival, Graham would be surrounded by other dance companies and their leaders, as well as experts on the future of music, American politics, literature, films on the "science of space," and cutting-edge premieres in theater.[9] Graham and her company showed a "tradition of innovation" in the United States, rather than an avant-garde phenomenon.[10] She was advertised as a "classical modernist," noted for her use of the three-act structure of a full-evening work with *Clytemnestra* and her history as a visionary, an "evangelical," with decades of dance under her belt.[11]

Once in Edinburgh, Graham went on the offense. She was not hosted at the typical embassy- or consulate-sponsored receptions. Adding to the slight, she was only asked to attend an old-fashioned "garden party" during which many other performers and producers were applauded.[12] Yet Graham took to the press and advertised *Phaedra*'s heightened eroticism; the surrounding critical attention could enable her to deflect from her failings and garner new approbation. *Phaedra* could become vital evidence of her essential relevance in charged times, thus avoiding the pitfalls of being "modern." This time, the plan worked. The explicit eroticism of Graham's technique and dramaturgy dominated the papers.[13] New York critic Clive Barnes concluded that Graham had interpreted the Greek myth more "in terms of Dr. Kinsey's report than Euripides or Racine," referring to the widely read work of Alfred Kinsey about sexual behaviors that many credited with sparking the sexual revolution of the 1960s.[14] Critic Richard Buckle noted that, for the public, "shock [was] usually followed by a glow of delight and admiration."[15] With *Phaedra*, Graham had demonstrated she was "truly modern."[16] A reporter noted that each year a particular artist or work gave the festival importance, and in 1963, *Phaedra* became "the moment everyone had waited for."[17] Graham fought hard and remade her mark, for the moment.

When Graham and her company landed in London after the conclusion of the festival, the now standard publicity shot with the dancers outside the airplane, neatly positioned on the steel stairs and tarmac, returned, once again leaving Graham at the back. Her impressively diverse company members looked straight into the camera, as they had been well-trained to do. Graham stood off center one row behind a well-coiffed, beautiful company member in a light cinched dress and delicate shoes. Graham, shoulders blanketed in black, looked far away into the distance.[18] Despite her comeback, she began to accept that she had to relinquish the center to perpetuate the legacy of her company and her work. But she could still mold the company image in her own.

The Edinburgh publicity for *Phaedra* encouraged critical opprobrium in London. While her company garnered praise, Graham continued to come under harsh scrutiny as a performer because of her age. A rampant ageism took hold of critics. Buckle wrote of Graham's work as Jocasta seducing her son in *Night Journey*: "She is older than the [Noguchi] rocks among which she sits."[19] At the same time, when Graham tried to do technical works from the 1940s, Barnes complained that she had passed her prime. Graham would speak out against such prejudices, yet she remained cognizant that the US government wanted to show off the finesse of her young dancers as a part of the American ethos that was infusing the decisions made by the export panel.

* * *

As the persona of Martha Graham grew less sturdy in the early 1960s—in spite of *Phaedra* and the debates it sparked—so did the Dance Panel's effectiveness. In the wake of ANTA's troubles in 1962 while Graham toured, a reconfigured ten-person export "advisory" panel in dance now included only four private-sector dance experts, with the remaining six members representing the State Department or USIS. In 1954, the Dance Panel had consisted of critics and experts, some practitioners, and only one identifiable State Department representative—although the configuration quickly changed. Inness-Brown mediated between government and the private sector as she had from 1954 as chair, representing government yet wearing a private-sector hat. *New York Herald Tribune* critic Walter Terry continued to serve on the board. Dance educator Martha Hill and publicist Isadora Bennett, who had attempted to produce a mixed-bill season of modern dance on Broadway, also sat on the committee. Former dancer William Bales, known for his potent mimetic technique and his humor, participated via his role as a dean of the now legendary Bennington Dance Department.[20] But the government officials had the power to dictate policy. And policy no longer favored high-art, elite-targeted exports. Trickle-down, cocktail-circuit diplomacy was being replaced by bottom-up, youth-targeted events.

At the first 1963 meeting, a State Department representative set the agenda with a review of the types of dance the department's "area specialists," cultural attachés, and USIS needed for export. Perhaps referring to an earlier study that concluded, "We are influenced, without wanting to imitate, by what the Russians are doing. The Russians sent circuses. They sent variety shows of their own. We think, without merely competing on their own terms, we can do much better. . . . We need a kind of variety show, high-class vaudeville, if you will."[21] The selections in order of preference were a musical comedy, a "Holiday on Ice" event, and other similar pop culture extravaganzas. However, the report noted, "Another thing. [The posts] want top-grade things." The State Department report suggested a "shopping list."[22] Dance was seventh on the list, with the earlier report stating, "One of the things which we hope may actually happen not too far in the future is that we can get a very good group of dancers who will portray American folk dancing, from the beginnings up to the present."[23] Thus in 1963, the committee expressed a preference for Americana in the form of a "national folk song and dance group." Moving to the highbrow, a government representative suggested, "Modern dancers have done a lot with folk material." He mused that a repertory group could go into the field with Graham's *Appalachian Spring* coupled with Sophie Maslow's *Folksay*. (Presumably, this official had not heard of Graham's contempt for the Maslow work.) Encouraged by his own idea, he then suggested combining the Graham and Maslow works with Alvin Ailey's "folk" works, perhaps referring to *Revelations*, in addition to pieces by Jerome Robbins that also had "folk" themes.[24] These works remained unidentified, and the title of this work was not indicated. He continued that a pickup team of dancers could be selected and deployed to perform these modern American masterpieces. Bennett objected, with good reason. The government officials had no knowledge of Bennett's many attempts to coordinate choreographers into a single season of mixed repertory, which had continually failed in New York. For her, it had seemed like herding clawed cats in some cases, an impossible "collaboration among divas."[25] An ensuing silence about Graham seemed to echo.

Graham remained in Europe, but a festering uproar over *Phaedra* in the United States suddenly escalated. Two members of Congress who had seen the work in Germany in 1962 and walked out in the middle, watching the eroticism unfold but not staying to view its dire consequences in the myth's dramatic end, attacked *Phaedra*'s explicit sexuality. Representative Peter Frelinghuysen, a Republican from New Jersey, traveling with Edna Kelly, Democrat of Brooklyn, took a publicity opportunity to discuss the "unfortunate" programming selection of *Phaedra* by government officials to represent the nation because *Phaedra* "dealt with the seamier side of life."[26]

The House Committee on Foreign Affairs launched an inquiry to ask "how the United States [was] doing on the cold war battle-ground of ideas."[27] During the meeting, entitled "Winning the Cold War: The U.S. Ideological Offensive," the committee chair steered the hearing toward "the projection of image" and inquired about the purpose, range, and efficacy of international cultural propaganda initiatives.[28] The committee launched into a discussion of history and the now famous "goodwill" tour by Vice President Nixon to Venezuela in 1958, during which his car was attacked and nearly overturned by heckling crowds, a striking contrast to the welcome that the New York Philharmonic received soon after in the nation's capital. Although one congressman, tongue in cheek and bored by the discussion, referenced the power of music and suggested that perhaps the Soviet Union could "stir up people" by having its orchestras play "Yankee Go Home," the committee agreed that cultural diplomacy remained a valuable part of American tactics, and what they called "propaganda." Although another congressman noted that using culture to project an image of America into the international arena was "nothing more than a form of selling," others underscored the larger importance of exchange, following Bronfman's testimony.[29] On September 9, 1963, using classically aspirational early Cold War rhetoric, the committee concluded that cultural exports "should display the highest artistic achievements of our free society" in order to "reach into the hearts and minds of men."[30]

Although Graham had neatly missed the HUAC trials in the late 1940s and the McCarthyite 1950s, this time she found herself under attack. Donderoism was back. In a further committee hearing called on the specifics of dance exports, Frelinghuysen betrayed his philistinism when he asked New York City Ballet star Melissa Hayden to explain the difference between dance exchanges and athletic exchanges between countries, explaining to the artist that dancers were actually just trained athletes. Another congressman jumped in to quip back, "Please, don't start on the opera singers."[31] Hayden elegantly explained to the committee that creativity in dance projected a different aspect of the nation than sports contests. The congresspeople listened but were ready to take the conversation to politics and zeroed in on the example of Graham's *Phaedra*.[32]

Having seen "the seamier side" of the American creative mind on display in Bonn, Germany, Kelly saw her opening and proclaimed that *Phaedra* was proof that Congress should be able to mold programming to suit a particular image of America created by dance.[33] "This is a matter of direction" in Cold War propaganda battles, she declared.[34] Frelinghuysen jumped in again and described *Phaedra* as "an act" with men in loincloths. He continued, "They had some couches which they reclined on with companions," adding, "The import was quite clear." He mirrored the fears of exporting "homosexuals" that had plagued the State Department and ANTA, invoking the "lavender scare" in Washington in which homosexuality had been tied to communism. He concluded, "I found it distasteful as to any kind of image of this country."[35] The two members of Congress used Graham's choreography to argue for strict government oversight of cultural exports, which others read as Donderoism at best, American censorship at worst.[36]

Graham's use of classical themes again shielded her. Taking the stand in Washington to defend Graham, Hy Faine of the American Guild of Musical Artists reminded the committee members that *Phaedra* was a story from antiquity. He acknowledged that the choreography was "erotic" but denied that it was "salacious." Eroticism, he said, "takes place in all forms of life." He cited the Bolshoi's performance of *Spartacus* in New York: "The reviews I saw stated that there was more eroticism in that ballet than Martha Graham's ballet."[37] Notably, he referred to both genres as "ballet." The lavish production had been panned by Walter Terry, who sat on the Dance Panel and new advisory panel, as "a faltering forward step of Russian dance on a winding path toward real modernism."[38] While Graham knew how to use sexuality for the purposes of high-art modernism, and had been so recognized internationally, the Russians had failed dismally. She remained, in the seasoned critical eye, good cultural ammunition.

The hearings became a cause célèbre, and Graham attracted media attention that elevated her profile, which surely pleased her. The *New York Times, New York Herald Tribune*, and *Washington Post* all reported on the House investigation. Joining them were newspapers in cities ranging from Chicago, Kansas City, and Minneapolis, to Pittsfield, Massachusetts; Elmira, New York; Hackensack, New Jersey; and Sunsbury, Pennsylvania, to name a few. The story was syndicated. The publicity was controversial, yet, as one expert said, "Bad publicity is better than no publicity." Graham had been seasoned to respond to criticism in her early career. The *Herald Tribune* and *Post* even published follow-up pieces, and the story went international. The *London Daily Express*, Montreal's *Star,* and the international edition of the *Herald Tribune* featured the debate. "Is Martha Too Sexy for Export?," asked a multipage spread in the famous *Life* magazine distributed by the Luce empire domestically and globally. The large, glossy black-and-white pictures featured the dancers and Graham in motion, rehearsing. When asked to comment on the American controversy from the United Kingdom, Graham declined. In divaesque style, she declared, "The public will defend me."[39,40]

Larger city newspapers indeed came to Graham's defense. The *Times* stressed that *Phaedra* was "an *allegedly* erotic dance." As one writer noted, some people were having a problem with the shenanigans described in the myth itself. "Anyway, it's a bit late to be trying to suppress the Phaedra story," one critic said, tongue in cheek, perhaps harking back to the congressional committee in the 1930s that had demanded to hear testimony from the sixteenth-century playwright Marlowe. "In the past few thousand years, it's kind of got around."[41] Yet another slyly added, "It's really rather late to start censoring 'Agamemnon' (458 BC)."[42] Reporters and critics poked fun at the philistinism of Kelly and Frelinghuysen, with articles citing Frelinghuysen's comment that he "couldn't quite make [the dance] out."[43] Indeed, aside from walking out of the performance before the story's fateful outcome was revealed, they also said that they had seen the work in Bonn, where the company had not performed *Phaedra*. Graham had only performed the work in Munich.

Artistic and political elites defined Graham's modernism and came to her defense. "Dance leaders and theater artists were both amused and irritated" by the dust-up over *Phaedra*, the *Herald Tribune* reported.[44] Lincoln Kirstein wrote a letter to the *Herald Tribune* defending Graham, saying, "Her analyses of time and spaces have altered the vision of all of us."[45] José Limón, who had led the first modern dance company to tour under government auspices in 1954, cabled the State Department from Manila, proffering his support.[46] Letters and telegrams flooded Kelly's office.[47] New York newspapers reminded readers that after Graham's Broadway appearance in October, she would be performing at Constitution Hall in Washington, DC, for President Kennedy and his first lady, who certainly understood high culture.

The European artistic community also supported Graham, happy to condemn American provincialism and lack of cultural sophistication, as well as the specter of censorship. *Variety* suggested that members of Congress could learn from European audiences.[48] A letter printed in the *New York Times* noted that the two members of the House had become "a laughing stock" in Europe.[49] Even more significant, the German Mary Wigman weighed in with a letter to the *New York Times*, noting that the desire to censor artists dated back to the Nazis. Wigman wrote that the government controversy over Graham was "quite a shock" because it took place in the United States, "the country in which freedom and liberty have always been written in capital letters." In addition to its international ironies, this could not have been more damning in the face of the American conflation of the Nazis with Soviet Communists. Mantras of freedom rang hollow if the US government suppressed artistic expression.[50]

Nonetheless, Kelly and Frelinghuysen garnered support from regional newspapers around the country, some of which viewed *Phaedra*, which reporters may not have actually seen, as evidence of American "sagging morality" and "national decadence."[51] In a twist on the power of dance symbolism and the significance assigned to Isadora Duncan's bared feet by both the early Soviets and the Americans, the *Binghamton Press* wrote, "We can see where [Graham technique] might give the erroneous impression that all Americans run around barefoot."[52]

Graham, the ever-tactful ambassador, seemed to remain above the fray and continued to decline comment, thus positioning herself anew as apolitical in London. Yet in late October, just as the press began to lose interest, she spoke. Breaking her avowed silence, she reminded the public that the two members of Congress had not even known in which city they had seen the dance, or stayed to see the end of the story, which she implied they may have not known. Regarding the men who were reclining on those onstage couches, she said that there was only one couch in *Phaedra*, that it was small and tilted, and that dancers could not possibly lounge around on it. She protected her male dancers and the expressions of sexuality embedded in the mythic piece, and reaffirmed her dedication to freedom of expression and the power of good modern art. Graham concluded that "all the arts disturb, or should."[53] However, she and her team then undermined her position as a respected defender of the US government. Graham's spokesman had emphasized her service to the nation as a performer and cultural ambassador and asserted, "Evil is in the eyes of the beholder."[54] She closed her press meeting by declaring that she "felt pawed by dirty hands."[55] In openly criticizing the US government during a tour it had helped fund, Graham had overstepped.

* * *

In late November 1963, Graham joined the international community in mourning the death of President Kennedy. Vice President Lyndon Johnson was sworn in, and in the new year the issue of civil rights took center stage. Jacqueline Kennedy, who had elegantly espoused high culture, moved out of the White House she had shown the world on television. Graham moved forward, privately maintaining her alliance with the former first lady, now in mourning.

The following month, another blow hit Graham and her company. The Ford Foundation granted $7 million to dance, and modern dance was largely left out, Graham glaringly so. The ballet companies associated with Lincoln Kirstein were given more than 75 percent of the allotment. Kirstein's long history with dance and diplomacy from its early days under Roosevelt paid dividends. In response to the large funding for ballet, however, Martha Hill, who served on the government's advisory board and trained dancers at Juilliard, "expressed dismay." Sol Hurok, who first presented the Isadora Duncan Dancers in 1916 and had worked closely with Graham, declared, "There are many others deserving support."[56] Luminaries from theater, the press, government, and fashion signed a petition demanding greater funding for American moderns.[57] Graham herself, speaking to the *New York Herald Tribune*, went on at length about her consternation. One black-and-white photo accompanying the article showed Balanchine, sponsored by Kirstein, looking toward the floor, contemplative and elegant. Another photo, to its left, presented Graham with her hand across her chest as though praying, not a hair out of place, looking upward, far beyond Balanchine. Under her picture lay her text: "I'll say flatly, I should have been included." She concluded by decrying that American-based dance had been left behind while a technique rooted in the "European" received funding (she did not mention that Balanchine was born in a Soviet bloc state): "That is my grief about it and my anger."[58] Despite the clear righteousness of her argument, speaking out against the establishment further diminished her value as an American ambassador in the field.

Yet Graham retained a cultural cachet that was much needed at the Johnson White House, even if she had not been given millions. In exchange activities with the Soviet Union, an agreement was signed in February 1964 for 1964–65. The report concluded that the most effective and "welcome" exports to the Soviet Union included composers, theatrical scene designers, choreographers, and professional women.[59] Martha Graham brought them all. In addition, the new president was not known as a sophisticate. Indeed, he had begun a conversation with Senator J. William Fulbright, who had sponsored cultural programs, bills, and funding from the start of export programming, by saying, "Well, you're so cultural, getting so much culture, that I can't talk to you."[60] Nonetheless, Johnson well understood its importance. The CIA had noted the political import of the performing arts center in the "cultural cold war"; the nation's capital needed a state theater. Johnson named the new Washington center for his slain predecessor. A Senate report for the president noted that the Soviet ballet was effective because "culture is the only international language. It is understood by all people, everywhere." It continued to emphasize dance: "In the battle for men's minds, now going on, this international language plays a vital role." The echoes of Graham's Asian tour of 1955 could still be heard in the chambers of the Senate, by the president, and under the watch of the CIA.[61]

Thus, Graham was invited to the White House for a reception honoring "presidential scholars"; she hobnobbed with celebrities and politicians, including Helen Hayes, Sidney Poitier, atomic scientist Robert Oppenheimer, federal appeals court judge Thurgood Marshall, FBI director J. Edgar Hoover, and the well-funded George Balanchine. Willem de Kooning, also in attendance, represented the modern arts along with Graham. Graham met the president's wife, Lady Bird Johnson, who had shown an interest in modern art. When the Museum of Modern Art reopened in New York after a period of renovation, Lady Bird cut the ribbon and sounded much like Graham when she spoke about the power of modern art: "For art is the window to man's soul."[62] Indeed, Johnson's files show her interest in the creation of the National Foundation on the Arts and the Humanities in 1965 as part of an overall White House priority of encouraging the arts.[63]

* * *

Although limping, however elegantly, in Washington, Graham became increasingly relevant in the international arena when she was named "artistic adviser" to Bethsabée de Rothschild's newly formed Batsheva Dance Company in Israel, which received both foundation and government support to demonstrate Israel's highly technical and sophisticated presence in the arts.[64] For those in charge, this seemed to depend on the deployment of the increasingly prevalent Graham technique as a training tool to firmly replace the Wigman-based approach by the German dancers who had escaped the Nazis by imigrating to Palestine, now Israel. Like the New York radicals at New Dance Group, the Jewish dancers had used Wigman's technique to form a new political approach. Modernized folk forms became central to create a politically inspired dance in the United States, Israel, India, the Soviet bloc nations, and the neutrals and anti-aligned. Yet Graham and Rothschild would have considered this "agricultural" if not abstracted. Graham brought high modernism with an American language that could train bodies to displace the German-born expressionist form with a "universal" approach promote the Americanization of freedom. "This was the idea," said one dancer. "To do good and high level [work], and do it perfectly like the Americans, not the Israeli way."[65] As the new nation established its geographic presence in the Middle East, empire by invitation was again at work on the cultural front.

Significantly, Graham not only allowed the Batsheva company to perform works that had not included her, such as *Diversion of Angels*, but also allowed dancers to take her own roles, which she had rarely done in the past. The performance of Jocasta and Clytemnestra by dancers other than Graham had been a source of great contention in the United States, particularly as critics called for her retirement. She was not willing to give these parts to Americans, but now she entrusted some parts to the Israeli women. Linda Hodes, a young star dancer featured during international tours in 1955 and 1962, settled in Tel Aviv to help direct the company and supervise the mounting of Graham's works. No other company in the world was allowed this privilege.[66]

As the company found its footing, critics cited the professionalism of the Israeli dancers and called for Batsheva to be made a part of the permanent state apparatus. While Graham's works were the repertory core, and Hodes became instrumental, Rothschild had her own agenda: after having performed great international works, the Israelis would make their own.[67] Training in professionalized "freedom of expression" ultimately planted seeds of dissent from a hegemon and a move away from the master, as they had with Graham at Denishawn and later in India during the Cold War. For the Americans, lessons of freedom's power would have their price.

* * *

In 1965, a group of noted scholars, political stars, and scientists gathered as Graham was awarded $30,000 by the Aspen Institute, which was publicly declared to be "impartial"—in marked contrast to the Ford Foundation's perceived caprice in denying awards to modern dance. However, Graham was cited not as an *avant* figure of the 1960s but as a "leader" who was "immortal."[68] Although Graham had always had an elliptical style of speech, her Aspen Award acceptance address seemed particularly disjointed. She thanked the distinguished guests and then rambled on to explain why her company hadn't done a *Nutcracker*-type ballet—perhaps because the now endowed Balanchine and Kirstein had sustained their New York City Ballet on *The Nutcracker*, garnering domestic students who pined to play Clara and paid for ballet lessons, and gathering ticket revenues from parents, grandparents, aunts, uncles, and awed friends of the children in the performance.[69] She defended herself for not having children, saying that many of her dancers did indeed become parents. Then, she oddly told the audience to examine their ears in the mirror to appreciate the miracle of the body. About receiving the award, she remarked, perplexingly, "It's not even a joy. It is a joy."[70] Despite Graham's ramblings, surely understood as artistic revelries, at a dinner in New York following the Aspen Award ceremony, the director of the Office of Cultural Presentations sat with Graham and discussed a tour in the fall of 1966.[71]

The Ford Foundation reviews of Graham's grant proposals in 1965 demonstrate the foundation's bias for ballet rather than the "so called modern dance," but also the consensus regarding her future. "Miss Martha Graham has only a short productive career remaining to her," the president of the Ford Foundation began. "It may well be that the programs she will offer in November [1965] in New York will be one of the last significant programs involving new repertoire." Indeed, Graham would continue to create new dances for decades. Although "The B. Rothschild Foundation" had funded a new work, Graham needed money to complete work on the Schuman score for *The Witch of Endor*. Ford granted her $6,000 under the condition that "the recording and the rights to the choreography . . . be made available to both established and developing choreographers and dancer in the field of modern dance."[72] Graham moved forward despite those who counted her days.

In 1965, Francis Mason, the cultural affairs officer for the American embassy in London, wrote a chatty note to Charles Ellison, director of cultural presentations in Washington, about Graham's performances in the wake of the 1962–63 disasters on tour. Graham's backers in London wanted her to perform because "the time now seems ready for American to get a great deal of extra prestige and . . . Miss Graham is very conscious of her duties as an American."[73] Mason reported on some subsequent "heart-to-heart talks" and added, "I think there is no doubt that this information might be useful to the Cultural Presentations Program." In these talks, it was "suggest[ed] that Graham gradually cease to dance." Mason continued, "This is of course a matter of such great delicacy that not even any member of the dance panel should know about it." The plan would be to tour and "mount some of Graham's older works on younger people." He warned, "Graham so far seems to be taking to this idea very well but there may well be trouble ahead."[74] Like Graham's mythic stage characters of the seer Tiresias in *Night Journey*'s story of Jocasta and Oedipus, or Cassandra's vain attempts to warn of impending doom in the three-act *Clytemnestra*, Mason's words should have rung loud.

In 1966, the National Council on the Arts bestowed grants of just under $500,000 for modern dance, with the largest two for Graham of $141,000 each. Although these grants were generous, the bias of the council became clear in the details. Announcing the decision on Valentine's Day, the

Washington Post reported that while José Limón, Alvin Ailey, Paul Taylor, and Merce Cunningham were offered grants as "choreographers," Graham was encouraged to stage "rehearsals" or "revivals" with the first offering. The second was a matching grant for domestic touring only, meaning that Graham had to find donors to cash in on government largesse. Typical of government programs, a domestic tour would provide publicity and test the touring mettle of a proposed company for the international market. In response to complaints from those who felt Graham was overindulged with the grants, Agnes de Mille proclaimed, "This was not an indulgence for her, but a need of the United States of America."[75] Always patriotic, de Mille was a reliable spokeswoman. At the end of the year, her supporters lobbied the government for an international festival appearance; the request was denied within days.[76]

The following year, it seemed that Graham's White House efforts might pay off: the Department of State wrote to embassies and consulates to say that it was arranging a six-week tour for the Graham company. After a sponsored season in London, under Rothschild and *Reader's Digest* founder Lila Acheson Wallace, she would again perform in Soviet bloc nations, repeating Yugoslavia and Poland, venturing into Hungary and Czechoslovakia, and adding Romania and Bulgaria. She would proceed through West Germany and Austria, one still divided and the other "neutral," both allied with the West. Firmly in Europe, Spain and Portugal followed in the plans. In Rome, she could meet the pope and perform there. The extravaganza would be bookended by Paris. "The Department's Dance Panel voted unanimously to nominate the Martha Graham Dance Company for this tour," and cables began.[77] European and Eastern European posts were told of Graham's recent Aspen Award.[78] The Dance Panel had approved Graham as their "first and only choice" for Kiev, Moscow, and St. Petersburg.[79] Included in the proposal was a total of fifty-five to sixty persons, including dancers, a conductor, the orchestra, as well as stage hands and assistants. News hit the streets: the *Washington Post* announced that the tour would again include a diverse group featuring female stars of American, Japanese, African American, and Jewish heritage.[80] The *New York Times* celebrated the importance of London because of its school of contemporary dance that featured Graham technique led by Graham dancers and thus encouraged "the growing trans-Atlantic interplay that is enriching both Europe and America."[81] The best of the British and Europeans in London would be sent to study with Graham herself in the cultural capital of the world, New York.

Francis Mason, now a cultural affairs officer at the embassy in London, wrote USIS that a confidential "heart-to-heart" with Graham might lead her to "gradually cease to dance" given the touring rigors and publicity. A State Department–sponsored London performance would succeed, he warned, only if it were "to mount some of Graham's older works on younger people." Although Graham initially seemed to be "taking to the idea," Mason reiterated: "There could be trouble ahead." The plans for the six-week extravaganza were left to individual embassies. Cable silence ensued.

Adding to Graham's decline, the government monitored Studs Terkel's well-publicized interview with her, which did not help her case as a cultural diplomat in Europe after the tour fizzled. During the live broadcast, although Graham told many familiar stories from her career and framed modern dance as a uniquely American innovation, she seemed garbled. Failing to use the rehearsed language she had used with Edward R. Murrow in 1962, however practiced, she now said, "And there comes a time when I . . . uh . . . I don't believe that you do much choosing. But of course you choose. But you do not choose with your will. It is very often that you are chosen. And you can make out of that what you want."[82] The interview rambled on in this manner. As time passed, trouble for Graham in New York continued, and a letter from Francis Mason from London to Washington ended, "I can not be encouraging." Mason was nominated by the government to act as an escort for her tour, but he was immersed in an intensive course to learn Russian.[83]

Reactions to the initial plans for 1967 occurred on all sides. The Russia and Ukraine performances were discussed with the Soviet Ministry of Culture, "and the reception of the idea was lukewarm." Even though "Martha Graham was not overly enthusiastic" about performing in Moscow, St. Petersburg, and Kiev, she remained confident about the other tour stops, as long as she remained center stage, performing.[84]

Other posts responded with a variety of reactions against the tour that spanned the political, practical, and aesthetic realms. On the political front, Budapest cabled the State Department, "No one knows what relations will be between the US government and the government of Hungary in April 1967, but as they exist now engagement by Graham troupe completely out of question," adding, "such decisions guided by political not cultural considerations."[85] After envoys in Romania described the Graham performances as a "calculated risk" in early September, Sofia, Bulgaria, telegrammed days later, "Acceptance not repeat not possible now because of prevailing political atmosphere."[86] On the practical front, budgets were being cut and the embassy in Poland did not feel that the expense justified the possible outcome. Austria also did not want to contribute from the embassy coffers.[87] Madrid and Paris looked for local sponsorship, which was not forthcoming. In Prague, the offer was met by a bit of confusion about Graham: "They requested publicity and background material—and the like—so that the decision makers can see in black and white exactly what troupe is and does."[88] From an aesthetic standpoint, the American embassy in Bonn summarized what many thought but would not put in print. "The Post appreciates the Department's offer of the Martha Graham Dance Company for the spring of 1967 but feels it would not be wise to avail itself of this opportunity," the memo opened politely. It immediately continued, "We have discussed the projected tour with a number of Germans knowledgeable in the field of modern dance and found unanimous reaction that such a tour might prove disastrous in a country which considers the Graham group, 'old hat.'" She could no longer fill even the smaller theaters with her "historic" and "outdated" modernism. It continued, "In Europe, especially, [modern dance] has progressed far beyond the stage of which Miss Graham's work is representative." In case Washington was not clear about the message, the memo concluded, "No reference is made to Miss Graham without such epitaphs as 'turgid,' 'bombastic,' 'old-fashioned,' 'corny,' etc." The 1962 tour had not been a success, and "We feel that a return engagement at this time would be counter-productive."[89] In response, Washington offered Bonn either Alvin Ailey or the Boston Symphony Orchestra "in view of the Post's objections to the Martha Graham Dance Company."[90]

Of key importance to the State Department was not only Graham's modernism but, as discussed by Mason, Martha Graham herself. A telegram from Belgrade, Yugoslavia, noted that the Graham company would be "tolerated" for a few days "provided Graham not performing." A later telegram emphasized the issue again: "May 10–17 [OK], provided Graham personally not repeat not performing."[91] In a letter to the files, the director of cultural presentations in Washington reported, "We and our posts had serious reservations about her attempting starring roles," although they could agree to "walk-on parts." According to the memo, Graham's own Board of Directors believed, "The problem will solve itself after a US tour of the company," because Graham might fail miserably, injure herself, and thus retire voluntarily. "If it does not [happen], and Miss Graham is unwilling to give up starring roles, the idea is to present the program as 'Martha Graham's last public appearances.'"[92] Indeed, Graham closed in Portugal, the only fully funded stop, with exactly this press.

On the positive side, local promoters in Lisbon, Portugal, encouraged Washington to fund performances in the São Carlos Theatre to be followed by a grand extravaganza performance of *Clytemnestra* in the Coliseum.[93] Indeed, the Lisbon National Theater delayed contract bookings with ballet companies in favor of Graham. The embassy cabled Washington, "Here [Graham] is the best known American name in field of dance. Leading Lisbon impresario states: 'Portugal has been waiting twenty years to see Martha Graham,'" noting that with various foundation, festival, embassy, and local support there would be "good financial arrangements."[94]

The official "recapitulation" for the files stated that the tour was cut to London, Paris, and Lisbon because of a sharp reduction in congressional funding for the program overall, with "the fact that response from countries in Eastern Europe less than satisfactory" as a secondary factor.[95] Eventually Paris was cut, as well. Money remained a trigger point. Typical of the Graham company's negotiating strategies, the company's demand for immediate fiscal renumeration and payment of fees thwarted possibilities of free and widespread popular publicity. Letters document haggling for a few thousand dollars from the government were augmented by accusations of broken promises, even after agreements were signed by all. While budgets show that Graham herself took 25 percent of the total pay for twenty dancers, plus weekly choreographic fees that equaled the cost of the conductor and wardrobe mistress combined, management was willing to cut the tour short or travel without the orchestra rather than cut the fee paid to Graham.[96] Money concerns bled the tour. The impresario hired by Graham was "incompetent," according to the State Department, and "demanded an exorbitant fee for the service he renders"; they concluded in a letter to Graham, "If no substitute is acceptable to you, then we will need to withdraw from the agreement." Graham management did not know that the reviews from posts did not augur well, and they continued with their hard-nosed letters. After relenting on the promoter, they continued to push for money, noting "slightly different recollections" about the deal.[97] In the end, Graham was offered $20,000 and was hosted in London at an embassy party courtesy of the ambassador's private funding and a government-supported press conference over a three-week season; financial support in Portugal over six days included an ambassadorial luncheon and initial funding for lecture-demonstrations that were canceled in the end.[98]

In London, Graham arrived for a long season with a packed repertory and more than twenty in cast and crew and performed with the esteemed

London Orchestra. Yet her age infused reviews. She refused to divulge her years, citing her "dignity." With reporters billing her season as a "peep show," she attempted to make age sexy and told reporters that "a fetish has been put upon age."[99] One author merged age and race, writing, "[Graham's] London season may strengthen old prejudices—that Negro people dance more freely than others [referencing Mary Hinkson] that the spinal crises of the mature [Graham] make less good dance spectacles."[100] The final post comment back to Washington merely noted that the company met with "warm reception" by an audience that was "60% youth" who were "devoted . . . to her as a personality."[101]

In Lisbon, Graham received mixed reviews that consistently linked her performances to US State Department sponsorship. Newspaper reporters clearly understood her season as a diplomatic mission. She arrived with corresponding fanfare; reporters cited her company of twenty dancers accompanied by the full London Orchestra, a sign of cachet. They made their debut at the São Carlos Theatre, Lisbon's grand opera house.[102] *Clytemnestra* received the most notable attention. Positive reviews cited the music and choreography, decor, or sets and costumes, all "stylistically unique—one of the reasons for the piece's strength." Yet Graham's age remained a thorn: "As a final note," one critic wrote, "we must say that, for us, it was disheartening to see the deficient physical condition in which Martha Graham currently finds herself, which removes all of the dramatic force from her work." He joked, "At the very least, we can still say for the near future that 'I saw Martha Graham dance!'"[103] On the final evening, Graham performed as Clytemnestra in a historic bullring, Coliseu dos Recreios, for an audience that reportedly shouted, "*Olê! Olê!*" as she danced. Despite the mixed reviews, she proclaimed that it was a crowning moment in her performing career.[104] In postperformance reports, the Lisbon office offered no direct comments but quoted *Diario Popular*, "You can like or dislike this type of dance," before finally calling it "genius."[105] In the end, little information on the State Department reviews exists beyond scant post reports. "Action copies of effectiveness reports on appearances of Martha Graham Dance Company cannot be found." Finally, the memo concluded, "The above two reports [on London and Lisbon] could be inadvertently misfiled."[106]

When Graham returned to New York, her decreasing value as a stage performer, deeply complicated by her drinking, became increasingly apparent. "[Graham] had to know that she was dancing a little too long and that it wasn't great," said Bertram Ross, who played Oedipus, Holofernes, and a myriad of other leading male roles. At the studio each day, in order to keep the repertory readied for performances, the company continually rehearsed in secret if she did not appear. One dancer recalled that when Graham arrived, "sometimes she would rehearse and get lost. Or sometimes she would rehearse, and it would work. You just didn't know."[107] Ross recalled, "It was very difficult to rehearse because she would come so drunk."[108] A younger dancer recalled of performances, "She'd do odd things onstage, hand right in her face sometimes; there were surprises that she didn't want."[109] She did not appear for the stage call of a New York performance of *Clytemnestra*. She was at home alone, drunk. The rehearsal director rushed over in a taxi and pulled her out of her apartment. After Graham was shepherded into the theater, she smacked the director's wife.[110] With coffee pumped into her, she made it onstage. Agnes de Mille summed it up: "She drank very heavily and it got worse, and worse and worse."[111] The company ceased touring internationally with public support.[112]

That spring, a Ford Foundation officer reflected on the state of modern dance and Martha Graham. Although the foundation had a $7.8 million balance to distribute to the art, Graham received just $144,000. Calling the "indigenous" genre the "so called modern (interpretive) dance," the report concluded that, in contrast to ballet, the lack of a single modern training vocabulary and its dependence on a single choreographer made it untenable in the long term, an artistic flash that would soon pass with its choreographers." It attributed Graham's longevity to "the lucky accident of financial stability made possible by her friend, Bethsabée de Rothschild." The report noted that even with Balanchine's death, ballet in the United States would flourish anyway. Although the moderns had current "seeming vitality," without Graham, Cunningham, and Taylor, their companies would perish. The Judson group was written off as a passing youthful fad. Graham received a grant only to film her works for posterity, and only if the eight films were offered to television stations and libraries for free with no copyright restrictions in order to give the public and scholars unrestricted access. Again, the terms would not be met by Graham in the end. Rockefeller would join with $25,000 in honor of "her last season," although Graham had not announced her retirement.[113]

* * *

While Graham struggled, in the United States covert funding for the arts and collusion with the government by artists came under scrutiny with the *Ramparts* scandal, which began when the *New York Times* reported that a student group had taken funds from the CIA according to an investigation by *Ramparts* magazine reporters. While a myriad of modern artists were "named" for their participation in CIA cultural espionage, Graham was not implicated.[114] Melvin Lasky, who had supported the Congress Hall opening that included Graham, and George Kennan, as the cultural diplomat who had boosted Graham as ambassador in Yugoslavia, both signed a letter to the *Times* that did not deny CIA funding for the cultural programming, but maintained that the cultural organizations that had been funded had operated with complete freedom. Indeed, the web of like-minded individuals who staffed the Ford and Rockefeller Foundations and numerous other institutions giving grants to artists had not needed specific guidance: they knew the targets and the message. Like the Congress Hall funding and opening ceremony apparatus, meetings often took place over lunch at exclusive clubs where men solidified ideological bonds that had been bred into them since prep school and in elite colleges. They understood themselves to be "pilot fish," or smaller fish who swam next to the shark to assist as needed while it dominated the sea and determined the course.[115] The CIA was subsequently banned from supplying funds to foundations. The drought of cultural funding had further implications for Graham.

Although Graham was not directly named, she, too, had relied on the CIA's largesse in the arts as the government's covert cultural ministry.[116] As noted, the CIA tracked Graham's 1955 landing in Indonesia, home of Bandung. After the first tour in 1955, the agency tracked her when she attended a summit on fighting communism and "foreign aspects of U.S. National Security." The Congress for Cultural Freedom had helped fund her export to Berlin in 1957. She and Aaron Copland had received grants from other front organizations. When her name appeared in journals, she was entered into the CIA database. When she was used as evidence to support supplemental appropriations for cultural exports by Congress, agents took note. As years passed, Graham would continue to hit the radar despite the government ban on covert funding for the arts. Here, the unrecognized power of dance for investigative reporters served Graham well, and would continue to do so during the Cold War. Yet both covert and overt government funding became scarce: in 1967, Congress cut the budget for cultural presentations by 42 percent for 1968. And Graham would have to compete in the open for government funds with the National Endowment for the Arts (NEA).

* * *

Nevertheless, Graham remained in the White House Rolodex. In October 1968, Lady Bird Johnson's East Wing booked Graham's dancers—if not Graham herself as a dancer—as entertainment for the prime minister of New Zealand and his wife. In a slight to the woman as ambassador, Graham was not invited to the state dinner.[117] Afterward, the guests went to the East Room to see *Diversion of Angels*. The mixed-race leads, Mary Hinkson and Bertram Ross, as the Woman in White and her lover, represented the purity of love. Photographs of the performance emphasize Johnson's dedication to civil rights legislation. Other dancers held hands onstage as Lady Bird greeted Graham: African American men held hands with Asian American women behind them. The cast stood, enraptured, as Lady Bird celebrated Graham alongside an audience filled with women dressed mostly in long shimmery gowns. Yet change was approaching for the well-coiffed: a few women wore their hair short and neatly cropped as they sported wide-sleeved blouses to offset tailored waists, more reminiscent of a hippie spin on elegance than one might expect. Graham stood near the president for photos, holding on to the earlier Cold War chic.

In 1968, the United States needed "acts" for the International Fine Arts Festival sponsored by the Mexican government surrounding the summer Olympics in Mexico City. As seen earlier, the government had mixed opinions about the effectiveness of festivals in showcasing the nation; however, Graham had fared well in Edinburgh, and perhaps her refusal to participate in a similar pre-Olympic festival in Berlin, 1936, would also seem to add currency for those who remembered their history. Several modern dance troupes performed, including Graham and Cunningham. Along with Graham's eight performances, which were not well attended, she and the company participated in five "off-stage activities" including dance classes and lecture-demonstrations, as well as the ever-important meetings with "local people at Embassy," an "Ambassador's reception," and a "Reception for press." While one government report stated the modern groups had performed without government support, a "recapitulation" report on 1968 states that Graham received "partial financial support," which "permitted this prestigious group to participate." In the end, while performances did not command full houses, Graham and her "prestige . . . help[ed] to underscore our friendship with that country."[118]

* * *

In 1969, Graham reluctantly retired from the stage. Aware of what was being written about her, she reflected, "At moments I think that it is time for me to stop. I think of Mallarmé's image of the swan, the beautiful swan who stayed too long in the winter water until the ice closed around his feet and he was caught." Performing while under the influence of alcohol must have been on her mind, since Mallarmé's poem opens, "Can the virgin, beautiful and day / Release this frosted and forgotten lake / With a drunk blow of wings." Graham described her loss as a performer, even as a dancer over seventy, as the "Ring of Dante's Hell, omitted."[119]

Once Graham left the stage, with no stage calls to get sober for, she had no mandate to stop drinking. She was hospitalized and fell into a coma—possibly induced, as can be medically mandated for those who quit drinking suddenly. Delirium, tremors, hallucinations, itching sweats, numbness, and the heart pounding out of the chest all require hospitalization. Some die.[120] Graham's official diagnosis was diverticulitis: a standard medical cover for alcohol-related liver damage. Agnes de Mille remembers being told, "You better hurry up and see her for she's not going to last long. She's dying of alcoholism."[121]

Initially, gifts of flowers adorned her room and luminaries visited. However, soon the trail of visitors trickled off, and Graham began to suffer from typical secondary side effects of withdrawal: depression, anxiety, and sleeplessness.[122] Doctors probably tried prescribing Valium, morphine-related drugs, or other painkillers that would mitigate these symptoms, and also help her now crippling arthritis. Graham let her signature jet-black hair turn gray at the roots.[123] According to de Mille, Graham rallied toward recovery in the moment that she saw the white streaks. Yet pride is often the flip side of guilt and denial for alcoholics, which can lead to a desire to soothe and medicate with the next good thing, doctor-prescribed pills. Although Graham famously is said to have written, "To stop drinking was easy for me," others saw a different story unfold.[124]

The road would remain difficult, as those in the foreign service observed. Even after hospitalizations, relapses haunt well over three-quarters of the hospitalized.[125] After Graham was released, Ben Garber—who had introduced Graham to her benefactor Lila Acheson Wallace, supported Graham financially, curated her makeup for galas, and put the finishing touches on her in her dressing room before she prepared for her last stage performance—took her into his elegant country home. Decrepit and swollen, she spent long hours sitting on a silk daybed covered with a duvet. Garber found glasses of whiskey hidden in his potted plants. Photographs reveal bruises on her limbs, and she was told by Garber's doctor that if she took another drink she would die. Following this much-needed warning, she recovered and returned to her apartment in Manhattan near the Graham school. She said she would not drink again, even if other medications soothed her pain.[126]

Enter Ron Protas full force, a dashing and debonair man who promised rejuvenation for Graham's career and her life. He would also become a powerful and problematic presence throughout her career and beyond. Protas grew up in Brooklyn and graduated from New York University in 1964 with honors. At Columbia Law School, his mentor was Hans Smit, who specialized in international arbitration, an area of expertise that served Protas well, both during his time with Graham and after her death in managing her legacy.[127] After leaving Columbia, he attempted to befriend numerous older female artists including de Mille, who shunned him. Graham dancers remember him first as an amateur photographer who "lurked about" well before she retired.[128] She largely ignored the handsome young man but allowed him to "flit" around.[129] As time passed, however, he served a distinct and burgeoning purpose in Graham's life. After she retired into drink, he visited her in the hospital when others peeled away. He took pictures of her with Garber in the flower garden and followed her back to her Upper East Side apartment.[130] He was charming with Graham, and she needed the kinds of support and adoration her offered, especially after she had undermined herself, center stage, as a performer.

Protas became an escort for the childless, familyless star. According to Linda Hodes, "Everybody around her had family and their own lives, and didn't want to spend their evenings with her. So I really saw the necessity that someone like Ron played in her life at that time." In addition, he served a purpose: "He was one of these guys that could tell a good story, could tell a joke." Hodes remembers dinners at which she and Protas would banter in Yiddish accents: "Martha used to say, 'You two stop it!'"[131] With Protas, Graham could recover some fun. Yet Protas also severed Graham from consistent contact with some friends and supporters considered not useful, and alienated longtime allies.[132]

Protas reminded Graham of her legacy and its vitality, and rebuilt her in the public eye as they appeared on the New York scene.[133] As he gained her trust over time, he began "insinuating himself in the creative process" in company matters.[134] He then attempted to dabble in the finances of the company and the school. Numerous individuals, administrators, and dancers found Protas controlling and repugnant. Company members who taught at the school and had developed the technique and repertory with Graham before Protas's arrival were instructed by him on matters of technique and artistry, yet also were often owed back pay. Many walked. A few just taught for free and walked past him in the hall to the studio as though he was not there. Some supporters, including Francis Mason, who would head her board, nonetheless remained loyal to Graham.[135] For Mason, Protas served distinct needs as he reinvented Graham as an icon.[136] A renewed, still unfolding legacy would establish an enduring place for her in the arts that would be solidified by her continued relationship with the White House. Yet Mason called it "a dance with the devil."[137] Although it required taking center stage with the devil in the wings, Graham, who had jokingly put herself onstage as God, could remain a cultural ambassador in a dance of diplomacy.

* * *

After having cut the budget for cultural presentations by 42 percent for 1968, Congress slashed it by another 25 percent for the next year. In addition, immediate politics interrupted plans for exchange: the State Department backed off from exporting overt Americana, as would Bush in 1989: "After the invasion of Czechoslovakia in August [1968], the Department decided to cancel anything of 'high visibility.'"[138] In 1970, Congress again reduced the budget for exchange by another 17 percent, "attack[ing] [the program] as being obsolete." The Advisory Committee on the Arts, including Nelson Rockefeller and the NEA director, Nancy Hanks, initially concluded, "A change in the administration is not likely to make a difference in this decision."[139] Yet Hanks went to work and lobbied 150 representatives, getting 100 to reverse their vote and fund government arts programs.[140]

Thus the Richard M. Nixon administration brought unexpected hope. Cultural diplomacy was particularly useful to Nixon because the process of detente, or the easing of tensions between the United States and the Soviet Union, took a significant move forward. Nixon, who had witnessed the effectiveness of the exportation of American arts as Eisenhower's vice president, had the State Department's Cultural Presentations Committee (CPC) reinstate the Dance Panel. The dance advisory panel began anew, convening in New York, 1970. Yet Nixon was not working alone. Henry Kissinger, then serving as Nixon's secretary of defense, had also worked with the Eisenhower administration and Rockefeller, special assistant to the president, who had exported dance under Roosevelt. In 1954–55, Kissinger, with a panel of eleven others, analyzed "the psychological aspects of US foreign strategy," including cultural exports, as Eisenhower was implementing his Emergency Fund and the CIA delved into cultural diplomacy projects of its own alongside foundations.[141] The report noted that art and philosophy were not cultural "contained compartments," but rather "linked" to economics and politics. The West brought the "respect for the individual, humanitarianism" that was missing in the USSR. "Cultural action" by the US government would "[eliminate] vulnerabilities to Communism" abroad. To replace "Hollywood films" and "comics," the report initially suggested the export of books.[142] Indeed, Rockefeller and the foundation had also been instrumental in establishing library programs before the start of the Cold War. After Eisenhower left office, Kissinger worked with the Rockefeller Foundation, Nelson Rockefeller, and Nancy Hanks on various studies published in 1961 as *Prospect for America*. He served as special adviser to Kennedy and Johnson, who, like Eisenhower, exported Graham. Kissinger would become Nixon's and Gerald R. Ford's secretary of state, heading the department that would tap Graham for export.

Moving forward and controlling outcomes, the Nixon administration configured the CPC Dance Panel membership so that votes could swing decisively to suit State Department needs, in line with the earlier iteration under Johnson, yet in a craftier manner. This time, twelve official members evenly represented the private sector and the State Department—six and six. Yet votes were also given to three official "observers"—two from State and one from the NEA, chaired by Nancy Hanks, whose earlier work connected her deeply with Nelson Rockefeller and Kissinger, with her study also appearing in *Prospect for America*. The newly configured Dance Panel pushed for Graham to perform in Russia.[143]

At subsequent meetings of the reconstituted Dance Panel, the NEA became an official force in international deployments, although the direct involvement had to be kept under wraps for Congress. Unlike ANTA, which had been chartered to work with the State Department and thus take on international work under Roosevelt, Congress had chartered the NEA in 1965 as an institution to promote "the encouragement and support of *national* progress and scholarship in the arts [emphasis added]."[144] The mandate was to serve the American domestic community and not fund cultural exports. When the CPC asked the NEA to fund companies internationally, the NEA representative noted that the institution, according to its charter, could not legally work in the international market; the CPC responded that if the NEA

supported a company domestically, then that group could tour internationally, because the resulting good reviews in the United States could be used
internationally by USIS as promotional materials and build credibility with
the posts.[145]

Even though the NEA was a good partner, the overall planning sys-
tems continued to rely on the historic "marriage" between business and
government—through program advertisements, personal relationships, or
corporate contributions. Minutes from the 1970 Dance Panel meetings show
how these connections were now made explicit. The panel members first decided that the organization should be more "canny" in fundraising and noted
that the Pepsi soft drink corporation "helped . . . enormously" in exporting
jazz to Africa because the company wanted to sell its products there.[146] One
phone call to IBM got Ailey to Paris.[147] They considered how to get oil companies to help in South America.[148] The panel openly attempted to identify
particular companies that had interests in the countries targeted by the State
Department for dance as a propaganda for export.

Business worked hand in hand with government to penetrate the Soviet
Union for communication objectives, and while the United States sought to
disseminate "facts" and "the truth" in order to achieve "peace," in the end,
government reports firmly stated, "Our short-term purpose is to find out as
much about the Soviet Union and its society as we can." Indeed, "The concrete achievement of the exchange program is the gain of information about
the Soviet Union and Eastern Europe."[149] In 1970, State noted that fiftieth-
anniversary celebrations in Russia were consuming the attention of its cultural officers. In February, the State Department managed "the shortest
negotiation in the history of the cultural-exchange program" with the Soviets
to expand the number of students and artistic groups that would participate
in cultural exchange. A report noted, "Being aware of what was happening
in Czechoslovakia and Poland and student unrest in several countries, the
Russians turned down all things recommended by the Advisory Committee
and the Panels, i.e. Martha Graham, jazz groups," adding, "All they wanted"
was "Holiday on Ice" and "things that were not controversial."[150]

Along with Holiday on Ice skaters and folk dancers, who had been
championed in earlier panel meetings, Alvin Ailey became the American
government's most promising modern dance export for Moscow, which
had criticized the United States about race relations, its "Achilles heel," for
decades.[151] He and his largely African American company had triumphed
in the Far East and Australia; his choreography used folk, gospel, strong

technique, and youthful bodies. His work *Revelations* showed sorrow, meditation, prayer, triumph, and jubilation with a closing that never failed to get audiences spontaneously to their feet. As a tour for 1970 was planned, racial injustices continued to plague the United States in the international markets, adding fuel for the Soviets. Ailey combined a positive spin on American racial politics and Cold War modernism.

The implementation of "rescue missions" for dance companies for export began, which engaged both domestic and international government offices. Just as USIS had relied on domestic reviews for publicity, the State Department would rely on new sources of domestic government funding, such as the NEA and local governments, to establish a company's footing for the international road. While identified as culturally vital in the international field, the Ailey company disbanded after its spring season because of uncertain finances. The NEA and the New York State Council on the Arts sprang into action with monies. The Ailey company was suddenly booked to perform in Washington, and it received State Department money to tour Africa over the summer; the domestic agencies made grants to keep the dancers employed through the fall, when they could leave for Moscow.[152]

In the Soviet Union, thirteen hundred "unrestrained" Russians in the audience cheered for the "swinging innovation" of the "American modern dance company." Ailey's reviews were triumphant: the show was "lively" but also "abstract, violent, humorous, and spiritual." While the American reporters called it "easily the most exciting evening of dance in Moscow this season," even the Russian press conceded that the performances were a success.[153]

While Ailey's integrated company led by an African American had clear propaganda intent, José Limón was a less obvious Soviet export for 1970, if ever the highly regarded diplomat and humanitarian. With Limón's *Dances for Isadora*, the State Department used programming to directly confront the Soviets and their politics. As discussed in earlier chapters, while Duncan had been heralded by dance historians as deeply American as one "Mother of Modern Dance," she had a strong early start in the Soviet Union, fueling Lenin's desire to create a dance for the proletariat. In 1969, as the Soviets prepared for their fiftieth anniversary, the legacy of Duncan initially proclaiming "I am Red" and dancing for Lenin, yet the Cold War troupe appearing alongside circus acts in small Russian towns, did not bode well for a pro-modern Soviet message. The State Department managed the program notes for *Dances for Isadora*, translated into Russian. Describing Duncan as "an American interpretive dancer," they hailed her as "one of the forerunners of modern dance." They continued, oddly, "Her dancing was largely improvisational."[154] They looked over Duncan's works such as *Dance of the Furies* and *Revolutionary Etude*, among others, that were choreographed with specific political intent, including dancers in red tunics flying with red flags across the stage and bearing Soviet-style fists to the audience.[155] Yet older Soviet audience members would have remembered Duncan's legacy; Duncan's school, then run by her daughter, was not shut down in the Soviet Union until 1949. After the death of Stalin, under Khrushchev former students asked the Ministry of Culture to reopen the school with a heartfelt political and artistic intent: "[Isadora Duncan's] dances, which, with the two funeral dances for the memory of Lenin, the girls of the Isadora Duncan School in Moscow have since danced all over Russia, across Siberia . . . are amazing in their effects on the audience. Quite apart from their revolutionary significance, they are all imbued with a real plastic beauty."[156] The request was denied with a curt explanation: "The plastic dance has lost its original significance for the Soviet audience."[157] Yet in 1970, Duncan held vital significance for the United States with its suppression of the communist Isadora who critics, choreographers, scholars, and government publicity rebuilt in the American way: revolutionary as a precursor to the modern, individualistic, and free voice in the arts, which had been stifled by Soviet totalitarianism.

The CPC relocated meetings from New York to Washington, further indicating the political mandate of cultural deployments in dance.[158] During the first DC-based meeting, arguments between government and private-sector experts began to take a bitter tone.[159] The government chair set the direction for the private sector experts when he asked them to give each dance company under consideration a grade of A, B, C, or F. Heated discussions ensued about "grading" criteria and even the idea of giving a work of art an academic mark, despite criteria established by Doris Humphrey in *The Art of Making Dances*. In addition, State representatives insisted that the dance experts refrain from suggesting particular dance groups for particular locations, although they had been allowed to add input to these considerations in the 1950s and 1960s. The CPC would make all "Area" decisions regarding dance troupes that got "passing" grades.[160] The political mandates for the project became paramount.

* * *

The Alvin Ailey tour had "erased" any questions about the effectiveness of dance as propaganda, and the White House looked to Asia next.[161] Nixon and his national security adviser, Kissinger, needed help as they prepared to open relations with mainland China and as they navigated an unpopular war in Vietnam. In late 1969, the *New York Times* reported on the American-led massacre in March 1968 in the Vietnamese village of My Lai, which would become a flashpoint for protests worldwide. "The troops dynamited [houses] made of brick and set fire to wooden structures," the *Times* reported. After the homes were destroyed, and women and their children fled outside, "the Vietnamese were gunned down where they stood." Villagers who survived had buried themselves under dead bodies. In 1970, Nixon authorized American troops to invade Cambodia to support the South Vietnamese, and met with political backlash in the private and public spheres. As for Graham, in 1955 she had volunteered to go to Cambodia, gotten her team through heated areas, and represented the nation as a cultural ambassador with excellence and aplomb in just the region where Nixon was failing, and where America's shaky Asian allies needed the most support.[162]

Although Nixon blamed what he called the world's "leader class" for global unrest, he knew the value of working to draw the allegiances of the elite to America's side: trickle-down diplomacy remained in play. The president understood the power of culture after being overshadowed by the New York Philharmonic years earlier in Latin America. The event had been remembered during congressional hearings in the 1960s, and became cultural lore for proponents of the arts as diplomacy. Henry Kissinger, himself a product of a family of teachers, many of whom perished in the Holocaust, was a potent advocate for cultural diplomacy. Intellectually, Kissinger felt comfortable "plunging into Hegel and Kant and Metternich and Dostoyevsky," despite his lack of interest in American politicians and American literary forebears like author Mark Twain. While assimilating to the United States as a young man, he understood the power of books, radio, and films.[163] Although he preferred not to highlight his Jewish background and the Nazi persecution and murder of his family members, or the ensuing turmoil in his life as his parents emigrated from Germany, Kissinger surely appreciated Martha Graham's anti-Nazi past, as well as her efforts in Berlin in 1957. She knew Asia and the Middle East. The 1950s "cocktail circuit of diplomacy" remained intact, if not central. If not for her crippling illness, Graham would have been an immediate choice for renewed efforts.[164]

As Nixon and Kissinger went to work to open China, Graham's Cold War dance and rhetoric could again converge with the policy and phrases propounded by American leaders. The intelligentsia still remembered Graham in Asia, where she had consistently spoken of "tapping into the hearts" of the people for whom she performed under Eisenhower, who was "competing for the hearts, minds and trust all over the world." In the 1970s, Nixon deployed what he called the "Hearts and Minds" strategy of diplomacy in Asia, language that Kissinger had adopted as well. No matter how "ingenious" foreign policy might be, Kissinger said, "it has no chance of success if it is born of the minds of a few and carried in the hearts of none."[165] A government representative told the Dance Panel that dance remained the second most important export behind music as a nonverbal tool, and thus deployments would be made "based on what we need." In response to violent protest movements internationally against US foreign policy, the government sought to target youth. American cultural propaganda needed to evolve in order to entice young leaders in people-to-people encounters with their carefully chosen, nonviolent American cultural counterparts. Smaller, younger, and less expensive dance companies could have greater appeal. Government representatives limited funding to only one large, established, "historically modern" company each year. Yet among the elite, the administration urgently needed goodwill in Asia.[166]

In 1972, the US government faced a cultural conundrum. Graham was backstage, perhaps sidelined. Among other established modern dance companies, inventory was low. The Judson Church choreographers who had emerged from the Cunningham studio had revolutionized dance and made it once again avant-garde. They advanced the cause of the youth and demonstrated that the United States continued to innovate, but their choreography took place anywhere except a Broadway stage and had included nudity, with a performer wrapped only in the American flag. Such irreverent dance leaders could not be trusted as ambassadors.[167] Thus, these young choreographers were not even discussed by the Dance Panel as potential cultural ambassadors. None of the modern dance alternatives to Graham seemed quite right for a tour of Asia. Merce Cunningham and Paul Taylor were possible exports: both were progeny of Graham. Although Cunningham's choreography proved "unquestionably that the United States is the world leader in modern dance," he did not embrace his role as ambassador at parties. Pictures show him standing in the corner of reception rooms looking past guests, observing them as he might a flock of birds. Cunningham received little funding even after he showed great public success in France.[168] The American embassy in Paris merely offered him $2,000 with the blessing of the State Department.[169] Taylor did not seem to be available. Another choice, the vigorous, even acrobatic choreographer Alwin Nikolais, was "rather elegant" and "awfully good at talking," and thus, like Graham, potentially a persuasive cultural representative. But the Dance Panel considered his work "theatrical gymnastics" rather than dance. Graham had established the depth of her authority in the form with the only modern dance three-act "ballet," *Clytemnestra*; she had created heralded new repertory since 1955, such as *Seraphic Dialogue*; and her established masterpieces, from *Night Journey* to *Diversion of Angels*, were remembered in Asia.[170] No one fit the bill for Asia like Graham.[171] According to the mandate, deployments would be made "based on what we need," and the Americans thought Asia needed modern dance.[172]

Yet financial deficits and internal unrest made the Graham enterprise seem unsustainable to some. Financial problems plagued even the school, which had typically been a source of income.[173] After examining the possibility of funding a tour to the Spoleto Festival in Italy, the Rockefeller Foundation pulled out. In 1971, the president of the Martha Graham Center resigned in response to the financial crisis.[174] The company manager, Leroy Leatherman, worked with star dancers Bertram Ross and Mary Hinkson to save the company. In order to restart, he lobbied the NEA as well as the Rockefeller and Ford Foundations, all of which offered only limited funding. In response, Ross and Hinkson arranged studio showings of works.[175] Leatherman planned to join a collaborative off-Broadway season with other companies such as those run by Twyla Tharp and Lar Lubovitch, new masters in the field, so that a "younger, larger company of dancers" could reinvigorate Graham's work. With this pitch, he wrote to the NEA to ask for funding to rebuild the company.[176] The Ford Foundation considered the idea. Again, the arrangement fell through.[177] After reviewing the company's barren financial statements, the Rockefeller and Ford Foundations pulled out entirely. State Department onlookers took note.[178]

After a two-year hiatus, the Dance Panel met again in 1972, and Henry Kissinger, who would become secretary of state the following year, followed the earlier calls for a "soft sell."[179] An official asked the Dance Panel if the Graham Company was ready.[180] "Not ready yet," replied the member, who then added, "It will be six to nine months before anyone has an opinion."[181] The panel then selected Limón as its modern dance touring company for the 1972–73 season. However, Jose Limón passed away suddenly in December just before the tour was set to begin.[182] Despite the loss of such a towering figure, star dancer Carla Maxwell would lead the company on a successful tour, representing the nation well during press conferences and radio shows.[183] But the fact remained that such tours needed a recognized American innovator as ambassador at the helm.

The question of which company would be sent on the next tour, in 1974, came to the table, yet Graham seemed further and further from government consideration.[184] With Protas at her side, Graham became furious with the new approaches taken by management to save the company. Because she had commanded Broadway seasons for her company that featured her name on the marquee, the informal showings in the studio context, arranged by Ross and Hinkson, violated Graham's mandate to maintain the company's high-art reputation. Regarding Leatherman's desire to include Graham repertory in evenings of shared programs, she declared, "I never share a stage" (in fact, between 1930 and 1955, she had participated in several joint concerts).[185] She announced to some members of the board that Leatherman would be leaving without having ever informed him. When he discovered that some people thought he had been fired, Leatherman followed with a memo defending his actions, writing, "None of us here imagines that during those years we have not made mistakes."[186] Despite Graham's furious objections, Leatherman's work had helped keep the company afloat. But under Graham's unrelenting assault, he resigned.[187] After Leatherman's departure, Ross served as acting manager and artistic director, but his position was doomed because of his contentious relationship with Protas.[188] When Ross resigned, Hinkson followed. The Woman in White saw red and walked out with him. The drama made the press: the *New York Times* reported that before Hinkson left, she "threw a dagger" at Graham—in fact, the "dagger" was a papier mâché prop for *Clytemnestra*, and Hinkson merely slammed it on a Noguchi bench in a rehearsal studio in a moment of frustration with Graham's demands.[189] Ross wrote Graham that Protas had "caused the leaving of a great many other loyal, devoted, competent, talented employees." Graham, as usual, remained silent. A *New York Post* article announced that the NEA was seeking a federal audit of Graham's books. Graham accused Ross of feeding information to the *Post* and hired a lawyer to demand that he cease and desist. The *New York Post* declared in a headline "A New Boss—and Dance Company Is Out of Step."[190] For many onlookers, the company seemed in no shape to tour.

Yet even with turnover and uproar, Graham remained a viable property, with Protas pushing opportunities and government still offering support. Former donor Bethsabée de Rothschild had slowly tapered off donations. While she remained on the board, her passion for dance now focused distinctly on Israel.[191] Lila Acheson Wallace had made significant investments in the company, but she did not match the early largesse of Rothschild. Yet government recognition brought a turnaround, surely inspired by Protas's letter-writing campaigns to public officials. In 1973, New York governor Nelson Rockefeller, the ardent supporter of government dance projects as cultural diplomacy in the interwar years, presided over a committee that granted Graham the New York State Council on the Arts Award. Graham was celebrated for her "original" yet also "enduring" contribution to the arts. Presumably to Graham's dismay, the honor framed her as a matriarch and not a cutting-edge artist.[192] Protas remained determined to depose the old guard and to position Graham as an icon of modern dance. She would take a position on her vaunted center stage—sitting in a director's chair like a throne.

In addition, her dancers were increasingly strong. For New York performances and touring, a group of magnificent dancers could be assembled and readied for work because the Graham technique thrived as a part of the academic canon. Dance Panel member Martha Hill had developed a rigorous curriculum at the Juilliard School, and dancers both domestically and internationally supplemented their Graham technique with ballet in schools from Tel Aviv and London to Tokyo. Dancers' bodies grew leaner, sleeker, and as airborne as Merce Cunningham had ever been. A young and technically exalted set of dancers assembled around Graham. Students played before class, spinning on a single hip bone to show off their skills. In the classrooms, legs extended higher, jumps flew into space, spines grew suppler, and single turns turned into doubles. Although the old guard complained that the weight was gone, that the dancers did not understand the power of bare feet hitting floor, that the legs were too high, that the breath formed shallow hollows, Graham could produce her now canonical repertory with dancers who would bring to it an even greater technical prowess.

Despite the *Post*'s declarations and notwithstanding complaints by historical critics of modern dance, the *New York Times* continued to support the company, and the government listened as it continued to look for a touring company for Asia. An April 1973 article in the *Times*, "The Monumental Martha," outlined Graham's career, celebrated her previous work, mentioned an upcoming tour, and noted her use of "Eastern" forms, which allied with government touring aims for old-fashioned modernist cultural convergences. Although Graham herself could no longer perform, she had firmly reemerged as the "Madame" and "Great Lady" of dance, as the *Times* called her. She had published her notebooks, which established the

longevity and brilliance of her work. Graham's established international sophistication and grace could remind leaders in Asia that the United States
remained a powerful yet nuanced and open-minded force. "Welcome back,"
the New York Times concluded.[193]

That same year, President Nixon offered Graham the Presidential Medal
of Freedom; ever savvy, she graciously refused it. Graham privately wrote to
Mason that she worried about corruption in the Nixon administration per-
petuated by Vice President Spiro Agnew. While Graham did not mention
Nixon himself to Mason in her letter, the Watergate scandal was breaking,
with congressional hearings and an independent prosecutor investigating
the June 1972 break-in at the Democratic National Committee offices and
whether the president was involved in the cover-up.[194] Agnew was charged
with extortion, bribery, and tax evasion, and he resigned in October 1973.
Graham well understood that if she accepted the award from Nixon, any
photo of the event would forever show her standing with him.[195]

In the mix, Mason alerted the Dance Panel that Graham was ready to take
the 1974 slot.[196] The CPC said that it wanted "the promise of trained, disciplined American youth working alongside the sophistication of its elders."[197]
With her dancers, Graham as Picasso and "God" could convey just this image.
And Asia was where the State Department and American embassies felt she
could most benefit the United States. Indeed, a request for funding from an
Asian post gushed, "Why a dance company?: Because the majority of Asian
posts have advised that modern dance is their first priority in the field of cultural presentations." Graham could again conquer the region where nearly
twenty years earlier she had been showered with flowers and celebrated with
fireworks. Because Mason had once warned of impending trouble, which
had come to pass with the oddly received 1967 tour, his vote carried weight
and credibility. Before the Dance Panel could meet to officially approve or
deny Graham tour funding, the State Department "locked in" Graham for
the 1974 tour.

As a "rescue mission" to enable a State Department tour, Graham secured
an NEA grant. Government agencies tied to commerce chipped in, as did
Reader's Digest and the ever-loyal Lila Acheson Wallace. Donations came
from heiress Doris Duke. Overseas posts in the field offered additional
funding; career cultural officers remembered her grandeur, glamour, and
Americanized sophistication that had played well in Asia. Nonetheless, other
government operatives remained wary of the Graham company management

and its shaky finances. The tour contract was sent directly to Mason—who had joined Graham's board—rather than to Protas, the more logical person from a day-to-day operational standpoint.[198]

In May 1974, the Martha Graham Dance Company reemerged on the domestic scene with a celebrated season in New York; the choreographer and charismatic star became the matriarch of a dazzling troupe ready to fight the next phase of the Cold War with an anticommunist message in Asia. Graham herself triumphed as a leader who took center stage, even if she was not dancing. In its review of the season, the *New York Times* emphasized both the youth and the timelessness of Graham's group and choreography: "Whatever it is, we all find Martha when we are young, and are best able to find her again when we are at our purest."[199] The reviewer noted that "the company has done good business, particularly, significantly enough, with the young audience."[200]

In addition, Cold War politics took "center stage": the renowned ballet dancer Rudolf Nureyev, who had defected from the Soviet Union in 1961, performed with the company, leading the *Times* to declare he "left the rusty artistic chains of Soviet Russia to find the freedom to breathe and the freedom to create [with Graham]."[201] In June, the resonance of Graham's work with Nureyev took on even greater import when the Soviet dancer Mikhail Baryshnikov defected in Canada. After working with Nureyev, Graham set her sights on working with Baryshnikov, who, like her male dancer Merce Cunningham as The Preacher in 1944, was known for his fantastic feats in the air. She could free the Soviet body.

Just months after the acclaimed season, the *New York Times* announced that Graham would lead her company on a State Department tour; the article opened with a discussion of Saigon. No American company had performed in the South Vietnamese capital since 1966, but Graham was headed for this contested region. The *Times* closed by noting that she was just returning from Israel, where she had created a new work for Batsheva.[202] The woman had risen like a phoenix from the ashes of modernism into an icon of America, however compromised by wars in the Middle East and Vietnam.

Just under three weeks before Graham was to leave on tour, President Nixon resigned, done in by the Watergate scandal. Graham's political instincts paid off well; she had worked with Washington without being shown beside the president. The *New York Times* the next morning brought her more good news on the front page. Along with "Ford Will Take Office Today," she could read underneath in smaller block letters, "Kissinger to Remain."[203] She remembered that Ford's wife, Betty, had been her student in New York before she had married—a political windfall for Graham. She was making her comeback, and now, potentially, with fresh attention and support from the White House.[204] Her connections at the State Department remained intact. Betty Ford was the new first lady. The future was set.

6

"Forever Modern"

From Ashes to Ambassador in Asia, 1974

On a warm summer day in August 1974, Martha Graham watched as Gerald R. Ford was sworn in as the thirty-eighth president of the United States. "My fellow Americans, our long national nightmare is over," the new president declared.[1] For Graham, having Ford in the White House and Henry Kissinger at the State Department promised to be a dream come true. The new first lady, Betty Bloomer Ford, had been Graham's student and performed with the company in her youth; Kissinger supported Graham's upcoming tour.[2] While Kissinger has been heralded for his power as a statesman and master of networks, often forgotten—except with the occasional scandal—was his ability to network with theatrical stars, particularly women.[3] Graham became a political bond in a moment of triage. Such an alliance could bring "decency" back to the White House in a propaganda move of redemption relying on a tested ambassador for freedom, truth, and democracy.

Ford entered the White House as the country's first unelected president, having been its first unelected vice president. His credibility as an international leader was at best untested. When it came to cultural diplomacy, his Midwestern upbringing and penchant for American football and golf did not suggest that he would command a sophisticated presence. Numerous cartoons immediately featured Ford with an oversized head running with a football as he tried to score yardage on global issues, or using a golfing iron to "putt" at problems.[4] As for the first lady, within hours of her husband's swearing-in, presidential aides debated how to frame her. Given her background as a Midwesterner, despite her years in New York as a model and dancer, she should shop at "middle class" department stores. With her history of teaching Sunday school and belief in equal rights, she should focus on "religion," "the blacks," and even "retarded children" to frame the West Wing.[5] Mentioned last: the arts. Betty needed her own friends, and remembered Graham fondly.

Martha Graham's Cold War. Victoria Phillips, Oxford University Press 2020. © Oxford University Press.
DOI: 10.1093/oso/9780190610364.001.0001

To counter some in the State Department who were dubious about Graham's foray into Asia on the heels of Nixon's resignation, and to soothe her East Wing White House staff, Betty Ford called Graham with words of support for the upcoming tour. The *New York Times* quickly celebrated Graham's connection to Ford, noting, "Miss Graham, who will leave with her company on August 22 on a two-month State Department tour of Asia, said she was especially pleased to be going on a Government-sponsored tour now that Mrs. Ford was the wife of the President."[6] Jumping at the opportunity, USIS repeatedly mentioned Ford's telephone calls in press releases sent to host countries.[7] Graham would arrive in Asia as the "First Lady" of American modern dance. Although her 1974 tour of Asia had been planned under Nixon, Graham "chirped" with Betty when discussing her previous encounters with the White House: "[The Nixon era] was a dreary time. A vicious time. I couldn't come here then."[8] While the connection between Graham and the Fords worked propaganda wonders to eliminate Nixon's White House legacy, it could also fray the facade that hers was an apolitical tour.

Just days before the company departed, Ron Protas wrote a letter to Betty Ford marked "Very Personal" and continued to use Graham's ability to fight the Cold War in his pleas for money. He referenced the first lady's supportive phone call to Graham regarding the upcoming tour to Asia and began planting seeds for his next fundraising initiative by noting that Graham had been facing "a rather gloomy afternoon" before the call because she was "facing financial and other matters." Protas described elaborate plans for the school, the company, and Graham. At the school, the dance curriculum would include ballet classes taught by ballet star Tanaquil le Clerq, Balanchine's former wife, and Margot Fonteyn, the famed British ballerina whose long career had been revitalized by her partnership with Rudolf Nureyev.[9] But, Protas warned, "unless our financial state improves we may not be able to [keep] open the school."[10] Protas pressed forward to describe future choreographic plans that could bring the first lady closer to dance's elite, and former Communists to Americana: "Martha has been hard at work putting together a version of 'The Scarlett [sic] Letter'; this would be the work Nureyev would do with her; although he has expressed an interest in doing the husbandman in 'Appalachian Spring.'" Nathaniel Hawthorne's *Scarlet Letter*, considered a masterpiece and set in seventeenth-century Puritan Massachusetts Bay Colony, made a perfect match for the Soviet defector who had renounced his citizenship because of a desire for artistic freedom. The moral allegory inspired by the Puritans, the red mark of the individual represented by a letter or an insignia, with a Russian at the helm of the drama, would show the time-less universality of Americana. *The Scarlet Letter* would reunite the creative team behind *Appalachian Spring*: both composer Aaron Copland and set de-signer Isamu Noguchi were on board to work with Graham, Protas assured the first lady (in fact, they were not). Protas continued, milking Graham's star power, "Margot as well wants to do a Graham piece." He concluded, "Well, the decision is in the lap of the Gods and Martha's Irish tongue," and prom-ised to keep Ford apprised of future developments. From a gloomy August day in the midst of financial doom, Protas painted a picture of future pros-perity for the tradition of Americana in dance with a Soviet defector in tow—if only Graham could receive the support she needed.[11]

As always, Graham's pre-tour New York season reviews served as fodder for USIS publicity abroad, which highlighted the youth and diversity of the troupe: "Martha Graham attracts world's young dancers." The multifac-eted company was "not unlike a mini United Nations," said one reviewer, repeating what Graham had said in Finland a decade earlier.[12] Graham not only featured African Americans but also brought Asian and Asian American dancers back to their forebears' homelands to dance the classical American modern dance masterpieces they had premiered in New York. The *New York Times* raved, "With the stunning debut of Takako Asakawa in Martha Graham's original 'Clytemnestra,' Miss Graham's full-length master-piece, the Graham Dance Company has entered into a new historic phase." According to the State Department, Graham provided something "gloriously made to order: high level and yet still associated with the youth."[13]

Before Graham left, USIS distributed a posed picture of Graham side by side with Rudolf Nureyev, along with the announcement that she would cho-reograph a new piece for the former Soviet as he continued to seek creative freedom in the West. Graham had the first lady and the secretary of state. She had a defector. She had a youthful company to represent a new post-Nixon America.

* * *

"A principal objective of the Graham visit is political," declared a State Department official. "Or politico-cultural," he then corrected himself.[14] Under the terms of the contract, Graham would begin in South Korea and then travel to Taiwan, Hong Kong, the Philippines, Indonesia, Singapore, Malaysia, Thailand, Burma, and South Vietnam.[15] She would also return to Japan, but since she was popular there, box office receipts would pay her way. The itinerary reflected Nixon and Kissinger's desire to soothe any mayhem regarding their desire to open China to the West, and their "one-China policy," which entailed recognizing the People's Republic of China and acknowledging Taiwan as a part of China, while also maintaining relations with Taiwan as a separate entity. Although Graham had retired, she remained "center stage" at arrivals and curtain calls, embassy parties, publicity shots, and lecture-demonstrations, which diplomats now referred to as "one of the great solo acts of the American theater."[16]

Cultural exchange with China under President Nixon had begun in 1971 with "ping-pong diplomacy," when nine American ping-pong players, two spouses, and several officials traveled from Hong Kong to mainland China. Although Chinese athletes had been allowed to travel abroad, no official US delegations had been invited into the country since 1949. The American athletes toured China and attended a Chinese ballet, acting in effect as diplomats beginning the process of opening relations between the two countries. Kissinger called the trip an "international sensation."[17] When Nixon himself visited China the following February, he saw the ballet *The Red Detachment of Women*, which included female ballerinas in battle fatigues brandishing guns, yet wearing European pointe shoes.[18] While initially dubious, Nixon ultimately appreciated the work and was reminded of the political power of women and dance.[19] Graham's female heroines, dancing barefoot while they expressed "the soul of mankind," could enact a cultural counterattack on the violent socialist Chinese ballet.

After landing in South Korea and proceeding to Taiwan and Hong Kong, Graham would proceed to the Philippines, Indonesia, Singapore, Malaysia, Thailand, and Burma, all countries where her company had performed in 1955–56. In the Philippines, Ferdinand Marcos, the president since 1965, had declared martial law in response to arms shipments to communist rebels and unrest. He curtailed press freedom, limited civil liberties, abolished the Philippine Congress, and ruled as a dictator. Opponents were arrested, killed, and disappeared.[20] Yet the Nixon administration had quietly supported Marcos, who had allowed the United States to use the Philippines for military bases.[21] Indonesia had been home to the largest Communist party outside China and the Soviet Union in 1965, but an anticommunist backlash after an attempted coup warmed relations with the West. In 1970, the increasingly pro-Western Indonesian president Suharto and his wife visited Disneyland as a guest of the State Department. According to the press, he was particularly impressed by the "America the Beautiful" exhibit. Following empire by invitation and soft-power initiatives, the Indonesian first lady decided to build a theme park in Jakarta, where Graham had performed in the 1950s and would land again under Nixon's State Department.[22] Other nations provided hope for the success of cultural Americanization; Graham would have been remembered by audiences from the earlier tour to Singapore, and was thus perhaps less threatening than a new entrant. In Malaysia, despite the restoration of democratic government, there was deep racial strife, poverty, and crisis. Thailand had been drawn into an alliance with the West and had been westernized by the Vietnam War. Dollars and American goods flooded the economy, and prostitution and drug abuse soared with US soldiers spending their leaves from Vietnam in Bangkok. Despite a ban on political meetings, student protests had begun in 1968 and were increasing over time. Relations with Burma had changed, and it had had no cultural exchange with the United States in twelve years. In 1962, a coup d'état had installed socialist leader General Ne Win, who was an isolationist; the Ford Foundation, Asia Society, and Fulbright fellows had been ordered to depart, and the US government had put a ban on future exchange programs.[23] The general's nominal retirement and, more important, his known fondness for things associated with the West—a result, in part, of a trip to London—left a small opening for exchange as the Graham tour was planned.[24] In all cases, the US government continued to battle the Communists, both the Chinese and the Soviets, while pursuing detente. Graham had been known to soothe relations where Nixon had inflamed crowds, and she brought the cultural sophistication that the golfing and former college football player president could not pull off.[25]

In a new political twist, the company would close the State Department tour in Saigon, South Vietnam. Although the United States had an increased military presence in Vietnam since the French left in 1954, the late 1960s would see a heavy escalation of US involvement, with the 1968 Tet Offensive, a battle named for the Vietnamese New Year, a major turning point. When it began, the North Vietnamese attack led to months of casualty-laden fighting. News photos appeared in the United States of the effects of chemical weapons in Vietnam, including Agent Orange, which burned the skin off children, and napalm, an incendiary gel that stuck to skin and burned to the bone. Journalists used television cameras to show jungle warfare as well as plastic body bags containing the corpses of some of the fifty thousand American soldiers.[26] Protests in the United States erupted, some violent. The Pentagon Papers, released in 1971, detailed a long series of public deceptions from the

Johnson and Nixon administrations. Although the Paris Peace Accords had been signed in 1973, fighting continued. A cultural attaché in Vietnam felt that cultural exports such as Graham might "give some balance to the overwhelming military presence especially in the wake of the Tet Offensive."[27]

At the end of the State Department tour, the Graham company would return to Japan, where Graham's government travels had started in 1955. Nearly twenty years later, Japan was deemed safe from any Communist threat, and Graham's work had become popular among the intelligentsia and the dance community. She had known Japanese stars performing in her iconic works. Japanese dancers who had gone on to train with Graham in the United States would return to Japan as stars in their home country, performing Graham's roles and showcasing an inclusive and internationalist America. Although the State Department did not fund this final leg of the tour, embassy memos about the tour start dispatched to "All Posts" included Tokyo.

* * *

The repertory was well planned to meet past expectations with modernist classics, yet also show how Graham remained relevant. Graham resurrected old works and choreographed new pieces, which were emphasized to meet specific diplomatic aims. The State Department asked Graham to provide the Office of Cultural Presentations (OCP) with "at least three different dance programs for approval," and then reviewed the list of available works in consultation with officers on the ground.[28] *Diversion of Angels* and myth-based works led the roster: "These various themes have been drawn upon by Martha Graham with great imagination to explore and express choreographically a wide spectrum of human emotions." *Night Journey, Cave of the Heart,* and *Errand into the Maze,* which used the Japanese American Isamu Noguchi's sets, Asian dancers, and the stories of classic mythology, fused the Western canon with Asian influences. Graham echoed the government's desire for humanity to shine through, declaring, "Mankind has been my inspiration."[29]

Americana would again demonstrate the power of the global archetypes that represented the United States and the power of freedom with *Appalachian Spring.* It reinforced what Graham had demonstrated under Eisenhower— that only the freedom offered by capitalistic democracy could develop a language that spoke to "the soul of mankind" or "the hearts and minds" through high-art archetypes. According to the State Department, the Graham company "illustrated in the most dramatic form possible the image of America."[30]

Americana had led programs on the 1955 Asia tour, but now because of American violence in the region, it had to be advertised less as a product of the frontier and more as a metaphor. Of *Appalachian Spring*, Graham had said on earlier tours, "You choose a piece of land; part of the house goes up. You dedicate it." *Appalachian Spring*, to Graham, was "essentially a dance of place." In 1974, by contrast, she would declare that it was "everyone's frontier," explaining, "It is not a frontier you can find on an atlas."[31] In 1955, the program in India had listed the credits across from a line drawing of George Washington looking west, suggesting a notion of American freedom and the possibilities of decolonization; in 1974, the page in the program opposite *Appalachian Spring*'s cast and crew merely described the next work to be performed. Whereas the biographical descriptions of Graham's life in 1955 emphasized her mother's tenth-generation ties to the *Mayflower*, the 1974 program dropped any mention of her heritage.

The character descriptions followed suit. In 1955 publicity, the Bride joined the men as an archetype; she embodied the struggle for freedom and the democratic right to build a new life, and just happened to be American and female. Now, the Bride merely represented "a bride or a mother-to-be," not a pioneer of manifest destiny. Regarding the frontier Husbandman, she reminded the audience of American scientific prowess via the NASA moon shot: the figure now could be "an astronaut or a scientist."[32]

Adhering to government wishes, the 1974 repertory plan also emphasized "religious themes," as in 1962. Although *Seraphic Dialogue* had been performed in 1955, religious works were given more promotional emphasis to reinforce a connection among American morality, human rights, "the soul," and the power of redemption—needed now considering the continuing news of past American atrocities in Vietnam. In addition, the power brokers in Vietnam with whom Graham would be mingling at embassy parties were largely Catholic converts. She brought *Embattled Garden*, the story of Adam and Eve. *El Penitente*, a trio about the Penitents sect in the American Southwest and its rites of purification, reflected her belief that people should be allowed to practice all religions.[33] USIS advertised *El Penitente* as another part of the American spectrum, both in the composition of its population and its religious character. It depicted a sect whose flagellant believers re-enacted the Passion of Jesus Christ at Easter. Graham had created *El Penitente* displaying an American ethnic and religious diversity not present in *Frontier* or *Appalachian Spring* (except in casting).[34] However, Graham remained "apolitical" in her religiosity, however prominently she featured Joan of Arc alongside Eve, the Virgin Mary, and the Preacher of *Appalachian Spring*.[35] As usual, she said that she wanted to "portray the soul's yearning," to reveal "the expression of man, the landscape of his soul."[36] During press conferences on this 1974 tour, Graham would profess her belief in God, although, as a denominationally neutral Cold War ambassador, she noted that she did not go to church.[37] "I am not a missionary," she would repeatedly state.[38] Graham sought to make her message universal and not tied to Christianity.[39]

Although Graham had employed eroticism in order to assert the cutting-edge nature of her work, she could not use that tactic in Asia. Graham's tour paralleled both the promise and the unrest that defined the United States in 1974 and had earned the country the title "Nervous Breakdown Nation."[40] While the new ABC network television comedy *Happy Days* brought an idealized 1950s into living rooms across America, student protesters burned the American flag, and oil prices sent the economy into a tailspin. The previous spring, heiress Patty Hearst was kidnapped in her gauzy 1950s nightgown and then photographed in combat fatigues brandishing a sawed-off M1 carbine in a bank holdup by the radical extremist group the Symbionese Liberation Army.[41] Even everyday clothing styles were in conflict. Graham's dancers toured wearing Cold War fashions, still replete with Mamie Eisenhower–like white gloves, yet they were thronged in airports by crowds expecting hip-looking dancers in blue jeans and beards. Graham would never allow such casual looks; even in hotel elevators or moving from room to room on the same floor, her women were to wear skirts and respectable shoes. Barbers were readied in case Graham's men might arrive with too much hair.

The *Phaedra* scandal and the current prevailing expectation that Americans would look like hippies had brought new attention to the issue of American depravity by domestic arbiters of taste. The CPC Dance Panel strongly discouraged explicit works: "exploitation," "flirtation with the audience," and "overdone" sexuality became taboo. Especially in Burma, but also elsewhere on tour, the company would have to stage dress rehearsals of all the works for local censors. Memos from the State Department expressed concern about the long hair of some of Graham's male dancers: it might make Asian audiences and Americans at diplomatic posts "wince." The government requested individual pictures of each dancer so that their appearance could be vetted. In Singapore, "unmarried" men and women sharing hotel rooms could be explained in a memo, but the practice would not be tolerated in Taipei, the Taiwanese capital, "although such living arrangements are fairly common among artists." Of particular note were "two men" whose accommodations needed to be separated. Ironically, given the sexual revolution in the United States, Martha Graham would have to be more delicately diplomatic than ever before as she hit closeted nations.[42]

USIS adopted one-size-fits-all company materials. Regional versions that USIS had used to fit local needs in 1955 were replaced by a single basic program featuring an unattributed black-and-white image of Graham's shadow. No matter the nation, the program covers featured Graham as a black-and-white silhouette perched on a stool.[43] USIS wrote that neither "age, nor change of country nor condition" could alter Graham's work.[44] However, publicity molded the elements of her image and choreography to reflect the changes in her persona and the way the dances were perceived in a new era— from modern dance revolutionary to classical matriarch.[45]

* * *

The company's first stop was supposed to be South Korea, but just as in 1955, the performances were canceled suddenly. On August 15, people had gathered in Seoul's National Theater, where Graham was to perform later that month, to witness President Park Chung-hee commemorate the anniversary of Korea's independence from Japan. He began his speech at the podium, with his wife, Yuk Young-soo, seated near him onstage, wearing her traditional ceremonial robe, her jet-black hair set in a halo around her head. A North Korean agent of Japanese descent rose from an orchestra seat brandishing a Japanese-made gun. He fired. The president ducked, a bodyguard opened fire from the stage, and a bullet hit the first lady. The audience watched as the woman fell. Later, angry South Koreans protested outside the Japanese embassy, screaming insults. The theater was closed and would not reopen for Graham. The geography of Graham's government tour remained precarious and unstable.[46]

Yet Graham took to the tarmac stage. "It is a great privilege to go back to Asia," she proclaimed. Still politically savvy, she added, "I know the Asia I will now see will be different." She understood the complexities of the war in Vietnam and the changed perspective toward America that she would face after an absence of almost twenty years.[47] After closing in Taipei, the company moved to Hong Kong in early September, and Graham's works brought politics directly into the dance. Neither representatives of the United States nor the pro-Communist press found the performances to be an unmitigated success. Hong Kong brought "triumph," and even some Communist reviewers had good words to say about Graham, contrasting her technique with the "bourgeois undercurrents" of ballet. However, not everyone was sanguine. A memo to Washington noted that works appeared "totally strange" to the audience and that applause petered out before the curtain descended. At the prompting of USIS for some culturally empathetic coverage, a local reporter explained to readers the characteristics that Chinese dance shared with American modern dance. Shooting back at this assumption, a reporter from a Chinese-language newspaper compared Graham unfavorably to Chinese modern dance; the Chinese form celebrated the masses, the journalist wrote, while American modernism was "directed by individual taste."[48]

As had been the case with Isadora Duncan in Russia, Wigman-inspired leftist dance movements in the 1930s, and dance movements in the 1950s in India and pre-Rothschild Israel, while freedom of expression suited the tenets of protest works, the centrality of the individual in a "free dance" did not support Marxist creeds. The paradox of modern dance as a statement of freedom of expression by the individual met with resistance when local audiences used the American form to protest against capitalism and the United States as a hot war hegemon. A politicized message embodied in an individual's holding of "center stage" sacrificed the power of group action.

As the tour progressed, the company seemed to be falling apart, which certainly would have been a fear given the reports on Graham from the 1960s. "Deeply regret that during first two weeks of tour immediate problems involving company is [sic] poor management, disorganization and inadequate pre-trip organization plus continuous logistics difficulties," noted a memo.[49] The matriarch herself was different as a purely diplomatic performer, and so was her dance company. Despite her "phoenix-like" recovery, government officers described her as "aged, fragile, ailing and crippled." Her powerful and youthful company was also raw and inexperienced in the politics and protocols of touring for the government. Infighting was notorious in the realm of Martha Graham; indeed, some in the company seemed to gain energy from internecine drama, as Graham had herself in her earlier years. Nonetheless, a State Department memo noted that the company members had the "discipline and taste" not to reveal internal dissent in public. To the outside onlooker, the company members were "representative of the youth of America" at their best, and "Madame herself a great lady, consummate actress/ artist of grace, poise and charm."[50] They persevered, as Graham always had.

Before Graham's arrival in the Philippines, American cultural officials there contacted the American embassy and asked for *Appalachian Spring* to be removed from the repertory. Despite changes in publicity to camouflage its pro-frontier, manifest destiny–based Americana, they feared the work would meet local backlash. The US embassy in Manila cabled the State Department, copying all posts where Graham would tour, demanding that if it had to remain in the repertory, it should only be performed at the Folk Arts Theatre. Nonetheless, the work remained in the repertoire. Such reactions did not bode well for the Americanist message. One writer complained that *Appalachian Spring* showed no joy or freedom and that the dancers' "self-conscious" and "neurotic" expressions crippled any sense of spontaneity. Another critic called it a "Surrealist fence act." A cable shot back defenses of the work. "Sophisticated audiences," USIS claimed, "would see beyond the fence." Some Americans disagreed: even for some sophisticates, the aging dramatics of Americana made Graham seem like an "old silent movie director."[51]

Despite the conflict around *Appalachian Spring* and management, Graham was paraded in the Philippines in the press and among pro-American dignitaries as a star when she was able. A cable back to the United States reported that the gala opening in Manila was attended by a "throng of notables," including President Marcos and his wife, ambassadors, cabinet members, and the diplomatic corps. "All three performances drew standing ovations and showers of confetti and flowers from adoring crowds," it continued. USIS knew how to work the modern world: aside from "daily announcements" in radio programming and print press, it used television. In Manila, Takako Asakawa, a star dancer, appeared on a popular TV talk show.[52] Pro-Western politicians embraced Graham: backstage, President Marcos congratulated Martha Graham, saying of *Appalachian Spring*, "That was excellent."[53]

Because of Graham's cultural impact, the State Department forgave the turmoil and conflict that beset the company early in the tour. While they were in Manila, the embassy tried to prevent Protas from speaking at a press conference and warned the Singapore embassy in a memo marked "Immediate" that it might be impossible to keep him from taking the mic. "Weak, erratic" company organization, direction, and management threatened to cause cancellations. A handwritten memo described allegations that the company manager had embezzled funds. Despite public displays of Graham-inspired protocol, when Protas had to eat in a hotel dining room with the company members and crew, "unpleasant confrontations" took place. He proved "the most burdensome, annoying, and time consuming" individual.[54] However, because of the vital role he served in supporting Graham personally, there seemed to be no way around him. Graham's absence from portions of the tour locations and performances only exacerbated matters. Whenever Graham was ill, company management revealed its lack of sophistication regarding local customs.[55] On days when she could not lead the troupe, "the company failed."[56]

While the Indonesian stop did not generate much press, the embassy in Jakarta was pleased that the Indonesian director of trade hosted a luncheon for Graham. She could influence those who would be making key economic decisions that would directly affect the United States. In turn, the American ambassador hosted a much-welcomed pool party for Graham and her dancers in the heat of early fall just before they left.[57]

In Singapore, USIS wrote a carefully worded and fact-specific report on the trials of the matriarch and the company: "Graham, with her crippled hands, is having trouble dressing, packing, and unpacking, etc." The memo asserted that audiences did not appreciate the works on opening night and that the company received "patted," or tepid, applause. Yet quoting the *Straits Times*, USIS reported to Washington that audiences appreciated the "brilliant and dynamic group of dancers," who made a "tremendous and unforgettable impact on all present." The lectures for local ballet teachers also made a strong impression: "The highly effective workshop was a display of the venerable Miss Graham at her most dynamic," and a "dazzling display of energy and insights that had even her own dancers impressed." USIS noted that the company's "final performance" met applause and had been appreciated by the "target population." Yet as in West Berlin in 1957, the performances were perceived as an elitist event: "Too many people came to be seen—rather than to see."[58] Graham was thus noted for her performance at the ambassador's reception: "Most important effect of visit was valuable assist in dispelling prevailing attitudes of American culture having little worth."[59]

After relative silence from Malaysia, in Thailand, Graham's company received strong advance press and many accolades, but not all in the audience were impressed by the performances themselves. In addition, management troubles accelerated, and the company's associate artistic director went "AWOL," according to an unnamed source in a handwritten memo, requiring that Graham attend all rehearsals and make all decisions alone. Yet Rick Grossman, an American reporter for a Bangkok paper, fulfilled USIS's hopes by announcing, "Miss Graham Never Fails to Astound." According to another journalist, *Seraphic Dialogue*'s depiction of the Catholic Joan showed a "universal dance language" that everyone in the audience understood. *El Penitente* also showed a "universal dance language" that had been "clearly understood by everyone in the audience."[60] However, in an article titled "Too Self Conscious," another local writer critiqued the company's biblical works, saying that if *Embattled Garden* was about Adam and Eve, it was news to him, and that he "was not very clear about the moral or purpose" of the performances writ large. For some, the Old Testament work seemed to carry no weight as an allegory of morality, let alone as Graham's "map of the human heart."[61]

Despite the mixed reviews of performances, the US embassy noted the political import of the presentation: "Royal command opening performance at National Theater Attended by His Majesty the King, Queen Ramphai Barni and other royalty was a sparkling success." During the second intermission, Ambassador William Kintner, a Ford appointee who was a staunch anticommunist and prolific author, escorted Graham alongside his wife to "the Royal Reception Room for [a] special audience with the King."[62] Graham wooed the elite with her persona; she remained center stage with kings and diplomats.

In Burma, Graham grew ill with bronchitis; Washington agreed with suggestions that she fly ahead to Tokyo with Ron Protas, thus skipping the performances in Saigon.[63] She had fulfilled her mission by showing up: a telegram from the embassy in Rangoon, Burma, asked that Graham's appearance be scheduled to preempt appearances by a Soviet dance troupe.[64] To further counter the Soviets, the CPC had recommended calling all dances "ballets," believing that the international public would have a better frame of reference and still understand that the American choreography was not "steeped in nineteenth-century tradition" but instead "innovative and contemporary."[65] Graham announced that she had not "rebelled" against ballet, but rather "used it." "She builds on it," one reporter added.[66] This framing of Graham's work painted her as a creative innovator who could expand upon the European-derived form without being bound to it like the Soviets. Distributed glossies of Graham with the Soviet ballet defector buttressed the idea with an image.

Before leaving the United States, Graham had expressed concern to the State Department about the political situation in Vietnam. Some observers claim that she did not go to Saigon because of these contested positions on the American involvement in Vietnam. Yet Graham was politically savvy, and clearly chose to take her company to the region where Washington needed political help.[67] She was frail, and Tokyo would bring experienced medical help to her immediately.

However, Graham's fears for her company proved prescient. There was a "sense of mounting crisis" on the political, economic, and military front, and the embassy representative said, "So having this ballet coming to appear, we thought it was a token of American support, of the American president, for the Republic of Vietnam."[68] Yet Vietnamese government vehicles stopped the company as it was traveling from the airport into downtown Saigon after the plane had landed in darkness. Armed officials searched under their cars and demanded that each dancer show papers. Shaken, they were allowed to proceed to the hotel. No other incidents occurred. In a moment of irony, a handwritten letter from Washington to Saigon noted, "After that, everything came up roses."[69]

Graham achieved what the State Department hungered for in Vietnam and in the tour overall: the seduction of Asian power brokers and perhaps some of the local youth to the American side. The elites at opening night in Saigon, including the South Vietnamese first lady herself, all "warmly applauded" for *Night Journey* and *Seraphic Dialogue*. Unexpectedly, the lay public also responded favorably. The walls of the backstage of the theater were made of heavy grates that allowed the uninvited to observe the performance if they scaled the iron. They shouted during *Diversion of Angels*: the mass celebration included cheering and banging on the metal grids in response to onstage falls, jumps, tilts, and contracted torsos. Dancers did not know whether to perform to the staid elite in the front, in their plush chairs, or to the enthusiastic crowds outdoors off to the sides, in the wings.[70]

While political realities preoccupied some of the country's anti-American elites in the audience and the press, Graham worked for some. Several Vietnamese politicians who had attended the performance did not attend the postperformance reception at the embassy because of what the press called "friction over Vietnamese issues." The party became limited to the Graham company and a smattering of diplomats; even the press did not attend.[71] The next day, observing a lecture-demonstration and taking a Graham class, a group of young Vietnamese seemed deeply impressed and inspired by the American way. "The Martha Graham Dance Group has sown the seeds of modern dance in Vietnam, which, of course, will reap brilliant results in the future," one local newspaper reported.[72] Old-fashioned empire by invitation seemed relevant, if only for the moment.

Yet other reporters saw through the propaganda unleashed by USIS proclaiming that Graham was an avatar of a sophisticated, humanistic America. In "Poor Clown, Light Actress," an article in *Tien Tuyen*, a daily printed by the South Vietnamese army and Information Service for both soldiers and civilians, the writer demanded to know whether the choreography was propaganda "aimed at promoting the Gospel." Backfiring, the religious works appeared to this writer to portray the American cause as proselytizing, particularly given the politico-religious legacy of Christianity in Vietnam as an imperialist project, and one that predated American imperialist interventions. The reference to the French warrior Joan of Arc as an anti-imperialist saint may also not have read well, given the country's long history of French colonization.[73] The author continued, "Does [the dance] have other missions, other than touring the world?" The acrid odor of propaganda was in the air.

USIS called a press conference in order to "dispel the suspicious atmosphere," another move that backfired. Graham herself was not present to respond to her critics or explain her dances. She became a symbol of an invisible imperialism that brought devastation, just as the military kind had. Reporters tied Graham to politics and used USIS publicity against the United States itself. If Graham had trained President Ford's wife, Betty Ford, then Graham must be connected to the White House, and thus to the State Department, and thus to Kissinger and Nixon, and thus to political decisions to engage in imperialist warfare.[74]

Despite cries of imperialism from some Vietnamese, American diplomats in Saigon raved about the season.[75] "My counterparts at the American consulates [in Vietnam] generally considered the USIA activities to be useless," recalls Wolfgang Lehmann, the chargé d'affaires. Elsewhere in South Vietnam, a movie promoting the Nixon-Kissinger opening to China had been shown with disastrous results. The very Vietnamese whom the United States wanted to woo with cultural offerings were repulsed by the idea of an American rapprochement with China. "They had arrested some people who were involved with that, and I had to get involved," Lehmann said. "This ballet was an exception. It was good."[76] Even as the front page of one paper condemned the unfolding failure of Kissinger's peace efforts under the headline "Reds Shell," its arts section announced that Graham's dance "stepped lightly into the heart" and demonstrated the "beauty of life and nature." Ostensibly apolitical, Graham's soft-power cultural diplomacy tempered political realities, at least for the moment.[77]

The tour's grandeur and success continued to be undermined by turmoil below—a dynamic that reached a culmination in Tokyo. Although the Nippon Cultural Centre had paid $50,000 to host the company and its crew of thirty-five, USIS remained involved with publicity.[78] However, by the time the company was ready to land outside Tokyo, plans for venues were crumbling, and lecture-demonstrations were sometimes proposed in the evenings. Although Graham had used vitamin B12 shots and shopping excursions to find relief from her illness and fatigue, she was fading. In a final frustrating blow to the embassy's plans, she refused to let the press photograph her. One State Department chronicler sympathized: "Surreal long flights really did take their toll on her physical strength and photogenic quality." Nonetheless, press was needed, and press conferences were at risk of being canceled "because the Japanese reporters show no interest if no photos." The report continued, "Please realize the seriousness of this and correct." Stock pictures from the 1950s tour had to compensate.[79]

When Graham was too weak to speak, a Japanese dancer in the company led the lecture-demonstrations. Despite the desire to show the cultural convergences between Asia and the United States with the company's "mini–United Nations," a memo to Washington complained that the Japanese dancer's accent was too strong when she spoke English. Another concluded with a Cold War trope, particularly ironic regarding the Japanese who were presenting American modern dance in Japan: "Americans should represent America."[80]

* * *

While racist attitudes bubbled under the surface for some cultural officers, Graham maintained an antiracist, apolitical stance that was publicly maintained by Washington. Because Graham was fighting the Cold War in Asia, advertising her attachment to Asian forms over European ones became critical. Referencing the early, Asian-influenced work of Ruth St. Denis and Ted Shawn, she declared that as a young woman she was "absorbed into the image and philosophy of the East."[81] However, the use of Denishawn publicity by USIS proved problematic for some State Department observers because both Denishawn and Graham seemed "campy."[82] One savvy commentator seemed uncomfortable with the conflation of "orientalist" forms in the promotion of Graham's tour in "The Orient." With Edward Said's book about cultural imperialism and "Orientalism" just years from publication, the theme had become a subject in the cultural conversation among the intelligentsia.[83] Yet a picture of Graham in a distinctly orientalist work by Denishawn was used repeatedly and even captioned with a quote from Graham: " 'It is a Great Privilege to Go Back to Asia.' "[84] In some ports, she added, "I feel closer to Southeast Asia than Europe." In Taipei, one reviewer had said that Graham transcended "American modern dance" by "integrating Oriental symbolic props and simple set pieces."[85] Further underscoring the Asianness of her work were Isamu Noguchi's widely admired sets.[86] According to another writer, Graham had "been greatly influenced by the study of Oriental culture and [had] incorporated into her work the kneeling, squatting, rising, sinking and sliding on the floor, which is an essential part of Oriental dancing."[87] USIS agreed, reporting to Washington that "many newspaper comments emphasized the important contribution of the visit to international understanding and friendship."[88]

As in 1955, tour publicity imagery directly addressed Soviet accusations that the United States did not bring freedom to all people, particularly African Americans. In the 1970s, these images were now expanded to direct pronouncements celebrating an internationally and racially diverse company: "She was the first to integrate her group racially, using Asians and Negros in the regular company."[89] Although Mary Hinkson had left the company on bad terms with Graham, USIS still used her picture as Mary, "Virgin, Magdalene, Mother," in press photos for El Penitente in order to promote Graham's racial inclusiveness. The American elites in 1974 were as roiled by race as their fellow citizens—indeed, at the 1972 Dance Panel meeting, one member said, "We must always face the fact that black today is not always beautiful," concluding, "It is exotic."[90] Yet publicity for the company showed that Graham's mythic women could be black, white, Asian, or Jewish, and thus of any color or faith, as could her archetypal pioneer woman, Matt Tierney.

Graham's meetings with women's groups had been an important part of her work as a cultural ambassador in 1955, but when it came to her self-identification as a woman, Graham's opinions did not necessarily coincide with the feminist movement. She remained politically unallied as a woman. On the domestic political scene, Republican Betty Ford joined Lady Bird Johnson and liberal women's groups to support the passage of the Equal Rights Amendment (ERA).[91] Yet Graham disdained the discussions surrounding the "Next Wave" of the American feminist movement, despite her connection to the first lady. While in the 1960s and 1970s, the feminist movement allied itself with the civil rights movement, which would have been a natural alliance for Graham, the desire for "workplace equality" did not seem to appeal to her. "Women in the movement would claim me as a women's liberationist. But I never think of myself in this way," she proclaimed. In this, she allied herself with Georgia O'Keeffe, Eleanor Dulles, and Clare Boothe Luce, and even the conservative anti-ERA activist Phyllis Schlafly. Graham continued, "I was baffled by [the feminist movement]. I had no affiliation with it."[92] American women had achieved suffrage when Graham was twenty-four, and she displayed the characteristics of what historians call the "paradox of feminism," the phenomenon in which the feminist movement seeks to improve conditions for all women but only a subset of women identify themselves as feminist.[93] Graham considered herself foremost as an individual, and not a political actor.

Graham also understood herself to be a part of a "universal" human phenomenon and did not relate this back to the political and social particularities of feminist movements. "Every woman has the quality of being a virgin, of being the temptress-prostitute, of being the mother," she said. "I feel that these, more than anything, are the common life of all women. Not politics."[94] While Graham pushed the limits of sexuality in her work, hers was an artistic venture and not a part of what in the 1970s was being called the feminist "Sex Wars."[95] Her female dancers still had to wear gloves; Graham certainly would not have them burn their bras. Instead, she wanted to be identified as speaking to a Jungian and universal "soul of mankind" that could be represented by a woman.[96]

During her 1955 Asian tour, USIS guides had advised that she remain seated with women at local teas and parties, and press photographs always showed her following gender-based protocol. In 1974, Graham resisted invitations to women's events, although she complied. Her connection to women continued to be a selling point for the embassies. In Rangoon, the wife of the president of Burma worked with the State Department to arrange a luncheon and tea with Graham and notable Burmese women—yet these women wanted to discuss Graham's career choices as a "modern woman," as they called her. Graham complained to State about the obligation to speak about the politics of being female. She found these meetings "particularly abhorrent."[97] Her "center stage" could host only one woman.

* * *

Although she had retired from the stage, Graham's age haunted her.[98] Back in New York, critic Clive Barnes had termed Graham and her work "forever modern," a locution USIS used in the field. The notion that once-revolutionary modernism was now a historic movement became conflated with Graham's venerable years. In a private memo, a government official suggested that Graham's modernism seemed overly "traditional."[99] Whereas some newspapers in the Philippines echoed USIS, praising Graham as a "living legend," others resorted to calling her the "Old Lady of Modern Dance."[100] A State Department telegram from Burma countered the notion that her age was a detriment, noting that Graham's age was a "distinction" there for which she was to be "venerated."[101] Newspapers took hold of her iconic status in Asia's former British colonies and called her the "Oriental Queen-Mother" of modern dance, who "held court from her throne" during interviews.[102]

Despite the recognition of the authority of age in Asia, in Graham's own self-generated publicity for the State Department she insisted on remaining "forever young" rather than "forever modern."[103] In Bangkok, Graham described herself as "a woman who doesn't believe in age." Critics made a "fetish" out of youth.[104] She described her return to Asia as a "rebirth."[105] Graham's insistence on eternal youth and rebirth backfired in some host countries. Multiple facelifts allowed her to claim that she looked like a young girl, yet reporters remarked on her "mask like face," gesturing to her facelifts that made youth a masquerade.[106] A leftist newspaper insisted on putting "Miss" in quotes around mentions of her last name, alluding to her 1954 divorce.[107] Another paper in Vietnam, one not translated for the State Department, examined the implications of the aged woman who was still a "Miss," asking in a headline, "Martha Graham—Loneliness in Old Age?"[108] Yet she claimed to be so young that she sent her mother a card on her birthday that year, "thanking her for giving me life."[109] In fact, Graham's mother died in 1958, when Graham was sixty-four.

Confusion about the "facts" of her age led to cables in which the State Department tried to reconcile what Graham had told them with actual documentation. An embassy telegram begged for clarification from Washington, even Kissinger himself: while Graham had claimed 1902 as her birth year, the tour manifest and her passport showed that she had been born in 1894.[110] While the claims led to momentary confusion, the facts won out. In 1974, USIS finally gave her age as eighty to the press.

To manage the problematic of an old modernist, USIS framed Graham's age in the context of her influence creating current leaders of avant-garde and postmodern dance. Despite the Dance Panel's historic unwillingness to support the avant-garde as an American export, USIS celebrated Graham for her influence on the American revolutionary dance generations coming after her: she had "changed the course of dance history."[111] The agency emphasized that Graham had singlehandedly inspired new, fresh choreographers in the United States, including Paul Taylor, Merce Cunningham, and even Yvonne Rainer, using a Lincoln Center publicity photograph. Cunningham, the original Preacher in *Appalachian Spring*, challenged her theatrics with movement emanating not from narratives but from chance. Taylor, who had starred as her young lover in *Clytemnestra*, made his independent mark by standing still onstage as the curtain went up, then down. Rainer saw Graham as the ultimate traditionalist whose codified contraction and release now harkened back to ballet's first position in the dance education canon.[112] With the rise of these artists, technique was no longer based on the dramatization of a woman's body or her "soul": life could be random.

* * *

Graham targeted and enticed the "leader class" into the American fold by bringing them into an imagined community of intellectual elites with choreographic works based on biblical and mythical stories that they, given their education and cultural sophistication, would know how to interpret. The State Department celebrated these stories, which had been "Grahamized and Americanized."[113] USIS expressed this directly in programs constructed for the tour: "Martha Graham, from early in her career, has had recognition from perceptive audiences."[114] Kissinger wrote the president that "her performances were hailed [by the intelligentsia] as one of the most significant cultural events to take place in years."[115] Yet a cable sent directly to Kissinger noted that "tepid applause" met the dancers. In some cases, the works were not effectively performed by government standards. A handwritten memo read, "While many of the themes Graham deals with are eternal, their treatment strikes reviewers as dated." Indeed, the theatricality seemed melodramatic and "occasionally approached the ridiculous," which was reflected by the "suppressed giggles" of some in the audience. The strong technique demonstrated by the dancers, however, led to "acceptable levels of applause" for technically demanding works such as *Diversion of Angels*. While the performances were "not a total disaster," the diplomatic mission was important.[116]

Graham's power as an ambassador for the United States, rather than as a visionary and venerable leader of a dance company, became the most successful element of her 1974 Asian tour in a cross-national elite bonding project. In a memorandum to Ford, Kissinger celebrated the fact that Graham performances commanded the elite.[117] With embassy events, meetings with ministers, awards, and flower petals, although her company might have ups and downs, Graham herself, when she was well, represented the nation as a cultural diplomat with aplomb.[118] Her charm, personality, anecdotes, and "old-fashioned courtesy" and her "almost intuitive feeling for the right gesture" made her an incomparable asset.[119] Graham's modern dance remained a potent export because of her unmatched rapport with the political elite.[120] A private memo from a State Department observer that harshly criticized modern dance as anything but new nonetheless celebrated Graham's brilliance during "protocol affairs."[121]

* * *

Only months after the Graham company left Saigon, just a few streets away from the theater in which she had performed, throngs of Vietnamese who had supported American policies lined up to crowd onto buses in an effort to evacuate the country as South Vietnam fell to the invading North. "There were desperate scenes of families separated and crying out for help, pleading not to be left behind, clutching at the last straw of hope," CBS News reported. At the embassy where her company had been fêted, US Marines in fatigues pointed rifles at Vietnamese citizens who tried to scale the steel barricades and find safety on US territory. Graham had closed her Saigon performance with *Appalachian Spring*, the story of the promise of freedom and the frontier. That tale would hold little promise for those left behind after the Americans departed.[122]

7

"Grahamized and Americanized"

The Defector Joins the First Lady on the Global Stage

Upon Graham's return to the United States, the State Department declared her a "very valuable asset."[1] As the "First Lady" of modern dance, Graham had "made a positive contribution to overall Department of State foreign relations objectives." Graham's modern dance "overcame national boundaries."[2] Performances "convinced everyone that modern American culture had made [an] important contribution to the development of the twentieth century."[3] Although one State official reflected that the problematic level of mismanagement at the company level required two or three further classified memos, which have not been found, Secretary of State Henry Kissinger signed a long document to President Ford detailing the trip in positive terms. Because Graham claimed to be apolitical, she had deep political import. Kissinger suggested to the president that Graham be invited to White House dinners with any head of state from the 1974 touring region in Asia because of "her contribution to international understanding."[4] While photographs of Graham and Kissinger show a mutual if stiff respect, Graham's principal alliance shifted to First Lady Betty Ford as Graham looked for White House invitations and financial support. Even as her company remained unstable, plagued by deficits that left it veering toward bankruptcy, Graham stayed on the government diplomatic resource list.[5] Graham tightened her alliance with the East Wing to solidify her attachment to the West.[6]

In her youth, Betty Ford showed tenacity, seeking to become a dancer while making her living in New York as a fashion model. Although sharply criticized in her hometown for her "bohemian" behavior, Betty Bloomer, a young Midwestern woman all by herself, moved to New York City amid the Great Depression to study with Graham, although her "active social life" got in the way of serious dance study. Like Graham, Betty relished men and drink, and she enjoyed the New York fashion scene. "I had talent as a dancer, but I wasn't a great dancer," she later reflected.[7] Despite the reputation of modern dance as being "free," even libertine, Graham wanted strong technical dancers;

Martha Graham's Cold War. Victoria Phillips, Oxford University Press 2020. © Oxford University Press.
DOI: 10.1093/oso/9780190610364.001.0001

according to Ford, "I couldn't get my knees straight enough."[8] When it came to Ford's raw talent, she recounted that her "confidence had always been shaky."[9] Measuring herself against the company's leader, she came up short.[10] Ultimately, Ford moved back home, concluding that she "hadn't been a huge success" as a Graham dancer.[11] She then took an acceptable "woman's career," also teaching Sunday School, where she again faced criticism for including African American students. She was married to her first husband, an alcoholic like her father, before she met the future president and got divorced.[12] Both Graham and Ford had potentially damaging pasts if framed by the wrong handlers, but both knew how to craft a successful presence.

The month after Graham returned from Asia, despite Ford's personal turmoil and her decision to use her political power to bring women's issues to the fore, she continued public support for Graham. In a precedent-shattering and controversial proclamation in a period when mastectomies were viewed as the end of one's femininity and something to be kept secret, Betty Ford announced to the public that she had breast cancer and would have a mastectomy. Although it might seem a wayward cause given the life-threatening issues of unexamined cancers, the MacDowell Colony, a well-respected artists' retreat, contacted Betty with news that it would be honoring Graham in November. Sponsors included Graham's longtime supporter Lila Acheson Wallace and the Reader's Digest Fund. William Schuman, who had composed the music for *Judith* and *Night Journey*, both of which had been core State Department exports, was chair of the MacDowell board. As typical of her nature, Ford agreed. "As one who has had the privilege of the benefit of Miss Graham's knowledge, perception, and expression," she wrote while recovering, "I enthusiastically applaud your giving her such a respected tribute and placing her among such distinguished artists. May your organization through further stimulation of contributions to our cultural heritage continue to inspire and to enrich our nation immeasurably."[13] Having witnessed the impact of her forthright acknowledgment of her cancer, the first lady was becoming well aware of her power to influence.

Graham and Protas remained in need of cash for the company, and the award could tap into political capital. Yet trouble ensued. While the duo seemed to expect the monies raised in her honor to land in the Graham company coffers, MacDowell used the funds to support its own internal programming. Graham then reported to Ford that the MacDowell award infuriated her—noting that the funds raised at the awards dinner went to MacDowell, not her—and derided the affair as a "publicity stunt."[14] Graham added, "There is one thing that I would like to say to you, and that is that I have never used your name or allowed it to be used with my knowledge to further any activity which would be a drain upon you or an encroachment upon your privacy or your commitments as the wife of the President." Hoping for a direct infusion of cash or perhaps another tour in the wings, Graham signed her letter to the first lady, "Love, Martha."[15]

Before Ford responded to Graham's letter, Nancy Hanks, a longtime associate of Nelson Rockefeller and heralded Nixon appointee for the National Endowment for the Arts (NEA), sent the first lady a highly curated package that reported on Graham's past tour. An informal note, handwritten, not on NEA stationery, accompanied a select group of official reports. She told the first lady that she thought Mrs. Ford would be proud of Graham. Although Graham was no longer dancing, her retirement added new promise to ventures. The package demonstrated the important connection between the NEA and the State Department. Although official reports and handwritten memos, as well as those classified, included details of failures as well as successes, the material forwarded to the East Wing showed only glowing reports that particularly emphasized the protocol events and Graham's grace as a diplomat. Americana had become a contested subject in 1974, and thus Hanks took special care to describe the company's presentation of *Appalachian Spring* in Manila, omitting the attempt to move the work to the Folk Arts Theater. She sent only the embassy report, which stated, "The Sultan of Masiu and his retinue of fifteen, travelled from Marawi City in Mindanao to see 'Appalachian Spring.'" As the NEA promoted the Graham performance funded by the State Department, it built credibility for increased funding for the Graham's home institution with the first lady. Americana remained onstage.[16]

Although it was almost a month before the first lady replied to Graham's letter, the recovery from her operation and pain medications alongside other prescriptions mixed with alcohol had interfered as well with the first lady's response. Betty Ford credited her training as a dancer for being a "great help" during her recovery in a letter to Graham. She continued, "No matter how long one stays away from the discipline of dancing, it is there as a reserve when one needs it." She provided a clear opening for Graham and Protas to engage with the White House: "I do hope that in the next few months, between your busy schedule and mine, we will be able to get together for a visit. The President joins with me in sending our very warmest regards." She signed her letter, "Fondly, Betty."[17] Graham responded with a present for the first lady: her routine yet coveted gift of jade from Asia. (She often offered these pieces she found in antique shops to dancers, wives of diplomats, and the intelligentsia.) Graham may have been unaware of the Ford administration's harsh crackdown on gifts after the Watergate scandal. Charmed nonetheless, Ford wrote back, "I shall treasure it always with warm thoughts of you and your inspirations which have been a guide for me throughout my life."[18] Graham then secured her own tour of the White House for her dancers, yet the company needed more support from the executive branch. Ford wrote that she hoped to see Graham in New York that June.

With plans to mount the new *Scarlet Letter* falling short, Graham and Protas floated the idea of the first lady's sponsorship of a partnership between Rudolf Nureyev and Margot Fonteyn to appear in a different new work by Graham. The biblical tale of Lucifer held promise with Nureyev as the star. Ford received information from Graham in order to secure a visa for Nureyev, who, although he was "considered essentially a citizen of the entire Western dancing world," was not a US citizen.[19] Graham's casting of these foreign-trained stars became an ideal Cold War trope, even if Americana was off the table for the moment. She could take the Soviet ballet–trained body and free it with her American modern dance. Indeed, Graham claimed that Nureyev had been inspired by her even before his defection. In addition, she reported to the press that in London the Russian sex symbol "used to come back to my dressing room and just look at me." Speaking of the traditional clash between ballet and modern dance, she proclaimed, "The war has ended."[20] And, with Nureyev as the cultural signal, American modern dance had won the Cold War. Nureyev, heralded for his ballet roles as nobles and princes, again proclaimed for the press that he wanted to perform Graham's modernist rendition of the American prince, the Husbandman in *Appalachian Spring*.[21] Nureyev would take on the title role in Graham's sparkling new *Lucifer*, as well as appearing as the Preacher in *Appalachian Spring*.

In June 1975, a week before a benefit gala for the Graham company's fiftieth anniversary, Betty Ford joined Graham in New York for a well-publicized public appearance.[22] Protas worked with the first lady's team in Washington to make the meeting seamless. According to those planning the trip for Ford, Protas was "wonderfully cooperative" with the White House.[23] The women sat like girlfriends chatting in Graham's dressing room in the Martha Graham Center townhouse, with the doyenne of modern dance draped in a dramatic red sheath. The two women took each other's hands while talking. Graham held up fabric for Betty to examine, checking the color of a purple-tinged-pink flowing gauze that Halston would fashion into a gown.[24] Ford was known for her love of fashion and couture.[25] Halston, the designer who made Graham's gowns and would design costumes for *Lucifer*, draped the fabric over the first lady. Once they moved to the studio where a group of invited guests had assembled, Graham and Ford gave speeches. Ford noted the appearance of the Soviet ballet star and addressed several points on her husband's agenda, including arts funding. She made clear, however, that the government was not paying for her ticket the following week, handing Graham a personal check as cameras popped. Then they watched the company rehearse *Lucifer*.[26]

Eight days later, the first lady arrived at the Presidential Suite at the Waldorf Astoria in New York, and Halston helped her into the gown. His work for the first lady would complement the *Lucifer* costumes. As the honorary chair of the benefit committee, Ford emerged from her limousine outside the Uris Theatre poised and ready for the photographers.[27] Just blocks away from the glittering spectacle, prostitutes and drug addicts roamed Times Square amid overflowing garbage bins and street rubbish as the city tottered near bankruptcy. The press had preannounced that the total value of Halston's costumes for the premiere reached $250,000, with various precious stones sewn into the cloth.[28] As Ford and guests were ushered through police barricades, reporters who had commented on the gold, jewels, and glitter of the costumes remarked on how the police on guard outside the theater would soon be laid off because of budget cuts in the city. A Democratic politician attending the gala remarked, "All this goes on while it's falling apart."[29] A few months later, President Ford would turn down the city's request for emergency financial assistance, provoking the infamous headline "Ford to City: Drop Dead."[30] As the city suffered, the elites walked past it, for the moment.

Once in the theater with Woody Allen at her side, the current first lady greeted political luminaries, and a woman in a kimono asked for an autograph. Politics was ever present: former first lady Jacqueline Kennedy (now Onassis) was listed as a "patron" and vice chair of the benefit.[31] Francis Mason sat next to Bethsabée de Rothschild.[32] The program opened with a brief solo from *Clytemnestra*, followed by *Seraphic Dialogue*. So that the audience could appreciate the radicalism of Graham's dance, Margot Fonteyn and Rudolf Nureyev performed the act 2 pas de deux from *Swan Lake*.[33]

Then came the premiere of *Lucifer*. The story demanded that audiences understand the Old Testament and Greek mythology; it was deeply human and gritty in its ultimately redemptive plot. The program quoted Isaiah 14:12, explaining, "This is a retelling of a mythical experience which is common to all mankind." The modern artist Joan Miró made original lithographs to commemorate the moment, and the posters were given to some attendees and dancers as gifts.[34] With *Lucifer*, the sequined black tutu and pointe shoes worn by Fonteyn and the prince's jacket and tights donned by Nureyev in *Swan Lake* just twenty minutes earlier faced off against a sheer, glimmering Halston unitard and Nureyev's bejeweled small costume. With Nureyev "naked save for the gold belted loincloth . . . his body an anatomical chart of protruding muscles," Ford's press secretary remarked that the dancer's "*'costume'* amounted to a bejeweled band aid!"[35] While Graham presented the potential of the modern dance to free the artistically enslaved body, she also took the opportunity to promote the sexuality, glamour, and pizzazz of American high fashion onstage and in the audience, where the first lady sat in a dress designed by Graham's costumer. After the curtain came down, Ford greeted Nureyev, Margot Fonteyn, and Graham onstage. They all joined hands to take a bow for the house, the audience on its feet. Nureyev stood, muscles rippled, beside the first lady.[36] Again, politics met performance.

Nureyev, Graham, and Ford had something in common: they all relished parties and the social scene.[37] Halston threw the postperformance party in his home, where "beautiful women were draping themselves all over the modern furniture in an architecturally perfect townhouse." The walls and the furniture were stark white, and the women's gowns gave the room splashes of color. Halston was a member in good standing of the Andy Warhol night-life crowd, as were many of the partygoers. Indeed, along with the iconic Campbell's Soup can, Warhol would paint Jackie Onassis and Graham, both at the party. Like pieces of live art, some guests just sat, "immobile."[38]

Back in Washington, Kissinger continued to advise Ford to show "appreciation to the grand lady of dance," and in the fall of 1975, Graham attended a state dinner at the White House for Emperor Hirohito and Empress Nagako of Japan, where Graham had launched her 1955 tour and concluded her most recent one. She arrived with Halston as her escort. As the emperor received her, she instinctively changed her body stance, bowing from the waist, straight-backed, deferential and alert.[39] Later, framed by the deep red and gilt-framed walls, Graham and Betty Ford stood together, with the first lady wearing the same Halston that she had worn to the New York Graham gala.[40] At the dinner, at two U-shaped tables sprinkled with red roses, Graham sat just eight guests away from Kissinger.[41] Afterward, he greeted her, now smiling.

Within a few weeks, the Graham team announced to the press that Nureyev and Fonteyn, the stars of her *Lucifer*, would reunite again to create a new work as part of a series in honor of the nation's bicentennial, in what it called an "Americana Evening." The series would feature *Appalachian Spring* and a revival of *Frontier*, the work Graham presented at the White House in 1937. Adding to the evening, Nureyev would play the lead in the long-planned *Scarlet Letter*, now funded by a $60,000 grant from the Phelps Dodge Corporation and featuring a score by Hunter Johnson, who had been brought in to replace Copland. Former first lady Jacqueline Kennedy Onassis would be event chair.[42]

The Scarlet Letter premiered in December 1975 at the third of three "galas" in New York, with repeated fanfare. Onassis was unable to attend this gala event; Betty Ford called Graham with a message read to the audience. The White House wanted a performance of the Russian star in a new American ballet for Washington's Kennedy Center, she said. Before the curtain rose on the Russian playing Dimmesdale, the Puritan priest, Graham uncharacteristically took to the stage to explain the work. Although not "endearing to Hawthorne scholars," the press asked, "how many times are you going to get a great choreographer to come out in front of a curtain before a premiere to explain explanations?"[43] Gone were claims of a "universal" language or understanding of archetypes through a language "that needs no words."

Although Clive Barnes, who dubbed Graham as "forever modern," appreciated the elements of a dance-off between genres, writing for the *Times*, "There is a feeling that modern dance can stand up to the seductive allure of classic ballet," reviews for the new work were decidedly mixed. Graham deployed sexuality to remain modern, but it seemed old-fashioned in the work as a study of "sex, sin, and retribution."[44] While Graham was applauded for expanding her range by featuring the angst of a male rather than her typical female-centric narrative, to one reviewer, the piece did "not really have the internal and personal ring of truth of Graham's best work." And Nureyev appeared to be an "outsider, stylistically speaking."[45] The costumes by Halston showed "stylized versions of Puritan attire," called by another reporter "costume[s] out of commedia dell'arte, which apparently inspired Halston's bizarre wardrobe." Hunter Johnson's score was greeted as a "nondescript 'modernistic'" piece with "vague references" to what the reviewer called "Americana."[46] A critic from Los Angeles firmly spoke his mind without the New York attachment to Graham's legacy when he wrote that Graham "seems to have lost her way in the labyrinth of symbolism where she was once mistress; her lost sense of continuity is aimless, diffuse dance movements." Noting that Graham's "creativity was on the wane," the journalist lamented that it was "sad" that the aged Nureyev was given "little dance movement," and thus "spent most of his time stalking and lurching around the stage . . . agonizing in the most undergraduate style."[47]

* * *

At the start of the bicentennial year of 1976, Graham and Betty Ford had a private lunch at the White House. Ford would become the chair of the continuing fiftieth-anniversary celebrations, with Graham pulling out anniversaries for more than twelve months, as would become the norm, despite the fact that Ford would be campaigning on behalf of her husband. Graham's events, which celebrated Graham herself and Americana, would continue to take the message of modern dance to international stages: the first performance of "the bare feet of modern dance" in London's Royal Opera House would take place. Nureyev would again perform in *Appalachian Spring*, now with Aaron Copland promised as the conductor.[48] Graham lunched in Washington, showing iconic pictures of herself to Ford in the East Wing sitting room. The first lady smiled with her, listening to her stories.[49]

Surely guided by Francis Mason, the Graham company's management astutely kept the State Department's now retitled Office of Cultural Affairs apprised of her upcoming independent European tours and available repertory. In 1976, the office contemplated sponsoring Graham in some additional Western European cities because she would already be performing there in June. State officials also considered a deployment dovetailing with the company's October season in Madrid and Paris.[50] Their findings paralleled reports from the field in 1974: the woman herself was the key to the success of this enterprise of cultural diplomacy. However, Graham's health was failing, and European intellectuals and dance experts increasingly viewed American modern dance as old-fashioned. Regarding the choreography, the dance community had become "overly familiar" with "Western cultural themes."[51] Graham's rewriting of these stories held little novelty. Like Germany, some cultures in Eastern Europe had developed their own forms and culturally resonant choreographic talent and training techniques. Ironically, it was the American insistence on the freedom of the individual that allowed the artistic intelligentsia in other nations to rebel against the Western canon deployed to free them.[52]

As Graham continued to solicit the first lady's patronage, Nureyev kept performing for her in the United States. She also enthusiastically recruited Mikhail Baryshnikov, who had defected from the Soviet Union in 1974. When Graham asked Baryshnikov to work with her, he called Nureyev, also a fellow "graduate" of what Baryshnikov called his "alma mater." Nureyev offered words of encouragement: "Oh it's great, you should do this, it's wonderful—and you should work hard because you know how she is."[53] Graham advertised that both Baryshnikov and Nureyev sought artistic freedom and found it in her dance. These handsome ballet superstars stood side by side with Graham and other stars in publicity photos taken in dance venues as well as in glamour shots with Halston at Manhattan hotspots.

When Graham's sister died, Ford wrote her a letter of condolence. Graham returned the gesture by sending Betty a letter on her birthday, in which she wrote, "May you be blessed by the love surrounding and enfolding you to meet with courage all those things life demands of you." She signed it, again, "Love, Martha." With the first lady having warmed to Graham, she in turn sent birthday wishes via telegram, signed, "All my love, Betty."

In the spring of 1976, Graham returned to the White House for a state dinner in honor of French president Valéry Giscard d'Estaing and his wife. On the White House reception line, Graham wore deep violet velvet and looked straight into the eyes of the coiffed diplomats.[54] Again, she confirmed State Department evaluations of her brilliance at "protocol affairs." When it came to "pre-planned" dinner seating, "There is rarely any spontaneity involved."[55] At dinner, the White House placed Graham at table number eleven with the first lady and next to the French president.[56] Graham talked cultural diplomacy with her dinner partner. She understood that the problems of politics, economics, and warfare did not suit. She could reign as an apolitical arbiter of compassion and unity. Graham ascertained that their nations' first ladies, Anne-Aymone Giscard and Betty Ford, shared an interest in dance and modern art, and allied herself accordingly.[57] Graham wrote Betty Ford the next day—ironically, from her room at the Watergate Hotel. Before asking for financial support for her company, Graham showed her friendship: "You looked radiant as usual, a little fragile, but beautiful." Perhaps Graham sensed Ford's rumored fight with alcohol and pain medications. Graham continued, "Try to preserve your precious strength as much as you can. I know that these are difficult times for you and my love and prayers are with you always."[58] Graham added a "P.S." that Protas would be sending her a lithograph by Miró inscribed to Ford.

Protas followed immediately with his own letter making "the ask." After thanking Ford for his invitation, he noted that as honorary chair of the fiftieth-year Graham celebration, Ford would automatically be included on a committee for Graham anniversary events in Paris—and could she and the president also enlist the French president and his wife? "Martha and I had thought after last evening with all the mentioning of the past, present, and future closeness of France and the United States that this would be a well chosen collaboration on the cultural level," he noted.[59] Adding to her solicitation of Betty Ford, Graham directly contacted the president to ask him and his wife to serve as chairs for the gala in Paris. The president agreed, as he noted, "because of Betty's friendship."[60]

In September, Graham's general manager, Cynthia Parker, sent Betty Ford a thick packet of the excellent reviews of Graham's London season. Never missing an opportunity to emphasize the political connections of Graham to Ford, she concluded in her note that everyone on the Graham team was thrilled with the "outcome of the convention," referring to the Republican convention the previous month where Ford had narrowly won the nomination in a heated contest with former California governor, and future Graham ally, Ronald Reagan. Parker wrote that all at Graham were "so proud to be able to count you as one of our alumnae."[61] Ford responded generously, "You were so thoughtful to remember me, and I am deeply grateful for your kind words."[62]

Early that fall, Graham arrived in the nation's capital to accept the Presidential Medal of Freedom from Gerald Ford. The first lady had lobbied her husband hard to give the award to Graham, whom the first lady now called "my idol."[63] While Graham never penned a letter to the White House to plead this case, others had joined the first lady. Indeed, the president's staff had urged Graham's supporters "not to push further."[64] Ford's team decided that giving Graham the award was not necessarily a clear "political plus" but that the "downside [did not have] many degrees of strength."[65] After the president approved the appointment, Betty Ford quickly insisted on a "Martha Graham Night," rather than holding the standard luncheon or doing a ceremony in which there would be a second award recipient. Graham was to be featured, center stage, as an ambassador.[66]

Supporting the arts could reap political benefits for President Ford, who was involved in the political battle of his life, and Graham became his conduit as well as his wife's. Now as vice president, Nelson Rockefeller, a longtime patron of dance as diplomacy, asserted in a long memo to the president,

Photo 1 Martha Graham identified in *Japanese Dance*, March 1, 1936. Associated Press.

Photo 2 Martha Graham in *Lamentation, No. 20,* c. 1939. Herta Moselsio Photographs of Martha Graham's *Lamentation*. Music Division, Library of Congress.

Photo 3 Martha Graham in *Frontier,* 1937. Barbara Brooks Morgan, photographer. Courtesy of the Wight Gallery Collection 1938–1967, UCLA.

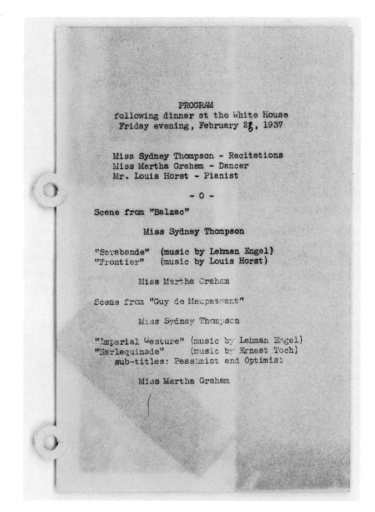

Photo 4 Program following dinner at the White House with Martha Graham performing *Frontier*, Feb. 27 (hand corrected to 26), 1937. Martha Graham Collection, Music Division, Library of Congress.

Photo 5 "At a dinner given by the Women's National Press Club, President Truman presents awards of achievement to six outstanding American professional women. Pictured (L-R) are: dancer Martha Graham; government official Dorothy Fosdick of the State Department; educator Pearl Wanamaker; President Truman; actress Olivia de Havilland; scientist Mildred Rebstock; and designer Claire McCardell," Washington, DC. O.D Mulligan, photographer. Credited to Bettmann, Getty Images; also photo 77-1237, for the International News Service, courtesy of Getty Images.

Photo 6 Bertram Ross, Stuart Hodes, Cameron McCosh (top row left to right), Mimi Cole, Mary Hinkson, Linda Hodes (bottom row left to right). The dancers responded to the press asking them to "do something" in their hotel lobby, Stockholm, 1954 European tour funded by Bethsabée de Rothschild. Courtesy of Linda Hodes.

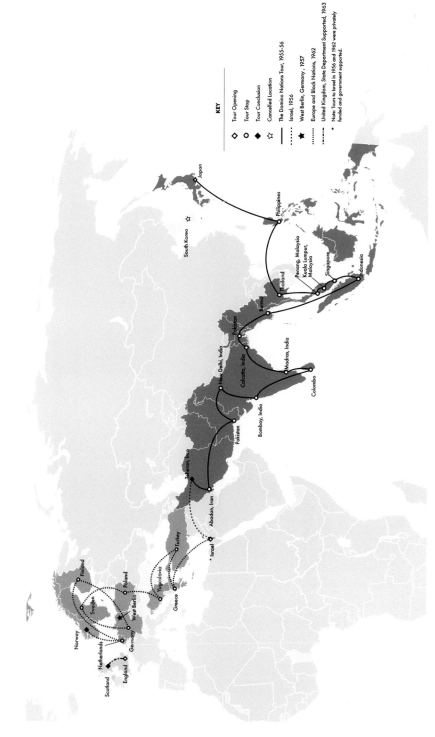

KEY

◇ Tour Opening
○ Tour Stop
◆ Tour Conclusion
☆ Cancelled Location

—— The Domino Nations Tour, 1955-56
········ Israel, 1956
★ West Berlin, Germany , 1957
········ Europe and Block Nations, 1962
········ United Kingdom, State Department Supported, 1963
* Note: Tours to Israel in 1956 and 1962 were privately funded and government supported.

Photo 7 Map 1 of tours, Laura Miner and Cassandra Nozil, with information provided by the FBI files of Martha Graham, Victoria Phillips Collection, Library of Congress, and augmented by other government documents at NARA and UAK.

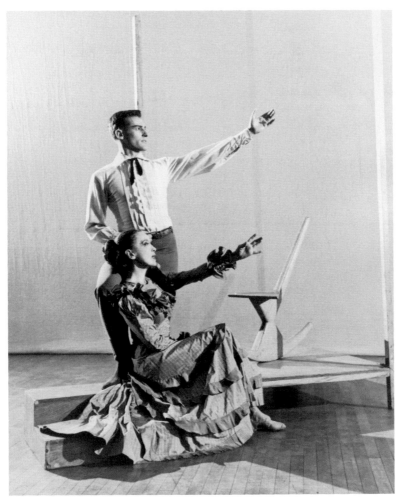

Photo 8 Martha Graham (Bride) with Stuart Hodes (Husbandman), *Appalachian Spring*, publicity photo, 1954/55. Martha Graham Collection, Music Division, Library of Congress.

Photo 9 Matt Turney as the Pioneer Woman in *Appalachian Spring*. Martha Swope, photographer. Courtesy of the *New York Times* and the New York Public Library for the Performing Arts.

Photo 10 Martha Graham, *Night Journey*, 1947. Arnold Eagle, photographer. Courtesy of the Music Division, Library of Congress; the New York Public Library for the Performing Arts; and Susan Goldman for the estate of Arnold Eagle.

Photo 11 Donald McKayle and Ethel Winter in publicity shot for the 1955–56 tour. K. Hayata, photographer. Ethel Winter and Charles Hyman Papers, Music Division Library of Congress.

Photo 12 Bertram Ross, Ethel Winter, Helen McGehee, and Bob Cohan shopping during the 1955-56 tour. Ethel Winter and Charles Hyman Papers, Music Division, Library of Congress .

Photo 13 The Martha Graham Dance Company in India, in front of the Taj Mahal, 1955–56 tour. Martha Graham Collection, Music Division, Library of Congress.

Photo 14 Martha Graham arriving in Israel, 1956. Martha Graham Collection, Music Division, Library of Congress.

Photo 15 "Night view of the Berlin Congress Hall—1957," Sept. 1957. Kongresshalle ("Benjamin-Franklin-Halle"). John-Foster-Dulles-Allee (Tiergarten), courtesy of the Landisarchive, Berlin.

Photo 16 Martha Graham talks with Eleanor Dulles, Berlin 1957. Bettmann Collection, Associated Press.

Photo 17 Martha Graham with Bob Cohan in *Clytemnestra*. No credit but attributed in pencil with "?" to Sam Frank, photographer. Martha Graham Collection, Music Division, Library of Congress.

Photo 18 Jacqueline Kennedy [Onassis] with Martha Graham at the Martha Graham Center of Contemporary Dance, 316 East Sixty-Third Street, New York, Studio One mirrors in the background. Martha Graham Collection, Music Division, Library of Congress.

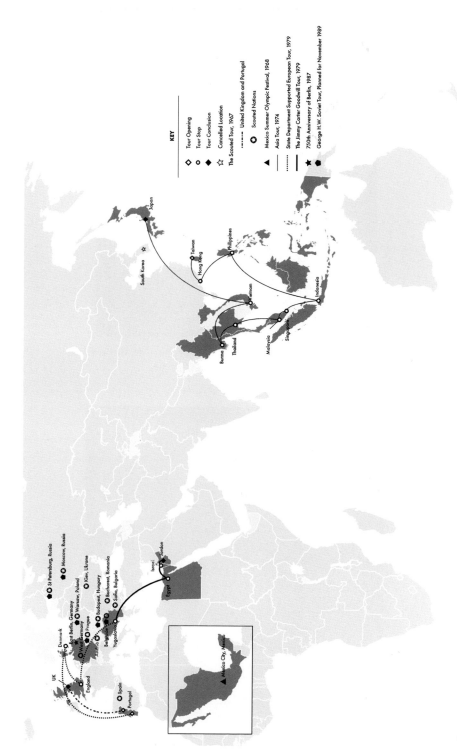

Photo 19 Map 2 of tours, Laura Miner and Cassandra Nozil, with information provided by the FBI files of Martha Graham, Victoria Phillips Collection, Library of Congress, and augmented by other government documents at NARA and UAK.

Photo 20 Robert Powell and Linda Hodes in *Phaedra,* publicity shot, 1969. Martha Swope, photographer. © The New York Public Library for the Performing Arts.

Photo 21 Mary Hinkson and Bertram Ross with Lady Bird Johnson and Martha Graham at the White House, Oct. 9, 1968. Robert Knudsen, photographer. Courtesy of the Lyndon B. Johnson Library and Museum.

Photo 22 Benjamin Garber applying makeup to Martha Graham for her final performance in *Cortege of Eagles*, 1969. Library of Congress, Benjamin Garber Papers, Music Division, Library of Congress.

Photo 23 "President Richard Nixon announcing during a press conference the entry of American soldiers in Cambodia," April 30, 1970. STF, photographer. Associated Press, APF Collection.

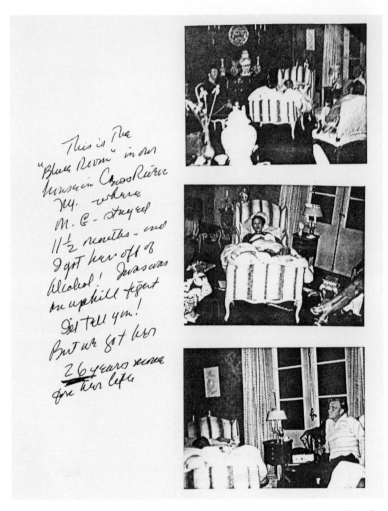

Photo 24 Martha Graham recuperating at the home of Benjamin Garber. His Polaroid photographs (also available in his Papers) were copied by Garber and ithe xeroxed page includes his handwritten notes. Benjamin Garber Papers, Music Division, Library of Congress.

Photo 25 Martha Graham and Henry Kissinger, with Nancy Kissinger and Alan Greenspan observing, Nov. 16, 1976. Karl Schumacher, photographer. Courtesy of the Gerald R. Ford Presidential Library and Museum.

Photo 26 Martha Graham with Betty Ford and Roy Halston at the Graham Studio in Graham's dressing room, June 11, 1975. The cloth draping Ford by Halston would be used to create Ford's dress for the upcoming gala. Karl Schumacher, photographer. Courtesy of the Gerald R. Ford Library and Museum.

Photo 27 Janet Eilber and Peter Sparling in *Diversion of Angels*, 1975. Martha Swope, photographer. © The New York Public Library for the Performing Arts.

Photo 28 "People scale over the wall surrounding the United States Embassy in Saigon, May 1975," May 1, 1975. Neal Ulevich, photographer. Associated Press.

Photo 29 Martha Graham with Betty Ford, Roy Halston, Elizabeth Taylor, and Liza Minelli outside Studio 54 at midnight, May 21, 1979. Ron Frehm, photographer. Associated Press.

Photo 30 Peggy Lyman with David Brown in *Frescoes*, publicity photo1978/79. Martha Graham Collection, Music Division, Library of Congress.

Photo 31 Takako Asakawa in *Judith* with George White, ca. 1985, No. 3. Martha Swope, photographer. © The New York Public Library for the Performing Arts.

Photo 32 Martha Graham with Pope John Paul II, summer 1984. Courtesy of Linda Hodes.

Photo 33 *Appalachian Spring* with Rudolf Nureyev (Preacher), Terese Capucilli (Bride), Mikhail Baryshnikov (Husbandman), and Maxine Sherman (Pioneer Woman), October 6, 1987. Robert R. McElroy, photographer. Archive Photos, Associated Press.

Photo 34 Martha Graham with Ronald Reagan at the White House, April 23, 1985. Terry Arthur, photographer. Courtesy of the Ronald Reagan Presidential Library and Museum.

Photo 35 Thea Narissa Barnes in *Frontier*, publicity shot, c. 1987. Martha Graham Legacy Collection, Music Division, Library of Congress.

Photo 36 "Martha Graham, center, with members of her company in 1990." Jim Wilson, photographer. *New York Times* Archives, courtesy of Redux Pictures.

Photo 37 "First Lady Barbara Bush visits with Martha Graham at the White House residence. Mrs. Bush's dog, Millie, looks on, as the First Lady shows Ms. Graham Millie's puppies," March 30, 1989. Carol Powers, photographer. Courtesy of the George H. W. Bush Presidential Library and Museum.

"Your leadership in this area [of funding for culture] has important political advantage."[67] A campaign adviser repeatedly told the president that there were "several requests for the President's position on the arts."[68] Honoring Graham would demonstrate his appreciation. In notes for Ford's Medal of Freedom speech, advisers told him that "more than half the American people would pay an additional $10 per year in support of the arts."[69] However, Ford had to stick to a fiscally responsible Republican platform and remained wary of expensive or extensive government sponsorship of the arts, such as the Soviets had: "I fear that total subsidization might bring with it the attendant philosophical problems of control and censorship."[70] He found a compromise with the government joining the private sector to fund the arts, a model Graham had used since the inception of her career. Thus in October, the president signed legislation that encouraged philanthropists and private foundations to work with a government "matching grant" program that gave one government dollar for each two dollars raised in the private market. And although the program was domestic, the White House distributed the facts of presidential funding initiatives to Voice of America to be broadcast internationally.[71] As an example of privatized success, Graham served the president's interests. And his remarks at the celebration of this American icon could be used to shore up his campaign and help to reverse his image regarding the arts and the Republican Party.

That fall, Graham telegrammed the president directly, also sending a copy to Betty Ford's press secretary, in order to encourage the coordination between the East Wing and West Wing to help with her publicity and thus funding opportunities in a show of support for his candidacy. "When I first danced at the White House there was a towel in my room which bore the lettering The President's House," she wrote. Actually, when she first performed at the White House in 1937, she did not stay overnight and thus did not have a room of her own. She had gone back to New York on the train after performing Frontier for the Roosevelts. Yet Graham continued, "My faith and prayers are that it will continue to be your house. Fondly Martha."[72] Graham had all to gain from Ford's successful bid for a full term as an elected president, and she could manufacture a memory to suit the occasion.

Preparations for Ford's speech honoring Graham adapted facts about her tours to suit White House needs. The first lady's staff put together a "Brief Summary of Martha Graham's International Tours" for the president, noting regions where she had toured under US government auspices, as well as those nations she had toured independently, such as Israel. Interestingly, they did not include South Vietnam, which by then had fallen to the Communist North, in the list of countries Graham had visited. The document lifted without attribution phrases from embassy cables and telegrams from the 1974 tour, such as "Her company illustrated in the most dynamic form possible the image of America as a culturally dynamic society." In Washington circularity, it also quoted newspapers that the diplomats had, in turn, quoted themselves. Her achievement was girded with statistics: "The Company gave 24 performances in 6 weeks, reached an audience of some 48,000 and gave 14 lecture-demonstrations with 18,000 participants."[73] Graham's value as an ambassador was underscored by an attached memo about the State Department cultural effort that began, "The world is a tinderbox where the firebugs often seem to outnumber the firefighters—this program produces firefighters." It continued, "U.S. capacity to constructively influence events is critically affected by relationships of trust between Americans and their counterparts in leading positions in and out of government around the world." The author stressed that a "*climate*" for diplomatic success was created by culture "especially [for] those in leadership positions" such as Martha Graham.[74] She was not only relevant—she was an entrenched leader for the United States.

Betty Ford's dedication to Graham showed during her hands-on involvement in the planning of the Medal of Freedom event. Nancy Hanks wrote the first lady that Graham "thinks 'money'" and wondered if it would be appropriate for the president to include a note in his remarks about the importance of private and public joint funding for the arts, and remind listeners about his legislation.[75] Ford worked directly with the NEA to construct a guest list that would encourage the much-needed funding for company operations from both government agencies and philanthropists in a matching-funds model. A handwritten note added the board chairman of Exxon to the list because he was "putting up money for M.G.," according to Hanks.[76]

While the Medal of Freedom was theoretically apolitical, like Graham, the guest list was not: the president was engaged in a tough campaign against his Democratic challenger, Jimmy Carter. With Election Day less than four weeks away, any edge that the event could provide would be welcome. One actor did not get an invitation after the presidential office noted it was "checking Carter affiliation" and did not like what it found.[77] William F. Buckley from the *National Review* was included, a penciled check next to his name, along with innovator Buckminster Fuller.[78] But international politics and money were also in play. Hoping for financial support from backers in the Middle East, Graham suggested that an invitation be sent to Prince Abdullah Ben

Saud, the son of the king of Saudi Arabia, "in his early 20's and much interested in the arts and dance." But his presence could cause a problem if Bethsabée de Rothschild, who was invited, also showed up. The first lady's office consulted with Brent Scowcroft, the National Security Advisor, about the invitation to the Saudi prince. The Saudis wanted to "avoid drama and confrontation."[79] The White House noted that while she promoted the prince as an invitee, "Miss Graham would understand if we could not include him."[80] In the end, the prince was not invited.

For the event, tables were set using the color of the gowns worn by the first lady and Graham at the New York gala. Bronze sculptures of dancers, on loan from a collection at the New York Public Library, were placed on the tables, on round mirrors that caught the light. Although most statues were of Graham or other American modern female dancers, the first lady gestured back to the anniversary gala and the Cold War by adding one of Nureyev.[81]

Graham wore a long, elegant gown in a deep rose, and Ford used the same hues but in a muted palette, allowing Graham center stage in color photographs.[82] While guests celebrated over cocktails, the president was late because he had been detained by the press, having just been cleared by a special prosecutor on issues surrounding his campaign and taxes.[83] President Ford was competitive with Carter in polls, but with twenty days left until the election, victory remained an elusive prospect. The Cold War had sneaked up on him: days earlier, a Cuban airplane crashed after CIA-linked terrorists exploded bombs on it, killing all passengers on board, including the Cuban national fencing team.[84] More damaging to his electoral prospects, during a debate with Carter, Ford had claimed that there was "no Soviet domination in Eastern Europe"; Democrats used that statement to question the president's fitness for office. While Ford's guests waited, he again had to defend his comment on the Soviet presence in Eastern Europe, explaining, "It depends on how you analyze the answer." He then compounded his gaffe by bringing up Poland as an example of a non-Soviet-dominated nation.[85]

When the president entered and took the podium, he apologized for arriving late to the ceremony. "Martha Graham's visits abroad have given the word real meaning: ambassador," Ford said, before linking her to the nation's bicentennial celebration.[86] As a choreographer and dancer, the president asserted, she transcended current events and showed how terms like "body language" were a part of the human condition. Despite youth movements and domestic unrest, her dancers demonstrated that "self-discipline is not an obstacle to creativity." Thanks to its "artistic and political freedom," America had flourished. Ford used this declaration of "freedom" as a segue into a discussion of arts funding and a presentation of his plan to ally the private sector with government agencies.

After Ford's speech, Graham took the stage, thanking the president for the award and declaring her support for his public-private matching grant legislation. It was clear that private funders joining with government had sustained her, and she specifically mentioned the importance of National City Bank in funding her early creative ambitions, despite the difficulties of obtaining bank loans during the Depression. While recognizing that the support foreign governments provided to the arts in their own countries was a model for what the United States could do, she remained ever the patriot. "America," she said, "has stood by me."[87]

Graham sat next to the president during the meal.[88] The after-dinner entertainment began with the now classically modernist *Lamentation* performed by Graham's own company. The second half of the program—a performance of *Frontier*—referenced Graham's career as a diplomat, which had begun just under forty years earlier. It had become an item of lore that, during the 1937 presentation of *Frontier* in the East Room, the sweep of Graham's leg had almost touched the chandelier when she performed as the pioneer on the American frontier for Franklin and Eleanor Roosevelt. With the Fords in the White House, Graham had brought the fence for *Frontier*, and she had it placed just under a chandelier and watched as her dancer took the stage. The audience held deep violet programs, complementing the first lady's decision of dress, flowers, and table settings to reference Graham, with the presidential seal embossed in gold. Inside, a line drawing showed the dancer looking westward next to the text: "The courage and excitement of the American frontier are captured in this dance."[89] Americana was now not pioneerism and early modernist expressions as with Roosevelt, but rather a bid to redemption with a nostalgia that engaged Americans with their past inventiveness to solve political problems.

After the 1937 performance of *Frontier* for the Roosevelts, Graham had returned to New York that night via train, as mentioned earlier. This time, she lingered for dancing and more celebration. Graham felt the energy of the bicentennial as the dancer who played the frontier woman, having changed from her bibbed pioneer dress into a bare-shouldered black sheath, waltzed with President Ford in front of a golden-framed mirror.[90] Although the attendees assumed that the heated press conference hours earlier, the Poland gaffe, and the tight presidential race would have constrained the evening, guests remarked that the president seemed "confident and cheerful."[91] Indeed, he broke out into the frug, a dance that had become a common phenomenon when official Washington let loose. When the DC elites danced, a reporter observed, "arms flail, hips swivel, faces sweat." Gerald Ford was known as an excellent dancer, even when frugging with a Graham star.[92] After Graham was escorted back to her hotel, guests stayed on into the night.[93]

A few weeks later, Graham wrote to Betty Ford from Paris, where she used some of the Phelps Dodge funding to stay at the elegant George V hotel. The marbled lobby and terraced rooms had hosted kings, queens, presidents, and now Graham. She wrote that her feelings were "too full for words to come out," yet she continued, saying, "Even though I have the beautiful medal on a sash and wonderful citations, as we walked past the guard into the room I kept thinking of my mother." Her mother knew in her "blood" that Graham was meant for greatness. She continued, referring to the upcoming election, "Keep your glorious smile, and know that wherever you are you are keeping intact the true meaning of 'The President's House'—I return the first week in November—all my prayers are with you both for that time. May you both have strength and faith and also assurance. With deep love, Martha."[94] She prayed for an outcome that would keep Betty in the East Wing.

Days later, Betty Ford, taking the podium in a crisp white top and tailored jacket, delivered her husband's concession speech for him. Ford had campaigned hard to close the slim margin between himself and Jimmy Carter, losing his voice at the end. A week and a half later, Graham met the president at the White House during her final visit of the Ford administration. Afterward, resting at a Washington hotel before her company's performance at a Kennedy Center gala that evening, Graham used the stationery to write one last note to Gerald Ford. She closed by thanking the president for "the image you have given to the world of the presidency," which he "elevated" with his "dignity and honesty."[95]

That evening, with Halston at her side, Graham arrived at the Kennedy Center with a crowd that boasted actress Eva Gabor, legend Paul McCartney, Secretary of State Kissinger, and chairman of the Council of Economic Advisers, Alan Greenspan. Unlike the Halston sheaths that the first lady had worn at other events, on this night Betty Ford looked older and more conservative in her high-necked top and long black skirt. Graham, always persevering, shimmered in silver inlaid cloth. The two women toasted each other, Graham holding up her tumbler to Ford's flute. The pair continued to work the room together, stopping to chat with Kissinger.[96] At the end of the evening, gathering her purse and her flowing black maxi coat, the first lady posed with Graham, smiling once more. Graham looked determinedly forward, just above the photographer, as though watching a bird in flight.[97]

8

"And Martha Knew How to Play That"

From Detente to Disco in Jimmy Carter's Middle East, 1979

It felt colder inside the glass-enclosed stone temple than outside in Central Park, despite the early December darkness. Waiting to enter as Cleopatra, the dancer stood in a shimmery gold Halston unitard, wrapped in a sleeping bag. The chill felt ancient to her. It was the opening night of Martha Graham's *Frescoes* in the Temple of Dendur at the Metropolitan Museum of Art, the centerpiece of the museum's newly opened Sackler Wing.[1] Although she had been strictly instructed not to touch the walls, Martha Graham's Cleopatra reached for the stone instinctually. "You felt the antiquity," she said. "You felt generations that had worshipped and witnessed the temple."[2] The temple was the stage she would dance on, a structure rescued by Western benefactors from the Aswan Dam project that would have flooded it, transported from Egypt piece by piece, reconstructed in New York City, surrounded by a pool of water that echoed the Nile, all of it bounded by a new geometric glass structure that allowed people outside to peer in at the glow of the sanctuary.

Yet outside, just due west of the Met in Central Park, Cleopatra's Needle was known as a marker to help locate the entrance to the Ramble, the wooded portion of the park where people wandered, shivering, scoring and doing drugs, then scouring the bushes for a quick "date." Fearing crime, those who were attending the gala event would not set foot into the park after dusk. While the people inside the park, bundled in jackets or blankets, were oblivious to the Cleopatra inside the glass, on the Fifth Avenue side of the building crowds stood close to the thick red ropes on the sides of the glowing steps leading into the museum on this exciting night late in 1978. Jacqueline Kennedy Onassis had helped bring the cultural greatness of ancient Egypt to New York; crowds would spot her in a glamorous French gown purchased at a Madison Avenue boutique. Women who seemed to glide up the steps were flanked by men in tuxedos: politicians, cultural leaders, businessmen,

Martha Graham's Cold War. Victoria Phillips, Oxford University Press 2020. © Oxford University Press.
DOI: 10.1093/oso/9780190610364.001.0001

people whose names would often appear in boldface in the society pages. But their names would not show up in relation to this event. Tonight's performance was considered by its creator to be so sacred that the press, although invited, was prohibited from publishing reviews of the new choreography.[3] This evening was to be relished and remembered with little trace it had ever happened. And for the onlookers, it was just the names, the dresses, and the sense of a gala that promised them and their city better times.

Martha Graham stood inside the glowing hall under the glass in her own shimmery Halston. *Frescoes* would have its official premiere in a Broadway theater; this performance was dubbed a preview. Graham had been persuaded to have three dancers perform her iconic *Lamentation* simultaneously on the evening's program as an "installation piece" in the museum, perhaps making it seem more modern. While not pleased, she remained charming with each person she greeted. Her escort, Ron Protas, stood at her side, ever watching, guarding, observing, and planning.

The evening began simply, without speeches.[4] Chairs for the audience had been strategically placed on either side of the space in front of the temple. Three dancers positioned themselves, two sitting on rocks and one in front of the ancient structure.[5] But in the moments before the dance began, it was the invited guests who appeared to be the real performers, the women dressed as they were in the glittery, draped, disco-inspired haute couture of the late 1970s, the men standing straight in their black tuxedos, seemingly timeless save a bit of modish length here and there in the jackets. Yet with Graham, American modernism's classical heritage was getting a new, glamorous twist. The music began. *Lamentation*, a solo some forty years old, now performed by three dancers simultaneously, had come to define the modern dance canon internationally. It was what had come to be called by a State Department observer "historic modernism," a black-tie, old-fashioned avant-garde museum event. Protas leaned into Graham to let her know the innovative staging was a success, and that they should think about doing it that way often, again. Graham responded simply, "If I had wanted it done that way, I would have."[6] But she knew the stakes were high and there was business to be done.

The audience held the program for *Frescoes*, which offered clues to the drama. Unlike *Lamentation*, *Frescoes* was based on a dramatic tale embedded in the temple itself. Graham quoted Shakespeare to introduce her heroine, Cleopatra: physically stunning, politically powerful, a warrior in love, ready to die from the bite of a snake at her breast.[7] The references went deep into Shakespeare and Egyptian history, archaeology, mythology, and the vocabulary of modernism. Those in the audience who didn't know the allusions would not let on to their neighbors.

Cleopatra exited the stone walls and struck her opening pose between the pillars. A barely audible gasp seemed to ricochet off the tall glass windows. The dancer seemed nude in the dulled light. But when she shifted, she shimmered, revealing a golden skintight stocking that hugged her perfect form as she moved.[8] Graham continued to use history to shock. The music opened.

After applauding at the end of the work, the audience adjourned to the main lobby of the museum with its grand ceilings and European flair. They had cocktails and broke off to dance, amid the conversations and negotiations that infused New York high-society cultural events. There began discussions between a State Department official and some Egyptian diplomats who relished Graham's choreography. With Jimmy Carter's efforts toward Middle East peace, the State Department considered sending the Graham company on another tour, with *Frescoes* as the centerpiece. With this dance set in the transplanted Temple of Dendur, American modern achievements stood for both political rapprochement and the power of new state alliances.

Eight months later, in August 1979, Graham would perform *Frescoes* in Egypt and tour in Jordan and Israel on what her dancers called the "Jimmy Carter Goodwill Tour," reflecting the president's achievements toward peace between Egypt and Israel as well as his broader aspirations for the region. In September 1978, the same month that the Temple of Dendur first opened to visitors, Carter had supervised the negotiations between Egypt and Israel at the presidential retreat Camp David that led to a historic peace treaty between the two nations.[9] After a meeting with President Anwar Sadat of Egypt, Carter beamed: "A shining light burst on the Middle East for me."[10]

Although the treaty was signed by the leaders of Egypt and Israel, its fate was determined by another country: Jordan.[11] King Hussein had expressed the same desire for peace that inspired Carter's foreign policy in the region.[12] However, Hussein had been tarnished by the *Washington Post's* disclosure of the money he had been receiving from the CIA, including for his personal needs. The scandal led the foreign minister of Egypt to conclude that "no one can sign any paper with the King."[13] Carter, however, articulated his desire for a relationship directly with Hussein during negotiations, stressing his need for the king's "strong personal support."[14] Relations with Hussein remained strained because he and Carter disagreed on how to achieve their goal for peace in the region, but progress seemed possible. In 1978, the king had married the American-born Lisa Halaby, who, as Queen Noor, became a cultural ambassador for her country and a popular figure in the United States.[15] She spoke publicly about advancing the place of women in her country and in society in general, and she supported Graham's work.[16] The Graham tour would articulate Carter's political aim of peace and reconciliation in the region.

Just months after the Camp David agreement was signed, diplomats went to work. Before the opening of new embassies, a number of joint committees lay the foundation for peaceful relations after thirty years of war.[17] Culture mattered: from tourism, culture, and youth, to commerce, customs, transport, agriculture, communications, and scientific cooperation, all seemed to offer hope.[18] In the fall, cultural officers in the region convened in Cairo and formulated a plan for "cultural normalization" between Israel and the rest of the region, including Egypt, Jordan, Lebanon, and Syria, in order to reinforce the "very fragile, very new peace."[19] Excitement was in the air. "Nothing like it had happened before," one diplomat noted. The plan involved touring plastic arts exhibits, performing arts, and exchange of professionals from physicians to scientists and archaeologists. Water experts would meet to discuss economic efforts, while dance company members worked on the ground. Exchange was key, whether it fostered collaborative problem-solving or simply the realization of common problems and shared humanity. According to Sally Coombs Cowal, the American cultural attaché in Tel Aviv, "Strong ties would be forged among the group participants which would transcend the historic enmities between people in the region."[20] All sides wanted to use culture as a way to build bridges, however rickety they seemed.

The Graham company tour was a key part of this blossoming of cultural exchange.[21] "Dance and music are always great because they speak to everyone," Coombs Cowal asserted, adding, "Dance is always great because it doesn't require language." Graham was an early entrant in a much larger project. Indeed, the political import was clear to the Graham dancers on the ground. When Graham arrived in Israel, newspapers reported that the company's tour had been organized by the US State Department "thanks to the new situation in the Middle East."[22] The fact that direct travel between these Middle Eastern countries was now possible often seemed more important to some government representatives than the performances themselves.[23]

Frescoes became a centerpiece of the tour. As always, Graham drew not only on the political moment but also on contemporary culture for inspiration. In 1978, "Egyptomania" had gripped the public and fashion houses in New York.[24] Crowds were "frenzied" about visiting museums, and the opening of the Temple of Dendur in the Sackler Wing drew massive crowds. Statistics celebrating the enormity of the temple reconstruction effort became part of its allure: 800 tons of the 1,993-year-old temple were packed into 640 crates that cost $875,000 to unpack, with every stone rebuilt complete with a 352,000-gallon moat for a mock river Nile in front of the 26-foot-high gateway—all of it with $16 million from the American government in a $9.5-million-dollar wing at the Met.[25] The Sackler Foundation was funded by medical advertising pioneer Arthur Sackler, who promoted pain medications to doctors, a strategy that would contribute to a national epidemic with OxyContin years later. The businessman-turned-philanthropist declared, "Great art and all culture belongs to all humankind."[26] Western civilization would bring the glass-enclosed Egyptian temple home to New York, where that modernized body would reign.

The opening of the blockbuster exhibit *Treasures of Tutankhamun* at the Metropolitan Museum followed Graham's *Frescoes*. In six cities throughout the United States, the King Tut exhibit drew record crowds willing to wait in line for ten hours or more.[27] The computerized ticketing company Ticketron sold places in line for the show, with reservations limited to four per person, as though it were a Broadway show or rock concert.[28] From California to Germany and Britain came the news flash: "Ancient Egypt Exhibits 'Hot.'"[29]

For all her espousal of the highest human goals and aspirations, Graham knew how to work with the trends of the moment, from the fad for ancient Egypt to the new prominence of high fashion as personified by the life and work of Halston, to the flash of the New York disco scene at the club Studio 54. With his couture dresses and costumes for Graham's *Frescoes*, Halston played on the bejeweled, draped fashions of traditional women's wear in the Middle East. Graham and Halston could be spotted with Betty Ford and Liza Minnelli at Studio 54, begowned, sitting on roped-off couches watching the dance floor and garnering drinks from bare-chested bartenders. The two Soviet defectors were spotted with Graham. Club owner Steve Rubell offered her the hotspot as the venue for her company's gala.[30] High-art modernism and Middle Eastern chic converged to become "irreverent exotica" according to a Graham official memo to the dancers as they prepared to tour with *Frescoes*.[31]

American interest in all things Middle Eastern provided opportunities for the United States to build upon the successes of Carter's diplomacy to reduce tensions in the Middle East. The Met exhibits came "just in time to provide

a visual tribute to the hoped-for accomplishments of the Camp David conference," as one reporter noted.[32] In the Met, which became known as "Little
Egypt," architecture, anthropology, and dance were weapons in the ever-
continuing Cold War.[33] Joan Mondale, the vice president's wife, who had
been dubbed "Joan of Arts" for her taking charge of all things cultural, was
featured in newspapers when she got an early glimpse of the temple.[34]

Mondale was a strong supporter of modern dance. In a letter supporting
NEA funding for modern dance, she included an unattributed quote from
Graham: "Modern Dance isn't anything except one thing in my mind; the
freedom of women in America."[35] Yet on a personal level, Mondale was more
interested in art in public spaces as well as the craft of Merce Cunningham.
Just before Mondale went to Israel as a part of the peace accords, Cunningham
wrote her a note thanking her for support and noting their shared interest in
Israel, with "the layers of time and mixtures of peoples."[36] Mondale would
then attend a Cunningham gala that concluded at Regine's, another more
European hotspot for New York's cultural elite. The event began with champagne and ended with the distribution of "disco bags" with Estée Lauder
party favors to guests as they prepared to leave.[37] Mondale promised to take
her prized "disco bag" "to only the most interesting places!," perhaps referencing her own trip to the Middle East.[38]

* * *

The ideological battles of the Cold War played out in the Middle East with
cultural diplomacy and architecture. Ever since the Eisenhower administration, the Aswan Dam, funded and engineered by the Soviet Union, and the
temple it would drown, had been a battleground in the cold and hot wars of
the Middle East. Because the Temple of Dendur had to be saved in response
to mishaps with the Aswan Dam, it immediately became an arena of conflict
for the United States and the Soviet Union and their proxies, Israel and the
Arab and Muslim countries it was fighting. The American preservation of the
Egyptian temple countered the Soviet portrayal of the United States as a bastion of uncivilized greed; indeed, it reversed the equation. Graham was fully
aware of this quarter century of controversy when she said, "*Frescoes* is about
the memories of stones, the indelible memories that are our inheritance."[39]

The Temple had a long Soviet-American Cold War history in the Middle
East as a part of the Israeli-Egyptian wars and eventual peace, however cold.
Following the Egyptian revolution in 1952 that toppled the king and installed

a civilian regime, the government sought to build the so-called High Dam at Aswan as a part of its modernization program. Both the United States and the Soviet Union became interested in participating in the project to prove their technical expertise and exert influence in the region.[40] The Suez Canal had been a prized possession of the British Empire for seventy-five years, serving as a military base and a way station for traders and diplomats en route to the Indian subcontinent.[41] In 1954, Egyptian president Gamal Abdel Nasser pressed the British to withdraw from the Suez base. In 1955, the recently formed state of Israel attacked Egyptian troops in Gaza, and Nasser sought relief from the Americans. When the United States refused, Nasser went to the Soviets for help. The Soviets were receptive: such an alliance suited their aims to bring nonaligned radical nations like Egypt into the communist fold.[42] The United States and Britain offered $270 million to build the dam in exchange for an Israeli-Arab peace negotiation. While Egypt brokered an arms deal with the Soviets, the State Department continued to support efforts to build the dam, albeit with less money. In 1956, when the project was viewed as "dead on arrival" by negotiators, the Soviet Union came forward with just over $1.2 billion.[43] The Aswan Dam became a clear example of Soviet support for modernization projects with money, machinery, and manpower.

Cold War turmoil in the region brought gunfire. That autumn of 1956, not long before the American presidential election, the Suez Crisis, in which France and Britain helped Israel invade Egypt after Nasser seized control of the canal from the two European nations, created a hot battle zone. With this incident coming at the same time as the Soviet rollback of a revolutionary movement in Hungary, tensions enveloped Europe and the Middle East. While Hungary seemed an obvious flashpoint, President Eisenhower recalled in his memoirs that the Soviets had "their eyes on the Middle East," where they wanted to "weaken Western civilization."[44] Washington went to work to woo the Saudis, Jordan's King Hussein, and the Christian leadership in Lebanon. Tensions in the region would continue to flare.[45]

By 1963, the Soviet-engineered and Soviet-funded dam had begun to submerge cultural monuments on the Nile, and international experts went to work to save them from the effects of economic modernization. Critics of the Aswan Dam positioned the removal of the monuments as a cultural salvation project.[46] A special committee of the United Nations Educational, Scientific, and Cultural Organization (UNESCO) spearheaded an international effort to relocate the monuments. The ancient monuments thus provided an opportunity to exercise the most literal kind of cultural diplomacy. According to experts, "Archeology as a facet of democracy building [was] validated by the concept of a common heritage of humankind."[47] Western democracy thus again brought "universal" tenets through cultural convergences and rescue missions. The 1945 UNESCO charter had underscored a "like-mindedness about cultural heritage" and "an intellectual and moral solidarity of humankind, which is instrumental in building peace in the minds of people."[48] The preservation of the monuments became an ideal Cold War political propaganda project because of its appeal to the cultural heritage of "humankind." Even more, it helped the United States to advance specific foreign policy objectives: renewing its bond with Egypt and the Arab world, taking some pressure off Israel, and undermining the Soviet presence in the region all at the same time.[49] Adding political and cultural cachet to the project, Jacqueline Kennedy became the honorary head of UNESCO.

In 1963, the Egyptian Department of Antiquities disassembled the temple and laid it out in blocks. But money was running low, so two years later, Egypt offered Dendur to the United States in exchange for financial assistance in saving the monument and the assurance that American philanthropists would build the temple a home.[50] President Lyndon B. Johnson created a commission to review proposals by American museums for the funding and placement of the temple, setting off a horse race described by the *New York Times* and the *Chicago Tribune* as the "Dendur Derby."[51] The Lila Acheson Wallace Curator in Egyptology at the Metropolitan Museum won the bid on behalf of the Metropolitan Museum.[52] Wallace had also been a longtime supporter of Graham's and surely alerted her to the artistic and publicity opportunity in the museum's curation of the Temple.

June 1967 brought the Six-Day War between Israel and the Arab states of Egypt, Syria, and Jordan, and the United States once again found itself on the opposite side of a nation it sought as an Arab ally against the Soviet Union.[53] The war, despite its brevity, proved cataclysmic, causing a realignment in power that continues to roil the region more than half a century later. Moscow lent firepower to the Egyptians, further enabling hot wars. Yet the temple's importance existed on a separate plane from current affairs: the Met's curator reported that even when "[Egyptian] forces were devastatingly attacked by Israel, and when diplomatic relations collapsed under the strain, there was never the slightest indication that the Egyptians would annul their gift [of the temple]."[54] The temple itself was the ultimate soft power cultural ambassador, a continuation of "architecture as diplomacy," even in the face of hard power and hot interventions in a Cold War.

The blocks of stone were carted to Manhattan and covered in thick off-white plastic under a bubble and stored outside in the Met parking lot on the edge of often-sketchy Central Park. Newspapers noted the "splendor" of the Fifth Avenue neighborhood in contrast to the "squalor of the slums" blocks away.[55] One journalist wondered if the temple would survive the city's "befouled air—not to mention all the unmentionable dangers to any fragile creature or thing standing outdoors for a protracted time in that town."[56] Letters to the editor of the *New York Times* flooded in: pedestrians grumbled and complained that they couldn't get in to see certain museum collections because of construction, and people demanded a playground in return for the parkland lost as the Sackler Wing expanded the museum's footprint.[57] To appease the public, the Met gave New York's children a $250,000 "ancient play garden." Designed to complement the temple, the playground had a sand-and-water motif and a series of fortresses, canals, and obelisks to simulate, in miniature, the environs of the ancient valley of the Nile.[58] Observers added, "Play teaches children lessons for living"; indeed, these children were learning to play nicely in the mock Middle East.

In 1970, Egypt's Nasser died suddenly and was replaced by the more pro-American Anwar Sadat, even as the 1973 Yom Kippur War soon brought Egypt and Israel into battle once more. American-led shuttle diplomacy eased tensions between Israel and Egypt, and the spring of 1974 brought hope with the end of the embargo by oil-producing nations angry at the West for its support of Israel. In New York during that time, the glass enclosure went up on the north side of the museum, and the Temple stones were moved in for painstaking reassembly. The building and assembly process moved slowly, drawing rolled eyes from New Yorkers who disdained the modernist easement attached to the grand museum.

Politics in the United States changed rapidly when Jimmy Carter replaced Ford as president, and Graham would seem to have been pushed out with Betty Ford, coupled with Joan Mondale's attachment to Cunningham. Graham had consistently worked as a freedom fighter against communism, while Carter initially felt that there was an "inordinate fear of communism" and set his sights on peace in the Middle East, despite skepticism.[59] In the spring of 1977, a series of meetings was arranged in Washington at the new president's behest, including with Israeli prime minister Yitzhak Rabin in March and Egypt's President Sadat and Jordan's King Hussein in April.[60]

Cyrus Vance, Carter's secretary of state, was assured that Arabs and Israelis "both now have full confidence in the U.S. and in President Carter to act as a mediator"—and on American soil.[61] In 1978, Sadat and Begin agreed to meet Carter at Camp David. They sat in Carter's wood-paneled office, the desk lamp slightly off-kilter, with the leaves outside yet to turn colors. That September, Carter, Begin, and Sadat stood in front of American-made mock-Grecian pillars of the White House shaking hands; that same month, as mentioned earlier, the Temple of Dendur opened to the public. Embedded in the opening of the Egyptian temple at the Met was a propaganda victory for the United States as well as a timely reminder of Carter's successes in the Middle East. Publicity proclaimed that the American cultural project saved "ancient sites" from being "submerged forever."[62]

Enter Martha Graham, with her experience as a global cultural ambassador, including the Middle East from the 1950s. The opening of *Frescoes* in the Sackler Wing once again positioned her as a modern artist who understood the integrity of her subject. At the Met, just as with Congress Hall, the doctrine of democratic American "transparency" demanded the innovative use of glass for spectacular effect. "On entering the rectangular Sackler Wing," one critic gushed, "the temple is seen bathed in natural light from the northern all-glass wall." At night, "the illuminated glass acts as a mirror reflecting the temple." Both structures employed modernist innovation: Congress Hall had a bowed roof that was once dubbed "Eleanor's Hat" but had since been rechristened "Jimmy Carter's Smile" in a wry nod to the ever-grinning president. The Sackler Wing rose like the single side of a glass pyramid.[63] Architecture again met the dance of American diplomacy.

The buildings in Germany and New York both used reflecting pools to double the architectural splendor. They boasted public participation. Congress Hall had become a place to convene, mail a letter, sit on the well-curated grass, and stroll into the German park. Architects of the Sackler Wing housed the temple in a glass casing with an unobstructed view from Central Park where "it can be seen from outside by strollers."[64] Both buildings highlighted cultural convergences. Congress Hall relied on the expertise of the German modernists who had found a home in America; the wing for the temple's stonework and surroundings was constructed "to evoke its ancient setting."[65] Architects designed the Dendur space to approximate the light and surroundings of the original location in Egypt, and oriented it from east to west to emulate the original temple.[66]

Echoing local complaints in Berlin about the American building in 1957 that looked like a "pregnant oyster," in 1978 some New Yorkers chided that it was "in very bad taste" to "display the ruins of a Roman temple in such a tremendous glass 'aquarium.'"[67] On opening night, a visiting Egyptologist threw a papier mâché crocodile into the reflecting pool, "as if to mock the synthetic character of the whole enterprise."[68] Critics called the building "an immense jewel casket" and derided it as "Hollywood-style kitsch."[69] Another concluded, "The Egyptian temple is tiny and delicate and the Sackler Wing is big and barren. It is like putting a desert flower in a gymnasium."[70]

Graham's choreography and her rhetoric as an ambassador reflected the same political mandates as the temple and its new home. As she had always done, she said that *Frescoes* "holds in its memory all matters of life."[71] Her now stock pronouncement that "movement never lies" and reveals the human "soul" was faithfully repeated in newspapers and served as an echo of President Carter's declarations about the "body and the spirit," and how governments should protect both. He spoke about the "soul" of his foreign policy.[72] Graham and Carter, it seemed, were speaking from the same missal, spreading the gospel that the human spirit could surmount human conflict, in the Middle East and beyond.

The inspiration for *Frescoes* sprang from the history of the Temple of Dendur, and the new work became made-to-order American high-art modernism for the tour on which Graham would soon embark. The temple was built by the Roman governor of Egypt about 15 BC and was dedicated to the Egyptian gods Isis and Osiris. Yet political historians knew its greater significance: it had been built as a peace offering of sorts, "a gesture of conciliation in exchange for military support."[73] On the outer stone walls, carvings of papyrus and lotus plants grow out of the Nile; inside, Emperor Augustus, "Caesar," prays and makes offerings to the gods. Mythology distilled with political power—Graham found a human universal that tied them to one another around the tragedy and endurance of love. Graham's couples danced the story of Isis and Osiris with Antony and Cleopatra in four sections: two for Isis and Osiris and two for Antony and Cleopatra. In order to understand the narrative and logic of *Frescoes*, an audience member would have to know how to read the temple's carvings and understand the dance's interwoven references to archaeology, mythology, Egyptian history, ancient drama, and Shakespeare.

Like *Lamentation*'s grief, *Frescoes*'s love was posited as an eternal human universal. Graham used the temple's references to Caesar to tell the story of the love between Antony and Cleopatra and to reward the intellectual sophistication of her audience. Graham used quotes from Shakespeare's *Antony and Cleopatra* to mark the sections in *Frescoes* in program notes. "Give me some music," Graham teased her viewers, alluding to the entrance of Cleopatra in act 2, scene 5. Graham introduces the "Fourth Fresco" with "Give me my robe, put on my crown," referencing the soliloquy delivered by Cleopatra in act 5, scene 2, before she commits suicide, embroiled in love, which had been a moment artists through the ages had represented. Elite knowledge would bring understanding: the seeming nudity of the dancer merely referenced a long lineage of visual art depicting the moment when the woman dresses herself. If scrutinized, Graham could aver that her audiences did not have to understand the historic and literary references to be moved by the stripped-down narrative. She was talking about love and redemption, and, thanks to her twentieth-century American language of the dance, the audience should feel that such virtues united people across national, political, and historical boundaries.

For *Frescoes*, reaching back to her Denishawn days, Graham had her dancers execute poses that mimed ancient Middle Eastern vases, and Cleopatra moved between positions that mimicked the friezes on the temple walls. As in the 1920s, fascination with all things Egyptian commanded the West's imagination via fashions, architecture, and dance. While Graham had studied with Ruth St. Denis as a young woman, people danced to the "Tutankhamun Rag" in popular halls. Ruth St. Denis choreographed works that fed on the frenzy. In the 1920s, the Metropolitan Museum had written in its *Bulletin* that the people "thrill deliciously at the very idea of buried treasure"; the 1970s were no different.[74] While the 1920s references in *Frescoes* might seem like a parody of the start of Graham's career, her elite early twentieth-century understanding of Egypt and its culture allowed her to ride the second wave of the popular fascination.[75]

In addition to relying on the resurgence of 1920s Tutmania that she understood from her Denishawn days, Graham built on successes she had with earlier modernist works, starting with *Lamentation* and extending through her full-length *Clytemnestra*. Cleopatra mourned the death of Antony while wearing a red sheath, reminiscent of the material and movements in *Lamentation*; she pulled it over her body as she wept. Few would miss the trope because the woman who played Cleopatra also performed *Lamentation* in the Met program. In the earlier section about the young couple, Graham accented the music with a playful, inviting, and even frolicking female figure reminiscent of the Woman in Yellow in *Diversion of Angels*. Using a flashback technique to set the tragedy in the context of past love, as in *Night Journey*, Graham accented Cleopatra's despair with her memories of happiness. In the stage work, the corps entered holding a sheath and spread it along the length of the stage, bringing *Cave of the Heart*'s technique into the choreography with its long fabric in which Medea wrapped her foe after killing her. In *Frescoes*, Graham's dancers moved the stage-length fabric so that it undulated like flowing water, or the Nile in front of the temple. In another section, Graham employed the *Clytemnestra*-like red fabric to cover the tormented body of Cleopatra after Antony's death.[76]

Graham was staging this work at a time when modernism was increasingly under attack by a new wave of artists and intellectuals, the postmodernists. The Sackler Wing, in particular, was a target of cultural critics, who found it "furiously academic in references to the past."[77] The *New York Times* noted that the postmodernists were giving the modernists their "lumps," asking, "Will modernism go down like the Titanic?"[78] Dance was implicated. Graham was historically modern, not avant-garde. After visiting the Sackler Wing, derided by some as modernist, Joan Mondale, the vice president's wife, went to a Merce Cunningham performance and chic benefit for his company, thus asserting her connection to new and daring forms.[79]

Graham could no longer rely on sex appeal to make herself contemporary. *Phaedra*-like, Graham fought back with *Frescoes* and gilded nudity, but reviewers said that Graham's "subjects had lost their taboo." The shimmery nudity of split-legged poses by her Cleopatra did not earn Graham a place at the table of contemporary choreographers.[80] She relied on the Egyptian fad. It was hot high art for hire.

* * *

Graham's 1979 State Department deployment to the Middle East followed the "pickup tour" model, as in 1956, 1962, 1969, and 1974. While this model helped defray costs and evade congressional oversight, under Carter arts funding was in turmoil. The president had been criticized by the press for not doing enough, and his staff became concerned. The White House considered a merger of the National Endowment for the Arts (NEA) and the National Endowment for the Humanities (NEH) with international agencies.[81] In the end, Carter combined USIS with the Bureau of Educational and Cultural Affairs of the Department of State into a new agency, the United States

International Communications Agency (USICA).[82] In the executive order announcing the consolidations, Carter wrote, "International and cultural policies and programs have become so increasingly important [as] a part of the foreign policy of the US" that programs must be coordinated. As a result, the State Department took direct control of USIS.[83] The goal of exports was to communicate "individual liberty and cultural diversity," and Carter took opportunities to write to artists and poets.[84] The United States could make its own contribution: Graham would be in the field already and could be funded to follow the president to the Middle East as a part of the Camp David Accords cultural exchange agreement.

The 1979 tour began in Western Europe before traveling into familiar "Communist territory" and then the Middle East. The company began its performances in Denmark in July. It then traveled to London and performed through early August. During the 1960s, Graham technique had become a part of the standard training curriculum at the London School of Contemporary Dance, which had been established by former Graham dancers.[85] In 1969, the State Department–supported tour had met with some critical attention, and ten years later, Graham had a following in London, which meant the company could fill theaters. No State Department funding was needed. Yet politics and national sensibilities influenced Graham's repertory. The company did not perform *Frescoes* in London because American government officials thought that European audiences would not appreciate "Egyptia."[86] *Frescoes*'s relevance as propaganda would be limited to the Middle East.

The company then proceeded to Yugoslavia, where its performances could have political impact. Graham had performed in Belgrade and Dubrovnik in 1962 while George Kennan had been ambassador. In the years since Kennan had left, Tito had been named president for life, and the country was undergoing an economic boom driven by a market socialism in which factory workers owned and also profited from the businesses that employed them. American artistic freedom had become linked to modernism, inspiring the Yugoslav population. New York's Museum of Modern Art had served in 1965 as the model for the Museum of Contemporary Art in Belgrade.[87] The following year, there was an American Pop Art exhibit. In 1968, students joined in the protests that had occurred worldwide that year. The following year, after productions in New York, London, Paris, and Munich, the hit rock-and-roll musical *Hair* arrived in Belgrade. American authors and films, and even Soviet dissident writers, could be found on the cultural landscape.[88] Adding to American hopes for cultural impact, more student protests emerged in 1970, and the global recession and Middle Eastern–led oil shock of 1973 hurt the nation economically, leading the government to borrow money from the West.[89] In 1974, a new constitution was ratified giving rights to the naturally fractious nation's distinctive provinces. Cultural exchange proved mutually beneficial, with the United States seeking to influence the elites of a Communist country and Yugoslavia seeking to portray itself as open and democratic on the international stage.[90]

Although Graham consistently rejected the idea of being a part of any dance production featuring other companies and choreographers, she agreed to perform at a festival in Dubrovnik in August. The State Department certainly encouraged the stop: the festival had a long history of artistic freedom of expression. Graham's American dance language would provide inspiration for the young dancers who flocked there for the "active exchange of personnel and ideas between ballet companies."[91] Graham's modernism was considered worthy of emulation, and not just because she was American or considered new or avant-garde. Indeed, Graham's *Appalachian Spring* became a centerpiece to demonstrate the festival's dedication to innovation in the context of tradition.[92]

* * *

Graham's dancers noted a distinct change when they landed in the Middle East with the Jimmy Carter Goodwill Tour.[93] The itinerary began with performances in Cairo. Because of customs issues, everyone in the company then received new passports and crossed into Israel using an American Army general's jet.[94] As in 1955, CIA operatives were surely party to this section of the tour. After performing in Israel, the company traveled by bus to the Mandelbaum Gate in Jerusalem.[95] The dancers carried their luggage over the Allenby Bridge to Jordan; soldiers with machine guns watched them closely on both sides.[96] They then performed in Amman.

Despite the serious nature of the Graham company's deployment, a staff memo offered dancers tongue-in-cheek written instructions about the countries, their politics, and local etiquette. Called "Aim for the Specific Edification and Amusement of the MGDC," the memo was subtitled, "Or Thoughts of a Not Necessarily Diplomatic Nature for a Diplomatic Tour."[97] The light tone reflected a confident moment in which the United States had scored a significant victory. The memo advised dancers of the politics and specific problems in each country. In Jordan, for example, the dancers received strict orders: "Don't discuss Israel. Period." In Egypt, there would be crowds and noise. Because they would be traveling during Ramadan, the Muslim holy month, their performances would take place late in the evening. The border crossing from Israel to Jordan would be "terrifying"; Israel would be a "militarized zone." Yet Amman would provide relief as a "sleepy town": "To quote an American Agency office, the Martha Graham Dance Company is the most exciting thing to happen in Amman for twenty years." As opposed to the raucous post-Ramadan celebrations in Egypt, in Amman the dancers could "expect no night life."[98] Amman, however, offered the most luxurious accommodations and glowing attention from the US embassy, as well as the king and queen. Queen Noor spoke to Graham extensively about her work, and the royal couple reportedly would attend performances.[99]

Aspirations for international exchange extended beyond the locations on the tour itself. American officials particularly wanted Syrian audiences to see *Frescoes*, which promoted the American attachment to Middle Eastern traditions, although coordinating this proved too difficult.[100] However, in cooperation with the Egyptian, Lebanese, and American officials, ten Lebanese dancers traveled to Jordan for the two-day run. Against all odds, a dance school in Beirut had remained open as the city's buildings were riddled by bullet holes during the Lebanese civil war that had begun in 1975. The director of the school even negotiated with armed rebels by offering them phone lines if they allowed her to keep the building and let the students continue to dance.[101] Although the civil war in Lebanon prevented the standing government from entering political negotiations, the Carter administration sought to cultivate future relations, particularly with the Christian Lebanese.[102] In a bid for cultural exchange and for an opportunity for the Americans to educate a larger Lebanese population, Peter Sparling, a principal with the Graham Company, gave a technique class to the Lebanese dancers once they arrived in Amman, enabling them to bring the American modernist system back to their school in Beirut. Lebanese dancers who went to Amman to see the Graham company viewed her as a symbol of the United States and its stability. Lebanese political leaders and the cultural intelligentsia shared the desire to restore national unity and re-establish international ties.[103] Although these dancers were well aware of Cunningham technique and the postmodern movement in New York, they worshipped Graham as the fount of modern dance.[104] She was a potent intermediary, able to reach those in countries the United States could not directly target.

Frescoes met with critical acclaim in every nation on the Jimmy Carter Goodwill Tour.[105] To a twenty-first-century viewer, the success of a work reliant on a mélange of "oriental" references and eroticism might seem improbable, yet in 1979, Graham's exotica was deeply appreciated in the Middle East because of its modernist abstraction and understanding of the universal compulsions of love. A principal dancer commented, "[*Frescoes*] was still abstract enough that we didn't feel that we were going over to Egypt to tell people what their history was like."[106] One reviewer specifically noted that Graham was not "aping" the "Orient," an indication that the elephant was, indeed, in the room.[107]

The press quoted Graham speaking about "the frescoes inside the skull, the unknown avenues upon which we paint our images."[108] One reviewer concluded that the work "instilled a driving force for the eternal drama of love by opposing joy to tragedy, youth to age, and gods to men."[109] Graham demonstrated her adoration of Egyptian heritage and archaeology, yet with her technique, she also displaced the colonial heritage of the nation by supplanting the French-Russian ballet with modernism, billed as apolitical and not attached to any nation, but rather the "human soul."[110] As one diplomat reflected, "Why should Egypt adopt foreign concepts that have no roots in the inner being of its people?"[111] Ironically, in an appeal to the elite, a reviewer writing in French applauded the work for its mixture of cultural references: "Martha Graham took care to keep the Egyptian frescoes theme recurring by having ancient Egyptian personages file by now and then, with a profiled face, front view chest and upper limbs, and profiled lower limbs, right in keeping with tradition."[112] Indeed, modernism, as a challenge to the French roots of ballet, would have been well understood by the elites.[113] One Lebanese dancer celebrated Graham's embrace of universal themes: "Graham's attention to the human condition was directly related to our own 5000-year history. Her universality struck a deep note in our history and in our hearts."[114] With Graham's status as the ultimate modernist so thoroughly established, her *Frescoes* could employ unmistakable and mimetic cultural references.

Graham's status as a revolutionary modernist continued to allow her to push the boundaries of sexuality onstage. *Frescoes* included physically explicit sexual passages and costuming; the press explained the eroticism as a product of Graham's modernist sensibility. Graham used her signature move, the contraction and release, to signify the culmination of sex. Cleopatra lengthens into a split-leg arabesque as she stretches over Antony's body. The dancers wore unitards fashioned by Halston that made their bodies look nude yet golden, drawing from the "brilliant spectacle" that painted the temple walls.[115] When they moved, they shimmered gold like the carved reliefs restored to their original luster. The women wore bejeweled headpieces and what resembled beaded thongs or codpieces. Preparing audiences for the performances, a reporter explained, "Through sexual statement she can lead us to feel the magnitude of the actions."[116] In Jordan, reviewers noted the "prevailing Symbolism."[117] Another review quoted Graham telling audiences that in order for them to understand the dance, they must comprehend that the human body is the "instrument through which all the primaries of experience are made manifest."[118] The article linked the heightened sexuality of *Frescoes* to Graham's classic work *Night Journey*: "The idiom is brutally explicit, from the moment when Oedipus plants his heel in Jocasta's groin, through the thickening and swelling of his limbs, to the fatal incestuous impregnation—but what stirs us is the sense of tragic destiny, not the physical events."[119]

One can easily frame the Jimmy Carter Goodwill Tour and Graham's orientalism as hegemonic projects of American empire—that critics, USICA, and Graham were conflating a distinctly American dance modernism with universality. However, because both the United States and its targeted countries participated in and celebrated the work, even a phrase like "empire by invitation" does not describe the nation-to-nation interactions that occurred. The project became a shared effort.

Ironically, at the same time as the American people were losing confidence in Carter, many people on this "goodwill" tour were celebrating the United States and its foreign policy. One dancer remembers people saying, "American? American? Jimmy Carter—love you, love you."[120] According to one Lebanese dancer in Jordan, "The Lebanese *loved* 'all things American.'"[121] The United States had established itself as the center of modernism; international elites who joined the American modern movement became attached to an international project of cultural sophistication.

In 1979, the idea of cultural convergences became the guiding principle with *Frescoes*, and yet the other components of Graham's aesthetic persona did not disappear. *Appalachian Spring*, still in the repertory, represented Americana, as it had on most tours. Some in the State Department found Graham to be an ideal deployment, with her combination of works of Americana alongside those that showed cultural convergences.[122] One diplomat remembered, "If [the artist] can do something, which is sort of

Americana like *Appalachian Spring*, suddenly it's better because it's the American story. That would be a two-for-one. You get the American programming, you get Frederick Jackson Turner's 'Frontier,' and you get Martha, and that's great. And Martha knew how to play that."[123] While Graham's promotion of the frontier as a lesson in democracy could seem overbearing propaganda on a State Department–sponsored tour, reviewers in Egypt and Jordan did not perceive the work as a moral and economic lesson. Nor were they thrilled with it.[124] In Jordan, reviewers felt that the ballet was poorly performed and old-fashioned. The *Jordan Times* reported that a British critic stated that *Appalachian Spring* came from "the golden age," and then added its own judgment that the performers "aren't the golden age Graham dancers."[125] The review found it "too strongly reminiscent of the discarded classical ballet with its romanticism, its epoch clothing." Usually praised for its modernism, the Noguchi set for *Appalachian Spring*, with its house, rocking chair, and fence, was called "appropriate scenery, even if just the suggestion of it." The audiences found its actual content "puzzling."[126]

In Israel, however, the audience greatly appreciated *Appalachian Spring*, perhaps because of its resonances with the issue of settlements and a "pioneering spirit." One reporter noted that Graham "created backwoods America—its ethos, its charm," and added that it was "the perfect picture, the perfect dance."[127] Graham was directly questioned about the piece and its "optimism and open frontier spirit." She immediately referenced the politics of modern warfare. "*Appalachian Spring* was done in 1944 in the mistaken belief that there would not be another war," she said. She concluded that it was a piece that showed promise for the future and for families.[128] In later negotiations about settlements, the Israeli prime minister evoked American rhetoric about expanding into new territory: "It was desert, untilled for so many years, but, of course, you can do something and we do something, in the pioneering spirit which you know so well from your own history." He added that, like the American frontier, the areas had few or no inhabitants: "The population is very small or doesn't exist at all."[129] During performances in Israel, there was no known Palestinian presence. Yasser Arafat, the Palestinian leader, was not on the guest list, and Graham would not be meeting with him. Reflecting back, one diplomat equated the separation of the people during the peace process with an *Appalachian Spring* marriage gone wrong: "The discussions were held by the best man (Egypt) and the bride (Israel) without the participation of the groom (the Palestinians)."[130] In the politics and the dance, despite the erection of political walls, frontiers were presented as uninhabited land that represented hope and promise for the future through land development and modernization brought by freedom and democracy.

The Lebanese dancers who were able to go to Jordan to see the Graham company explicitly understood the political message of the frontier and embraced it as a symbol of American strength that they could emulate. According to a teacher who would bring Graham technique back to her school in war-torn Beirut, "*Appalachian Spring* represented the spirit of America which is what we most admired—its voracity, its daring, sense of exploration, the sense of nationhood—as the Bride and Husband embraced their future together."[131] While *Appalachian Spring* brought mixed enthusiasm overall; the Lebanese dancers who longed for the reunion and democratization of their divided nation saw it as a dance of jubilation and of hope.

* * *

In Egypt, newspaper articles indicated that while most in the audience would not have understood anything about what they were seeing in Graham's dances, the country's cultural leaders fully participated in the works and their meanings. Starting in the 1960s, classical ballet had become an important part of Egyptian cultural life, which led journalists to define modern dance in terms of the classical form: "In contrast to the traditional ballet is the modern style, leaving complete freedom for a choreographer to bring out his creative abilities."[132] Music and costuming were outlets for artistic freedom.[133] While Graham's works were said to be a product of the United States, newspapers reported that she used Egyptian composers to inspire her work, connecting Egyptian culture with New York's art scene.[134] The elites both imported and sanctioned the project: Jalal al-Sharafawy, the head of the Egyptian Ballet Troupe, and his son, as well as another dance leader, attended the performance and met with Graham beforehand.[135] In Egypt, Graham met with leaders, lectured to groups, and held press conferences, and the company was hosted by the embassy alongside diplomats and the cultural intelligentsia. Martha Graham became the cultural symbol of the alliance between Egypt and the United States with the American *Frescoes* set in the Egyptian Temple of Dendur rescued by the Americans.

Graham went sightseeing with the company, despite political turmoil. For the press, she expounded on the Nile, on which the Temple of Dendur had once rested: "It is so implacable, so full of life and the legends of life."[136] She added, "Minute by minute the river changes."[137] Diplomats knew they could rely on her. "Martha knew what these folks in the State Department wanted her to say and do."[138] Graham well knew how to speak, and where to go, even if she took chances. Visiting Egypt's ancient sites, the dancers encountered a student demonstration that was met with tear gas, which stung the performers' eyes even as officials loaded them into the vehicles that took them back to their hotels.[139]

In the Middle East, travel between countries became political news because it was an integral part of the cultural project.[140] While Graham had easily landed in Cairo, getting the company to Israel proved difficult and mirrored larger geopolitical issues of trade and exchange between nations. Although a charter company had at first agreed to take Graham, the London-based firm backed out at the last minute "for political reasons." The US ambassador in Cairo cabled to Washington that any airline with direct flights between the two nations could become a target of terrorism. Travel bookings fell through.[141] There was thought of having the dancers travel through the desert by bus, but Graham's age militated against that. In the end, Graham was loaded into a general's plane with her company. "She arrived in style," a newspaper announced. Graham recounted her experience on the general's "VIP plane" for the press.[142]

Although the company had now gotten to Israel, a problem remained: the sets and costumes, which weighed about 6.5 tons.[143] Thus the suitcases and sculptures were loaded into a truck in Cairo, driven through the Sinai, and met by another truck at the border of Israel. The trucks backed up, as close to each other as possible, but the wheels never crossed the border. Piece by piece, a group of Egyptians workers handed their Israeli counterparts the deconstructed sets and the trunks containing the costumes. After joining together to get the job done, they sat in the heat and drank Coca-Colas.[144] The press later announced, "Both Egyptian and Israeli crews worked together loading the trucks."[145] The abstracted farmhouse on the frontier and the American rocking chair were handed across.[146]

The trip to Israel, which included performances in Tel Aviv, Haifa, and Jerusalem, was a diplomatic coup, with Graham scheduled to meet with Prime Minister Menachem Begin on the last day of performances in Jerusalem. Yet it may have been personally uncomfortable for Graham, who had ended her friendship with Bethsabée de Rothschild over the politics and emotions of dance competitions in Israel. As mentioned earlier, Rothschild had founded the Batsheva Dance Company with Graham's repertory and her blessing; Linda Hodes became key to the project.[147] Yet by 1975, the Israeli

dance world was in disarray. Rothschild had formed a second company, Bat-
Dor, headed by Jeanette Ordman. Ordman had strong ballet training, and
Graham refused to teach her the repertory. Rothschild supported both companies at first; when she threatened to remove funding for Batsheva, the government intervened. Modern dance and the company displayed the cultural
prowess of the Jewish people.[148] Rothschild became infuriated at government suggestions that she merge the companies; while supporting the state,
she was a private individual. Graham, incensed with Rothschild, promised
to never come to Israel again.[149] Yet Graham returned to Israel in 1974 with
a grant that came not from Rothschild but rather from the America-Israel
Foundation and the American embassy. It was the first time she would create
a work for a company other than her own, according to the press. There was
no mention of Rothschild when they reported that Graham "helped found"
Batsheva. Graham said she had chosen to present works with a biblical theme
that would honor the desert, a "place of terror and enchantment."[150]

Because of the Batsheva company, Israeli audiences understood the
Graham repertory, and thus critics reviewed the American dancers as
interpreters of these works rather than unique innovators. One performer
"danced well" but was not "sensuous enough." Her partner "was strong-
limbed, sexy," however, "One lover does not a love affair make."[151] In Israel,
critics and audiences evaluated the specifics of the performers, their technical finesse, and their star quality because their familiarity with the work
gave them a sophisticated evaluative eye.

Yet politics were never left far behind. A reporter in Israel asked Graham
about her political feelings. Graham replied, "I still have them." When asked
to elaborate, she referenced her refusal to go to the 1936 Olympics, but also
mentioned that she had been asked to blacklist a German dancer, which she
refused to do.[152] Other newspapers reported extensively on the 1936 refusal, and Graham went into greater detail than she had done in the United
States with reporters in earlier years. In Israel, she noted to reporters that
when she informed the Nazi organizers that half her dancers were Jewish,
they responded, "Whoever will come with Graham will be welcomed,
their American passport will protect them." Graham said she replied, "Still
I cannot come, if only because of the prospects for Jewish artists who do not
hold American passports."[153]

In Jordan, however, Graham's technique and choreography had not been
previously seen, which allowed an opportunity for the nation's elite to demonstrate their cultural erudition. Two articles in the *Jordan Times* celebrated

Graham as a figure associated with dance of international importance. She arrived "laden with honours and knee-deep in laurels," as "the doyenne of American modern dance."[154] Graham was not seen as an export sent by Jimmy Carter; rather, the performances were framed as taking place "at the invitation" of Jordan's Ministry of Culture.[155] King Hussein and the American-born Queen Noor hosted Graham. As on other occasions, these social moments were of key importance. The US embassy in Amman used the Graham evenings to make political connections. For diplomats, these events always offered "a chance to meet in a situation where you weren't particularly noticed because you were both in the same place."[156] As had been during the early Cold War in Asia and the Middle East, "it was a neutral ground.... [that] would also give political, CIA and Defense people a chance to meet these people off the record—no listening devices, you weren't in their office. So it's an opportunity to do the business that you are there to do in a lovely setting."[157] Even if individuals had listening devices, they would likely be foiled because of the loud music and chatter.[158] The embassy in Amman cabled Washington that King Hussein was "in a good mood" because of the postponement of a vote on the "Palestinian issue." American and Jordanian diplomats met at the Martha Graham gala to discuss like interests further.[159] The final night in Amman closed with Graham receiving the first order of the Jordanian Medal of Freedom, which the king bestowed not just on cultural figures but on government officials, foreign military officers, physicians, and authors.[160] Graham and the company received a rapturous standing ovation.

* * *

The company returned to New York at the end of a hot summer, the city still enmeshed in haze. Graham was exhausted. A diplomat recalled that by the time Graham had reached Israel, she was "not altogether *compos mentis*."[161] Even near Graham's Upper East Side apartment, garbage piled in the streets smelled like a baked sweetmeat just a day out, or old beer. Central Park's earth came through in brown patches. People put out folding tables in front of real estate brokerage stores peddling their impossible wares—apartments, attached houses, an empty lot with a fence.[162] Graham recovered in her antique-filled apartment with new pieces of jade and other exotic gifts.

The company toured in the United States that fall, performing *Frescoes* and other works in half-filled theaters. In the new work, American critics saw an old-fashioned modernism, and noted references to past dances and repeated tropes, particularly from *Primitive Mysteries*, Graham's 1931 work set on the American frontier.[163] *Frescoes* was called "an interesting throwback." Graham's desire to appeal to a "contemporary" public was merely "Miss Graham's contribution to Tutmania."[164] Graham remained dedicated to the mystery of the moment, telling the press that she spent the summer in Egypt, "standing between the paws of the Sphinx in the moonlight."[165] But the moment was fading; next to the Metropolitan Museum, the King Tut children's playground sandbox quickly filled with used needles discarded by junkies.

Undeterred, in December 1979 Graham stood in Washington, DC, with Aaron Copland to be honored at the Kennedy Center. Before the evening began, she was received at the White House.[166] As she entered the building, surely she could recall her first visit there to perform *Frontier* more than forty years earlier. While Franklin D. Roosevelt's Office of Protocol wondered about her bare feet, here she was offered champagne from a cut glass flute. She graciously declined. First Lady Rosalyn Carter greeted her with reverence.[167] But the president was noticeably absent. Although it was only the second year of the Kennedy Center awards, a show that would be broadcast on national television for all Americans to see, Jimmy Carter did not attend. He and his State Department were embroiled in the Iranian hostage crisis. The first lady apologized to Graham on behalf of the president.[168]

Carter had allowed the deposed Shah of Iran into New York to enjoy the fruits of modern American medical expertise. In 1956, Graham had danced for him during her first tour. She had closed in Iran as the Bride in *Appalachian Spring*. But in November 1979, protesters had stormed the American embassy in Tehran, where Graham had once been received as a cultural diplomat. Pictures flooded the press of students scaling the embassy fence while others stood outside with fists raised. They took those in the embassy prisoner, fifty-two soldiers and diplomats.[169] The prisoners were blindfolded and marched in haggard clumps for the cameras and for "the Great Satan Carter." In the United States, people took to the streets to protest, shouting "Deport Iranians!"

Yet even as the hostage crisis dragged into its second month, at the Kennedy Center Graham recalled the allure of the Middle East and wore a green and black chiffon Halston.[170] Film star and Hollywood dancer Gene Kelly introduced Graham: despite her upbringing in a wealthy suburb, he depicted her as one "who was born in the shadow of the Appalachian Hills," conflating her biography with the story of *Appalachian Spring*. He concluded with a nod, the lights went down, and the audience heard the wind, not music, that opened *Frescoes*. Rather than an excerpt from her work with Copland, Graham had chosen selections from the glittering *Frescoes* to show off her company onstage, and remind the audience of her status as a cultural ambassador to the Middle East. At the conclusion, two thousand bejeweled women and somber men applauded politely, eager to get off to the party. In the Hall of Nations, they were seated according to protocol.[171] The next day, Graham packed up and went home.

* * *

Graham continued forward, undaunted by the nation's increasingly grim political situation. The previous July, Carter had spoken to the country like a doctor to a patient, diagnosing what he called "a crisis of confidence," or malaise. His White House staff wrote memos on the internal "morale issues" within the administration and looked for solutions in an eleven-point analysis that included suggestions like "a party for the whole staff ASAP," "luggage tags," "squawk-boxes" for desks, and "inexpensive T.V.'s" to distribute to staff."[172] But Graham seemed in the best of psychic health, venturing out to be seen. Studio 54 roared, and she sat behind velvet ropes night after glamorous night with Halston, Liza Minnelli, and Betty Ford, joined by Andy Warhol and Elizabeth Taylor as they watched the crowds dance. Dressed in her Halston gowns, she said that she saw "a return to elegance" and "a pride in the body" at the disco.[173] And the Temple of Dendur became a destination location for elite candlelit parties and Hollywood blockbuster movie openings.[174]

Graham would witness the end of humanitarianism as a way of political life. The Soviet Union invaded Afghanistan just after Christmas 1979, and Carter became a hardened Cold Warrior. In Afghanistan, Carter was confronted with a direct manifestation of the Cold War. Already, the once promising ideas of "normalization" between Israel and Egypt had become known as a "cold peace."[175] Then had come the Iranian crisis, followed by Afghanistan.[176] Human rights as an agenda and its concurrent cultural diplomacy rang hollow and weak in the face of hot aggression. Yet Carter would not meet the expansionist Soviet moves with hot power. Instead, he halted American participation in the 1980 Olympics and shut down cultural exchange, believing this would punish the Russians and make a powerful statement of moral principle.[177] Athletes and artists became symbols, silenced.[178]

Ever promotional and undeterred, Graham remained ready, telling a reporter, "One has to be hungry for life. You have to eat it. Taste it." She continued, with a pause, "Sometimes it is bitter." Meanwhile, Ronald Reagan was again emerging on the national scene from California, with his 1940s-cowboy-movie-star self-readied to fight the Communists with what he had called a "crusade for freedom" when he worked as an actor. Graham seemed charmed. In April 1980, as Reagan was eliminating opponents for the Republican presidential nomination, Carter attempted to use physical force to free the hostages, and two American helicopters crashed; the mangled tentacles of helicopter blades and the news of dead soldiers symbolized the failure of American power.[179]

In the end, diplomatic representatives maintained hope, and they again gathered in Cairo that May. With Graham and other projects at their backs, they signed the 1980 "Cultural Agreement between the State of Israel and the Arab Republic of Egypt," thus "desiring to normalize and promote relations between the two countries in accordance with the Treaty of Peace done at Washington D.C." They sought to consolidate "a just and comprehensive peace in the area" with "cultural relations" to "promote cooperation in the cultural, artistic and scientific fields." Visiting experts would traverse borders to encourage "a better understanding of the civilization and culture of the other country" with artists, medical experts and scientists, archaeologists, and academics, and through television and radio programming. The agreement was to hold for five years and renew automatically. The document was finally published in Hebrew and Arabic, with the English text prevailing in the archives.[180] Although Graham had set a course for diplomacy, the Carter presidency seemed to be crumbling.

By midsummer, with Reagan running against Carter, Graham saw an opening. Reagan, like Graham, had a charisma that Carter could not match. Although Betty Ford and Nancy Reagan were foes, Graham could attach herself to the East Wing with frontierism. Relishing her syllables, Graham added to her anecdote about surviving the job of living, "Sometimes, it's very, very sweet."[181]

9

Dancing along the Wall

Graham, Reagan, and the Reunification of Berlin, 1987–1989

"You Are Leaving the American Sector," signs read in three languages as Graham and her dancers crossed out of West Berlin at Checkpoint Charlie in February 1987; the guards at Checkpoint Friedrichstraße in the East attempted to wrestle passports from their grips to examine them, as others shone flashlights under the bus transporting the group into communist terrain. The company had moved from the color-filled West to the East, where the buildings seemed gray, devoid of flashy advertisements. As they drove deeper into the city, "the air smelled of brown coal and two-stroke petrol."[1] Martha Graham arrived in the East to join the celebration of Berlin's 750th anniversary; the East German government sought reunification under the mantra of brotherhood and peace. Initially reluctant to join the celebration, the West perceived the bid as typical of communist peace propaganda dating back to Stalin. Ever the apolitical diplomat, Graham declared to the East German press that it was a "great honor" for her to be in Berlin because "dancing is a bond that connects all countries." She acknowledged the power of "brotherhood." Graham did not utter the word "peace" in any of her public statements, but that did not prevent the East Germans from asserting that "for the 1987 season [Graham] used the motto, 'For peace in the world.'"[2,3] With the entrance of Martha Graham into communist territory, they co-opted her rhetoric as "peace," "reunification," and the promise of "human bonds" became political weapons.[4]

The previous month, history had repeated itself in the new year when the East Germans inaugurated the 750th anniversary celebration of the city of Berlin and announced a slew of festivals and events to celebrate "peace and reunification."[5] The German Democratic Republic (GDR) invoked the Soviet rhetoric that had infused early Cold War German politics with the "Stalin Note" incident in 1952. Sent from East Germany, Stalin's "note" proposed a "peace treaty" and the reunification of Germany with the understanding that

Martha Graham's Cold War. Victoria Phillips, Oxford University Press 2020. © Oxford University Press.
DOI: 10.1093/oso/9780190610364.001.0001

it would remain militarily neutral. In return, Stalin promised all Germans "the rights of man and basic freedoms, including freedom of speech, press, religious persuasion, political conviction, and assembly," as well as democratic rights including a multiparty system. On the propaganda front, the Soviet Union claimed to bring peace among peoples in a united communist brotherhood, and contrasted communism with capitalism led by the "war mongering" United States that had dropped the bomb on Japan. Suspecting a bluff, yet caught in a propaganda quagmire, the United States and the allies in Berlin considered their reply. After discussions, the West Germans concluded it was yet another Stalinist scheme, but notes were exchanged to test the offer. After the fourth Stalin note, negotiations failed that year. However, among policymakers and historians in Europe and the United States, debates continued about the notes as the possibility of a "missed chance," whether for "peace and reunification" or the Soviet domination of Europe with a united communist Germany in its sphere.[6]

These debates about "peace" activities influenced dance as diplomacy in Europe well before the Stalin notes regarding Germany. In 1947, Graham had withdrawn from the youth conference in Prague along with most others on the committee to send dance, mirroring government sentiment that communist peace talk was propaganda. The Soviet Union sent ballet stars; amateur folk dancers represented the United States. The State Department seemed inept. Although the United States initially claimed that peace-lovers were communists or duped by the Kremlin propaganda, after 1947 the stance backfired as it had in Prague. Confronting the "Note" incident and relentless peace propaganda from Moscow, in 1953 Eisenhower battled to retake the term in his "Atoms for Peace" speech in front of the United Nations, and launched the Atoms for Peace program domestically and abroad with atomic seeds for better gardens, mobile information trucks, Disney television programs, books, and toys for children. Yet American political groups calling for peace and arms reductions continued to be subject to McCarthyite investigations, and as the American Century continued as the Vietnam War's figure of movie star "Hanoi Jane" Fonda hit the press. By 1983, President Ronald Reagan became infuriated by Soviet "peace" propaganda, which he called "the antithesis of peace." A Reagan commission on the "peace problem" quoted a Johns Hopkins University publication from the 1950s on "psychwar" and the conduct of propaganda operations: "The Communists seem to have followed the lead of Humpty Dumpty, who explained to Alice, 'When I use a word it means just what I choose it to mean.'"[7] Thus in

1987, Berlin's birthday seemed to some to be a well-rehearsed plot of Soviet expansionism.

In response to the need for propaganda offensives, Reagan became the first president since Eisenhower to use Voice of America broadcasts to make himself known as president behind the Iron Curtain. Thirty years earlier, he had worked with Eisenhower on the "crusade for freedom" campaign to raise "truth dollars" for Radio Free Europe (each "truth dollar" donated purchased one hundred words of "truth" to be broadcast into Eastern Europe).[8] Reagan invoked his past when he spoke about his own "crusade for freedom" to the UK Parliament while president. The reference did not go unnoticed. "The phrase that he chose to characterize his new program, a crusade for freedom, was drawn from the Presidential campaigns of Dwight D. Eisenhower," reported the *New York Times*.[9] After a thaw in US-Soviet relations following a summit meeting in Geneva in 1985, tensions escalated again in October 1986, when Soviet premier Mikhail Gorbachev requested that talks about missiles include the deployment of "Star Wars," Reagan's new nuclear deterrent scheme that sounded straight out of a Hollywood movie, and the antithesis of peace. Regan seemed the warmonger. Thus the East Germans countered with more propaganda around peace and unification, a rhetoric that seemed to be winning the campaign in Western minds. Now, to balance out the propaganda with an American viewpoint, Graham, who had worked for Eisenhower to fight the Soviets, would tour for Reagan to battle the East Germans with ideas of "human bonds" that asserted the power of freedom and would dismantle fences and boundaries to unite nations as a part of that crusade.

Graham fit nicely with Reagan's quietly renewed emphasis on cultural diplomacy. Upon entering office, even if he seemed to use hard power threats against the Soviets with talk of the "evil empire" and a cold war that seemed nuclear in 1983, the former film star understood the importance of cultural diplomacy, soft power, and broadcasting freedom: he unwound Carter's reorganization of the State Department's cultural offices and put a family friend, Charles Wick, in charge of the reset United States Information Agency (USIS). Although known to some as a minor television producer, Wick would later be considered "the man who brought our International Communications Agency into the twentieth century." Reagan increased federal funding for Voice of America and supported the creation of Radio Martí, a new station to fight Fidel Castro.[10] Under Reagan, the budget for public diplomacy increased significantly in real dollar terms.[11]

Graham's all-American aura and celebrity status converged nicely with Ronald Reagan's cowboy nationalism. Reaching back to the promise of the American dream, Reagan offered hope, however romantic. He channeled the frontier thesis of Frederick Jackson Turner, as Graham had earlier. Running for president in 1980, he had adopted the musical theme "California Here I Come," reminding the public of the promise of the West and the nation's forward expansion. After his 1981 inauguration, Reagan ignited a new wave of nationalism with an aggressive interventionism and a promise to be an international "hard cop."[12] Graham immediately fell into Reagan's circle when the company performed in Washington, DC, in February 1981, introduced by Betty Ford, "National Honorary Patron" of the gala. Betty Ford had socialized with Secretary of State Alexander Haig and his wife, Pat.[13] Graham sidled up to the Republicans easily, with the Haigs listed in the Washington program just under Ford in large type as "Honorary Patrons."[14] The gala also included Halston, Liza Minnelli, Andy Warhol, and the "diplomatic corps." Graham took the stage to open the performance, not to explain the new works or her technique, but to explain "that we are trying to reach each other across a gulf." The program included *Appalachian Spring* for the Washington crowd. Graham premiered *Acts of Light*, based on an Emily Dickinson quote that recognizes good friends, with a stunning section in which the company performs the classroom exercises as choreography in glittering Halston unitards in the closing section, "Ritual to the Sun." Because Graham had used a Dutch composer, the postperformance party took place at the Dutch embassy. Just over a month after the event, a would-be assassin shot Reagan, and in the uncertain hours afterward, Haig appeared before the press and proclaimed, "I'm in charge here!"—a declaration that would help force him out of the administration. But he had served his function for Graham: she had captured the attention of people close to the Reagans and "held the Kennedy Center's audience in her hand."[15]

The symbolism of Graham's work resonated for export: Graham's East Berlin repertory featured *Frontier*, the same work of Americana that she and her company had danced at the White House in 1937 and then more recently under Ford. Old-fashioned cowboy nationalism could be revived for export. Unlike Graham's pioneer woman with the fence behind her as she looked out to the promise of freedom and the West, East Berliners stood in front of a wall, a barbed-wire fence; Graham's dancer envisioned an expansionist future—not a stopping point. "The girl is seeing a great landscape, untrammeled," Graham said of her pioneer woman. "It's the appetite for space, which is one of the characteristics of America. It's one of the things that has made us pioneers."[16] She would repeat these well-practiced mantras in East Berlin. Reagan and Graham, with their ease with grand and idealistic notions of American freedom and opportunity, worked in tandem to bring East Germany into the Western fold.

* * *

"Martha Graham was a woman whose style was larger than life," declared the style editor of the *New York Times Magazine*.[17] Graham accepted her status as a "living legend."[18] Despite the company's dire finances, she appeared at events erect and proud in her bejeweled cape-like Halston dresses, with her "masklike" face pulled by multiple facelifts. In her company, the sleek and talented young dancers performed *Diversion of Angels* with ever-vertical split-leg tilts never before seen in the history of dance. Although Graham contended with her image as a grande dame of dance, she capitalized on it with the help of her lieutenant Ron Protas, who took an ever more important role in the Graham Foundation and school, as well as in questions of promotion and artistic direction. "She *had* to be on everyone's lips," said dance critic Clive Barnes. "It was essential for her to get the large sums of money she needed to create."[19]

As experienced cultural diplomats, Graham—and Protas—contacted the president and his wife through Senator Barry Goldwater soon after the election. While the Haigs were more moderate Republicans of the Ford type, and thus one step from the Reagans, Goldwater was an ideological father of sorts to the new president. Reagan had made his public career as an unrelenting anticommunist with a forthright faith that the United States and its values of freedom could surmount communism and bring nations to the side of the West. Goldwater then invited Nancy Reagan to become "Honorary Chairman" for a Graham event that would take her and the company to Phoenix, Arizona, for the winter. Although the first lady declined, Goldwater had put Graham on the radar.[20]

Like Ronald and Nancy Reagan—the first lady also had acted in movies— Graham had her own connections to Hollywood. She had trained numerous actors at Neighborhood Playhouse; her legacy harkened back to Lillian Gish and Katherine Cornell; and she hobnobbed around New York with Elizabeth Taylor (a friend of the Reagans) and Liza Minnelli, boasted numerous ties to Gregory Peck, often seen at the White House, and Gene Kelly, who had toasted her under Ford at the Kennedy Center. In manner and style, both the Reagans and Graham shared a love for the theatrics of showbiz that the public appreciated. Despite the first lady's refusal, deals could be done.

In 1983, Reagan launched a full-out call to expand public diplomacy. Under the National Security Council, the president set up a task force to address the "international 'war of words'" between the Americans and the Soviets. He recommended a heightened role for USIS. Above all, the task force called for "awareness at the highest levels of American government that public diplomacy is an essential ingredient in the conduct of foreign affairs." The report recommended that USIS strengthen the American cultural and political presence abroad through an expanded program of exhibits and performances. USIS engaged artists with a new program called Artistic Ambassadors. The president scheduled a meeting with four "Artistic Ambassadors," and what the government called the "culture press" covered the event.[21]

Recognizing Graham's fluency in "protocol affairs," Reagan invited Graham to a state dinner in October 1983 with the West German president Karl Carstens and his wife, Veronica. Wearing a white gown with a sequined overlay, Graham once again stood in the official White House receiving line. During cocktails, Graham and Nancy Reagan stood together, appearing to chat like well-heeled girlfriends as they smiled at each other, taking each other's hand.[22]

Despite Graham's gracious exterior, she had been deeply wounded by Washington: she had been excluded from the president's new Artistic Ambassadors program; the month before her dinner invitation, the National Endowment for the Arts (NEA) had denied Graham funding despite her "great contribution to American dance." The rejection letter concluded, "More recent reports in the last year or two have, as you are aware, raised questions about the current caliber of the company's work." The NEA questioned "the stability and strength of [the] company's board, management, and administration" and its ability to raise money and to engage in "long-range plans."[23] Graham had taken to the public stage in protest. In an "appeal to the American public," she accused the NEA of age discrimination, claiming that there were no valid charges against her based on artistic merit, although her recent works had been questioned.[24] Reagan had received letters from the Joffrey Ballet, actor Gregory Peck, and others decrying the Graham rejection as "a serious mistake." In a telegram, Peck cabled the president, "Please help Martha. She is deeply hurt by this undeserved rebuke."[25]

Now in the White House, Graham worked the room with a heightened diplomatic aplomb.

In New York, Graham continued, seemingly unabated. She went to work creating a piece for an upcoming international tour supported by private funding. Announcing her ninetieth birthday celebration, she held a press conference. Rudolf Nureyev, the great Soviet defector who had been so appreciated by Betty Ford, would continue his work with Graham in *Phaedra's Dream*, which would be performed in Paris. The press announced she would choreograph *The Rite of Spring*. The work held special import for Graham. She had performed the lead role early in her career to great acclaim, but it was also the work that had led to Wigman's triumph over her in Berlin in 1957. "I started on *Rite of Spring* with reluctance and fear," she told reporters, continuing, in her best diva voice, "I had to let that fear go." In addition, she announced the creation of the Martha Graham Institute at the University of California, Los Angeles, the Reagans' hometown educational institution. The chairman of Pan American airlines, which would partially fund her international tour, stood by calling Graham and her dancers "brilliant ambassadors of American culture and international understanding." When the press asked Graham about the NEA issue, she refused to comment.[26]

The following year, in 1984, Graham and Ronald Reagan began corresponding regularly, and Graham often wrote to the first lady as well. Swiftly embracing the popular pioneer-cowboy persona that united herself and the president, Graham held forth on their shared passion for the nation's westward expansion. "My childhood in Santa Barbara has made me feel a deep tie to California no matter how many years since that time in my life has taken me from my first home," she wrote to the president. (In fact, Graham's family didn't move to California until she was fourteen.) She reminded him and Nancy of the glory of the Western expanse, and how she had trained in Santa Barbara as a dancer. She then asked them to become honorary chairs of a Graham company season in New York, writing that it would be a "California night" because "one of the ballets came in an inspiration from the childhood years growing up in Santa Barbara." The inspiration for *Primitive Mysteries* had, in truth, come from not from her youth in California but from her trips to the pueblos in New Mexico, her experience of the Native American ritual dances, and a desire to join the cultural salons in the 1920s and 1930s. Nonetheless, she continued, crediting the California landscape for her inspiration: "The story is that my young sisters and I would often go into our garden by candlelight to watch and listen to the night blooming ceres' flowers open. I was so taken by these luminous white blossoms I resolved that one day I would make a costume like that." Finally, to tie the project to current-day politics, she let the couple know that Nureyev would join her.[27] Meanwhile, a White House staffer received a note promoting Graham to the president; enclosed with it was a picture of Graham with Nureyev.[28] Although the Reagans did not accept the invitation, the president sent a long letter praising Graham in grand, flowery language. While he would not be able to attend, he lauded her for "set[ting] the course of modern dance for the entire century" and "look[ed] forward to future years of creativity, innovation, and inspiration."[29]

Not to be daunted, and surely encouraged by the president's effusive letter even if it did note a "century" of "modern" dance, Graham tried again, asking Reagan and the first lady to become honorary chairs for the opening of her institute at UCLA, adding, "It would mean so much to me personally." She reminded them about their ties to the movie industry, perhaps intending to invoke the telegram of support Gregory Peck had sent, and concluded by sending her "fondest greetings." Again, the Reagans declined, this time not writing the letter themselves; the director of presidential scheduling and appointments sent their regrets.[30]

However, after the turndown, the NEA intervened and asked the first lady to reconsider, perhaps needing White House cover for its denial of funding.[31] That summer, the NEA relented and funded Graham with a special grant to preserve her works; particularly noted was the preservation of a film of Graham herself dancing *Frontier*.[32] President Reagan acquiesced and sent another letter. "Dear Martha," he began. "It is a great honor for Nancy to serve as Honorary Chairman." After mentioning the recent NEA grant, he closed, "Your name has become synonymous with masterpieces of American Dance, and we look forward to more brilliant works in the years ahead. We wish we could be with you at this Gala Dinner, and we join with your friends and colleagues to toast an exceptional career and an extraordinary woman."[33] The program announcement featured Nancy Reagan as honorary chair, with Elizabeth Taylor, Gregory Peck, Halston, and Betty Ford on the gala committee.[34] Although Nancy did not appear, the chair of the NEA read remarks approved by the White House on Reagan's behalf at the event that would include *Acts of Light*.[35] Graham sent a glossy book about her company to the first lady. Nancy Reagan replied, citing the "grace and charm" of Graham and her dancers.[36]

In the same year, Reagan's general counsel launched a long vetting of Graham in anticipation of a nomination to the National Council on the Arts, a body of appointees who advised the NEA chair, or a National Medal of the Arts, established in 1984 to offer the highest honor to American artists or patrons by the government. Theoretically, her FBI file included mention of her activities to support the pro-Communist, antifascist side in the Spanish Civil War in the 1930s, as well as her support of Soviet ballerinas in 1943, but these records disappeared.[37] The FBI conducted interviews. The questions about her use of alcohol and drugs were framed in the context of "abuse," and not "use," enabling the silence among those who were aware of Graham's addictions. In a series of documents spanning almost a hundred pages, everyone interviewed, including a mistakenly unredacted interview with Betty Ford, responds negatively to the question of whether Graham had ever abused alcohol or drugs. One person, whose name was cut out, noted that she had an alcohol problem "twenty years ago," meaning in 1964. One interviewee did mention Graham's use of prescription painkillers.[38] All those in the know knew more than they told the government.

The president's office sent Graham a questionnaire, which went unanswered. Repeated requests finally brought responses. When Graham was asked if she had ever been subject to a lawsuit, she responded that she had lost one to a dance student who had accused her of punching her in the stomach, "in the 40s or early 50s."[39] Indeed, the year was 1963, and she lost: she was initially required to pay $49,000, a large sum at the time. Graham's violence and temper were legendary. "Martha was volatile," reported Pearl Lang, who played the part of the Woman in Red in *Diversion of Angels*. Indeed, one dancer alleged that Graham had kicked a famed American Ballet Theatre choreographer at a cocktail party. When she was not in the White House or in elegant embassies over the globe, she could hit or slap her dancers or competitors.[40] The judge in the 1963 lawsuit commented that "the jury had apparently been resentful over 'the lack of humility and modesty of Miss Graham'": she had repeatedly referred to herself as being of the "genius class." Graham ultimately settled with the former dancer for $25,000, still a tidy sum.[41] Despite the reporting of the lawsuit in newspapers, the presidential reports overlooked these sorts of incidents in a personal past that Graham had so carefully curated.

In March 1985, Reagan awarded Graham the National Medal of the Arts.[42] "It is impossible to measure the profound impact your work has had on the development of modern dance, not only in this nation but throughout the world," Reagan told Graham at the White House ceremony. He continued, "The numerous tributes and awards bestowed upon you by institutions and governments all over the world attest to the appreciation and acknowledgment of your contribution to dance." While she had to share the stage with other recipients that year, including Lincoln Kirstein and Georgia O'Keeffe, later that spring Graham spent time with actor Clint Eastwood and other Hollywood Republicans at the White House and was placed at the head table next to the president himself. While others talked, Graham smiled like a schoolgirl, with Reagan bending in to listen.[43] Her jet-black hair matched his. Hers was offset by her pure white top and the yellows and oranges of the flowers arranged at the center of the table. Graham's grace and light elegance seemed choreographed for the moment.

Following protocol, Graham sent a letter thanking the president for his "acts of light," referencing the quote on which the choreography for her own *Acts of Light* had been based—premiered in Washington, DC, and performed on the evening for which Nancy Reagan had served as honorary chair. She noted the NEA funding, although it had been offered for preservation and distinctly not for invention. She continued of the White House support, "It acts as an example to the world when a great nation backed by a discerning President establishes such a symbol of recognition. Such an act of faith."[44]

Graham continued to woo the president with messages that summer. "This is just a word to tell you how much I admire your courage and how much you mean to the world in general. This strength that carries you through this awesome time is inspiring," she wrote. After mentioning the awards and honors Reagan was bestowing on her, she concluded, still smarting from the NEA conclusion, "Live through any criticism and live through the strength of the world that is backing you."[45] The letter paid dividends. The president sent Graham a pictorial record of his diplomatic tour earlier that spring. He had started in Germany for an economic summit and then attended ceremonies relating to the fortieth anniversary of the end of World War II. In her letter thanking him, Graham continued to flatter the president: "I know the trip must have been very difficult and, frankly, I do not see how you endure with such generosity and purity of presence." She signed the letter, "Love, Martha Graham."[46]

In 1986, Reagan wrote Graham again, applauding her in a seemingly unprompted letter: "Sixty years at your craft, and you still dazzle the dance world and charm your audiences with your unique style and daring artistic vision . . . a tribute to your brilliance." He continued, "We look forward to many more years of dazzling terpsichorean and theater magic." Before signing off, he added a clean, single sentence in his own handwriting: "God bless you."[47] In her next correspondence Graham signed her letter to the first couple, "Bless you."

In the same year, Graham solidified her stature as an American archetype when Andy Warhol, whose depiction of American cultural products included Campbell's soup, Marilyn Monroe, and Jackie Kennedy, made a set of three lithographs of Graham. Warhol chose cultural images that had once been new, formidable, and sexy and turned them into American artifacts and commodities. The silk-screened and neon-colored images could be replicated and sold, and the Graham company auctioned the lithographs at a benefit.[48] Despite newfound vigor, the company remained in desperate need of cash. Modernism was ossifying, yet Graham persisted in trying to vivify it.

Just as Graham was reasserting her artistic relevance, Ronald Reagan was doubling down on the importance of cultural diplomacy, something that had historically served Graham well. In April 1986, Reagan expressed his support for cultural exchange in an address on US-Soviet relations in the wake of the Geneva Summit. He said the Americans and the Soviets had found a "common vision of a world at peace" and that he saw "new possibilities for a fresh start in U.S.-Soviet relations." Cultural exchange was key to making sure this new start would not "falter": "Our governments have worked hard and successfully to promote exchanges. . . . The Kirov Ballet will soon come to Washington and Vladimir Horowitz has performed in the USSR."[49] Although the president proceeded to discuss nuclear proliferation and chemical warfare in the next sentences, he clearly understood the direct import of dance, music, and the nonverbal arts.

Although Ronald Reagan is today remembered for his demand for German reunification, early in his administration a National Security Council memo called the idea of reunification a "half-baked proposal"; it "horrified" the State Department.[50] Following up on the East German proposal to promote reunification, Edwin Meese, adviser to the president, noted that Wick had launched "Project Truth" alongside a strong public affairs program "geared especially to European audiences." It would include the State Department and embassies. Any propaganda that targeted the idea of reunification would be closely examined.[51]

On New Year's Day, 1987, the East German Office for National Anniversaries and Memorial Holidays opened the Berlin birthday festivities with a concert attended by the country's political elite. East German chancellor Erich Honecker announced that the celebration would constitute "an outstanding political event of national and international significance."[52] East Berlin, as the capital of the GDR, demonstrated the enduring power of socialism. The socialist paper *Neues Deutschland* treated the anniversary events as front-page news. More than one thousand exhibitions, concerts, theatrical events, congresses, and conferences were planned throughout the year, and even UNESCO, the Paris-based institution that had overseen the Temple of Dendur's move to New York, would hold a meeting in East Berlin.[53] City planners and architects would "give the city a facelift," according to the press, with new construction and renovation. From restorations of the Ephraim Palace and the German State Opera House to the building of "the most attractive shopping street," the GDR was determined to advertise itself as a culturally sophisticated bastion of plenty. Its Berlin would be "imaginative, inventive, and open to the world."[54]

American agencies were initially at odds over how best to respond to the East German celebration of the divided city. To give it credence would be to admit the Communists' claims that they were the harbingers of "peace." Yet the propaganda was taking hold. "A day does not pass without there being some mention in the official media of the 750th anniversary," Radio Free Europe (RFE) noted in reports.[55] News of the aggressive East German propaganda effort would have made it to the circle of advisers around Reagan, and perhaps to the president himself. Radio Free Europe added that the celebrations gave the GDR "an opportunity to stress its achievements, reinforce its political position, and to promote international prestige."[56] It was generally agreed that claims from the East could not go unchallenged.

The State Department moved to respond. The government found a strategic advantage in noting that in Honecker's announcement of the anniversary celebration, he had strayed from the Soviet party line, acknowledging that there were two Germanys and arguing that the borders "are not what they should be." He had concluded his speech by declaring that one day "the borders will no longer divide us, but unite us."[57] While Honecker's words might have seemed a boilerplate declaration that communism would eventually triumph in a reunited Germany, young people in the GDR believed that the speech "signaled the obsolescence of the Berlin Wall."[58] Adding to this momentum, the West Berlin newspaper *Der Tagesspiegel* began to print a regular report on the history of Berlin from Frederick the Great to the present. In a barely indirect reference to the current totalitarian rule of the

Communists, stories focused most heavily on the years 1933 through 1936 with pictures of Nazi rallies in front of the Reichstag and the Brandenburg Gate, both a part of the East Berlin landscape. Articles emphasized the destruction of the German people by totalitarian rule, equating Nazism with communism.

Although there was no official American response to the 750th birthday celebrations, by mid-January 1987, memos were circulating about Graham's upcoming performances in the East, and not the West. Packets of promotional materials made their way internationally: "In 1926 Martha Graham Knocked the Ballet Shoes Off American Dance." The brochure continued, "In 1986, See How Far She's Come." Then at the bottom of the page, the publicity managers quoted *Life* magazine from 1963: "Is Martha Graham Too Sexy for Export?"[59] The consulate in West Berlin noted that Graham's visit would "arouse considerable interest locally [in East Berlin]" and that the GDR would likely try to "get the most out of the visit as a contribution to *their* 750th program." But officials wanted to understand strategy in light of official nonrecognition policy: "We would be interested in specifically [in the present instansic] in learning of Washington pitch to Graham and her company." The Graham company certainly was not traveling to East Berlin on its own, but its appearance was not immediately overseen by the government, which worried American diplomats in West Germany, including the ambassador in Bonn. The memo continued, "Assume both agencies [USIS and State] have considered briefing U.S. cultural groups participating in East Berlin 750th on political aspects." It was, of course, still a communist project. Complicating the matter were the statuses of the different capitals of West and East Germany. While the East Germans had kept Berlin as their capital, Bonn was the capital of West Germany and where other nations had their embassies. Her arrival and the cultural presentation contradicted the standing American policy of nonengagement with East Germany. Finally, the US embassy in Bonn deferred to the State Department and USIS, and the woman and the company would be hosted at a reception in East Berlin.[60] In February, the Graham company would open in the Metropol Theatre, and close at the Komische Opera. The outside of the opera house had been squared off in a renovation in the Soviet aesthetic, but inside, the walls retained their gilded and ornate status.[61]

Enter Martha Graham. Focused now on promoting its founder as a legend, the Martha Graham company developed a program, surely with the assistance of USIS, that demonstrated her choreographic genesis. Program notes began with a list of international awards she had won, other dancers she had trained, and famous actors who had taken her movement classes. Of her legacy, it concluded, "Only a few people are able to become monuments in their own time. Martha Graham is one of these few."[62] Her technique, however codified, retained legitimacy as something that brought new life to dance: "Its productivity has still not been exhausted." Summing up the historical significance of what by 1987 was a traditional form of art, the program declared, "Modern dance has the characteristics of a historical and thus a 'classic' phenomenon."[63] Even with her highly stylized persona and status as an aggressively American figure, Graham continued to be a living symbol of the possibilities that Western innovation had brought.

Graham's persona was mapped by publicity to appeal to the East Germans and promote American aims. Unlike programs in the United States, the notes fashioned for the GDR introduced her as a scion of her father, "a psychiatrist and neurologist," rather than her mother, a tenth-generation descendant of the *Mayflower*. Her "characters looked back on their lives in moments of crisis [and] were influenced by psychoanalytical achievements embraced in America."[64] Communist nations did not embrace psychoanalysis because of its individualistic focus. In contrast, Graham's work showed the power of the individual as she delved into the psyche. Graham's dances also featured powerful women in direct rebuke to Communist propaganda that had long attacked America for suppressing women. Graham presented herself as a powerful and emotionally charged woman who was unafraid in both her choreography and her diplomatic performances as an ambassador.

To combat the East German oppression of religious freedom, the program noted that Graham had grown up following both the Protestant and Roman Catholic religions; her mother was an American Protestant, and her father was Irish Catholic. Her very heritage demonstrated America's commitment to freedom of religion. Accenting this, USIS announced that another new ballet, *Song*, was inspired by the New Testament, while other works were derived from the Old.[65] The program also prominently featured a recent visit Graham had with Pope John Paul II, which was not a typical narrative explored in domestic program notes. Graham was proud of this moment, but, more important, it fit Reagan's political agenda to open and strengthen diplomatic relations with the pope and his aggressively anticommunist Vatican.[66] Twenty-five years after presenting her string of religious works in John Paul's native Poland, Graham was revisiting the Cold War battleground of religion—again promoting Americanized freedom.

Graham's "European" influence presented an opportunity for the West in publicity that linked her to the German Mary Wigman—this time, with Graham the prevailing figure. Program notes portrayed Graham's and Wigman's modernism as concurrent artistic outcomes of the same impulse: to oppose the ballet. That Wigman's innovation came first, while Graham was still performing "exotic" works at Denishawn, was conveniently left out. Wigman "introduced a fundamental, sometimes radically conducted process of rethinking and paved the way for the creation of *Ausdruckstanz* [expressionist dance] in Germany and other parts of Europe."[67] Not in the United States. The publicity indicated that Graham went one step further: she developed a codified, "universal" technique that brought freedom and truth.[68] She created "what is now summarized as existing as modern dance in America, exerting influence globally."[69] Wigman did not.

As the audience held these crafted programs, opening night in East Berlin began with *Diversion of Angels*, Graham's internationally acclaimed abstract work, inspired by a subversive artist, however old-fashioned as a modernist. Wassily Kandinsky's work had been banned by the Nazis as degenerate art. The East German government did not encourage abstract visual art. Audiences cheered the dance. After that strong opening, *Lamentation* brought Graham's status as an innovator into high relief. The opening night slate culminated with *Frontier*, here subtitled the "American Perspective and the Prairie." The program described the work as a "tribute to the vision and the independence of the American pioneer woman, her strength and tenderness, her determination and her exultation in having overcome the dangers of the new land that she loved."[70] The dance movements corresponded with the enlarging horizon of the stage to transmit a sense of distance and courage: the dancer performs in front of the fence, the barrier, the Wall. With *Frontier*, Graham had started her series of what programs again called "Americana," a word that had not been seen in USIS Graham publicity for decades.

The casting of the dances once again combated international charges of American racism. Graham was promoted as the first company leader who accepted Asian and "colored" people (although the latter word was a term that harkened back to an earlier age in the United States, it was familiar at that time in Berlin to some, and not considered derogatory).[71] Indeed, continuing a tradition (the role had been played by an African American on early tours and in a film exported into the international market), Thea Narissa Barnes, an African American dancer, played the Pioneering Woman in East Berlin.[72] While Graham had long cast her dances based on talent, and without regard to color, subtle messages could still be conveyed via the diversity of the performers in lead roles. When planning the 1985 Geneva Summit with Soviet premier Mikhail Gorbachev, USIS had written about "Soviet Public Themes" and the problem of racism in America in "Public Diplomacy Strategy." For Reagan, direct "pressure on 'human rights' [in the Soviet Union] is hypocritical—since the U.S. is plagued by racism, inequality."[73] The government still needed African American casting for publicity purposes, as Graham and Reagan certainly knew.

On other evenings, Graham's full-length *Clytemnestra* testified to the ability of her choreography to match that of any Russian choreographer of full-length ballets. *Acts of Light* showcased the company's impeccable technique; *Temptations of the Moon* proclaimed the power of American male and female equality.[74]

In the face of the relentless Americana of the prepublicity and program notes, the GDR used Graham for its own publicity purposes.[75] Reporters insisted that Graham was a guest of East Berlin and "not part of any Western export program."[76] The GDR was inviting "modern" Western cultural figures into a city that had been advertised as closed. Once in the East, she could be appropriated, which she was. The East German newspaper *Neues Deutschland* framed Graham as a historical figure of great import: "She once provided important impulses for modern stage dance and contributed substantially to the extension of artistic expression to Modern Dance."[77] But, in a second article the following day, the paper explicitly wrote that as the "Grand Old Lady of Modern Dance" she was a reflection of an outdated American style.[78] Indeed, the East Germans differentiated between what they called "modern stage dance," or their more contemporary choreographers, and what they defined, in the English language and with initial capital letters, as "Modern Dance." Seeking to separate her from her rugged-individual American frontier stance, they finally claimed that Graham demonstrated the individual angst that was created and deeply encouraged by capitalism. She "grapples with the alienation and estrangement of the individual in the highly [capitalistic] industrialized society." Further framing her as a good socialist, state reporters praised Graham's "dance [that] attacks [American] hypocrisy."[79] An East German woman's magazine noted that Graham fought against the "stagnation and emptiness" of women in America."[80] According to pro-exchange press, Graham's performances were met with "rapturous applause for an evening of great dance art."[81] A review announced "ovations for the guest performance of the world-famous dance company of the USA," adding, "Brilliant dance art became an unforgettable experience."[82] Graham's dancers, who are perhaps more reliable narrators, do not recall such an effusive reception.[83]

The Graham company dancers had been well trained by their leader to present themselves in public as good emissaries for the United States, and that had always been well briefed by USIS. However, this time they had not been advised before they left home about the physical conditions they would encounter. A German dancer in the company had attempted to educate Graham's staff about what they would experience in the GDR: "They didn't believe me, so they went without their tissues, without their soaps. I said, 'It's not there. You've got to bring it—if you need this you've got to bring it.'"[84] Stories of how to wrangle bath toiletries or tissues to wipe off makeup became company lore: "There was a reception at the embassy, and we just raided the bathrooms and took every roll of toilet paper we could put our hands on."[85] Each dancer received a GDR cash stipend, although it seemed impossible to buy anything. Some could secure fur scarves and hats in the freezing weather. One dancer recalled of the trip overall, "East Berlin was *really* depressing. Everything seemed to be in a state of decay."[86] But despite the dancers' sentiments about useless currency, shortages, and unremarkable audience reactions, the GDR press reported on their excitement over the trip and their love for the city of East Berlin.

Graham, well aware of her age on this tour at ninety, did not feel comfortable in Communist East Germany and departed early, claiming illness. A staunch freedom fighter, she remembered the totalitarianism of Hitler. A dancer who rode back to the West in Graham's limousine recalled, "She did not like going [to East Germany]. She talked all the time there about the ground being covered in blood."[87] Yet if Graham had reservations about the trip, she did not show them in public or within the walls of the White House. She remained the consummate diplomat.

* * *

After Graham departed for New York, Western celebrations of Berlin's 750th anniversary began in earnest, with architecture again involved as diplomacy. The new Deutsches Historisches Museum (German Historical Museum) told the story of all Germany, and its architectural footprint faced the Reichstag, mirroring the placement of Congress Hall, the "shining beacon of peace" that Graham had opened in 1957.[88] As an unfortunate legacy of the contested architectural plan for the building—as Eleanor Dulles pushed the project forward, engineers argued about the weight of the bowed structure—the white roof of Congress Hall had collapsed in 1980. Rebuilt and reopening during the 750th-anniversary year, Congress Hall was renamed Haus der Kulturen der Welt (House of World Cultures) and became a community space with international shows, symposia, concerts, and other events. It had transcended its distinctly American heritage while also retaining a respect for its historical roots.[89]

In June 1987, the Americans formally acknowledged the 750th anniversary of Berlin with a presidential proclamation. President Reagan spoke of the city as a reflection of the "human spirit" in the potential for renewal, "to strive and seek, to build anew and create, and, most of all, to hope." That hope would be born of the "attachment of its people to freedom," their "freedom-loving spirit" that will "ensure a future of freedom for all mankind." Again referencing religiosity, he said that the city was "close to the spiritual center of the Western world." He ended on a celebratory note, calling upon citizens back home "to join in celebrating and honoring the 750th anniversary with appropriate ceremonies and activities."[90]

The next month, the president appeared in front of cheering crowds in West Berlin wearing a crisp suit and waving at the throng with his genial movie-star ease. In preparation, Western news had featured the Reagans in front of a tiered birthday cake to celebrate Berlin.[91] Two days before Reagan appeared, David Bowie, the Eurythmics, and New Model Army had performed a "Rock 'im Roll" concert at the Wall for three hundred thousand attendees.[92] The broadcast station Radio in the American Sector was accused of pointing speakers east, toward four thousand listeners standing on the other side of the wall at the "border security facility" in East Berlin. At the end of the program, they shouted, "The Wall must go!" and threw explosives and fireworks at police. In newspapers, a spokesman for the East Germans responded that the youth were merely "very energetic."[93] In his speech, possibly using unscripted rhetoric, perhaps inspired by the young people's chants a day earlier, in the East, Reagan demanded, "Mr. Gorbachev, tear down this wall." The following day, the newspapers showed Nancy Reagan, appearing in a cowboy hat next to her husband, who wore blue jeans and a rancher's belt, totems of the frontier that Graham had evoked in her dances.

After the president returned to Washington, Graham wrote the first couple, seizing the Americana moment. For her upcoming season, *Appalachian Spring* would be her centerpiece with Mikhail Baryshnikov and Rudolf Nureyev performing in her signature work as Husbandman and Preacher.

Graham reminded the Reagans that the work was "considered the most American of ballets." Noting that the score had been composed by Pulitzer Prize winner Aaron Copland, she mentioned his original title for the work, "Ballet for Martha." She continued, hinting at the work's power as anti-Soviet propaganda: "I know it would mean so much to Misha" if the anti-Soviet president and first lady were to attend the defector's performance as the frontier Husbandman.[94] Graham and the ballet superstar had grown closer to one another, sharing meals, traveling to California for gala performances to support Betty Ford's hospital, and to Washington, DC, to seek funding for Graham herself. Baryshnikov deeply admired Graham, the training, her wit and humor, her memory.[95] Indeed, Graham remained canny with her invitation, citing "Misha," who had petitioned the Senate Appropriations Committee members with Graham and her hired lobbyists. In addition, she was being considered for another NEA grant, "a controversial issue," according to a presidential adviser. The president could not tip his hat. The Reagans did not respond personally, and the White House appointments director declined, writing, "It is a great disappointment for them that they will not be able to attend the affair due to a previous commitment."[96]

Not to be deterred, during the season Graham featured two Soviet defectors and a current star of the Bolshoi. The "celebrity studded gala" hit the press. It marked the first time a Soviet citizen had performed on-stage alongside defectors. In *Appalachian Spring*, Baryshnikov played the Husbandman, entering to Copland's sparse tones that signaled the "gift to be free," and gazed at his abstracted house, stroking its panels. He was a new homeowner, a husband-to-be on the frontier. Of playing the Husbandman, he recalls, "Her favorite position was stillness. No matter how you stand and what your position is, you need to have an internal life in you. . . . But a man and a woman standing—you have to deliver something. And she was famous for that stillness, perhaps the most difficult movement there is. Being modest and at the same time being very powerful and delivering your part—that was what she asked of the dancer."[97] Nureyev played the Preacher, with his mania calmed by the Pioneering Women just before he wed the new couple. The crowd of luminaries included Jacqueline Kennedy Onassis, who rose with the audience to give the dancers fifteen curtain calls. Maya Plisetskaya, prima ballerina assoluta of the Bolshoi, who had been given permission by the Kremlin to perform with the Graham Company, performed a reconstruction of Ruth St. Denis's *The Incense*.[98] Soviet premier Gorbachev's glasnost, or openness policy, was now enacted on Martha Graham's stage.

Yet on the day the season closed, the New York Times reported on Graham's political work in Washington to get funding, and ballet's star was in tow. Indeed, the paper reported that Baryshnikov and Graham had traveled to the nation's capitol "several times" to meet with members of the Senate Appropriations Committee in search of funding. The NEA, much like the Ford Foundation in earlier years, was not forthcoming with large monies seemingly because modern dance would have no future without its leaders. So Graham and her team attempted to circumvent the NEA and went straight to Congress. New York City Ballet's Lincoln Kirstein called modern dance "a kind of irrelevant heterodoxy" and summed up the issue: "For the Government to back it seems to me like a waste of money." Protas, in his own interview with the Times, equated modern dance and Graham technique to ballet, gesturing over his "large broom closet" of an office, according to the reporter, saying that you could feel like you were at the Kirov.[99]

With the Senate deliberating, the Graham Foundation drafted a letter to gala donors, quoted critics, and celebrated Graham's hold on the elite. "Even the intermissions were amazing," the letter gushed. In an early draft, the letter writer added that it was an evening that "New York society will not soon forget," but then edited out the word "society." The letter concluded with a bow to modernism and its paradoxes in dance: "The movement that formed the root and influenced virtually all of modern and contemporary dance as we know it today."[100] While Graham claimed never to have used the term "modern dance," she and the State Department found the term productive. That tension, long evident in how the diplomats defined her dances and how an aging Graham sought to maintain her cultural immediacy, continued to manifest itself in Graham's last years.

In addition, the company was plotting another tour "behind the Iron Curtain," this time to include Poland and Czechoslovakia.[101] Yet particularly in Germany and Poland, where Graham had been seen before, the American-led idea that Graham was at "the root" of all contemporary dance seemed as hollow as in the late 1950s in Berlin when she went up against Mary Wigman, and again in the 1960s, even with the uproar around the sexuality in Phaedra. The tour did not take place, but Graham and Protas continued to plan.

The 1987 presentation of Graham dances in the GDR, the voices of the youth, and Reagan's demand that the Berlin Wall come down—none of these indicated that the fall of the Wall was imminent. Although the Wall would come down in just two years, for the Graham performers in East Berlin, the situation looked "very bleak."[102] One dancer remembered, "I didn't feel any sense of *hope*, or impending, looking forward to something that was percolating positively at all."[103] However dated they might seem with their frontier narratives and cowboy hats, for a particular time in the Cold War, both Graham and Reagan represented to many the American ideal of freedom, however idealized, simplistic, and sentimental it seemed. The American ideal meant walls had to come down. Those who built "barriers" were totalitarian, fearful of freedom, and hostile to creative thinking and new ideas. Indeed, the German Wigman had joined with Graham to defend freedom of expression even when the Wall was still standing. Graham kept summoning audiences into a free, ever-renewing, ever-American frontier.

Coda

American Document and American Icons: "Grahamizing and Americanizing" the Russians for the Soviet Stage

On March 30, 1989, just months before the fall of the Berlin Wall, First Lady Barbara Bush received Martha Graham at the White House for a social call and a discussion of Graham's upcoming tour, again "behind the Iron Curtain." They exchanged gifts, as etiquette would demand. Yet they also broke with protocol as they played with the Bush dogs; a relaxed familiarity infused the women's smiles as the new pups jumped on Graham's lap.[1] Millie, the mother, would became "the most famous White House dog in history" when in 1992 Barbara Bush proclaimed that Millie understood more about foreign policy than her husband's political opponent, Bill Clinton, who would win the presidency after Graham's death. But in the moment, Graham reigned. Barbara Bush, who suffered no fools, sang the modernist's praises: "Her remarkable talent, grace, and beauty is still evident in everything she does."[2] Upon arriving home in New York, Graham sent the first lady the requisite piece of jade from an earlier tour, a necklace, with "a very special note." In May, Bush wrote to Graham as "My dear friend." Although the letter was typewritten, Bush added in her own hand, "[The jade necklace] is so lovely . . . especially because it came from you. Thanks."[3]

By June, the Graham company tour seemed assured: the dancers would return to Poland and Yugoslavia, perform in Czechoslovakia and Hungary as Graham had proposed in earlier years, and then move into Russia, appearing in St. Petersburg and the political center of the Soviet Union, Moscow.[4] The tour would return to two old haunts, despite newly released books in Poland that called Graham's 1962 performance of *Phaedra* "old-fashioned," even compared with works presented by American Ballet Theatre (ABT) and Jerome Robbins's Ballets USA.[5] While Robbins "introduced a new path," Graham was stuck in old-fashioned modernism: "[Graham] was educated and started her artistic career [in the 1930s]—and as far as technical measures are concerned—she goes back to that time." Another Polish author called Graham "a hot-headed modern American dance priest."[6] Yet

Martha Graham's Cold War. Victoria Phillips, Oxford University Press 2020. © Oxford University Press.
DOI: 10.1093/oso/9780190610364.001.0001

in Yugoslavia, Graham had a strong reputation with her performances and festival appearances in the 1960s. For the State Department, Czechoslovakia and Hungary continued to show political promise as disruptive states for the Soviets, and Radio Free Europe (RFE) programming could promote Graham. Russia would pose the most difficulties, although other companies had been celebrated in the two cities, including Lucia Chase's ABT, Kirstein and Balanchine's New York City Ballet (NYCB), and, in the realm of modern dance, Alvin Ailey Dance Theater. Indeed, the Soviet ballet defectors remembered performances of NYCB and Ailey there and commented on their importance.

Technical difficulties could be overcome and negotiated for Graham and others. The stages were raked, a common technical hurdle for ballet companies, and the angle made the tilts in *Diversion of Angels* a particular gravitational challenge, yet the company had tested experience in Europe. The biggest challenge offered by the touring was appropriate housing for Graham; in Moscow, officials insisted that Graham live in a well-appointed apartment, but that would require the ninety-five-year-old woman to climb several long flights of stairs. While Linda Hodes sorted out the details as had Craig Barton in the 1950s as Graham's "advance man," plans seemed to be shaping up. Although full funding had not been secured, private donors had fallen in with government programming in the past. Moscow seemed ripe with opportunity: McDonald's had arrived with great fanfare, and burger diplomacy was hot.[7] Waiting in the airport, Hodes spotted another American. Striking up conversation, he told her that he, too, was a scout. He worked for real estate titan Donald Trump and was looking for deals. "Golf courses," he said to Hodes.[8] Yet like Graham and McDonald's, he had bigger plans for Americana in Russia with his own trickle-down diplomacy, government and private-sector partnerships, and the architecture of diplomacy.

Like Graham with Baryshnikov, Trump, too, would be dancing with the Russians in Moscow in the late 1980s. It also began with elite people-to-people exchange and partnerships. "A prominent business man who does a lot of business in Russia calls to keep me posted on a construction project in Moscow," Trump wrote in his datebook one Wednesday at 2:30 p.m. in 1987.[9] He continued, with government meeting the private sector, "The idea got off the ground after I sat next to the Soviet ambassador, Yuri Dubinin, at a luncheon." The daughter of the host encouraged the project and, "One thing led to another and now I'm talking about building a large luxury hotel . . . in partnership with the Soviet Government."[10] Unlike Graham, Trump was offered a suite in the National Hotel; indeed, Lenin had slept there.[11] Like Dulles's Congress Hall, he, too, had his eye on the Kremlin, with the hotel site "across the street." He also considered several sites near Red Square.[12] And as with Graham, relentless planning continued.

As Graham planned her tour, Americana would be featured next to the renewed and vigorous repertory, all with the aura of theatrical glamour and glitz with Liza Minnelli on the touring team. Most important, Graham was bringing the Russian ballet star back to the Soviet Union, with Mikhail Baryshnikov starring—if only on film. In a bold move at ninety-five years of age, Graham declared that she would be coming out of retirement as a dancer to film herself performing with Baryshnikov in *Acrobats of God*. She explained that it was "not terribly much movement for me," and that the Soviet defector would be by her side. "Will I be able to encompass it?," she asked, as though recalling the State Department reports from the 1960s, and replied to her own question, "It is in the lap of the Gods." Liza Minnelli would also join the company and narrate a documentary of the tour, which would be shown back in the United States.[13]

Graham wrote to Barbara Bush, asking if the first lady would become honorary chair of yet another upcoming gala. Graham referenced the company's "deep [financial] trouble" and emphasized the importance of the upcoming Soviet performances.[14] Bush would join the likes of Jacqueline Kennedy Onassis, Betty Ford, and Nancy Reagan. In order to fund the diplomatic tour, Graham needed domestic cash.

In a letter to Bush, Graham called the gala program "In the American Grain" and proposed works inspired by the American Southwest, *El Penitente* and *Primitive Mysteries*, along with Americana, *Frontier* and *Appalachian Spring*.[15] Graham proclaimed that she would add *American Document*, billed to Bush as a "world premiere," even though Graham had, in fact, premiered the work in 1938. Ironically, the original subject matter of *American Document* and its late 1930s newspaper reviews could easily have associated its creator with the Depression-era Communist Party. Graham's first premiere used the words of Walt Whitman (following Duncan and Shawn), Abraham Lincoln, and the Declaration of Independence to show "proud episodes in American history," but it was not all celebratory. The four sections of the work knowingly "presented a cycle through *shameful*—as well as proud—episodes in American history."[16] In 1938, Graham lamented the fate of Native Americans, racial injustice, and the predicament of impoverished Americans during the Depression. Indeed, when the leftist *Daily Worker* interviewed Graham in 1938, she said she had constructed the work to engage common people, fighting her reputation on the left as bourgeois. She used the spoken word in a modern dance, which had been successfully deployed in earlier protest works by Jane Dudley, including *Time Is Money*, set to a poem by a communist writer decrying the oppression of the worker by the "financiers." The New Dance Group's *Van der Lubbe's Head*, referencing the German communist martyr, had been celebrated by both John Martin in the *New York Times* and the Workers Dance League, which offered it the Lenin Prize, including a bronze statue of the revolutionary leader. The use of the spoken word to accompany dance achieved aesthetic and political power. Reviewers and judges specifically cited the work's use of words. Following critical appreciation for the use of spoken language in a protest work, Graham featured known leftist and even Communist dancers for her piece. In the end, however, the work celebrated democracy in its promise, if not its realization. "I refer to such a word as democracy that reminds us of rights we have, but *may not* avail ourselves of," she said in the 1930s. Ironically, her Depression-era words signaled her own manufactured history in the Cold War anti-Soviet era. "As the line goes in the script of the dance," she had said to the *Daily Worker*, " 'We forget too much.' "[17]

With "forgetting" a signal characteristic as the company struggled to survive, Graham billed *American Document* as a "world premiere" and a "new American ballet . . . with lines from great American documents: The Emancipation Proclamation, The Declaration of Independence, and American Indian sayings."[18] Gone were the criticisms of racial injustice with the new narrative of triumph in the post–civil rights era, and of the treatment of Native Americans, now imagined on Graham's frontier as a blank slate in *Appalachian Spring* or with her works that celebrated their traditions in a distinctly orientalist manner. In the 1980s, Native Americans spoke, if only through their "sayings." Workers didn't need discussion, nor did the left. The legacy of Vietnam, cuts in social welfare programs in housing and healthcare under Reaganomics, persistent racism, drug addiction, the collapse of the Equal Rights Amendment for women, the AIDS epidemic, and a myriad of international atrocities did not make it onto Graham's stage.

In a grand Cold War move, Graham cast Baryshnikov as the lead male in the new celebratory ballet that emphasized an escape from tyranny and celebrated democracy with "The Declaration of Independence." The political import, however, did not resonate with the dancer himself. Baryshnikov recalls, "I wasn't that much interested in the political aspects [of *American*

Document]. She asked me to do things, and I did them. I don't remember the details. I was interested in dance. She asked me to do it for some fundraising event, and I did it. That was it."[19] He rehearsed the work, showing her his grand leaps, suspended in the air, but also practiced reciting from celebratory American documents, in English, with a still discernible Russian accent, in anticipation of a star-studded New York showing, branded American by the White House, to support an upcoming tour of the Soviet Union. With Bush on the gala marquee on Broadway, Graham could finance a tour to the Soviet Union and bring Baryshnikov back to the Russian people with a work that showed the promise of America and its frontier freedoms under Graham's teachings. Baryshnikov discovered the power of stillness as he performed as the Husbandman, as a man dedicated to artistic renewal. In 1938, the narrator had proclaimed the "Americanness" of immigrants in the United States who embraced the ideals of democracy and freedom.[20] Baryshnikov would be happy with the dance's agenda, having declared, "I am an individualist and there [in the USSR] it is a crime."[21] He told the press that as a boy he "fantasized about freedom."[22] Graham announced to the press that the American words of Lincoln and the nation's leaders "last forever," and that the appearance of the Soviet Baryshnikov in the American context "gives new life and animation."[23]

Although the first lady had agreed to let her name appear on the program, the Bushes dodged the gala-chairing appearance because of their "committed schedules."[24] In the fall of 1989, in a series of confused declarations and responses, Ron Protas again contacted the White House seeking further support for what he again called "The World Premiere of [Graham's] 179th Ballet *American Document* with Mikhail Baryshnikov."[25]

The White House received another letter from Protas the day of the 1989 premiere of the work in New York, causing much confusion. Protas offered seats in New York to the president, first lady, and White House staff, noting that Gregory Peck would be there and that if the president and the first lady would attend, they could sell out the house.[26] Protas also asked the first couple for a telegram to be read at the "premiere gala" of *American Document* in which they would announce they had agreed to be honorary chairs of Graham's upcoming full-year celebration in honor of her ninety-fifth year. A White House representative called Protas to decline.

After the gala, Protas graciously thanked the first lady, writing that her "lending her name" had helped them clear $230,000.[27] Protas was also working with the *New York Times* on an article, and he asked the first lady for a quote.[28] Bush agreed: "One of the greatest pleasures of my life is to meet extraordinary people, and that is how I feel about Martha Graham." She concluded, making the support resonate in diplomatic fields, "This is a very special American woman."[29] As under Ford, the tour now seemed assured by diplomatic approval, the press backing by the White House, and cash in the coffers.

Yet the Graham apparatus, ever relentless, kept pushing for White House attention. Protas wrote both the East Wing and the West Wing requesting that the president and his wife chair a season for Graham's ninety-*sixth* year. In response, notes by White House aides read, "The President has already wished her a Happy B-day on May 11, 1989 as she began her 95th year," adding, "I don't think we need to do this." Several other aides agreed, writing in black, red, and green pens.[30] Yet President Bush sent Graham a gracious letter in which he declared that the "new" ballet *American Document* "had thrilled [Graham's] fans and added another memorable chapter to the history of dance."[31] It was history remade, ready for the making in the Soviet Union.

In early November, within two weeks of the response to Protas by the East and West Wings of the White House, the Berlin Wall fell, and with it the ideological battle of the Cold War began to draw to an end. As youth took to the streets in bloc nations, political mayhem ensued in Moscow. President Bush admirably remained quiet and did not blow triumphalist capitalistic horns, despite the call from many, including prominent Democrats, to do so.[32] As Graham well knew, Cold War anti-communism crossed the aisle. Graham had performed in Warsaw in 1962 under Democratic president John F. Kennedy; important uprisings were now taking place there. The Bush administration understood that the revolutions against Moscow could destabilize Kremlin reformers who would bring the East to the West.[33] Thus for Bush, Americana, at such a volatile moment, could seem heavy-handed and even destructive to the ultimate realization of American goals. Under the elegant, diplomatically discerning Bush administration, the tour never took place.

Like a true warrior, Graham persevered, still hopeful, even after the cancellation of the tour and the dissolution of Moscow's political power over bloc states. Despite the graphic pictures of students taking down the Wall in Berlin, smashing concrete with pick-hammers, Poland followed by Hungary had set the stage for the "Tale of Two Revolutions," and the "Velvet Revolution." Czechoslovakia followed.[34] Protas wrote to the White House, once again reminding the Bushes of Graham's birthday. Graham received a formal typed birthday letter from the president and his wife, signed but without handwritten notes. Behind the scenes, jotted memos from East Wing staffers imply that the president did not enjoy Graham's modern dance and was tired of the repeated requests for gala attendance and birthday salutations. So ended correspondence. At the start of 1991, "mayhem" ensued in Moscow, where Graham had aspired to bring home her Russian in works of Americana refashioned for the period.[35] Indeed, because of "internal mayhem" causing the "end" of the Cold War, she had lost her relevance as a cultural diplomat with Americana as propaganda in tow. She would be preaching to the converted. Old-fashioned 1930s modernism had been replaced by a vision of the youth climbing over the crumbling Wall, and taking to the streets in bloc nations. The State Department, embassies, and consulates kept the Ailey company but otherwise looked for programming that took dance to the streets, with performances on city cobblestones and sidewalks, and classes in dance and choreography for the everyperson rather than the elite-trained bodies. Martha Graham died on April 1, 1991. On the day after Christmas that year, the hammer and sickle flag was lowered for the last time over the Kremlin.

Just after Graham's death on April Fool's Day, Doubleday published Graham's autobiography, edited by former first lady Jacqueline Kennedy Onassis. Using the first person "I," Graham told a triumphalist narrative of the East Berlin performance of *Frontier*. Ever apolitical, she never mentioned her connection to the Reagans. Instead, she invoked the Wall, recalling that a woman in the audience could not understand the concept presented by *Frontier* because she believed that "when you reach the frontier, you've reached a barrier." Mirroring Reagan and the beliefs that had become inscribed into her legacy, Graham said that she explained to the East German that the frontier signaled the "spirit of man and union of man."[36] Graham spoke from the grave to the power of the American land frontier, which would reflect the frontier of the spirit and bring nations together, as long as walls were not erected.

Martha Graham had begun her career-long engagement with the executive branch of the US government when she opened in *Frontier* at the White House in 1937; fifty years later, unbeknownst to her at the time, she closed the chapter with the same work two years before the Cold War barrier was taken down. The only international event that could silence her Americana as an executive branch export was the end of the Cold War itself. The relic that is Checkpoint Charlie, through which Graham crossed in her limousine

speaking of spilled blood, has since been moved to a location more conven-
ient for tourists. "Certified real" chunks of the Berlin Wall are sold in gift
shops alongside Berlin Noodlin, pasta that is shaped like the Brandenburg
Gate, where Reagan told Gorbachev to tear down the wall. Nearby, on a posh
street in the former Communist sector, royal red Cartier backdrops show off
sparkling gems. Yet nostalgia for a lost past echoes in the streets.

From Franklin Roosevelt through George H. W. Bush, every sitting president either sent Martha Graham abroad or received her at the White House.
From Eisenhower through Bush, each administration planned to deploy
Graham as cultural ambassador and her dances as cultural propaganda.
Although she publicly denied her attachment to politics, her connections to
the US government were active and calculated. Despite the Americana and
its signals with the Soviets on the frontier, stories of empire, imperialisms,
and democracy's contested hegemony have to be renegotiated. Theoretically,
Graham and her work demonstrated freedom of expression that was available only in a democracy in which artists were not tools of the state and
thus not subject to totalitarian intervention or suppression, be it Nazi or
Soviet. Western modernism, retold as a victor's history, was derived from
an abstracted approach to humanism and "universalism." It was available
only as a byproduct of the freedom of the individual, and it was readable
by all people despite cultural differences, because it embedded and enacted
cultural convergences. Graham's dances used a hybrid American–German–
Asian–Middle Eastern technique, orientalist in fruition, to highlight the
potency of the Western canon in America, as well as its pioneering frontier spirit. During her international tours, Graham promised to join elites
in an imagined cultural community that served American diplomatic aims.
She could persuade elite international leaders to join the American government to enact its foreign policy objectives, through her choreography
and her company, but, most important, also through her own position at
center stage. Graham's *Frontier* told the story of a pioneer woman marking
her space in a new land full of promise. Although the political implications
of the dance would shift over the decades—from redemptive during the
Depression under Roosevelt, to hokey during the "Frontiers of Freedom"
and Reagan cowboy era—her persona and her choreography remained
poignant and persuasive to government officials and dancegoers alike, as
an example of American innovation, however traditional it became. It became a suspect product of a hegemonic empire working with Foucauldian

soft-power imperialism to train the international body in the "universal" American modern ways.

In the summer of 2010, the Martha Graham Dance Company staged a series in New York titled "Dance Is a Weapon," presenting the works of Depression-era Communists and Graham. In this, the company took the title from the famous 1932 Moscow delegation's declaration upon its return to the United States, "Art Is a Weapon." Graham's antifascist work was brilliantly revived and indeed seems to have become a "crowd pleaser." Reminiscent of the Depression era, just two years earlier the famous banking conglomerate Lehman Brothers had filed for bankruptcy, the largest bankruptcy in history, and the global financial system seemed on the verge of implosion because of the collapse of financial products, packaged and repackaged, based on individual home mortgages. Although governments working with a few "financiers" averted a full-fledged meltdown on Wall Street, people lost their homes and their jobs. They had taken out mortgages, and now they were left with paper and personal debt. In 2009, Bernie Madoff pleaded guilty to one of the largest investment Ponzi schemes. In the midst of reverberating shocks, audience members celebrated the Graham series that revived Jane Dudley's *Time Is Money*; its closing echo of the word "financiers" now held more than historic interest. It had personal meaning. New Dance Group works found renewed fame with the depiction of the homeless onstage. Yet the Graham company closed with *Appalachian Spring*, to the shock of some. "How dare they?," demanded an audience member who had just lost her home as she stared into my eyes in the lobby. As a historian of the New Dance Group, I stood, mute. In contrast to Graham's perpetual elocutional elegance, I had no response. For some, Graham's Americana smacked of a celebratory American exceptionalism and a presumptuous appropriation of universalist claims on behalf of one world superpower, which had just nearly felled a global system with greed and its iterations.

Graham always saw the tragic and evil, if in her telling she found the redemptive at the end. What she said she was not—political, a modernist, feminist, missionary—brought the best of what these container words represent: cultural exchange, friendships across borders, political softening, the pursuit of curiosity and innovation, technical excellence and discipline, empowerment for all women as they choose. She remained the bearer of ideals such as truth and freedom, however old-fashioned they may seem in the twenty-first century. Graham understood the futility of physical walls and totalitarian rule, as well as the antihumanist implications of the wall as a metaphor. She expressed this in her own narrative of the falling of the Berlin Wall: "I saw it go up and now I have seen it come down. It makes me feel triumphant to think that nothing lasts but the spirit of man and the union of man." She used the trope of the Wall to criticize narrow-minded thinking and showed it to be the legacy of a totalitarian future that promises its citizens sure repressions and their destructive, even fatal fallout. She concluded, ever redemptive, "People cross the border from East to West to shake the hands of those they have not seen before. In a way, they have become each other's frontier."[37] As she had crossed from East to West Germany, past the Wall, Graham recalled the atrocities inspired by Hitler, who came to power rapidly, who many thought was a passing fad and the product of a man who would soon be gone, and who consolidated power using the politics of fear, nationalism, and "the other" in what today would be called by some, "rule by executive decree."[38] She felt the blood spilled in Germany in her bones, the "blood memory." Graham wrote that each person "carries thousands of years of that [human] blood and its memory." She concluded, "We are the carriers of lives and legends."[39]

As I was sagely advised by one of her stars, the ever-famous Woman in Red, "Never forget: Martha is a genius."[40]

Acknowledgments

Never go anywhere without your gang.

—Blanche Wiesen Cook

I must first express my deep gratitude to Martha Graham for her genius, and for inspiring me to push beyond what I thought possible in both my youth and my advanced age as a dancer and then as a historian.

A long list of mentors and professors at Columbia University and professionals outside my home institution, colleagues, friends, and family have encouraged me and added significantly to what would have been a small study of a single series of performances in the 1950s. Eric Foner and Lynn Garafola never seemed to doubt the power of my research tenacity. Initially, I sought to write about Graham in India in 1955, and Eric pressed me to write about all the tour locations and all her tours; little did we know the scope. When I came to him, proclaiming my fear of dilettantism and my uncertainty about how to cover more than twenty-five countries, he merely said, "Nonsense. You're a tourist." He gave me permission to persevere. Most importantly for this project, he consistently pointed out his wall of past students' books that he said he cherished. As I advise my own students, the advice offered by Eric Foner and Lynn Garafola remains invaluable. Perhaps one of my proudest moments was when I gave a presentation on Graham's religious works as Cold War propaganda at a conference and Lynn tilted her head and said, "I never thought of that"; I was flabbergasted. Lynn knows everything. The following fall, I presented my own students at a conference at which Dr. Garafola was honored. I will always remain grateful for their mentorship, which included the deep understanding of my responsibility to inspire future generations.

The other members of my dissertation committee have been mentors well beyond the call of duty. Carol Gluck challenged me to push beyond the constructed borders I had put on my abilities. She unfailingly demanded that I become a better historian and teacher than I thought possible. Just when the work seemed to be spiraling out of control, she could see the bones of it.

Teaching next to her for several semesters at Columbia showed me the internal workings of a master. In the classroom, rarely does a month pass that I don't quote her wise sayings. As her teaching fellow, I understood the power of primary documents, and thus launched the Cold War Archive Research (CWAR) project at Columbia University. And, to boot, she offered me her home and friendship in the hardest of times. Without Carol Gluck, the book would still be a hope and a dream. I will always value her wise counsel.

I have had the honor of teaching foreign policy for Anders Stephanson, having him on all my PhD committees, working with him on CWAR, and sharing emails. He took me on as a teaching assistant although I had no background in foreign policy whatsoever. I have had the pleasure of working for him and with him on several conferences at Columbia University and West Point Military Academy. In all cases, he has generously volunteered his expertise and insightful commentary. Anders brings this piercing critical eye to my work; he has helped me to understand the joys of Fredric Jameson. I remain ever grateful as I close this chapter and pursue the next projects.

Victoria de Grazia commands "center stage" with Miss Graham. During my first semester as an elderly graduate student, she taught a class on empires and imperialism. Although I was committed to exploring the interwar communist dancers, the Graham archives opened during this semester, and I used the newly available material for a seminar paper. As I struggled with the final draft, she said, "You can't write it because it's your dissertation." I did not know it at the time, but she was, as always, spot on. A formative part of my development took place during a conference at Aarhus University in Denmark, where she took me as her student. We have been fortunate to receive funding for the European Institute's Cultural Initiative, which allows me to design courses in cultural diplomacy at Columbia and funds CWAR. Vicky has allowed me to think beyond what seemed possible and to enact programs I had only imagined. She has provided critical support for this book with edits, suggestions, and good walks on the beach.

Along with Victoria de Grazia, I thank the European Institute, and particularly François Carrel-Billiard. When I came up with a variety of seemingly hare-brained academic schemes to take students to archives and teach courses that raised eyebrows, he was always present to encourage and discipline the ideas. I would have been much more cautious without his encouragement and finesse. I rely on him with each new step to guide my work and practice. In addition, Adam Tooze welcomes my ideas, despite my training as an "Americanist." Sharon Kim keeps us all going in the right direction and brings her keen intelligence and creativity to all projects.

The Oral History Research Center at Columbia University and Mary Marshall Clark have provided vital support and training, without which this book would not have been possible. While working on my MA at New York University, I took my first class with Mary Marshall Clark, which was one of the highlights of my academic career. Under her guidance, I began interviewing dancers. While some are no longer with us, we have their stories in collections at Columbia, the Library of Congress, and the New York Public Library, and on tape at Martha Graham Resources. They have, in many cases, "made history." Mary Marshall taught me one of the greatest skills I rely on daily as a historian: to let the silence linger. Pauses mean people are thinking. She taught me that, as with paper documents, what is *not* said—and the silences—are as important, if not more so, as the record.

The chair of my committee, Alice Kessler-Harris, was the second professor I met before I applied to the PhD program in history at Columbia University. One of the early struggling drafts of my dissertation was written for Kessler-Harris during a seminar on women and gender. As I grappled with the ideas and the archives, she remained tolerant of my ramblings. As I tussle with my women who disavow their feminism, she has helped me to sort through its meaning and focus my thoughts.

The number of other Columbia University professors who have influenced the book is an embarrassment of riches. They have included Americanists, Europeanists, and scholars of Asia, the Middle East, journalism, and religion, as well as dance, culture, diplomacy, and the Cold War. In this, I am sure to forget someone, and for this I apologize. Elizabeth Blackmar was an instant inspiration in my first-semester literature review course; when she learned of my knowledge of dance, we even did a French minuet in her office. Mark Mazower contributed to my research, scholarship, and development as a practitioner. Rashid Khaledi tolerated and even welcomed my naïve questions, suggested books and advice, and has kept his office door open to me. As a teaching assistant for Ken Jackson, I still proudly wear my New York City bike ride T-shirt, and have benefited immensely from the now suspended seminars at the Lehman Center for American History. He always greets me with kindness, and Lisa Keller always met me with a warm welcome and a book. I first got to know Matthew Connelly in Aarhus, and since then, I have always learned from our dialogue and his approach to archival material. I cannot thank Richard John enough for his support of my students and of CWAR, and for getting me a seat on the bus to Washington in a pink hat. Mary Boys offered me the distinct honor of being accepted as part of the student body of Union Theological Seminary as I explored the history of religion as a master's student, yet again. Euan Cameron has provided me with new inspiration in a quiet and studied examination of the personal and the political during the religious Cold War.

Volker Berghahn has been a mentor and guiding presence, although I have never taken his class or worked for him. This is typical of Volker's presence at Columbia; he is the grand master of generosity. I cannot thank him enough for his wise words during coffees while I was a student and lecturer at Columbia, and his mentorship as a junior yet old faculty member both in the United States and "across the pond" at the London School of Economics. His books and lectures never cease to inspire, and his guidance fuels my plans for future research.

Working for Alan Brinkley was an honor and a privilege, and I miss him dearly. I studied under him, and he invited me to assist him in his seminars on American conservatism and the American liberal tradition. There has not been a semester of teaching in which he goes unmentioned; he deeply influences my students and will continue to do so. When I don't understand a problem, I follow his wise guidance: "Write a syllabus." He thus inspired me to create and teach a course on women in the Cold War to understand women in politics in 2020. I offered a paper in his honor at the Berkeley First Inaugural Right-Wing Studies Center conference in 2019. Whenever I feel a bit glum, I remember the sparkle in his eye.

It is an honor to work for Columbia University and to teach in the History Department and for its joint programs, and I have been adopted by the Harriman Institute. Line Lillevik is an inspiration and a friend, and is always at the batting plate for me. The Department of History administrators and staff have shown me bright smiles in difficult times as a PhD candidate and as an instructor. The Harriman Institute and Kimberly Martin have been a continued source of professional support and friendship. Alex Cooley, Istvan Deak, Alan Timberlake, and Christopher Caes have all been extremely generous and supportive of my work and CWAR with advice, funding, and translations. I received a generous grant from PEPSICO through Harriman that contributed to the findings on religion as propaganda in Eastern Europe, and publication of this book was made possible with a grant from the Harriman Institute. The book has been generously included in the Studies of the Harriman Institute Series.

Too numerous to mention are the professors from other institutions who have offered formative insights into my work as I struggled to write articles and present at conferences, and many are mentioned in the endnotes. Mark Franko, Joellen Meglin, and Barbara Palfry have published my work, mentored me, and provided editorial support while they tolerated my writing. Naima Prevots is the founder of us all, and met me early in my career on a bench in DC to discuss my project. She gave me key documents. Gregg Brazinsky at the George Washington University not only critiqued my work at two conferences but also invited me to come to the George Washington University and speak, which resulted in new thinking about Asia. His guidance in Germany made research possible because he found my eyes and ears, students who shared their language and research skills with me. In addition, Penny von Eschen, one of the mothers of us all in cultural diplomacy, has acted as commentator during panels at both the Society of Historians of American Foreign Relations and the American Historical Association. Her insights both during the conferences and after have furthered the work. Laura Belmonte offered wonderful support after I presented my work on the Camp David Accords. A. Ross Johnson has provided deeply enriching support for CWAR, my work, and my students.

Julia Foulkes, the New School, and Gay Morris have contributed significantly to the thinking that guides the work and supported my work when I was first a PhD candidate with coffee and sage council. While in Berlin, Madeline Ritter, Tanzplan Deutschland, provided evenings of conversation and guidance. They have provided mentorship, advice, support, and hospitality. The London team has also been ever present: Henrietta Bannerman would not cease and desist until missing documents appeared on her desk; Victoria Thoms, Stacey Prickett, Lise Uytterhoeven, and other dance scholars helped with documents, conferences, museum visits, coffee, and great dinners.

Lauren Erin Brown, Marymount College, has been a good friend and stalwart colleague from the start.

International institutions have provided key resources. Csaba Békés and his Cold War Research Center at Corvinus University have deeply supported my scholarship and my students. Professor Békés has hosted my CWAR group at his Cold War Conference from 2016 to 2019, and we look forward to 2020 and beyond. His dedication to free speech and academic freedom is infectious, and I am honored to teach at Corvinus with him. At the Vera and Donald Blinken Open Society Archives, my students and I have been welcomed and funded by István Rév; our deep gratitude is offered to Robert

Parnica, who guides us through the archives, its history, and the documents, meeting with us at the conclusion of each day to guide the next. I thank my cohort at Women Writing Women's Literature, and particularly Blanche Wiesen Cook, quoted in the epigraph to this section. I thank all those nationally and internationally with whom I have presented and worked, listed at www.victoria-phillips.global.

My teaching "gap year" as an exchange faculty member of the Department of International History at the London School of Economics has transformed the book and my teaching. When I was a PhD student, I was honored to be accepted for a conference hosted in London by the London School of Economics, Stanford University, and Columbia. Then, Nigel Ashton helped me with the chapter on the Camp David Accords as I searched for Graham in Jordan. Little did I know that within a decade I would see his office light from my own. Taylor Sherman made my office seem like a home and offered ever-sage advice as we planned the year from across the "pond." I would also like to thank Matthew Jones, who is ever supportive and offered numerous insightful comments on the manuscript. I'm sure he and others will find missed opportunities and Cold War errors, and for this I apologize in advance. Piers Ludlow has shown great support, and I deeply appreciate the generosity of Roham Alvandi, who left me tea and an office that I shall miss. We look forward to sharing Amagansett again. Vladislav Zubok offered sage advice on my next project and a knowing glance as he saw me wrestling with a stack of thick books on Bandung as I entered Sardinia House with a daunting task: "I have to sum this up in a paragraph." It has been an honor to work with the many whose scholarship is also acknowledged in the endnotes. Members of the Cold War cluster, working groups, Cumberland House, and Thursday seminars have provided insights into history and the international Cold War that are incomparable. Indeed, having met other fellows at LSE, the department's spirit of intellectual exchange has led to the creation of a working group to study women and diplomacy internationally; thanks to Johanna Gehmacher, Susanna Erlandsson, Flako Schnicke, and the German Historical Institute. The LSE first-floor support staff always warmly welcomed me with expert professional advice and patiently answered the silliest Internet questions. I look forward to a continued relationship with the department.

In all the institutions in which I have taught, including Columbia University and the London School of Economics, Barnard and Marymount Colleges, with special thanks to Katie Langan, I have been consistently inspired by my students. I start all seminars with the mandate that with their final essays, "Tell me something I don't know." We have all read the books, and a book report earns a C at best. To excel, find a primary document and an archive; read the literature of the fields. Create a thesis statement that is not written in stone. Write. Put it in a drawer. Edit for "throat clearing" and "verbal ticks" (thank you, Carol Gluck). Draft. Finish. Nearly to a student over a decade, they have filled the mandate. They have inspired my scholarship. Although some are acknowledged in the endnotes when I used their papers and theses directly, most are not cited by name. Dear All, you know who you are, and I thank you.

Archivists have been my lifeblood, and many have become good friends. James Smith at the Rockefeller Archive Center has offered his power as a scholar to both critique the work and shape me as a scholar. His reminders to remain focused and disciplined as I wander through archives, only to discover some new detail, have been instrumental in revising and finishing the manuscript. Yet he has always encouraged me to go one step further, and thus it is because of him that I have a to-do list for the future. He has let me see that I will be taken out of the profession "feet first," as the saying goes.

The archivists with whom I have had the pleasure of working have provided invaluable support in the United States, Germany, Israel, Poland, Hungary, and other nations found in the endnotes. Without fail, these people, the gatekeepers, have not only welcomed me but also brought me documents I did not know existed. Charles Perrier at the New York Public Library, Jerome Robbins Dance Division, brought me an invaluable cardboard box, now cataloged. The National Security Archive provided an extra two pages of the Martha Graham FBI file that led me to previously undocumented tours. Mary Daniels at the Hugh Stubbins Archive, Harvard University, and Vera Ekechukwu, and now Melanie Griffith, Special Collections, University of Arkansas, contributed significantly as the welcoming force in the first and last archive I visited. Other archivists at the Truman, Eisenhower, Kennedy, Nixon, Ford, Reagan, and Bush presidential libraries have provided on-the-spot responses and sent thousands of pages of documents. Although I wish to name the people involved, one by one, this would take pages. Yet I do have to thank, in particular, the archivists at the Gerald Ford Library. Because of their dedication, I was able to create a new chapter of the book, as well as inspiration for future publication. Gerald R. Ford and his wife provide a foundational mantra to our nation with the dignity they brought back to the White House. I am proud to be a small part of their legacy. Yet others abound: the archivists are our inspiration.

Despite funding cuts and the inevitable problems of government, the professionals at the National Archives in Washington, DC, and in College Park, Maryland, helped me find the best approach to the wealth of material that seemed unconquerable. There were disputes, but in the end, even if I was told "we have nothing," we always found something. And my students did as well—with the blessings and cooperation of the archivists.

Archivists in European institutions have been extremely helpful despite my language fumblings. In particular, I wish to thank Siglinde Tuschy, who was Director of Programs at the Haus der Kulturen der Welt (Congress Hall). She has shown me items from the institution's archive; arranged for me to present my work at the Haus, which provided invaluable feedback on Graham's 1957 performance; and become a valued friend. In addition, she has inspired my next book project.

I have been honored to receive a Visegrad Fellowship from the Open Society Archives in Budapest, Hungary. The archivists there have been generous with me and with my students, where we have worked for five summers. The funding allowed me to probe more deeply into the radio programming that supplemented the dance performances, and to explore general policy in the realm of culture during the Cold War in Eastern Europe. I am honored to continue teaching in Eastern Europe with this background.

I have been blessed with wonderful research assistants in Germany, Eastern Europe, Israel, and Poland, and in Spanish and Portuguese archives, including Julia Sittman, Natalija Dimic, Uri Turkenich, and especially Marek Dąbrowski and Conor Lane. They are all fine hunters, gatherers, translators, and scholars in their own right.

Of course, I must thank the numerous US-based researchers and editors who have helped me through the process both in the United States and in Europe. I must give special recognition to Tinatin Japaridze and Sarah Roth, who both started as students and CWAR fellows, and are now colleagues as we present at conferences. We traveled back to our hotel from the Eisenhower archives in the summer rush hour of Abilene, Kansas, with no cars, and then in the heart of busy Budapest, where we ate plates of goulash. Ms. Japaridze has been an invaluable TA, a fine scholar in her own right, and a good friend. Ms. Roth continually inspires my work with her archival tenacity and good cheer. Both contributed to this book as research assistants and key advisers. In addition, Lotte F. M. Houwink ten Cate has heightened my understanding of gender as a CWAR fellow, colleague, and friend. I thank Jonathan Cohn, a stalwart editor and adviser. He has edited every article I have published and worked with me on this manuscript for nine years in various forms. Special thanks to Laura Heimert, who introduced me to David Groff—an unparalleled editor who made me give up an aversion to drama and adjectives, and led me to understand the power of Martha, advising, "Never leave a paragraph without Graham." Trent Duffy brought up the rear in fine force. Alexandra Cook built the book website and explained the value of blogs when I asked, "What's a blog?" Nick Cohen brings in the future.

Because official documents have been lost or destroyed, in some cases at the wish of Martha Graham herself, members and former members of the Martha Graham Dance Company and Foundation have been invaluable guides to the woman, the work, and the tours through oral histories and documents they pulled from underneath their beds and, in many cases, contributed to the Library of Congress or the New York Public Library. Janet Eilber, Artistic Director of the Graham company, initially allowed me to archive and photograph the company's documents and provided me with tapes of performances. I remain saddened that I cannot name the Martha Graham Dance Company as an archive because of its current practice of charging a significant entry fee to scholars. Without open access, I am not able to cite its sources. While I have proposed various solutions, they remain corporate papers available only to wealthy scholars or, uncitable for old-fashioned scholars who rely on stable documents, via the company's Google Cultural Institute (https://www.google.com/culturalinstitute/beta/partner/martha-graham-center-of-contemporary-dance). Although the effort to bring documents and ideas to the public space is essential and meets today's trends, hard documents, physical access, and these citations are the stuff of historians who make arguments for generations.

Yet for historians, adversity brings opportunity. When sorting out how to obtain pictures at an affordable cost, I realized that any picture taken of Graham with a politician would be held by both Graham Resources and the politician. It was this realization that led me to query every presidential library, Roosevelt through Bush. In addition to finding a plethora of photographic materials, and wonderful archivists, I unearthed new documents that revealed an intimate relationship between Graham and those living in the White House over decades and administrations, Republican and Democratic. Thus, I am thankful for barriers erected because ultimately these obstacles make us stronger and more resourceful as historians.

Although I cannot name them all, I would like to specifically thank dancers who contributed to this book and have passed: Ethel Winter,

Mary Hinkson, Pearl Lang, Mimi Cole, and David Zurak. They remain lost friends, and yet I can hear their voices guiding and warning me as I work. The first oral history I ever conducted was with Ethel Winter. Years later, when she was hospitalized, she sternly told nurses to let me in because I was her daughter. "Basically," she said under her breath to me. Mary Hinkson, the iconic Woman in White in *Diversion of Angels*, provided insights and became one of my closest friends. I miss her deeply, daily. When Pearl Lang was in the hospital, I brought her a stuffed pink dog, the first stuffed animal anyone had ever given her, she said. From her bed, which we all expected her to sweep out of, she wisely advised me, "Never forget. Martha is a genius." David Zurak is deeply missed, and we always smiled and laughed together at political antics.

Of the vital living, Linda Hodes's oral histories have deeply influenced my thinking and research to understand the tours and company dynamics. She, too, has become an important mentor, guide, and friend. Because of Linda, two new chapters emerged. Martha Hodes, her daughter and world-renowned scholar named for Martha, has provided sound guidance. Peggy Lyman offered documents to me and the Metropolitan Museum archive that literally "made history." Terese Capucilli has the most important archive on Graham after 1974, and she opened her apartment door and allowed me to document her complete records of the 1979 and 1987 tours, meticulously cataloged, neither of which can be found in any public repository. She and Christine Dakien always return phone calls and emails about the smallest details. Ellen Graff and Mimi Thomas are well noted and joyful in conversation. Miki Orihara always lent me wise counsel. Yuko Giannakis has remained a stalwart supporter. Nejila Yatkin demonstrates the continuing power of dance and politics. Many others who have offered stories, anecdotes, and color to the book are listed in the endnotes; I only wish I could thank them one by one.

Because of Graham's legacy of "Sturm und Drang" that gave her creative power, yet simultaneously undermined her work, her legacy, and the relationships among dancers as she pitted one against another on the home front for dramatic effect onstage, some of my professional partnerships and friendships have been taken hostage by this book project. We marvel: from Israel to New York, women who danced the same roles brush by, barely speaking. I have not named these good people who have helped further this work and are lost as associates and friends. I offer gratitude for your help along the way.

Lieutenant Colonel Greg Tomlin has provided unparalleled support for my work outside of Columbia University alongside West Point Military Academy. Although I hardly consider myself a peer because of his experience and work in the US military, I know he generously welcomes me as a part of his cohort. After Greg's presentation at the Society of Historians of American Foreign Relations on Edward R. Murrow, he mentioned that he had set up a radio show while serving on the ground. Never again will I conduct research without going to military records. Because of Greg and others at West Point, including John Melcon and the Center for the Study of Civil Military Operations (CSCMO) at West Point, and with the continued support of LTC MIL USA USMA Gail Yoshitani, I have had the distinct honor of guiding cadets in Budapest and through international archives via CWAR and teaching on the subject of women in the military. In addition to having the honor of calling Greg a colleague, I am proud to call Greg and his wife, Elizabeth, friends. We are blessed to have people like Greg and the West Point Military Academy cadets I have worked with serve our nation.

I wish to personally thank all the diplomats and members of the press who provided interviews and are named in the endnotes. The chapters that include Israel would not have been possible without Barry Swersky's relentless dedication to this project. Ambassador Robert Finn and Helena Finn are without compare. Arthur Zegelbone has watched the project unfold and guided my thinking for almost a decade. Our nation has been fortunate to have had them in our service abroad.

Members of my cohort, future colleagues, and friends have challenged me to be the best that I can be intellectually in the classroom. In particular, I remain indebted to Thai Jones, Michael Woodsworth, Ben Lyons, and Yuki Oda; we served in the trenches as teaching assistants at Columbia. Thai Jones remains a constant source of inspiration as a writer, teacher, archivist, and ever-present friend. I would particularly like to single out Seth Anzika, who has shared his knowledge of Carter and Reagan with me, met me in Lebanon, and made sure I was always well cared for in Israel and the Middle East. If not for his "What about Israel?" question, the book would be very different.

I like to refer to the core of my female PhD cohort as "Historically Brunette" versus "Legally Blonde," following the tale of Elle Woods at Harvard Law School. Jessica Adler, Tamara Mann, Melissa Borja, and I not only have become colleagues but also have grown together and cried together as we conquered our early years as PhD candidates, as well as authors and professionals. We join with other Columbia scholars Joanna Dee Das, Ana

Keilson, and Elizabeth Schwall. Although we may not think of ourselves as feminists or even scholars who are distinctly female, we have shared the joys and trials of being wives, mothers, and professional women. While blonde, Elizabeth Leake has been an addition to these Columbia women in my life as a scholar, adviser, roommate, and friend.

Jens Richard Giersdorf renders me wordless. When I believed I might become too ill to finish the book, I gave it to Jens. Ned's chair in Amagansett is never the same without Ned sitting in it, reading. And Emma's room will always be in Brooklyn with my grandmother's canopy bed waiting, Amagansett, London, or wherever I am—she has been in my heart from the moment I saw her. Welcome, Mabel. Be nice to Cecily, please.

I thank the town of Amagansett, New York, and all those I have met there who provide me with a glorious "room of one's own." If not for Phyllis Sank and Patrick McBrien, I would not have had a place to write. Mike O'Rourke has kept me sane from Hurricane Sandy to the present, feeding me when I forgot to eat. Salman Somjee, Pele Ritter supported me deeply through Hurricane Sandy and returning to paint murals on the reconstructed walls. Dozens others remain unnamed.

As a book project that has taken many years, there have been illnesses, cancer, various hospitals, and thus physicians and professionals. I cannot thank the physicians enough who watch over me: Dr. Shari Medoneck and her group, Dr. Michael Cantor, Dr. Robert Gelfand, and, in London, Dr. Madeline Clarke, as well as Dr. Guy Northridge and Dr. Feng Chao. Also, John, Bow Tie, Randal, Mary, and the team. Without them, the book would not have made it to publication. I thank all those who serve us from New York to London with scientific creativity (much needed in my case) and integrity as healers. They are backed by friends who help keep the everyday going—Murph, David, Cindy, London SoHo friends, those by the ocean where we swim and talk, and those who spent hours with me in hospitals and provided food, good cheer, sage advice, and quiet comfort, including Peggy Gilder, Lauren Brown, Chris Anderson, and John Viso.

As a former dancer, sitting at a desk is not my first instinct. Tim O'Donnell practices contact improvisation, the polar opposite of Graham, and he makes sure that I can stand up and walk away for a bit. Keeping me sane, perhaps limping, I thank Robbie McMillin and Barry's Bootcamp for their national and global workouts. Danny Nichols and the men and women at Mendez Boxing keep me focused on the important fights. As an unlikely fighter, I am forever "The Secret" as I enter the ring for the next round. This inspires my work as I return to the historical trenches. In London, Ellie Ioannidow and her team get me back on my legs when I'm down or hobble in on a cane. Susan and Babs continue the work with me in Florida.

Richard Gilder's influence has reached me personally and professionally, and his dedication to history reaches far beyond my work. On a personal level, I would not have had the confidence in my analytic abilities without Dick's belief in my work. While I worked for him on Wall Street, no matter how disastrous my recommendation seemed in the moment, if I was sure, he was sure. There was nothing I loved more than a great disaster, and Dick heartily agreed if the work relied on the fundamental analysis of documents, shifts in trends, and interviews. It is just these skills that I have relied on to research this work. Dick trained me and believed in me. His commitment to the study of history has contributed significantly to the public recognition of the importance of the discipline and its practitioners. He not only has supported the project with his philanthropy but also has drawn others into significant funding projects. He has recognized the preeminent scholars in the field; he encourages budding grade school students and their teachers. This is irreplaceable.

Travis Anderson, a longtime colleague from Wall Street when we both worked at Gilder, Gagnon, and Howe, LLC, now my husband, even reads my footnotes. Carol Gluck turned to him when I was a PhD student and said, "You have to read everything she writes because you don't know anything." He now knows everything about Miss Graham, and sometimes remembers things I have written and forgotten. Dedicated to history, honesty, integrity, and truth, in the quietest way, he has read almost every draft, word for word, letter by letter. I could not have done it without him.

My daughters—Amanda, Nancy, and Brammy— all began the process with me and suffered the slings and arrows of living with a PhD candidate. As I attempted to negotiate a professional and personal life, after not having worked for nineteen years and never thinking that the PhD program was a full-time job, much less a twenty-four-hour commitment, I cannot thank them enough for their love and understanding. I hope they will feel proud as they read this book knowing that they were formative in its creation and foundational in its realization.

Joyce Kennedy, my daughters' nanny and my spiritual grandmother, led me into an understanding of motherhood and has become both a social model and a source of prayer and strength. She always said I would go to Washington, DC, from the time I held Amanda in my arms. As always, so be it.

I also thank Buzzy Geduld for his loving support and for making the research "road trips" possible. Irwin, now passed away, and other Gedulds will always be family with memories of Passover and Florida. We continue with holidays and talks.

I must thank the Anderson clan, all thirty of whom gathered as a testament to the power of family in the summer of 2017 as I finished the manuscript (or so I thought at the time) on a beach vacation. George Anderson, my husband's father, who worked fearlessly in the diplomatic corps during the Cold War, read portions of the manuscript. I have promised to bring him a copy in Iowa. Eleanor, Travis's mother, has inspired me to study and contribute to the legacy of diplomatic women and wives. I deeply admire her.

My grandmother Nancy, my grandfather known to all as "The General" because he was one, and my nanny, now all departed, serve as constant reminders of grace, elegance, bootstrap determination, and the power of creativity. Nancy's famous sayings serve me well in archives and while buying shoes: "Why honey, when in doubt, do both." Her eye for great art and iconic dresses, pure charm, elegance, and unconditional love for me have consistently pushed me forward as she did through illnesses and cancer, always dressing for lunch. I have attempted to emulate her, my grandfather ("If you're on time, you're ten minutes late"), the daughters they produced, including my mother, Maryanne, whom I adore, and Little Nancy, taken too early by cancer. My nanny, Miss Ruth Schindelin, taught me to play and plant and revel in my doll house.

My father is my hero. Although he was my "Dr. Doomsday" along with my mother, "The Queen of the Obscure," he has been there for me with his warmth and unmitigated support, no matter what mess I had gotten myself into, which have been quite a few. And we both love London. One of the disasters I seemed to have gotten myself into in the 1970s was studying with Graham and refusing to attend college. My father hadn't seen me in months and came to observe company class. I always took class near the piano, playing with the reverberations on the floorboards. After entering, Martha Graham invited my father to sit with her at the front of the room on the Noguchi sculpture. As she taught and spoke, I danced, blind to the moment of configuration. Later, he remarked that as a descendant of those on the boat just after the *Mayflower*, he clearly understood Graham's Puritanical rhetoric and Protestant work ethic. I only knew the dance. That would change.

This book is dedicated to two Elizabeths, Elizabeth Aldrich and Dr. Elizabeth A. R. Brown. Elizabeth Aldrich called me after she bravely went to bat with the Office of the General Council at the Library of Congress to have the Graham Foundation papers opened. This work is dedicated to her— a mentor, colleague, and good friend. Her tireless pursuit of open archives has furthered the potential for new historical scholarship long beyond our lives. She inspires the imagination. I have had the honor of working with her in the back recesses at the Library of Congress as a fellow, making trips to acquire new collections, conducting oral histories, presenting at conferences, curating exhibits, and working in Germany. Yet we share more than the love of archives. I am deeply touched to be able to have her as one of my closest friends. Between daily emails that allow me to be irate, sassy, distraught, and ebullient, and our yearly archival "road trips," she is a gem.

The second Elizabeth is a scholar first, and also my mother. I understand that she typed her dissertation in part while she recovered from giving birth to me in the hospital. My little jumps to the rhythm of the steel hitting the paper and the sound of the old-fashioned return lever are lore among female historians. Her dedication is clear-cut and trailblazing. She was one of the first women to become a teaching fellow at Harvard after she challenged those who believed that women had nothing to teach men. She relies on French archives from the fourteenth and fifteenth centuries; this history that has earned its mettle with enduring debates. My historical evidence includes subjects who are often alive, and the debates are just beginning. Yet we are similar: hers is "Big Man" history, and mine is "Big Women," both of which are out of sync with historical moves into the everyday. She has taught me to adore the archives, whether documents or images, hers stained glass and mine moving. Her article on feudalism tore at the core of the boundaries of periodization and "isms," into which I too easily fall despite her training and legacy. As I came into consciousness, I only wish I had better understood her dedication to her profession and her bravery as a woman. As offbeat as it sounds, after my year in London, we had a mother-daughter reunion at Auschwitz and walked the grounds as the sun set, inconceivably, beautifully, over the barracks of Birkenau. After many years of not understanding, I honor her. I only hope my daughters will find the same forgiveness as they approach my work. And of course, I must thank my editor Norman Hirschy, project manager Ayshwarya Ramakrishnan, copyeditor Susan Ecklund, and publisher Oxford University Press. The anonymous readers gave their time and thoughtful comments. Without Norm and OUP, this would all be black on white, useless sitting on my hard drive.

Even with all this support, the mistakes are surely many as I traverse the globe as an advanced tourist yet self-proclaimed dilettante. The errors are wholly attributable to me. I look forward to a dialogue with colleagues and future scholars to correct the problematics and argue the points. That is the point.

Choreographic Works by Martha Graham (Ballets)

Acrobats of God, premiered April 3, 1958, music by Carlos Surinach, set by Isamu Noguchi, costumes by Martha Graham.[1]

Acts of Light, premiered February 26, 1981, music by Carl Nielsen, costumes by Halston.

Alcestis, premiered April 29, 1960, music by Robert Starer, set by Rouben Ter-Arutunian, costumes by Martha Graham.

American Document, premiered August 6, 1938, music by Ray Green, spoken text, set by Arch Lauterer, costumes by Edythe Gilfond; revival premiered October 3, 1989, with excerpts from the original and spoken text.

Appalachian Spring, premiered December 30, 1944, music by Aaron Copland, set by Isamu Noguchi, costumes by Edythe Gilfond.

Cave of the Heart, premiered May 10, 1946, music by Samuel Barber, set by Isamu Noguchi, costumes by Edythe Gilfond.

Chronicle, premiered December 20, 1936, music by Wallington Riegger, set by Isamu Noguchi, costumes by Martha Graham.

Clytemnestra, premiered April 1, 1958, music by Halim El-Dabh, set by Isamu Noguchi, costumes by Martha Graham.

Deaths and Entrances, premiered July 18, 1943, music by Hunter Johnson, set by Arch Lauterer, costumes by Edythe Gilford.

Deep Song, premiered December 19, 1937, music by Henry Cowell, costumes by Edythe Gilfond.

Diversion of Angels, premiered August 13, 1948, music by Norman Dello Joio, set by Isamu Noguchi, costumes by Martha Graham.

El Penitente, premiered August 11, 1940, music by Louis Horst, set by Arch Lauterer, redesigned and set seen on tour by Isamu Noguchi, costumes by Edythe Gilfond.

Embattled Garden, premiered April 3, 1958, music by Carlos Surinach, set by Isamu Noguchi, costumes by Martha Graham.

Errand into the Maze, premiered February 28, 1947, music by Gian-Carlo Menotti, set by Isamu Noguchi, costumes by Martha Graham.

Every Soul Is a Circus, premiered December 27, 1939, music by Louis Horst, set by Philip Stapp, costumes by Edythe Gilfond.

Figure of a Saint, premiered January 24, 1929, music by George Frideric Handel, costume by Martha Graham.

A Florentine Madonna, premiered May 28, 1926, music by Sergei Rachmaninoff, costumes by Erle Franke, premiered as *From a XII Century Tapestry*, April 18, 1926.

Frescoes, premiered September 24, 1978, music by Samuel Barber, set in the Sackler Wing, Museum of Modern Art, costumes by Halston.

Frontier, see *Perspectives—Frontier*.

Gypsy Portrait, or *Portrait—After Federico Beltrán-Masses,* premiered April 18, 1926, music by Manuel de Falla, costume by Martha Graham.

Heretic (A Faith), premiered April 14, 1929, music credited "to an old Breton song," costumes by Martha Graham.

Judith, premiered January 4, 1950, music by William Schuman, set by Charles Hyman and revised by Isamu Noguchi (1951), costumes by Martha Graham, revised by Isamu Noguchi (1951).

Lamentation, premiered January 8, 1930, music by Zoltán Kodály, costume by Martha Graham.

The Legend of Judith, premiered October 25, 1962, music by Mordecai Seter, set by Dani Caravan, costumes by Martha Graham.

Letter to the World, premiered August 11, 1940, music by Hunter Johnson, set by Arch Lauterer, costumes by Edythe Gilfond.

Lucifer, premiered June 20, 1975, music by Halim El-Dabh, set by Leandro Locsin, costumes by Halston.

Night Journey, premiered ay 3, 1947, music by William Schuman, set by Isamu Noguchi, costumes by Martha Graham.

Perspectives—Frontier, premiered February 28, 1935, music by Louis Horst, set by Isamu Noguchi, costumes by Martha Graham.

Phaedra, premiered March 5, 1962, music by Robert Starer, set by Isamu Noguchi, costumes by Martha Graham.

Primitive Mysteries, premiered February 2, 1931, music by Louis Horst, costumes by Martha Graham.

The Rite of Spring, premiered February 29, 1984, music by Igor Stravinsky, set uncredited, costumes by Halston.

The Scarlet Letter, premiered December 22, 1975, music by Hunter Johnson, set by Marisol Escobar, costumes by Halston.

Secular Games, premiered August 17, 1962, music by Robert Starer, set by Jean Rosenthal.

Seraphic Dialogue, premiered May 8, 1955, music by Norman Dello Joio, set by Isamu Noguchi, costumes by Martha Graham.

Strong, Free, Joyous Action: Nietzsche, premiered January 20, 1929, music by Arthur Honegger, costume by Martha Graham.

A Study in Lacquer, premiered April 18, 1926, music by Marcel Bernheim, costume by Martha Graham.

Three Gopi Maidens, premiered April 18, 1926, music by Cyril Scott, costumes by Norman Edwards.

The Triumph of St. Joan, premiered December 5, 1951, music by Norman Dello Joio, set by Frederick Kiesler, costumes by Martha Graham.

The Real Ambassadors (selections)

Music, lyrics, and book by Iola Brubeck with Louis Armstrong

> Who's the real ambassador?
> It is evident we represent American society,
> Noted for its etiquette, its manners, and sobriety.
> We have followed protocol with absolute propriety.
> We're Yankees to the core.
> We're the real ambassadors,
> Though we may appear as bores.
> We are diplomats with our proper hats;
> Our attire comes habitual along with all the ritual.
> The diplomatic corps has been analyzed and criticized by NBC and CBS.
> Senators and Congressmen are so concerned they can't recess;
> The State Department stands and all your coup d'etats have met success;
> They caused this great uproar.
> Who's the real ambassador.
> Yeah, the real ambassador?

"Cultural Exchange"

> The State Department has discovered Jazz.
> It reaches folks like nothing ever has.
> Like when they feel that jazzy rhythm,
> They know we're really with 'em.
> That's what we call cultural exchange.
> No commodity - is quite so strange
> As this thing called cultural exchange.
> Say that our prestige needs a tonic.
> Export the Philharmonic.
> That's what we call cultural exchange.
> We put *Oklahoma!* in Japan.

South Pacific, we gave to Iran,
And when our neighbors call us vermin,
We sent out Woody Herman.
That's what we call cultural exchange.
Gershwin gave the Muscovites a thrill (with *Porgy & Bess!*).
Bernstein was the darling of Brazil.
Just to stop internal mayhem,
We dispatched Martha Graham.
That's what we call cultural exchange
    . . . and if the world goes wacky,
We'll get John to send out Jackie -
"You mean Jackie Robinson?!
No man, I mean the First Lady!"
That's what we call cultural exchange.
That's what we call cultural exchange.

Archival Abbreviations

AMSZ: Archiwum Ministerstwa Spraw Zagranicznych RP, the Polish Diplomacy Archive, National Archive, Warsaw, Poland.

AY: Archives of Yugoslavia (Архив Југославије), 318 (Federal Education and Culture Secretariat), 240, Senjak, Belgrade, Serbia.

BRC: Bertram Ross Papers, 1910–2006, New York Library of the Performing Arts, Jerome Robbins Dance Division, New York, NY.

BUSH: George H. W. Bush Presidential Library, College Station, TX.

CARTER: Jimmy Carter Library, Atlanta, GA.

DDE: Dwight D. Eisenhower Presidential Library, Abilene, KS.

DDRS: Declassified Documents Reference System, accessed through Columbia University Library System, http://www.gale.cengage.com/pdf/facts/ddrs.pdf.

DP/IEP: International Exchange Program, "Dance Panel Meeting," UAK.

DTK: Martha Graham, Clippings File, the Deutsches Tanzarchiv Köln, Im Mediapark 7, D-50670 Köln, Germany. Note all translations from this archive were done by Heidi Ziegler, New York University.

EHC-LOC: Erick Hawkins Collection, 1940–1993, Library of Congress, Music Division, Library of Congress, Washington, DC.

ELD/DDE: Eleanor Lansing Dulles Papers, 1880–1973, Dwight D. Eisenhower Presidential Library, Abilene, KS.

ELD/GWU: Eleanor Lansing Dulles Papers, Special Collections Research Center, the George Washington University, Washington, DC.

ELD/PU: Eleanor L. Dulles Papers, 1863–1989, Mudd Manuscript Library, Princeton University Library, Princeton, NJ.

FORD: Gerald R. Ford Presidential Library, Ann Arbor, MI.

FWC-LOC-MD: Frances G. Wickes Papers, Manuscript Division, Library of Congress, Washington, DC. Note that these letters are undated.

GFK-PUSK: George F. Kennan Papers (MC 076) unless otherwise noted, Public Policy Papers, Department of Rare Books and Special Collections, Seeley G. Mudd Manuscript Library, Princeton University Library, Princeton, NJ.

HSA: Hugh Stubbins Archive: The Early Years Collection, uncataloged, Special Collections, Frances Loeb Library, Graduate School of Design, Harvard University, Cambridge, MA.

HSTL: Harry S. Truman Library, Independence, MO.

IDA: The Israeli Dance Archive at Beit Ariela, Tel Aviv, Israel.

JFK: John F. Kennedy Presidential Library and Museum, Columbia Point, Boston, MA.

JRDD-NYPL: New York Public Library for the Performing Arts, Jerome Robbins Dance Division, Lincoln Center, New York, NY.

LA: Landesarchiv aus dem Aktenbestand, Eichborndamm 115-121, 13403, Berlin, Germany.

LBJ: Lyndon Baines Johnson Library, Austin, TX.

LOC: Library of Congress, Music Division, Library of Congress, Washington, DC.

LOC-MD: Library of Congress, Manuscript Division, Washington, DC.

McCREA: Grace McCrea Collection, Music Division, Library of Congress, Washington, DC.

META: Metropolitan Museum of Art Archives, New York, NY.

MGC-LOC: Martha Graham Collection, Music Division, Library of Congress, Washington, DC.

MGC-MGF: Martha Graham Collection, Martha Graham Foundation, New York City, uncataloged collection, files available from author if documents have been destroyed in the 2013 flood with the permission of the foundation in writing to the author.

MGLC-LOC: Martha Graham Legacy Collection, Music Division, Library of Congress, Washington DC.

MONDALE: Joan Mondale Personal Papers, Minnesota Historical Society, St. Paul, MN.

MWA: Mary-Wigman-Archiv, Akademie der Künste, Tanz Archiv, Berlin.

NARA: National Archives and Records Administration, College Park, MD.

NARPF: Nelson A. Rockefeller, Personal Files.

NSA: National Security Archive, Washington, DC.

NWRP: Nancy Wilson Ross Papers, Harry Ransom Center Archives, Austin, TX.

NYU-TAM: Elmer Holmes Bobst Library, Tamiment Library and Robert F. Wagner Archives, New York University, New York, NY.

OSA: Open Society Archives, Budapest, Hungary.

PAA: Politisches Archiv des Auswärtigen Amtes, Berlin. Note all translations, when needed, and research guidance was done by Elisabeth Engel, Freie Universität Berlin, Germany.

RAC: Rockefeller Archive Center, Sleepy Hollow, NY.

RBTC: Robert Breen Theater Collection (ANTA), Special Collections and Archives, George Mason University Libraries, Arlington, VA.

RG: Record Group

RRL: Ronald Reagan Library, Simi Valley, CA.

RSTC: Robert Schnitzer Theatre Collection, Special Collections and Archives, George Mason University Libraries, Arlington, VA.

SAI—State Archives of Israel, Jerusalem, Israel.

TLA: Tanzarchiv Leipzig e.v., Leipzig University Library (Albertina), Special collections, Beethovenstraße, Leipzig, Germany. Note all translations from this archive were done by Julio Decker, Freie Universität Berlin, Germany.

UAK: Bureau of Education and Cultural Affairs Historical Collection (CU MC468), group II (Cultural Presentations Program). Special Collections, University of Arkansas Libraries, Fayetteville, AK.

WAR: Warsaw Public Library–Central Library of the Masovian Voivodeship, Warsaw, Poland.

Notes

Introduction

1. "Japan: Contacts," Memo, Oct. 17–Nov. 5, box 2, folder 5, "Japan, 1956, part 2," Martha Graham Dance Company Tour Records, 1941–1957, JRDD-NYPL; "Amazing Fighting Spirit," *Sankei Shimbun* (Evening Edition), Oct. 18, 1956, United States Information Agency (USIS) translation, box 336, scrapbooks, MGC-LOC.
2. "Martha Graham to Visit Japan: American Modern Dance Fanatic Popularity in the United States," *Sankei Evening*, Sept. 5, 1955, scrapbooks 333, MGC-LOC.
3. Nick Kapur, "Mending the 'Broken Dialogue': U.S.-Japan Alliance Diplomacy in the Aftermath of the 1960 Security Treaty Crisis," *Diplomatic History* 41, no. 3 (June 2017): 491n5, quoted from Sayuri Shimizu, *Creating People of Plenty: The United States and Japan's Economic Alternatives, 1950–1960* (Kent, OH: Kent State University Press, 2001), 27. The quote appeared in the *Kansas City Times*, June 23, 1954, 1, and Eisenhower said that the "communist lake" should be an "American pond."
4. To: Department of State, Fr: AmEmbassy Tokyo, RE: Evaluation Report, Dec. 28, 1954, box 318, folder 16, UAK.
5. Martin J. Medhurst, "Eisenhower and the Crusade for Freedom: The Rhetorical Origins of a Cold War Campaign," *Presidential Studies Quarterly* 27, no. 4 (1997): 646; Richard Cummings, *Radio Free Europe's "Crusade for Freedom": Rallying Americans Behind Cold War Broadcasting, 1950–1960* (Jefferson, NC: McFarland, 2009); "'Dancing Picasso' Visited Japan," *Nikkan Sports*, Oct. 19, 1955, USIS translation, box 336, scrapbooks, MGC-LOC.
6. George Kennan, "International Exchange in the Arts," *Perspectives USA* 16 (Summer 1956): 6–14 (note that digitized versions list page numbers as 9–14). NB: The CIA used the National Committee for Free Europe as "a conduit for funds," supporting universities in Asia, Iran, and Indonesia, and the Congress for Cultural Freedom, noting that "[Allen] Dulles is our primary point of contact." The Ford Foundation considered taking CIA funds for projects that included support for defectors, West Germany programs, and other cultural projects including literature and magazines. Finally, the foundation did not accept these secret monies for specific projects. Yet in response to CIA discussions, Ford did initiate Program One, with Kennan as a participant, to fund projects to fight the Soviets with psychwar in line with the CIA cultural projects, including magazines such as *Perspectives USA*. Program One was "fought, at least in part, in the minds of men," utilizing culture and "spiritual, doctrinal and psychological factors" in order to "influence men's attitudes and minds, and thereby their conduct" (H. Rowan Gaither, To: Paul Hoffman, "Memorandum: Some Operating Guides for Project One," Dec. 4, 1950, Some operating guidelines for Program One

[Reports 010528], 1950, Ford Foundation records, Catalogued Reports, Reports 9287-11774, 1936-2005, RAC). The Ford Foundation referred to its role as "pilot fish," also known as "follow ships," that congregate near sharks and rays. Sea tales also assert that pilot fish would, in the end, navigate a ship to its desired course (Ford Foundation records, Office of the President, Office Files of H. Rowan Gaither [FA621], Series I: Area I: Establishment of Peace, Box 1, Folder 1: CIA [Central Intelligence Agency], 1951 April–1951 May). Special thanks to Volker Berghahn for his research guidance. See also Greg Barnhisel, "*Perspectives USA* and the Cultural Cold War: Modernism in Service of the State," *Modernism/modernity* 14, no. 4 (November 2007): 729–54.

7. LeRoy Leatherman, "A Question of Image: The Dance-Theater of Martha Graham," *Perspectives USA* 4 (Summer 1955): 46–48.

8. Note the use of the acronym USIS versus USIA because the Agency was called "the United States Information Service" in the field and referred to as "USIS."

9. "U.S. and Soviet Competition in Dancing: Graham and Ulanova," *Jiji Shimpo*, Oct. 17, 1955, Scrapbooks, MGC-LOC. Note the veiled reference to Revelation 3:8.

10. Linda Hodes, email to author, July 6, 2017.

11. Jennifer Dunning, "$250,000 Film Grant to Miss Graham," *New York Times*, July 19, 1984, Section C, 13, also found in Appointment Process Personal Interview Record, March 14, 1985, Counsel to the President: Appointment Files, CFOA 901–908, box 11, folder Martha Graham, RRL.

12. "Martha Graham to Visit Japan."

13. "U.S. and Soviet Competition in Dancing."

14. "U.S. and Soviet Competition in Dancing."

15. "U.S. and Soviet Competition in Dancing."

16. "U.S. and Soviet Competition in Dancing."

17. "'Dancing Picasso' Visited Japan."

18. "To 'New Classic': Miss Graham Interviewed," *Asahi Shimbun, Evening Edition*, Oct. 18, 1955, translation, scrapbook 336, MGC-LOC.

19. "To 'New Classic': Miss Graham Interviewed."

20. "A Study of USIA Operating Assumptions," UM-5, Dec. 1954, Records of the United States Information Agency (USIA), Office of Research, Special Reports, 1953–63, RG 306, WNRC Acc. No. 306-69A3445, 159, box 7, NARA.

21. Note the influence of Christina Klein's "Global Imaginary of Integration" in *Cold War Orientalism: Asia in the Middlebrow Imagination, 1945–1961* (Berkeley: University of California Press, 2003). While Klein examines "middlebrow" cultural expressions with the theme of "Getting to know all about you" in the *King and I*, for example, she largely examines how these products worked in the United States for its citizens. Here, I extend the concept to show how "highbrow" and modernist cultural products, with Graham's dance as the example, was purposefully chosen for export to engage foreign elite audiences, in regions including but not limited to Asia, to experience culture and thus argue for political commonalities in the host country through American cultural figures. Also included in "cultural convergences" is the embedded Cold War ideology of "universalism" that binds people together despite language and national borders.

22. "'Dancing Picasso' Visited Japan."

23. "Martha Graham to Visit Japan."

24. Emiko Tokunaga, *Yuriko: An American Japanese Dancer* (New York: Tokunaga Dance Ko, 2008), 12, 15–16.

25. Tokunaga, *Yuriko*, 16. Yuriko recalled having seen Kreutzberg in Japan and mentioned that the dance students were thrilled by the performer.

26. "Martha Graham to Appear," *Ongaku Shimbun*, Feb. 10, 1955, scrapbooks, box 326, MGC-LOC.

27. Special thanks to Arthur Zegelbone, retired program officer, State Department, who made this observation.

28. "Martha Graham and Dance Company," box 3, folder 7 (Iran), Helen McGehee and Umaña Collection of Dance Materials, Music Division, LOC.

29. "'Dancing Picasso' Visited Japan."

30. See photographs of the dancers shopping in the Ethel Winter and Charlie Hyman Papers, box 1, folder 10, LOC; also see author interviews with Ethel Winter and Linda Hodes (transcripts available upon request with permission).

31. Scrapbooks, box 331, MGC-LOC. The names of countries are based on 1955 geography as listed in "Project Title: Martha Graham Dance Troupe; Description: (Completed)," National Security Council Staff Papers, Operations Coordinating Board (OCB) Central File Series, Cultural Presentations Staff: Papers, 1948–1961, President's Fund Program [FY1955], box 14, DDE. Naima Prevots, *Dance for Export: Cultural Diplomacy and the Cold War* (Middletown, CT: Wesleyan University Press, 1999), 8.

32. Donald T. Critchlow, *Phyllis Schlafly and Grassroots Conservatism: A Woman's Crusade* (Princeton, NJ: Princeton University Press, 2005), 146. Schlafly speaks about the "cocktail party circuit," which is mirrored in "A Study of USIA Operating Assumptions," 1954, and later regarding the "cocktail circuit of diplomacy" in "To: State Department, From Amcongen, Damascus," June 12, 1962, RG 59, CDF, box 1047, NARA.

33. "Impression of Miss Graham," *Sankei Shimbun* (Evening Edition), Oct. 18, 1955, USIS translation, scrapbooks, box 336, MGC-LOC.

34. Interview with Linda Hodes, Jan. 25, 2016 (transcript upon request with permission).

35. Benedict R. Anderson, *Imagined Communities: Reflections on the Origin and Spread of Nationalism* (New York: Verso, 1991).

36. "Amazing Fighting Spirit," *Sankei Shimbun* (Evening Edition), Oct. 18, 1956, United States Information Agency (USIS) translation, box 336, scrapbooks, MGC-LOC.

37. "Graham Grips Audience," *Nippon Times*, Nov. 4, 1955, scrapbooks, box 337, MGC-LOC.

38. *Sixth Quarterly Report: President's Emergency Fund for Participation in International Affairs*, Oct. 1–Dec. 31, 1955, DDE Library White House Office, National Security Council Staff Papers 1948–61, OCB Central File Series, box 15, OCB 007, [Cultural Activities] (File #3) (3) [December 1955–May 1956], DDE.

39. Ethel Winter and Charles Hyman Papers, box 1, folder 10, LOC.

40. "U.S. and Soviet Competition in Dancing"; "Brilliant Finale: Martha Graham Troupe Most Successful," *Sankei Jiji Shimbun*, Nov. 8, 1955, translation, scrapbook 336, MGC-LOC.

41. "Martha Graham to Mrs. Wickes," nd, FWC-LOC-MD.
42. *Sixth Quarterly Report.*
43. Robert Trumbull, "Hiroshima Prays on Day of Bomb," *New York Times*, Aug. 6, 1955, 3.
44. Michel Foucault, "Truth and Power," in *Power/Knowledge: Selected Interviews and Other Writings, 1972–1977*, ed. Colin Gordon (New York: Pantheon, 1980), 109–33; Geir Lundestad, "Empire by Invitation?: The United States and Western Europe, 1945–1952," *Journal of Peace Research* 23, no. 3 (September 1986): 263–77; Joseph S. Nye Jr., *Soft Power: The Means to Success in World Politics* (New York: Public Affairs, 2004).
45. "Brilliant Finale."
46. "Graham Grips Audience."
47. "Pure Art of Dancing Heart," *Sankei Jiji*, Nov. 2, 1955, USIS translation, scrapbook 336, MGC-LOC.
48. Untitled clipping, *Manila Times*, Nov. 19, 1955, Scrapbooks, MGC-LOC.

Introduction

1. Prevots, *Dance for Export*, 51. See author's interview with Ethel Winter, dancer, and Charles Hyman, stage manager, regarding the 1955–56 tour, fall 2006; portions of the transcript is available through the Ethel Winter and Charles Hyman Papers, box 1, folder 10, LOC.
2. Martha Graham, Federal Bureau of Investigation file, requested 2006, Victoria Phillips Collection, Performing Arts Division, LOC; Federal Bureau of Investigation (FBI) Personality Files, Michael Ravnitzky Donation, box 12, Martha Graham, NSA. Note that dance historians Victoria Thoms and Camelia Lenart have demonstrated that the government supported and watched Graham's tours to Europe in the 1950s; see Camelia Lenart, "Turning the Tide and Reconstructing the Politics: A New Perspective on Martha Graham's Tours to Britain in 1954 and the Response to Its Political and Artistic Complexity," *Dance History: Politics, Practices and Perspectives Conference Proceedings*, Mar. 13, 2010, https://www.academia.edu/267220/Conference_Proceedings_Compilation_Dance_History_Conference (accessed January 27, 2017); see also Victoria P. Geduld, "Dancing Diplomacy," *Dance Chronicle* 33, no. 1 (2010): 44–81, which credits Thoms's archival research. Although Lenart asserts that historians have not taken the early Graham tours to Europe (1950, 1954) under the funding of Bethsabée de Rothschild into consideration, indeed more recently historians have viewed them as a precursor to direct government involvement along with this author; see Clare Croft, *Dancers as Diplomats: American Choreography in Cultural Exchange* (New York: Oxford University Press, 2015), Mark Franko, *Martha Graham in Love and War: The Life in the Work* (New York: Oxford University Press, 2012), and Victoria Phillips Geduld "Dancing Diplomacy," *Dance Chronicle* 33, no. 1 (2010): 44–81; note also pictures of Eleanor Roosevelt at Graham's Paris performances, 1954, box 264, folder 6, MGC-LOC.

3. Dave and Iola Brubeck, Louis Armstrong, "Cultural Exchange" (4:38) and "The Real Ambassadors" (3:08), in *The Real Ambassadors* (soundtrack album), Columbia, 1962.
4. "Foreign Service Digest—Unofficial USIS, Djakarta," marked "Republication Prohibited," VIII- #146, 2" and "USIS Report," December 9, 1955, box 11, folder 5, BRC. The digest quotes local newspaper articles.
5. Greg Castillo, "Domesticating the Cold War: Household Consumption as Propaganda in Marshall Plan Germany," *Journal of Contemporary History* 40, no. 2 (April 2005): 265.
6. Eric Foner, *The Story of American Freedom* (New York: W. W. Norton, 1998), xiii.
7. "Transcript of Proceedings," Bureau of Educational and Cultural Affairs, Office of Cultural Presentations, Dance Panel Meeting, November 23, 1970, box 101, folder 22, 102, UAK.
8. See the work of Max Kozloff, Eva Cockroft, David and Cecile Shapiro, Serge Guilbaut, and Frances Stonor Saunders quoted in Greg Barnhisel, *Cold War Modernists: Art, Literature, and American Cultural Diplomacy* (New York: Columbia University Press, 2015), 4.
9. William E. Daugherty and Morris Janowitz, "Introduction," in *The Psychological Warfare Casebook* (Baltimore: Johns Hopkins University Press, Operations Research Office, 1958), 2–3.
10. Barnhisel, *Cold War Modernists*, 5n7, 259, quoting Max Kozloff, "American Painting during the Cold War," *Artforum*, May 1973, 44.
11. Foner, *The Story of American Freedom*.
12. "Nikita Khrushchev, Conversation at the Manege Exhibit, December 1, 1962," as reported as a conversation in *Encounter* 20, no. 4 (April 1963): 102–3.
13. "Nikita Khrushchev."
14. Barnhisel, *Cold War Modernists*; Melvyn P. Leffler, "The Cold War: What Do 'We Now Know'?" *American Historical Review* 104, no. 2 (April 1999): 501–24; Penny M. Von Eschen, Satchmo Blows Up the World: Jazz Ambassadors Play the Cold War (Cambridge, MA: Harvard University Press, 2004); "Special Forum: Musical Diplomacy: Strategies, Agendas, Relationships," *Diplomatic History* 36, no. 1 (January 2012): 17–75; Andrew L. Yarrow, "Selling a New Vision of America to the World: Changing Messages in Early U.S. Cold War Print Propaganda," *Journal of Cold War Studies* 11, no. 4 (Fall 2009): 3–45; Reinhold Wagnleitner and Elaine Tyler May, eds., *"Here, There and Everywhere": The Foreign Politics of American Popular Culture* (Hanover, NH: University Press of New England, 2000); Uta G. Poiger, Jazz, Rock, and Rebels: Cold War Politics and American Culture in a Divided Germany (Berkeley: University of California Press, 2000); David Caute, *The Dancer Defects: The Struggle for Cultural Supremacy during the Cold War* (New York: Oxford University Press, 2003); Yale Richmond, *Cultural Exchange and the Cold War: Raising the Iron Curtain* (University Park: Pennsylvania State University Press, 2003); Sabina Mihelj, "Negotiating Cold War Culture at the Crossroads of East and West: Uplifting the Working People, Entertaining the Masses, Cultivating the Nation," *Comparative Studies in Society and History* 53, no. 3 (July 2011): 509–39; Volker R. Berghahn, *America and the Intellectual Cultural Cold Wars in Europe* (Princeton, NJ: Princeton

University Press, 2001); Tony Shaw and Denise J. Youngblood, *Cinematic Cold War: The American and Soviet Struggle for Hearts and Minds* (Lawrence: University Press of Kansas, 2014); Stephen Wagg and David Andrews, *East Plays West: Sport and the Cold War* (New York: Routledge, 2006); Margaret Peacock, *Innocent Weapons: The Soviet and American Politics of Childhood in the Cold War* (Chapel Hill: University of North Carolina Press, 2014); Danielle Fosler-Lussier, *Music in America's Cold War Diplomacy* (Berkeley: University of California Press, 2015); Deborah Cohen, "Regionalism and U.S. Nationalism in William Faulkner's State Department Travels," in *Creating and Consuming the U.S. South*, ed. Martyn Bone, Brian Ward, and William A. Link (Gainesville: University Press of Florida, 2015), 248–67; Daniel J. Leab, *Orwell, Subverted: The CIA and the Filming of Animal Farm* (University Park: Pennsylvania State University Press, 2007); Clare Croft, "Ballet Nations: The New York City Ballet's 1962 US State Department Sponsored Tour of the Soviet Union," *Theater Journal* 61, no. 3 (2009): 421–42; Catherine Gunther Kodat, "Dancing through the Cold War: The Case of the 'Nutcracker,'" *Mosaic* 33, no. 3 (2000): 1–17; Melinda Copel, "Modern Dance Humanism and the State Department's Agenda: Raising U.S. Status in the World Community during the Cold War," in *Congress on Research in Dance Papers*, ed. Ninotchka Bennahum and Tresa M. Randall (Tallahassee: Florida State University2005), 31–41. See also the fine work on the Soviet Union by Serge Zhuk, including *Rock and Roll in the Rocket City: The West, Identity, and Ideology in Soviet Dniepropetrovsk, 1960–1985* (Baltimore: Johns Hopkins University Press, 2010), and Gleb Tsipursky, *Socialist Fun: Youth, Consumption, and State-Sponsored Popular Culture in the Soviet Union, 1945–1970* (Pittsburgh: University of Pittsburgh Press, 2017), both of whom have been invaluable advisers to the author.

15. Michael F. Hopkins, "Continuing Debate and New Approaches in Cold War History," *Historical Review* 50, no. 4 (2007): 913–34.

16. Fredric Jameson, *A Singular Modernity: Essay on the Ontology of the Present* (New York: Verso, 2002), 13. Thanks to Professor Anders Stephanson for encouraging the author to explore the links to Jameson's work.

17. Martha Graham, *Blood Memory* (New York: Doubleday, 1991), 237. Note that my own work challenges the accuracy of Graham's quotes in *Blood Memory* (Victoria Phillips, "Martha Graham's Gilded Cage: *Blood Memory—An Autobiography*," *Dance Research Journal* 45, no. 2 [August 2013]: 63–84). Transcripts of her testimony given for the book demonstrate that her words were edited by Jacqueline Kennedy Onassis, Graham's editor at Doubleday, as well as others. The author only quotes those passages in which a facsimile of the idea exists in transcripts, on television, during radio interviews, or according to oral testimony given by dancers, because Graham's sentences and syntax are often disjointed and difficult to grasp.

18. "Nikita Khrushchev."

19. George F. Kennan, "Draft—Opening Speech," box 302, folder 32, GFK-PUSK.

20. "Nikita Khrushchev."

21. Kennan, "Draft—Opening Speech,".

22. Graham, *Blood Memory*, 200–202.

23. Graham, *Blood Memory*, 202.

24. Dagmar Herzog, *Cold War Freud: Psychoanalysis in an Age of Catastrophes* (New York: Cambridge University Press, 2016); Rebecca Reich, *State of Madness: Psychiatry, Literature and Dissent after Stalin* (DeKalb: Northern Illinois University Press, 2018).

25. Graham, *Blood Memory*, 30.

26. Nils Gilman, *Mandarins of the Future: Modernization Theory in Cold War America* (Baltimore: Johns Hopkins University Press, 2003), 1.

27. Odd Arne Westad, *The Cold War: A World History* (New York: Basic Books, 2017), 8–9.

28. Westad, *The Cold War*, 7.

29. Gilman, *Mandarins of the Future*, 2.

30. Emily S. Rosenberg, "Considering Borders," in *Explaining the History of American Foreign Relations*, 3rd ed., ed. Frank Costigliola and Michael J. Hogan (New York: Cambridge University Press, 2016), 190; Mary Louise Pratt, *Imperial Eyes: Travel Writing and Transculturation* (New York: Routledge, 2008).

31. "Report on Indonesia," [Craig Barton], Martha Graham, box 2, folder 10, Kuala Lumpur, 1955, "Programs, Kuala Lumpur," Martha Graham, box 2, folder 10, Kuala Lumpur, 1955, Martha Graham Dance Company Tour Records, 1941–1957, JRDD-NYPL.

32. "Dancing in the East and West," January 3, 1956, scrapbooks, box 334, MGC-LOC.

33. "Interview with Charles Weidman," conducted by Agnes de Mille, June 25, 1974, JRDD-NYPL.

34. Graham, *Blood Memory*, 201.

35. Graham, *Blood Memory*, 200–202.

36. Edward P. Crapol, "Introduction," in *Women and American Foreign Policy: Lobbyists, Critics, and Insiders*, 2nd ed. (New York: Rowman and Littlefield, 1992), 3.

37. "Martha Graham—Radio Speech—Iran—6 Feb. 1956," box 3, folder 8, Abadan, Martha Graham Dance Company Tour Records, 1941–1957, JRDD-NYPL.

38. Phillips, "Martha Graham's Gilded Cage," 63–84.

39. Westad, *The Global Cold War*.

40. "A Study of USIA Operating Assumptions," December 1954, Vol. 1, p. O-21, RG 306, box 36, fn. 564, NARA.

41. Note that the term "domestic cultural diplomacy" has been established by Gleb Tsipursky in "Domestic Cultural Diplomacy and Soviet State-Sponsored Popular Culture in the Cold War, 1953–1962," *Diplomatic History* 41, no. 5 (November 2017): 985–1009.

42. Graham, *Blood Memory*, 202.

Chapter 1

1. "A Study of USIA Operating Assumptions," Dec. 1954, Vol. 1, record group 306, "Records of the United States Information Agency (USIA), Office of Research, Special Reports, 1953–63," box 7, RC 5, NARA, P-4.

2. "Martha Graham," *Sunday Times* [Philippines], Nov. 13, 1955, scrapbooks, box 335, MGC-LOC.

3. Daniel Immerwahr, *How to Hide an Empire: A History of the Greater United States* (New York: Farrar, Straus and Giroux, 2019).

4. Margaret Lloyd, *The Borzoi Book of Modern Dance* (New York: Alfred A. Knopf, 1949), xvii. Special thanks to Jens Richard Giersdorf and Ana Isabel Keilson for their help with this chapter. For a clear understanding of the political emergence of Mary Wigman, see Ana Isabel Keilson, "Making Dance Modern: Knowledge, Politics, and German Modern Dance, 1890–1927" (PhD diss., Columbia University, 2017); see also Maaike Bleeker, "Lecture Performance as Contemporary Dance," in *New German Dance Studies*, ed. Susan Manning and Lucia Ruprecht (Champaign: University of Illinois Press, 2012), 234. See also Michael Huxley, *The Dancer's World, 1920–1945: Modern Dancers and Their Practices Reconsidered* (New York: Palgrave Macmillan, 2015), 45n13. In addition, Huxley quotes Susan A. Manning to underscore the way in which the German artists moved from an idea of a "universal" to the "Volk"; while this is contested, see the important work of Manning, including *Ecstasy and the Demon: Feminism and Nationalism in the Dances of Mary Wigman* (Berkeley: University of California Press, 1993). Note also Huxley's use of Elizabeth Selden, who wrote about the Germans and used the term "Free Dance" in the early 1930s: Huxley, *The Dancer's World*, 38, quoting Elizabeth Selden, "The New German Credo," in *The Dancer's Quest* (Berkeley: University of California Press, 2011), 25–32.

5. Isadora Duncan, "I See American Dancing," *New York Herald Tribune*, Oct. 2, 1927, SM16.

6. Important new work on colonization and freed dance expression is taking place globally and is yet unpublished. See, for example, Cécile Bushidi, "Old and New Dances in the Making of Communities: Settler Colonialism, Nationalist Politics, and Moralities in Colonial Central Kenya, 1937–1963," paper presented in Studies in Dance Seminar, Mar. 11, 2019, Columbia University, New York.

7. Harold Bergsohn and Isa Partsch-Bergsohn, *The Makers of Modern Dance in Germany: Rudolf Laban, Mary Wigman, Kurt Jooss* (Hightstown, NJ: Princeton Book Company, 2003), 12; Maggie Odom, "Mary Wigman: The Early Years, 1913–1925," *Drama Review* 24, no. 4 (December 1980): 81–92.

8. John V. Maciuika, *Before the Bauhaus: Architecture, Politics, and the German State, 1890–1920* (Cambridge: Cambridge University Press, 2005), 233.

9. Bergsohn and Partsch-Bergsohn, *The Makers of Modern Dance in Germany*, 12; Odom, "Mary Wigman," 81–92.

10. Bergsohn and Partsch-Bergsohn, *The Makers of Modern Dance in Germany*, 15; Alexandra Kolb, *Performing Femininity: Dance and Literature in German Modernism* (New York: Peter Lang, 2009).

11. John Martin, "The Dance: Tamiris' Art," *New York Times*, Feb. 5, 1928, 11; Martin, "Ito Pleases in Dances," *New York Times*, Mar. 19, 1928, 20; Mary-Jean Cowell and Satoru Shimazaki, "East and West in the Work of Michio Ito," *Dance Research Journal* 26, no. 2 (Autumn 1994): 11–23; Margaret Lloyd, "An Oracle Speaks Simply," *Christian Science Monitor*, Mar. 17, 1936, 303, box 311, MGC-LOC.

12. Martha Graham quoted in Clive Barnes, "For Martha Graham, A Resurgence," *New York Times*, May 5, 1974, Arts1.

13. Elizabeth Souritz, "Isadora Duncan's Influence on Dance in Russia," *Dance Chronicle* 18, no. 2 (1995): 281–91.

14. Souritz, "Isadora Duncan's Influence on Dance in Russia," 281–91.

15. Isadora Duncan, *My Life* (London: Boni and Liveright, 1927; reprint, New York: W. W. Norton, 1955), 254.

16. Ann Daly, *Done into Dance: Isadora Duncan in America* (Middletown, CT: Wesleyan University Press, 1995).

17. Souritz, "Isadora Duncan's Influence on Dance in Russia," 289.

18. Souritz, "Isadora Duncan's Influence on Dance in Russia," 287.

19. Lynne Conner, *Spreading the Gospel of Modern Dance: Newspaper Dance Criticism in the United States, 1850–1934* (Pittsburgh: University of Pittsburgh Press, 1997).

20. Duncan, "I See America Dancing."

21. "Denishawn: The Ruth St. Denis School of Dancing and Its Related Arts, Second Season, Summer 1916," box 1, folder 51, McCREA.

22. Graham, *Blood Memory*, 98; note that Graham recalled the event of seeing her first modernist works differently in taped interviews in "Martha Graham—Reel #2—Side B—December 7, 1971," box 240, folder 6, 3, Lucy Kroll Collection–LOC. See footnote 87, in Victoria Phillips, "Martha Graham's Gilded Cage: Blood Memory—An Autobiography (1991)," *Dance Research Journal* 45, no. 2 (August 2013): 80.

23. Wassily Kandinsky, *Concerning the Spiritual in Art*, trans. M. T. H. Sadler (New York: Dover, 1977); this is an unabridged republication of Wassily Kandinsky, *The Art of Spiritual Harmony* (London: Constable, 1914), 36.

24. Program, nd, India, box 1, folder 53, McCREA.

25. "Ruth St. Denis—Ted Shawn and Their Denishawn Dancers in the Orient, Bulletin Number 5 from Southern India, Ceylon, Malay Peninsula and Java," box 1, folder 53, McCREA; Souvenir Program, Denishawn, Oct. 1926, box 2, folder 9, McCREA.

26. For details on the location of letters, contact Martha Graham Resources, New York City, NY. The author holds photographs and transcripts of the letters that were obtained via permission before the company move from Sixty-Third Street to Westbeth Artists Community, and the subsequent flood that destroyed some materials. The author does not have permission to share these documents, although other primary sources have been donated to the Metropolitan Museum of Art Archives with permission.

27. Baron Ishimoto, *Japan Advertiser*, Sept. 22, 1925, quoted in "Ruth St. Denis, Ted Shawn & their Denishawn Dancers. Transcontinental American Tour beginning December 1926 following eighteen months of unprecedented triumph in Near and Far East," box 1, folder 47, McCREA.

28. "Ruth St. Denis, Ted Shawn & their Denishawn Dancers."

29. "Ruth St. Denis—Ted Shawn and their Denishawn Dancers in the Orient, Bulletin Number 5 from Southern India, Ceylon, Malay Peninsula and Java," box 1, folder 53, McCREA.

30. Program, India, nd, India, McCREA; Grace McCrea, "Calcutta: First Night Free," handwritten notes, box 1, folder 52, McCREA.

31. McCrea, "Calcutta: First Night Free."

32. "Bulletin No. 4: The Denishawn Pictoral: Ruth St. Denis, Ted Shawn and Their Denishawn Dancers," box 1, folder 53, McCREA.

33. Program, nd, India.

34. "The Musings of a Punjabee (H. V. Dugvekar)," *Lahore Sunday Times*, nd, quoted in "Bulletin No. 4: The Denishawn Pictoral: Ruth St. Denis, Ted Shawn and Their Denishawn Dancers," MCREA.

35. Program, nd, India, McCREA.

36. Baron Ishimoto, *Japan Advertiser*, Sept. 22, 1925, McCREA.

37. Although other critics had reviewed dance before reviewers began writing for the *New York Herald Tribune, New York Times*, and *Christian Science Monitor*, they were not dance critics per se.

38. John Martin, "Over America the Dance Wave Sweeps," *New York Times*, Apr. 8, 1928, SM3.

39. John Martin, "The Dance Is Attuned to the Machine," *New York Times*, Feb. 24, 1929, 79.

40. Martin, "The Dance Is Attuned to the Machine," 79.

41. See Kimerer L. LaMothe, *Nietzsche's Dancers: Isadora Duncan, Martha Graham, and the Revaluation of Christian Values* (New York: Palgrave Macmillan, 2006).

42. Martin, "Over America the Dance Wave Sweeps."

43. John Martin, "Graham Dance Recital: Artist More Eloquent When She Is Lyrical Than When Dramatic," *New York Times*, Feb. 13, 1928, X9.

44. John Martin, "Kreutzberg Superb in Dance Recital," *New York Times*, Jan. 21, 1929, 22.

45. Martin, "Graham Dance Recital."

46. Dore Ashton, *Noguchi East and West* (Berkeley: University of California Press, 1992), 121.

47. John Martin, "The Dance: Kreutzberg," *New York Times*, Jan. 27, 1929, X8; John Martin, "The Dance: Diaghileff Still in Revolt," *New York Times*, Aug. 4, 1929, X9; Martin, "The Dance Is Attuned to the Machine."

48. In describing the choreography, the *New York Telegraph* (Apr. 16, 1929) noted, "*Heretic* presented a black circle of relentless figures, toward which an angelic soul draped in white cried and pleaded. As the plea registered with the merciless circle they rose to their fullest height and turned menacingly upon the priestess." The reviewer added, "Because of these group compositions, I regard this Martha Graham recital the best ensemble program of the entire season." See Library of Congress, https://www.loc.gov/item/ihas.200182599 (accessed June 1, 2017).

49. John Martin, "The Dance: Modernism," *New York Times*, Dec. 22, 1929, X9.

50. John Martin, "The Dance: Mary Wigman's Art," *New York Times*, Aug. 3, 1930, 101.

51. John Martin, "The Dance: New Standards," *New York Times*, June 1, 1930, X6.

52. Marcia B. Siegel, "Modern Dance before Bennington: Sorting It All Out," *Dance Research Journal: Congress on Research in Dance* 19, no. 1 (Summer 1977): 3.

53. John Martin, "Project of Michio Ito for Theatre Building Is Taking Shape," *New York Times*, June 10, 1928, 109; John Martin, "Old and New Ways for Showing Dance Figures by Notation," *New York Times*, June 24, 1928, X6; Helen Caldwell, *Michio Ito: The Dancer and His Dances* (Berkeley: University of California Press, 1977), 174.

54. Ted Shawn, *The American Ballet* (New York: Henry Holt, 1926).

55. Graham, *Blood Memory*, 119.

56. "Martha Graham Gives Delightful Dance," *New York Times*, Jan. 12, 1930, 30; "Martha Graham Gives Dance without Music," *New York Times*, Jan. 9, 1930, 28; John Martin, "The Dance: A Week of Unique Programs," *New York Times*, Jan. 5, 1930, 9.

57. Oliver M. Sayler, ed., *Revolt in the Arts: A Survey of the Creation, Distribution, and Appreciation of Art in America* (New York: Brentano's, 1930).

58. Martha Graham, "Seeking an American Art of the Dance," in *Revolt in the Arts*, 249–50.

59. Graham, "Seeking an American Art of the Dance," 250.

60. Martha Hill, *Interview with Martha Hill*, conducted by Agnes de Mille, 2 sound cassettes, 100 min., Jan. 18, 1984, cassette 2, JRDD-NYPL.

61. John Mack Faragher, "A Nation Thrown Back upon Itself: Frederick Jackson and the Frontier," in *Rereading Frederick Jackson Turner: The Significance of the Frontier in American History and Other Essays*, edited by John Mack Faragher (New Haven, CT: Yale University Press, 1994), 2.

62. Graham, *Blood Memory*, 219.

63. Shawn, *The American Ballet*, 9.

64. Shawn, *The American Ballet*, 10–11.

65. John Martin, "The Dance: American Art," *New York Times*, Nov. 16, 1930, X4; Martin, "The Dance: Mary Wigman's Art."

66. Mary Wigman, "Die Amerika-Tourneen," in Ein Vermächtnis (Zurich: Florian Noetzel Verlage, 1986), 119.

67. Wigman, *Ein Vermächtnis*, 135; Mary Mayer, "Mary Wigman's Dance Principles Explained," *Los Angeles Times*, Dec. 6, 1931, B18; special thanks to Jens Richard Giersdorf for his insights.

68. John Martin, "Martha Graham, Dancer, Is Cheered," *New York Times*, Dec. 7, 1931.

69. Martin, "Martha Graham, Dancer, Is Cheered."

70. Eleanor King, *Transformations: A Memoir by Eleanor King of the Humphrey-Weidman Era* (Brooklyn, NY: Dance Horizons, 1978), 52; John Martin, "The Dance: Miss Graham: To a Performer, Now High in Her Art," *New York Times*, Feb. 18, 1931, 109.

71. Peter M. Rutcoff and William B. Scott, *New School: A History of the New School for Social Research* (New York: Free Press, 1986), 38, 42.

72. See authors in part II, "Dancing Interventions," in *The Oxford Handbook of Dance and Politics*, ed. Rebekah J. Kowal, Gerald Siegmund, and Randy Martin (New York: Oxford University Press, 2017), 396.

73. Rutcoff and Scott, *New School*, 79–80.

74. John Martin, *The Modern Dance* (New York: A. S. Barnes, 1933; reprint, New York: Dance Horizons, 1972), 7.

75. Michael Denning, *The Cultural Front: The Laboring of American Culture in the Twentieth Century* (New York: Verso, 1997). Special thanks to Professor Denning, who commented on my first presentation at an academic conference in 2006; his encouragement gave me invaluable confidence early in my career. See also William Francis McDonald, *Federal Relief Administration and the Arts: The Origins and Administrative*

History of the Arts Projects of the Works Progress Administration (Columbus: Ohio State University Press, 1969), 491; Charlotte M. Canning, "'In the Interest of the State': A Cold War National Theater for the United States," *Theater Journal* 61, no. 3 (October 2009): 407–20; see Ellen Graff, *Stepping Left: Dance and Politics in New York City, 1928–1942* (Durham, NC: Duke University Press, 1997), for the foundational work on politics and dance, as well as the work by this author published as Victoria Phillips Geduld for the origins of the phrase "Dance Is a Weapon."

76. Martin, *The Modern Dance*, 53.

77. Ronald H. Carpenter, "Style in Discourse as an Index of Frederick Jackson Turner's Historical Creativity: Conceptual Antecedents of the Frontier Thesis in His 'American Colonization,'" *Huntington Library Quarterly* 40, no. 3 (May 1977): 276.

78. Carpenter, "Style in Discourse," 273–74.

79. Martha Graham, *Interview with Martha Graham: The Early Years*, conducted by Walter Terry, 2 sound cassettes, 55 min., 1973, cassette 2, JRDD-NYPL.

80. David Pietrusza, *1932: The Rise of Hitler and FDR—Two Tales of Politics, Betrayal, and Unlikely Destiny* (New York: Rowman and Littlefield, 2016); William L. Shirer, *The Rise and Fall of the Third Reich: A History of Nazi Germany* (New York: Simon and Schuster, 1990), 35, 146.

81. John Martin, "Martha Graham in Dance Recital: Cheers Meet Performers at Guild Theatre—'Frontier' Feature of Evening," *New York Times*, Nov. 11, 1935, 21.

82. Margaret Lloyd, "Dance History in the Making," *Christian Science Monitor*, Aug. 24, 1935, 10.

83. Laurie Lisle, *Portrait of an Artist: A Biography of Georgia O'Keeffe* (New York: Seaview Books, 1980; reprint, New York: Washington Square Press, 1997), 72.

84. Martha Graham, "Platform for the American Dance," in *I See America Dancing: Selected Readings, 1685–2000*, ed. Maureen Needham (Champaign: University of Illinois Press, 2002), 204. This essay can also be found in in *The Modern Dance*, ed. Merle Armitage and Virginia Stewart (New York: Dance Horizons, 1935; reprint, 1975).

85. Martha Graham, "Platform for the American Dance," 203.

86. Bergsohn and Partsch-Bergsohn, *The Makers of Modern Dance in Germany*, 92; Melissa Ragona, "Ecstasy, Primitivism, Modernity: Isadora Duncan and Mary Wigman," *American Studies* 35, no. 1 (Spring 1994): 57; Mary Wigman, *Deutsche Tanzkunst* (Dresden: C. Reisner, 1935), 43.

87. Walter Sorell, *Hanya Holm: The Biography of an Artist* (Middletown, CT: Wesleyan University Press, 1969). See also a large body of recent literature on Holm available at http://www.danceheritage.org/holm.html (accessed April 1, 2019).

88. McDonald, *Federal Relief Administration and the Arts*; Caning, "'In the Interest of the State.'"

89. "Exchange of Remarks between the President and Martha Graham," Oct. 14, 1976, box 27, folder "Martha Graham," Office of the Press Secretary, David Gergen File, 1974–77, FORD.

90. "Charter—The ANTA, 1935," box 3, folder 1935, RBTC. Incorporation took place under the 74th Cong., 1st Sess., pt. 2, P.L. 199, July 5, 1935.

91. "The American National Theatre and Academy: Chartered by the Congress," July 1936, box 34, folder 3, RBTC.

92. John Martin, *America Dancing: The Background and Personalities of the Modern Dance* (Brooklyn, NY: Dance Horizons, 1968), 64.

93. Martin, *America Dancing*.

94. Margaret Lloyd, "An Oracle Speaks Simply," *Christian Science Monitor*, Mar. 17, 1936, 24, box 311, MGC-LOC.

95. Joseph Goebbels, *Reichsminister für Volksaufklärung und Propaganda*, Dr. Th. Lenald, Prasident des Organisations-Komitees fur die XL Olympiade Berlin, 1936, and Rudolf von Laban to Martha Graham, Feb. 29, 1936, box 311, MGC-LOC.

96. David Clay Large, *Nazi Games: The Olympics of 1936* (New York: W. W. Norton, 2007).

97. Frederic Spotts, *Hitler and the Power of Aesthetics* (New York: Overlook Press, 2002), 151–68; Lilian Karina and Marion Kant, *Hitler's Dancers: German Modern Dance and the Third Reich* (New York: Berghahn Books, 2003).

98. For the story of Jesse Owens, see Jeremy Schapp, *Triumph: The Untold Story of Jesse Owens and Hitler's Olympics* (New York: Mariner Press, 2007).

99. Martha Graham to Rudolf von Laban, Mar. 14, 1936, box 311, MGC-LOC.

100. "Martha Graham Rejects Olympics Dance Part," *New York Post*, Mar. 13, 1936; "Martha Graham Declines Bid to German Festival," *Chicago Tribune*, Mar. 14, 1936; "Dancer Turns Down Bid to Nazi Festival," *Daily Worker*, Mar. 16, 1936; "An Oracle Speaks Simply," *Christian Science Monitor*, Mar. 17, 1936, all box 311, MGC-LOC.

101. Schapp, *Triumph*.

102. Mary Wigman, "Choreographic Sketchbook, 1930–1961: Munich-Leipzig-Mannheim-Berlin," AP87350, W659, C5, NB9, HW5128, MWA; Karina and Kant, *Hitler's Dancers*.

103. Michael Kimmelman, "The Art Hitler Hated," *New York Review of Books*, June 19, 2014, 25–26.

104. Stephanie Barron, ed., *"Degenerate Art": The Fate of the Avant-Garde in Nazi Germany* (New York: Harry N. Abrams, 1991), 9.

105. Alfred H. Barr Jr., "Is Modern Art Communistic? On the Contrary, Says an Expert, It Is as Damned in Soviet Russia as It Was in Nazi Germany," *New York Times*, Dec. 14, 1952, SM22. Note the relationship between Barr and Rockefeller in the context of tirades against "Donderoism" by Barr in the press.

106. Eleanor Roosevelt, "My Day," May 22, 1936, https://www2.gwu.edu/~erpapers/myday/displaydoc.cfm?_y=1936&_f=md054337 (accessed April 1, 2017).

107. Camelia Lenart, "A Trustworthy Collaboration: Eleanor Roosevelt and Martha Graham's Pioneering of American Cultural Diplomacy," *European Journal of American Studies* 12, no. 1 (Spring 2017): 7.

108. Graham, *Blood Memory*, 44.

109. Janet Mansfield Soares, *Louis Horst: A Musician in a Dancer's World* (Durham, NC: Duke University Press, 1992), 131.

110. Soares, *Louis Horst*, 131.

111. Eleanor Roosevelt, "My Day," Mar. 1, 1937, https://www2.gwu.edu/~erpapers/myday/displaydoc.cfm?_y=1937&_f=md054579 (accessed April 1, 2017).

112. Note that Lenart writes about the enduring collaboration of Graham and Roosevelt in "A Trustworthy Collaboration." Although Lenart cites an invitation for Graham to present *American Document*, this was a group work and would not have been possible given the constrained space in the State Dining Room. In addition, it did not have its premiere until the following year, 1938.

113. Nicholas J. Cull, *The Cold War and the United States Information Agency: American Propaganda and Public Diplomacy, 1945–1989* (New York: Cambridge University Press, 2008), 13.

114. Cull, *The Cold War and the United States Information Agency*, 11.

115. "First Phase—Axis Penetration," box 7, folder 59, Series O, RG 4, FA350, Nelson A. Rockefeller personal papers, RAC; Walter Hixson, *Parting the Curtain: Propaganda, Culture, and the Cold War, 1945–1961* (New York: St. Martin's Press, 1998); Kenneth Osgood, *Total Cold War: Eisenhower's Secret Propaganda Battle at Home and Abroad* (Lawrence: University Press of Kansas, 2006); Laura A. Belmonte, *Selling the American Way: U.S. Propaganda and the Cold War* (Philadelphia: University of Pennsylvania Press, 2008).

116. Rebecca Stein, interview with author, May 2005 (transcript available upon request); Oscar Saul, *Revolt of the Beavers* (New York: Dramatists Play Service, 1936).

117. "Address Delivered by President Franklin D. Roosevelt in a Nation-Wide Broadcast Which Marked the Opening of the Museum's New Building on May 8, 1939," box 9, folder 76, Series O, RG 4, FA350, Nelson A. Rockefeller personal papers, RAC.

118. "Address Delivered by President Franklin D. Roosevelt in a Nation-Wide Broadcast Which Marked the Opening of the Museum's New Building on May 10, 1939."

119. Graff, *Stepping Left*, 130, fig. 44, n. 103 cites *Dance Observer*, May 1939.

120. "Department of State, For the Press, No. 537," Nov. 7, 1941, box 9, folder 70, Box 9, Series O, RG 4, FA350, Nelson A. Rockefeller personal papers, RAC.

121. "Office for Emergency Management: Office of the Coordinator of Commercial and Cultural Relations between the American Republics," July 25, 1941, box 9, folder 70, Series O, RG 4, FA350, Nelson A. Rockefeller personal papers, RAC; Council of National Defense, Coordinator of Commercial and Cultural Relations between the American Republics," July 15, 1941, box 5, folder 37, Series O, RG 4, FA350, Nelson A. Rockefeller personal papers, RAC; Nelson A. Rockefeller to Dr. Carl H. Milam, American Library Association, Jan. 30, 1940, box 207, folder 2468, Series 200R, RG 1.1, Projects, FA386, Rockefeller Foundation records, RAC; "Department of State, For the Press, 537"; Jennifer L. Campbell, "Creating Something Out of Nothing: The Office of Inter-American Music Committee (1940–1941) and the Inception of a Policy for Musical Diplomacy," Diplomatic History 36, no. 1 (January 2012): 29–39.

122. Martin Duberman, *The Worlds of Lincoln Kirstein* (New York: Alfred A. Knopf, 2007); Richard Norton Smith, *On His Own Terms: A Life of Nelson Rockefeller* (New York: Random House, 2014).

123. "General Report to the Coordinator of Commercial and Cultural Relations between the American Republics, RE: Contract No. NDCar-50, Effective March 17th, 1941," box 101, folder 966, Series L, RG 4, FA348, Nelson A. Rockefeller personal papers, RAC.

124. "General Report to the Coordinator of Commercial and Cultural Relations between the American Republics, RE: Contract No. NDCar-50, Effective March 17th, 1941," box 101, folder 966, Series L, RG 4, FA348, Nelson A. Rockefeller personal papers, RAC. Note that Martha Graham and her company performed in Havana, Cuba, just after Roosevelt's declaration of war in Dec. 1941. Sophie Maslow reported, "We were greeted with joy." I have not found evidence of government support for this tour, yet further research may uncover funding or support. See Russell Freedman, *Martha Graham: A Dancer's Life* (New York: Clarion Books, 1988), 94. Special thanks to Elizabeth Schwall for this citation.

125. Victoria Phillips with Conor Lane, "Political Partnering: The Dance of Latin American Diplomacy from the Interwar to into the Cold War," in *Making Friends? U.S. Public Diplomacy Strategies in Latin America in the Cold War*, ed. Lorenzo Delgado, Benedetta Calandra, and Francisco Rodríguez Jiménez (forthcoming).

126. "Inter-American Beginnings of U.S. Cultural Diplomacy, 1936–1948," J. Manuel Espinosa, Group XIV, Series 1, box 308, folder 3, UAK.

127. "Inter-American Beginnings of U.S. Cultural Diplomacy, 1936–1948."

128. "Four Years of War in the Americas," box 7, folder 59, Series O, RG 4, FA350, Nelson A. Rockefeller personal papers, RAC.

129. Osgood, *Total Cold War,* 29–30.

130. "Inter-American Beginnings of U.S. Cultural Diplomacy, 1936–1948."

131. "Appalachian Spring: Piano Rehearsal Copy No. 2," box 10, MGC-LOC; Programs, Ethel Winter and Charles Hyman Papers, LOC.

132. Both quotes from Graham, "Dance Libretto," box 35, MGC-LOC.

133. Michael Neiberg, *Potsdam: The End of World War II and the Remaking of Europe* (New York: Basic Books, 2015).

134. Elaine Tyler May, *Homeward Bound: American Families in the Cold War Era* (New York: Basic Books, 1988); Svetlana Alexievich, *War's Unwomanly Face* (Moscow: Progress Publishers, 1988; reprint, New York: Random House, 2017); Emily Yellin, *Our Mother's War: American Women at Home and on the Front during World War II* (New York: Free Press, 2004); Keith Lowe, *Savage Continent: Europe in the Aftermath of World War II* (New York: St. Martin's Press, 2012).

135. Alan L. Heil Jr., *Voice of America: A History* (New York: Columbia University Press, 2003), 35; Cull, *The Cold War and the United States Information Agency,* 14; Belmonte, *Selling the American Way,* 23.

136. Dear Gladys, signed Martha, from Santa Barbara, Calif., Aug. 23, 1946, typewritten, box 1, folder 1945, Correspondence, EHC-LOC.

137. Edward Alden Jewell, "Eyes to the Left," *New York Times,* Oct. 6, 1946, X8.

138. "Modern Art to Be Seen: State Department Display to Open at Metropolitan Friday," *New York Times,* Sept. 29, 1946, 63.

139. "Marshall Cancels Tour Abroad of State Department Modern Art," *Herald Tribune Bureau,* Apr. 5, 1947, 1A, 12.

140. Alfred H. Barr, Jr. to Nelson A. Rockefeller, May 3, 1947, box 154, folder 1540, Series O, RG 4, FA350, Nelson A. Rockefeller personal papers, RAC.

141. "Speech of Hon. George A. Dondero of Michigan: Communist Conspiracy in Art Threatens American Museums," Congressional Record, Proceedings and Debates of the 82nd Cong., 2nd sess., in *Modern Art Shackled to Communism: Speech of Hon. George A. Dondero of Michigan in the House of Representatives, Tuesday, August 16, 1949* (Washington, DC: Government Offprint, 1949).

142. "Marshall Cancels Tour Abroad of State Department Modern Art"; "Radical Art Shows Again Laid to U.S.: Dondero Cites 'Left-Wing' Exhibit at St. Albans," *New York Herald Tribune*, Mar. 12, 1949, 11; Arthur Miller, "Art Critics Work Best in Climate of Freedom," *Los Angeles Times*, June 11, 1949, A4.

143. Graham, FBI File, NSA.

144. George Kennan, "Long Telegram," http://nsarchive.gwu.edu/coldwar/documents/episode-1/kennan.htm (accessed May 30, 2017).

145. Barr, "Is Modern Art Communistic?"

146. Ludmilla B. Turkevich, "The Second Congress of Soviet Writers," *Books Abroad* 30, no. 1 (Winter 1956): 31–34; Michael Walter, "Music of Seriousness and Commitment," in *The Cambridge History of Twentieth-Century Music*, vol. 1, ed. Nicholas Cook and Anthony Pople (Cambridge: Cambridge University Press, 2004), 288.

147. Solomon Volkov, *Shostakovich and Stalin: The Extraordinary Relationship between the Great Composer and the Brutal Dictator* (New York: Alfred A. Knopf, 2004), 9, 288.

148. Larissa Vasilieva, *Kremlin Wives: The Secret Lives of the Women behind the Kremlin Walls—from Lenin to Gorbachev*, trans. Cathy Porter (New York: Arcade, 2015), 234; Caute, *The Dancer Defects*, 20.

149. George F. Kennan, *Memoirs: 1925–1950* (Boston: Little, Brown, 1967), 289–90.

150. Kennan, *Memoirs*, 273.

151. Prevots, *Dance for Export*, 19.

152. "Excerpts from a Letter Written by Mr. Benton to an Associate," Mar. 19, 1947, box 2, folder 9, Series O, RG 4, FA350, Nelson A. Rockefeller personal papers, RAC.

153. "Excerpts from a Letter Written by Mr. Benton to an Associate," Mar. 19, 1947, box 2, folder 9, Series O, RG 4, FA350, Nelson A. Rockefeller personal papers, RAC.

154. "'OIC Budget for Fiscal Year 1948 and Analysis of Requested $25 Million Increase,' Addressed to Frances Jamieson, Rockefeller Foundation, from Oliver McKee, Special Assistant to the Secretary of State," Mar. 24, 1947, box 2, folder 9, Series O, RG 4, FA350, Nelson A. Rockefeller personal papers, RAC.

155. Mary Ann Caws, "Editor's Preface," in *Stéphane Mallarmé: Selected Poetry and Prose* (New York: New Directions, 1982).

156. Richard H. Pells, *The Liberal Mind in a Conservative Age: American Intellectuals in the 1940s and 1950s* (Hanover, NH: University Press of New England, 1985; reprint, Middletown, CT: Wesleyan University Press, 1989), 122–23.

157. John Martin, "The Dance: Program," *New York Times*, June 1, 1947, 10; "Walter Terry, Chairman, to Morton Baum," on the Letterhead of the Continuations Committee of the American Dance Committee of the Youth Festival, Dec. 15, 1947, folder 266, Morton Baum Papers, 1938–1968, JRDD-NYPL.

158. "World Youth Festival," in *The Bright Face of Peace* (New York: World Festival of Youth and Students for Peace and Friendship, 1947), 17, 19, file folder, "Publications relating to World Festival of Youth and Students for Peace and Friendship," NYU-TAM.

159. "Red Issue Splits Youth Delegate," *New York Times*, Oct. 7, 1947, 5; "World Youth Festival," 19; "Rift of U.S. Group in Budapest Noted," *New York Times*, Sept. 3, 1949, 3.

160. Rebecca Rosenberg, interview with author, New York City, 2006.

161. Lloyd, *The Borzoi Book of Modern Dance*, xvii, 11–12, 16, 21, 23, 37, 49, 303.

162. "Martha Graham and Her Company," *Le Monde*, June 29, 1950, in translation, scrapbook 326, MGC-LOC.

163. "From Martha Graham's Ballets to Those of the Opera," *Le Parisien Libéré*, June 30, 1950, in translation, scrapbooks, box 326, MGC-LOC; See picture of Roosevelt at the Paris performance, nd, © D.M. Bernard, Paris, box 264, MGC-LOC.

164. "Paris Dazed by Graham; Dance Too Advanced," *Variety*, clippings service, July 12, 1950, scrapbooks, box 326, MGC-LOC.

165. Robert Schnitzer to Robert Breen and Blevins Davis, Nov. 22, 1950, box 2, folder 1, RSTC.

166. Fr: Harry S. Truman, to Miss Venable, Director, The National Ballet, May 18, 1950, Official File, box 476, file 80-A, HSTL; USIS Report, volume 2, O-110, RG 306, entry A1-1066, NARA.

167. Attachment to a letter to Mr. President, Fr: Blevins Davis, June 2, 1950, Official File, box 476, file 80-A, HSTL.

168. Fr: William D. Hassett, Secretary to the President, To Mr. Blevins Davis, July 8, 1950, Official File, box 476, file 80-A, HSTL; USIS Report, volume 2, O-110.

169. Box 2, folder 1, and box 4, folder 2, for plans and reactions sent to the Department of State by Schnitzer regarding American National Ballet Theatre, RSTC; USIA Report, vol. 1, O-25.

170. Telegram Fr: William D. Hassett, To: Blevins Davis, July 20, 1950, Attachment to a letter to Mr. President, Fr. Blevins Davis, June 2, 1950, Official File, box 476, file 80-A, HSTL.

171. To: Matthew Connelly, William Hassett, James Webb, Fr: Blevins Davis, Re: "Brief Resume of Background and Immediate Action To Be Taken," nd, see also Fr: R.B. Landry, "Memorandum for Lt. Colonel Floyd J. Gudgel, ODC/S, USAF, Aug. 17, 1950, Official File, box 476, file 80-A, HSTL.

172. To: Matthew Connelly, William Hassett, James Webb, Fr: Blevins Davis, Re: Brief Resume of Background and Immediate Action To Be Taken.

173. To: Mr. Secretary (Hassett), Fr: Louis Johnson, Secretary of Defense, June 28, 1950, Official File, box 476, file 80-A, HSTL.

174. Fr: Robert Schnitzer, To: The White House, Aug. 18, 1950, Official File, box 476, file 80-A, HSTL.

175. "Truman's Pose with Women Award Winners," *Chicago Daily Tribune*, Apr. 16, 1950, 7; Drew Pearson, "Washington Merry-Go-Round," *Mirror*, May 30, 1948, both on scrapbooks, box 311, MGC-LOC.

176. Martha Graham to Eric Hawkins, handwritten and undated; Martha Graham to Eric Hawkins, typewritten, August 1946, both box 3 of 3, folder 1939-1940, EHC.

177. Proposed Press Release on Mr. Rockefeller's Proposals, box 49, folder 374, Series D, Civic Interests, Office of Mssrs. Rockefeller, FA313, RAC; Kimie Hara, "Introduction," in *The San Francisco System and Its Legacies: Continuation, Transformation, and Historical Reconciliation in the Asia-Pacific*, ed. Kimie Hara (New York: Routledge, 2014), 1–20.

178. Yujiro Iwai to Nelson A. Rockefeller, Feb. 21, 1951, box 49, folder 373, Series D, Civic Interests, Office of Mssrs. Rockefeller, FA313, RAC.

179. From: John D. Rockefeller, 3rd, To: Ambassador Dulles, "Subject: United States-Japanese Cultural Relations," Confidential, Apr. 16, 1951, box 49, folders 372, 72–73, 77, 79, Box 49, Series D, Civic Interests, Office of Mssrs. Rockefeller, FA313, RAC.

180. USIS Report, vol. 2, P-43.

181. From: John D. Rockefeller, 3rd, To: Ambassador Dulles, "Subject: United States-Japanese Cultural Relations," Confidential, Apr. 16, 1951, box 49, folders 372, 15, Series D, Civic Interests, Office of Mssrs. Rockefeller, FA313, RAC.

182. C. P. Trussell, "Red Plot Laid to Artists' Equity As 'Using' Party Line in Museums," *New York Times*, Mar. 18, 1952, 24.

183. Roland Végsö, *The Naked Communist: Cold War Modernism and the Politics of Popular Culture* (New York: Fordham University Press, 2012), 93; John Merryman, *Law, Ethics, and the Visual Arts* (London: Kluwer Law International. 2002), 537.

184. Barr, "Is Modern Art Communistic?"

185. Belmonte, *Selling the American Way*, 65.

186. Dwight D. Eisenhower to Nelson A. Rockefeller, Dec. 16, 1954, *The American Presidency Project*, ed. Gerhard Peters and John T. Woolley http://www.presidency.ucsb.edu/ws/?pid=10157 (accessed March 22, 2013).

187. Lincoln Kirsten to Nelson A. Rockefeller, June 17, 1955, box 80, folder 615, Series O, RG 4, FA350, Nelson A. Rockefeller personal papers, RAC. Note that ANBT toured the United States as Ballet Theatre during this period, and Eisehnower would request that it be called American Ballet Theatre (ABT), which it remains in 2020.

188. "A Brief on the Work of the American National Theatre and Academy (ANTA)," March 1950, box 1, folder 36, 4, RBTC.

189. Fr: President Dwight D. Eisenhower, To: Lucia Chase, American Ballet Theatre Corporate Offices, New York, NY.

190. Hixson, *Parting the Curtain*, 25.

191. "Terms of Reference for Working Group on Cultural Activities," October 8, 1954, DDRS; "Fifth Quarterly Report, July 1, 1955–September 30, 1955," box 80, folder 618, Series O, RG 4, FA350, Nelson A. Rockefeller personal papers, RAC.

192. "Summary of Progress Report on Activities of the Operations Coordinating Board Cultural Presentation Committee Covering Period 1/1-6/30/55," July 13, 1955; "Memorandum for Members of the OCB Cultural Presentations Committee," Sept. 21, 1955, all DDRS. Note that at times the OCB is called the Operations Coordinating Board, and at other points is referred to as the Operation Coordination Board (emphasis mine). Both receive the acronym OCB in this book.

193. "Progress Report on Activities of the OCB Trade Fair Committee," Feb. 28, 1956, DDRS.

194. "Fourth Quarterly Report, April 1, 1955–June 1955 30," box 80, folder 618, Series O, RG 4, FA350, Nelson A. Rockefeller personal papers, RAC.

195. Prevots, *Dance for Export*, 24.

196. Prevots, *Dance for Export*, 24; for a deeper consideration of the problem of speaking Spanish to audiences in Brazil, see Phillips and Lane, "Political Partnering."

197. Martha Graham to Frances Wickes, [nd], FWC-LOC-MD.

198. Lenart, "Turning the Tide and Reconstructing the Politics," 7.

199. USIA to Department of State, despatch no. 6, unsigned, received Oct. 1, 2008, reference #NWCT2R-CB-08-10292 from Connie Beach, Archives II Section, Textual Reference Division, NARA, courtesy of Victoria Thoms.

200. "Summary of Progress Report on Activities of the Operations Coordinating Board."

201. "A Study of USIA Operating Assumptions," vol. 1, 4; vol. 1, AA-22, vol. 2, T 10–16.

202. USIS Summary of reviews, Apr. 3, 1954, box 218, MGC-LOC.

203. William E. Daugherty and Morris Janowitz, *The Psychological Warfare Casebook* (Baltimore: Johns Hopkins University Press, Operations Research Office, 1958), 682.

204. Daugherty and Janowitz, *Psychological Warfare Casebook*, 722.

205. "Memorandum for the Operations Coordinating Board," Mar. 8, 1955, box 80, folder 618, Series O, RG 4, FA350, Nelson A. Rockefeller personal papers, RAC.

206. "Memorandum for the Operations Coordinating Board."

207. Justice Georges Abi-Saab, "Foreword," in *Bandung Global History, and International Law: Critical Pasts and Pending Futures*, ed. Luis Eslava, Michael Fakhri, and Vasuki Nesiah (New York: Cambridge University Press, 2017), xxx.

208. Luis Eslava, Michael Fakhri, and Vasuki Nesiah, "Understanding Bandung," in Eslava, Fakhri, and Nesiah, *Bandung, Global History, and International Law*, 4.

209. Robert Young, "Postcolonialism: From Bandung to the Tricontinental," *Historein* 11 (2005): 14, quoted in Eslava, Fakhri, and Nesiah, "Understanding Bandung," 13n41.

210. Tillman Durdin, "Richard Wright Examines the Meaning of Bandung," *New York Times*, Mar. 18, 1965, quoted in Ibrahim J. Gassama, "Bandung 1955: Deceit and the Conceit," in Eslava, Fakhri, and Nesiah, *Bandung, Global History, and International Law*, 131n14.

211. Eslava, Fakhri, and Nesiah, "Understanding Bandung," 5.

212. Eslava, Fakhri, and Nesiah, "Understanding Bandung," 4.

213. Matthew Jones, "A 'Segregated' Asia? Race, the Bandung Conference, and Pan-Asianist Fears in American Thought and Policy, 1954–1955," *Diplomatic History* 29, no. 5 (November 2005): 844.

214. Gregg A. Brazinsky, *Winning the Third World: Sino-American Rivalry during the Cold War* (Chapel Hill: University of North Carolina Press, 2017), 91–95.

215. Jones, "A 'Segregated' Asia?," 844.

216. Brazinsky, *Winning the Third World*, 97.

217. Jones, "A 'Segregated' Asia?," 852.

218. Jones, "A 'Segregated' Asia?," 844.

219. Eslava, Fakhri, and Nesiah, "Understanding Bandung," 5.

220. For a specific discussion of modernization in this context, see Eslava, Fakhri, and Nesiah, "Understanding Bandung," 21.

221. Zoran Oklopcic, "A Triple Struggle: Nonalignment, Yugoslavia, and National, Social, and Geopolitical Emancipation," in Eslava, Fakhri, and Nesiah, *Bandung, Global History, and International Law*, 276–77.

222. Fr: AmEmbassy Tehran, To: Department of State, Su: Educational Exchange, Nov. 27, 1956, box 318, folder 5, UAK.

223. Fr: AmEmbassy Tel Aviv, To: Department of State, USIA, CIA, Ref: Foreign Service Educational Exchange Circular No. 6, Dec. 11, 1953, July 10, 1956, box 318, folder 10, UAK.

224. Osgood, *Total Cold War*, 136.

225. DP/IEP, October 21, 1954, 2, UAK; "Memorandum for the Operations Coordinating Board."

226. "Memorandum for the Operations Coordinating Board."

227. Serge Guilbaut, *How New York Stole the Idea of Modern Art: Abstract Expressionism, Freedom and the Cold War*, trans. Arthur Goldhammer (Chicago: University of Chicago Press, 1983); Greg Barnhisel, *Cold War Modernists: Art, Literature, and American Cultural Diplomacy* (New York: Columbia University Press, 2015).

228. "Virginia Inness-Brown, 89," Obituaries, *New York Times*, Aug. 8, 1990, http://www.nytimes.com/1990/08/08/obituaries/virginia-inness-brown-arts-advocate-89.html (accessed May 30, 2017).

229. John Martin, "The Dance: Diplomacy: Limón Makes Conquest in South America," *New York Times*, Jan. 25, 1955, X11.

230. See Duberman, *The Worlds of Lincoln Kirstein*; Alex C. Ewing, *Bravura! Lucia Chase and the American Ballet Theatre* (Gainesville: University Press of Florida, 2009); DP/IEP, March 1954.

231. DP/IEP, Oct. 21, 1954, 1–2, UAK.

232. "Third Quarterly Report, January 1, 1955–March 31, 1955," box 80, folder 618, Series O, RG 4, FA350, Nelson A. Rockefeller personal papers, RAC.

233. "Chronology, 7 January 1954–20 January 1954," *Chronology of International Events* 10, no. 2 (1954): 37–63.

234. Betty S. Anderson, *The American University of Beirut: Arab Nationalism and Liberal Education* (Austin: University of Texas Press, 2011), 142; "News in Brief," *Universal-International News*, Apr. 5, 1954, Beirut, Lebanon, 50 sec., clip #65675045469, Critical Past, https://www.criticalpast.com/video/65675045469_students_students-protest_American-university_Turkey-Pakistan-defense-pact (accessed August 25, 2019).

235. Ran Kochan, "Israel in Third World Forums," in *Israel in the Third World*, ed. Michael Curtis and Susan Aurelia Gitelson (New York: Routledge, 1976), 245. Special thanks to Xinyi Chen for her work on this subject in her master's dissertation in the London School of Economics/Columbia University Dual Master's Program, 2019.

236. Kochan, "Israel in Third World Forums," 246.

237. Kochan, "Israel in Third World Forums," 246.

238. Kochan, "Israel in Third World Forums," 247.

239. Kochan, "Israel in Third World Forums," 248.

240. Kochan, "Bandung: The Gate Is Down," in *Israel in the Third World,* 252.

241. "Martha Graham and Dance Company," box 3, folder 7 (Iran), Helen McGehee and Umaña Collection of Dance Materials, Music Division, LOC.

242. "Report—Abadan," box 3, folder 8, Abadan, Martha Graham Dance Company Tour Records, 1941-1957, JRDD-NYPL.

243. "Report—Tehran (continued)," box 3, folder 9, Tehran, Martha Graham Dance Company Tour Records, 1941-1957, JRDD-NYPL.

244. "D/APM," May 5, 1955, 2, UAK.

245. Bertram Ross, "Martha (Draft)," [nd], box 10, folder 10, BRC.

246. DP/IEP, Oct. 21, 1954, 2, UAK.

247. "Fifth Quarterly Report, July 1, 1955–September 30, 1955," box 80, folder 618, Series O, RG 4, FA350, Nelson A. Rockefeller personal papers, RAC.

248. DP/IEP, March 1954; Samuel Zipp, *Manhattan Projects: The Rise and Fall of Urban Renewal in Cold War New York* (New York: Oxford University Press, 2012), 196.

249. "Correspondence—Tour Operations," box 10, folder 10, RBTC.

250. Laura McEnaney, "Personal, Political, and International: A Reflection on Diplomacy and Methodology," *Diplomatic History* 36, no. 4 (September 2012): 770; Frank Costigliola, "Pamela Churchill, Wartime London, and the Making of the Special Relationship," *Diplomatic History* 36, no. 1 (September 2012): 753–63.

Chapter 2

1. DDE Library White House Office, National Security Council Staff Papers 1948–61, (File #3) (3) OCB Central File Series, box 15, OCB 007, [Cultural Activities] [Dec. 1955–May 1956], DDE.

2. Scrapbooks, box 331, MGC-LOC. The names of countries are used based on 1955 geography as listed in "Project Title: Martha Graham Dance Troupe; Description: (Completed)," National Security Council Staff Papers, Operations Coordinating Board (OCB) Central File Series, Cultural Presentations Staff: Papers, 1948–1961, President's Fund Program [FY1955], box 14, DDE; Prevots, *Dance for Export,* 8.

3. Memo, nd, box 2, folder 10, Kuala Lumpur, Martha Graham Dance Company Tour Records, 1941–1957, JRDD-NYPL.

4. "(Deleted) The Asia Foundation," document number (FOIA) 0001088617, https://www.cia.gov/library/readingroom/document/deleted-asia-foundation (accessed April 1, 2017).

5. "Debriefing, March 21, 1956, March 28, 1956," To: IFS, Fr: IES, SU: box 318, folder 22, UAK.

6. Mao Zedong, "The Chinese People Have Stood Up!," Opening Address by Mao Zedong, Chairman of the Chinese Communist Party, at the First Plenary Session of the Chinese People's Political Consultative Conference, Sept. 21, 1949, http://web.

international.ucla.edu/institute/article/18179 (accessed November 4, 2009); David Halberstam, *The Coldest Winter: America and the Korean War* (New York: Hyperion, 2007), 631–33; Arissa H. Oh, To Save the Children of Korea: The Cold War Origins of International Adoption (Palo Alto, CA: Stanford University Press, 2015).

7. "Debriefing, March 21, 1956, March 28, 1956."

8. Beverly Gaillard to Mr. Robert Schnitzer, Eighth Army Entertainment, July 1, 1955, box 2, folder 10, Kuala Lumpur, Martha Graham Dance Company Tour Records, 1941–1957, JRDD-NYPL.

9. "Debriefing, March 21, 1956, March 28, 1956."

10. Box 2, folder 7, Seoul, Martha Graham Dance Company Tour Records, 1941–1957, JRDD-NYPL.

11. "95. Memorandum, Fr: Assistant Secretary of State for Far Eastern Affairs (Robertson) to the Under Secretary of State (Hoover), Washington, Oct. 18, 1955," in "Korea (Foreign Relations of the United States, 1955–1957, Vol. XXIII, Part 2)," Office of the Historian, Bureau of Public Affairs, United States Department of State, XXIII.2, 701.

12. "98. Memorandum Fr: Assistant Secretary of State for Far Eastern Affairs (Robertson) to the Under Secretary of State (Hoover), Washington, November 9, 1955, SUBJ: President Rhee," in "Korea (Foreign Relations of the United States, 1955–1957, Vol. XXIII, Part 2)," Office of the Historian, Bureau of Public Affairs, United States Department of State, XXIII.2, 720.

13. Box 2, folder 7, Seoul, Martha Graham Dance Company Tour Records, 1941–1957, JRDD-NYPL.

14. Stanley Karnow, *In Our Image: America's Empire in the Philippines* (New York: Random House, 1989); Luis H. Francia, *A History of the Philippines: From Indos Bravos to Filipinos* (New York: Overlook Press, 2013).

15. *Manila Times*, Nov. 14, 1955, scrapbooks, box 335, MGC-LOC.

16. "Graham Dancers Were Great," *Singapore Tiger Standard*, Dec. 5, 1955, scrapbooks, box 331, MGC-LOC.

17. Pearl Lang, interview with author, taped at the Martha Graham School of Contemporary Dance, MGF-MGC.

18. Wassily Kandinsky, *Concerning the Spiritual in Art*, trans. M. T. H. Sadler (New York: Dover, 1977), an unabridged republication of *The Art of Spiritual Harmony* (London: Constable, 1914); Pearl Lang, interview with author; Graham, *Blood Memory*, 98. Note that the Woman in White had originally been costumed in blue, but when Mary Hinkson took the role Graham changed the color to white.

19. Sept. 17, 1955, scrapbooks, box 336, MGC-LOC.

20. "Living Goddess of Beauty: Martha Graham," Oct. 24, 1955, box 336, MGC-LOC.

21. Diane Kirby, ed., *Religion and the Cold War* (New York: Palgrave Macmillan, 2002; reprint 2003).

22. William Inboden, *Religion and American Foreign Policy, 1945–1960: The Soul of Containment* (New York: Cambridge University Press, 2008), 2, quotes President Harry Truman, "Address the Public during a Cornerstone Laying at the New York Avenue Presbyterian Church," Apr. 3, 1951, http://www.presidency.ucsb.edu/ws/?pid=14048 (accessed February 10, 2017).

23. Andrew Preston, *Sword of the Spirit, Shield of the Faith: Religion in American War and Diplomacy* (New York: Random House, 2012); Inboden, *Religion and American Foreign Policy*, 241; Eisenhower, " 'UNDER GOD' " in Pledge to Flag [June 14, 1954]," "Convenience" File, 1945–1969, A70-41, Papers, Post Presidential, box 1, DDE; Osgood, *Total Cold War*, 55.

24. Hill, *Interview with Martha Hill*, conducted by Agnes de Mille.

25. Ernestine Stodelle, *Deep Song: The Dance Story of Martha Graham* (New York: Schirmer Books, 1984), 173.

26. Stodelle, *Deep Song*, 173.

27. Stodelle, *Deep Song*, 173.

28. Stodelle, *Deep Song*, 220.

29. Hill, *Interview with Martha Hill*, conducted by Agnes de Mille.

30. Rachel L. Halloway, " 'Keeping the Faith': Eisenhower Introduces the Hydrogen Age," in *Eisenhower's War of Words: Rhetoric and Leadership*, ed. Martin J. Medhurst (Ann Arbor: University of Michigan Press, 1994), 51.

31. Daniel Hobbins, "Introduction," in *The Trial of Joan of Arc*, ed. and trans. Daniel Hobbins (Cambridge, MA: Harvard University Press, 2005), 30.

32. Hobbins, ed. and trans., *The Trial of Joan of Arc*, Saturday, Mar. 17, 113.

33. Robert S. Alley, *So Help Me God: Religion and the Presidency, Wilson to Nixon* (Louisville, KY: John Knox Press, 1972), 82.

34. For further analysis, see Victoria Phillips, "Cold War Modernist Missionary: Martha Graham Takes Joan of Arc and Catherine of Siena 'Behind the Iron Curtain,'" in *Dancing the Cold War: An International Symposium*, 65, https://harriman.columbia.edu/event/dancing-cold-war-international-symposium (accessed April 1, 2019).

35. Matthew Connelly, A Diplomatic Revolution: Algeria's Fight for Independence and the Origins of the Post–Cold War Era (New York: Oxford University Press, 2002), 211.

36. Belmonte, *Selling the American Way*, 102.

37. Programs, Ethel Winter and Charles Hyman Papers, LOC.

38. Philippines, caption under picture, nd, scrapbooks, box 335, MGC-LOC.

39. "Extracts from press clippings on the Martha Graham dance troupe," Vicente Rivera Jr., "Martha Graham's Art," *Evening News*, Nov. 17, 1955, scrapbooks, box 337, MGC-LOC.

40. *Sixth Quarterly Report: President's Emergency Fund for Participation in International Affairs*, Oct. 1–Dec. 31, 1955, DDE Library White House Office, National Security Council Staff Papers 1948–61, OCB Central File Series, box 15, OCB 007 [Cultural Activities] (File #3) (3) [December 1955–May 1956], DDE.

41. *Sixth Quarterly Report*.

42. Lee Leatherman to American Consulate Calcutta, box 3, folder 8, Abadan, Martha Graham Dance Company Tour Records, 1941–1957, JRDD-NYPL.

43. Author interviews with Linda Hodes, Marni Thomas, and Ellen Graff (transcripts available upon request with written permission of Thomas, Graff, and Hodes).

44. John Curtis Perry, *Singapore: Unlikely Power* (New York: Oxford University Press, 2017).

45. To: SecState Wash DC 1276, From: Singapore, Info: USIA WashDC and Bangkok, Hong Kong, Jakarta, Kuala Lumpur, Manila, Rangoon, Saigon, Taipei, Oct. 1, 1974, Elizabeth Betty Ford White House Papers Box 39, Graham, Martha—Dance Company (2), FORD; "A Study of USIA Operating Assumptions," Dec. 1954, vol. 1, P-5.

46. To: SecState Wash DC 1276, From: Singapore.

47. To: SecState Wash DC 1276, From: Singapore.

48. To: SecState Wash DC 1276, From: Singapore.

49. *Sixth Quarterly Report.*

50. Adrian Vickers, *A History of Modern Indonesia*, 2nd ed. (New York: Cambridge University Press, 2013).

51. "1957-05-22 Technical Landing Right—Indonesia," Stories of Sacrifice and Dedication, 520037a0993294098d51744c, Freedom of Information Act Reading Room, Central Intelligence Agency, NARA, also https://www.cia.gov/library/readingroom/document/520037a0993294098d51744c (accessed June 2, 2019).

52. Peter G. Boyle, ed., *The Eden-Eisenhower Correspondence, 1955–1957* (Chapel Hill: University of North Carolina Press, 2005), 63.

53. "1957-05-22 Technical Landing Right—Indonesia."

54. *Sixth Quarterly Report.*

55. "Foreign Service Digest."

56. Lundestad, "Empire by Invitation?," 263–77.

57. "Report on Djakarta," Nov. 11, 1955, box 2, folder 11, Djakarta, Martha Graham Dance Company Tour Records, 1941–1957, JRDD-NYPL.

58. *Sixth Quarterly Report.*

59. "Progress Report on the Activities of the OCB Cultural Presentation Committee," Oct. 4, 1956, DDRS.

60. *Sixth Quarterly Report.*

61. Michael W. Charney, *A History of Modern Burma* (New York: Cambridge University Press, 2009).

62. Eric D. Pullin, "The Bandung Conference: Ideological Conflict and the Limitations of US Propaganda," in *Neutrality and Neutralism in the Global Cold War: Between or within the Blocs?*, ed. Sandra Bott, Jussi M. Hanhimäki, Janick Marina Schaufelbuehl, and Marco Wyss (New York: Routledge, 2016).

63. Author interview with Ethel Winter, Ethel Winter and Charles Hyman Papers, LOC.

64. Author discussion with Charles Hyman, stage manager, while examining his paperwork; author interview with Ethel Winter.

65. *Sixth Quarterly Report.*

66. Author interview with Linda Hodes.

67. Author interview with Linda Hodes, Ethel Winter, and Charles Hyman.

68. Robert J. McMahon, *The Cold War on the Periphery: The United States, India, and Pakistan* (New York: Columbia University Press, 1994), 183.

69. Reports contained in "USIS Propaganda Policy in India," Foreign Service Despatch, 511.91, May 7, 1952, RG 59, box 25, NARA.

70. McMahon, *The Cold War and the Periphery*, 225.

71. Reports contained in "USIS Propaganda Policy in India."
72. "Library Readership Study Conducted in India," Feb. 4, 1953, 4, enclosure 1, Fr: New Delhi, "Reports and Studies, 1948–53, India and Iran," RG 306, box 32, NARA.
73. "Some Clarification of the Word 'Americana,'" New Delhi India Despach No. 1442, Dec. 19, 1952, "Reports and Studies, 1948–53, India and Iran," RG 306, box 32, NARA. Note original spelling of "despatch."
74. "Some Clarification of the Word 'Americana,'" 1.
75. "Some Clarification of the Word 'Americana,'" 2.
76. "Indian Ambassador of Goodwill," Times of India, Apr. 23, 1935, 3.
77. "Uday Shankar in London: A Great Artiste," Times of India, Mar. 17, 1937, 15.
78. Paul Hume, "Sense of Immediacy Fills Shankar Hindu Dance Moves," Washington Post, Feb. 15, 1950, 18.
79. A Ballet Critic, "Martha Graham's Dance Recital," Statesman, Dec. 28, 1955, scrapbooks, box 334, MGC-LOC.
80. Lalita Uberoi, "Martha Graham Good Showmanship, but . . . ," Woman's Viewpoint, scrapbooks, box 334, MGC-LOC.
81. See Prarthana Purkayastha, Indian Modern Dance, Feminism and Transnationalism (London: Palgrave Macmillan, 2014). Special thanks to Ms. Purkayastha for her fine insights into the work of nationalism in Graham's presentations in India, which she offered during the panel presentation "Performing Nationalisms: Outsiders, Revolutions, Locales," chaired by Susan Manning, at the 2009 meeting of the Society of Dance History Scholars at Stanford University.
82. Prarthana Purkayastha, "Bodies beyond Borders: Modern Dance in Colonial and Postcolonial India" (PhD diss., Roehampton University, 2008), 130, 149, 158.
83. Purkayastha, "Bodies beyond Borders," 141.
84. Folksay, choreography Sophie Maslow, music Woody Guthrie and Earl Robinson, premiere November/December 1942 (exact date unknown), Central High School, New York, NY; note first review by John Martin, "The Dance, Americana: Stability of the Native Art as Evidenced by Sophie Maslow's 'Folksay,'" New York Times, Dec. 6, 1942, X5 (Martin notes the performance as "last week").
85. Author interview with Janet Eilber, New York, May 1, 2012.
86. Clipping, na, Statesman, Jan. 21, 1956, 1955–1956 Tour, box 3, folder 6, Helen McGehee and Umaña Collection of Dance Materials, Music Division, LOC.
87. Na, nt, Statesman, Jan. 21, 1956, scrapbooks, box 337, MGC-LOC.
88. Na, nt, Statesman, Jan. 21, 1956.
89. Associated National Press, "Martha Graham Dance Company Set for Japan," Los Angeles Sentinel, Sept. 22, 1955, 11.
90. Prevots, Dance for Export, 51.
91. From [unsigned] to Barrett, Jan. 28, 1956, box 3, folder 9, Teheran, Martha Graham Dance Company Tour Records, 1941–1957, JRDD-NYPL
92. Gowri Ramnarayan, "Memories of Madras—Stepping Back in Time," The Hindu, June 8, 2010, updated Nov. 18, 2016, http://www.thehindu.com/features/friday-review/history-and-culture/Memories-of-Madras-Stepping-back-in-time/article16241880.ece (accessed November 20, 2017).

93. A Staff Reporter, "Miss M. Graham Impressed: Indian Dancing," *Times of India*, Jan. 15, 1956, 3. Many thanks to Dr. Arshiya Sethi and her work with Gina Lalli for this recounting of the reception of Graham in India.

94. Box 2, folder 5, Japan, 1955, Martha Graham Dance Company Tour Records, 1941–1957, JRDD-NYPL.

95. Box 2, folder 5, Japan, 1955, Martha Graham Dance Company Tour Records, 1941–1957.

96. Christopher de Bellaigue, *Patriot of Persia: Muhammad Mossadegh and a Tragic Anglo-American Coup* (New York: Harper, 2012).

97. "Report—Teheran (continued)," box 3, folder 9, Teheran, Martha Graham Dance Company Tour Records, 1941–1957, JRDD-NYPL.

98. See pictures and assorted invitations in scrapbooks, boxes 334 and 338, MGC-LOC.

99. Fr.: Leroy Leatherman, To: Mrs. Wickes, nd, box 2, folder "Martha Graham," FWC-LOC-MD.

100. Fr.: Leroy Leatherman, To: Mrs. Wickes.

101. "Report—Teheran (continued)," box 3, folder 9, Teheran, Martha Graham Dance Company Tour Records, 1941–1957, JRDD-NYPL.

102. "Martha Graham—Radio Speech—Iran," Feb. 6, 1956, 2, box 3, folder 8, Abadan, Martha Graham Dance Company Tour Records, 1941–1957, JRDD-NYPL.

103. "Martha Graham—Radio Speech—Iran," Feb. 6, 1956, 2.

104. "Martha Graham—Radio Speech—Iran," Feb. 6, 1956, 4.

105. Ida Meftahi, *Gender and Dance in Modern Iran: Biopolitics on Stage* (New York: Routledge, 2016), 9, 24, 41, 45. Note that Meftahi does not mention the influence of Martha Graham or dance modernism as a Western-derived form.

106. Fr: AmEmbassy Tel Aviv, To: Department of State, USIA, CIA, Ref: Foreign Service Educational Exchange Circular No. 6, Dec. 11, 1953, sent on July 10, 1956, box 318, folder 10, UAK.

107. "Gertrude Macy, 79: Broadway Producer, Writer, and Manager," *New York Times*, Oct. 19, 1983; Gertrude Macy to Lee Eastman, Feb. 22, 1955, box 3, folder 10, Israel, Martha Graham Dance Company Tour Records, 1941–1957, JRDD-NYPL.

108. "Edward Norman Dead," *Jewish Telegraphic Authority, Daily News Bulletin*, June 21, 1955, XXII.119, 4.

109. Obituary, "Leroy Leatherman, Novelist," *New York Times*, Apr. 12, 1984, D27.

110. Martha Graham, "Faith and Trust, in Dance," 1, attachment to application to perform, To: The Council of Movies and Plays in Israel, Internal Affairs Office, Fr: Administration of Habima Theatre, Request Form: Martha Graham Performance, Feb. 8, 1956, SAI.

111. Fr.: Gertrude Macy, To: Craig Barton, Jan. 25, 1956, box 3, folder 10, Israel, Martha Graham Dance Company Tour Records, 1941–1957, JRDD-NYPL.

112. See box 3, folder 10, Israel, Martha Graham Dance Company Tour Records, 1941–1957, JRDD-NYPL.

113. Ruth Eshel, "Ausdrucktanz in Eretz Yisrael," "Losing Faith: Israeli *Ausdrucktanz* Meets American Dance," and "Bringing in the New World: American Dance in Israel," in *Dance Spreads Its Wings: The Fascinating Story of Israeli Concert Dance*,

1920–2000, trans. Uri Turkenich (Tel Aviv: Israel Dance Diaries, 2016), 45–68, 75–101.

114. Author interview with Ruth Eshel, May 16, 2017, Tel Aviv (transcript available from the author with the written permission of Ruth Eshel).

115. Author interview with Ruth Eshel; Eshel, *Dance Spreads Its Wings*.

116. Haim Ganzu, "The Choreographic Art of Martha Graham," *Haaretz*, Feb. 24, 1956, 2, scrapbooks, box 326, MGC-LOC.

117. Author interview with Ruth Eshel; Eshel, *Dance Spreads Its Wings*.

118. Clipping, na, *Haaretz*, nd, scrapbooks, box 337, MGC-LOC.

119. Fr: AmEmbassy Tel Aviv, To: Department of State, Ref: Foreign Service Educational Exchange Circular No. 6, Dec. 11, 1953.

120. AmEmbassy Tel Aviv, To: Department of State, Ref: Educational Exchange, Dec. 11, 1953.

121. Drew Pearson, "Washington Merry-Go-Round," *Sunday Mirror*, July 29, 1956, scrapbooks, box 337, MGC-LOC.

122. Agnes de Mille, "Dance Magazine Awards," *Dance Magazine* 30 (April, 1956): 25.

123. Author interview with Francis Mason, Aug. 15, 2008.

124. Helen McGehee, "Our Recent Dance Tour," nd, 1, box 10, folder 10, Helen McGehee and Umaña Collection of Dance Materials, Music Division, LOC.

125. Notes on CU History, CU History Project, CU and the CIA, nd, box 308, folder 23, UAK.

126. Charlotte M. Canning, *On the Performance Front: U.S. Theater and Internationalism* (London: Palgrave Macmillan, 2015), 179.

127. DP/IEP, Nov. 17, 1955, UAK.

128. DP/IEP, Mar. 1, 1956, 3; Jan. 19, 1956, 2, UAK.

129. Eleanor Roosevelt, "My Day," May 22, 1956, https://www2.gwu.edu/~erpapers/myday/displaydoc.cfm?_y=1956&_f=md003490 (accessed June 2, 2017).

130. Eleanor Roosevelt, "My Day," July 17, 1956, https://www2.gwu.edu/~erpapers/myday/displaydoc.cfm?_y=1956&_f=md003538 (accessed June 2, 2017).

131. Walter Terry, "Dancing Her Way to Victory," *New York Herald Tribune*, Jan. 15, 1956, D1.

Chapter 3

1. "Date Book," *Evening News* (Manila), Nov. 15, 1955, Martha Graham Collection, Scrapbooks, box, 330, MGC-LOC; Graham, *Blood Memory*, 65; Editorial Board, "Ein Symbol der freien Welt," *Telegraf*, Sept. 20, 1957, 5, LA (translations from German by Julio Decker, who also worked as a research assistant in the archive, and Elizabeth Engel).

2. "Protokoll der Aufsichtsratsitzung der Benjamin Franklin Stiftung," May 24, 1957, B.Rep. 166-02, Nr. 14; "Minutes of the Meeting of the Benjamin Franklin Foundation, January 26, 1956," Rep 166-02, Nr. 11, LA.

3. "Martha Graham Here for 5 Performances," *Liberty Monday* (Bangkok), nd, (1955 tour), scrapbooks, box 330, MGC-LOC; Graham, *Blood Memory*, 242; Scrapbook

1, 35, HSA; Steffen de Rudder, "A Building as Propaganda: The Berlin Congress Hall and the Cold War," in *The House. The Cultures. The World: Fifty Years: From the Congress Hall to the House of World Cultures*, ed. Bernd M. Scherer, trans. Matthew Gaskins (Berlin: Nicolai, 2006; reprint, 2007), 30–31.

4. *Berliner Morgenpost*, Sept. 19, 1957, USIS translation, scrapbooks, 340, MGC-LOC; "Die Weihe der Kongreßhalle," *Telegraf*, Sept. 21, 1957, 23, LA.

5. Editorial Board, "Ein Symbol der freien Welt," *Telegraf*, Sept. 20, 1957; see also HSA/Scrapbooks 1, 35; Graham, *Blood Memory*, 153; DP/IEP, Oct. 17, 1956, UAK.

6. Employment records, box 12, ELD/DDE; box 21, folder 8, ELD/GWU; box 19, ELD/DDE; Congress Hall, Berlin, 1957 (1), boxes 13, ELD/DDE; Eleanor Lansing Dulles, *Chances of a Lifetime: A Memoir* (Englewood Cliffs, NJ: Prentice-Hall, 1980), 242. For other works that discuss the propaganda value of the building, see also Barbara M. Lane, "The Berlin Congress Hall 1955–1957," *Perspectives in American History*, 1 (1984): 131–85; Jane C. Loeffler, *The Architecture of Diplomacy: Building American Embassies* (New York: Princeton Architectural Press, 1998; reprint, 2010), 10, 81–83; Ron T. Robin, *Enclaves of America: The Rhetoric of American Political Architecture Abroad, 1900–1965* (Princeton, NJ: Princeton University Press, 1992).

7. See Petra Goedde, *GIs and Germans: Culture, Gender, and Foreign Relations* (New Haven, CT: Yale University Press, 2003); Daniel F. Harrington, *Berlin on the Brink: The Blockade, the Airlift, and the Early Cold War* (Lexington: University Press of Kentucky, 2012).

8. Dulles, *Chances of a Lifetime*, 284.

9. D. M. Giangreco and Robert E. Griffin, *Airbridge to Berlin: The Berlin Crisis of 1948, Its Origins and Its Aftermath* (New York: Presidio, 1988); Dulles, *Chances of a Lifetime*, 183; see also Leonard Mosley, *Dulles: A Biography of Eleanor, Allen, and John Foster Dulles and Their Family Network* (New York: Dial Press, 1978); Lynne K. Dunn, "Joining the Boys' Club: The Diplomatic Career of Eleanor Lansing Dulles," in *Women and American Foreign Policy: Lobbyists, Critics, and Insiders*, ed. Edward P. Crapol, 2nd ed. (New York: Rowman and Littlefield, 1992).

10. Mariusz Czepczyński, *Cultural Landscapes of Post-Socialist Cities: Representations of Powers and Needs* (London: Ashgate, 2008), 90.

11. Armin Grünbacher, *Reconstruction and Cold War in Germany, 1948–1961* (London: Ashgate, 2004).

12. Dulles, *Chances of a Lifetime*, 255–56.

13. "Official Correspondence and Reports, 1931–1968," "Clippings," box 11, folder 1953, ELD/DDE; Christian F. Ostermann and Malcom Byrne, *Uprising in East Germany, 1953: The Cold War, the German Question, and the First Major Upheaval behind the Iron Curtain* (Washington, DC: Central European University Press, 2003), 138, 163; Alison Smale, "60 Years Later, Germany Recalls Its Anti-Soviet Revolt," *New York Times*, June 18, 2013, A4; Bernard Wasserstein, Barbarism and Civilization: A History of Europe in Our Time (New York: Oxford University Press, 2007), 494.

14. David Reynolds, *The Origins of the Cold War in Europe: International Perspectives* (New Haven, CT: Yale University Press, 1994), 13.

15. Hope M. Harrison, *Driving the Soviets Up the Wall: Soviet–East German Relations, 1953–1961* (Princeton, NJ: Princeton University Press, 2003). Special thanks to Professor Harrison, who encouraged my early work.

16. Ursina Bentele and Sacha Zala, "Neutrality as a Business Strategy: Switzerland and Latin America in the Cold War," in *Neutrality and Neutralism in the Global Cold War: Between or within the Blocs?*, ed. Sandra Bott, Jussi M. Hanhimäki, Janick Marina Schaufelbuehl, and Marco Wyssf (New York: Routledge, 2016); Rinna Kullaa, *Non-alignment and Its Origins in Cold War Europe: Yugoslavia, Finland and the Soviet Challenge* (New York: I. B. Tauris, 2012); Jussi M. Hanhimäki, *Scandinavia and the United States: An Insecure Friendship* (New York: Twayne, 1997).

17. Frederick Taylor, *The Berlin Wall: A World Divided, 1961–1989* (New York: Harper Perennial, 2008), 37–38; Godfrey Hodgson, "Obituary: Eleanor Dulles," Independent, Nov. 6, 1996; "Eleanor L. Dulles of State Department Dies at 101," *New York Times*, Nov. 4, 1996, B10.

18. Dulles, *Chances of a Lifetime*, 256; H. P. Storl and Hugh Stubbins, *Berlin Baut 2— The Congress Hall: History, Collapse, Reconstruction* (Berlin: Senat Department for Building and Housing, 1987), 73.

19. Dulls, *Chances of a Lifetime*, 261.

20. Dulles, *Chances of a Lifetime*, 265.

21. "Minutes of the Meeting of the German Members of the Board of Directors of the Benjamin Franklin Stiftung, October 2, 1956," B Rep 166-02, Nr. 12, LA.

22. Dulles, *Chances of a Lifetime*, 251–253.

23. "Minutes of the Meeting of the German Members of the Board of Directors of the Benjamin Franklin Stiftung, September 4, 1956," B Rep 166-02, Nr. 12; "Minutes of the Meeting of the German Members of the Board of Directors of the Benjamin Franklin Stiftung, October 2, 1956."

24. de Rudder, "A Building as Propaganda," 31.

25. Opening Ceremonics Program, Congress Hall/Kongresshalle, B Rep. 166-02, Nr. 30, LA.

26. Eleanor Dulles, "The Influence of Modern Communications on the Conduct of Foreign Policy," box 29, folder 8, Oct. 29, 1954, ELD/DDE.

27. Dulles, *Chances of a Lifetime*, 256; for a description of the intention of the Department of State, see "Minutes of the Meeting of the Benjamin Franklin Foundation, Jan. 24, 1956," Rep 166-02, Nr. 11, LA.

28. de Rudder, "A Building as Propaganda," 30–31.

29. "Minutes of the Meeting of the German Members of the Board of Directors of the Benjamin Franklin Stiftung, October 2, 1956."

30. Program announcement, B Rep. 166-02, Nr. 30, PAA; Dulles, *Chances of a Lifetime*, 261.

31. Program announcement, B Rep. 166-02, Nr. 30, PAA; "Meeting Minutes," Dec. 12, 1955, Enclosure 3 to Despatch 989, B Rep 166-02, Nr. 11, LA; Dulles, *Chances of a Lifetime*, 261.

32. Congress Hall, Berlin 1957 (1), box 13, ELD/DDE; Frances Stonor Saunders, *The Cultural Cold War: The CIA and the World of Arts and Letters* (New York: New Press, 2001; reprint, 2013), 44.

33. To: Eleanor Dulles, Fr: Marvin Lasky, nd, Correspondence, box 20, folder 1956, Congress Hall, ELD/DDE; "Memo," nd, 1956, "Congress Hall," B.Rep.166 02, Nr. 219/12, LA.

34. Dulles, *Chances of a Lifetime*, 262; Correspondence, box 20, folder 1956, Congress Hall, ELD/DDE; "Memo," nd, 1956, "Congress Hall," B.Rep.166 02, Nr. 219/12, LA.

35. "Minutes of the Meeting of the German Members of the Benjamin Franklin Stiftung, May 6, 1957," B Rep 166-02, Nr. 14, LA.

36. Dulles, *Chances of a Lifetime*, 261.

37. DP/IEP, May 1957, UAK; John Foster Dulles Papers, Telephone Conversations Series, box 3, folder 4, Mar. 15, 1955, DDE.

38. "Contemporary Arts," *Spectator*, Oct. 12, 1956, 20.

39. DP/IEP, Jan. 16, 1958, UAK.

40. DP/IEP Oct. 17, 1957, UAK.

41. DP/IEP, May 1957.

42. DP/IEP, April 1957; Prevots, *Dance for Export*, 8.

43. *Der Abend*, Sept. 10, 1957, USIS translation, folder Sept. 1957 (1), Congress Hall Scrapbook, box 13, ELD/DDE; "Radio Symphony Orchestra Program Notes," folder Congress Hall, Berlin 1957 (1), box 13, ELD/DDE; *Der Abend*, Sept. 10, 1957, USIS translation; Dulles, *Chances of a Lifetime*, 261.

44. Sylvia Jukes Morris, *Price of Fame: The Honorable Clare Boothe Luce* (New York: Random House, 2014), 312–436; Morris, "Clare, in Love and War," *Vanity Fair*, July 2014, https://www.vanityfair.com/style/society/2014/07/clare-boothe-luce-marriage-ambassadorship (accessed August 24, 2017).

45. Leon Chamberlin to Mr. Ralph Walker, Oct. 9, 1958, B Rep. 166-02, Nr. 1, LA; [CU] to the Secretary, RE: Virginia Inness Brown Award, on Department of State letterhead, Nov. 9, 1967, "Award Programs, Virginia Inness-Brown," box 49, folder 24, UAK.

46. Program Announcement, Berlin B Rep. 166-02, Nr. 30, LA.

47. John Martin, "Stravinsky's Ballet: 'Le Sacre du Printemps' is to be . . . ," *New York Times*, Apr. 20, 1930, 106.

48. Giles Scott-Smith, *The Politics of Apolitical Culture: The Congress for Cultural Freedom and the Political Economy of American Hegemony, 1945–1955* (London: Routledge, 2001), 93; Saunders, *The Cultural Cold War*, 142.

49. Scrapbook 1, HSA.

50. "Protokoll der Aufsichtsratsitzung der Benjamin Franklin Stiftung."

51. Note that the Ronald Reagan "Freedom Bell" that looms over Haus der Kulturen der Welt, rebuilt in 1987 during the 750th anniversary of Berlin, during which time Graham's company performed, plays the Shaker tune of "Simple Gifts" on some days, reminding some of *Appalachian Spring*'s score.

52. Melvyn P. Leffler, *For the Soul of Mankind: The United States, the Soviet Union, and the Cold War* (New York: Hill and Wang, 2008), 353; Evan Thomas, *Ike's Bluff: President Eisenhower's Secret Battle to Save the World* (New York: Little, Brown, 2012), 43; Martin J. Medhurst, *Eisenhower's War of Words: Rhetoric and Leadership* (East Lansing: Michigan State University Press, 1994), 47.

53. "Theologie, Geschichte und Literatur," *Die Neue Zeit*, Sept. 3, 1957, LA.

54. de Rudder, "A Building as Propaganda," 35; Matt. 5:16, "Let your light shine before men in such a way that they may see your good works and glorify your Father who is in heaven," King James Bible, Cambridge edition, 2012.

55. Scrapbook 1, HSA; box 13, ELD/DDE; author visits to Haus der Kulturen der Welt, 2010, 2012, 2017; "Minutes of the Meeting of the German Members of the Board of Directors of the Benjamin Franklin Stiftung, October 2, 1956."

56. Graham, *Blood Memory*, 194.

57. Graham, *Blood Memory*, 4.

58. Loeffler, *The Architecture of Diplomacy*.

59. Author conversation with Sieglinde Tuschy, Director of Programs, 2015, Haus der Kulturn der Velt.

60. Graham, scrapbooks, box 311, MGC-LOC; author discussion with Claudia Jeschke, 2010 (notes available on request).

61. Program: Congress Hall, Berlin B Rep. 166-02, Nr. 30, PAA.

62. Shimon Redlich, "Khrushchev and the Jews," *Jewish Social Studies* 34, no. 4 (October 1972): 343–53.

63. Ronald Taylor, *Berlin and Its Culture: A Historical Portrait* (New Haven, CT: Yale University Press, 1997), 371.

64. Martha Graham to William Schuman, Nov. 10, 1984, box 130, folder 8, William Schuman Papers, New York Public Library, NYC.

65. Bertram Ross, "Martha (Draft)" nd, box 10, folder 10, BRC.

66. See Werner Roelens's photographs of Graham in Berlin on stage at Congress Hall, box 247, folder 13, MGC-LOC. According to Rena Gluck and Pearl Lang during informal discussions with the author, Graham believed that a visual recording was made of the performance. Despite attempts by dancers and scholars, the footage has not yet been found.

67. "Bekenntnis zum deutschen Tanz zum ersten Mal in Deutschland: Martha Graham," *Berliner Morgenpost*, Scpt. 20, 1957, LA.

68. *Berliner Morgenpost*, Sept. 19, 1957, USIS translation, scrapbooks, 340, MGC-LOC.

69. Scrapbooks 1, 36, HSA.

70. DP/IEP, May 1957; Dulles, *Chances of a Lifetime*, 46; "Fairy Tale Magic," *Nachtdepesche*, Sept. 20, 1957, 57, USIS translations for ELD, Congress Hall Scrapbook, Sept. 1957 (2), box 13, ELD/DDE.

71. A search at Landesarchiv in Berlin of *Der Morgen, National-Zeitung, Die Wahrheit, Die Tribüne,* and *Neues Deutschland* showed no response to Congress Hall. East German newspapers in 1957 ignored the event, which signals its significance.

72. Kongresshalle, B Rep. 166-02, Nr. 1, LA.

73. Stuart Oderman, *Lillian Gish: A Life on Stage and Screen* (Jefferson, NC: McFarland, 2000), 290; Clippings (1), box 22, ELD/DDE; Dulles, *Chances of a Lifetime*, 257.

74. Stephen Kinzer, The Brothers: John Foster Dulles, Allen Dulles, and Their Secret World War (New York: Henry Holt, 2013), 202; "Congress Hall," items 80-36-324, 325, 330, Audiovisual Collection, DDE. Note that *The Devil's Chessboard: Allen*

Dulles, the CIA, and the Rise of America's Secret Government by David Talbot (New York: HarperCollins, 2017), which features Eleanor Dulles, does not mention Congress Hall or Kongresshalle in Berlin.

75. Clare Boothe Luce, "Berlin, Symbol of the West," Sept. 19, folder 4, box 688, Clare Boothe Luce Papers, Manuscript Division, LOC.

76. Congress Hall, Berlin, 1957 (1), box 13, ELD/DDE; Congress Hall, 80-36-772-75, Audiovisual Collection, EPL.

77. "Berlins neues Wahrzeichen—Ein bleibendes Symbol deutsch-amerikanischer Zusammenarbeit" *Telegraf*, Sept. 22, 1957, 32, LA; "Die Weihe der Kongreßhalle," *Telegraf*, Sept. 21, 1957, 23, LA.

78. Editorial Board, "Die neue Kongreßhalle, eine Schöpfung der Benjamin-Franklin-Stiftung soll, wie die Eröffnungsfeier schon bewies, eine Stätte der Begegnung, der Aussprache, eine Denkmal des Geistes und der Muse sein," *Telegraf*, Sept. 20, 1957, 35, LA.

79. *Telegraf*, Sept. 19, 1957, 30, LA.

80. This is based on my time as a dancer at the Martha Graham School of Contemporary Dance, 1976–80, with Kenny Pearl, Armgard von Bardeleben, Linda Hodes, and, most important, Martha Graham. I wish to thank Kenny Pearl for his contributions to my understanding of Graham technique and his friendship, and give a salute to Armgard von Bardeleben in memory of her contributions to the legacies of Graham and Wigman in her work and oral histories with the author. See also Graham, *Blood Memory*, 1.

81. "Erste Begegnung mit Martha Graham," *Der Tagespiegel*, Sept. 25, 1957, 29; author interview with Armgard von Bardeleben, March 2010 (transcript available upon request with permission from her estate).

82. Interviews with unnamed audience members who wish to remain anonymous. This description is contested by some in the audience who assert that the applause was hearty immediately, yet all agreed that no standing ovation took place until Wigman took the stage with Graham.

83. "Orchestra and Dance," *Telegraf*, Sept. 24, 1957, 35, LA; "Guests from America: Martha Graham," *Der Abend*, Sept. 23, 1957, 30; "Erste Begegnung mit Martha Graham," *Der Tagespiegel*, Sept. 25, 1957, 29; "American Music at the Congress Hall," *Der Tagesspiegel*, Sept. 24, 1957, all USIS translations for ELD, Congress Hall Scrapbook, Sept. 1957 (2), box 13, ELD/DDE; "Amerikanische Musik" and "Orchestermusik getanzt: Begegnung mit Martha Graham," *Berliner Morgenpost*, Sept. 25, 1957, 25, LA; Bertram Ross, "Draft—Martha Graham's Biography," and "Notes About Maryha Graham," box 10, folders 19, 21, BRC; Harry Gilroy, "Berlin Observes Culture of U.S.," *New York Times*, Sept. 29, 1957, 85; B.Z., "Congress Hall: Listen, Look, and Be Amazed," Sept. 21, 1957, 57, USIS translations for ELD, Congress Hall Scrapbook, Sept. 1957 (2), box 13, ELD/DDE.

84. See HSA for USIS pictures of the ceremonies also in *Berliner Morgenpost, Der Kurier, Telegraf*, and *Der Tagesspiegel*, Sept.–Oct., LA.

85. Graham, scrapbooks, box 340, MGC-LOC.

86. Graham, *Blood Memory*, 127–30.

87. Graham, *Blood Memory*, 137.
88. Graham, *Blood Memory*, 131.
89. Graham, *Blood Memory*, 231, 251.
90. Graham, scrapbooks, box 340, MGC-LOC; Albert Goldberg, "Wigman Choreography for Ballet Exciting," *Los Angeles Times*, Feb. 4, 1958, 7.
91. To: Allen Dulles, Fr: Eleanor Dulles, nd, box 32, folder 1957, ELD/DDE. Note that when Dulles wrote to her brothers, communications were generally quite formal, and you would not immediately grasp that they were siblings.
92. Eleanor Dulles to Martha Graham, Sept. 23, 1957, Graham, scrapbooks, box 340, MGC-LOC.
93. Fr.: Eleanor Lansing Dulles, To: Martha Graham, Sept. 23, 1957, received Sept. 27, 1957, Graham, scrapbooks, box 340, MGC-LOC.
94. DP/IEP, Oct. 17, 1957.
95. Graham, scrapbooks, box 340, MGC-LOC; Bertram Ross, Manuscript Draft "Clytemnestra," 1991, box 10, folder 13, 17, BRC; author interview with Miki Okihara, 2015.
96. The author saw an annotated three-act version with subtitles in New York and Washington, DC, in 2009. Accounts of the full ballet, unredacted and translated, have been described using Siegel's *Shapes of Change* and Stodelle's *Deep Song*, as well as informal discussions with dancers who saw the original production.
97. John Martin, "American Modern Dance," in *The Dance Encyclopedia*, rev. ed., ed. Anatole Chujoy and P. W. Manchester (New York: Simon and Schuster, 1967), 48.
98. John Martin, "Graham; 'Clytemnestra' an Epic Full-Evening Work by a Modern Master," *New York Times*, Apr. 6, 1958, X12.
99. Walter Terry, "Graham Triumph," *New York Herald Tribune*, June 5, 1958, scrapbooks, box 341, MGC-LOC.
100. Trudy Goth, "The New York Music Season," *Athens News*, June 4, 1958, scrapbooks, box 341, MGC-LOC.
101. John Martin, "Dance: Graham," *New York Times*, Apr. 6, 1958, X12; Walter Terry, "Graham: Monumental Dance," *New York Herald Tribune*, Apr. 6, 1958, D6; John Martin, "Dance: Graham," *New York Times*, Apr. 13, 1958, X12; Seymour Peck, "Graham: Explorer of Dance Frontiers," *New York Times*, Mar. 30, 1958, SM22.

Chapter 4

1. Bethsabée de Rothschild quoting Martha Graham, "Program Notes," Batsheva, Dec. 16, 1964, quoted in Rena Gluck, *Batsheva Dance Company, 1964–1980: My Story* (Tel Aviv: Internet Publication, 2006, renagluck@gmail.com and available via Kindle at Amazon.com), 61; program also available at IDA.
2. To Miss Martha Graham, from Eric Johnson, The White House, Washington DC, 4 Feb. 1958, Scrapbooks, Box 343, MGC-LOC.
3. Mr. R. Gordon Arneson, Director, Office of Cultural Exchange, "Current Report on Cultural Presentations Program," Jan. 11, 1961, box 85, folder 15, UAK.

4. Arneson, "Current Report on Cultural Presentations Program."
5. "Footnotes: Graham," *New York Times*, Oct. 28, 1962, 27; Mary Blume, "Martha Graham Completes Another Triumphant Journey," *New York Herald Tribune*, Paris issue, Dec. 29, 1962, scrapbooks, box 354, MGC-LOC.
6. "Martha Graham's Intn'l Troupe to Dance for Habimah," *Jerusalem Post*, Aug. 18, 1958, scrapbooks, box 342 MGC-LOC; note that ambassadors often had discretionary funds that could be used without direct congressional or State Department approval for a project.
7. To: "Eyes Only for the President," Fr: Richard Goodwin, "Top Secret," Nov. 1, 1961, http://nsarchive.gwu.cdu/bayofpigs/19611101.pdf (accessed June 10, 2017).
8. Communications between Kennedy and Khrushchev, Documents 9 and 10, 1961, United States Department of State, FRUS (Washington, DC: US Office of the Historian), http://history.state.gov/historicaldocuments/frus1961-63v06/d9n, http://history.state.gov/historicaldocuments/frus1961-63v06/d10 (accessed April 9, 2019).
9. Sandra Bott, Jussi M. Hanhimäki, Janick Marina Schaufelbuehl, and Marco Wyss, "Introduction," in *Neutrality and Neutralism in the Global Cold War: Between or within the Blocs*, ed. Sandra Bott, Jussi M. Hanhimäki, Janick Marina Schaufelbuehl, and Marco Wyss (New York: Routledge, 2016), 4.
10. Harrison, *Driving the Soviets Up the Wall*.
11. Frederick Kempe, *Berlin 1961* (New York: Penguin Group, 2011), 251.
12. Kempe, *Berlin 1961*, 225–27.
13. Harrison, *Driving the Soviets Up the Wall*.
14. Svetozar Rajak, "'Companions in Misfortune': From Passive Neutralism to Active Un-commitment—the Critical Role of Yugoslavia," in Bott et al., *Neutrality and Neutralism in the Global Cold War*, 72–89.
15. Robert B. Rakove, *Kennedy, Johnson, and the Nonaligned World* (New York: Cambridge University Press, 2013).
16. Bott et al., "Introduction," and Jussi M. Hanhimäki, "Non-aligned to What? European Neutrality and the Cold War," 17–22, both in Bott et al., *Neutrality and Neutralism in the Global Cold War*.
17. Rinna Kullaa, "Roots of the Non-Aligned Movement in Neutralism: Yugoslavia, Finland and the Soviet Political Border with Europe 1948–1961," in Bott et al., *Neutrality and Neutralism in the Global Cold War*; Jim Clash, "Nuclear Adventure," *Forbes*, Dec. 26, 2015.
18. Conor Lane, "American Exceptionalism Redux: How President John F. Kennedy Repurposed Frederic Jackson Turner's Frontier Thesis to Promote the Alliance for Peace Program," conference paper and essay, Cold War Power, London School of Economics HY480, 2019.
19. Note this was the term used by David Halberstam in his book about the Kennedy "whiz kids" and foreign policy from 1960, *The Best and the Brightest* (New York: Random House, 1972). Halberstam said that he got the title from English bishop and hymn writer Reginald Heber in his "Hymns. Epiphany" (1822): "Brightest and best of the sons of the morning, / Dawn on our darkness and lend us thine aid."

20. "Department of State: For the Press," No. 653, Sept. 21, 1961, box 312, folder 1, Group XIV, Series 4, UAK.

21. "Office of the White House Press Secretary: Remarks of the President at the Ceremonies in the Rose Garden in Connection with the 15th Anniversary of the Fulbright Act," Aug. 1, 1961, box 312, folder 1, Group XIV, Series 4, UAK.

22. George Kennan, excerpted by Chester E. Bowles, "The Place of Modern Art in the World Today," March 1961, Press Archives, Museum of Modern Art, 145, https://www.moma.org/momaorg/shared/pdfs/docs/press_archives/2772/releases/MOMA_1960_0170_145.pdf?2010 (accessed June 10, 2017); Graham, *Blood Memory*, 8, 65.

23. Croft, *Dancers as Diplomats*, 42–43.

24. Author discussion with Ellen Graff and Marni Thomas, Mar. 21, 2016, New York City (transcript available with permission of Graff and Thomas).

25. Ellen Graff, author discussion with Ellen Graff and Marni Thomas.

26. Doris Humphrey, *The Art of Making Dances*, ed. Barbara Pollack (New York: Dance Horizons, 1959; reprint, 1987).

27. "Martha Graham as Phaedra," *New York Herald Tribune*, Feb. 18, 1962, C8.

28. Walter Terry, "Martha Graham," *New York Herald Tribune*, Mar. 5, 1962, 11.

29. Walter Terry, "Graham Dances: Sensuous, Tragic," *New York Herald Tribune*, Mar. 11, 1962, C4.

30. Terry, "Graham Dances," C4.

31. Terry, "Martha Graham."

32. Terry, "Graham Dances."

33. Terry, "Martha Graham."

34. "Martha Graham: Evaluation," USIS Report, scrapbooks, box 354, MGC-LOC.

35. H.K., nt, *Hufvudstadsbladet* (Helsinki), Dec. 11, 1962, USIS Translation, scrapbooks, box 354, MGC-LOC.

36. H.K., nt, *Hufvudstadsbladet* (Helsinki).

37. Souvenir Program, Helsinki, scrapbooks, box 354, MGC-LOC.

38. Walter Terry, "Martha Graham's Vivid Art," *New York Herald Tribune*, May 8, 1960, D4.

39. P. W. Manchester, "Noted Dancer Offers Two World Premières," *Christian Science Monitor*, May 7, 1960, 6; this review would be directly exported by USIS and its wording adopted by Finnish critics.

40. John Martin, "Graham: Thoughts in Gratitude for a Notable Season," *New York Times*, May 8, 1960, X10.

41. Hixson, *Parting the Curtain*, 42; Inboden, *Religion and American Foreign Policy*, 21.

42. Tony Shaw, "'Martyrs, Miracles and Martians': Religion and Cold War Cinematic Propaganda in the 1950s," in *Religion and the Cold War*, ed. Dianne Kirby (New York: Palgrave Macmillan, 2003; reprint, 2013), 214n11.

43. Shaw, "'Martyrs, Miracles, and Martians,'" 214, fn 10.

44. Inboden, *Religion and American Foreign Policy*, 19, quoting Will Herberg, *Protestant, Catholic, Jew: An Essay in American Religious Sociology* (Chicago: University of Chicago Press, 1955; reprint, 1983); Shaw, "'Martyrs, Miracles, and Martians,'"

211–31; Dianne Kirby, "The Religious Cold War," in *The Oxford Handbook of the Cold War*, ed. Richard H. Immerman and Petra Goedde (New York: Oxford University Press, 2016), 551.

45. Inboden, *Religion and American Foreign Policy*, 21.
46. Graham, *Blood Memory*, 39.
47. Graham, *Blood Memory*, 41, 52, 53, 176. Note that Graham recalls also going to church while on tour with Denishawn (*Blood Memory*, 86).
48. Graham, *Blood Memory*, 15.
49. Graham, *Blood Memory*, 37.
50. "Martha Graham: Biographical Data," Office of War Information, RG 208. 5.2, 2.A, Records of the News and Features Bureau, NARA.
51. Kirby, "The Religious Cold War," 548.
52. Kirby, "The Religious Cold War," 545.
53. "Martha Graham's Dance Theater," *Ilta-Sanomat*, Dec. 11, 1962, scrapbooks, box 354, MGC-LOC.
54. "Martha Graham Evening," *Suomen Sosialidemokraatti*, Dec. 13, 1962, scrapbooks, box 354, MGC-LOC.
55. Romans, 4:20–21: "He staggered not at the promise of God through unbelief; but was strong in faith, giving glory to God; And being fully persuaded that, what he had promised, he was able also to perform." Abraham is justified by faith, not works. Jews and Gentiles are thus blessed as the same under God.
56. "This I Believe," RG 306, 306.TIB.79A, nd, 22 min.; also 306VOA.TIB 45B, 23/33/2, NARA. The interview would have been taped in preparation for the tour while Murrow was at USIS, before 1963. As always, with special thanks to Greg Tomlin for his guidance and support; see Greg Tomlin, *Murrow's Cold War: Public Diplomacy for the Kennedy Administration* (Lincoln, NE: Potomac Books, 2016).
57. John F. Kennedy, Democratic National Convention, July 15, 1960, CBS Motion Picture, Accession Number: TNC: 191-E5, http://www.jfklibrary.org/Asset-Viewer/AS08q5oYz0SFUZg9uOi4iw.aspx (accessed July 20, 2017). This speech later became known as "The New Frontier."
58. Margareta Sjögren, nt, *Svenska Dagbladet*, Dec. 5, 1962, USIS translation, scrapbooks, box 354, MGC-LOC.
59. Author interview with Rina Schenfeld, May 15, 2017, at the Schenfeld studio, Tel Aviv, Israel.
60. Author interview with Rina Schenfeld; Gluck, *Batsheva Dance Company*, 37–38.
61. Gluck, *Batsheva Dance Company*, 38; author interview with Ruth Eshel, May 17, 2017, Tel Aviv, Israel.
62. Author interview with Rina Schenfeld.
63. Thomas G. Paterson, *Kennedy's Quest for Victory: American Foreign Policy, 1961–1963* (New York: Oxford University Press, 1989), 156.
64. To: Mordacai Seter, Fr: Martha Graham, June 28, 1962, Seter, 111.6.4, IDA.
65. To: Mordacai Seter, Fr: Martha Graham, June 28, 1962.
66. To: Mordacai Seter, Fr: Martha Graham, June 28, 1962.
67. To: Mordacai, Fr: Martha, Aug. 31, 1962, Seter, 111.6.4, IDA.

68. Dani Karavan, *Dani Karavan: Dialogue with the Environment, Resonance with the Earth* (Tokyo: Asahi Shimbun, 1997). Further work on the influence of Japanese art on this sculptor must be conducted.

69. To: Mordacai Seter, Fr: Martha Graham, June 28, 1962.

70. Gluck, *Batsheva Dance Company*, 41.

71. Blume, "Martha Graham Completes Another Triumphant Journey," 5; also scrapbooks, box 354, MGC-LOC.

72. *Dance Magazine*, December, 1962, Box 354, MGC-LOC.

73. Marni Thomas, author discussion with Marni Thomas and Ellen Graff, Mar. 21, 2016, New York City (transcript available with permission of Graff and Thomas).

74. "Martha Graham: Evaluation."

75. Author interview with George Anderson and Travis Anderson, June 2017; Judith Cody, *Vivian Fine: A Bio-bibliography* (Westport, CT: Greenwood Press, 2002), 208; Sheldon M. Stern, *The Cuban Missile Crisis in American Memory: Myths versus Reality* (Stanford, CA: Stanford University Press, 2012).

76. Author discussion with Marni Thomas and Ellen Graff.

77. Blume, "Martha Graham Completes Another Triumphant Journey."

78. Prime Minister Constantine Caramanlis in a Toast to President John F. Kennedy at a State Luncheon, Apr. 17, 1961, Public Papers of the President, John F. Kennedy, 1961 (US Government Printing Office), 128. Also in Papers of John F. Kennedy, Presidential Papers, White House Central Subject Files, CO:94, JFKWHCSF-0057-007, Series 07, John F. Kennedy Presidential Library and Museum, Columbia Point, Boston, MA, http://www.jfklibrary.org/Asset-Viewer/Archives/JFKWHCSF-0057-007.aspx (accessed June 10, 2017).

79. Author interview with Linda Hodes, Feb. 19, 2016 (transcript available with the permission of Linda Hodes).

80. Blume, "Martha Graham Completes Another Triumphant Journey."

81. "Martha Graham: Evaluation."

82. "Martha Graham: Evaluation."

83. "Critical Comments on Martha Graham Performances from Posts," Jan. 9, 1963, scrapbooks, box 354, MGC-LOC.

84. Daniele Ganser, *NATO's Secret Armies: Operation Gladio and Terrorism in Western Europe* (New York: Routledge, 2004).

85. Canan Inaloglu, "Social Corner," *Daily News*, Nov. 15, 1962, scrapbooks, box 350, MGC-LOC.

86. Inaloglu, "Social Corner."

87. "Martha Graham," *The Week* (Ankara), Nov. 16, 1962, np, year 11, No. 46, scrapbooks, box 350, MGC-LOC.

88. "Martha Graham," *The Week* (Ankara).

89. Dr. Adel Safty, *The Cyprus Question: Diplomacy and International Law* (Bloomington, IN: iUniverse, 2011), 81, 88; James Edward Miller, *The United States and the Making of Modern Greece: History and Power, 1950–1974* (Chapel Hill: University of North Carolina Press, 2012).

90. Marni Thomas, author discussion with Marni Thomas and Ellen Graff.

91. To: Martha Graham, Fr: Francis Mason, Munich, Dec. 17, 1957, box 220, correspondence, MGC-LOC. Thanks to Camelia Lenart, who quotes this letter in "Dancing Art and Politics behind the Iron Curtain: Martha Graham's 1962 Tours to Yugoslavia and Poland," *Dance Chronicle* 39, no. 2 (2016): 197–217n1, 212 (when Lenart worked at LOC, the letter was in box 339—note the box change). Also with deepest thanks to Libby Smigel, dance curator, Music Division, Library of Congress, who found this letter and scanned it for me. Lenart inspired me to use archival materials from Yugoslavia and Poland to unpack the vital differences between these two countries and their policies on the arts, culture, and politics. Questions about the influence of Soviet "soft power" become vital because of the shifting definition of the "Iron Curtain" and Yugoslavia's position. Special thanks to Ryan D. Eavenson, Columbia University, European Institute, for his work on these issues. See also Patryk Babiracki, *Soviet Soft Power in Poland: Culture and the Making of Stalin's New Empire, 1943–1957* (Chapel Hill: University of North Carolina Press, 2015). I would like to express deep gratitude to Patryk Babiracki, who met with me in Berlin in 2017 to discuss his work.

92. Author interview with Francis Mason, Aug. 15, 2008, selections published as Victoria Phillips Geduld, "This American Manifestation," *Ballet Review* 39, no. 2 (Summer 2011): 40–49.

93. George F. Kennan Papers (MC 076), box 302, folder 23, GFK-PUSK.

94. Anders Stephanson, *Kennan and the Art of Foreign Policy* (Cambridge, MA: Harvard University Press, 1989); John Lewis Gaddis, *George F. Kennan: An American Life* (New York: Penguin Books, 2011); Grace Kennan Warnecke, *Cold War Daughter* (Pittsburgh: University of Pittsburgh Press, 2018). Special thanks to Grace Kennan Warnecke for this line of thinking about the modern arts and diplomacy under her father's watch.

95. Emily Genauer, "Embassy of Good Will: A U.S. Show in Red Poland," *New York Herald Tribune*, June 20, 1962, 20.

96. Anne Applebaum, *Iron Curtain: The Crushing of Eastern Europe, 1944–1956* (New York: Doubleday, 2012), 254.

97. Robert Vitalis, "The Midnight Ride of Kwame Nkrumah and Other Fables of Bandung (Bandoong)," *Humanith: An International Journal of Human Rights, Humanitarianism, and Development* 4, no. 2 (2013): 277; Jason Parker, "Cold War II: The Eisenhower Administration, the Bandung Conference, and the Reperiodization of the Postwar Era," *Diplomatic History* 30, no. 5 (2006): 867–92; Eric Gettig, "'Trouble Ahead in Afro-Asia': The United States, the Second Bandung Conference, and the Struggle for the Third World, 1964–1965," *Diplomatic History* 39, no. 1 (2015): 126–56; Westad, *The Global Cold War*.

98. John Foster Dulles, "The Cost of Peace," June 9, 1956, *Department of State Bulletin* 39, no. 886 (June 18, 1956): 1001.

99. Rinna Kullaa, "Roots of the Non-Aligned Movement in Neutralism," 34–38, 48.

100. Svetozar Rajak, "'Companions in Misfortune': From Passive Neutralism to Active Un-Commitment—the Critical Role of Yugoslavia," in *Non-alignment and Its Origins in Cold War Europe*, 83.

101. "The US Propaganda in Yugoslavia," Oct. 24, 1962, 7–11, translated and annotated by Natalija Dimic (transcript available from the author upon request), AY.
102. Ruth Montgomery, "Tito Handout Helps Cuba," *Boston Record-American*, Sept. 23, 1963, in Yugoslavia: General 1962–1963, Presidential Papers, President's Office Files, Series 09, JFK.
103. Kullaa, "Roots of the Non-Aligned Movement," 45; Jussi M. Hanhimäki, *Containing Coexistence: America, Russia, and the "Finish Solution,"* 1945–1956 (Kent, OH: Kent State University Press, 1997).
104. Hanhimäki, "Non-aligned to What?," 17–22; Hanhimäki, *Scandinavia and the United States*; Westad, *The Global Cold War*.
105. Eric D. Pullin, "The Bandung Conference: Ideological Conflict and the Limits of US Propaganda," in Bott et al., *Neutrality and Neutralism in the Global Cold War*, 60.
106. Pullin, "The Bandung Conference," 61.
107. Pullin, "The Bandung Conference," 67.
108. "The US Propaganda in Yugoslavia," 2
109. "The US Propaganda in Yugoslavia."
110. "The US Propaganda in Yugoslavia."
111. "Belgrade Entertainment Guide," Nov. 13, 1962, scrapbook 350, MGC-LOC.
112. George F. Kennan Papers (MC 076), Diaries, 1962, subseries 4C, box 235, folder 1, for Nov. 16, 1962, GFK-PUSK.
113. "Guest List for Ambassador's Reception for Martha Graham," Nov. 16, 1962, scrapbook 350, MGC-LOC.
114. Marni Thomas, author discussion with Marni Thomas and Ellen Graff.
115. For Engle from Conly, "Herewith Translation of 'Borba' and 'Politica' Reviews of November 18, 1962," Belgrade 4, scrapbooks, box 350, MGC-LOC.
116. For Engle from Conly, "Herewith Translation of 'Borba' and 'Politica' Reviews of November 18, 1962."
117. For Engle from Conly, "Herewith Translation of 'Borba' and 'Political' Reviews of November 18, 1962."
118. "Guest Performance of the American Ballet Ensemble of Martha Graham: A Long Story of the Dance," *Politika*, Nov. 19, 1962, scrapbooks, box 350, MGC-LOC.
119. "The Perfect Culture of Movement: Guest Performance of the Martha Graham Company in Belgrade," USIS translation, 1962, 221.2.2.2, IDA.
120. Blume, "Martha Graham Completes Another Triumphant Journey."
121. "Ovations for Martha Graham," USIS translation, Daily, 7, *Večernji*, Nov. 21, 1962, 221.2.2.2, IDA.
122. 71/3140/0, Przedsiębiorstwo Państwowe Polska Agencja Artystyczna "Pagart" w Warszawie, Archiwum m.st. Warszawy, sygn. 23, Reports for 1962, 19. The report was filed by the Polish Artistic Agency, PAGART, which reported to the Ministry of Culture and Arts and "served Polish socialist culture and implemented the principles of the country's cultural policy." It was particularly engaged with targeting the youth. The Polish Artistic Agency PAGART also booked foreign groups for the ministry. It's 1962 financial report (71/3140/0, Przedsiębiorstwo Państwowe Polska Agencja Artystyczna "Pagart" w Warszawie, Archiwum m.st. Warszawy, sygn. 23,

Financial Settlements for 1962, 93) reported, "Ballet Martha Graham from the USA, costs 189 184, 45 zlotys, receipts (income) 199 700, 00 zlotys." Special thanks to Iwona Surleta at The Institute of Music and Dance in Warsaw who identified, Irena Ostrowska, *Bibliografia zagadnień sztuki tanecznej z lat 1961–1962* ["Bibliography of dance art issues from 1961–1962"] (Warsaw: CPARA, 1964). Using this resource, Marek Dąbrowski was able to trace numerous documents and articles.

123. Author interview with Linda Hodes, Feb. 19, 2016.

124. Babiracki, *Soviet Soft Power in Poland*, 8n25, quoting Jan C. Behrends, *Die erfundene Freundschaft: Propaganda für die Sowjetunion in Polan und in der DDR* (Köln: Böhlau Verlag, 2006), 167; see also Magdalena Sirecka-Wołodko, *Zagraniczna polityka kulturalna Polski w latach, 1956–1970* (Toruń, Poland: Wydawnictwo MADO, 2011); Andrej Antoszek and Kate Delaney, "Poland: Transmissions and Translations," in *The Americanization of Europe: Culture, Diplomacy, and Anti-Americanism after 1945*, ed. Alexander Stephan (New York: Berghahn Books, 2006).

125. Babiracki, *Soviet Soft Power in Poland*, 197, 193.

126. "Poland: Rebellious Compromiser," *Time*, Dec 10, 1956, http://content.time.com/time/magazine/article/0,9171,808728-1,00.html (accessed November 20, 2017).

127. "Poland: Rebellious Compromiser."

128. Babiracki, *Soviet Soft Power in Poland*, 301n25, Evgenii Taranov, "'Raskachaem Leninskie Gory!' Iz istorii 'vol'nodumstva v Moskovskom Universitete, 1955–1956," *Svobodnaia mysl'* 10 (1993): 94–103, 102, 231.

129. Antoszek and Delaney, "Poland," 221.

130. Antoszek and Delaney, "Poland," 221.

131. Antoszek and Delaney, "Poland," 222–23.

132. John F. Kennedy, "Speech of Senator John F. Kennedy, Polish-American Congress, Chicago, IL," Oct. 1, 1960, http://www.presidency.ucsb.edu/ws/?pid=25896 (accessed June 13, 2016).

133. Pawel Machcewicz and Maya Latynski, *Poland's War on Radio Free Europe, 1950–1989* (Palo Alto, CA: Stanford University Press, 2015).

134. Babiracki, *Soviet Soft Power in Poland*, 232.

135. Raport organizacyjny Ambasady PRL w Waszyngtonie za 1961 r., Department III, 6_6w1, file 1, POL-S, AMSZ (translation by Marek Dąbrowski).

136. Raport organizacyjny Ambasady PRL w Waszyngtonie za 1961 r.

137. Dokument dot. zniszczonych akt ws Inness Brown, wiceprzewodniczącej ANTA, Department III, 30_65w9, file 77, POL-S, AMSZ; note that Inness-Brown also visited Poland in 1963 as part of an ANTA delegation.

138. Babiracki, *Soviet Soft Power in Poland*, 302n37.

139. See Babiracki, *Soviet Soft Power in Poland*, n123, and scrapbooks, box 354, MGC-LOC.

140. Sukces "Mazowsza" w Nowym Jorku (Telefon od stałego korespondenta), TC 17 XI 1961, WP_20170620_09_21_34_Pro, Department III, 6_66w18, file 57b, POL_ part 1-2, AMSZ (translation by Marek Dąbrowski).

141. Marthy Graham: w Warszawie," *Kurier Polski*, nd, 1962, scrapbooks, box 352, MGC-LOC.

142. Author discussion with Linda Hodes.

143. Author discussion with Linda Hodes.

144. Author discussion with Linda Hodes.

145. "The Martha Graham Ballet," *Trybuna Ludu*, no. 331, Nov. 29, 1962, USIS translation, scrapbooks, box 352, MGC-LOC; see also interviews with Hodes, Thomas, and Graff.

146. Marni Thomas, author discussion with Marni Thomas and Ellen Graff.

147. Babiracki, *Soviet Soft Power in Poland*, 201, 211n114, Fik, "Kultura Polska," 266.

148. Confidential source, "Radio Warsaw Listeners Demand Religious Program," Dec. 18, 1956, HU OSA 300-1-2-77444; Records of Radio Free Europe/Radio Liberty Research Institute: General Records: Information Items; in French, "Early December 1956," Item No 11325/56, OSA.

149. Martha Graham in the spoken introduction to *Acrobats of God*, in *3 by Martha Graham*.

150. "The Stage: The Martha Graham Ballet," *Życie Warszawy*, no. 283, Nov. 28, 1962, USIS translation, scrapbooks, box 352, MGC-LOC.

151. Tadeusz Kaczyński, "The Ballet (Freedom through Discipline)," *Sztandar Młodych*, no. 282, Warsay, Nov. 26, 1962, USIS translation, scrapbooks, box 352, MGC-LOC.

152. Kaczyński, "The Ballet (Freedom through Discipline)."

153. Kaczyński, "The Ballet (Freedom through Discipline)."

154. *Svenska Dagbladet*, Dec. 6, 1962, USIS translation, scrapbooks, box 354, MGC-LOC; Margareta Sjögren, nt, *Svenska Dagbladet*, Dec. 5, 1962, USIS translation, scrapbooks, box 354, MGC-LOC.

155. Author discussion Linda Hodes, with the accounts corroborated by Marni Thomas and Ellen Graff.

156. Hanna Szczawińska, "Gry na wyspie tańca," *Kierunki*, 9 XII 1962, 49, 10, The National Library of Poland in Warsaw (translated by Marek Dąbrowski).

157. "American Ballet in Warsaw" [cable], Nov. 23, 1962, scrapbooks, box 352, MGC-LOC.

158. N.K., "Martha Graham's Team," *Nowa Kultura* ["The New Culture Magazine"], 48.662, Year XIII, Dec. 2, 1962, WAR; speciał thanks to Dr. Christopher J. Caes, Columbia University, for his help with the translation. Marek Dąbrowski found this article and immediately realized its importance because it had not been cited by me in my dissertation, by Croft in *Dancers as Diplomats*, or by Lenart in "Dancing Art and Politics behind the Iron Curtain." Because of the dramatic nature of this review, I had multiple translations done to extract nuance from the report. Professor Caes provided the final source. Again, thanks to Linda Hodes, who believes that Graham did not see this review.

159. Jerzy Waldorff, "Towary na eksport," *Świat*, 9 XII 1962, 49, 5, The National Library of Poland in Warsaw (translated by Marek Dąbrowski).

160. Author interview with Linda Hodes.

161. TO: Chargé, All Offices, From: P&C, Subject: Martha Graham, "Office Memorandum," scrapbooks, box 352, MGC-LOC.

162. Hanhimäki "Non-aligned to What?," 22.

163. Robin Hood (pseudonym for Bengt Idestam-Almquvist), nt, *Stockhollms-Tidningen*, Dec. 5, 1962, USIS translation, scrapbooks, box 352, MGC-LOC.

164. Scrapbooks, box 352, MGC-LOC.

165. Marni Thomas, author discussion with Marni Thomas and Ellen Graff.

166. Margareta Sjögren, nt, *Svenska Dagbladet*, Dec. 5, 1962, USIS translation, scrapbooks, box 354, MGC-LOC.

167. "Kölner Stadt Anzeiger] (USIS)," Nov. 30, 1962, Amerika-Haus Köln, scrapbooks, box 352, MGC-LOC.

168. Author interview with Armgard von Bardeleben, New York City, Nov. 29, 2011.

169. Susan Laikin Funkenstein, "Engendering Abstraction: Wassily Kandinsky, Gret Palucca, and 'Dance Curves,'" *Modernism/modernity* 14, no. 3 (September 2007): 389–406.

170. "Die Statthalterin des freien Tanzes," *Der Mittag* (Düsseldorf), Dec. 3, 1962, clippings file, Martha Graham, DTK.

171. Gerhard Schön, "Mit der Seele suchend," *Rheinische Post* (Düsseldorf), Dec. 1962, clippings file, Martha Graham, DTK.

172. "Getanzte Psychoanalyse," *Stuttgarter Zeitung*, Dec. 7, 1962, scrapbooks, box 350, MGC-LOC.

173. "Martha Graham: Evaluation."

174. Carolus Heibe, "Hohepriesterin des modernen Tanzes," 1962, clippings file, Martha Graham, DTK.

175. Marni Thomas, author discussion with Marni Thomas and Ellen Graff.

176. Helen McGhee to Umaña, Handwritten Letter, Nov. 30, 1962, box 9, folder 21, Helen McGehee and Umaña Collection of Dance Materials, LOC.

177. Helen McGhee to Umaña,

178. Marni Thomas, author discussion with Marni Thomas and Ellen Graff.

179. Rikki Korppi-Tommola, "Politics Promote Dance: Martha Graham in Finland, 1962," *Dance Chronicle* 33, no. 1 (2010): 93.

180. Rinna Kullaa, "Roots of the Non-Aligned Movement in Neutralism," 48; Hanhimäki, "Non-aligned to What?," 22, 23.

181. Vladislav Zubok, "The Soviet Union and European Integration from Stalin to Gorbachev," *Journal of European Integration History* 2, no. 1 (1996): 89; Vladislav Zubok and Constantine Pleshakov, *Inside the Kremlin's Cold War: From Stalin to Khrushchev* (Cambridge, MA: Harvard University Press, 1996), 182–86. Again, special thanks to Vladislav Zubok.

182. Korppi-Tommola, "Politics Promote Dance," 91n31, Kimmo Rentola, "Suojelupoliisi kylmässä sodassa 1949–1991," in *Ratakalu 12, Suojdupoliisi 1949–2009*, ed. Matti Simola (Helsinki: WSOY, 2009), 30–46, 94.

183. Hanhimäki "Non-aligned to What?," 26.

184. Rakove, *Kennedy, Johnson, and the Nonaligned World*; "Arrival Ceremonies for Urho Kekkonen, President of Finland," Oct. 16, 1961, AR6842-B, JFK.

185. Kullaa, "Roots of the Non-Aligned Movement in Neutralism"; Clash, "Nuclear Adventure."

186. Roy Allison, *Finland's Relations with the Soviet Union, 1944–84* (New York: St. Martin's Press, 1985), 45–50.

187. Korppi-Tommola, "Politics Promote Dance," 91, bottom page note references Rentola, "Suojelupoliisi kylmässä sodassa 1949–1991," 43, 272–73, for the reperiodization of this event based on US documents at NARA.

188. "Congratulatory Remarks on the Re-election of President Kekkonen," Feb. 16. 1961, Papers of John F. Kennedy, Presidential Papers, National Security Files, Finland: General, December 1961–April 1962, JFKNSF-070-004, series 1, JFK, http:// www.jfklibrary.org/Asset-Viewer/Archives/JFKNSF-070-004.aspx (accessed June 14, 2017).

189. Korppi-Tommola, "Politics Promote Dance."

190. Aino Kekkonen, "Dance in Finland," and Martha Bröyer Collection (TeaMA 1152), Theater Museum Archives, Helsinki, Finland.

191. Korppi-Tommola, "Politics Promote Dance," 85–86.

192. Korppi-Tommola, "Politics Promote Dance," 102n69, Tarkkailija [pseudonym], "Näyttämöiltä nähtyä ja kuultua," Etelä Suomi, Dec. 18, 1962, np [translation by Korppi-Tommola].

193. Korppi-Tommola, "Politics Promote Dance."

194. Korppi-Tommola, "Politics Promote Dance," 94.

195. Korppi-Tommola, "Politics Promote Dance," 95n44, Tarkkailija, "Yhdistyneet kansakunnat' tanssillisessa mielessä," Helsingin Sonat, Dec. 10, 1962, np.

196. Korppi-Tommola, "Politics Promote Dance," 95.

197. Korppi-Tommola, "Politics Promote Dance," 88.

198. H.K., Hufvudstadsbladet, Helsinki, Finland, Dec. 11, 1962, box 354, MGC-LOC.

199. H.K., Hufvudstadsbladet.

200. H.K., Hufvudstadsbladet.

201. H.K., Hufvudstadsbladet.

202. Korppi-Tommola, "Politics Promote Dance," 101n67, Mäkinen, "Martha Graham taide on tanssiteatterinsa," Hufvudstadsbladet, Dec. 11, 1962.

203. Korppi-Tommola, "Politics Promote Dance," 102n69, Tarkkailija [pseudonym], "Näyttämöiltä nähtyä ja kuultua."

204. Korppi-Tommola, "Politics Promote Dance," 102n69.

205. H.K., Hufvudstadsbladet.

206. "Translated Excerpts of Press Reviews on Netherlands Tour of Martha Graham Dance Company, December 13–16, 1962," USIS translations, "Martha Graham, 'First Lady' of the American Dance," De Groene Amsterdammer, Dec. 22, 1962, scrapbooks, box 350, MGC-LOC.

207. "Translated Excerpts of Press Reviews on Netherlands Tour of Martha Graham Dance Company."

208. "Translated Excerpts of Press Reviews on Netherlands Tour of Martha Graham Dance Company," "Graham Dance Style Seems to Be Imperishable," Het Parool and Het Deutschland [unclear], Dec. 14, 1962; "Translated Excerpts of Press Reviews," from Algemaan Handelsblad, Dec. 14, 1962, scrapbooks, box 354, MGC-LOC; "Translated Excerpts of Press Reviews on Netherlands Tour of Martha Graham Dance Company, 13–16 Dec. 1962," from De Groene Amsterdammer, Dec. 2, 1962, scrapbooks, box 354, MGC-LOC; "Translated Excerpts of Press Reviews on Netherlands Tour of Martha Graham Dance Company, 13–16 Dec. 1962," from Het Vrije Volk, Dec. 15, 1962, scrapbooks, box 354, MGC-LOC.

209. "Martha Graham: Evaluation."
210. Ethel A. Kuhn to Mr. Craig Barton, Cultural Affairs Officer, US Information Service, the Foreign Service of the United States of America, Mar. 22, 1963, scrapbooks, box 352, MGC-LOC. Note the opportunity for further study for a scholar with access to the archives and oral histories in Norway.
211. Hanhimäki "Non-aligned to What?," 21, 25.
212. Marni Thomas, author discussion with Marni Thomas and Ellen Graff.
213. Author in private discussions with Graham dancers.
214. Clive Barnes, "Martha in Europe," *Dance and Dancers*, Jan. 1963, 18, scrapbooks, box 354, MGC-LOC.
215. John Chamberlain, "The Embattled Dancers," clipping, Jan. 22, 1963, scrapbooks, box 354, MGC-LOC.
216. "Artists Give Views of Audiences Abroad," Washington, DC [unreadable], Mar. 12, 1963, scrapbooks, box 354, MGC-LOC.
217. Arthur Todd, "Dance: Riches: The Art of the American Negro Is One of Our Foremost National Treasures, *New York Times*, July 2, 1961, X6.
218. "Martha Graham Baffles and Fascinates," scrapbooks, box 354, MGC-LOC.
219. "Critical Comments on Martha Graham Performances from Posts."
220. "Martha Graham: Evaluation."
221. "Critical Comments on Martha Graham Performances from Posts."
222. Author interview with Linda Hodes, Feb. 19, 2016.

Chapter 5

1. DP/IEP, Mar. 25, 1963, UAK.
2. Michael Kuhar, *The Addicted Brain: Why We Abuse Drugs, Alcohol, and Nicotine* (Upper Saddle River, NJ: Financial Times Press, 2015).
3. "Martha Graham: Evaluation," USIS Report, scrapbooks, box 354, MGC-LOC.
4. "Manifesto of the Congress for Cultural Freedom," June 30, 1950, MS 2395/4, Arthur Koestler Papers, University of Edinburgh, Edinburgh, UK, quoted in footnote 10, Sarah Miller Harris, *The CIA and the Congress for Cultural Freedom in the Early Cold War: The Limits of Making Common Sense* (New York: Routledge, 2016).
5. "Virginia Royall Inness-Brown," box 49, folder 24, UAK.
6. Edgar M. Bronfman, "Culture and the Struggle for Men's Minds," Congressional Record—Senate, Oct. 8, 1963, 18061, CIA Release 2003/10/10, RDP65B00383R00200170013-0 (accessed June 5, 2017).
7. Scrapbooks, box 357, MG-LOC.
8. To: CU, FR: CU/CP, SUJ: Cultural Presentations, "CU/CP International Festivals," Aug. 27, 1962, box 85, folder 25, UAK.
9. For references to the importance of music as a cultural product with deeply political implications at present, see Ludovic Hunter-Tilney, "ISIS Hates Music for Its Power over Our Minds and Bodies," *Financial Times*, May 29, 2017, 9.
10. "Spotlight: Festival Exhibition," *British Vogue*, Aug. 1963, 5, scrapbooks, box 357, MGC-LOC.

11. Kenneth Tynan, "Martha Graham: Holy Acrobat," *Observer*, Aug. 18, 1963, 18, also *New York Times*, Aug. 27, 1963; scrapbooks, box 357, MGC-LOC.

12. "Festival Guild," in the program Edinburgh International Festival, Royal Scottish Museum, nd, Festival Guild, scrapbooks, box 357, MGC-LOC.

13. G.C.S., "Graham the Appetizer," *Evening Dispatch*, Aug. 8, 1963, scrapbooks, box 357, MGC-LOC.

14. Clive Barnes, "Edinburgh Hails Graham Dancers," *New York Times*, Aug. 27, 1963, 28, scrapbooks, box 347, MGC-LOC.

15. Richard Buckle, "The Voice from the Cave," Sunday Times, Sept. 6, 1963, scrapbooks, box 357, MGC-LOC.

16. Susan Lester, "Approach to Martha Graham," *Sunday Telegraph*, Sept. 1, 1963, scrapbooks, box 357, MGC-LOC.

17. G.C.S., "Graham the Appetizer"; "Ballet Causes Controversy," *Jewish Chronicle*, Aug. 30, 1963, scrapbooks, box 357, MGC-LOC.

18. Susan Lester, "Approach to Martha Graham," *Sunday Telegraph*, Sept. 1, 1963, scrapbooks, box 357, MGC-LOC.

19. Buckle, "The Voice from the Cave."

20. Jennifer Dunning, "William Bales, Dancer, Is Dead; Choreographer and Educator, 80," *New York Times*, Sept. 11, 1990, http://www.nytimes.com/1990/09/11/obituaries/william-bales-dancer-is-dead-choreographer-and-educator-80.html (accessed June 12, 2017).

21. Mr. R. Gordon Arneson, Director, Office of Cultural Exchange, "Current Report on Cultural Presentations Program," Jan. 11, 1961, box 85, folder 15, UAK.

22. Arneson, "Current Report on Cultural Presentations Program."

23. Arneson, "Current Report on Cultural Presentations Program."

24. DP/IEP, July 23, 1963, UAK.

25. Victoria Phillips Geduld, "Collaboration Among Icons: The New York City Dance Theatre, 1949," *Ballet Review* 38, no. 4 (Winter 2011): 40–56 (see box 7, folder 8, BRC, for a copy of the article); Victoria Geduld, "Collaborations among Divas: Modern Dance Repertory Seasons, 1930–1968" (MA thesis, Gallatin School of Individualized Study, New York University, 2006).

26. *Winning the Cold War: The U.S. Ideological Offensive: Hearings before the Subcommittee on International Organizations and Movements of the Committee on Foreign Affairs*, House Subcommittee on International Organizations and Movements of the House Committee on Foreign Affairs, 88th Cong., 1st Sess., May 1, 1963, 421.

27. *Winning the Cold War*, 13.

28. *Winning the Cold War*, 171.

29. *Winning the Cold War*, 418.

30. *Winning the Cold War*, 389A.

31. *Winning the Cold War*, 435.

32. "Criticism Rebutted by Graham Troupe," *New York Times*, Sept. 11, 1963, 5.

33. *Winning the Cold War*, 436–37.

34. *Winning the Cold War*, 421.

35. *Winning the Cold War*, 438.

36. David K. Johnson, *The Lavender Scare: The Cold War Persecution of Gays and Lesbians in the Federal Government* (Chicago: University of Chicago Press, 2006). Future studies may also consider Jerome Robbins's testimony in front of HUAC in this context, particularly since his Ballets USA was an important export by the US government that has yet to be fully explored by scholars.

37. *Winning the Cold War*, 438–39.

38. Simon Morrison, *Bolshoi Confidential: Secrets of the Russian Ballet from the Rule of the Tsars to Today* (New York: W. W. Norton, 2016).

39. Tom Prinkley, "Is Martha Too Sexy for Export?," *Life*, 1963, Martha Graham Collection, scrapbooks, box 355, MGC-LOC. Note that through the 1980s, Graham used this quote in her own promotional materials. This reinforces the argument that she herself understood the allure of "sex appeal" to make herself modern. For example, she used the slogan in Israel in 1986 to promote her company; see "In 1926, Martha Graham Knocked the Ballet Shoes Off American Dance," promotional mailed leaflet, Martha Graham Dance Company, Martha Graham, 221.2.2.2, IDA.

40. Allen Hughes, "Miss Graham Back from Tour; 'Startled' by Criticism of Dance," *New York Times*, Sept. 17, 1963, 30.

41. "Not Bubbles," *Baltimore Sun*, Sept. 13, 1963, scrapbooks, box 355, MGC-LOC; "Guest Editorials Not Bubbles: Editorial," *Chicago Tribune*, Sept. 11, 1963, 20.

42. "The Trojan, Not the Cold War," *New York Times*, Sept. 11, 1963, 42.

43. "Congressmen Call Graham Dance Erotic," *Chicago Tribune*, Sept. 10, 1963, scrapbooks, box 355, MGC-LOC.

44. "Dance World Rallies," *New York Herald Tribune*, Sept. 11, 1963, scrapbooks, box 355, MGC-LOC.

45. Lincoln Kirsten to John Whitney, Sept. 17, 1963, scrapbooks, box 355, MGC-LOC.

46. José Limón to United States Department of State, Sept. 11, 1963, scrapbooks, box 355, MGC-LOC.

47. Baird Hastings to Edna Kelly, Sept. 15, 1963, scrapbooks, box 355, MGC-LOC.

48. "Washington 'Star' Raps Rep. Kelly on Proposed Censorship of Culture," *Variety*, Sept. 25, 1963, scrapbooks, box 355, MGC-LOC.

49. Arthur Todd, "Letter to the Editor," *New York Times*, Sept. 24, 1963, scrapbooks, box 355, MGC-LOC.

50. "'Phaedra' Shocks U.S. Legislators," *New York Times*, International Edition, Sept. 11, 1963, scrapbooks, box 355, MGC-LOC; "Criticism Rebutted by Graham Troupe."

51. "Not Bubbles."

52. "Just a Moment," *Binghamton Press*, Sept. 28, 1963, scrapbooks, box 355, MGC-LOC.

53. Walter Terry, "Martha Graham's Critics," *Twin City Sentinel* (Winston-Salem, NC), Oct. 27, 1963, scrapbooks, box 355, MGC-LOC.

54. "'Phaedra' Shocks U.S. Legislators"; "Criticism Rebutted by Graham Troupe."

55. "'Phaedra' Shocks U.S. Legislators."

56. "Ford Grants Stir Dance Comment," *New York Times*, Dec. 17, 1963, 46.

57. Dr. Henry T. Herald, Ford Foundation, Jan. 8, 1964, scrapbooks, box 358, MGC-LOC.

58. "Ford Grants $4,425,000 to Balanchine Ballets Here," *New York Herald Tribune*, Dec. 16, 1963, 21, scrapbooks, box 358, MGC-LOC.

59. Soviet and Eastern European Exchanges Staff, Department of State, "A Summary Report on the United States Exchanges Program with the Soviet Union," Apr. 18, 1964, box 320, folder 26, UAK.

60. Lyndon B. Johnson with William Fulbright, telephone conversation #11603, sound recording, Mar. 1, 1967, 3:00 p.m., Recordings and Transcripts of Telephone Conversations and Meetings, LBJ, http://www.discoverlbj.org/item/tel-11603 (accessed January 24, 2017).

61. "Vietnam Must Change or Forfeit Aid," Oct. 8, 1963, CIA-RDP65B00383R000200170013-0, General CIA Records, https://www.cia.gov/library/readingroom/document/cia-rdp65b00383r000200170013-0 (accessed June 11, 2017).

62. Audio diary and annotated transcript, Lady Bird Johnson, May 25, 1964 (Monday), Lady Bird Johnson's White House Diary Collection, LBJ, http://www.discoverlbj.org/item/ctjd-19640525 (accessed January 24, 2017).

63. Folder title list, White House Central Files, Subject Files, Arts (AR), LBJ, http://www.discoverlbj.org/item/ftl-whcf-ar (accessed January 24, 2017).

64. Gluck, *Batsheva Dance Company*, 43. The premiere of the company took place on December 16, 1964, in Tel Aviv (Gluck, *Batsheva Dance Company*, 57).

65. Author interview with Rina Schenfeld, May 15, 2017.

66. Gluck, *Batsheva Dance Company*, 47, 57. See also author interviews with Ethel Winter regarding her performances of *Salem Shore* in the 1940s and Mary Hinkson as she learned *Clytemnestra* more than a decade later.

67. Gluck, *Batsheva Dance Company*, 58–59, 76.

68. US Congress, Congressional Record: Proceedings and Debates of the 89th Cong., 1st Sess., vol. III, Washington, Aug. 13, 1965, 149.

69. Jennifer Fisher, *Nutcracker Nation: How an Old World Ballet Became a Christmas Tradition in the New World* (New Haven, CT: Yale University Press, 2003).

70. Martha Graham, "Acceptance Speech of the Aspen Award," July 31, 1964, scrapbooks, box 329, MGC-LOC.

71. Charles M. Ellison, Director, Office of Cultural Presentations, To: Mr. Robin Howard, June 29, 1965, box 64, folder 28, UAK.

72. To: Mr. Henry T. Heald, From: W. McNeil Lowry, Su: Grant out of Appropriation, Sept. 7, 1965, MGSchool of Contemporary Dance 065003600000, 1965 Sept. 23–1965 Sept. 22, 4–6, Grants FA732H, Series Reel 0948, Ford Foundation Records, RAC.

73. Robin Howard, to Mr. Charles Ellison, Mar. 1, 1965, box 64, folder 28, UAK.

74. Francis S. Mason, Cultural Affairs Office, To: Mr. Charles Ellison, Chief of Cultural Presentations, Mar. 5, 1965, box 64, folder 28, UAK.

75. Leroy F. Aarons, "Martha Graham Gets 2 Top Arts Grants," *Washington Post*, February 14, 1966, State Department file, box 64, folder 28, UAK.

76. Mr. Robin Howard, Acting Director, London School of Contemporary Dance, To: Lawrence E. Norrie, Special Assistant, Office of Cultural Presentations, Dec. 13, 1966, return letter Dec. 19, 1966, box 64, folder 28, UAK.

77. To: Belgrade, Bonn, Bucharest, Budapest, Prague, Sofia, Warsaw, Info: Lisbon, London, Madrid, Paris, Rome, Vienna, Fr: Department of State, "Tour of Martha Graham Dance Company," Aug. 4, 1966, box 64, folder 7, UAK.

78. Charles M. Ellison, Director, Office of Cultural Presentations, To: Craig Barton, Manager, Martha Graham Dance Company, July 14, 1965; "Tour of Martha Graham Dance Company."

79. "Report on Status of Martha Graham Tour," nd, box 64, folder 28, UAK.

80. Jean Battey, "Martha Graham Due Here in October," *Washington Post*, Sept. 11, 1966, State Department clippings, box 64, folder 28, UAK.

81. Clive Barnes, "Dance: American Export," *New York Times*, Aug. 9, 1966, State Department clippings, box 64, folder 28, UAK.

82. Studs Terkel interview with Martha Graham on "Riverside," nd, RG 306, Local Identification: 306-EN-R-T-7808, NARA. From the conversation, the taping must have taken place after 1963 and the "*Phaedra* scandal," to which Graham alludes. Because of references to a forthcoming engagement in Chicago, the tape can be dated to April 1966 (the company would perform in Chicago for the first time in seventeen years that October, opening with *Seraphic Dialogue*). See Thomas Willis, "Graham and Dancers Back after 17 Years," *Chicago Tribune*, Oct. 23, 1966, G9.

83. Mr. Robin Howard, To: Mr. Charles M. Ellison, Director, Office of Cultural Presentations, June 13, 1966, and return correspondence, box 64, folder 28, UAK.

84. "Report on Status of Martha Graham Tour."

85. Fr: O'Shaughnessy, Budapest, To: Secretary of state, Sept. 17, 1966, "Cancelled," Ref: CA-1022, State 43785, box 64, folder 7, UAK.

86. Airgram, To: Department of State, FR: American Embassy, Bucharest, SU: Tour of Martha Graham Company, Sept. 6, 1966; Telegram, To: SecState WashDC, FM, AmLegation Sofia, Sept. 28, 1966, all box 64, folder 67, UAK.

87. Telegrams, Aug. 26 and Sept. 14, 1966, box 64, folder 28, UAK.

88. Telegram, TO: SecState WashDC, FR: AmEmbassy Prague, Aug. 12, 1966, box 64, folder 28, UAK.

89. Airgram, To: Department of State, USIA WashDC, From: AmEmbassy Bonn, REF: Tour of Martha Graham Company, Aug. 23. 1966, box 64, folder 7, UAK.

90. TO: AmEmbassy Bonn, FR: Department of State, REF: Tour of Martha Graham Dance Company, Aug. 31, 1966, box 64, folder 7, UAK.

91. Telegram, FR: Belgrade, To: Secretary of State, SU: Action SecState, Information Zagreb, Sept. 22, 1966, box 64, folder 28, UAK.

92. To: CU/CP – For the Files, Fr: CU/CP, Subject: Martha Graham Dance Company, Aug. 23, 1966, box 64, folder 28, UAK.

93. Telegram, To: SecState WashDC Priority, Fm: AmEmbassy Lisbon, Apr. 14, 1967, box 64, folder 28, UAK.

94. Telegram, To: SecState WashDC, FM: AmEmbassy Lisbon, Aug. 19, 1966, box 64, folder 28, UAK.

95. Recapitulation, Martha Graham Dance Company, UK/Portugal, Apr. 4–May 1, 1967, box 97, folder 7, UAK.

96. "Weekly Salaries, Staff and Artists," box 64, folder 7, UAK; see also "Correspondence," Graham, Martha, Dance Company, 1966–67, box 64, folder 28, UAK.

97. "Correspondence."

98. Itinerary, Martha Graham Dance Company, box 97, folder 7, UAK.

99. "First Lady of Dance in Britain," *Los Angeles Times*, Apr. 4, 1967, C10; Ashton Applewhite, *This Chair Rocks: A Manifesto against Ageism* (London: Melville House, 2016); Patricia Cohen, *In Our Prime: The Invention of Middle Age* (New York: Scribner, 2012); Todd D. Nelson, Yoav S. Bergman, Maria Clara P. Couto, Dirk Wentura, and Michael S. North, *Ageism: Stereotyping and Prejudice against Older Persons* (Cambridge, MA: MIT Press, 2016).

100. David Authur, "Lighter Graham: Ballet," *Observer*, Apr. 16, 1967, 24.

101. For the Files, I.C., July 2 [1967], box 64, folder 28, UAK.

102. "Martha Graham and Her Company Debut Tonight at São Carlos Theatre," *Diário de Lisboa*, first ed., "Diversões," 4/32, translated by Conor Lane. The author wishes to thank Conor Lane for his research excellence and tenacity in finding these reports on a previously underrecognized series of performances. The author hopes that these findings will inspire new work by future historians.

103. "Martha Graham's Company at São Carlos," *Diário de Lisboa*, first ed., "Diversões," 19/32, translated by Conor Lane.

104. Russell Freedman, *Martha Graham: A Dancer's Life* (New York: Clarion Books, 1988), 133. Unfortunately, no reviews of this performance can be found in Portuguese newspapers, and Freedman cites no source. Alberto de Lacerda interviewed Graham for *Diário de Notícias*, April 27, and this could contain the quote. See "Final Show of Ballet Season at São Carlos," *Diário de Lisboa*, first ed., "Diversões," 6/36, translated by Conor Lane.

105. Final Evaluation Reports, Post Comments, Martha Graham Dance Company, box 97, folder 7, UAK.

106. For the Files, I.C., July 2 [1967], box 64, folder 28, UAK.

107. Marni Thomas, author interview with Marni Thomas and Ellen Graff, Nov. 11, 2004, and Mar. 21, 2016, New York City (transcript available with permission of Graff and Thomas).

108. Bertram Ross, *American Masters*, season 8, episode 2, "Martha Graham: The Dancer Revealed," aired May 13, 1994, on PBS.

109. Patricia Birch, *American Masters*, season 8, episode 2, "Martha Graham: The Dancer Revealed," aired May 13, 1994, on PBS.

110. Thomas, author interview with Marni Thomas and Ellen Graff, Nov. 11, 2004, and Mar. 21, 2016.

111. Agnes de Mille, *American Masters*, season 8, episode 2, "Martha Graham: The Dancer Revealed," aired May 13, 1994, on PBS.

112. "Critical Comments on Martha Graham Performances from Posts," Jan. 9, 1963, USIS memo, scrapbooks, box 354, MGC-LOC; FBI File, Martha Graham.

113. To: Mr. McGeorge Bundy, Fr: W. McNeil Lowry, Division: Humanities and Arts, Grants out of Appropriation, Performance and Preservation of the Repertoire of the Modern Dance, May 22, 1968, 2–7, MGCenter for Contemporary Dance 06800621, 1968 June 14–1969 Dec., Grants L–N (FA732E), Series Reel 2176, Ford Foundation Records, RAC.

114. Tity de Vries, "The 1967 Central Intelligence Scandal: Catalyst in a Transforming Relationship between State and People," *Journal of American History* 98, no. 4 (March 2012): 1075–92.

115. Note the Ford Foundation correspondence during which the foundation agrees not to take CIA funds directly; however, in immediate response, it initiates "Program One." See Richard Magat, "Swimming for 25 Years as a Pilot Fish at the Ford Foundation," Reports 019683, Sept. 23, 1982, memo addressed to Frank Sutton, 019683; Ford Foundation Records, Office of the President, H. Rowan Gaither, FA621, Series 1, box 1, folder 1, 1–2; "Some Operating Guides for Program One," To: Paul Hoffner, Fr: H. Rowan Gaither, Jr., Dec. 4, 1950, 01528, all Ford Foundation, RAC. These Ford Foundation discussions are also queried by Olivier Zunz, *Philanthropy in America: A History* (Princeton, NJ: Princeton University Press, 2011).

116. "Foreign Aspects of U.S. National Security; Conference Report and Proceedings," Feb. 25, 1958, declassified 2013/05/08, CIA-RDP67-00318R000100370001-7 (accessed January 25, 2017); "Supplemental Appropriations, 1956," *Congressional Record—House*, July 14, 1955, declassified 2006/11/09, CIA-RDP63T00245R000100120004-3 (accessed January 25, 2017); "Hindemith—Early and Late," *New Republic*, Apr. 6, 1963, 26, CIA-RDP80B01676R003100210030-4 (accessed June 5, 2017); National Council on the Arts, "Federal Funds and Services for the Arts," nd, Graham, 11, declassified 2004/10/13, CIA-RDP88-01315R000300620001-3 (accessed January 25, 2017); Saunders, *The Cultural Cold War*, 142, 291.

117. Lady Bird Johnson's Daily Diary entry, Oct. 9, 1968, Lady Bird Johnson's White House Diary Collection, LBJ, http://www.discoverlbj.org/item/ctjd-ctjdd-19681009 (accessed January 24, 2017); Lyndon B. Johnson, Remarks of Welcome at the White House to Prime Minister Holyoake of New Zealand, Oct. 9, 1968, http://www.presidency.ucsb.edu/ws/?pid=29163 (accessed January 24, 2017).

118. Martha Graham Dance Company, Latin America, Recapitulation, box 97, folder 2, UAK.

119. Helen McGehee to Umaña, Nov. 30, 1962, box 9, folder 21, McGehee and Umaña Collection of Dance Materials, LOC; Harold J. Smith, "The Bird and the Mirror: A Reading of Mallarmé's 'Le Vierge,'" *French Review* 63, no. 1 (October 1989): 57–65; Graham, *Blood Memory*, 200, 237, 380–81; *Martha Graham: The Dancer Revealed* (New York: Criterion Collection, 1991); Agnes de Mille, *Martha: The Life and Work of Martha Graham* (New York: Random House, 1991), 380.

120. Louis A. Trevisan, MD, Nashaat Boutros, MD, Ismene L. Petrakis, MD, and John Krystal, MD, "Complications of Alcohol Withdrawal: Pathophysiological Insights," *Alcohol Health and Research World* 22, no. 1 (1998): 61–66.

121. de Mille, *Martha*, 237, 380; Graham, *Blood Memory*, 237.

122. Trevisan et al., "Complications of Alcohol Withdrawal."

123. Graham, *Blood Memory*, 237; de Mille, *Martha*, 237.

124. Phillips, "Martha Graham's Gilded Cage."

125. Trevisan et al., "Complications of Alcohol Withdrawal."

126. Patrick Radden Keefe, "The Family That Built an Empire of Pain," *New Yorker*, Oct. 30, 2017. Note that Keefe opens this article at the Temple of Dendur, where Graham would premiere *Frescoes* in 1979.

127. Unnamed source; "Hans Smit Celebrated as 'Leading Light' at Law School," *Columbia Law School Magazine*, www.law.columbia.edu/magazine/61837 (accessed June 8, 2017); email with unnamed classmate.

128. Author interview with Mary Hinkson, Mar. 3, 2015 (transcript available upon request with the permission of Mary Hinkson's estate)..

129. Author interview with Mary Hinkson.

130. Author interview with Linda Hodes, Jan. 25, 2016 (transcript available upon request with permission of Hodes).

131. Author interview with Linda Hodes.

132. Author interview with Linda Hodes.

133. Ron Protas, *American Masters,* season 8, episode 2, "Martha Graham: The Dancer Revealed," aired May 13, 1994, on PBS.

134. Author interview with Linda Hodes.

135. The characterization of Protas's relationships with people and dancers who were close to Graham is based on oral histories with numerous dancers and friends who wish to remain anonymous.

136. To Ben, from Martha Graham, 1970, box 1, see notes in folders 24, 25; still photographs, Polaroids, box 3, folders 26, 27, both from the Ben Garber Papers, LOC.

137. Author interview with Francis Mason, Aug. 15, 2008.

138. "Status of Program for FY 1970, Report on US-USSR Exchanges Agreement," Dec. 5, 1969, box 97, folder 24, UAK.

139. Summary Minutes of Meeting, Advisory committee on the Arts, Nov. 1, 1968, box 97, folder 2, 1, UAK.

140. Wolfgang Saxon, "Nancy Hanks Is Dead at 55," *New York Times,* Jan. 8, 1983, 17.

141. "Psychological Aspects of United States Strategy," Panel Report HR70-14, Nov. 1, 1955, in CIA General Records, "CIA Rockefeller Approved on Relbase 2007/ 01/17," CIA-13WP86B00269R000300120001-4 (FOIA) /ESDN (CREST): CIA-RDP86B00269R000300120001-4, Original Classification: Secret; also Panel Report HR70-14, Submitted by Major General Frederick L. Anderson (USAF) to Nelson A. Rockefeller, Special Assistant to the White House, November 1955, Nelson A. Rockefeller Vice Presidential Records, Foreign Affairs and National Security, Series 19 (FA385), box 15, folder 376, RAC.

142. "Psychological Aspects of United States Strategy."

143. "Status of Program for FY 1970, Report on US-USSR Exchanges Agreement."

144. Mark Bauerlein and Ellen Grantham, eds., *National Endowment for the Arts: A History, 1965–2008* (Washington, DC: National Endowment for the Arts, 2009), 18.

145. "Brief Summary of Martha Graham's International Tours," 66; "Transcript of Proceedings," 1970, 33, 35, 1974, box 65, folder 4, UAK; Bauerlein and Grantham, *National Endowment for the Arts,* 19; "Transcript of Proceedings," 1970, 32.

146. "Transcript of Proceedings," 1970, 18.

147. "Transcript of Proceedings," 1970, 19.

148. "Transcript of Proceedings," 1970, 18.

149. Achievements of Exchanges, the United States Exchange Program with the Soviet Union and Eastern Europe, Review of Exchanges, July 15, 1961, box 320, folder 26, UAK.

150. "Status of Program for FY 1970, Report on US-USSR Exchanges Agreement."

151. Peter Grose, "Moscow and U.S. Widen Exchanges: Reach Swift Agreement on 1970–1971 Cultural Pact," *New York Times*, Feb. 11, 1970, 9.

152. "Ailey Troupe Saved by State Department," *New York Times*, June 9, 1970, 25.

153. James F. Clarity, "Moscow Audience Hails Ailey Dancers," *New York Times*, Oct. 23, 1970, 30; Charlotte Saiikowski, "Modern Dance Captures Moscow: Beyond Orthodoxy," *Christian Science Monitor*, Oct. 26, 1970, 5; Jean Battey Lewis, "Ovation for Ailey: Dance Notes," *Washington Post*, Nov. 7, 1970, C6.

154. Proposed Programs, Jose Limon Dance Company, Soviet Tour, and ". . . notes on Dances for Isadora," box 68, folder 7, UAK.

155. See reconstructions by Lori Belilove, the Isadora Duncan Dance Company, and "Dance Is a Weapon" series, Martha Graham Dance Company. https://isadoraduncan.org/foundation/, http://www.marthagraham.org/history/ (accessed September 1, 2019).

156. Ilya Ilyich Schneider, Isadora Duncan: The Russian Years (New York: Harcourt, Brace and World, 1969), quoted in Nadia Chilkovsky Nahumck, Nicholas Nahumck, and Anne M. Moll, *Isadora Duncan: The Dances* (Washington DC: National Museum of Women in the Arts, 1994), http://www.isadoraduncanarchive.org/repertory/29/.

157. "I Am Red: Isadora Duncan's Moscow Life through Photos and Recollections," *moscow.ru*, Mar. 13, 2019, https://www.mos.ru/en/news/item/52113073/ (accessed September 1, 2019).

158. "Transcript of Proceedings, Dance Panel," Nov. 23, 1970, box 101, folder 22, 5, UAK.

159. "Transcript of Proceedings," DPM/IEP, May 25, 1972, box 101, folder 22, 29–32, see also 38, UAK.

160. "Transcript of Proceedings," DPM/IEP, May 25, 1972.

161. "Transcript of Proceedings," Nov. 23, 1970, 33.

162. Henry Kamm, "Vietnamese Say G.I.'s Slew 567 in Town," *New York Times*, Nov. 17, 1969, 1; Horst Faas, photographer, Phouc Vinh airstrip in South Vietnam. Picture taken on the Phouc Vinh airstrip, South Vietnam, June 18, 1965, of 173 Airborne Brigade Battalion member Larry W. Chaffin, syndicated; Richard Melanson, *American Foreign Policy since the Vietnam War: The Search for Consensus from Richard Nixon to George W. Bush* (New York: M. E. Sharpe, 2005), 48.

163. Walter Isaacson, *Kissinger* (New York: Simon and Schuster, 2005), 31, 36.

164. Graham, *Blood Memory*, 237; de Mille, *Martha*, 380–84; Cadra Peterson McDaniel, *American-Soviet Cultural Diplomacy: The Bolshoi Ballet's American Premiere* (Lanham, MD: Rowman & Littlefield Publishing Group, 2015), 207; Stanley I. Kutler, *The Wars of Watergate: The Last Crisis of Richard Nixon* (New York: W. W. Norton, 1990), 60; To: State Department, Fr: Damascus, RG 59, Central Decimal Files (CDF), box 1047, NARA; "Transcript of Proceedings," DP/IEP, Nov. 23, 1970, box 101, folder 22, 5, UAK.

165. Dwight D. Eisenhower, "Address at the Cow Palace on Accepting the Nomination of the Republican National Convention," Aug. 23, 1956; Gerhard Peters and John T. Woolley, *The American Presidency Project*, http://www.presidency.ucsb.edu/ws/?pid=10583 (accessed June 13, 2017); George Rising, *Stuck in the*

Sixties: Conservatives and the Legacy of the 1960s (New York: Xlibris, 2010), 183; Noam Kochavi, *Nixon and Israel: Forging a Conservative Partnership* (Albany: State University of New York Press, 2009), 57.

166. "Fifth Quarterly Report, 1 July 1955–30 September 1955," Nelson Rockefeller Personal Files, RG 4, Special Assistant to the President, Cultural Activities, box 80, folder 618, 1, RAC; "Transcript of Proceedings," Nov. 23, 1970, 1–2, 29–32; "Transcript of Proceedings," DP/IEP, May 25, 1972, box 101, folder B-48, 52, UAK.

167. "Transcript of Proceedings," 1972, 33; Yvonne Rainer, "Flag Dance, 1970," in *Work, 1961–73* (Halifax: Press of Nova Scotia College of Art and Design, 1974), 171–72; *I See America Dancing: Selected Readings 1685–2000*, ed. Maureen Needham (Champaign: University of Illinois Press, 2002), 220–22; Bauerlein and Grantham, *National Endowment for the Arts*, 18–19; "Transcript of Proceedings," 1970, 33.

168. "Transcript of Proceedings," 1970, 31.

169. "Transcript of Proceedings," 1970, 30.

170. "Transcript of Proceedings," 1970, 30, 32, 45, 195.

171. "Transcript of Proceedings," 1970, 145.

172. "Transcript of Proceedings," 1972, 40.

173. Martha Graham to Nancy [Ross], Mar. 31, 1971, "Martha Graham Center of Contemporary Dance, Inc., and Martha Graham School of Contemporary Dance, Inc., Statement of Estimated Receipts and Expenditures, 1972," Series 5, box 87, folder 5, NWRP.

174. To: Members of the Board of the Martha Graham Center of Contemporary Dance, Inc., Fr: Jeanette Roosevelt, Oct. 4, 1971, Series 5, box 87, folder 7, NWRP.

175. To: Members and Directors of the Martha Graham Center, Inc., and the Martha Graham School, Inc., Fr: LeRoy Leatherman, Series 5, box 87, folder 5, NWRP.

176. LeRoy Leatherman to Members of the Martha Graham Dance Company, Sept. 22, 1972, Series 5, box 87, folder 6, NWRP.

177. LeRoy Leatherman to Nancy Hanks, National Endowment for the Arts, June 15, 1971, 2, Series 5, box 87, folder 5, NWRP.

178. William B. McHenry to Nancy Wilson Ross, Jan. 14, 1974, Series 5, box 87, folder 9, NWRP; LeRoy Leatherman to Nancy Hanks, National Endowment for the Arts, June 15, 1971, 2, Series 5, box 87, folder 5, NWRP; Martha Graham to Nancy Ross, Mar. 31, 1971; "Martha Graham Center of Contemporary Dance, Inc., and Martha Graham School of Contemporary Dance, Inc., Statement of Estimated Receipts and Expenditures, 1972," Series 5, box 87, folder 5, NWRP; Martha Graham to Nancy Ross, Mar. 31, 1971; "Martha Graham Center of Contemporary Dance, Inc., and Martha Graham School of Contemporary Dance, Inc., Statement of Estimated Receipts and Expenditures, 1972," Series 5, box 87, folder 5, NWRP; Jeanette Roosevelt to Members of the Board of the Martha Graham Center of Contemporary Dance, Inc., Oct. 4, 1971, Series 5, box 87, folder 7, NWRP.

179. "Transcript of Proceedings," 1972, B-48, B-52.

180. "Transcript of Proceedings," 1972, 64.

181. "Transcript of Proceedings," 1972, 65.

182. Lynn Garafola, introduction to *José Limón: An Unfinished Memoir*, by José Limón (Middletown, CT: Wesleyan University Press, 2001); "Transcript of Proceedings," 1970, 65, 102; Prevots, *Dance for Export*, 24.

183. Carla Maxwell, "Dancing the Cold War: An International Symposium," Feb. 18, 2017, Harriman Institute, Columbia University in the City of New York, http://harriman.columbia.edu/event/dancing-cold-war-international-symposium (accessed June 13, 2017).

184. "Transcript of Proceedings," 1972, B-83.

185. Don McDonagh, *Martha Graham: A Biography* (New York: Praeger, 1973), 293–95; author interview with Charles Reinheart, 2006; Victoria Phillips Geduld, "Collaboration among Icons: The New York City Dance Theatre, 1949," *Ballet Review* 38, no. 4 (Winter 2011): 40–56; if *Ballet Review* is unavailable, see box 7, folder 8, BRC.

186. LeRoy Leatherman to Members of the Martha Graham Company, Sept. 22, 1972, Series 5, box 87, folder 6, NWRP.

187. McDonagh, *Martha Graham*, 293–95; author interview with Charles Reinheart, 2006; Geduld, "Collaboration among Icons," 40–56; LeRoy Leatherman to Members of the Martha Graham Company.

188. LeRoy Leatherman to Nancy Hanks, National Endowment for the Arts, Sept. 22, 1972, Series 5, box 87, folder 7, NWRP.

189. Author oral history with Mary Hinkson, Mar. 3, 2005 (closed except with the permission of Mary Hinkson's family).

190. Bertram Ross to Martha Graham, Dec. 4, 1973, Series 5, box 87, folder 7, NWRP; William Slattery, "A New Boss—and Dance Company Is Out of Step," *New York Post*, Dec. 17, 1972, 2; Arnold Weissberger to Bertram Ross, nd, Series 5, box 87, folder 10, NWRP; Anna Kisselgoff, "Amid Discontent, Tour of Europe Is Planned by Graham Dancers," *New York Times*, Dec. 13, 1973, also in Series 5, box 87, folder 11, NWRP; author oral history with Mary Hinkson, Mar. 3, 2005 (closed except with the permission of Mary Hinkson's family).

191. Gluck, *Batsheva Dance Company*, 169.

192. Nelson A. Rockefeller to Miss Martha Graham, Mar. 13, 1973, scrapbooks 231, folder 1973, NWRP.

193. Deborah Jowitt, "The Monumental Martha," *New York Times*, Apr. 29, 1973; John Richardson Jr. to George S. Springsteen, Sept. 11, 1973, box 65, folder 2, UAK; Martha Graham, *The Notebooks of Martha Graham* (New York: Harcourt, 1973).

194. Carl Bernstein and Bob Woodward, "Five Held in Plot to Bug Democratic Offices Here," *Washington Post*, June 18, 1972, 1, http://www.washingtonpost.com/wp-srv/politics/special/watergate/part1.html (accessed November 28, 2016).

195. Justin P. Coffey, *Spiro Agnew and the Rise of the Republican Right* (Santa Barbara, CA: ABC-CLIO, 2015), 169.

196. John Richardson Jr. to George S. Springsteen, Sept. 11, 1973, box 65, folder 2, UAK.

197. "Transcript of Proceedings," 1973, 63.

198. TO: CU—Mr. Fox, FR: CU/CP Mark Lewis, RE: Request for Funding, Apr. 23, 1974, box 65, folder 3, UAK; "Transcript of Proceedings," 1973, 53; "Transcript of

Proceedings," 1970, 8; Embassy Saigon to Department of State, telegram, nd, 1974, box 65, folder 4, UAK; "Brief Summary of Martha Graham's International Tours," nd, 112–14, box 65, folder 2, UAK; Mark B. Lewis, Director, Office of Cultural Presentations, to Francis Mason, May 28, 1974, box 237, folder 3, MGC-LOC.

199. Clive Barnes, "For Martha Graham, a Resurgence," *New York Times*, May 5, 1974, D18.
200. See also Anna Kisselgoff, "Graham Rebellion Still Lures Young," *New York Times*, Apr. 24, 1974, 30.
201. Barnes, "For Martha Graham, a Resurgence."
202. Kisselgoff, "Asian Tour Slated by Martha Graham."
203. John Herbers, "Nixon Resigns," *New York Times*, Aug. 8, 1974, 1.
204. Martha Graham to Francis Mason, Dec. 5, 1973, box 235, folder "Correspondence," Lucy Kroll Papers, Manuscript Division, LOC.

Chapter 6

1. Gerald R. Ford, "Remarks upon Taking the Oath of Office as President," Aug. 9, 1974, https://www.fordlibrarymuseum.gov/library/speeches/740001.asp (accessed June 13, 2017).
2. I had the opportunity to ask Dr. Kissinger about his memory of the tours and their significance. He generously looked directly into my eyes and said, "You will tell me."
3. Niall Ferguson, *The Square and the Tower: Networks and Power, From Freemasons to Facebook* (New York: Penguin Press, 2017), 284–299; Tony Allen-Mills, "Mafia Lawyer Shares Actress with Kissinger," *The Sunday Times of London*, Sept. 24, 2006, https://www.thetimes.co.uk/article/mafia-lawyer-shared-actress-with-kissinger-zn698wjgmn9 (accessed September 5, 2019); WWD Staff, "Henry Kissinger in the Swinging Seventies," *Women's Wear Daily*, https://wwd.com/fashion-news/fashion-features/celebrating-henry-kissinger-6967416/ (accessed September 5, 2019).
4. See file folder, "Ford, Gerald Randolph, Cartoons, Satire, etc., 1974," Reading Room, FORD.
5. For: Jerry Jones, Fr: David Parker, Re: Schedule Suggestions for the First Lady, Aug. 15, 1974, David Hoopes Files, box 9, folder "First Lady's Office—General (1)," FORD.
6. Anna Kisselgoff, "Martha Graham Recalls Years with Former Pupil, Betty Ford," *New York Times*, Aug. 10, 1974, 19, First Lady's Staff, Sheila Weidenfeld Files, 1974–77, General Subject File, box 36, clippings files, "Betty Ford, Arts, Dance," FORD.
7. Henry Kissinger to Gerald Ford, Sept. 6, 1974, box 65, folder 2, UAK; John Robert Greene, *Betty Ford: Candor and Courage in the White House* (Lawrence: University Press of Kansas, 2004), 9; "Brief Summary of Martha Graham's International Tours"; "Martha on Private Life," *Nation*, Sept. 8, 1974, np, box 65, folder 6, UAK.
8. Greene, *Betty Ford*, 89.
9. Jack Anderson, "Rudolf Nureyev, Charismatic Dancer Who Gave Fire to Ballet's Image, Dies at 54," *New York Times*, Jan. 7, 1993, A1.

10. To: Mrs. Ford, From: Ron Protas, Aug. 21, 1974, Elizabeth "Betty" Ford White House Papers, box 39, folder, Graham, Martha—Dance Company (1), FORD.

11. To: Mrs. Ford, From: Ron Protas, Aug. 21, 1974.

12. Letty Magsanoc, "Modern Dance 'High Priestess' and Troupe Here," *Bulletin Today*, Sept. 11, 1974, 8, box 65, folder 5, UAK; Anna Kisselgoff, "Dance: An Unusual Turn," *New York Times*, May 2, 1974, 64; Anna Kisselgoff, "Dance: Graham Protégée," *New York Times*, Apr. 19, 1974, 22; Clive Barnes, "For Martha Graham, a Resurgence," *New York Times*, May 5, 1974, C2.

13. Barnes, "For Martha Graham, a Resurgence"; "Brief Summary of Martha Graham's International Tours"; "Transcript of Proceedings," 1972, 63.

14. Embassy Rangoon to Department of State, telegram, May 4, 1974, box 65, folder 4, UAK.

15. "Prepatory Agreements," Mark B. Lewis, Director, Office of Cultural Presentations, To: Francis Mason, Martha Graham Dance Company, Grant Agreement No. SCC-1069-477023, May 28, 1974, Company Correspondence, box 237, folder 3, MGC-LOC. The grant offered just over $124,000 for the thirty-five members of the company and crew. They would fly from New York to Seoul (canceled), Taipei, Hong Kong, Manila, Jakarta, Singapore, Kuala Lumpur, Bangkok, Rangoon, Saigon, and back to New York. The Graham Company arranged a privately sponsored tour to Japan.

16. "Brief Summary of Martha Graham's International Tours."

17. Margaret MacMillan, *Nixon and Mao: The Week That Changed the World* (New York: Random House, 2007; reprint, 2008), 179.

18. MacMillan, *Nixon and Mao*, photo insert, 278, 282.

19. Celeste Chan, "Was Ping Pong Diplomacy a Man's Game?," final paper, Women as Cold War Weapons, HISTGU4217, Columbia University, New York, NY, Fall 2017.

20. Rigoberto D. Tiglao, "Enrile: CPP-NPA and China—Provoked," *Manila Times*, Mar. 31, 2017, 1.

21. Raymond Bonner, *Waltzing with a Dictator: The Marcoses and the Making of American Policy* (New York: Times Books, 1987); James Hamilton-Paterson, *America's Boy: A Century of United States Colonialism in the Philippines* (New York: Henry Holt, 1999).

22. David Shaw, "Indonesia's President Given Tourist's View of Disneyland," *Los Angeles Times*, June 1, 1970, 3.

23. Robert Trumbull, "Burma Banning Fulbright Men, Ford and Asia Fund Advisors," *New York Times*, Apr. 20, 1962, 2.

24. Jack Foisie, "Lonely Burma's Closed Society Shows Signs of Relaxation," *Los Angeles Times*, Aug. 13, 1972, k7.

25. Donald P. Gregg, *Pot Shards: Fragments of a Life Lived in CIA, the White House, and the Two Koreas* (Washington, DC: New Academia Publishing, 2014), 165; FR: AmEmb Seoul, TO: SecStateWasDC, RE: Martha Graham Dance Company, telegram, Oct. 1, 1974, box 65, folder 4, UAK.

26. Marilyn Young, *The Vietnam Wars, 1945–1990* (New York: HarperCollins, 1991). Dr. Young helped support this work with her personal time, attention, and support, and hosted me at New York University's Cold War Center. She found delight in my explanation of "an abstracted folk dance" in *Appalachian Spring* that ultimately led

me to just show a tape of the section on film. Robert M. Neer, *Napalm: An American Biography* (Cambridge, MA: Belknap Press, 2013); thanks to Bob for all his support throughout our Ph.D. years at Columbia and beyond.

27. "Brief Summary of Martha Graham's International Tours"; Von Eschen, *Satchmo Blows Up the World*, 221; Gary J. Bass, *The Blood Telegram: Nixon, Kissinger, and a Forgotten Genocide* (New York: Alfred A. Knopf, 2013). Note that Graham's final stops in Japan were monitored by the State Department but not officially funded.

28. "Preparatory Arrangements."

29. "Preparatory Arrangements."

30. "Graham to Choreograph for Nureyev," Times Journal, Oct. 1, 1974, box 65, folder 5, UAK; "Martha Graham Company Opens Manila Engagement September 12," *Philippines Daily Express*, Sept. 9, 1974, folder 5, box 65, UAK; "Brief Summary of Martha Graham's International Tours."

31. "Martha on Private Life"; "Martha Graham Tour Begins in Triumph," USIS press release, Sept. 19, 1974, box 65, folder 7, UAK; "Graham Technique Currently on Show," *Business Day*, Sept. 13, 1974, box 65, folder 5, UAK.

32. "Martha on Private Life"; "Martha Graham Tour Begins in Triumph"; "Graham Technique Currently on Show."

33. "Famed Martha Graham Dance Company to Perform in Saigon," USIS Vietnamese Press #6808, Sept. 22, 1974, MGC-MGF; Jeremi Suri, "Détente and Its Discontents," in *Rightward Bound: Making America Conservative in the 1970s*, ed. Bruce J. Schulman and Julian E. Zelizer (Cambridge, MA: Harvard University Press, 2008), 231; Sarah E. Ruble, *The Gospel of Freedom and Power: Protestant Missionaries in American Culture after World War II* (Chapel Hill: University of North Carolina Press, 2012), 9, 15, 79.

34. "Martha Graham Tour Begins in Triumph."

35. Graham, *Blood Memory*, 4; "Bridging the Past and the Future," *Bangkok Post*, Sept. 28, 1974, box 65, folder 6, UAK; "Martha Graham's 'Rebirth,'" Nation (Bangkok), Sept. 27, 1974, box 65, folder 6, UAK; Lewis Grossbeyer, "Martha Graham: Back to Work," *Indonesian Observer*, Sept. 16, 1974, MGC-MGF. Note that the Graham Company records do not have location records. These files are available from the author with the written permission of the Martha Graham Dance Company, Martha Graham Resources. Otherwise, there is a fee to search for the records in New York City.

36. "Martha Graham Company Opens Manila Engagement September 12," *Philippines Daily Express*, Sept. 9, 1974, 15, box 65, folder 5, UAK.

37. Grossbeyer, "Martha Graham: Back to Work."

38. Grossbeyer, "Martha Graham: Back to Work"; "Bridging the Past and the Future," *Bangkok Post*, Sept. 28, 1974, box 65, folder 6, UAK; "Martha Graham's 'Rebirth,'" *The Nation*, Sept. 27, 1974, box 65, folder 6, UAK.

39. Graham, *Blood Memory*, 4; Grossbeyer, "Martha Graham: Back to Work"; "Bridging the Past and the Future"; "Martha Graham's 'Rebirth.'"

40. Jeffrey Toobin, *American Heiress: The Wild Saga of the Kidnapping, Crimes and Trial of Patty Hearst* (New York: Doubleday, 2016), 13.

41. Toobin, *American Heiress*, 1, 118.

42. "Brief Summary of Martha Graham's International Tours"; FR: AmEmbSingapore, TO: SecState WashDC, RE: Martha Graham Dance Company, Aug. 21, 1974, box 65, folder 4, UAK; FR: AmEmbTaipei, TO: AmEmbBangkok, RE: Martha Graham Dance Company, Aug. 30, 1974, box 65, folder 4, UAK.

43. Folder 6, box 65-UAK; scrapbooks, box 373, MGC-LOC.

44. "Martha Graham Dance Tour."

45. Magsanoc, "Modern Dance 'High Priestess' and Troupe Here"; "Martha Graham Dance Tour."

46. Gregg, *Pot Shards*, 165; "S. Korean First Lady Assassinated 1974," http://www.military.com/video/operations-and-strategy/assassination/s-korean-first-lady-assassinated/2507728485001 (accessed December 17, 2016); FR: AmEmb Seoul, TO: SecStateWasDC, RE: Martha Graham Dance Company, telegram, Oct. 01, 1974, box 65, folder 4, UAK.

47. "Martha Graham Company Opens Manila Engagement September 12."

48. "Brief Summary of Martha Graham's International Tours"; "Martha Graham Company Receiving High Praise during Southeast Asian Tour," USIS Report Bangkok and Hong Kong, Oct. 3, 1974, MGC-MGF; "Martha Graham," *Shih Chieh Jit Pao*, Sept. 27, 1974, folder 6, box 65, UAK; "Martha Graham" and "Watching the Martha Graham Dance Company," USIS excerpts of the *Song Than*, Oct. 12, 1974, MGC-MGF.

49. FR: AmConsulHongKong, TO: AmEmbassy Bangkok, Jakarta, Kuala Lumpur, Rangoon, Singapore, Saigon, INFO: AmSecState WashDC, Sept. 9, 1974, box 65, folder 4, UAK.

50. From: AmEmbassyRagoon, TO: SecStateWashDC, INFO: Bangkok, Saigon, Tokyo, SUBJ: Martha Graham Dance Company, telegram, 094184, box 65, folder 4, UAK; "Brief Summary of Martha Graham's International Tours."

51. Embassy Philippines to Department of State, cable, cc'ed all posts, nd, 1974, box 65, folder 4, UAK; "Martha Graham Tour Begins in Triumph"; Martha Graham Dance Company program labeled "Martha Graham Dance Tour," USIA Programs, 1970–1978, RG 306, box 1, NARA.

52. To: Dept. of State—CU/CP, From: Embassy, Manilla [Sullivan], Info: USIA/IEA and All IEA Posts, Airgram 327, Sept. 26, 1974, Elizabeth "Betty" Ford White House Papers, box 39, Graham, Martha—Dance Company (2), FORD.

53. To: SecState Wash, Fr: AmEmb Manila, Info: USIA WashDC, All Posts, Sept. 14, 1974, Elizabeth "Betty" Ford White House Papers, box 39, Graham, Martha—Dance Company (2), FORD.

54. "Brief Summary of Martha Graham's International Tours."

55. "Brief Summary of Martha Graham's International Tours"; Embassy Tokyo to Department of State, telegram, Sept. 4, 1974, box 65, folder 4, UAK; Embassy Manila to Embassy Singapore, Sept. 13, 1974, box 65, folder 3, UAK; Embassy Singapore to Department of State, telegram, nd, 1974, box 65, folder 4, UAK.

56. "Brief Summary of Martha Graham's International Tours."

57. To: SecState Wash, From: AmEmb Jakarta [Newsom], Info: AmEmb Tokyo, Taipei, consulate Hong Kong, Manila, Singapore, Kuala Lumpur, Rangoon, Bangkok, Saigon,

NOTES 379

Oct 1, 1974, Elizabeth "Betty" Ford White House Papers, box 39, Graham, Martha—Dance Company (2), FORD.

58. FR: AmEmbSingapore, TO: Bangkok, Rangoon, Saigon, RE: Martha Graham Dance Company, Sept. 23, 1974, box 65, folder 4, UAK; "Martha Graham Company Receiving High Praise during Southeast Asian Tour"; "Brief Summary of Martha Graham's International Tours."

59. To: SecState Wash DC 1276, From: AmEmb Singapore, Info: USIA WasDC and Bangkok, Hong Kong, Jakarta, Kuala Lumpur, Manila, Rangoon, Saigon, Taipei, Oct. 1, 1974, Elizabeth "Betty" Ford White House Papers, box 39, Graham, Martha—Dance Company (2), FORD.

60. Rick Grossman, "Miss Graham Never Fails to Astound," Bangkok Post, Sept. 19, 1974, box 65, folder 6, UAK.

61. Grossman, "Miss Graham Never Fails to Astound"; J.L., "Too Self-Conscious," clipping, nd, box 65, folder 6, UAK; Graham, Blood Memory, 134; FR: AmEmbSaigon, TO: AmEmb Tokyo, RE: Martha Graham Dance Company, Oct. 1, box 65, folder 4, UAK.

62. From: AmEmbassy Bangkok, To: SecState Wash DC, Priority 7167, Info: USIA WashDC, AmEmb Rangoon, Saigon, Oct. 1 despatch (Sept. 74), Elizabeth "Betty" Ford White House Papers, box 39, Graham, Martha—Dance Company (2), FORD; "Brief Summary of Martha Graham's International Tours"; "Martha Graham Tour Begins in Triumph."

63. Clare Croft, "Too Sexy for Export or Just Enough? Martha Graham Dance Company on Tour," in Dancers as Diplomats, 105–42. Note that Croft largely discounts the later Graham tours under President Jimmy Carter in 1979 because the touring apparatus was moved from the State Department to USIA under his administration in 1978. Croft cites the end of the Cold War as taking place "in the 1980s" (142). While historians debate the "end" of the Cold War, this study follows the trajectory of the Cold War well through the Reagan presidency and President George H. W. Bush and the dissolution of the Soviet Union in 1991. Graham showed continued value as government "propaganda" in the age of the "evil empire" and a 1983 "war scare," which historians are just beginning to explore (see John Prados, "The War Scare of 1983," in The Cold War: A Military History, ed. Robert Cowley [New York: Random House, 2006], 438–54). Indeed, the 1980s brought heightened tensions before the fall of the Berlin Wall in 1989, and the ultimate collapse of the Soviet Union in 1991.

64. Department of State, FR Embassy Rangoon, telegram, May 4, 1974, box 65, folder 4, UAK.

65. "Transcript of Proceedings," 1970, 6.

66. Leonor Orosa-Goquingco, "Graham Extrapolates Emotion," Bulletin Today, Sept. 14, 1974, box 65, folder 5, UAK.

67. Note that Croft outlines ideas put forward that Graham was staging a political protest when she elected not to go to Vietnam. As Croft states, official government memos and dancers noted Graham's illness. Since Graham and the government representatives in the United States worked together to mold repertory and tour planning, certainly Graham would have been vocal about political views before the itinerary was

set. Anna Kisselgoff also used the stop in Saigon as a featured part of her announce-ment in the *Times*. Indeed, as voiced by Lyman in *Dancers as Diplomats*, the com-pany members saw the tour stop as an honor. They would not have worked against Graham's wishes—indeed, they almost always mirrored them. In addition, the hand-written memo cited in these notes, "Brief Summary of Martha Graham's International Tours," documented the details of her health and poor lungs, and available photos show her weakened state. This surely accounts for her ban of candid pictures in Japan, to the chagrin of USIS.

68. Author interview with Wolfgang Lehmann, via telephone, Feb. 14, 2017.

69. "Martha Graham Tour Begins in Triumph"; "Brief Summary of Martha Graham's International Tours."

70. "First Lady Presides over Performance of Martha Graham Dance Company," Official Government News Agency translation, Oct. 6, 1974, MGC-MGF. During my inter-view with Eilber, she spoke about the metal grates, as she did with Croft. However, in a telephone interview with Wolfgang Lehmann, the chargé d'affaires at the American embassy in Saigon in 1974 who introduced the company on stage, he stated that the grates were not there; the theater was fully enclosed. He also recalls hearty applause at the end. Eilber then clarified and wrote in an email (Apr. 1, 2017) that the grates were at the side of the theater backstage, thus further confusing dancers who had to project to audiences both in front and directly to the side of them.

71. Author interview with Lehmann.

72. "Martha Graham Dance Group Has Sown Seeds of Modern Dance in Vietnam," USIS translation labeled "Chinese Press Reaction to Martha Graham Dance Group," *Vien Dong Daily*, Oct. 15, 1974, MGC-MGF; "First Lady Presides over Performance of Martha Graham Dance Company."

73. Young, *The Vietnam Wars*, 300–301.

74. "Poor Clown, Light Actress," USIS excerpts of *Tien Tuyen*, Oct. 12, 1974, MGC-MGF; author interview with Janet Eilber, February 19, 2009. Additional interviews with Eilber were conducted in March 2008, March 2010, and May 2011. Eilber has been too consumed with company management as artistic director to grant further interviews requested in 2016-2019 regarding Ron Protas.

75. Author interview with Lehmann.

76. Author interview with Lehmann.

77. Author interview with Eilber, Feb. 19, 2009. Note that Eilber recounted a similar story about the Saigon performance cited by Croft, *Dancers as Diplomats*, 136. See also "Martha Graham Tour Begins in Triumph"; nt, *Saigon Post*, Oct. 14, 1974, MGC-MGF; "Watching the Martha Graham Dance Company," USIS excerpts of *Song Than*, Oct. 12, 1974, MGC-MGF; Hai Vien, "We Were in a Kind of 'Alice in Wonderland' World," USIS excerpts of *Viet Hoa Daily*, Oct. 16, 1974, MGC-MGF.

78. "Agreement," Company Correspondence, 1974, box 239, folder 3, MGC-LOC.

79. FR: AmEmbTokyo, TO: AmEmbSingapore Priority, RE: Martha Graham Dance Company, Sept. 20, 1974, box 65, folder 4, UAK; "Brief Summary of Martha Graham's International Tours."

80. "Brief Summary of Martha Graham's International Tours"; Embassy Tokyo to Department of State, telegram, Sept. 4, 1974, box 65, folder 4, UAK; Embassy Manila to Embassy Singapore, Sept. 13, 1974, box 65, folder 3, Embassy Manila to Embassy Singapore, Sept. 13, 1974, box 65, folder 3, both UAK; Embassy Singapore to Department of State, telegram, nd, 1974, box 65, folder 4, UAK.

81. "Brief Summary of Martha Graham's International Tours"; FR: USIS Manila, TO: USINFO WasDC, Sept. 12, 1974, box 65, folder 3, UAK; "Graham Dance School: Strong Eastern Roots," *Times Journal: Business Day*, Sept. 14, 1974, 20, box 65, folder 5, UAK.

82. "Brief Summary of Martha Graham's International Tours."

83. Edward W. Said, *Orientalism* (New York: Pantheon, 1978).

84. "'It Is a Great Privilege to Go Back to Asia'—Martha Graham," *Philippines Evening Express*, Sept. 7, 1974, box 65, folder 5, UAK.

85. "Taipei All Praise for Graham Dancers," *Times Journal*, Sept. 8, 1974, box 65, folder 5, UAK.

86. "Brief Summary of Martha Graham's International Tours."

87. "Martha Graham and Dance Company Sets 3 Manila Performances," *Philippines Evening Express*, Aug. 17, 1974, 8, box 65, folder 5, UAK.

88. William D. Miller Jr., Acting Public Affairs Officer, US Information Service Taipei to USIA Washington, SU: The Martha Graham Dance Company, Sept. 24, 1974, Message No. 14, Elizabeth "Betty" Ford White House Papers, box 39, Graham, Martha—Dance Company (2), FORD.

89. "Manila Visit of Martha Graham Dance Company," *Bulletin Today*, Aug. 18, 1974, 25, box 65, folder 5, UAK.

90. "Transcript of Proceedings," 1970, 23.

91. Marjorie J. Spruill, *Divided We Stand: The Battle over Women's Rights and Family Values That Polarized American Politics* (New York: Bloomsbury, 2017), 43–46. Note that Ford's association with Graham as a "professional dancer" in New York is used by authors to frame her as a powerful and independent woman.

92. Graham, *Blood Memory*, 25.

93. Nancy Cott, *The Grounding of Modern Feminism* (New Haven, CT: Yale University Press, 1989); Myra Jehlen, "Archimedes and the Paradox of Feminist Criticism," *Signs* 6, no. 4 (Summer 1981): 575–601.

94. Graham, *Blood Memory*, 26.

95. Lisa Duggan and Nan D. Hunter, *Sex Wars: Sexual Dissent and Political Culture* (New York: Routledge, 1996).

96. Embassy Rangoon to Department of State, telegram, 1974, box 65, folder 4, UAK; *Hein Chung Yuan Pao*, Sept. 17, 1974, box 65, folder 6, UAK; "Brief Summary of Martha Graham's International Tours."

97. "Brief Summary of Martha Graham's International Tours."

98. Special thanks to Victoria Thoms for her work here.

99. "Brief Summary of Martha Graham's International Tours."

100. "'It Is a Great Privilege to Go Back to Asia'—Martha Graham."

101. Department of State, FR Embassy Rangoon, telegram, Oct. 4, 1974, box 65, folder 4, UAK.
102. Orosa-Goquingco, "Graham Extrapolates Emotion."
103. "Brief Summary of Martha Graham's International Tours."
104. Heather Miller, "A Woman Who Doesn't Believe in Age," *Bangkok Post*, Sept. 28, 1974, box 65, folder 6, UAK.
105. "Martha Graham's 'Rebirth.'"
106. Magsanoc, "Modern Dance 'High Priestess' and Troupe Here."
107. "Poor Clown, Light Actress."
108. *Prachachart*, Sept. 29, 1974, MGC-MGF.
109. "Martha on Private Life."
110. Embassy Singapore to Department of State, telegram, nd, 1974.
111. Sally Banes, "The Birth of the Judson Dance Theatre: 'Concert Dance' at Judson Church, July 6, 1962," *Dance Chronicle* 5, no. 2 (1982): 167–212; Jane Ram, "Legend in Her Time," *South China Morning Post*, Sept. 4, 1974, MGC-MGF.
112. See "Yvonne Rainer and 'Martha Graham' (Richard Move) in *Trio A*," http://www.dailymotion.com/video/x2ortnv (accessed August 25, 2017). Note the link has been removed in the United States, but access to the video can be obtained for a fee in the US and free of charge in some international markets.
113. "Martha Graham Tour Begins in Triumph."
114. "Martha Graham Dance Tour."
115. "Brief Summary of Martha Graham's International Tours."
116. Magsanoc, "Modern Dance 'High Priestess' and Troupe Here"; Embassy Taipei to Department of State, telegram, nd, 1974, box 65, folder 4, UAK; "Brief Summary of Martha Graham's International Tours"; clipping, na, nt, *Hsin Chung Yuan Pao*, Sept. 24, 1974, box 65, folder 6, UAK.
117. "Brief Summary of Martha Graham's International Tours"; FR: USIS Manila, TO: USINFO WasDC, Sept. 12, 1974, box 65, folder 3, UAK; "Graham Dance School: Strong Eastern Roots," 20.
118. Embassy Singapore to Department of State, telegram, nd, 1974; "Martha Graham Company Receiving High Praise during Southeast Asian Tour"; "Brief Summary of Martha Graham's International Tours"; press photo caption, *Daily Express*, Sept. 4, 1974, 1, box 65, folder 5, UAK; author interview with Eilber; "Brief Summary of Martha Graham's International Tours"; FR: USIS Manila, TO: USINFO WasDC, Sept. 12, 1974, box 65, folder 3, UAK; "Graham Dance School: Strong Eastern Roots."
119. "Brief Summary of Martha Graham's International Tours."
120. "Martha Graham Dance Tour."
121. "Brief Summary of Martha Graham's International Tours"; Singapore to Department of State, telegram, 1974, box 65, folder 4, UAK.
122. Ed Bradley, "CBS Evening News," aired Apr. 30, 1975, CBS News Archives, http://www.cbsnews.com/videos/1975-flashback-evacuation-of-saigon/ (accessed June 13, 2017).

Chapter 7

1. "Brief Summary of Martha Graham's International Tours." Note that this memo quotes, "To State Department, from Embassy (Jakarta)," 1974, box 198, folder 14, MGC-LOC; identical memo, box 65, folder 6, UAK.

2. Embassy Rangoon to Department of State, telegram, Oct. 4, 1974; Embassy Jakarta to State Department, nd, 1974, box 198, folder 14, MGC-LOC; identical memo, box 66, folders 6 and 2, UAK; "Taipei All Praise for Graham Dancers," *Times Journal* (Taipei), Sept. 8, 1974, box 65, folder 5, UAK; "Martha Graham Gets Warm Reception," *Bulletin Today*, Sept. 6, 1974, box 65, folder 5, UAK; Embassy Jakarta to State Department, 1974, box 198, folder 14, MGC-LOC, identical memo, box 66, folders 6 and 2, UAK.

3. "Brief Summary of Martha Graham's International Tours."

4. "TO: The President, FR: Henry A. Kissinger, SUBJECT: White House Appearance," Sept. 6, 1974, MC468, box 65, folder 2, UAK.

5. Fr: Tom Kerrigan, "Fact Sheet," June 19, 1975, Betty Ford Papers, Trip File, 1974–1977, box 10, folder 6/19–20, New York, Martha Graham (1), FORD.

6. Tsipursky, "Domestic Cultural Diplomacy and Soviet State-Sponsored Popular Culture in the Cold War," 985.

7. Betty Ford with Chris Chase, *Betty: A Glad Awakening* (New York: Doubleday, 1987), 35.

8. Greene, *Betty Ford*, 9–13.

9. Ford with Chase, *Betty*, 35.

10. Ford with Chase, *Betty*, 36.

11. Ford with Chase, *Betty*, 35.

12. Greene, *Betty Ford*, 12–13, 17.

13. To: Dear Friends, From: Betty Ford, Oct. 29, 1974, benefit brochure, the MacDowell Colony, Nov. 1974, Elizabeth Betty Ford White House Papers, box 39, Graham, Martha—Dance Company (1), FORD.

14. To: Mrs. Gerald Ford, Fr.: Mary-Lucy Smith, Benefit Chairman, the MacDowell Colony, Nov. 14, 1974, Elizabeth Betty Ford White House Papers, box 39, Graham, Martha—Dance Company (1), FORD.

15. Fr.: Martha, To: Betty, Dec. 17, 1974, Elizabeth Betty Ford White House Papers, box 39; folder, Graham, Martha—Dance Company (2), FORD.

16. To: Betty, Fr.: Nancy, envelope received by the White House Nov. 30, 1974, To: Dept of State—CU/CP, Fr: Embassy, Manilla [Sullivan], Info: USIA/IEA and All IEA Posts, Airgram 327, Sept. 26, 1974, Elizabeth Betty Ford White House Papers, box 39, Graham, Martha—Dance Company (2), FORD.

17. To: Martha, Fondly: Betty, Jan. 22, 1975, Elizabeth Betty Ford Papers, box 55, folder, Graham, Martha, FORD.

18. To: Martha, Fr.: Betty, April 18, 1975, Elizabeth Betty Ford White House Papers, box 39, Graham, Martha—Dance Company (1), FORD.

19. Anderson, "Rudolf Nureyev"; "Rudolf Nureyev Information; Fr.: Martha Graham," nd, Elizabeth Betty Ford White House Papers, box 39, Graham, Martha—Dance Company (1), FORD.

20. Anna Kisselgoff, "Fonteyn, Nureyev to Join Martha Graham in Benefit," *New York Times*, Apr. 18, 1975, 22.

21. Anderson, "Rudolf Nureyev."

22. "White House Photographs—Martha Graham," Rolls/Digital Files A5012–A5015, June 11, 1975, Photographer: Karl Schumacher, binder 52, FORD. Although publicity often stated that Ford "danced with Graham," implying that she had been a member of the company, in fact Graham's publicity stated that Ford studied with Graham in the late 1930s and early 1940s, and appeared with the company as a part of the "Assistant Dance Group" in 1938 for *American Document*. See Fr.: Tom Kerrigan, nd, "Betty Ford and Martha Graham: Background," Betty Ford Papers, Trip File, 1974–1977, box 10, folder 6/19-20, New York, Martha Graham (1), FORD.

23. To: Peter Sorum, Fr.: Susan Porter, "Action Memo," May 27, 1975, Betty Ford Papers, Trip File, 1974–1977, box 10, folder 6/19–20, New York, Martha Graham (1), FORD.

24. Note that a picture was taken with Ursula Reed, Graham's dresser.

25. Sheila Rabb Weidenfeld, *First Lady's Lady: With the Fords at the White House* (New York: G. P. Putnam's Sons, 1979), 35.

26. "Aspirations of the Past: *The Washington Post*," *Digest*, June 12, 1975, Betty Ford Papers, Trip File, 1974–1977, box 10, folder 6/19–20, New York, Martha Graham (2), FORD.

27. "Proposed Schedule: Mrs. Ford's Visit to New York City," June 13, 1975, Betty Ford Papers, Trip File, 1974–1977, box 10, folder 6/19–20, New York, Martha Graham (1); "White House Photographs—Martha Graham," Rolls/Digital Files A5145–A5149, June 19, 1975, Photographer: Karl Schumacher, binder 51, FORD.

28. "First Lady in Town for Gala Evening," *Daily News*, June 20, 1975, Betty Ford Papers, Trip File, 1974–1977, box 10, folder 6/19–20, New York, Martha Graham (2), FORD.

29. Judy Bachrach, "A Black Tie, Sneakers, and the First Lady on His Arm," *Washington Post*, June 21, 1975, C2, Betty Ford Papers, Trip File, 1974–1977, box 10, folder 6/19–20, New York, Martha Graham (2), FORD.

30. Kim Phillips-Fein, *Fear City: New York's Fiscal Crisis and the Rise of Austerity Politics* (New York: Henry Holt, 2017), 1. Note that I argue that Ford's Republican position on arts funding as a collaboration between government and the private sector can be seen as the seed of the transformation of the New York State Theater to the Koch Theater, and the like.

31. "It's an Historic Night for Dance," 50th Anniversary Celebration Catalogue, Martha Graham Dance Company, Betty Ford Papers, Trip File, 1974–1977, box 10, folder 6/19–20, New York, Martha Graham (1), FORD.

32. "Uris Theater Seating," nd, Betty Ford Papers, Trip File, 1974–1977, box 10, folder 6/19–20, New York, Martha Graham (1); "Statement from Martha Graham," attachment to a memo from Cynthia Parker, Sept. 24, 1976, for President and Mrs. Ford, Maria A. Downs Files, 1974–1977, Entertainment Files, 1974–1977, box 23, folder Martha Graham, FORD. This document includes a summary of donors (NEA, New York State Council on the Arts, Phelps Dodge, Mellon Foundation, Lila Acheson Wallace Fund [*Reader's Digest*], and other named and unnamed trustees and friends).

33. "Proposed Schedule: Mrs. Ford's Visit to New York City," June 13, Betty Ford Papers, Trip File, 1974–1977, box 10, folder 6/19–20, New York, Martha Graham (1), FORD.

34. "It's an Historic Night for Dance."

35. Bachrach, "A Black Tie, Sneakers, and the First Lady on His Arm"; Weidenfeld, *First Lady's Lady*, 148.

36. "White House Photographs—Martha Graham," Rolls/Digital Files A5145–A5149, June 19, 1975, photographer, Karl Schumacher, binder 51, FORD.

37. Anderson, "Rudolf Nureyev."

38. Weidenfeld, *First Lady's Lady*, 149.

39. "White House Photographs—Martha Graham," Rolls/Digital Files A6726, Oct. 2, 1975, photographer, Thomas, binder 68, FORD.

40. "White House Photographs—Martha Graham," Rolls/Digital Files A6721, Oct. 2, 1975, photographer, Kurt Schumacher, binder 68, FORD.

41. "White House Photographs—Martha Graham," Rolls/Digital Files A6749, Oct. 2, 1975, photographer, Fitz-Patrick, binder 68, FORD.

42. From: Tom Kerrigan, press release, MGDC, Oct 28, 1975, Elizabeth Betty Ford Papers, box 55, folder Graham, Martha, FORD.

43. Clive Barnes, "Dance: Miss Graham's Scarlet Letter," *New York Times*, Dec. 24, 1975, 11.

44. Alan M. Kriegsman, "A Legacy," *Washington Post*, Dec. 24, 1975, B1 and B2, 5.

45. Nancy Goldner, "Scarlet Letter—A 'Natural' for Martha Graham's Troupe," *Christian Science Monitor*, Dec. 29, 1975, 28.

46. Kriegsman, "A Legacy," B1 and B2, 5.

47. Frederick M. Winship, "Dance Review: Nureyev Performs," *Los Angeles Times*, Jan. 2, 1976, E11.

48. From: Tom Kerrigan, press release, MGDC.

49. "White House Photographs—Martha Graham," Rolls/Digital Files A8377, Feb. 16, 1976, photographer, Schumacher, binder 84, FORD; Greene, *Betty Ford*, 121, 144n8; see also John Pope, "Betty Ford," in *Modern First Ladies: Their Documentary Legacy*, ed. Nancy Kegan Smith and Mary C. Ryan (Washington, DC: Smithsonian Press, 1989), 553.

50. From Cynthia Parker, Martha Graham School of Contemporary Dance, to Beverly Gerstein, State Department Office of Cultural Affairs, June 4, 1976, MC 468, box 65, folder 2, UAK.

51. "Brief Summary of Martha Graham's International Tours."

52. "Brief Summary of Martha Graham's International Tours."

53. Author discussion with Mikhail Baryshnikov, Dec. 11, 2017. Transcript available with the permission of Mr. Baryshnikov. I offer deepest thanks to Joe and Diana Dimenna, Georgiana Pickett, and Vernon Scott for their thorough understanding of the issues involved with the planned tour, and their help obtaining the interview with Mr. Baryshnikov.

54. "White House Photographs—Martha Graham," Rolls/Digital Files A9865, May 17, 1976, photographer, Schumacher, binder 99, FORD.

55. Weidenfeld, *First Lady's Lady*, 130–31.

56. "White House Photographs—Martha Graham," Rolls/Digital Files A9866, May 17, 1976, photographer, Schumacher, binder 99, FORD.

57. Fr: Anne-Aymone Giscard d'Estaing, To: Mrs. Ford, via Department of State, Division of Language Services (Translation), Mar. 25, 1976, attachment to itinerary, First Lady's Staff, Maria Downs Files, 1974–1977, Social Events File, 1974–1977, box 4, Social Events File 1975/05/15, folder "Event—Reception 5/15/75," FORD; "White House Photographs—Martha Graham," Rolls/Digital Files A9882, May 18, 1976, photographer, Schumacher, binder 99, FORD.

58. To: Betty, Fr.: Martha, sent from the Watergate Hotel, nd (dinner was May 17, 1976), Elizabeth Betty Ford Papers, box 55, folder Graham, Martha; see also the same note on Graham Foundation stationery, typed, nd, Gerald and Betty Ford, Special Materials, box B2, folder Graham, Martha, FORD.

59. To: Mrs. Ford, Fr.: Ron Protas, May 18, 1976, Elizabeth Betty Ford Papers, box 55, folder Graham, Martha, FORD.

60. To: Miss Graham, Fr.: Gerald R. Ford, Aug. 30, 1976, Office of the Press Secretary, David Gergen Files, 1974–1977, Medal of Freedom Name File, 1973–1976, box 27, folder "Martha Graham," FORD; To: My Dear Betty, Fr.: Martha, May 12, 1976, Gerald and Betty Ford Special Materials, box B2, folder Graham, Martha, FORD.

61. To: Betty Ford, Fr.: Cynthia Parker, Sept. 3, 1976, Elizabeth Betty Ford Papers, box 55, folder Graham, Martha, FORD; For: President and Mrs. Ford, Fr.: Cynthia Parker, Sept. 24, 1976, Maria A. Downs Files, 1974–1977, Entertainment Files, 1974–1977, box 23, folder Martha Graham, FORD.

62. To: Betty Ford, Fr.: Cynthia Parker, Sept. 3, 1976.

63. Jean Libman Block, "The Betty Ford Nobody Knows," *Good Housekeeping*, May 1974, Sheila R. Weidenfeld Files (1924) 1974–1977, General Subject File, 1974–1977, box 36, clippings file, FORD.

64. To: Peter McPherson, Fr.: Susan Porter, Dec. 12, 1975, David Gergen Files, 1974–1977, David Gergen's Medal of Freedom Name Files, 1974–1977, box 27, folder "Martha Graham," FORD.

65. WWW, handwritten comments, Sept. 3, 1976, on a memorandum to William Nicholson from Susan Porter, Maria Downs Files, 1974–1977, Social Events File, 1974–1977, box 11, folder "Medal of Freedom," 1976/10/14, and 1976/07/22, FORD.

66. To: Paul Thesis, Fr.: Susan Porter, March 24, 1975; For: Dave Gergen, Fr.: Judy Muhlberg, Re: Martha Graham, July 27, 1976, David Gergen Files, 1974–1977, David Gergen's Medal of Freedom Name Files, 1974–1977, box 27, folder "Martha Graham," FORD.

67. Fr.: The Vice President, To: The President, Re: Presidential Initiative in the Arts, Sept. 14, 1976, Sarah C. Massengale Files, 1974–1977, Cultural Affairs File, 1975–1977, box 27, folder "Commission of Fine Arts," FORD.

68. Fr.: Jim Cannon, For: Phil Buchen, Robert T. Hartmann, Jack Marsh, Max Friedersdorf, Jim Lynn, Oct. 6, 1976, Sarah C. Massengale Files, 1974–1977, Cultural Affairs File, 1975–1977, box 27, folder "Commission of Fine Arts," FORD.

69. Handwritten note from "Massengale, approved by OMB," and "Fact Sheet: Cultural Challenge Grants Program," Sarah C. Massengale Files, 1974–1977, Cultural Affairs File, 1975–1977, box 27, folder "Commission of Fine Arts," FORD.

70. See Office of the White House Press Secretary, "Statement by the President, Oct. 10, 1976," Sarah C. Massengale Files, 1974–1977, Cultural Affairs File, 1975–1977, box 27, folder "Commission of Fine Arts," FORD. Also "Draft Statement on the President's Policy on the Arts," Fr: Jim Cannon, For: Phil Buchen, Robert T. Hartmann, Jack Marsh, Max Friedersdorf, Jim Lynn, Oct. 6, 1976, same folder "Commission of Fine Arts," FORD.

71. Distribution list attached to handwritten note from "Massengale, approved by OMB," "Fact Sheet: Cultural Challenge Grants Program," folder "Commission of Fine Arts—Policy on the Arts," Domestic Council, Sarah C. Massengale Files, 1974–1977, Cultural Affairs File, 1975–1977, box 27, folder "Commission of Fine Arts," FORD.

72. To: President Gerald R. Ford, Attn: Sheila Weidenfeld, From: Martha, Oct. 8, 1976, Elizabeth Betty Ford Papers, box 55, folder Graham, Martha, FORD.

73. To: Ms. Linda Baker, Fr.: Patricia S. Lindh, Department of State, "Brief Summary of Martha Graham's International Tours," Oct. 13, 1976, box 23, First Lady's Staff, Maria A. Downs Files, 1974–1977, Entertainment File, Events 1976/7/20, folder "Entertainment Events: Martha Graham," FORD.

74. Attachment to Linda Baker memo, To: Ms. Linda Baker, Fr.: Patricia S. Lindh, Department of State, "Brief Summary of Martha Graham's International Tours," attachment, Oct. 13, 1976, box 23, First Lady's Staff, Maria A. Downs Files, 1974–1977, Entertainment File, Events 1976/7/20, folder "Entertainment Events: Martha Graham," FORD. The word "climate" was underlined in the original.

75. Fr.: Nancy Hanks, For: Mrs. Ford, Re: Martha Graham Award, Oct. 3, 1976, Betty Ford Files, Local Events File, 1974–1977, box 7, folder 10-14-76 (2), FORD.

76. Betty Ford, handwritten note on "The White House" notepaper included with formal guest list, nd, Betty Ford Files, Local Events File, 1974–1977, box 7, folder 10-14-76 (2), FORD.

77. To: Mrs. Ford, Fr.: Maria Downs, "Guest List," handwritten note by Downs, Sept. 30, 1976, Betty Ford Files, Local Events File, 1974–1977, box 7, folder 10-14-76 (1), FORD.

78. "Proposed Guest List for Presidential Medal of Freedom Dinner," nd, Betty Ford Files, Local Events File, 1974–1977, box 7, folder 10-14-76 (2), FORD.

79. Henry Kissinger, *Years of Renewal: The Concluding Volume of His Memoirs* (New York: Touchstone, 1999), 373–74.

80. "Proposed Guest List for Presidential Medal of Freedom Dinner."

81. "Calligraphy Card Information, 10/14/76," Maria A. Downs Files, 1974–1977, Décor File, 1974-77, box 27, folder "Events 1976/10/14, Martha Graham," FORD; "Martha Graham: Biographical Information," Oct. 8, 1976, Betty Ford Files, Local Events File, 1974–1977, box 7, folder 10-14-76 (2), FORD.

82. "White House Photographs—Martha Graham," Rolls/Digital Files B1866, Oct. 15, 1976, Photographer: Schumacher, binder 119, FORD.

83. Gerald R. Ford, "The President's News Conference-898," Oct. 14, 1976, John Wooley and Gerhard Peters, *The American Presidency Project*, http://www.presidency.ucsb.edu/ws/index.php?pid=6462 (accessed June 13, 2017).

84. Dion E. Phillips, "Terrorism and Security in the Caribbean: The 1976 Cubana Disaster off Barbados," *Studies in Conflict and Terrorism* 14, no. 4 (1991): 211.

85. Ford, "The President's News Conference-898."

86. "Brief Summary of Martha Graham's International Tours"; Henry Kissinger to President Gerald Ford, Sept. 6, 1974, MC468, box 65, folder 2, UAK; Han Xu to Martha Graham, nd, box 231, folder 6, MGC-LOC; Gerald R. Ford, "Remarks upon Presenting the Presidential Medal of Freedom to Miss Martha Graham," Oct. 14, 1976, 4, Presidential Speeches: Reading Copies, FORD.

87. "Exchange of Remarks between the President and Martha Graham," Oct. 14, 1976, Office of the Press Secretary, David Gergen File, 1974–1977, Medal of Freedom Name File, 1973–1976, box 27, folder "Martha Graham," FORD.

88. "White House Photographs—Martha Graham," Rolls/Digital Files B1867, Oct. 15, 1976, Photographer: Karl Schumacher, binder 119, FORD.

89. "In Honor of Miss Martha Graham," The White House, Oct. 14, 1976, Maria A. Downs Files, 1974–1977, Entertainment File Events 1976/7/20, box 23, folder "Entertainment—Events: Martha Graham," FORD. The line drawing was taken from a picture of Peggy Lyman in *Frontier* sent by the Graham Company, picture #606-33, box 23, Maria A. Downs Files.

90. "White House Photographs—Martha Graham," Rolls/Digital Files B1871, Oct. 15, 1976, photographer, Schumacher, binder 119, FORD.

91. "An 'Overwhelming Moment'"; "White House Photographs—Martha Graham," Rolls/Digital Files B1871, Oct. 15, 1976, photographer, Schumacher, binder 119, FORD; see specifically frames with Janet Eilber, photographer, Schumacher, binder 119, FORD.

92. Joy Billington, "Everyone's Doing the Celebrity Hop," *Washington Star*, Aug. 3, 1975, F3, Sheila R. Weidenfeld Files (1924) 1974–1977, General Subject File, 1974–1977, box 36, clippings file, FORD.

93. For: Mrs. Ford, Fr: Maria Downs, "Dinner in Honor of Martha Graham," Oct. 14, 1976, Betty Ford Files, Local Events Files, 1974–1977, box 7, folder 10-14-76 (1). Graham sent the Ford administration a "Statement" during which she discussed finances and her creative patterns. She concluded, "For I have a firm belief and commitment towards the future of the works and my Company as an ongoing artistic entity." Martha Graham, "Statement from Martha Graham," attachment to a memo from Cynthia Parker, Sept. 24, 1976, for President and Mrs. Ford, Maria A. Downs Files, 1974–1977, Entertainment Files, 1974–1977, box 23, folder Martha Graham, FORD.

94. Handwritten to Betty, Fr.: Martha, Hotel George V stationery, postmarked Nov. 3, 1976, Elizabeth Betty Ford Papers, box 55, folder Graham, Martha, FORD.

95. To: Mr. President, Fr.: Martha Graham, Nov. 21, 1976, Gerald and Betty Ford Special Materials, box A5, folder Graham, Martha, FORD.

96. "White House Photographs—Martha Graham," Rolls/Digital Files B2271, Oct. 15, 1976, photographer, Schumacher, binder 123, FORD.

97. "White House Photographs—Martha Graham," Rolls/Digital Files B2271, Nov. 16, 1976, photographer, Schumacher, binder 123, FORD. Ford had to remain a Republican and not support government sponsorship of the arts, but rather he encouraged philanthropists and private foundations to give with the government "matching grant" embedded in H.R. 12838. He had initially planned to say, "I fear that total subsidization might bring with it the attendant philosophical problems of control and censorship," which was deleted in the end. See Office of the White House Press Secretary, "Statement by the President," Oct. 10, 1976, Sarah C. Massengale Files, 1974–1977, Cultural Affairs File, 1975–1977, box 27, folder "Commission of Fine Arts," FORD. Also "Draft Statement on the President's Policy on the Arts." He mentions that Betty Ford helped him understand the importance of the arts. Also note that Ron Protas pushed for a press photo of Ford and Graham for the benefit, but the White House said it wasn't necessary. To: Sheila Weidenfeld, Fr.: Susan Porter, June 2, 1975, Sheila R. Weidenfeld Files (1924) 1974–1977, Trip File, 1974–77, box 16, folder "6/11/75—New York City Martha Graham Benefit," FORD; also see box 11, folder "11/16/76—Kennedy Center—Martha Graham." A growing tension between the White House and Protas seems to have consistently been deflected by the grace, presence, and charisma of Graham herself.

Chapter 8

1. Author interview with Peggy Lyman, New York, Dec. 3, 2010, New York, NY; "At the Dedication of the Sackler Wing in the Metropolitan Museum of Art, The Martha Graham Dance Company Presents Lamentation and Frescoes, December 9, 1978, New York," program with thanks to the Arthur M. Sackler Foundation Archives, Stephanie Morillo. This program is also deposited at the Metropolitan Museum of Art Archive as an addendum to box 90, Exhibitions, 1978, folder 1, Temple of Dendur (Opening) 1978, Historical Clippings and Ephemera, 1880–1980, META. Note that the program can also be obtained for a fee through the Martha Graham Dance Company records by contacting Martha Graham Resources. A copy of the Graham Resources program has been deposited at the Metropolitan Museum of Art Archive by the author with the permission of Janet Eilber, and free access is offered by that archive.
2. Author interview with Lyman.
3. "Sackler Wing of Art Museum Is Dedicated," Register (Mobile, AL), Dec. 11, 1978, in box 90, Exhibitions, 1978, folder 1, Temple of Dendur (Opening) 1978, Historical Clippings and Ephemera, 1880–1980, META.
4. Associated Press, "Graham Troupe Opens Met Wing," Clarion Ledger (Jackson, MS), Dec. 12, 1978; "Sackler Wing of Art Museum Is Dedicated."
5. Author interview with Lyman.
6. Author conversation and email with Linda Hodes.
7. William Shakespeare, Antony and Cleopatra, act 2, scene 5.
8. Ronald H. Fritze, Egyptomania: A History of Fascination, Obsession and Fantasy (London: Reaktion Books, 2016), 343–46; Lucy Hughes-Hallett, Cleopatra: Histories, Dreams and Distortions (New York: Harper and Row, 1990).

9. William L. Cleveland and Martin Bunton, *A History of the Modern Middle East*, 4th ed. (New York: Perseus Books, 2009), 379; see also Salim Yaqub, *Imperfect Strangers: Americans, Arabs, and U.S.–Middle East Relations in the 1970s* (Ithaca, NY: Cornell University Press, 2016).

10. Gaddis Smith, *Morality, Reason and Power: American Diplomacy in the Carter Years* (New York: Hill and Wang, 1986), 161.

11. Nigel John Ashton, "Taking Friends for Granted: The Carter Administration, Jordan, and the Camp David Accords, 1977–1980," *Diplomatic History* 41, no. 3 (June 2017): 620–45.

12. Nigel John Ashton, *King Hussein of Jordan: A Political Life* (New Haven, CT: Yale University Press, 2008), 197.

13. Bob Woodward, "CIA Paid Millions to Jordan's King Hussein," *Washington Post*, Feb. 18, 1977, A1; Ashton, "Taking Friends for Granted," 629.

14. Ashton, *King Hussein of Jordan*, 203.

15. Ashton, *King Hussein of Jordan*, 208.

16. Ashton, *King Hussein of Jordan*, 256.

17. Ephraim Dowek, *Israeli-Egyptian Relations, 1980–2000* (London: Frank Cass, 2001), 160.

18. Dowek, *Israeli-Egyptian Relations*, 111.

19. Author interview with Sally Coombs Cowal, May 2, 2017, Washington, DC (transcript and recording available upon request). During the interview, she echoed other interviews, saying, "Nothing like that has happened since." In my interview with Ambassador Haim Koren, May 22, 2017, Jerusalem, Israel, he expressed deep hope for the future through music groups.

20. Dowek, *Israeli-Egyptian Relations*, 111, 120–22. Note that the efforts seemed to become "dead-letter diplomacy" within years of signing, with strains hitting the process of normalization during the cold peace. While it has been argued that the project of cultural exchange with troupes such as Graham's, art shows, and orchestras has achieved little, indeed the roadblocks put up by nations to thwart exchange testify to its power. If there were not potency, and there were not fears that the youth would absorb ideas from various nations, governments surely would not have been so eager to undermine projects. Author interview with Ephraim Dwork, May 22, 2017, Israel. Deep thanks to Yirael Medad and Rami Shtivi at the Begin Center, Jerusalem, Israel, who worked to find archival documents.

21. Sally Coombs Cowal, email with author and Barry Swersky, Apr. 25, 2017; author interview with Coombs Cowal.

22. Clippings file, nt, Aug. 10, 1979, Martha Graham 1984–1985, 221.2.1.5, IDA.

23. Author interview with Eilber.

24. Sylvia Hochfield, "Egyptomania in New York," *ARTnews*, Dec. 1978, in box 90, Exhibitions, 1978, folder 1, Temple of Dendur (Opening) 1978, Historical Clippings and Ephemera, 1880–1980, META.

25. Associated Press, "Ancient Temple Highlights Museum Exhibits," *Morning Avalanche-Journal* (Lubbock, TX), Sept. 16, 1978; "Temple Built in 15 B.C. Unveiled in New York," Baltimore Morning Sun, Sept. 16, 1978, both in box 90, Exhibitions,

1978, folder 1, Temple of Dendur (Opening) 1978, Historical Clippings and Ephemera, 1880–1980, META.

26. "Temple Built in 15 B.C. Unveiled in New York." Note that Arthur Sackler's language mirrors the 1954 Hague Convention's statement on "Cultural Heritage" and the protection of culture, and later UNESCO's declarations. See Janet Ulph and Ian Smith, *The Illicit Trade in Art and Antiquities: International Recovery and Criminal and Civil Liability* (Oxford: Heart Publishing, 2012), 5, 31, 33; Sam Quinones, *Dreamland: The True Tale of America's Opiate Epidemic* (New York: Bloomsbury, 2015; reprint, 2016), 28–30, 232–35.

27. Associated Press, "New York Art Museum Unveils an Ancient Temple from Egypt," *Plain Dealer* (Cleveland, OH), Sept. 17, 1978, in box 90, Exhibitions, 1978, folder 1, Temple of Dendur (Opening) 1978, Historical Clippings and Ephemera, 1880–1980, META.

28. Associated Press, "Egyptian Temple Unveiled," *Sunday Record* (Hackensack, NJ), Sept. 16, 1978, box 90, Exhibitions, 1978, folder 1, Temple of Dendur (Opening) 1978, Historical Clippings and Ephemera, 1880–1980, META.

29. Byron Belt, "On the Arts," *Newhouse News Service*, nd, box 90, Exhibitions, 1978, folder 1, Temple of Dendur (Opening) 1978, Historical Clippings and Ephemera, 1880–1980, META.

30. http://www.gettyimages.com/event/martha-graham-benefit-at-studio-54-june-22-1978-75121052?#doris-duke-during-martha-graham-benefit-at-studio-54-june-22-1978-at-picture-id105592274 (accessed June 14, 2017).

31. "Thoughts of a Not Necessarily Diplomatic Nature about a Diplomatic Tour," "Israel," private archives of Terese Capucilli, New York, NY. Special thanks to Ms. Capucilli, who has been so generous with her papers and time in support of this project.

32. Newhouse News Service, "Ancient Egypt Exhibits 'Hot,'" *Fresno Bee*, Sept. 24, 1978, in box 90, Exhibitions, 1978, folder 1, Temple of Dendur (Opening) 1978, Historical Clippings and Ephemera, 1880–1980, META.

33. Harriet Senie, "Shades of Egypt: A Temple in the Met," *New York Post*, Dec. 28, 1978, in box 90, Exhibitions, 1978, folder 1, Temple of Dendur (Opening) 1978, Historical Clippings and Ephemera, 1880–1980, META.

34. Jerry Adler, "Joan of Arts Tours City's Little Egypt," *New York Daily Press*, Sept. 28, 1978, in box 90, Exhibitions, 1978, folder 1, Temple of Dendur (Opening) 1978, Historical Clippings and Ephemera, 1880–1980, META.

35. Joan Mondale to Susan Weil, Program Director, Dance Program, NEA, June 30, 1977, Public Affairs Center, box 35, 154.I.19.B, Folder AR 1-2, Dancers, 1977–1980, MONDALE.

36. From Merce Cunningham to Joan Mondale, Sept. 26, 1978, Public Affairs Center, box 7, ID:144.E.6.1B, folder "Merce Cunningham Dance Company," July 2, 1978, MONDALE.

37. Fr: Mondale, to Mrs. Eugene M. Schwartz, Oct. 5, 1978, Public Affairs Center, box 7, ID:144.E.6.1B, folder "Merce Cunningham Dance Company," July 2, 1978, MONDALE.

38. To Ronald and Jo Carol Lauder, Oct. 13, 1978 Fr: Mondale, Public Affairs Center, box 7, ID:144.E.6.1B, folder "Merce Cunningham Dance Company," July 2, 1978, MONDALE.

39. Linda Winer, "Martha Graham: 'Only Constant Is Change,'" *Chicago Tribune*, Nov. 16, 1979, B2.

40. Sanjeev Khagram, *Dams and Development: Transnational Struggles for Water and Power* (Ithaca, NY: Cornell University Press, 2004), 82.

41. Douglas Little, "The Cold War in the Middle East: Suez Crisis to Camp David Accords," in *The Cambridge History of the Cold War*, vol. 2, *Crisis and Détente*, ed. Melvyn P. Leffler and Odd Arne Westad, (New York: Cambridge University Press, 2010), 306.

42. Little, "The Cold War in the Middle East," 307.

43. Little, "The Cold War in the Middle East," 307; Dale Whittington and Giorgio Guariso, *Water Management Models in Practice: A Case Study of the Aswan High Dam* (London: Elsevier Science, 1983), 34.

44. Little, "The Cold War in the Middle East," 310.

45. Little, "The Cold War in the Middle East," 312.

46. Cyril Aldred, *The Temple of Dendur* (New York: Metropolitan Museum of Art, 1978), 67.

47. Christina Luke and Morag Kersel, *U.S. Cultural Diplomacy and Archaeology: Soft Power, Hard Heritage* (New York: Routledge, 2012), 7.

48. Luke and Kersel, *U.S. Cultural Diplomacy and Archaeology*, 8; Canning, *On the Performance Front*, 15.

49. Luke and Kersel, *U.S. Cultural Diplomacy and Archeology*, 9, 10; note the "growing body of scholarship that explores the linkages between archeology and foreign relations" (15).

50. Aldred, *The Temple of Dendur*, 67.

51. Milton Esterow, "Metropolitan Due to Get Temple of Dendur," *New York Times*, Apr. 26, 1967, 1; "LBJ Sets Group to Pick Temple Site," *Chicago Tribune*, Jan. 23, 1967, A2.

52. Aldred, *The Temple of Dendur*, 67.

53. Isabella Ginor and Gideon Remez, *The Soviet-Israeli War, 1967–1973: The USSR's Military Intervention in the Egyptian-Israeli Conflict* (New York: Oxford University Press, 2017).

54. Dr. Henry G. Fischer, Curator of Egyptian Art, the Metropolitan Museum of Art, "The Temple of Dendur Comes to New York City [Draft]," for *ARAMCO Magazine*, 14, in box 90, Exhibitions, 1978, folder "Dendur Temple—Clippings and Press Releases," Historical Clippings and Ephemera, 1880–1980, META.

55. United Press International, "Then and Now," *The Youngstown Vindicator*, nd, in box 90, Exhibitions, 1978, folder 1, Temple of Dendur (Opening) 1978, Historical Clippings and Ephemera, 1880–1980, META.

56. Franz Schulze, "Art: Dendur Shines in Tut's Shadow," *Sun Times* (Chicago, IL), Dec. 24, 1978, 2, box 90, Exhibitions, 1978, folder 1, Temple of Dendur (Opening) 1978, Historical Clippings and Ephemera, 1880–1980, META.

57. Sarah Lansdell, "Gift Temple from Egypt to Open at Metropolitan," *Louisville Courier-Journal*, Sept. 3, 1978, box 90, Exhibitions, 1978, folder 1, Temple of Dendur (Opening) 1978, Historical Clippings and Ephemera, 1880–1980, META.

58. "The Play's the Thing," *Newsweek*, Dec. 27, 1971, 30, box 90, Exhibitions, 1978, folder 1, Temple of Dendur (Opening) 1978, Historical Clippings and Ephemera, 1880–1980, META.

59. Julian E. Zelizer, "Conservatives, Carter, and the Politics of National Security," in *Rightward Bound*, ed. Bruce J. Schulman and Julian E. Zelizer, (Cambridge, MA: Harvard University Press, 2008), 270.

60. Seth Anziska, "Camp David's Shadow: The United States, Israel, and the Palestinian Question, 1977–1993" (PhD diss., Columbia University in the City of New York, 2015); also Anziska, *Preventing Palestine: A Political History from Camp David to Oslo* (Princeton, NJ: Princeton University Press, 2018).

61. Memorandum of Conversation, Cairo, Feb. 17, 1977, 7–8:45 PM, Doc 10, *FRUS, 1977–1980*, vol. 8, 52, quoted in Anziska, *Camp David's Shadow*, 264.

62. Aldred, *The Temple of Dendur*, 67.

63. Aldred, *The Temple of Dendur*, 71.

64. Associated Press, "Temple of Dendur Unveiled at the Met," *Star* (Newark, NJ), Sept. 28, 1978, box 90, Exhibitions, 1978, folder 1, Temple of Dendur (Opening) 1978, Historical Clippings and Ephemera, 1880–1980, META; Aldred, *The Temple of Dendur*, 77.

65. Associated Press, "Temple of Dendur Unveiled at the Met."

66. Aldred, *The Temple of Dendur*, 78.

67. Maximillian Gottlieb, "Ridiculous Display," *New York Post*, Oct. 18, 1978, box 90, Exhibitions, 1978, folder 1, Temple of Dendur (Opening) 1978, Historical Clippings and Ephemera, 1880–1980, META.

68. Franz Schulze, "Art: Dendur Shines in Tut's Shadow," *Sun Times* (Chicago), Dec. 24, 1978, 2, box 90, Exhibitions, 1978, folder 1, Temple of Dendur (Opening) 1978, Historical Clippings and Ephemera, 1880–1980, META.

69. Schulze, "Art: Dendur Shines in Tut's Shadow," 2, box 90, Exhibitions, 1978, folder 1, Temple of Dendur (Opening) 1978, Historical Clippings and Ephemera, 1880–1980, META; Hochfield, "Egyptomania in New York."

70. Ada Louise Huxtable, "On Architecture," *New York Times*, Dec. 31, 1978, 21.

71. Jenab Tutunji, "Martha Graham Dance Company to End World Tour with Performance in Amman," Jordan Times, Aug. 11, 1979, clippings, from the private archives of Georgette Gebara.

72. Jimmy Carter, "Universal Declaration of Human Rights Remarks at a White House Meeting Commemorating the 30th Anniversary of the Declaration's Signing," Dec. 6, 1978, http://www.presidency.ucsb.edu/ws/?pid=30264 (accessed November 19, 2016).

73. "A Nubian Temple from the First Century B.C. Finds a 20th-Century Home at the Metropolitan Museum," *Architectural Record*, Oct. 1978, box 90, Exhibitions, 1978, folder 1, Temple of Dendur (Opening) 1978, Historical Clippings and Ephemera, 1880–1980, META.

74. Fritze, *Egyptomania*, 237.

75. Fritze, *Egyptomania*, 240.

76. I was allowed free access to a taped version of the work performed at the Kennedy Center in Washington, DC, in December 1979. Unfortunately, access to that recording is no longer available. For an hourly fee, scholars can see the film through the Martha Graham Dance Company.

77. Adler, "Joan of Arts."

78. Huxtable, "On Architecture."

79. Adler, "Joan of Arts."

80. Linda Winer, "Graham Dances Retain Their Overwhelming Potency," *Chicago Tribune*, Nov. 19, 1979, A6.

81. For Bess Abell, FR: Peter N. Kyros, Jr., Office of the Vice President, July 18, 1977, Folder: AR-Confidential; To: Jamie Wyeth, FR: Jimmy, Jan. 25, 1977, box AR-1, folder: AR Executive 1/20/77–2/28/77, White House Central File, Subject File, Arts, CARTER.

82. Cull, *The Cold War and the United States Information Agency*, 358–68.

83. For: The President, FR: Bert Lance, SU: Approach to Congress Concerning the Reorganization of International Exchange and Information Programs, Aug. 26, 1977, box 6, folder, USIA, Barry Jagoda Papers, Donated Historical Materials, Special Projects, CARTER.

84. Jimmy Carter, Executive Order (International Communication Agency), Feb. 14, 1978, box 178, folder: Cultural Affairs [O/A 6235], Staff Offices, Domestic Policy Staff, Stuart Eizenstat, CARTER; To Abdalla El Ghareeb Ahmed, FR Carter, box AR-1, folder: AR Executive 1/1/79–1/20/80, White House Central File, Subject File, Arts, CARTER.

85. Sally Banes, ed., *Reinventing the Dance in the 1960s: Everything Was Possible* (Madison: University of Wisconsin Press, 2003), 151. Note that Mary Hinkson first traveled to the British capital to teach, but the establishment of the London School of Contemporary Dance has been credited to other dancers who taught in London, including Ethel Winter. The most influential director of the school who taught Graham technique was Jane Dudley.

86. Author interview with Eilber; author interview with Lyman.

87. Radina Vučetić, *Koka-Kola Socijalizam* (Beograd: Službeni Glasnik, 2012), 224–304, translated for the author by Natalija Dimic.

88. Maja Bezjak, "Balet, atraktivni gost Dubrovačkih ljetnih igara!," in *Dubrovačke ljetne igre 1950–1989* (Zagreb: Festival Dubrovnik, 1989), 3, translated for the author by Natalija Dimic.

89. Jörg Baten, *A History of the Global Economy: From 1500 to the Present* (New York: Cambridge University Press, 2016), 64.

90. Vučetić, *Koka-Kola Socijalizam*, 24.

91. Bezjak, "Balet, atraktivni gost Dubrovačkih ljetnih igara!"

92. Bezjak, "Balet, atraktivni gost Dubrovačkih ljetnih igara!"

93. Author interview with Lyman; author interview with Eilber.

94. Winer, "Martha Graham."

95. Author interview with Georgette Gebara, former director of Beirut School of Dance, July 18, 2012, Beirut, Lebanon.

96. Author interview with Lyman; "Thoughts of a Not Necessarily Diplomatic Nature about a Diplomatic Tour," "Israel," private archives of Terese Capucilli, New York, NY; Bat Dor Dance Company, press release, Aug. 15, 1979, Martha Graham 1984–1985, 221.2.2.2, IDA.

97. "Thoughts of a Not Necessarily Diplomatic Nature about a Diplomatic Tour."

98. "Thoughts of a Not Necessarily Diplomatic Nature about a Diplomatic Tour."

99. Author interview with Lyman. In 2012, the author tried to interview Queen Noor about the performances, but, according to her assistant, she did not recall the events.

100. Fawzia Mai, "Martha Graham Dance Class Brings N.Y. Style to Amman," *Jordan Times*, Aug. 29, 1979, clipping, private archives of Georgette Gebara.

101. Author interview with Gebara.

102. Cleveland and Bunton, *A History of the Modern Middle East*, 373.

103. Cleveland and Bunton, *A History of the Modern Middle East*, 386.

104. Mai, "Martha Graham Dance Class Brings N.Y. Style to Amman."

105. Winer, "Martha Graham."

106. Author interview with Eilber.

107. Fawzia Mai, "Two Evenings with Martha Graham," *Jordan Times*, nd, 1979, clipping, the private papers of Georgette Gebara.

108. Tutunji, "Martha Graham Dance Company to End World Tour."

109. Mai, "Two Evenings with Martha Graham."

110. For a nuanced understanding of the French impact on cultural diplomacy with Egypt, see Dowek, *Israeli-Egyptian Relations*, 22–23.

111. Dowek, *Israeli-Egyptian Relations*, 25.

112. "Un Evenement Qui Attire Aussi Beaucoup de Libanais," *Le Orient-Le Jour*, Aug. 7, 1979, clipping, private archives of Georgette Gebara.

113. Author interview with Hiam Koren, May 22, 2017, Jerusalem, Israel.

114. "Martha Graham Dance Company Perform in Cairo Soon," *Egyptian Gazette*, Aug. 2, 1979, 4, clipping, private archives of Georgette Gebara; Gebara, email exchange with author, July 16, 2012.

115. Hochfield, "Egyptomania in New York."

116. Tutunji, "Martha Graham Dance Company to End World Tour."

117. Mai, "Two Evenings with Martha Graham."

118. Tutunji, "Martha Graham Dance Company to End World Tour."

119. Tutunji, "Martha Graham Dance Company to End World Tour."

120. Author interview with Lyman.

121. Author interview with Gebara.

122. Author interview with Coombs Cowal.

123. Author interview with Coombs Cowal.

124. Usama al-Mansi, "Martha Graham Inspires American Ballet in Cairo," *Rose-al-Yousef*, Aug. 7, 1979, clipping in USIS translation, MGC-MGF.

125. Tutunji, "Martha Graham Dance Company to End World Tour."

126. Mai, "Two Evenings with Martha Graham."

127. Dora Sowden, "Martha Graham's Magic," *Jerusalem Post*, Aug. 24, 1979, 6.

128. Martha Graham quoted, newspaper clipping, nt, Martha Graham 1984–1985, 221.2.1.4, IDA.
129. "Meeting between Committee on Autonomy, Chairman Dr. J. Burg, Minister of Interior and USA Secretary of State, Mr. Alexander Haig, Jan. 28, 1982, 8:10 AM, Cabinet Room, Government Secretariat, Prime Minister's Office, Jerusalem," MFA-6898/8, ISA.
130. Dowek, *Israeli-Egyptian Relations*, 226.
131. Marianne Hirabi, email to author, May 15, 2012.
132. Barbara Farrar Karkabi, "Choreography in Cairo: Classical Ballet Comes to Egypt," *Saudi Aramco World* 28, no. 2 (March/April 1977); al-Mansi, "Martha Graham Inspires American Ballet in Cairo."
133. al-Mansi, "Martha Graham Inspires American Ballet in Cairo."
134. al-Mansi, "Martha Graham Inspires American Ballet in Cairo."
135. "What Says Martha Graham to Najwa Fouad?," *Al-Akhbar*, Aug. 6, clipping in USIS translation, MGC-MGF.
136. Winer, "Martha Graham."
137. Winer, "Martha Graham."
138. Author interview with Coombs Cowal.
139. Author interview with Eilber.
140. Dowek, *Israeli-Egyptian Relations*, 168.
141. FR: AmEmbassy Cairo, To HQ USAF, Department of State, SU: Request for Use of Air Force Plane, Oct. 1, 1979, 16340 120950Z, Central Foreign Policy Files, 1973–79/Electronic Telegrams, RG 59: General Records of the Department of State, National Archives, https://www.archives.gov/ (accessed May 15, 2017).
142. Dora Sowden, "VIP Plane Brought Martha Graham Here," *Jerusalem Post*, nd, clipping, GV1702, SOW (1977–1981), DA-I.
143. Bat Dor, press release.
144. Author interview with Coombs Cowal.
145. Bat Dor, press release.
146. Author interview with Coombs Cowal.
147. Author interview with Hodes.
148. Eshel interview with Rothschild.
149. Benham interview with Gluck.
150. Rita Delfiner, "A Biblical Theme for Graham in Israel," *New York Post*, May 31, 1974, box 372, clippings, MGC-LOC.
151. Dora Sowden, "Martha Graham's Magic," *Jerusalem Post*, Aug. 24, 1979, 6.
152. Martha Graham quoted, newspaper clipping, nt, Martha Graham 1984–1985, 221.2.1.4, IDA.
153. Clippings, nt, July 20, 1979, Martha Graham 1984–1985, 221.2.1.5, 221.2.1.6, IDA.
154. Mai, "Two Evenings with Martha Graham."
155. Tutunji, "Martha Graham Dance Company to End World Tour."
156. Author interview with Coombs Cowal.
157. Author interview with Coombs Cowal.
158. Author interview with Coombs Cowal.

159. AmEmbassy Amman to Secretary of State, SU: King Hussein's Interest in Meeting Prior to Departure to Havana, Secret, Oct. 1, 1979, 05341 271412Z, Central Foreign Policy Files, 1973–79/Electronic Telegrams, RG 59: General Records of the Department of State, National Archives, https://www.archives.gov/ (accessed May 15, 2017).

160. "The Independence Medal in Jordan is in five degrees (one to five). The first degree medal is granted to people of the level of Prime Ministers and Ministers, the second degree is granted to Secretary Generals and Head of Departments, the rest of the degrees are granted to employees of lower level ranks." See *Official Website of Jordan, Laws and Regulations,* http://www.lob.gov.jo/ui/main.html (accessed May 1, 2016).

161. Author interview with Coombs Cowal.

162. Jen Carlson, "Flashback: New York City, 1978–1980," *Gothamist,* Jan. 31, 2011, photo by Frank Florianz, http://gothamist.com/2011/01/31/flashback_new_york_city_1978-1980.php#photo-21 (accessed June 15, 2017).

163. Linda Winer, "Graham Dances Retain Their Overwhelming Potency," *Chicago Tribune,* Nov. 19, 1979, A6.

164. Stephen Godfrey Hamilton, "Martha Graham: Dance Power Stays," *Toronto Globe and Mail,* Nov. 27, 1979, 17.

165. Winer, "Martha Graham."

166. "Top Stars among Artists in 'The Kennedy Center Honors,'" *Afro-American,* Dec. 29, 1979, 11.

167. Barbara Gamarekian, "Kennedy Center Honors Five for Life Achievements in Arts," *New York Times,* Dec. 3, 1979, C14.

168. Gamarekian, "Kennedy Center Honors Five for Life Achievements in Arts."

169. Zelizer, "Conservatives, Carter, and the Politics of National Security," 280–81.

170. Gamarekian, "Kennedy Center Honors Five for Life Achievements in Arts"; "Top Stars among Artists in 'The Kennedy Center Honors.'"

171. Gamarekian, "Kennedy Center Honors Five for Life Achievements in Arts."

172. TO: Hamilton Jordan, FR: Len Hirsch, Betty Rainwater, Bill Simpson, Jan Esbeck, RE: Morale Issues, Oct. 18, 1979; FR: Leonard Hirsch, TO: Betty Rainwater, Bill Simpson, Jan Esbeck, Oct. 25, 1979, box 207, Subject Files, White House Morale Issues, Staff Offices: Chief of Staff, Len Hirsch, CARTER.

173. Winer, "Martha Graham."

174. Dana Taylor, "CBS 2 News Sunday," *WCBS-TV,* New York City, May 18, 2003.

175. Yitshak Shamir, "Foreword," in Dowek, *Israeli-Egyptian Relations,* xii.

176. Zelizer, "Conservatives, Carter, and the Politics of National Security," 278–79.

177. Zelizer, "Conservatives, Carter, and the Politics of National Security," 283.

178. Anziska, *Preventing Palestine.*

179. Zelizer, "Conservatives, Carter, and the Politics of National Security," 285–86.

180. "Cultural Agreement between the State of Israel and the Arab Republic of Israel," May 8, 1980, signed Eliahu Ben Elissar [First Israeli Ambassador to Egypt], and unrecognizable signature [J.G.] "For the Government of the Arab Republic of Egypt," Treaties Department, Ministry of Foreign Affairs, National Archive, Israel. Note that Saad Mortada was the Egyptian ambassador to Israel at the time. Received via email.

181. Winer, "Martha Graham."

Chapter 9

1. Patrick Major, *Behind the Berlin Wall: East Germany and the Frontiers of Power* (New York: Oxford University Press, 2010), 1.
2. "Neue Berliiner Illustrierte" *Neues Deutschland*, Feb. 16, 1987, 1, LA; "Graham Company im Metropol," *Neues Deutschland*, Feb. 18, 1987, LA.
3. "Graham Company im Metropol."
4. Petra Goedde, *The Politics of Peace: A Global Cold War History* (New York: Oxford University Press, 2019).
5. Andrew J. Webber, *Berlin in the Twentieth Century: A Cultural Topography* (Cambridge: Cambridge University Press, 2008), 14; Dirk Verheyen, *United City, Divided Memories? Cold War Legacies in Contemporary Berlin* (Lanham, MD: Lexington Books, 2010), 216; Ernst Diehl, *Komitee der Deutschen Demokratischen Republik zum 750 jährigen Bestehen von Berlin* (Berlin: Dietz, 1986); Diehl, *750 Years of Berlin: A Selection of Events from the 1987 Anniversary Programme* (East Berlin: Panorama, 1987).
6. Rolf Steininger, *The German Question: The Stalin Note of 1952 and the Question of German Reunification* (New York: Columbia University Press, 1990).
7. "1983 Report of the United States Advisory Commission on Public Diplomacy," 12, Robert R. Reilly Files, box 19, folder OA 12421, RRL.
8. Cummings, *Radio Free Europe's "Crusade for Freedom"*; Monique Kil, "A Penny for Every Word: Radio Free Europe's Call for 'Truth Dollars'" (paper presented at the *Radio Free Europe/Radio Liberty Conference*, European Institute and Harriman Institute, Columbia University in the City of New York, March 24, 2017).
9. R. W. Apple Jr., "President Urges Global Crusade for Democracy," *New York Times*, June 9, 1982.
10. Ronald Reagan, Charles Wick Testimonial Dinner, Thursday, Nov. 17, 1988, Presidential Handwriting File, Series III, Presidential Speeches, 9/27/88–12/31/88, box 34, folder 688, RRL.
11. "1983 Report of the United States Advisory Commission on Public Diplomacy," 13.
12. Taylor, *The Berlin Wall: A World Divided*, 385.
13. Ford with Chase, *Betty*, 201.
14. Martha Graham: Program, Kennedy Center, Washington, DC, Feb. 1981, box 31, 144.G.11.4F, Folder, Dance 1981–1983, MONDALE.
15. Anna Kisselgoff, "Dance: Martha Graham Presents 'Acts of Light,'" Feb. 27, 1981, *New York Times*, C18.
16. "Martha Graham: The Dancer Revealed," *American Masters* (season 8, episode 2), PBS, aired May 13, 1994.
17. Holly Brubach, interview in "Martha Graham: The Dancer Revealed," *American Masters*, aired May 13, 1994.
18. Author interview with Janet Eilber, February 19, 2009.
19. Clive Barnes, interview in "Martha Graham: The Dancer Revealed," *American Masters*, aired May 13, 1994.

20. Dearest Nancy [Reagan], Fr Barry [Goldwater], Dec. 11, 1981, WHORM, Subject File, PR 014-12, box 2, file 053119, RRL.

21. To: Frederick J. Ryan, Jr., Fr: Faith Whittlesey, RE: Presidential Appointments, Schedule Proposal, Oct. 27, 1983, Robert R. Reilly Files, box 19, folder transition file, OA 12421, RRL; 1983 Report of the United States Advisory Commission on Public Diplomacy, 1, 10, 9, 11.

22. C125-75, Fitz-Patrick, Dinner for the Carsens, Oct. 4, 1983, AV Department, RRL.

23. To: Miss Martha Graham, Fr: F. S. M. Hodsoll, Sept. 13, 1983, WHORM Alpha File, box 28, folder Martha Graham, RRL.

24. Anna Kisselgoff, "Dance View: Graham Protests," *New York Times*, Sept. 18, 1983, 2–12 (also in Appointment Process Personal Interview Record, Mar. 14, 1985, Counsel to the President: Appointment Files, CFOA 901-908, box 11, folder "Martha Graham," RRL).

25. To: Mr. Ronald Reagan, Fr: Jonathan McPhee, Nov. 8, 1983, WHORM Subject File FA (Federal Aid), 002 (Arts), box 24, folder 191000-199999, 191151; To: President and Mrs. Ronald Reagan, Fr: Gregory Peck, Oct. 6, 1983, WHORM Subject File, FA 002, box 24, folder 160000-190999, 174164, RRL.

26. Jennifer Dunning, "Martha Graham's Year," *New York Times*, Dec. 7, 1983, C25 (also in Appointment Process Personal Interview Record, Mar. 14, 1985, Counsel to the President: Appointment Files, CFOA 901-908, box 11, folder Martha Graham, RRL).

27. Dear President and Mrs. Reagan, Sincerely, Martha [Graham], Feb. 12, 1984, WHORM Subject File, ME (Messages), ME-001, folder 2088552, RRL.

28. To: Ms. Dodie Livingston, Fr: Diana D. Aldridge, Feb. 23, 1984, WHORM Subject File, ME (Messages), ME-001, folder 2088552, RRL.

29. Dear Martha, Fr: Ronald Reagan, Feb. 24, 1984, WHORM Subject File, ME (Messages), ME-001, folder 2088552, RRL.

30. To: President & Mrs. Ronald Reagan, Fr: Martha Graham, Apr. 17, 1984; Dear Miss Graham, Fr: Frederick J. Ryan, Jr., WHORM Subject File, PR (Public Relations), 014-12, box 10, folder 239161, RRL.

31. For: Theresa Elmore, Fr: Frank Hodsoll, June 27, 1984, Office of the First Lady, Projects Office: Records, OA18761, box 14, folder Martha Graham Dance Co. 15th Anniversary [NB date mistake on file], 9/15/1984.

32. Jennifer Dunning, "250,000 Film Grant to Miss Graham," *New York Times*, July 19, 1984, C13 (also in Appointment Process Personal Interview Record, Mar. 14, 1985, Counsel to the President: Appointment Files, CFOA 901-908, box 11, folder Martha Graham, RRL). Note that the grant funded the filming of the dances, voice-overs added to existing films, oral histories and interviews, and adding music to the silent film of *Frontier*. Although the films and interviews would be freely opened to the public at both UCLA and the Graham Center in New York, the terms of the grant have not been met, with the access to these projects limited to scholars who can afford to gain access to the materials in New York, when produced, 2017.

33. Dear Martha, Sincerely Ronald Reagan, Sept. 11, 1984, WHORM Subject File, ME (Messages), 001, box 80, folder 256157, RRL.

34. "Los Angeles Tribute to Martha Graham," flyer, Office of the First Lady, Projects Office: Records, OA18761, box 14, folder Martha Graham Dance Co. 15th Anniversary [NB date mistake on file], 9/15/1984.

35. To: Donna Blume, Fr: Jeanne Rhinelander, RE: Presidential Letter to Arrive No Later Than September 13, 1984, Sept. 7, 1984, WHORM Subject File, ME 001, box 80, folder 256157, RRL.

36. To Miss Martha Graham, Fr: Nancy Reagan, Sept. 10, 1984, WHORM Subject File, GI, 002, folder 255892, RRL.

37. Federal Bureau of Investigation (FBI) Personality Files (Michael Ravnitzky Donation), box 12, Martha Graham file, NSA; also found in the Victoria Phillips Collection, LOC, with a later request date. Note that the Ravintzky file is the most complete and ordered earlier.

38. Federal Bureau of Investigation (FBI) Personality Files.

39. "Martha Graham, Personal Data Statement," nd, attachment to "Appointment Process Personal Interview Record," Mar. 14, 1985, Counsel to the President: Appointment Files, CFOA 901-908, box 11, folder Martha Graham, RRL.

40. Pearl Lang, interview in "Martha Graham: The Dancer Revealed," *American Masters* (season 8), PBS, aired May 13, 1994.

41. "Suit against Martha Graham by Ex-Dancer Is Settled," *New York Times*, Nov. 15, 1963, 25.

42. The White House, Office of the Press Secretary, Mar. 21, 1985, WHORM Subject File, ME (Messages), 001, box 98, folder 308380, RRL.

43. C285-36, Potus & Flotus at Arts and Humanities Luncheon, Apr. 23, 1985, AV Department, RRL.

44. Dear Mr. President, Fr. Martha, nd, WHORM Subject File, ME (Messages), 001, box 98, folder 308380, RRL; also Presidential Handwriting File, Series II: Presidential Records, 3/1/85–5/28/85, box 12, folder 308380, RRL.

45. Dear Mr. President, Sincerely Martha Graham, July 25, 1985, WHORM Alpha File, box 28, folder "Martha Graham," RRL.

46. Dear President Reagan, Love Martha Graham, Oct. 4, 1985, WHORM Subject File, GI 001, box 12, folder 342171, RRL.

47. From Ronald Reagan to Martha, May 27, 1986, WHORM Alpha File, ME (Messages), 002, box 28, folder 415259, RRL.

48. See "In 1926, Martha Graham Knocked the Ballet Shoes Off American Dance," promotional mailed leaflet, Martha Graham Dance Company, Martha Graham 1984–1985, 221.2.2.2, IDA.

49. "Presidential Address on U.S.-Soviet Relations," Apr. 8, 1986, Jack F. Matlock Papers, box 44, folder USSR Relations, folder 1998 [*sic*], RRL.

50. For: Richard V. Allen, Fr: James M. Rentschler, Su: Reunification of Germany, etc. (Phil Crane), Oct 30, 1981, WHORM Subject, CO 054-01 (Germany), box 74, file Begin 099999, RRL.

51. Dear Phil [Crane], Fr: Edwin Meese, III, Nov. 20, 1981, CO 054-01, box 74, folder Begin 099999, RRL.

52. Erhard Krack, "Local Politics for the Well-Being of Our Citizens," *Einheity*, Jan. 1987, quoted in Barbara Donovan, "East Berlin's 750th Birthday Celebrations," RAD Background Report/34, Germany, for Radio Free Europe, Mar. 13, 1987, box 27, folder 4, report 118, OSA.

53. "Festliches Konzert im Schauspielhaus gab den Auftakt zur 750-Jahr-Feier Berlins," *Neues Deutschland*, Jan. 1, 1987, 1, LA.

54. "Nachrichten und Kommentare," *Neues Deutschland*, Jan. 2, 1987, 2, LA; Taylor, *The Berlin Wall: A World Divided*, 396.

55. Donovan, "East Berlin's 750th Birthday Celebrations."

56. Donovan, "East Berlin's 750th Birthday Celebrations."

57. Taylor, *The Berlin Wall: A World Divided*, 391.

58. Mike Dennis, *The Rise and Fall of the German Democratic Republic, 1945–1990* (New York: Longman, 2000), 180.

59. "In 1926, Martha Graham Knocked the Ballet Shoes Off American Dance."

60. Fr.: EM, Berlin, To: SecState WashDC Immediate, USIA WashDC, Immediate, Info: Am Embassy Bonn, US Mission Berlin, Su: Martha Graham Dance Company, Jan. 1987, Doc No. CO5160043, declassified and sent to author under FOIA, released 12/20/2013, US Department of State Case No. F-2009-04692, document available upon request from author.

61. "Graham Company im Metropol."

62. "Martha Graham: USA, 750 Jahre Berlin, 1987," program courtesy of Jens Giersdorf, available from author upon request.

63. "Martha Graham: USA, 750 Jahre Berlin, 1987."

64. "Martha Graham: USA, 750 Jahre Berlin, 1987."

65. "Martha Graham: USA, 750 Jahre Berlin, 1987."

66. Fr: Ronald Reagan, To: George Shultz, RE: Establishment of Diplomatic Relations with the Vatican," nd, Robert Reilly Files, box 12421, folder "Vatican-U.S. Diplomatic Relations," RRL.

67. "Martha Graham: USA, 750 Jahre Berlin, 1987."

68. "Tänzerin und Choreographin von epochaler Bedeutung," *Neue Zeit*, Feb. 24, 1987, in LA.

69. "Martha Graham: USA, 750 Jahre Berlin, 1987."

70. "Martha Graham: USA, 750 Jahre Berlin, 1987."

71. "Martha Graham: USA, 750 Jahre Berlin, 1987."

72. Author interview with Peggy Lyman, Dec. 3, 2010 (transcript available with written permission of Lyman). I wish to thank Lyman for her dedication to "making history" with her contributions to archives at the Metropolitan Museum of Art, New York.

73. "Public Diplomacy Strategy, 1986 Reagan-Gorbachev Summit," nd, Jack F. Matlock, Jr. Files, Series II, Subject File, USSR, box 44, folder, USIA Conference on Peace, RRL.

74. Lewis Segal, "Dance Review: Power of Martha Graham Carries San Diego," *Los Angeles Times*, Mar. 16, 1992, 32; Anna Kisselgoff, "Dance: Martha Graham Offers World Premiere," *New York Times*, May 28, 1986, C19.

75. "Tänze der Hoffnung," *Neues Deutschland*, Feb. 23, 1987, 7-A-3, in LA.

76. "Berliner Zeitung," *Neues Deutschland*, 7-A-3; and various reviews in East German newspapers, all in LA.

77. "Brillante Tanzkunst, die zum unvergeblichen Erlebnis wurde," *Neues Deutschland*, Feb. 20, 1987, in LA.

78. Eberhard Rebling, "Exzellente Darbietungen des berühmten Ensembles," *Neues Deutschland*, Feb. 21, 1987, in LA.

79. Eberhard Rebling, "Ovationen beim Gastspiel der weltberühmten Graham Dance Company aus den USA," *Neues Deutschland*, Feb. 21, 1987, in LA.

80. "Für Dich," *Neues Deutschland*, Feb. 26, 1987, 7-A-3, "Tänze der Hoffnung," 7-A-3, in LA.

81. "Graham Dance Company zu Gast," Feb. 18, 1987, clipping labeled *BZ am Abend*, Berlin, *Globus VEB Zeitungsausschnittdienst*, "Martha Graham," box 21, folder A4, TLA.

82. Eberhard Rebling, "Künstler aus den USA gastieren zum Berlin Jubiläum," *Neues Deutschland*, Weeked Edition, February 21–22, 1987; for a positive summary of the season, see "Huldigung für Martha Graham," *Tribüne*, Feb. 21, 1987, in LA.

83. Author interview with Lyman; Author interview (via telephone) with Thea Narissa Barnes, 2011.

84. Oral history conducted by author with Armgard von Bardeleben, Nov. 29, 2011, New York, closed without permission.

85. Oral history conducted by author with von Bardeleben.

86. Author interview with Lyman.

87. Author interview with Lyman.

88. Rosmarie Beir-de Hann, "Deutsches Historisches Museum: Rethinking German History Against the Background of a Burdened Past and New Challenges for the 21st Century," *Entering the Minefields: the Creation of New History Museums in Europe*, conference proceedings from EuNaMus, European National Museums: Identity Politics, the Uses of the Past and the European Citizen, Brussels, Jan. 25 2012, Bodil Axelsson, Christine Dupont & Chantal Kesteloot, eds. (Linköping University Electronic Press: EuNAMus, Report no. 9): 55–70, http://www.ep.liu.se/ecp_home/index.en.aspx?issue=083 (accessed September 12, 2019).

89. Michael S. Cullen, "Berlin's Congress Hall, a.k.a. the House of World Cultures," in Bernd, *The House. The Cultures. The World* (Berlin: Nicolai Verlag, 2007), 48–49.

90. Document No. 330-809, June 5, 1987, White House Staff Members and Office Files, Anne Higgins Files, Series V: Proclamations, Working Papers, box 63, folder, 750th Anniversary of the City of Berlin, 1987, RRL. See also Series IV, Presidential Proclamations, 1981–1989, 1987, N-Y, box 82, folder, 1987—750th Anniversary of Berlin, RRL.

91. "Geburtstags—Party auf amerikanisch," *Sonnabend*, June 13, 1987, 3, in LA.

92. "Rockstars gratulieren zum Fest," *Berliner Morgenpost*, June 10, 1987, in LA.

93. Elizabeth Janik, *Recomposing German Music: Politics and Musical Tradition in Cold War Berlin* (Boston: Brill Academic Publications, 2005), 297.

94. To: President and Mrs. Ronald Reagan, Fr.: Martha Graham, Aug. 20, 1987, WHORM Subject File, IV (Invitations), 087, box 8, folder 510445, RRL.

95. Author discussion with Mikhail Baryshnikov, Dec. 11, 2017 (transcript available with the permission of Mr. Baryshnikov).
96. Cover note to letter, Dear Ms. Graham, Sincerely Frederick J. Ryan, Jr., Sept. 21, 1987, WHORM Subject File, IV (Invitations), 087, box 8, folder 510445, RRL.
97. Author discussion with Baryshnikov.
98. "The 61st Anniversary Season of the Martha Graham Dance Company," box 212, folder 10, "1987 Cake Sale Gala," MGC-LOC.
99. Eva Resnikova, "Graham's Company Plays the Capitol," Oct. 25, 1987, *New York Times*, H33.
100. "The 61st Anniversary Season of the Martha Graham Dance Company."
101. "The 61st Anniversary Season of the Martha Graham Dance Company." Special thanks to Gens Giersdorf, who provided insights into this performance.
102. Author interview with Lyman.
103. Author interview with Lyman.

Coda

1. Contact Sheet P01725, Mar. 30, 1989, BUSH.
2. "Proposed Quote for Martha Graham," Bush Presidential Records, Records Management, White House Office of (WHORM), Alphabetical file, Graham, Martha, BUSH. Deepest thanks to the George H. W. Bush archivists for identifying these documents, reviewing and declassifying them, and then sending copies to me. Without their dedication, this tour would not have been uncovered as anything more than "a joke, or maybe it was Ron's suggestion" [unattributed expert].
3. Dear Martha, Warmly Barbara, May 19, 1989, cc: Gift Unit, George Bush Presidential Collection, Records Management, White House Office of (WHORM), Case Number ME001 08051, BUSH.
4. Dear Barbara, With Love and Blessings, Martha, June 14, 1989, George Bush Presidential Collection, Records Management, Records Management, White House Office of (WHORM), Case Number ME001 08051, BUSH.
5. Irena Turska, "Martha Graham," in *Krótki zarys historii baletu i tańca* (Warsaw: Polskie Wydawnictwo Muzycnze, 1983), 232–34, translated for the author by Marek Dąbrowski.
6. Tacjana Wysocka, "Martha Graham," in *Dzieje baletu* (Warsaw: P.I.W., Rok wydania, 1970), translated for the author by Marek Dąbrowski.
7. Tinatin Japaridze, "The Taste of Capitalist Soft Power: American 'Burger Diplomacy' in the U.S.S.R.," Feb. 15, 2016, HIST W4470, *Cold War Power: "Hot," "Soft," and "Hard" Diplomacy*, Dr. Victoria Phillips, Spring 2016, Columbia University, New York. Special thanks to Ms. Japaridze for drawing my attention to the intricacies of cultural exchange in Moscow and Mr. Trump's memoir.
8. Linda Hodes and Martha Hodes, conversation with author, Dec. 9, 2017.
9. Donald J. Trump with Tony Schwartz, *Trump: The Art of the Deal* (New York: Random House, 1987), 26.

10. Trump with Schwartz, *Trump*, 364.

11. Trump with Schwartz, *Trump*, 364.

12. Trump with Schwartz, *Trump*, 364.

13. Dear Barbara, With Love and Blessings, Martha, June 14, 1989.

14. Dear Barbara, With Love and Blessings, Martha, June 14, 1989.

15. Dear Barbara, With Love and Blessings, Martha, June 14, 1989.

16. Julia Foulkes, *Modern Bodies: Dance and American Modernism from Martha Graham to Alvin Ailey* (Chapel Hill: University of North Carolina Press, 2002), 148–51.

17. *American Document*, choreographed by Martha Graham, see Miles Kastendieck, "Graham Presents 'American Document,'" Oct. 9, 1938, box 314, folder 95, MGC and https://www.loc.gov/item/ihas.200182818 (accessed September 11, 2019).

18. Dear Barbara, With Love and Blessings, Martha, June 14, 1989.

19. Author discussion with Baryshnikov.

20. Foulkes, *Modern Bodies*, 148.

21. Nicci Gerrard, "Balancing Acts: Mikhail Baryshnikov Was Just Once a Great Soviet Dancer. Then He Moved On," *Observer* (London), Aug. 4, 1996, C5; Mikhail Baryshnikov, *New Statesman*, quoted by Diego Giolitto, "Mikhail Baryshnikov: Dancing Away," *HuffPost United Kingdom*, Oct. 10, 2014, http://www.huffingtonpost.co.uk/diego-giolitti/mikhail-baryshnikov-dancing-away_b_5995450.html (accessed August 8, 2017).

22. Carole Mallory, "Free, Even to Fail: What Was Mikhail Baryshnikov's Greatest Gain When He Defected to the U.S.?," *Baltimore Sun*, Oct. 8, 1989, 26.

23. Jack Anderson, "Words of Beauty and Terror Inform a Graham Classic," *New York Times*, Oct. 1, 1989, H8.

24. To: Mr. Protas, From: Joseph W. Hagin II, Oct. 27, 1989, The White House Correspondent Tracking Sheet, George Bush Presidential Collection, Records Management, Records Management, White House Office of (WHORM), Case Number ME001 08051, BUSH.

25. To: President Bush, Fr: Ronald Protas, Sept. 27, 1989, received Oct. 3, 1989, George Bush Presidential Collection, Records Management, Records Management, White House Office of (WHORM), Case Number ME001 08051, BUSH.

26. To: Tony, Fr.: Ron Protas, nd, received Oct. 3, 1989, George Bush Presidential Collection, Records Management, Records Management, White House Office of (WHORM), Case Number ME001 08051, BUSH.

27. Dear Mrs. Bush, Sincerely Ron Protas, nd, George Bush Presidential Collection, Records Management, Records Management, White House Office of (WHORM), Case Number ME001 08051, BUSH.

28. To Laurie, from Celeste, May 8, 1989, George Bush Presidential Collection, Records Management, Records Management, White House Office of (WHORM), Case Number ME001 08051, BUSH.

29. "Proposed Quote for Martha Graham," given to Ron Protas by Laurie, May 9, 1989 [morning], George Bush Presidential Collection, Records Management, Records Management, White House Office of (WHORM), Case Number ME001 08051, BUSH.

30. To: Shirley Green, Fr.: Unidentified Source [Linda W.], Oct. 2, 1989, George Bush Presidential Collection, Records Management, Records Management, White House Office of (WHORM), Case Number ME001 08051, BUSH.

31. To: Shirley Green, Fr.: Unidentified Source [Linda W.], Oct. 2, 1989, with notes by "Sy" and Julie Cooke, George Bush Presidential Collection, Records Management, Records Management, White House Office of (WHORM), Case Number ME001 08051, BUSH; To: Martha Graham, Fr.: George Bush, Oct. 8, 1989, George Bush Presidential Collection, Records Management, Records Management, White House Office of (WHORM), Case Number ME001 08051, BUSH.

32. Robert Service, *The End of the Cold War, 1985–1991* (New York: Perseus, 2015), 416.

33. Service, *The End of the Cold War*, 416.

34. Ronald Grigor Suny, "The Empire Falls: The Revolutions of 1989: The Story of Communism's Rise and Fall in Eastern Europe Is a Tale of Two Revolutions," *Nation*, Oct. 28, 2009.

35. Service, *The End of the Cold War*, 482.

36. Graham, *Blood Memory*, 219, also quoted from Graham's early written manuscripts in her own hand for the book, box 227, folders 5–8, MGC-LOC.

37. Graham, *Blood Memory*, also referenced in interviews, box 227, folders 5–8, MGC-LOC.

38. Volker R. Berghahn, *Journalists between Hitler and Adenauer: From the Inner Emigration to the Moral Reconstruction of West Germany* (Princeton, NJ: Princeton University Press, 2019), final lecture, Lehmann Center, Columbia University, Apr. 23, 2019.

39. Graham, *Blood Memory*, 1, also quoted from Graham's early written manuscripts in her own hand for the book, box 227, folders 5–8, MGC-LOC.

40. Pearl Lang, personal discussion with author, Feb. 20, 2009.

Appendix 1

1. Through 1945, premiere dates have been accessed from the LOC database, Elizabeth Aldrich, "Martha Graham Timeline: 1894–1945," http://lcweb2.loc.gov/diglib/ihas/loc.natlib.ihas.200154832/ (accessed March 24, 2012), and hard copy available from the author. Graham scholars have misstated premiere dates because the MGC-LOC did not open until 2006. Premiere dates and information between 1945 and 1984 from Ernestine Stodelle, *Deep Song: The Dance Story of Martha Graham* (New York: Macmillan, 1984), 298–317. Premiere dates and details after 1984 are gathered from newspapers.

Bibliography

Acharya, Amitav, and Tan See Seng, eds. *Bandung Revisited: The Legacy of the 1955 Asian-African Conference for International Order*. Chicago: University of Chicago Press, distributed for National University of Singapore Press, 2008.

Adam, Thomas, ed. *Germany and the Americas: Culture, Politics and History*. Santa Barbara, CA: ABC-CLIO, 2005.

Aldred, Cyril. *The Temple of Dendur*. New York: Metropolitan Museum of Art, 1978.

Alexievich, Svetlana. *War's Unwomanly Face*. Moscow: Progress Publishers, 1988. Reprint, New York: Random House, 2017.

Allegheny City Society. *Allegheny City, 1840–1907*. Chicago: Arcadia Publishing, 2007.

Alley, Robert S. *So Help Me God: Religion and the Presidency, Wilson to Nixon*. Louisville, KY: John Knox Press, 1972.

Allison, Roy. *Finland's Relations with the Soviet Union, 1944–84*. New York: St. Martin's Press, 1985.

Ambrose, Stephen E. *Eisenhower: Soldier and President*. New York: Touchstone, 1990.

Andaya, Barbara Watson, and Leonard Y. Andaya. *A History of Malaysia*. 3rd ed. New York: Palgrave, 2017.

Anderson, Benedict R. *Imagined Communities: Reflections on the Origin and Spread of Nationalism*. New York: Verso, 1991.

Anderson, Betty S. *The American University of Beirut: Arab Nationalism and Liberal Education*. Austin: University of Texas Press, 2011.

Anderson, Jack. Introduction to *The Dance in Theory*, by John Martin, i–xiv. Princeton, NJ: Princeton Book Company, 1989.

Anderson, Sheldon. *A Cold War in the Soviet Bloc: Polish–East German Relations: 1945–1962*. Boulder, CO: Westview Press, 2001.

Antoszek, Andrej, and Kate Delaney. "Poland: Transmissions and Translations." In *The Americanization of Europe: Culture, Diplomacy, and Anti-Americanism after 1945*, edited by Alexander Stephan, 218–250. New York: Berghahn Books, 2006.

Anziska, Seth. *Preventing Palestine: A Political History from Camp David to Oslo*. Princeton, NJ: Princeton University Press, 2018.

Applebaum, Anne. *Iron Curtain: The Crushing of Eastern Europe, 1944–1956*. New York: Doubleday, 2012.

Appy, Christian G., ed. *Cold War Constructions: The Political Constructions of the United States, 1945–1966*. Amherst: University of Massachusetts Press, 2000.

Armitage, Merle, ed. *Martha Graham: The Early Years*. 1937. Reprint, New York: Da Capo Press, 1978.

Armitage, Merle, and Virginia Stewart, eds. *The Modern Dance*. New York: Will A. Kistler, 1935. Reprint, New York: Dance Horizons, 1975.

Arndt, Richard. *The First Resort of Kings: American Cultural Diplomacy in the Twentieth Century*. 2005. Reprint, Dulles, VA: Potomac Books, 2007.

Ashton, Dore. *Noguchi East and West*. Berkeley: University of California Press, 1992.

Ashton, Nigel John. *King Hussein of Jordan: A Political Life*. New Haven, CT: Yale University Press, 2008.

Ashton, Nigel John. "Taking Friends for Granted: The Carter Administration, Jordan, and the Camp David Accords, 1977–1980." *Diplomatic History* 41, no. 3 (June 2017): 620–45.

Auten, Brian J. *Carter's Conversion: The Hardening of American Defense Policy*. Columbia: University of Missouri Press, 2008.

Babiracki, Patryk. *Soviet Soft Power in Poland: Culture and the Making of Stalin's New Empire, 1943–1957*. Chapel Hill: University of North Carolina Press, 2015.

Banes, Sally. "The Birth of the Judson Dance Theatre: 'Concert Dance' at Judson Church, July 6, 1962." *Dance Chronicle* 5, no. 2 (1982): 167–212.

Banes, Sally. *Dancing Women: Female Bodies on Stage*. New York: Routledge, 1998.

Banes, Sally, ed. *Reinventing the Dance in the 1960s: Everything Was Possible*. Madison: University of Wisconsin Press, 2003.

Barnhisel, Greg. *Cold War Modernists: Art, Literature, and American Cultural Diplomacy*. New York: Columbia University Press, 2015.

Barnhisel, Greg. "Perspectives USA and the Cultural Cold War: Modernism in Service of the State. *Modernism/modernity* 14, no. 4 (November 2007): 729–54.

Barrett, James R. *William Z. Foster and the Tragedy of American Radicalism*. Urbana: University of Illinois Press, 2001.

Barron, Stephanie, ed. *"Degenerate Art": The Fate of the Avant-Garde in Nazi Germany*. New York: Harry N. Abrams, 1991.

Bass, Gary J. *The Blood Telegram: Nixon, Kissinger, and a Forgotten Genocide*. New York: Alfred A. Knopf, 2013.

Bauerlein, Mark, and Ellen Grantham, eds. *National Endowment for the Arts: A History, 1965–2008*. Washington, DC: National Endowment for the Arts, 2009.

Behrends, Jan C. *Die erfundene Freundschaft: Propaganda für die Sowjetunion in Polen und in der DDR*. Köln: Böhlau Verlag, 2006.

Bellman, Samuel I. *Constance M. Rourke*. Boston: Twayne, 1981.

Belmonte, Laura A. *Selling the American Way: U.S. Propaganda in the Cold War*. Philadelphia: University of Pennsylvania Press, 2008.

Berghahn, Volker R. *America and the Intellectual Cold War in Europe*. Princeton, NJ: Princeton University Press, 2001.

Berghahn, Volker R. "American Social Scientists and the European Dialogue on Social Rights, 1930–1970." Lecture. April 2009. Department of History, Columbia University, New York, NY.

Berghahn, Volker R., *Journalists between Hitler and Adenauer: From the Inner Emigration to the Moral Reconstruction of West Germany*. Princeton, NJ: Princeton University Press, 2019.

Bergsohn, Harold, and Isa Partsch-Bergsohn. *The Makers of Modern Dance in Germany: Rudolf Laban, Mary Wigman, Kurt Jooss*. Highstown, NJ: Princeton Book Company, 2003.

Bezjak, Maja. *Dubrovačke ljetne igre 1950–1989*. Zagreb: Festival Dubrovnik, 1989.

Beir-de Hann, Rosmarie. "Deutsches Historisches Museum: Rethinking German History Against the Background of a Burdened Past and New Challenges for the 21st Century." In *Entering the Minefields: the Creation of New History Museums in Europe*, conference proceedings from EuNaMus, European National Museums: Identity Politics, the Uses of the Past and the European Citizen, Brussels Jan. 25 2012, Bodil Axelsson, Christine

Dupont & Chantal Kesteloot, eds. Linköping University Electronic Press: EuNAMus, Report no. 9: 55–70.

Biess, Frank. *Homecomings: Returning POWs and the Legacies of Defeat in Postwar Germany*. Princeton, NJ: Princeton University Press, 2006.

Bird, Dorothy. *Bird's Eye View: Dancing with Martha Graham and on Broadway*. Pittsburgh: University of Pittsburgh Press, 1977.

Blake, Caesar R., ed. *The Recognition of Emily Dickinson: Selected Criticism since 1890*. Ann Arbor: University of Michigan Press, 1964.

Bleeker, Maaike. "Lecture Performance as Contemporary Dance." In *New German Dance Studies*, edited by Susan Manning and Lucia Ruprecht, 232–46. Champaign: University of Illinois Press, 2012.

Bloom, Harold. *The Western Canon: The Books and School of the Ages*. New York: Harcourt Brace, 1994.

Bonner, Raymond. *Waltzing with a Dictator: The Marcoses and the Making of American Policy*. New York: Times Books, 1987.

Bott, Sandra, Jussi M. Hanhimäki, Janick Marina Schaufelbuehl, and Marco Wyss, eds. *Neutrality and Neutralism in the Global Cold War: Between or within the Blocs?* New York: Routledge, 2016.

Bouwsma, William J. "From History of Ideas to History of Meaning." *Journal of Interdisciplinary History* 12, no. 2 (Autumn 1981): 279–91.

Boyle, Peter G., ed. *The Eden-Eisenhower Correspondence, 1955–1957*. Chapel Hill: University of North Carolina Press, 2005.

Brazinsky, Gregg A. *Winning the Third World: Sino-American Rivalry during the Cold War*. Chapel Hill: University of North Carolina Press, 2017.

Brinkman, Reinhold, and Christoph Wolff, eds. *Driven into Paradise: The Musical Migration from Nazi Germany to the United States*. Berkeley: University of California Press, 1999.

Buckley, Sandra. *The Encyclopaedia of Contemporary Japanese Culture*. New York: Routledge, 2001.

Burt, Ramsay. *Alien Bodies: Representations of Modernity, "Race" and Nation*. New York: Routledge, 1998.

Bush, Barbara. "Gender and Empire: The Twentieth Century." In *Gender and Empire*, edited by Philippa Levin, 77–111. New York: Oxford University Press, 2004.

Caldwell, Helen. *Michio Ito: The Dancer and His Dances*. Berkeley: University of California Press, 1977.

Campbell, Jennifer L. "Creating Something Out of Nothing: The Office of Inter-American Music Committee (1940–1941) and the Inception of a Policy for Musical Diplomacy." *Diplomatic History* 36, no. 1 (January 2012): 29–39.

Canning, Charlotte M. "'In the Interest of the State': A Cold War National Theater for the United States." *Theater Journal* 61, no. 3 (October 2009): 407–20.

Canning, Charlotte M. *On the Performance Front: US Theater and Internationalism*. London: Palgrave Macmillan, 2015.

Carpenter, Ronald H. "Style in Discourse as an Index of Frederick Jackson Turner's Historical Creativity: Conceptual Antecedents of the Frontier Thesis in His 'American Colonization'" *Huntington Library Quarterly* 40, no. 3 (May 1977): 269–77.

Carroll, Mark. *Music and Ideology in Cold War Europe*. New York: Cambridge University Press, 2003.

Castillo, Greg. "Domesticating the Cold War: Household Consumption as Propaganda in Marshall Plan Germany," *Journal of Contemporary History* 40, no. 2 (April 2005): 261–88.

Castillo, Greg. *Cold War on the Home Front: The Soft Power of Midcentury Design.* Minneapolis: University of Minnesota Press, 2010.

Castor, Helen. *Joan of Arc: A History.* New York: Harper Perennial, 2015.

Caute, David. *The Dancer Defects: The Struggle for Cultural Supremacy during the Cold War.* New York: Oxford University Press, 2003.

Caws, Mary Ann. "Editor's Preface." In *Stéphane Mallarmé: Selected Poetry and Prose,* i–iv. New York: New Directions, 1982.

Chakrabarty, Dipesh. "The Muddle of Modernity." In "Historians and the Question of 'Modernity.'" *American Historical Review* 116, no. 3 (June 2011): 663–75.

Chang, Alexandra. *Envisioning Diaspora: Asian American Visual Arts Collectives from Godzilla, Godzookie to the Barnstormers.* Beijing: Timezone 8 Editions, 2009.

Charney, Michael W. *A History of Modern Burma.* New York: Cambridge University Press, 2009.

Chujoy, Anatole, and P. W. Manchester, eds. *The Dance Encyclopedia.* New York: Simon and Schuster, 1967.

Clark, Mark W. *Beyond Catastrophe: German Intellectuals and Cultural Renewal after World War II.* Lanham, MD: Lexington Books, 2006.

Clark, Mary E. *Ariadne's Thread: The Search for New Modes of Thinking.* New York: Palgrave, 1989.

Cleveland, William L. and Martin Bunton. *A History of the Modern Middle East.* 4th ed. New York: Perseus Books, 2009.

Cody, Judith. *Vivian Fine: A Bio-bibliography.* Westport, CT: Greenwood Press, 2002.

Coffey, Justin P. *Spiro Agnew and the Rise of the Republican Right.* Santa Barbara, CA: ABC-CLIO, 2015.

Cohen, Deborah. "Regionalism and U.S. Nationalism in William Faulkner's State Department Travels." In *Creating and Consuming the U.S. South,* edited by Martyn Bone, Brian Ward, and William A. Link, 248–67. Gainesville: University Press of Florida, 2015.

Connelly, Matthew. *A Diplomatic Revolution: Algeria's Fight for Independence and the Origins of the Post–Cold War Era.* New York: Oxford University Press, 2002.

Conner, Lynne. *Spreading the Gospel of Modern Dance: Newspaper Dance Criticism in the United States, 1850–1934.* Pittsburgh: University of Pittsburgh Press, 1997.

Cooper, Andrew Scott. "Showdown at Doha: The Secret Oil Deal That Helped Sink the Shah of Iran." *Middle East Journal* 62, no. 4 (Autumn 2008): 567–91.

Cooper, Elizabeth. "Tamiris and the Federal Dance Theatre, 1936–1939: Socially Relevant Dance amidst the Politics of a New Era." *Dance Research Journal* 29, no. 2 (Autumn 1997): 23–48.

Cooper, Frederick, and Ann Laura Stoler. "Between Metropole and Colony: Rethinking a Research Agenda." In *Tensions of Empire: Colonial Cultures in a Bourgeois World,* edited by Frederick Cooper and Ann Laura Stoler, 1–57. Berkeley: University of California Press, 1997.

Cooper, James Ford. *On the Finland Watch: An American Diplomat in Finland during the Cold War.* Claremont, CA: Regina Books, 2000.

Copel, Melinda. "Modern Dance Humanism and the State Department's Agenda: Raising U.S. Status in the World Community during the Cold War." In *Congress on Research in*

Dance: Conference Papers, edited by Ninotchka Bennahum and Tresa Randall, 31–41. Tallahassee: Florida State University, 2005.

Corn, Wanda M. "Coming of Age: Historical Scholarship in American Art." *Art Bulletin* 70, no. 2 (June 1988): 188–207.

Costigliola, Frank. "Pamela Churchill, Wartime London, and the Making of the Special Relationship." *Diplomatic History* 36, no. 4 (September 2012): 753–63.

Costigliola, Frank, and Michael J. Hogan, eds. *Explaining the History of American Foreign Relations.* 3rd ed. New York: Cambridge University Press, 2016.

Cott, Nancy F. *The Grounding of Modern Feminism.* New Haven, CT: Yale University Press, 1989.

Cowell, Mary-Jean. "Michio Ito in Hollywood: Modes and Ironies of Ethnicity." *Dance Chronicle* 24, no. 3 (2001): 263–305.

Cowell, Mary-Jean, and Satoru Shimazaki. "East and West in the Work of Michio Ito." *Dance Research Journal* 26, no. 2 (Autumn 1994): 11–23.

Crapol, Edward P. *Women and American Foreign Policy: Lobbyists, Critics, and Insiders.* 2nd ed. New York: Rowman and Littlefield, 1992.

Critchlow, Donald T. *Phyllis Schlafly and Grassroots Conservatism: A Woman's Crusade.* Princeton, NJ: Princeton University Press, 2005.

Croft, Clare. "Ballet Nations: The New York City Ballet's 1962 US State Department Sponsored Tour of the Soviet Union." *Theater Journal* 61, no. 3 (2009): 421–42.

Croft, Clare. *Dancers as Diplomats: American Choreography in Cultural Exchange.* New York: Oxford University Press, 2015.

Cronon, William. "Revisiting the Vanishing Frontier: The Legacy of Frederick Jackson Turner." *Western Historical Quarterly* 18, no. 2 (April 1987): 157–76.

Cull, Nicholas J. *The Cold War and the United States Information Agency: American Propaganda and Public Diplomacy, 1945–1989.* New York: Cambridge University Press, 2008.

Cummings, Richard H. *Radio Free Europe's "Crusade for Freedom": Rallying Americans behind Cold War Broadcasting 1950–1960.* Jefferson, NC: McFarland, 2010.

Curtis, Michael, and Susan Aurelia Gitelson, eds. *Israel in the Third World.* New York: Routledge, 1976.

Czepczyński, Mariusz. *Cultural Landscapes of Post-socialist Cities: Representations of Powers and Needs.* London: Ashgate, 2008.

Daiber, Hans. *Deutsches Theater seit 1945: Bundesrepublik Deutschland, Dt. Demokrat. Republik, Österreich, Schweiz.* Stuttgart: Reclam, 1976. Translation for author by Julia Sittman.

Dallek, Robert. *Nixon and Kissinger: Partners in Power.* New York: HarperCollins, 2007.

Daly, Ann. *Done into Dance: Isadora Duncan in America.* Middletown, CT: Wesleyan University Press, 1995.

Danto, Arthur C. *Andy Warhol.* New Haven, CT: Yale University Press, 2009.

Daugherty, William E., and Morris Janowitz. *The Psychological Warfare Casebook.* Baltimore: Johns Hopkins University Press, Operations Research Office, 1958.

de Bellaigue, Christopher. *Patriot of Persia: Muhammad Mossadegh and a Tragic Anglo-American Coup.* New York: Harper, 2012.

De Grazia, Victoria. *Irresistible Empire: America's Advance through Twentieth-Century Europe.* Cambridge, MA: Harvard University Press, 2005.

de Mille, Agnes. *Martha: The Life and Work of Martha Graham.* New York: Random House, 1991.

Denning, Michael. *The Cultural Front: The Laboring of American Culture in the Twentieth Century*. New York: Verso, 1997.

Dennis, Mike. *The Rise and Fall of the German Democratic Republic, 1945–1990*. New York: Longman, 2000.

de Vries, Tity. "The 1967 Central Intelligence Scandal: Catalyst in a Transforming Relationship between State and People." *Journal of American History* 98, no. 4 (March 2012): 1075–92.

Diehl, Ernst. *Komitee der Deutschen Demokratischen Republik zum 750 jährigen Bestehen von Berlin*. Berlin: Dietz, 1986.

Diehl, Ernst. *750 Years of Berlin: A Selection of Events from the 1987 Anniversary Programme*. Berlin: Panorama, 1987.

Dils, Ann. "The Federal Dance Project (FDP, 1936–1939)." Dance Heritage Coalition (New York): 1–4. http://new.danceheritage.org/html/treasures/fdp_essay_dils.pdf. Accessed March 18, 2017.

Douglas, Ann. *Terrible Honesty: Mongrel Manhattan in the 1920s*. New York: Farrar, Straus and Giroux, 1996.

Dowek, Ephraim. *Israeli-Egyptian Relations, 1980–2000*. London: Frank Cass, 2001.

Duberman, Martin. *The Worlds of Lincoln Kirstein*. New York: Alfred A. Knopf, 2007.

Duggan, Lisa, and Nan D. Hunter. *Sex Wars: Sexual Dissent and Political Culture*. New York: Routledge, 1996.

Dulles, Eleanor Lansing. *Chances of a Lifetime: A Memoir*. Englewood Cliffs, NJ: Prentice-Hall, 1980.

Duncan, Isadora. *My Life*. London: Boni and Liveright, 1927. Reprint, New York: W. W. Norton, 1955.

Dunn, Lynn. "Joining the Boys' Club: The Diplomatic Career of Eleanor Lansing Dulles." In *Women and American Foreign Policy: Lobbyists, Critics, and Insiders*, edited by Edward P. Crapol, 2nd ed, 119–35. New York: Rowman and Littlefield, 1992.

Duus, Masayo. *The Life of Isamu Noguchi: Journey without Borders*. Translated by Peter Duus. Princeton, NJ: Princeton University Press, 2004.

Duus, Peter, and Kenji Hasegawa, eds. *Rediscovering America: Japanese Perspectives on the American Century*. Berkeley: University of California Press, 2011.

El-Khazen, Farid. *The Breakdown of the State in Lebanon, 1967–1967*. Cambridge, MA: Harvard University Press, 2000.

Emling, Shelley. *Setting the World on Fire: The Brief, Astonishing Life of Catherine of Sienna*. New York: St. Martin's Press, 2016.

Engerman, David, Nils Gilman, Mark H. Haefele, and Michael E. Latham. *Staging Growth: Modernization, Development, and the Global Cold War*. Amherst: University of Massachusetts Press, 2003.

Engerman, David C., Nils Gilman, Michael E. Latham, Amy Sayward, Catherine V. Scott, and Corinna R. Unger. "Roundtable 3–4 on *The Right Kind of Revolution: Modernization, Development, and U.S. Foreign Policy from the Cold War to the Present*." H-Diplo, and H-Net: Humanities and Social Sciences Online, III, no. 4 (2011), https://issforum.org/ISSF/PDF/ISSF-Roundtable-3-4.pdf. Accessed August 24, 2019.

Eshel, Ruth. *Dance Spreads Its Wings: The Fascinating Story of Israeli Concert Dance, 1920–2000*. Translated for the author by Uri Turkenich. Tel Aviv: Israel Dance Diaries, 2016.

Eslava, Luis, Michael Fakhri, and Vasuki Nesiah, eds. *Bandung, Global History, and International Law: Critical Pasts and Pending Futures*. New York: Cambridge University Press, 2017.

Ewing, Alex C. *Bravura! Lucia Chase and the American Ballet Theatre*. Gainesville: University Press of Florida, 2009.

Faragher, John Mack. "'A Nation Thrown Back upon Itself': Frederick Jackson Turner and the Frontier." In *Rereading Frederick Jackson Turner: "The Significance of the Frontier in American History" and Other Essays*, edited by John Mack Faragher, 1–10. New Haven, CT: Yale University Press, 1994.

Ferguson, Niall. *The Square and the Tower: Networks and Power, from Freemasons to Facebook*. New York: Penguin Press, 2017.

Finney, Gail. *Women in Modern Drama: Freud, Feminism, and European Theater at the Turn of the Century*. Ithaca, NY: Cornell University Press, 1991.

Fisher, Jennifer. *Nutcracker Nation: How an Old World Ballet Became a Christmas Tradition in the New World*. New Haven, CT: Yale University Press, 2003.

Fitzgerald, Frances. *The Evangels: The Struggle to Shape America*. New York: Simon and Schuster, 2017.

Fitzpatrick, Shanon, and Emily Rosenberg, eds. *Bodies/Nations: The Global Realms of U.S. Body Politics in the Twentieth Century*. Durham, NC: Duke University Press, 2014.

Foglesong, David S. *The American Mission and the "Evil" Empire*. New York: Cambridge University Press, 2007.

Foner, Eric. "Fighting for the Four Freedoms." In *Give Me Liberty! An American History*, 3rd ed, 902–45. New York: W. W. Norton, 2011.

Foner, Eric. *The Story of American Freedom*. New York: W. W. Norton, 1998.

Ford, Betty, with Chris Chase. *Betty: A Glad Awakening*. New York: Doubleday, 1987.

Fosler-Lussier, Danielle. *Music in America's Cold War Diplomacy*. Berkeley: University of California Press, 2015.

Foucault, Michel. *Power/Knowledge: Selected Interviews and Other Writings, 1972–1977*. Edited by Colin Gordon. New York: Pantheon, 1980.

Foulkes, Julia. *Modern Bodies: Dance and American Modernism from Martha Graham to Alvin Ailey*. Chapel Hill: University of North Carolina Press, 2002.

Francia, Luis H. *A History of the Philippines: From Indos Bravos to Filipinos*. New York: Overlook Press, 2013.

Franko, Mark. *Dancing Modernism/Performing Politics*. Bloomington: Indiana University Press, 1995.

Franko, Mark. *Martha Graham in Love and War: The Life in the Work*. New York: Oxford University Press, 2012.

Freedman, Russell. *Martha Graham: A Dancer's Life*. New York: Clarion Books, 1988.

Frey, Marc. "Tools of Empire: Persuasion and the United States's Modernizing Mission in Southeast Asia." *Diplomatic History* 27, no. 4 (September 2003): 543–68.

Frieberg, Annika. "The Project of Reconciliation: Journalists and Religious Activists in Polish-German Relations, 1956–1972." PhD diss., University of North Carolina, 2008.

Friend, Theodore. *Indonesian Destinies*. Cambridge, MA: Harvard University Press, 2003.

Fritze, Ronald H. *Egyptomania: A History of Fascination, Obsession and Fantasy*. London: Reaktion Books, 2016.

Funkenstein, Susan Laikin. "Engendering Abstraction: Wassily Kandinsky, Gret Palucca, and 'Dance Curves.'" *Modernism/modernity* 14, no. 3 (September 2007): 389–406.

Gaddis, John Lewis. *The Cold War*. New York: Penguin Books, 2005.

Gaddis, John Lewis. *George F. Kennan: An American Life*. New York: Penguin Books, 2011.

Ganser, Daniele. *NATO's Secret Armies: Operation Gladio and Terrorism in Western Europe*. New York: Routledge, 2004.

Garafola, Lynn. *Diaghilev's Ballets Russes*. New York: Oxford University Press, 1989.

Garafola, Lynn. Introduction to *José Limón: An Unfinished Memoir*, by José Limón, xix–xx. Middletown, CT: Wesleyan University Press, 2001.

Garafola, Lynn. "Lincoln Kirstein, Modern Dance, and the Left: The Genesis of an American Ballet." *Dance Research: The Journal of the Society for Dance Research* 23, no. 1 (Summer 2005): 18–35.

Garafola, Lynn. Review of *Blood Memory*, by Martha Graham. *The Drama Review* 37, no. 1 (Spring 1993): 167–73.

Gardner, Howard. "Martha Graham: Discovering the Dance of America." In *Creating Minds: An Anatomy of Creativity as Seen through the Lives of Freud, Einstein, Picasso, Stravinsky, Eliot, Graham, and Gandhi*, 247–88. New York: Basic Books, 1993.

Geduld, Victoria Phillips. "Collaboration among Icons: The New York City Dance Theatre, 1949." *Ballet Review* 38, no. 4 (Winter, 2011): 40–56. See box 7, folder 8, BRC.

Geduld, Victoria Phillips. "Dancing Diplomacy." *Dance Chronicle* 33, no. 1 (2010): 44–81.

Geduld, Victoria Phillips. "This American Manifestation." *Ballet Review* 39, no. 2 (Summer 2011): 40–49.

Genter, Robert. *Late Modernism: Art, Culture, and Politics in Cold War America*. Philadelphia: University of Pennsylvania Press, 2010.

Gettig, Eric. "'Trouble Ahead in Afro-Asia': The United States, the Second Bandung Conference, and the Struggle for the Third World, 1964–1965." *Diplomatic History* 39, no. 1 (2015): 126–56.

Giangreco, D. M., and Robert E. Griffin, *Airbridge to Berlin: The Berlin Crisis of 1948, Its Origins and Its Aftermath*. New York: Presidio Press, 1988.

Giersdorf, Jens. *The Body of the People: East German Dance since 1945*. Madison: University of Wisconsin Press, 2013.

Giersdorf, Jens. *Choreographing Socialism : Bodies and Performance in East Germany before, during and after the Fall of the Wall*. Riverside: University of California Press, 2001.

Gilman, Nils. *Mandarins of the Future: Modernization Theory in Cold War America*. Baltimore: Johns Hopkins University Press, 2003.

Ginor, Isabella, and Gideon Remez. *The Soviet-Israeli War 1967–1973: The USSR's Military Intervention in the Egyptian-Israeli Conflict*. New York: Oxford University Press, 2017.

Gitelman, Claudia. *Dancing with Principle: Hanya Holm in Colorado, 1941–1983*. Boulder: University of Colorado Press, 2001.

Gluck, Carol. "The End of Elsewhere: Writing Modernity Now." In "Historians and the Question of 'Modernity.'" *American Historical Review* 116, no. 3 (June 2011): 676–87.

Gluck, Rena. *Batsheva Dance Company, 1964–1980: My Story*. Tel Aviv: Internet Publication, 2006, Kindle at Amazon.

Gluck, Sherna B., and Daphne Patai, eds. *Women's Worlds: The Feminist Practice of Oral History*. New York: Routledge, 1991.

Goedde, Petra. *GIs and Germans: Culture, Gender, and Foreign Relations*. New Haven, CT: Yale University Press, 2003.

Goedde, Petra. *The Politics of Peace: A Global Cold War History*. New York: Oxford University Press, 2019.

Graff, Ellen. *Stepping Left: Dance Politics in New York City, 1928–1942*. Durham, NC: Duke University Press, 1997.

Graham, Martha. "The American Dance." In *The Modern Dance*, edited by Merle Armitage and Virginia Stewart, 53–58. New York: Will A. Kistler, 1935. Reprint, New York: Dance Horizons, 1970.

Graham, Martha. *Blood Memory—An Autobiography*. New York: Doubleday, 1991.

Graham, Martha. *Interview with Martha Graham: The Early Years*. Conducted by Walter Terry. Audiocassette, 2 sound cassettes, 55 min. New York Public Library: Jerome Robbins Dance Division, 1973.

Graham, Martha. *The Notebooks of Martha Graham*. Introduction by Nancy Wilson Ross. New York: Harcourt, 1973.

Graham, Martha. "Platform for the American Dance." In *I See America Dancing: Selected Readings, 1685–2000*, edited by Maureen Needham, 203–4. Champaign, IL: University of Illinois Press, 2002.

Graham, Martha. "Seeking an American Art of the Dance." In *Revolt in the Arts: A Survey of the Creation, Distribution and Appreciation of Art in America*, edited by Oliver M. Sayler, 249–55. New York: Brentano's, 1930.

Greene, John Robert. *Limits of Power: The Nixon and Ford Administrations*. Bloomington: University of Indiana Press, 1992

Greene, John Robert. *Betty Ford: Candor and Courage at the White House*. Lawrence: University Press of Kansas, 2004.

Gregg, Donald P. *Pot Shards: Fragments of a Life Lived in CIA, the White House, and the Two Koreas*. Washington, DC: New Academia Publishing, 2014.

Grunbacher, Armin. *Reconstruction and Cold War in Germany, 1948–1961*. London: Ashgate, 2004.

Guha, Ramachandra. *India after Gandhi: The History of the World's Largest Democracy*. New York: HarperCollins, 2007.

Guilbaut, Serge. *How New York Stole the Idea of Modern Art: Abstract Expressionism, Freedom, and the Cold War*. Translated by Arthur Goldhammer. Chicago: University of Chicago Press, 1983.

Halberstam, David. *The Best and the Brightest*. New York: Random House, 1972.

Halberstam, David. *The Coldest Winter: America and the Korean War*. New York: Hyperion, 2007.

Halloway, Rachel L. "'Keeping the Faith': Eisenhower Introduces the Hydrogen Age." In *Eisenhower's War of Words: Rhetoric and Leadership*, edited by Martin J. Medhurst, 1–24. Ann Arbor: University of Michigan Press.

Hamilton, Paula, and Linda Shopes, eds. *Oral History and Public Memories*. Philadelphia: Temple University Press, 2008.

Hamilton-Paterson, James. *America's Boy: A Century of United States Colonialism in the Philippines*. New York: Henry Holt, 1999.

Hanhimäki, Jussi M. *Containing Coexistence: America, Russia, and the "Finnish Solution," 1945–1956*. Kent, OH: Kent State University Press, 1997.

Hanhimäki, Jussi M. *Scandinavia and the United States: An Insecure Friendship*. New York: Twayne, 1997.

Hara, Kimie. "Introduction." In *The San Francisco System and Its Legacies: Continuation, Transformation, and Historical Reconciliation in the Asia-Pacific*, edited by Kimie Hara, 1–20. New York: Routledge, 2014.

Harrington, Daniel F. *Berlin on the Brink: The Blockade, the Airlift, and the Early Cold War*. Lexington: University Press of Kentucky, 2012.

Harris, Sarah Miller. *The CIA and the Congress for Cultural Freedom in the Early Cold War: The Limits of Making Common Sense*. New York: Routledge, 2016.

Harrison, Hope. *Driving the Soviets Up the Wall: Soviet–East German Relations, 1953–1961*. Princeton, NJ: Princeton University Press, 2003.

Hawass, Zahi. *The Mysteries of Abu Simbel: Ramses II and the Temples of the Rising Sun.* Cairo: American University in Cairo Press, 2000.

Heil, Alan L., Jr. *Voice of America: A History.* New York: Columbia University Press, 2003.

Helpern, Alice, ed. *Martha Graham: A Special Issue of the Journal 'Choreography and Dance.'* 5, no. 2. New York: Routledge, 1999.

Herberg, Will. *Protestant, Catholic, Jew: An Essay in American Religious Sociology.* Chicago: University of Chicago Press, 1955. Reprint, 1983.

Herring, George C. *From Colony to Superpower: United States Foreign Policy since 1776.* New York: Oxford University Press, 2008.

Herzog, Dagmar. *Cold War Freud: Psychoanalysis in an Age of Catastrophes.* New York: Cambridge University Press, 2016.

Hill, Martha. *Interview with Martha Hill.* Conducted by Agnes de Mille, January 18, 1984. Audiocassette, 2 sound cassettes, 100 min. New York Public Library: Jerome Robbins Dance Division.

Hixson, Walter L. *Parting the Curtain: Propaganda, Culture, and the Cold War, 1945–1961.* New York: St. Martin's Press, 1998.

Hobbins, Daniel. "Introduction." In *The Trial of Joan of Arc*, translated by Daniel Hobbins, 1–32. Cambridge, MA: Harvard University Press, 2005.

Hobsbawm, Eric. *The Age of Extremes: A History of the World, 1914–1991.* New York: Pantheon, 1994.

Hopkins, Michael F. "Continuing Debate and New Approaches in Cold War History." *Historical Review* 50, no. 4 (2007): 913–34.

Horosko, Marian. *May O'Donnell: Modern Dance Pioneer.* Gainesville: University Press of Florida, 2005.

Horst, Louis. *Interview with Louis Horst.* Conducted by Jeanette S. Roosevelt. 1959–60. Audiocassette, 8 sound cassettes, 13 hours, transcript 211 pages. New York Public Library: Jerome Robbins Dance Division.

Horst, Louis, and Carroll Russell. *Modern Dance Forms in Relation to the Other Modern Arts.* San Francisco: Impulse Publications, 1961. Reprint, New York: Dance Horizons, 1987.

Howe, Irving. *The Idea of the Modern in Literature and the Arts.* New York: Horizon Press, 1967.

Hughes-Hallett, Lucy. *Cleopatra: Histories, Dreams and Distortions.* New York: Harper and Row, 1990.

Humphrey, Doris. *The Art of Making Dances.* Edited by Barbara Pollack. New York: Dance Horizons, 1959. Reprint 1987.

Humphrey, Doris. *New Dance: Writings on Modern Dance.* Edited by Charles Humphrey Woodford. Highstown, NJ: Princeton Book Company, 2008.

Huxley, Michael. *The Dancer's World, 1920–1945: Modern Dancers and Their Practices Reconsidered.* New York: Palgrave Macmillan, 2015.

Huxley, Michael. "European Early Modern Dance." In *Dance History: An Introduction*, 2nd ed., edited by Janet Adshead-Lansdale and June Layson, 151–68. New York: Routledge, 1994.

Immerwahr, Daniel. *How to Hide an Empire: A History of the Greater United States.* New York: Farrar, Straus and Giroux, 2019.

Inboden, William. *Religion and American Foreign Policy, 1945–1960: The Soul of Containment.* New York: Cambridge University Press, 2008.

Isaacson, Walter. *Kissinger: A Biography.* New York: Simon and Schuster, 2005.

Ito, Michio. "No Time for the Arts." In *Rediscovering America: Japanese Perspectives on the American Century*, edited by Peter Duus and Kenji Hasegawa, 216–17. Berkeley: University of California Press, 2011.

Jameson, Fredric. *The Modernist Papers*. New York: Verso, 2007.

Jameson, Fredric. *A Singular Modernity: Essay on the Ontology of the Present*. New York: Verso, 2002.

Janik, Elizabeth. *Recomposing German Music: Politics and Musical Tradition in Cold War Berlin*. Boston: Brill Academic Publications, 2005.

Jehlen, Myra. "Archimedes and the Paradox of Feminist Criticism." *Signs* 6, no. 4 (Summer 1981): 575–601.

Jensen, Robert. *Marketing Modernism in Fin-de-Siècle Europe*. Princeton, NJ: Princeton University Press, 1994.

Johnson, David K. *The Lavender Scare: The Cold War Persecution of Gays and Lesbians in the Federal Government*. Chicago: University of Chicago Press, 2006.

Johnson, Ross A., and Eugene R. Parta. *Cold War Broadcasting: Impact on the Soviet Union and Eastern Europe*. Budapest: Central European Press, 2012.

Jones, Matthew. "A 'Segregated' Asia? Race, the Bandung Conference, and Pan-Asianist Fears in American Thought and Policy, 1954–1955." *Diplomatic History* 29, no. 5 (November 2005): 841–68.

Jowitt, Deborah. *Time in the Dancing Image*. New York: William Morrow, 1988.

Kandinsky, Wassily. *Concerning the Spiritual in Art*. Translated by M. T. H. Sadler. New York: Dover, 1977. An unabridged republication of Wassily Kandinsky, *The Art of Spiritual Harmony*, London: Constable, 1914.

Kandinsky, Wassily. "Über die Formfrage" in *Der Blaue Reiter*. Munich: R. Piper, 74–100. 1912. Transl. Kenneth Lindsaych as "On the Problem of Form." *Theories of Modern Art: A Source Book by Artists and Critics*, ed. Herschel B. Chipp, 155–58. Berkeley, CA: University of California Press, 1968. Reprint, 1998.

Kapur, Nick. "Mending the 'Broken Dialogue': U.S.-Japan Alliance Diplomacy in the Aftermath of the 1960 Security Treaty Crisis." *Diplomatic History* 41, no. 3 (June 2017): 489–517.

Karavan, Dani. *Dani Karavan: Dialogue with the Environment, Resonance with the Earth*. Tokyo: Asahi Shimbun, 1997.

Karina, Lilian and Marion Kant. *Hitler's Dancers: German Modern Dance and the Third Reich*. New York: Berghahn Books, 2003.

Karkabi, Barbara Farrar. "Choreography in Cairo: Classical Ballet Comes to Egypt." *Saudi Aramco World* 28, no. 2 (March/April 1977): 16–23.

Karnow, Stanley. *In Our Image: America's Empire in the Philippines*. New York: Random House, 1989.

Kasprzak, Michal. "Radio Free Europe and the Catholic Church in Poland during the 1950s." *Canadian Slavonic Papers/Revue Canadienne des Slavistes* 46, nos. 3/4 (September–December 2004): 315–27.

Keefe, Patrick R. "The Family That Built an Empire of Pain." *New Yorker*, October 30, 2017.

Keilson, Ana Isabel. "Making Dance Modern: Knowledge, Politics, and German Modern Dance, 1890–1927." PhD diss., Columbia University, 2017.

Kennan, George F. *Memoirs: 1925–1950*. Boston: Little, Brown, 1967.

Kent, Richard J. "Keynes's Lectures at the New School for Social Research." *History of Political Economy* 36, no. 1 (Spring 2004): 196–206.

Khagram, Sanjeev. *Dams and Development: Transnational Struggles for Water and Power.* Ithaca, NY: Cornell University Press, 2004.

King, Eleanor. *Transformations: A Memoir by Eleanor King of the Humphrey-Weidman Era.* Brooklyn, NY: Dance Horizons, 1978.

Kinzer, Stephen. *The Brothers: John Foster Dulles, Allen Dulles, and Their Secret World War.* New York: Henry Holt, 2013.

Kirby, Dianne. "The Religious Cold War." In *The Oxford Handbook of the Cold War,* edited by Richard H. Immerman and Petra Goedde, chapter 31. New York: Oxford University Press, 2013. Reprint 2016.

Kissinger, Henry. *Years of Renewal: The Concluding Volume of His Memoirs.* New York: Touchstone, 1999.

Klein, Christina. *Cold War Orientalism: Asia in the Middlebrow Imagination, 1945–1961.* Berkeley: University of California Press, 2003.

Klein, Kerwin Lee. *Frontiers of Historical Imagination: Narrating the European Conquest of Native America, 1890–1990.* Berkeley: University of California Press, 1997.

Kochavi, Noam. *Nixon and Israel: Forging a Conservative Partnership.* Albany: State University of New York Press, 2009.

Kodat, Catherine Gunther. "Dancing through the Cold War: The Case of the 'Nutcracker." *Mosaic* 33, no. 3 (2000): 1–17.

Kolb, Alexandra, ed. *Dance and Politics.* New York: Peter Lang, 2011.

Kolb, Alexandra. *Performing Femininity: Dance and Literature in German Modernism.* New York: Peter Lang, 2009.

Korppi-Tommola, Rikki. "Politics Promote Dance: Martha Graham in Finland, 1962." *Dance Chronicle* 33, no. 1 (2010): 82–112.

Kowal, Rebekah J. *How to Do Things with Dance: Performing Change in Postwar America.* Middletown, CT: Wesleyan University Press, 2010.

Kowal, Rebekah J., Gerald Siegmund, and Randy Martin, eds. *The Oxford Handbook of Dance and Politics.* New York: Oxford University Press, 2017.

Kraut, Anthea. *Choreographing Copyright: Race, Gender, and Intellectual Property Rights in American Dance.* New York: Oxford University Press, 2016.

Kreutzberg, Harald. "The Modern Dance." In *The Modern Dance,* edited by Merle Armitage and Virginia Stewart, 29–34. New York: Will A. Kistler, 1935. Reprint, New York: Dance Horizons, 1970.

Kuhar, Michael. *The Addicted Brain: Why We Abuse Drugs, Alcohol, and Nicotine.* Upper Saddle River, NJ: Financial Times Press, 2015.

Kullaa, Rinna. *Non-alignment and Its Origins in Cold War Europe: Yugoslavia, Finland and the Soviet Challenge.* New York: I. B. Tauris, 2012.

Kurth, Peter. *Isadora: A Sensational Life.* Boston: Little, Brown, 2001.

Kutler, Stanley I. *The Wars of Watergate: The Last Crisis of Richard Nixon.* New York: W. W. Norton, 1992.

LaMothe, Kimerer L. *Nietzsche's Dancers: Isadora Duncan, Martha Graham, and the Revaluation of Christian Values.* New York: Palgrave Macmillan, 2006.

Lane, Barbara M. "The Berlin Congress Hall 1955–1957." *Perspectives in American History,* n.s., 1 (1984): 131–85.

Large, David Clay. *Nazi Games: The Olympics of 1936.* New York: W. W. Norton, 2007.

Latham, Michael E. *Modernization as Ideology: American Social Science and "Nation Building" in the Kennedy Era.* Chapel Hill: University of North Carolina Press, 2000.

Laville, Helen. *Cold War Women: The International Activities of American Women's Organizations.* 2002. Reprint, New York: Manchester University Press, 2009.

Leab, Daniel J. *Orwell, Subverted: The CIA and the Filming of Animal Farm*. University Park: Pennsylvania State University Press, 2007.

Lean, Eugenia. *Public Passions: The Trial of Shi Jianqiao and the Rise of Popular Sympathy in Republican China*. Berkeley: University of California Press, 2007.

Leatherman, LeRoy. "A Question of Image: The Dance-Theater of Martha Graham." *Perspectives USA* 4 (Summer 1955): 46–48.

Leatherman, LeRoy. *Martha Graham: Portrait of the Lady as an Artist*. New York: Alfred A. Knopf, 1966.

Leffler, Melvyn P. "The Cold War: What Do 'We Now Know'?" *American Historical Review* 104, no. 2 (April 1999): 501–24.

Leffler, Melvyn P. *For the Soul of Mankind: The United States, the Soviet Union, and the Cold War*. New York: Hill and Wang, 2008.

Leffler, Melvyn P., and Odd Arne Westad, eds. *The Cambridge History of the Cold War*. Vol. 2. Cambridge: Cambridge University Press, 2010.

Lenart, Camelia. "A Trustworthy Collaboration: Eleanor Roosevelt and Martha Graham's Pioneering of American Cultural Diplomacy," *European Journal of American Studies* 12, no. 1 (Spring 2017): article 5 (https://journals.openedition.org/ejas/11972); "Thinking Modern, Dancing Modern: Eleanor Roosevelt and Martha Graham's Collaboration in the Pioneering of the American Cultural Diplomacy." In *The Global Citizen: Eleanor Roosevelt's Views on Diplomacy and Democracy*, edited by Anya Luscombe and Dario Fazzi. Forthcoming. London: Palgrave, 2019.

Lenart, Camelia. "Dancing Art and Politics behind the Iron Curtain: Martha Graham's 1962 Tours to Yugoslavia and Poland." *Dance Chronicle* 39, no. 2 (2016): 197–217.

Lenart, Camelia. "Turning the Tide and Reconstructing the Politics: A New Perspective on Martha Graham's Tours to Britain in 1954 and the Response to Its Political and Artistic Complexity." *Dance History: Politics, Practices and Perspectives Conference Proceedings*, March 13, 2010, https://www.academia.edu/267220/Conference_Proceedings_ Compilation_Dance_History_Conference. Accessed January 27, 2017.

Lenti, Vincent A. *The Eastman School of Music*. Rochester, NY: Rochester Public Library, 1996.

Lenti, Vincent A. *For the Enrichment of Community Life: George Eastman and the Founding of the Eastman School of Music*. Rochester, NY: Meliora Press, 2004.

Lisle, Laurie. *Portrait of an Artist: A Biography of Georgia O'Keeffe*. New York: Seaview Books, 1980. Reprint, New York: Washington Square Press, 1997.

Little, Douglas. "The Cold War in the Middle East: Suez Crisis to Camp David Accords." In *The Cambridge History of the Cold War*. Vol. 2, *Crisis and Détente*, edited by Melvyn P. Leffler and Odd Arne Westad, 305–26. New York: Cambridge University Press, 2010.

Lloyd, Margaret. *The Borzoi Book of Modern Dance*. New York: Alfred A. Knopf, 1949.

Loeffler, Jane C. *The Architecture of Diplomacy: Building American Embassies*. New York: Princeton Architectural Press, 1998. Reprint, 2010.

Lowe, Keith. *Savage Continent: Europe in the Aftermath of World War II*. New York: St. Martin's Press, 2012.

Lower, Wendy. *Hitler's Furies: German Women in the Nazi Killing Fields*. New York: Houghton, Mifflin, Harcourt, 2013. Reprint, 2014.

Luce, Henry. *The American Century*. Comments by Dorothy Thompson, Quincy Howe, John Chamberlain, Robert G. Spivack, and Robert E. Sherwood. New York: Farrar and Rinehart, 1941.

Luke, Christina, and Morag Kersel. *U.S. Cultural Diplomacy and Archaeology: Soft Power, Hard Heritage*. New York: Routledge, 2012.

Lundestad, Geir. "Empire by Invitation? The United States and Western Europe, 1945–1952. *Journal of Peace Research* 23, no. 3 (September 1986): 263–77.

Machcewicz, Pawel, and Maya Latynski. *Poland's War on Radio Free Europe, 1950–1989.* Palo Alto, CA: Stanford University Press, 2015.

Maciuika, John V. *Before the Bauhaus: Architecture, Politics, and the German State, 1890–1920.* Cambridge: Cambridge University Press, 2005.

MacMillan, Margaret. *Nixon and Mao: The Week That Changed the World.* New York: Random House, 2007. Reprint, 2008.

Maier, Charles S. *Among Empires: American Ascendancy and Its Predecessors.* Cambridge, MA: Harvard University Press, 2006.

Major, Patrick. *Behind the Berlin Wall: East Germany and the Frontiers of Power.* New York: Oxford University Press, 2010.

Manning, Susan. *Ecstasy and the Demon: Feminism and Nationalism in the Dances of Mary Wigman.* Berkeley: University of California Press, 1993.

Martin, John. *America Dancing: The Background and Personalities of the Modern Dance.* Brooklyn, NY: Dance Horizons, 1968.

Martin, John. "American Modern Dance." In *The Dance Encyclopaedia*, revised and enlarged edition, edited by Anatole Chujoy and P. W. Manchester, 43–49. New York: Simon and Schuster, 1967.

Martin, John. *John Martin's Book of the Dance.* New York: Tudor Publishing, 1963.

Martin, John. *The Modern Dance.* New York: A. S. Barnes, 1933. Reprint, New York: Dance Horizons, 1972.

Matthews, Jean V. *The Rise of the New Woman: The Women's Movement in America, 1875–1930.* New York: Rowman and Littlefield, 2004.

May, Elaine Tyler. *Homeward Bound: American Families in the Cold War Era.* New York: Basic Books, 1988.

McCaughey, Robert. *Stand, Columbia: A History of Columbia University in the City of New York.* New York: Columbia University Press, 2003.

McDaniel, Cadra Peterson. *American-Soviet Cultural Diplomacy: The Bolshoi Ballet's American Premiere.* Lanham, MD: Rowman & Littlefield Publishing Group, 2015.

McDonagh, Don. *The Complete Guide to Modern Dance.* Garden City, NY: Doubleday, 1976.

McDonagh, Don. *Martha Graham: A Biography.* New York: Praeger, 1973.

McDonald, William F. *Federal Relief Administration and the Arts: The Origins and Administrative History of the Arts Projects of the Works Progress Administration.* Columbus: Ohio State University Press, 1969.

McEnaney, Laura. "Personal, Political, and International: A Reflection on Diplomacy and Methodology." *Diplomatic History* 36, no. 4 (September 2012): 769–72.

McMahon, Robert J. *The Cold War on the Periphery: The United States, India, and Pakistan.* New York: Columbia University Press, 1994.

McMurry, Ruth Emily, and Muna Lee. *The Cultural Approach: Another Way in International Relations.* Chapel Hill: University of North Carolina Press, 1947. Reprint, Port Washington, NY: Kennikat Press, 1972.

Mead, V. H. "More Than Mere Movement: Dalcroze Eurhythmics." *Music Educators Journal* 82, no. 4 (1996): 38–41.

Medhurst, Martin J. *Eisenhower's War of Words: Rhetoric and Leadership.* East Lansing: Michigan State University Press, 1994.

Medhurst, Martin J. "Eisenhower and the Crusade for Freedom: The Rhetorical Origins of a Cold War Campaign." *Presidential Studies Quarterly* 27, no. 4 (1997): 646–61.

Meftahi, Ida. *Gender and Dance in Modern Iran: Biopolitics on Stage.* New York: Routledge, 2016.

Melanson, Richard A. *American Foreign Policy since the Vietnam War: The Search for Consensus from Richard Nixon to George W. Bush.* New York: M. E. Sharpe, 2005.

Merryman, John. *Law, Ethics, and the Visual Arts.* London: Kluwer Law International, 2002.

Mieczkowski, Yanek. *Gerald Ford and the Challenges of the 1970s.* Lexington: University Press of Kentucky, 2005.

Mihelj, Sabina. "Negotiating Cold War Culture at the Crossroads of East and West: Uplifting the Working People, Entertaining the Masses, Cultivating the Nation." *Comparative Studies in Society and History* 53, no. 3 (July 2011): 509–39.

Miles, Rosie. *Victorian Poetry in Context.* New York: Continuum, 2013.

Miller, James Edward. *The United States and the Making of Modern Greece: History and Power, 1950–1974.* Chapel Hill: University of North Carolina Press, 2009.

Mills, Dana. *Dance and Politics: Moving beyond Boundaries.* Manchester, UK: Manchester University Press, 2016.

Moeller, Robert G. *Protecting Motherhood: Women and Family in the Politics of Postwar Germany.* Berkeley: University of California Press, 1993.

Morris, Gay. *A Game for Dancers Performing Modernism in the Postwar Years, 1945–1960.* Middletown, CT: Wesleyan University Press, 2006.

Morris, Sylvia Jukes. *Price of Fame: The Honorable Clare Boothe Luce.* New York: Random House, 2014.

Morrison, Simon. *Bolshoi Confidential: Secrets of the Russian Ballet from the Rule of the Tsars to Today.* New York: W. W. Norton, 2016.

Mosley, Leonard. *Dulles: A Biography of Eleanor, Allen, and John Foster Dulles and Their Family Network.* New York: Dial Press, 1978.

Muehlenbeck, Philip. *Religion and the Cold War: A Global Perspective.* Nashville, TN: Vanderbilt University Press, 2012.

Munroe, Alexandra. *The Third Mind: American Artists Contemplate Asia, 1860–1989.* New York: Guggenheim Museum, 2009.

Neer, Robert M. *Napalm: An American Biography.* Cambridge, MA: Belknap Press, 2013.

Neiberg, Michael. *Potsdam: The End of World War II and the Remaking of Europe.* New York: Basic Books, 2015.

Neuman, Robert. "The Use of Psychology in History." *Psychohistory Review* 25 (1996): 10–21.

Nguyen, Viet Thanh. *Nothing Ever Dies: Vietnam and the Memory of War.* Cambridge, MA: Harvard University Press, 2016.

Nietzsche, Friedrich. *The Portable Nietzsche.* Translated by Walter Kaufmann. New York: Penguin Books, 1976.

Nye, Joseph S., Jr. *Soft Power: The Means to Success in World Politics.* New York: Public Affairs, 2004.

Oderman, Stuart. *Lillian Gish: A Life on Stage and Screen.* Jefferson, NC: McFarland, 2000.

Odom, Maggie. "Mary Wigman: The Early Years 1913–1925." *The Drama Review* 24, no. 4 (December 1980): 81–92.

Oh, Arissa H. *To Save the Children of Korea: The Cold War Origins of International Adoption.* Palo Alto, CA: Stanford University Press, 2015.

Osborne, Robin. *Athens and Athenian Democracy.* New York: Cambridge University Press, 2010.

Osgood, Kenneth Alan. *Total Cold War: Eisenhower's Secret Propaganda Battle at Home and Abroad*. Lawrence: University Press of Kansas, 2006.

Ostermann, Christian F., and Malcom Byrne, *Uprising in East Germany, 1953: The Cold War, the German Question, and the First Major Upheaval behind the Iron Curtain*. Washington, DC: Central European University Press, 2003.

Ostrowska, Irena. *Bibliografia zagadnień sztuki tanecznej z lat 1961–1962*. Warsaw: CPARA, 1964. Translated for the author by Marek Dąbrowski.

Parker, Jason. "Cold War II: The Eisenhower Administration, the Bandung Conference, and the Reperiodization of the Postwar Era." *Diplomatic History* 30, no. 5 (2006): 867–92.

Partsch-Bergsohn, Isa. *Modern Dance in Germany and the United States: Crosscurrents and Influences*. New York: Routledge, 1995.

Paterson, Thomas G. *Kennedy's Quest for Victory: American Foreign Policy, 1961–1963*. New York: Oxford University Press, 1989.

Pattanaik, Devdutt. *Indian Mythology: Tales, Symbols, and Rituals from the Subcontinent*. Rochester, VT: Inner Traditions International, 2003.

Peacock, Margaret. *Innocent Weapons: The Soviet and American Politics of Childhood in the Cold War*. Chapel Hill: University of North Carolina Press, 2014.

Pells, Richard H. *The Liberal Mind in a Conservative Age: American Intellectuals in the 1940s and 1950s*. Hanover, NH: University Press of New England, 1985. Reprint, Middletown, CT: Wesleyan University Press, 1989.

Pells, Richard H. *Radical Visions and American Dreams*. New York: Harper and Row, 1973.

Perks, Robert, and Alistair Thomson. *Oral History Reader*. New York: Routledge, 1998.

Perry, John Curtis. *Singapore: Unlikely Power*. New York: Oxford University Press, 2017.

Phillips, Dion E. "Terrorism and Security in the Caribbean: The 1976 Cubana Disaster off Barbados." *Studies in Conflict and Terrorism* 14, no. 4 (1991): 209–19.

Phillips, Victoria. "Martha Graham's Gilded Cage: *Blood Memory—An Autobiography* (1991)." *Dance Research Journal* 45, no. 2 (August 2013): 63–84.

Pietrusza, David. *1932: The Rise of Hitler and FDR—Two Tales of Politics, Betrayal, and Unlikely Destiny*. New York: Rowman and Littlefield, 2016.

Pigman, G. W. "Freud and the History of Empathy." *International Journal of Psychoanalytics* 76, no. 2 (April 1995): 237–56.

Poiger, Uta G. *Jazz, Rock, and Rebels: Cold War Politics and American Culture in a Divided Germany*. Berkeley: University of California Press, 2000.

Polisi, Joseph. *American Muse: The Life and Times of William Schuman*. Milwaukee, WI: Amadeus Press, 2008.

Pomeranz, Kenneth. "Empire and Civilizing Missions Past and Present." *Daedalus* 134, no. 2 (Spring 2005): 32–45.

Prados, John. "The War Scare of 1983." In *The Cold War: A Military History*, edited by Robert Cowley, 438–54. New York: Random House, 2006.

Pratt, Mary Louise. *Imperial Eyes: Travel Writing and Transculturation*. New York: Routledge, 1992. Reprint, 2008.

Preston, Andrew. "Bridging the Gap between the Sacred and the Secular in the History of American Foreign Relations." *Diplomatic History* 30, no. 5 (2006): 783–812.

Preston, Andrew. *Sword of the Spirit, Shield of the Faith: Religion in American War and Diplomacy*. New York: Random House, 2012.

Prevots, Naima. *Dance for Export: Cultural Diplomacy and the Cold War*. Middletown, CT: Wesleyan University Press, 1999.

Pritchard, Jane. *Rambert: A Celebration of the Company's First Seventy Years.* London: Rambert Dance Company, 1996.

Purkayastha, Prarthana. "Bodies beyond Borders: Modern Dance in Colonial and Postcolonial India." PhD diss., Roehampton University, 2008.

Purkayastha, Prarthana. *Indian Modern Dance, Feminism and Transnationalism.* London: Palgrave Macmillan, 2014.

Quinones, Sam. *Dreamland: The True Tale of America's Opiate Epidemic.* New York: Bloomsbury, 2015. Reprint, 2016.

Rainer, Yvonne. *Work, 1961–73.* Halifax: Press of Nova Scotia College of Art and Design, 1974.

Ragona, Melissa. "Ecstasy, Primitivism, Modernity: Isadora Duncan and Mary Wigman." *American Studies* 35, no. 1 (Spring 1994): 47–62.

Rakove, Robert B. *Kennedy, Johnson, and the Nonaligned World.* New York: Cambridge University Press, 2013.

Rambert, Marie. *Quicksilver: The Autobiography of Marie Rambert.* London: St. Martin's Press, 1972.

Redlich, Shimon. "Khrushchev and the Jews." In *Jewish Social Studies* 34, no. 4 (October 1972): 343–53.

Reich, Rebecca. *State of Madness: Psychiatry, Literature and Dissent after Stalin.* DeKalb: Northern Illinois University Press, 2018.

Reynolds, David. *The Origins of the Cold War in Europe: International Perspectives.* New Haven, CT: Yale University Press, 1994.

Reynolds, Nancy. *Repertory in Review: 40 Years of the New York City Ballet.* New York: Dial Press, 1977.

Richmond, Yale. *Cultural Exchange and the Cold War: Raising the Iron Curtain.* University Park: Pennsylvania State University Press, 2003.

Robin, Ron. *Enclaves of America: The Rhetoric of American Political Architecture Abroad, 1900–1965.* Princeton, NJ: Princeton University Press, 1992.

Roeder, George Holzshu. *Forum of Uncertainty: Confrontations with Modern Painting in Twentieth-Century American Thought.* Ann Arbor: University of Michigan Research Press, 1980.

Rohrer, Karen M. "If There Was Anything You Forgot To Ask ... The Papers of Betty Ford." In *Modern First Ladies: Their Documentary Legacy*, edited by Nancy Kegan Smith and Mary C. Ryan, 131–42. Washington, DC: Smithsonian Press, 1989.

Rosenberg, Emily S. "Considering Borders." In *Explaining the History of American Foreign Relations*, 3rd ed., edited by Frank Costigliola and Michael J. Hogan, 188–202. New York: Cambridge University Press, 2016.

Ross, Dorothy. "American Modernities, Past and Present." In "Historians and the Question of 'Modernity.'" *American Historical Review* 116, no. 3 (June 2011): 702–14.

Rourke, Constance. *American Humor: A Study of the National Character.* New York: Harcourt and Brace, 1931. Reprint, New York: NYRB Classics, 2004.

Ruble, Sarah E. *The Gospel of Freedom and Power: Protestant Missionaries in American Culture after World War II.* Chapel Hill: University of North Carolina Press, 2012.

Rudnick, Lois Palken. *Intimate Memories: The Autobiography of Mabel Dodge Luhan.* Albuquerque: University of New Mexico Press, 1999.

Rudnick, Lois Palken. *Mabel Dodge Luhan: New Woman, New Worlds.* Albuquerque: University of New Mexico Press, 1991.

Rudnick, Lois Palken. *Utopian Vistas: The Mabel Dodge Luhan House and the American Counterculture*. Albuquerque: University of New Mexico Press, 1996.

Rutcoff, Peter M., and William B. Scott. *New School: A History of the New School for Social Research*. New York: Free Press, 1986.

Safty, Adel. *The Cyprus Question: Diplomacy and International Law*. Bloomington, IN: iUniverse, 2011.

Said, Edward W. *Culture and Imperialism*. New York: Alfred A. Knopf, 1993.

Said, Edward W. *Orientalism*. New York: Pantheon, 1978.

Saul, Oscar. *Revolt of the Beavers*. New York: Dramatists Play Service, 1936.

Saunders, Frances Stonor. *The Cultural Cold War: The CIA and the World of Arts and Letters*. New York: New Press, 2001.

Sayler, Oliver, ed. *Revolt in the Arts: A Survey of the Creation, Distribution, and Appreciation of Art in America*. New York: Brentano's, 1930.

Schapp, Jeremy. *Triumph: The Untold Story of Jesse Owens and Hitler's Olympics*. New York: Mariner Press, 2007.

Scherer, Bernd M., ed. *The House. The Cultures. The World: Fifty Years: From the Congress Hall to the House of World Cultures*. Translated by Matthew Gaskins. Berlin: Nicolai, 2006. Reprint, 2007.

Scholl, Tim. *From Petipa to Balanchine: Classical Revival and the Modernization of Ballet*. New York: Routledge, 1994.

Scott-Smith, Giles. *The Politics of Apolitical Culture: The Congress for Cultural Freedom and the Political Economy of American Hegemony 1945–1955*. London: Routledge, 2001.

Seachrist, Denise A. *The Musical World of Halim El-Dabh*. Kent, OH: Kent State University Press, 2003.

Seib, Philip. *Religion and Public Diplomacy*. New York: Palgrave Macmillan, 2013.

Selden, Elizabeth. "The New German Credo." In *The Dancer's Quest: Essays on the Aesthetic of the Contemporary Dance*, 25–32. Berkeley: University of California Press, 2011.

Service, Robert. *The End of the Cold War, 1985–1991*. New York: Perseus, 2015.

Shamir, Yitshak. "Foreword." In *Israeli-Egyptian Relations, 1980–2000*, by Ephraim Dowek, xi–xiii. London: Frank Cass, 2001.

Shaw, Tony. "'Martyrs, Miracles and Martians': Religion and Cold War Cinematic Propaganda in the 1950s." In *Religion and the Cold War*, edited by Dianne Kirby, 211–31. New York: Palgrave Macmillan, 2003. Reprint, 2013.

Shaw, Tony, and Denise J. Youngblood. *Cinematic Cold War: The American and Soviet Struggle for Hearts and Minds*. Lawrence: University Press of Kansas, 2014.

Shawn, Ted. *The American Ballet*. New York: Henry Holt, 1926.

Shawn, Ted. *Ruth St. Denis, Pioneer and Prophet*. Vol. 1, *Being a History of Her Cycle of Oriental Dances*. San Francisco: J. Howell, 1920.

Sherman, Jane. *Denishawn: The Enduring Influence*. Boston: Twayne, 1983.

Sherman, Jane. *The Drama of Denishawn*. Middletown, CT: Wesleyan University Press, 1979.

Shimizu, Sayuri. *Creating People of Plenty: The United States and Japan's Economic Alternatives, 1950–1960*. Kent, OH: Kent State University Press, 2001.

Shirer, William L. *The Rise and Fall of the Third Reich: A History of Nazi Germany*. New York: Simon and Schuster, 1990.

Sickels, Robert. *The 1940s*. Westport, CT: Greenwood Press, 2004.

Siegel, Marcia B. "Modern Dance before Bennington: Sorting It All Out." *Dance Research Journal: Congress on Research and Dance* 19, no. 1 (Summer 1987): 3–9.

Siegel, Marcia B. *The Shapes of Change: Images of American Dance.* Boston: Houghton Mifflin, 1979.

Sirecka-Wołodko, Magdalena. *Zagraniczna polityka kulturalna Polski w latach, 1956–1970.* Toruń, Poland: Wydawnictwo MADO, 2011.

Skrabec, Quenton R. *H. J. Heinz: A Biography.* Jefferson, NC: McFarland, 2009.

Smith, Gaddis. *Morality, Reason and Power: American Diplomacy in the Carter Years.* New York: Hill and Wang, 1986.

Smith, Harold J. "The Bird and the Mirror: A Reading of Mallarmé's 'Le Vierge.'" *French Review* 63, no. 1 (October 1989): 57–65.

Smith, Richard Norton. *On His Own Terms: A Life of Nelson Rockefeller.* New York: Random House, 2014.

Soares, Janet M. *Louis Horst: A Musician in a Dancer's World.* Durham, NC: Duke University Press, 1992.

Soares, Janet M. *Martha Hill and the Making of Modern Dance.* Middletown, CT: Wesleyan University Press, 2009.

Soley, Lawrence. *Radio Warfare: OSS and CIA Subversive Propaganda.* New York: Praeger, 1989.

Sorell, Walter. *Hanya Holm: The Biography of an Artist.* Middletown, CT: Wesleyan University Press, 1969.

Souritz, Elizabeth. "Isadora Duncan's Influence on Dance in Russia." *Dance Chronicle* 18, no. 2 (1995): 281–91.

Sowell, Debra Hickenlooper. *Christensen Brothers: An American Dance Epic.* London: Routledge, 1998.

"Special Forum: Musical Diplomacy: Strategies, Agendas, Relationships." *Diplomatic History* 36. no. 1 (January 2012): 17–75.

Spector, Irwin. *Rhythm and Life: The Work of Emile Jaques-Dalcroze.* Stuyvesant, NY: Pendragon Press, 1990.

Spielvogel, Jackson J. *Western Civilization.* 8th ed. New York: Cengage Learning, 2011.

Spotts, Frederic. *Hitler and the Power of Aesthetics.* New York: Overlook Press, 2002.

Spruill, Marjorie J. *Divided We Stand: The Battle over Women's Rights and Family Values That Polarized American Politics.* New York: Bloomsbury, 2017.

Stansell, Christine. *American Moderns: Bohemian New York and the Creation of a New Century.* New York: Metropolitan Books, 2000.

Steininger, Rolf. *The German Question: The Stalin Note of 1952 and the Question of German Reunification.* New York: Columbia University Press, 1990.

Stephanson, Anders. "Cold War Degree Zero." In *Uncertain Empire: American History and the Idea of the Cold War,* edited by Joal Isaac and Duncan Bell, 19–50. New York: Oxford University Press, 2012.

Stephanson, Anders. *Kennan and the Art of Foreign Policy.* Cambridge, MA: Harvard University Press, 1989.

Stephanson, Anders. *Manifest Destiny: American Expansion and the Empire of Right.* New York: Hill and Wang, 1995.

Stern, John Allen. *C. D. Jackson: Cold War Propagandist for Democracy and Globalism.* Lanham, MD: University Press of America, 2012.

Stern, Sheldon M. *The Cuban Missile Crisis in American Memory: Myths versus Reality.* Stanford, CA: Stanford University Press, 2012.

Stodelle, Ernestine. *Deep Song: The Dance Story of Martha Graham.* New York: Schirmer Books, 1984.

Stoler, Ann Laura. *Race and the Educating of Desire: Foucault's History of Sexuality and the Cultural Order of Things*. Durham, NC: Duke University Press, 1995.

Stolps, Sven. *The Maid of Orleans: The Life and Mysticism of Joan of Arc*. San Francisco: Ignatius Press, 2014.

Storl, H. P., and Hugh Stubbins. *Berlin Baut 2—The Congress Hall: History, Collapse, Reconstruction*. Berlin: Senat Department for Building and Housing, 1987.

Suri, Jeremi. "Détente and Its Discontents." In *Rightward Bound: Making America Conservative in the 1970s*, edited by Bruce J. Schulman and Julian E. Zelizer, 227–45. Cambridge, MA: Harvard University Press, 2008.

Swayne, Steve. *Orpheus in Manhattan: William Schuman and the Shaping of America's Musical Life*. New York: Oxford University Press, 2011.

Symes, Carol. "When We Talk about Modernity." In "Historians and the Question of 'Modernity.'" *American Historical Review* 116, no. 3 (June 2011): 715–26.

Taber, Sara Mansfield. "My Saigon Summer, before the Fall: A Spy's Daughter Remembers Life during Wartime." *Literary Hub* via *The American Scholar* (July 16, 2015), http://lithub.com/saigon-summer/. Accessed August 11, 2017.

David Talbot. *The Devil's Chessboard: Allen Dulles, the CIA, and the Rise of America's Secret Government*. New York: HarperCollins, 2017.

Taranov, Evgenii. "'Raskachaem Leninskie Gory!' Iz istorii 'vol'nodumstva v Moskovskom Universitete, 1955–1956." *Svobodnaia mysl'* 10 (1993): 94–103.

Taylor, Frederick. *The Berlin Wall: August 13, 1961–November 9, 1989*. London: Bloomsbury, 2009.

Taylor, Frederick. *The Berlin Wall: A World Divided, 1961–1989*. New York: Harper Perennial, 2008.

Taylor, Ronald. *Berlin and Its Culture: A Historical Portrait*. New Haven, CT: Yale University Press, 1997.

Terry, Walter. *Frontiers of Dance: The Life of Martha Graham*. New York: Crowell, 1975.

Thomas, Evan. *Ike's Bluff: President Eisenhower's Secret Battle to Save the World*. New York: Little, Brown, 2012.

Thomas, Helen. *Dance, Modernity and Culture*. New York: Routledge, 1995.

Tokunaga, Emilio. *Yuriko: An American Japanese Dancer*. New York: Tokunaga Dance Ko, 2008.

Tomlin, Greg. *Murrow's Cold War: Public Diplomacy for the Kennedy Administration*. Lincoln, NE: Potomac Books, 2016.

Toobin, Jeffrey. *American Heiress: The Wild Saga of the Kidnapping, Crimes and Trial of Patty Hearst*. New York: Doubleday, 2016.

Tracy, Robert. *Goddess: Martha Graham's Dancers Remember*. New York: Limelight Editions, 1997.

Trevisan, Louis A., MD, Nashaat Boutros, MD, Ismene L. Petrakis, MD, and John Krystal, MD. "Complications of Alcohol Withdrawal: Pathophysiological Insights." *Alcohol Health and Research World* 22, no. 1 (1998): 61–66.

Tsipursky, Gleb. "Domestic Cultural Diplomacy and Soviet State-Sponsored Popular Culture in the Cold War, 1953–1962." *Diplomatic History* 41, no. 5 (November 2017): 985–1009.

Tsipursky, Gleb. *Socialist Fun: Youth, Consumption, and State-Sponsored Popular Culture in the Soviet Union, 1945–1970*. Pittsburgh: University of Pittsburgh Press, 2017.

Tudda, Chris. *The Rhetorical Diplomacy of Dwight D. Eisenhower and John Foster Dulles*. Baton Rouge: Louisiana State University Press, 2006.

Turkevich, Ludmilla B. "The Second Congress of Soviet Writers." *Books Abroad* 30, no. 1 (Winter 1956): 31–34.

Turska, Irena. *Krótki zarys historii baletu i tańca*. Warsaw: Polskie Wydawnictwo Muzyczne, 1983.

Ulph, Janet, and Ian Smith. *The Illicit Trade in Art and Antiquities: International Recovery and Criminal and Civil Liability*. Oxford: Heart Publishing, 2012.

Undset, Sigrid. *Catherine of Siena*. Oslo: H. Aschehoug and Company, 1951. Reprint, San Francisco: Ignatius Press, 2009.

Undset, Sigrid. *Men, Women, and Places*. New York, Alfred A. Knopf, 1939.

United States Committee for the World Youth Festival. *The Bright Face of Peace: The Story of American Participation in the World Youth Festival, Prague, July–August, 1947*. New York: US Committee for the World Youth Festival/American Youth for a Free World, 1947.

Vasilieva, Larissa. *Kremlin Wives: The Secret Lives of the Women behind the Kremlin Walls—from Lenin to Gorbachev*. Translated by Cathy Porter. New York: Arcade, 2015.

Végső, Roland. *The Naked Communist: Cold War Modernism and the Politics of Popular Culture*. New York: Fordham University Press, 2012.

Verheyen, Dirk. *United City, Divided Memories? Cold War Legacies in Contemporary Berlin*. Lanham, MD: Lexington Books, 2010.

Vickers, Adrian. *A History of Modern Indonesia*. 2nd ed. New York: Cambridge University Press, 2013.

Vitalis, Robert. "The Midnight Ride of Kwame Nkrumah and Other Fables of Bandung (Bandoong)." *Humanith: An International Journal of Human Rights, Humanitarianism, and Development* 4, no. 2 (2013): 261–88.

Volkov, Solomon. *Shostakovich and Stalin: The Extraordinary Relationship between the Great Composer and the Brutal Dictator*. New York: Alfred A. Knopf, 2004.

Von Eschen, Penny. *Satchmo Blows Up the World: Jazz Ambassadors Play the Cold War*. Cambridge, MA: Harvard University Press, 2004.

Von Laban, Rudolf. *A Life for Dance Reminiscences*. New York: Theatre Arts Book, 1948. Reprint, New York: Routledge, 1975.

Vučetić, Radina. *Koka-Kola Socijalizam*. Beograd: Službeni Glasnik, 2012.

Wagg, Stephen, and David Andrews. *East Plays West: Sport and the Cold War*. New York: Routledge, 2006.

Wagnleitner, Reinhold, and Elaine Tyler May, eds. *"Here, There and Everywhere": The Foreign Politics of American Popular Culture*. Hanover, NH: University Press of New England, 2000.

Walter, Michael. "Music of Seriousness and Commitment: The 1930s and Beyond." In *The Cambridge History of Twentieth-Century Music*. Vol. 1, edited by Nicholas Cook and Anthony Pople, 286–306. Cambridge: Cambridge University Press, 2004.

Ware, Susan, ed. *Notable American Women: A Biographical Dictionary*. Vol. 5. Cambridge, MA: Harvard University Press, 2005.

Ware, Susan. *Letter to the World: Seven Women Who Shaped the American Twentieth Century*. New York: W. W. Norton, 1998.

Warnecke, Grace Kennan. *Cold War Daughter*. Pittsburgh: University of Pittsburgh Press, 2018.

Wasserstein, Bernard. *Barbarism and Civilization: A History of Europe in Our Time*. New York: Oxford University Press, 2007.

Webber, Andrew J. *Berlin in the Twentieth Century: A Cultural Topography.* New York: Cambridge University Press, 2008.

Westad, Odd Arne. *The Cold War: A World History.* New York: Basic Books, 2017.

Westad, Odd Arne. *The Global Cold War: Third World Interventions and the Making of Our Times.* New York: Cambridge University Press, 2005.

White, Eric Walter. *Stravinsky: The Composer and His Works.* 1966. Reprint, Berkeley: University of California Press, 1985.

Whittington, Dale and Giorgio Guariso. *Water Management Models in Practice: A Case Study of the Aswan High Dam.* London: Elsevier Science, 1983.

Weidenfeld, Sheila Rabb. *First Lady's Lady: With the Fords at the White House.* New York: G. P. Putnam's Sons, 1979.

Wigman, Mary. *Deutsche Tanzkunst.* Dresden: C. Reisner, 1935.

Wigman, Mary. "Dance and Modern Woman." In *The Mary Wigman Book: Her Writings,* edited and translated by Walter Sorell, 104–6. Middletown, CT: Wesleyan University Press, 1973.

Wigman, Mary. "Stage Dance—Stage Dancer." In *The Mary Wigman Book: Her Writings,* edited and translated by Walter Sorell, 107–15. Middletown, CT: Wesleyan University Press, 1973.

Wilber, Donald. "CIA Clandestine Service History, Overthrow of Premier Mossadeq of Iran, November 1952–August 1953." CIA Report. March 1954. Published March 1969. National Security Archive, George Washington University, Washington, DC. http://www.gwu.edu/~nsarchiv/NSAEBB/NSAEBB28/#documents. Accessed July 28, 2008.

Winsor, Justin. *The History of the House of Duxbury, Massachusetts with Genealogical Registers.* Boston, 1849.

Winter, Ofir. "Israel in the Egyptian Stamp Album." Institute for National Security Studies. http://www.inss.org.il/publication/?pauthor=61442. Accessed June 30, 2017.

Winther-Tamaki, Bert. *Art in the Encounter of Nations: Japanese and American Artists in the Postwar Years.* Honolulu: University of Hawaii Press, 2001.

Wolin, Richard. "'Modernity': The Peregrinations of a Contested Historiographical Concept." In "Historians and the Question of 'Modernity.' " *American Historical Review* 116, no. 3 (June 2011): 740–51.

Wong, Yutian. "Artistic Utopias: Michio Ito and the Trope of the International." In *Worlding Dance,* edited by Susan Leigh Foster, 144–62. London: Palgrave Macmillan, 2009.

Wright, Lawrence. *Thirteen Days in September: The Dramatic Story of the Struggle for Peace.* London: Oneworld Publications, 2015.

Wysocka, Tacjana. *Dzieje baletu.* Warsaw: P.I.W., Rok wydania, 1970.

Yaqub, Salim. *Imperfect Strangers: Americans, Arabs, and U.S.–Middle East Relations in the 1970s.* Ithaca, NY: Cornell University Press, 2016.

Yarrow, Andrew L. "Selling a New Vision of America to the World: Changing Messages in Early U.S. Cold War Print Propaganda." *Journal of Cold War Studies* 11, no. 4 (Fall 2009): 3–45.

Yellin, Emily. *Our Mother's War: American Women at Home and on the Front during World War II.* New York: Free Press, 2004.

Yeoh, Seng Guan, Wei Leng Loh, Salma Nasution Khoo, and Neil Khor, eds. *Penang and Its Region: The Story of an Asian Entrepôt.* Singapore: National University of Singapore, 2009.

Young, Marilyn Blatt. *The Vietnam Wars, 1945–1990.* New York: HarperCollins, 1991.

Zelizer, Julian E. "Conservatives, Carter, and the Politics of National Security." In *Rightward Bound: Making America Conservative in the 1970s*, edited by Bruce J. Schulman and Julian E. Zelizer, 265–87. Cambridge, MA: Harvard University Press, 2008.

Zhuk, Serge. *Rock and Roll in the Rocket City: The West, Identity, and Ideology in Soviet Dniepropetrovsk, 1960–1985*. Baltimore: Johns Hopkins University Press, 2010.

Zipp, Samuel. *Manhattan Projects: The Rise and Fall of Urban Renewal in Cold War New York*. New York: Oxford University Press, 2012.

Zubok, Vladislav. "The Soviet Union and European Integration from Stalin to Gorbachev." *Journal of European Integration History* 2, no. 1 (1996): 85–98.

Zubok, Vladislav, and Constantine Pleshakov. *Inside the Kremlin's Cold War: From Stalin to Khrushchev*. Cambridge, MA: Harvard University Press, 1996.

Zunz, Olivier. *Philanthropy in America: A History*. Princeton, NJ: Princeton University Press, 2012.

Index